Praise for *Core Python Programming*

"The long-awaited second edition of Wesley Chun's *Core Python Programming* proves to be well worth the wait—its deep and broad coverage and useful exercises will help readers learn and practice good Python."
—Alex Martelli, author of *Python in a Nutshell* and editor of *Python Cookbook*

"There has been lot of good buzz around Wesley Chun's *Core Python Programming*. It turns out that all the buzz is well earned. I think this is the best book currently available for learning Python. I would recommend Chun's book over *Learning Python* (O'Reilly), *Programming Python* (O'Reilly), or *The Quick Python Book* (Manning)."
—David Mertz, Ph.D., IBM DeveloperWorks®

"I have been doing a lot of research [on] Python for the past year and have seen a number of positive reviews of your book. The sentiment expressed confirms the opinion that *Core Python Programming* is now considered the standard introductory text."
—Richard Ozaki, Lockheed Martin

"Finally, a book good enough to be both a textbook and a reference on the Python language now exists."
—Michael Baxter, *Linux Journal*

"Very well written. It is the clearest, friendliest book I have come across yet for explaining Python, and putting it in a wider context. It does not presume a large amount of other experience. It does go into some important Python topics carefully and in depth. Unlike too many beginner books, it never condescends or tortures the reader with childish hide-and-seek prose games. [It] sticks to gaining a solid grasp of Python syntax and structure."
—http://python.org bookstore Web site

"[If] I could only own one Python book, it would be *Core Python Programming* by Wesley Chun. This book manages to cover more topics in more depth than *Learning Python* but includes it all in one book that also more than adequately covers the core language. [If] you are in the market for just one book about Python, I recommend this book. You will enjoy reading it, including its wry programmer's wit. More importantly, you will learn Python. Even more importantly, you will find it invaluable in helping you in your day-to-day Python programming life. Well done, Mr. Chun!"
—Ron Stephens, Python Learning Foundation

"I think the best language for beginners is Python, without a doubt. My favorite book is *Core Python Programming*."
—s003apr, MP3Car.com Forums

"Personally, I really like Python. It's simple to learn, completely intuitive, amazingly flexible, and pretty darned fast. Python has only just started to claim mindshare in the Windows world, but look for it to start gaining lots of support as people discover it. To learn Python, I'd start with *Core Python Programming* by Wesley Chun."
—Bill Boswell, MCSE, Microsoft Certified Professional Magazine Online

"If you learn well from books, I suggest *Core Python Programming*. It is by far the best I've found. I'm a Python newbie as well and in three months time I've been able to implement Python in projects at work (automating MSOffice, SQL DB stuff, etc.)."
—ptonman, Dev Shed Forums

"Python is simply a beautiful language. It's easy to learn, it's cross-platform, and it works. It has achieved many of the technical goals that Java strives for. A one-sentence description of Python would be: 'All other languages appear to have evolved over time—but Python was designed.' And it was designed well. Unfortunately, there aren't a large number of books for Python. The best one I've run across so far is *Core Python Programming*."
—Chris Timmons, C. R. Timmons Consulting

"If you like the Prentice Hall Core series, another good full-blown treatment to consider would be *Core Python Programming*. It addresses in elaborate concrete detail many practical topics that get little, if any, coverage in other books."
—Mitchell L Model, MLM Consulting

core

PYTHON

programming

Second Edition

PRENTICE HALL
CORE SERIES

core

PYTHON

programming

Second Edition

WESLEY J. CHUN

PRENTICE
HALL

Upper Saddle River, NJ • Boston • Indianapolis • San Francisco • New York
Toronto • Montreal • London • Munich • Paris • Madrid • Capetown
Sydney • Tokyo • Singapore • Mexico City

Many of the designations used by manufacturers and sellers to distinguish their products are claimed as trademarks. Where those designations appear in this book, and the publisher was aware of a trademark claim, the designations have been printed with initial capital letters or in all capitals.

The author and publisher have taken care in the preparation of this book, but make no expressed or implied warranty of any kind and assume no responsibility for errors or omissions. No liability is assumed for incidental or consequential damages in connection with or arising out of the use of the information or programs contained herein.

The publisher offers excellent discounts on this book when ordered in quantity for bulk purchases or special sales, which may include electronic versions and/or custom covers and content particular to your business, training goals, marketing focus, and branding interests. For more information, please contact:

U.S. Corporate and Government Sales
(800) 382-3419
corpsales@pearsontechgroup.com

For sales outside the United States, please contact:
International Sales
international@pearsoned.com

This Book Is Safari Enabled

The Safari® Enabled icon on the cover of your favorite technology book means the book is available through Safari Bookshelf. When you buy this book, you get free access to the online edition for 45 days.

Safari Bookshelf is an electronic reference library that lets you easily search thousands of technical books, find code samples, download chapters, and access technical information whenever and wherever you need it.

To gain 45-day Safari Enabled access to this book:

- Go to http://www.prenhallprofessional.com/safarienabled
- Complete the brief registration form
- Enter the coupon code F5JI-KJ2L-9DLR-BWK1-7QBM

If you have difficulty registering on Safari Bookshelf or accessing the online edition, please e-mail customer-service@safaribooksonline.com.

Visit us on the Web: www.prenhallprofessional.com

Library of Congress Cataloging-in-Publication Data
Chun, Wesley.
    Core Python programming / Wesley J. Chun. – 2nd ed.
        p. cm.
    Includes bibliographical references and index.
    ISBN 0-13-226993-7 (pbk. : alk. paper)
    1. Python (Computer program language) I. Title.
    QA76.73.P98C48 2006
    005.13'3–dc22
                                    2006019559

ISBN 0-13-226993-7
Text printed in the United States on recycled paper at Courier in Stoughton, Massachusetts.
First printing, September 2006

To my parents,
    who taught me that everybody is different.
And to my wife,
    who *lives* with someone who is different.

Contents

x   **Contents**

Preface

Welcome to *Core Python Programming!*

We are delighted that you have engaged us to help you learn Python as quickly and as in-depth as possible. Learning the syntax is one goal of this book; however, we also believe that if you learn how Python works under the covers, you won't just be able to *program* in Python, but you will write more *effective* Python applications even as a beginner to the language. As you know, just because you learn a language's syntax does not make you competent in it right away.

Throughout the book, you will find many examples that you can try right in front of your computer. To hammer the concepts home, you will also find fun and challenging exercises at the end of every chapter. These easy and intermediate exercises are meant to test your learning and push your Python skills. There simply is no substitute for experience. We believe you should not only pick up Python programming skills but also be able to master them in as short a time period as possible.

About This Book

This book differs from other Python books on the market by presenting a broad range of topics, providing numerous examples, and going in-depth where necessary. This book does not require a specific background such as prior knowledge of C or object-oriented programming. It is also not a large case study book that does not facilitate picking up the language quickly. Finally, this book is not a pure reference nor is it meant to be a quick "dive" into Python. What we have is an extremely comprehensive introduction to the core features of the language (Part I) followed by a set of chapters that delve into specific areas of intermediate Python programming.

This book is 40 percent introductory, 40 percent intermediate to advanced, and 20 percent reference. It is targeted toward technical professionals who are already familiar with programming in one other high-level language, as well as university/college and secondary students. Because Python is used in larger solutions such as Zope, Plone, MailMan, and Django, this book may be used by principals developing, managing, maintaining, or integrating with those systems.

With regards to the code in this book, about a third of the first edition readers sent in complaints that there were not enough large, full-fledged applications in the book, or that the code examples were not long or comprehensive enough. Everyone else wrote that they loved the short, easy-to-understand examples and were not bored of page after page of mind-numbing code. The philosophy behind more short examples is to give you the ability to look at a piece of code and grasp its entirety. These turn into building blocks to understanding and then can be incorporated into larger applications as well. There are line-by-line explanations for most of the larger programs in the book. The abundant interpreter code snippets scattered throughout the book are there for you to try on your computer as you are learning Python—use the interactive interpreter as much as possible. You not only learn and improve your Python from using it, but you can also benefit from working out bugs in your code *before* you paste it into your source file.

Because you cannot learn Python well without practice, you will find the exercises at the end of every chapter to be one of the greatest strengths of this book. They will test your knowledge of chapter topics and definitions, as well as get you to code as much as possible. There is no substitute to learning a programming language faster and more effectively than by building applications. You will find easy, intermediate, and difficult problems to solve. It is also here that you may have to write one of those "large" applications that many readers wanted to see in the book, but rather than having me do it, you gain the most from such exercises. Appendix A features answers to selected problems from each chapter.

Another set of first edition readers remarked how useful the reference tables were throughout the book, and how they meticulously copied them for reference. Well, instead of flipping through each chapter looking for the tables, we have summarized the most highly used ones in Appendix B. Thanks for all of your feedback. I encourage you to keep talking to us and help us make a third edition possible and better than its predecessors!

Finally, both the "Other References" appendix and the CD-ROM from the first edition are not included with this edition. You would not believe how quickly Web links can become obsolete in six months much less six years! The most up-to-date source code and Python interpreters can easily be downloaded for offline use at the book's Web site, so there really is no reason to include a CD-ROM.

About the Reader

This book is meant for you if you are a programmer completely new to Python or already know some Python but want to know more and improve your Python skillset. Python is used in many fields, including engineering, information technology, science, business, entertainment, and so on. This means that the list of Python users (and readers of this book) includes but is not limited to:

- Software engineers
- Hardware design/CAD engineers
- QA/testing and automation framework developers
- IS/IT/system and network administrators
- Scientists and mathematicians
- Technical or project management staff
- Multimedia or audio/visual engineers
- SCM or release engineers
- Web masters and content management staff
- Customer/technical support engineers
- Database engineers and administrators
- Research and development engineers
- Software integration and professional services staff
- Collegiate and secondary educators
- Web service engineers
- Financial software engineers
- And many others

Some of the most famous companies using Python include Google, Yahoo!, NASA, Lucasfilm/Industrial Light and Magic, Red Hat, Zope, Disney, Pixar, and Dreamworks.

The Author's Experience with Python

I discovered Python over a decade ago at a company called Four11. At the time, the company had one major product, the Four11.com White Page directory service. Python was being used to design our next product: the Rocketmail Web-based e-mail service that would eventually evolve into what today is Yahoo!Mail.

It was fun learning Python and being on the original Yahoo!Mail engineering team. I helped rearchitect the address book and spell checker. At the time, Python also made its way as part of a number of other Yahoo! sites, including People Search, Yellow Pages, and Maps and Driving Directions, just to name a few. I was the lead engineer for People Search.

Although Python was new to me then, it was fairly easy to pick up—much simpler than other languages I had learned in the past. The scarcity of textbooks at the time led me to primarily use the Library Reference and Quick Reference Guide as my tools in learning, and also led to the motivation for the book you are reading right now.

Since my days at Yahoo!, I have been able to use Python in all sorts of interesting ways at the jobs that followed. In each case, I was able to harness the power of Python in solving the problems at hand and in a timely manner. I have also developed several Python courses and have used this book to teach those classes, truly eating my own dogfood.

Not only is *Core Python Programming* a great book to *learn* Python from, but it is also the best book to *teach* Python with! As an engineer, I know what it takes to learn, understand, and apply a new technology. As a professional instructor, I also know *what is needed to deliver the most effective sessions for clients*. This provides the experience necessary to be able to give you real-world analogies and tips that you cannot get from someone who is "just a trainer" or "just a book author."

About the Author's Writing Style: Technical, Yet Easy Reading

Rather than strictly a "beginners" book or a pure, hard-core computer science reference book, my instructional experience indicates that an easy-to-read, yet technically oriented book serves our purpose the best, which is to get you up to speed on Python as quickly as possible so that you can apply it to your tasks *posthaste*. We will introduce concepts coupled with appropriate examples to expedite the learning process. At the end of each chapter you will find numerous exercises to reinforce some of the concepts and ideas acquired in your reading.

We are thrilled and humbled to be compared with Bruce Eckel's writing style (see the reviews to the first edition at the book's Web site (http://corepython.com). This is not a dry college textbook. As the author, I am having a conversation with you, as if you were attending one of my well-received Python training courses. As a lifelong student, I constantly put myself in my student's shoes and tell you what you need to hear in order to learn the concepts as quickly and as thoroughly as possible. You will find reading this book fast and easy, without losing sight of the technical details.

As an engineer, I know what I need to tell you in order to teach you a concept in Python. As a teacher, I can take technical details and boil them down into language that is easy to understand and grasp right away. You are getting the best of both worlds with my writing and teaching styles, but you will enjoy programming in Python even more.

About This Second Edition

At the time the first edition was published, Python was entering its second era with the release of version 2.0. Since then, the language has seen significant improvements contributing to the overall continuing success and acceptance of the language. Deficiencies have been removed and new features added that bring a new level of power and sophistication to Python developers worldwide. We are thrilled to be able to update this book yet still deliver easy reading along with comprehensive coverage of the exciting new features. This book includes changes to Python 2.5, released in the fall of 2006, and even some pre-announced features of 2.6 and beyond. As in the first edition, we aim to keep all of the topics relevant for readers regardless of the Python version you are using, extending the lifetime of this book, retarding its obsolescence.

Python is slowly going to be transitioning to the next big version change with a release affectionately called "Python 3000" by its creator, Guido van Rossum. This is just the marketing name for Python 3.0, or "Py3K" for short. It will be developed in parallel with the remaining 2.x releases. There will be some incompatibilities with older versions of Python; however, the core team will work hard to ensure that code will be backwards-compatible for the most part. (This is in tradition with any new Python release.) Look mostly for interesting additions to the language as well as the disappearance of old design flaws and deprecated features.

We will continue to update the book's Web site with white papers, updates, and other related articles to keep *Core Python Programming* as contemporary as possible, regardless of which new release of Python you have migrated to.

The new topics we have added to this edition include:

- Boolean and set types (Chapters 5 and 7)

- New-style classes (Chapter 13)
  - Subclassing built-in types
  - Static methods and class methods
  - Slots
  - Properties
  - Descriptors
  - Metaclasses

- Functions (Chapter 11)
  - Generators
  - Function (and method) decorators
  - Statically nested scoping
  - Inner functions
  - Closures
  - Currying and partial function application

- Looping constructs (Chapter 8)
  - Iterators
  - List comprehensions
  - Generator expressions

- Extended import syntax (Chapter 12)
  - `as` keyword
  - Multi-line import
  - Absolute importing
  - Relative importing

- Improved exception handling features (Chapter 10)
  - `with` statement
  - `try-except-finally` statement

In addition, we are proud to introduce three new chapters to the book: "Internet Client Programming" (Chapter 17), "Database Programming" (Chapter 21), and "Miscellaneous" (Chapter 23). These are a few intermediate areas where Python is used quite often. All existing chapters have been refreshed and updated to the latest versions of Python. Please see the chapter guide that follows for more details.

Chapter Guide

This book is divided into two main sections. The first part, taking up about two-thirds of the text, gives you treatment of the "core" part of the language, and the second part provides a set of various advanced topics to show what you can build using Python.

Python is everywhere—sometimes it is amazing to discover who is using Python and what they are doing with it—and although we would have loved to produce additional chapters on such topics as Java/Jython, Win32 programming, CGI processing with HTMLgen, GUI programming with third-party toolkits (wxWidgets, GTK+, Qt, etc.), XML processing, numerical and scientific processing, visual and graphics image manipulation, and Web services and application frameworks (Zope, Plone, Django, TurboGears, and so on), there simply wasn't enough time to develop these topics into their own chapters. However, we are certainly glad that we were at least able to provide you with a good introduction to many of the key areas of Python development including some of the topics mentioned previously.

Here is a chapter-by-chapter guide.

Part I: Core Python

Chapter 1—Welcome to Python!

We begin by introducing Python to you, its history, features, benefits, and so on, as well as how to obtain and install Python on your system.

Chapter 2—Getting Started

If you are an experienced programmer and just want to see "how it's done" in Python, this is the right place to go. We introduce the basic Python concepts and statements, and because many of these will be familiar to you, you can simply learn the proper syntax in Python and get started right away on your projects without sacrificing too much reading time.

Chapter 3—Syntax and Style

This section gives you a good overview of Python's syntax as well as style hints. You will also be exposed to Python's keywords and its memory management ability.

Your first Python application will be presented at the end of the chapter to give you an idea of what real Python code looks like.

Chapter 4—Python Objects

This chapter introduces Python objects. In addition to generic object attributes, we will show you all of Python's data types and operators, as well as show you different ways to categorize the standard types. Built-in functions that apply to most Python objects will also be covered.

Chapter 5—Numbers

In this chapter, we discuss Python's main numeric types: integers, floating point numbers, and complex numbers. We look at operators and built-in and factory functions which apply to all numbers, and we also briefly discuss a few other related types.

Chapter 6—Sequences: Strings, Lists, and Tuples

Your first meaty chapter will expose you to all of Python's powerful sequence types: strings, lists, and tuples. We will show you all the built-in functions, methods, and special features, which apply to each type as well as all their operators.

Chapter 7—Mapping and Set Types

Dictionaries are Python's mapping or hashing type. Like other data types, dictionaries also have operators and applicable built-in functions and methods. We also cover Python's set types in this chapter, discussing their operators, built-in and factory functions, and built-in methods.

Chapter 8—Conditionals and Loops

Like many other high-level languages, Python supports loops such as `for` and `while`, as well as `if` statements (and related). Python also has a built-in function called `range()` which enables Python's **for** loop to behave more like a traditional counting loop rather than the "foreach" iterative type loop that it is. Also included is coverage of auxiliary statements such as **break**, **continue**, and **pass**, as well as a discussion of newer constructs like iterators, list comprehensions, and generator expressions.

Chapter 9—Files and Input/Output

In addition to standard file objects and input/output, this chapter introduces you to file system access, file execution, and persistent storage.

Chapter 10—Errors and Exceptions

One of Python's most powerful constructs is its exception handling ability. You can see a full treatment of it here, instruction on how to raise or throw exceptions, and more importantly, how to create your own exception classes.

Chapter 11—Functions and Functional Programming

Creating and calling functions are relatively straightforward, but Python has many other features that you will find useful, such as default arguments, named or keyword arguments, variable-length arguments, and some functional programming constructs. We also dip into variable scope and recursion briefly. We will also discuss some advanced features such as generators, decorators, inner functions, closures, and partial function application (a more generalized form of currying).

Chapter 12—Modules

One of Python's key strengths is its ability to be extended. This feature allows for "plug-and-play" access as well as promotes code reuse. Applications written as modules can be imported for use by other Python modules with a single line of code. Furthermore, multiple module software distribution can be simplified by using packages.

Chapter 13—Object-Oriented Programming

Python is a fully object-oriented programming language and was designed that way from the beginning. However, Python does not require you to program in such a manner—you may continue to develop structural/procedural code as you like, and can transition to OO programming anytime you are ready to take advantage of its benefits. Likewise, this chapter is here to guide you through the concepts as well as advanced topics, such as operator overloading, customization, and delegation. Also included is coverage of new features specific to new-style classes, including slots, properties, descriptors, and metaclasses.

Chapter 14—Execution Environment

The term "execution" can mean many different things, from callable and executable objects to running other programs (Python or otherwise). We discuss these topics in this chapter, as well as controlling execution via the operating system interface and different ways of terminating execution.

Part II: Advanced Topics

Chapter 15—Regular Expressions

Regular expressions are a powerful tool used for pattern matching, extracting, and search-and-replace functionality. Learn about them here.

Chapter 16—Network Programming

So many applications today need to be network-oriented. You have to start somewhere. In this chapter, you will learn to create clients and servers, using TCP/IP and UDP/IP, as well as get an introduction to `SocketServer` and Twisted.

Chapter 17—Internet Client Programming

In Chapter 16, we introduced network programming using sockets. Most Internet protocols in use today were developed using sockets. In this chapter, we explore some of these higher-level libraries, which are used to build clients of such Internet protocols. In particular, we focus on FTP, NNTP, SMTP, and POP3 clients.

Chapter 18—Multithreaded Programming

Multithreaded programming is a powerful way to improve the execution performance of many types of application. This chapter ends the drought of written documentation on how to do threads in Python by explaining the concepts and showing you how to correctly build a Python multithreaded application.

Chapter 19—GUI Programming

Based on the Tk graphical toolkit, Tkinter is Python's default GUI development module. We introduce Tkinter to you by showing you how to build simple sample GUI applications (say that ten times, real fast!). One of the best ways to learn is to copy, and by building on top of some of these applications, you will be on your way in no time. We conclude the chapter by presenting a more complex example, as well as take a brief look at Tix, Pmw, wxPython, and PyGTK.

Chapter 20—Web Programming

Web programming using Python takes three main forms: Web clients, Web servers, and the popular Common Gateway Interface applications that help Web servers deliver dynamically-generated Web pages. We will cover them all in this chapter: simple and advanced Web clients and CGI applications, as well as how to build your own Web server.

Chapter 21—Database Programming

What Python does for application programming carries to database programming as well. It is simplified, and you will find it fun! We first review basic database concepts, then introduce you to the Python database application programmer's interface (API). We then show you how you can connect to a relational database and perform queries and operations with Python. Finally, if you want hands-off using the Structured Query Language (SQL) and want to just work with objects without having to worry about the underlying database layer, we will introduce you to a few object-relational managers (ORMs), which simplify database programming to yet another level.

Chapter 22—Extending Python

We mentioned earlier how powerful it is to be able to reuse code and extend the language. In pure Python, these extensions are modules, but you can also develop lower-level code in C, C++, or Java, and interface those with Python in a seamless fashion. Writing your extensions in a lower-level programming language gives you added performance and some security (because the source code does not have to be revealed). This chapter walks you step-by-step through the extension building process.

Chapter 23—Miscellaneous

This new chapter consists of bonus material that we would like to develop into full, individual chapters in the next edition. Topics covered here include Web Services, Microsoft Office (Win32 COM Client) Programming, and Java/Jython.

Optional Sections

Subsections or exercises marked with an asterisk (*) may be skipped due to their advanced or optional nature. They are usually self-contained segments that can be addressed at another time.

Those of you with enough previous programming knowledge and who have set up their Python development environments can skip the first chapter and go straight to Chapter 2, "Getting Started," where you can absorb Python and be off to the races.

Conventions

All program output and source code are in Courier font. Python keywords appear in **Courier-Bold** font. Lines of output with three leading greater than signs, >>>, represent the Python interpreter prompt.

"Core Notes" are highlighted with this logo.

"Core Style" notes are highlighted with this logo.

"Core Module" notes are highlighted with this logo.

"Core Tips" notes are highlighted with this logo.

New features to Python are highlighted with this logo. The version(s) of Python these features first appeared in is given inside the logo.

2.5

Book Resources

I welcome any and all feedback: the good, the bad, and the ugly. If you have any comments, suggestions, kudos, complaints, bugs, questions…anything at all, feel free to contact me at corepython@yahoo.com.

You will find errata source code, updates, upcoming talks, Python training, downloads, and other information at the book's Web site located at:

http://corepython.com

Acknowledgments

Acknowledgments for the Second Edition

Reviewers and Contributors

Shannon -jj Behrens (lead reviewer)
Michael Santos (lead reviewer)
Rick Kwan
Lindell Aldermann (co-author of the new Unicode section in Chapter 6)
Wai-Yip Tung (co-author of the Unicode example in Chapter 20)
Eric Foster-Johnson (co-author of *Beginning Python*)
Alex Martelli (editor of *Python Cookbook* and author of *Python in a Nutshell*)
Larry Rosenstein
Jim Orosz
Krishna Srinivasan
Chuck Kung

Inspiration

My wonderful children and pet hamster.

Production

Mark Taub and Debra Williams-Cauley (Acquisitions Editors)
Lara Wysong (Project Editor)
John Fuller (Managing Editor)
Sam RC (Project Manager at International Typesetting and Composition)

Acknowledgements for the First Edition

Reviewers and Contributors

Guido van Rossum (creator of the Python language)
Dowson Tong
James C. Ahlstrom (co-author of *Internet Programming with Python*)
S. Candelaria de Ram
Cay S. Horstmann (co-author of *Core Java* and *Core JavaServer Faces*)
Michael Santos
Greg Ward (creator of `distutils` package and its documentation)
Vincent C. Rubino
Martijn Faassen
Emile van Sebille
Raymond Tsai
Albert L. Anders (co-author of MT Programming chapter)
Fredrik Lundh (author of *Python Standard Library*)
Cameron Laird
Fred L. Drake, Jr. (co-author of *Python & XML* and editor of the official Python documentation)
Jeremy Hylton
Steve Yoshimoto
Aahz Maruch (author of *Python for Dummies*)
Jeffrey E. F. Friedl (author of *Mastering Regular Expressions*)
Pieter Claerhout
Catriona (Kate) Johnston
David Ascher (co-author of *Learning Python* and editor of *Python Cookbook*)
Reg Charney
Christian Tismer (creator of Stackless Python)
Jason Stillwell
and my students at UC Santa Cruz Extension

Inspiration

James P. Prior (my high school programming teacher)
Louise Moser and P. Michael Melliar-Smith (my graduate thesis advisors at UCSB)
Alan Parsons, Eric Woolfson, Andrew Powell, Ian Bairnson, Stuart Elliott, David Paton, all other Project participants, and fellow Projectologists and Roadkillers (for all the music, support, and good times)

I would also like to thank my family, friends and the Lord above, who have kept me safe and sane during this crazy period of late nights and abandonment. And finally, I would like give a big thanks to all those who believed in me (you know who you are!)—I couldn't have done it without you. Those who didn't ... well, you know what you can do! :-)

Finally, I would like to thank you, my readers, and the Python community at large. I am excited at the prospect of teaching you Python and hope that you enjoy your travels with me, on our second journey.

Wesley J. Chun
Silicon Valley, CA
(It's not as much a place as it is a state of sanity.)
July 2006

Part I

CORE PYTHON

WELCOME TO PYTHON!

Chapter Topics

Chapter 1

Our introductory chapter provides some background on what Python is, where it came from, and what some of its "bullet points" are. Once we have stimulated your interest and enthusiasm, we describe how you can obtain Python and get it up and running on your system. Finally, the exercises at the end of the chapter will make you comfortable with using Python, both in the interactive interpreter and also in creating scripts and executing them.

1.1 What Is Python?

Python is an elegant and robust programming language that delivers both the power and general applicability of traditional compiled languages with the ease of use (and then some) of simpler scripting and interpreted languages. It allows you to get the job done, and then read what you wrote later. You will be amazed at how quickly you will pick up the language as well as what kind of things you can do with Python, not to mention the things that have *already* been done. Your imagination will be the only limit.

1.2 Origins

Work on Python began in late 1989 by Guido van Rossum, then at CWI (Centrum voor Wiskunde en Informatica, the National Research Institute for Mathematics and Computer Science) in the Netherlands. It was eventually released for public distribution in early 1991. How did it all begin? Like C, C++, Lisp, Java, and Perl, Python came from a research background where the programmer was having a hard time getting the job done with the existing tools at hand, and envisioned and developed a better way.

At the time, van Rossum was a researcher with considerable language design experience with the interpreted language ABC, also developed at CWI, but he was unsatisfied with its ability to be developed into something more. Having used and partially developed a higher-level language like ABC, falling back to C was not an attractive possibility. Some of the tools he envisioned were for performing general system administration tasks, so he also wanted access to the power of system calls that were available through the Amoeba distributed operating system. Although van Rossum gave some thought to an Amoeba-specific language, a generalized language made more sense, and late in 1989, the seeds of Python were sown.

1.3 Features

Although it has been around for well over fifteen years, some feel that Python is still relatively new to the general software development industry. We should, however, use caution with our use of the word "relatively," as a few years seem like decades when developing on "Internet time."

When people ask, "What is Python?" it is difficult to say any one thing. The tendency is to want to blurt out all the things that you feel Python is in one breath. Python is   (fill-in-the-blanks here) . Just what are some of those features? For your sanity, we will elucidate each here . . . one at a time.

1.3.1 High Level

It seems that with every generation of languages, we move to a higher level. Assembly was a godsend for those who struggled with machine code, then came FORTRAN, C, and Pascal, which took computing to another plane and created the software development industry. Through C came more modern compiled languages, C++ and Java. And further still we climb, with powerful, system-accessible, interpreted scripting languages like Tcl, Perl, and Python.

Each of these languages has higher-level data structures that reduce the "framework" development time that was once required. Useful types like Python's lists (resizeable arrays) and dictionaries (hash tables) are built into the language. Providing these crucial building blocks in the core language encourages their use and minimizes development time as well as code size, resulting in more readable code.

Because there is no one standard library for heterogeneous arrays (lists in Python) and hash tables (Python dictionaries or "dicts" for short) in C, they are often reimplemented and copied to each new project. This process is messy and error prone. C++ improves the situation with the standard template library, but the STL can hardly compare to the simplicity and readability of Python's built-in lists and dicts.

1.3.2 Object Oriented

Object-oriented programming (OOP) adds another dimension to structured and procedural languages where data and logic are discrete elements of programming. OOP allows for associating specific behaviors, characteristics, and/or capabilities with the data that they execute on or are representative of. Python is an object-oriented (OO) language, all the way down to its core. However, Python is not *just* an OO language like Java or Ruby. It is actually a pleasant mix of multiple programming paradigms. For instance, it even borrows a few things from functional languages like Lisp and Haskell.

1.3.3 Scalable

Python is often compared to batch or Unix shell scripting languages. Simple shell scripts handle simple tasks. They may grow (indefinitely) in length, but not truly in depth. There is little code-reusability and you are confined to small projects with shell scripts. In fact, even small projects may lead to large and unwieldy scripts. Not so with Python, where you can grow your code from project to project, add other new or existing Python elements, and reuse code at your whim. Python encourages clean code design, high-level structure, and "packaging" of multiple components, all of which deliver the flexibility, consistency, and faster development time required as projects expand in breadth and scope.

The term "scalable" is most often applied to measuring hardware throughput and usually refers to additional performance when new hardware is added to a system. We would like to differentiate this comparison with ours here, which tries to reflect the notion that Python provides basic building blocks on which you can build an application, and as those needs expand and grow, Python's pluggable and modular architecture allows your project to flourish as well as maintain manageability.

1.3.4 Extensible

As the amount of Python code increases in your project, you will still be able to organize it logically by separating your code into multiple files, or modules, and be able to access code from one module and attributes from another. And what is even better is that Python's syntax for accessing modules is the same for all modules, whether you access one from the Python standard library, one you created just a minute ago, or even an extension you wrote in another language! Using this feature, you feel like you have just "extended" the language for your own needs, and you actually *have*.

The most critical portions of code, perhaps those hotspots that always show up in the profiler or areas where performance is absolutely required, are candidates for being rewritten as a Python extension written in C. But again, the interface is exactly the same as for pure Python modules. Access to code and objects occurs in exactly the same way without any code modification whatsoever. The only thing different about the code now is that you should notice an improvement in performance. Naturally, it all depends on your application and how resource-intensive it is. There are times where it is absolutely advantageous to convert application bottlenecks to compiled code because it will decidedly improve overall performance.

This type of extensibility in a language provides engineers with the flexibility to add-on or customize their tools to be more productive, and to develop in a shorter period of time. Although this feature is self-evident in mainstream third-generation languages (3GLs) such as C, C++, and even Java, the ease of writing extensions to Python in C is a real strength of Python. Furthermore, tools like PyRex, which understands a mix of C and Python, make writing extensions even easier as they compile everything to C for you.

Python extensions can be written in C and C++ for the standard implementation of Python in C (also known as CPython). The Java language implementation of Python is called Jython, so extensions would be written using Java. Finally, there is IronPython, the C# implementation for the .NET or Mono platforms. You can extend IronPython in C# or Visual Basic.NET.

1.3.5 Portable

Python can be found on a wide variety of systems, contributing to its continued rapid growth in today's computing domain. Because Python is written in C, and because of C's portability, Python is available on practically every type of platform that has an ANSI C compiler. Although there are some platform-specific modules, any general Python application written on one system will run with little or no modification on another. Portability applies across multiple architectures as well as operating systems.

1.3.6 Easy to Learn

Python has relatively few keywords, simple structure, and a clearly defined syntax. This allows the student to pick up the language in a relatively short period of time. What may perhaps be new to beginners is the OO nature of Python. Those who are not fully versed in the ways of OOP may be apprehensive about jumping straight into Python, but OOP is neither necessary nor mandatory. Getting started is easy, and you can pick up OOP and use when you are ready to.

1.3.7 Easy to Read

Conspicuously absent from the Python syntax are the usual mandatory symbols found in other languages for accessing variables, code block definition, and pattern-matching. These include dollar signs ($), semicolons (;), tildes (~), and so on. Without all these distractions, Python code is much more clearly defined and visible to the eye. In addition, much to many programmers' dismay (and relief), Python does not give as much flexibility to write obfuscated code compared to other languages, making it easier for others to understand your code faster and vice versa. Readability usually helps make a language easy to learn, as we described above. We would even venture to claim that Python code is fairly understandable even to a reader who has never seen a single line of Python before. Take a look at the examples in the next chapter, "Getting Started," and let us know how well you fare.

1.3.8 Easy to Maintain

Maintaining source code is part of the software development lifecycle. Your software usually continues to evolve until it is replaced or obsoleted. Quite often it lasts longer than a programmer's stay at a company. Much of Python's success is that source code is fairly easy to maintain, dependent, of course, on size and complexity. However, this conclusion is not difficult to draw given that Python is easy to learn and easy to read. Another motivating advantage of Python is that upon reviewing a script you wrote six months ago, you are less likely to get lost or pull out a reference book to get reacquainted with your software.

1.3.9 Robust

Nothing is more powerful than allowing a programmer to recognize error conditions and provide a software handler when such errors occur. Python provides "safe and sane" exits on errors, allowing the programmer to be in the driver's seat. When your Python crashes due to errors, the interpreter dumps out a "stack trace" full of useful information such as why your program crashed and where in the code (file name, line number, function call, etc.) the error took place. These errors are known as exceptions. Python even gives you the ability to monitor for errors and take an evasive course of action if such an error does occur during runtime.

These exception handlers can take steps such as defusing the problem, redirecting program flow, perform cleanup or maintenance measures, shutting down the application gracefully, or just ignoring it. In any case, the debugging part of the development cycle is reduced considerably. Python's robustness is beneficial for both the software designer and the user. There is also some accountability when certain errors occur that are not handled properly. The stack trace that is generated as a result of an error reveals not only the type and location of the error, but also in which module the erroneous code resides.

1.3.10 Effective as a Rapid Prototyping Tool

We've mentioned before how Python is easy to learn and easy to read. But, you say, so is a language like BASIC. What more can Python do? Unlike self-contained and less flexible languages, Python has so many different interfaces to other systems that it is powerful enough in features and robust enough that entire systems can be prototyped completely in Python. Obviously, the same systems can be completed in traditional compiled languages, but Python's simplicity of engineering allows us to do the same thing and still be home in time for supper. Also, numerous external libraries have already been developed for Python, so whatever your application is, someone may have traveled down that road before. All you need to do is "plug-and-play" (some assembly required, as usual). There are Python modules and packages that can do practically anything and everything you can imagine. The Python Standard Library is fairly complete, and if you cannot find what you need there, chances are there is a third-party module or package that can do the job.

1.3.11 A Memory Manager

The biggest pitfall with programming in C or C++ is that the responsibility of memory management is in the hands of the developer. Even if the application has very little to do with memory access, memory modification, and memory management, the programmer must still perform those duties, in addition to the original task at hand. This places an unnecessary burden and responsibility upon the developer and often provides an extended distraction.

Because memory management is performed by the Python interpreter, the application developer is able to steer clear of memory issues and focus on the immediate goal of just creating the application that was planned in the first place. This leads to fewer bugs, a more robust application, and shorter overall development time.

1.3.12 Interpreted and (Byte-) Compiled

Python is classified as an interpreted language, meaning that compile-time is no longer a factor during development. Traditionally, purely interpreted languages are almost always slower than compiled languages because execution does not take place in a system's native binary language. However, like Java, Python is actually byte-compiled, resulting in an intermediate form closer to machine language. This improves Python's performance, yet allows it to retain all the advantages of interpreted languages.

CORE NOTE: File extensions

Python source files typically end with the .py *extension. The source is byte-compiled upon being loaded by the interpreter or by being byte-compiled explicitly. Depending on how you invoke the interpreter, it may leave behind byte-compiled files with a* .pyc *or* .pyo *extension. You can find out more about file extensions in Chapter 12, "Modules."*

1.4 Downloading and Installing Python

The most obvious place to get all Python-related software is at the main Web site at http://python.org. For your convenience, you can also go to the book's Web site at http://corepython.com and click on the "Install Python" link to the left—we have organized a grid with most contemporary versions of Python for the most platforms, with a focus, of course, on the "Big Three." Unix, Win 32, MacOS X.

As we alluded to earlier in Section 1.3.5, Python is available on a wide variety of platforms. They can be broken down into these basic categories and available platforms:

- All Unix flavors (Linux, MacOS X, Solaris, FreeBSD, etc.)
- Win32 (Windows NT, 2000, XP, etc.)
- Older platforms: MacOS 8/9, Windows 3.x, DOS, OS/2, AIX
- Handhelds (PDAs/phones): Nokia Series 60/SymbianOS, Windows CE/Pocket PC, Sharp Zaurus/arm-linux, PalmOS
- Gaming consoles: Sony PS2, PSP; Nintendo GameCube
- Real-Time platforms: VxWorks, QNX
- Alternative implementations: Jython, IronPython, stackless
- Others

The most recent versions of Python will likely be found only on "the Big Three." In fact, current versions of Linux and MacOS X already come with Python installed—you'll have to check to see which Python release it is. Other versions will be older 2.x releases while some have yet to progress beyond 1.5. Some come with binaries to install directly while others require you to build Python manually before installation.

Unix (Linux, MacOS X, Solaris, *BSD, etc.)

As mentioned above, your Unix-based system may already have Python installed. The best way to check is to run Python from the command line and see if it is both in your path and available. Just type:

```
myMac:~ wesley$ python
Python 2.4 (#4, Mar 19 2005, 03:25:10)
[GCC 3.3 20030304 (Apple Computer, Inc. build 1671)] on darwin
Type "help", "copyright", "credits" or "license" for more information.
">>>"
```

If starting Python fails, it doesn't mean it's not installed, just that it's not in your path. Hunt around for it, and if you're unsuccessful, try building it manually, which isn't very difficult (see "Build It Yourself" on the next page). If you're using certain versions of Linux, you can get the binary or source RPMs.

Windows/DOS

Download the `.msi` file from python.org or corepython.com as described previously (i.e., `python-2.5.msi`) and execute it to install Python. If you are planning on doing any kind of Win32 development, such as with COM, MFC, or need any of the Win32 libraries, we also strongly suggest that you download and install the Python for Windows Extensions. You can then run Python from a DOS command window or via one of the IDEs, IDLE, the default Python IDE, or PythonWin, the IDE that comes with the Windows Extensions distribution.

Build It Yourself

For most other platforms, download the `.tgz` file,. extract the files, and go to the main directory. Build Python by performing the following:

1. `./configure`
2. `make`
3. `make install`

Python is usually installed in a standard location so you can find it rather easily. It has become quite commonplace for systems today to have multiple versions of Python installed. While it is easy to find the binary executable, you also have to deal with where the libraries are installed.

On Unix machines, the executable is usually installed in `/usr/local/bin` while the libraries are in `/usr/local/lib/python2.x` where the `2.x` is the version of Python you are using. For MacOS X, Python is installed in `/sw/bin` and/or `/usr/local/bin`, and the libraries are in `/sw/lib`, `/usr/local /lib`, and/or `/Library/Frameworks/Python.framework/Versions`.

On Windows, the default installation area is `C:\Python2x`. Try to avoid installing Python in `C:\Program Files`. Yes, we know it's the general place to put installed programs, but DOS does not support those types of long names; it is usually aliased as `Progra~1`. This may also lead to problems running some programs, so it's best to avoid it. So, let's say you installed Python in `C:\Python`, then the standard library files are typically installed in `C:\Python\Lib`.

1.5 Running Python

There are three different ways to start Python. The simplest way is by starting the interpreter interactively, entering one line of Python at a time for execution. Another way to start Python is by running a script written in Python. This is accomplished by invoking the interpreter on your script application. Finally, you can run from a graphical user interface (GUI) from within an integrated development environment (IDE). IDEs typically feature additional tools such as an integrated debugger, text editor, and support for a wide range of source code control tools such as CVS.

1.5.1 Interactive Interpreter from the Command Line

You can enter Python and start coding right away in the interactive interpreter by starting it from the command line. You can do this from Unix, DOS, or any other system that provides you a command-line interpreter or shell window. One of the best ways to start learning Python is to run the interpreter interactively. Interactive mode is also very useful later on when you want to experiment with specific features of Python.

Unix (Linux, MacOS X, Solaris, *BSD, etc.)

To access Python, you will need to type in the full pathname to its location unless you have added the directory where Python resides to your search path. Common places where Python is installed include `/usr/bin` and `/usr/local/bin`.

We recommend that you add Python (i.e., the executable file `python`, or `jpython` if you wish to use the Java version of the interpreter) to your search path because you do not want to have to type in the full pathname every time you wish to run interactively. Once this is accomplished, you can start the interpreter with just its name.

To add Python to your search path, simply check your login startup scripts and look for a set of directories given to the `set path` or `PATH=` directive. Adding the full path to where your Python interpreter is located is all you have to do, followed by refreshing your shell's path variable. Now at the Unix prompt (`%` or `$`, depending on your shell), you can start the interpreter just by invoking the name `python` (or `jpython`), as in the following.

```
$ python
```

Once Python has started, you'll see the interpreter startup message indicating version and platform and be given the interpreter prompt ">>>" to enter Python commands. Figure 1–1 is a screen shot of what it looks like when you start Python in a Unix (MacOS X) environment.

Windows/DOS

To add Python to your search path, you need to edit the `C:\autoexec.bat` file and add the full path to where your interpreter is installed. It is usually either `C:\Python` or `C:\Program Files \Python` (or its short DOS name

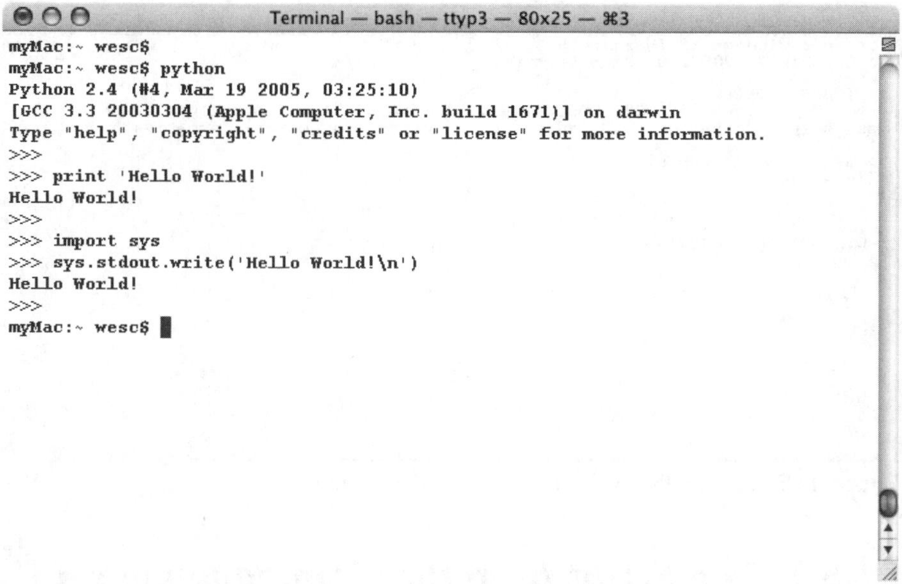

```
  ○ ○ ○              Terminal — bash — ttyp3 — 80x25 — ⌘3
myMac:~ wesc$
myMac:~ wesc$ python
Python 2.4 (#4, Mar 19 2005, 03:25:10)
[GCC 3.3 20030304 (Apple Computer, Inc. build 1671)] on darwin
Type "help", "copyright", "credits" or "license" for more information.
>>>
>>> print 'Hello World!'
Hello World!
>>>
>>> import sys
>>> sys.stdout.write('Hello World!\n')
Hello World!
>>>
myMac:~ wesc$ ▮
```

Figure 1–1 Starting Python in a Unix (MacOS X) window

equivalent `C:\Progra~1\Python`). From a DOS window (either really running in DOS or started from Windows), the command to start Python is the same as Unix, `python` (see Figure 1–2). The only difference is the prompt, which is `C:\>`.

```
    C:\> python
```

Command-Line Options

When starting Python from the command-line, additional options may be provided to the interpreter. Here are some of the options to choose from:

`-d`	Provide debug output
`-O`	Generate optimized bytecode (resulting in `.pyo` files)
`-S`	Do not run importsite to look for Python paths on startup
`-v`	Verbose output (detailed trace on **import** statements)
`-m mod`	run (library) `module` as a script
`-Q opt`	division `options` (see documentation)
`-c cmd`	Run Python script sent in as `cmd` string
`file`	Run Python script from given file (see later)

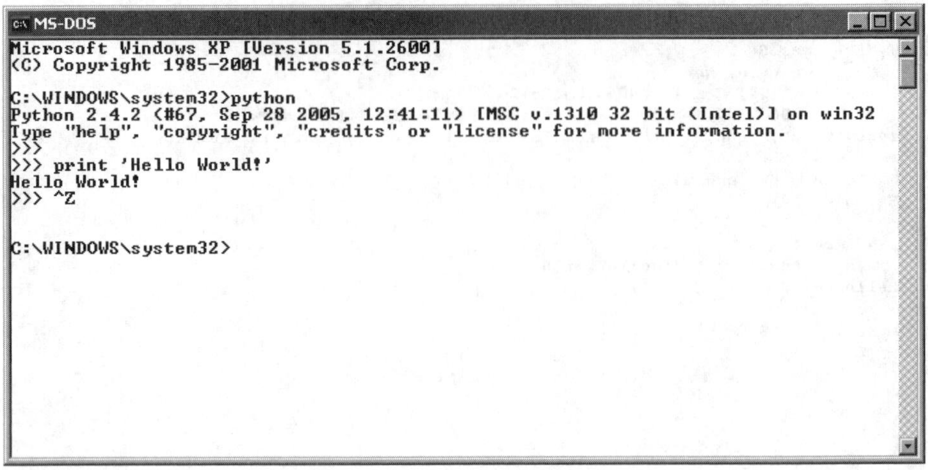

```
c:\ MS-DOS                                                          _ □ X
Microsoft Windows XP [Version 5.1.2600]
(C) Copyright 1985-2001 Microsoft Corp.

C:\WINDOWS\system32>python
Python 2.4.2 (#67, Sep 28 2005, 12:41:11) [MSC v.1310 32 bit (Intel)] on win32
Type "help", "copyright", "credits" or "license" for more information.
>>>
>>> print 'Hello World!'
Hello World!
>>> ^Z

C:\WINDOWS\system32>
```

Figure 1-2 Starting Python in a DOS/command window

1.5.2 As a Script from the Command Line

Unix (Linux, MacOS X, Solaris, *BSD, etc.)

From any flavor of Unix, a Python script can be executed by invoking the interpreter on your application from the command line, as in the following:

```
$ python script.py
```

Python scripts end with a file extension of .py, as indicated above.

It is also possible in Unix to automatically launch the Python interpreter without explicitly invoking it by name from the command line. If you are using any Unix-flavored system, you can use the shell-launching ("sh-bang") first line of your program:

```
#!/usr/local/bin/python
```

The file path, the part that follows the #!, is the full path location of the Python interpreter. As we mentioned before, it is usually installed in /usr/ local/bin or /usr/bin. If not, be sure to get the exact pathname correct so that you can run your Python scripts. Pathnames that are not correct will result in the familiar Command not found error message.

As a preferred alternative, many Unix systems have a command named env, installed in either /bin or /usr/bin, which will look for the Python interpreter in your path. If you have env, your startup line can be changed to something like this:

```
#!/usr/bin/env python
```

or, if your `env` is located in `/bin`,

```
#!/bin/env python
```

`env` is useful when you either do not know exactly where the Python executable is located, or if it changes location often, yet still remains available via your directory path. Once you add the proper startup directive to the beginning of your script, it becomes directly executable, and when invoked, loads the Python interpreter first, then runs your script. As we mentioned before, Python no longer has to be invoked explicitly from the command. You only need the script name:

```
$ script.py
```

Be sure the file permission mode allows execution first. There should be an 'rwx' permissions getting for the user in the long listing of your file. Check with your system administrator if you require help in finding where Python is installed or if you need help with file permissions or the `chmod` (CHange MODe) command.

Windows/DOS

The DOS command window does not support the auto-launching mechanism; however, at least with WinXP, it is able to do the same thing as Windows: it uses the "file type" interface. This interface allows Windows to recognize file types based on extension names and to invoke a program to handle files of predetermined types. For example, if you install Python with PythonWin, double-clicking on a Python script with the `.py` extension will invoke Python or PythonWin IDE (if you have it installed) to run your script. Thus, running the following will have the same effect as double-clicking on it:

```
C:\> script.py
```

So now both Unix-based and Win32 systems can launch Python scripts without naming Python on the command line, but you can always fall back on it if just calling the script leads to an error like "command is not recognized."

1.5.3 In an Integrated Development Environment

You can run Python from a graphical user interface (GUI) environment as well. All you need is a GUI application on your system that supports Python. If you have found one, chances are that it is also an IDE (integrated development environment). IDEs are more than just graphical interfaces. They typically have source code editors and trace and debugging facilities.

Unix (Linux, MacOS X, Solaris, *BSD, etc.)

IDLE is the very first Unix IDE for Python. It was also developed by Guido van Rossum and made its debut in Python 1.5.2. IDLE stands for IDE with a raised "L," as in Integrated DeveLopment Environment. Suspiciously, IDLE also happens to be the name of a Monty Python troupe member. Hmmm. . . . IDLE is Tkinter-based, thus requiring you to have Tcl/Tk installed on your system. Current distributions of Python include a minimal subset of the Tcl/Tk library so that a full install is no longer required.

Also, if Python was automatically installed on your system or if you have a Python RPM, chances are it does not include IDLE or Tkinter, so look for both before trying to run IDLE. (There is actually a separate Tkinter RPM that you can download along with the Python one if you want it.) If you build Python yourself and Tk libraries are available, then Tkinter will be automatically built along with Python, and both Tkinter and IDLE will be installed when Python is.

If you want to run IDLE, you will find it where your standard library is installed: `/usr/local/lib/python2.x/idlelib/idle.py`. If you build and install Python yourself, you may find a shortcut script called `idle` in `/usr/local/bin` allowing you to just launch IDLE from your shell command-line prompt. A screen shot of IDLE in Unix appears in Figure 1–3.

MacOS X is very Unix-like (based on the Mach kernel with BSD services). Python is now compiled for MacOS X with the traditional Unix build tools. The MacOS X distributions come with a compiled Python interpreter; however, none of the special Mac-oriented tools (i.e., GNU readline, IDE, etc.) are installed. The same applies for Tkinter and IDLE.

You tend to go download and build your own, but be careful: sometimes it is tricky to decouple your new Python install from the Apple factory version. Do your research carefully first. You can also get Python for MacOS X from Fink/FinkCommander and DarwinPorts:

> http://fink.sourceforge.net/
> http://darwinports.org

For the most up-to-date Mac stuff and information for Python, visit:

> http://undefined.org/python
> http://pythonmac.org/packages

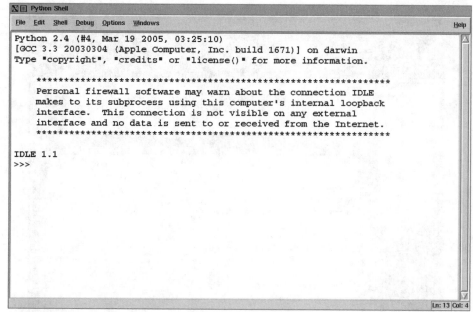

```
Python Shell

File  Edit  Shell  Debug  Options  Windows                                    Help

Python 2.4 (#4, Mar 19 2005, 03:25:10)
[GCC 3.3 20030304 (Apple Computer, Inc. build 1671)] on darwin
Type "copyright", "credits" or "license()" for more information.

        ********************************************************************
        Personal firewall software may warn about the connection IDLE
        makes to its subprocess using this computer's internal loopback
        interface.  This connection is not visible on any external
        interface and no data is sent to or received from the Internet.
        ********************************************************************

IDLE 1.1
>>>



                                                                    Ln: 13 Col: 4
```

Figure 1–3   Starting IDLE in Unix

Another option would be to download a MacOS X Universal binary from the Python Web site. This disk image (DMG) file requires at least version 10.3.9 and will run on both PowerPC- and Intel-based Macs.

Windows

PythonWin is the first Windows interface for Python and is an IDE with a GUI. Included with the PythonWin distribution are Windows API, and COM (Component Object Model, a.k.a. OLE [Object Linking and Embedding] and ActiveX) extensions. PythonWin itself was written to the MFC (Microsoft Foundation Class) libraries, and it can be used as a development environment to create your own Windows applications. You can download and install it from the Web sites shown on the next page.

PythonWin is usually installed in the same directory as Python, in its own subdirectory, `C:\Python2x\Lib\site-packages\pythonwin` as the executable `pythonwin.exe`. PythonWin features a color editor, a new and improved debugger, interactive shell window, COM extensions, and more. A screen snapshot of the PythonWin IDE running on a Windows machine appears in Figure 1–4.

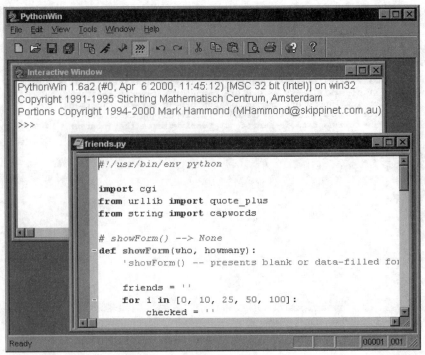

Figure 1–4 PythonWin environment in Windows

You can find out more about PythonWin and the Python for Windows Extensions (also known as "win32all") at the following locations organized by Mark Hammond:

http://starship.python.net/crew/mhammond/win32/
http://sourceforge.net/projects/pywin32/

IDLE is also available on the Windows platform, due to the portability of Tcl/Tk and Python/Tkinter. It looks similar to its Unix counterpart (Figure 1–5).

From Windows, IDLE can be found in the `Lib\idlelib` subdirectory where your Python interpreter is found, usually `C:\Python2x`. To start IDLE from a DOS command window, invoke `idle.py`. You can also invoke `idle.py` from a Windows environment, but that starts an unnecessary DOS window. Instead, double-click on `idle.pyw`. Files ending in `.pyw` will not open a DOS command window to run the script in. In fact, your author just creates a shortcut to `C:\Python2x\Lib\idlelib\idle.pyw` on the desktop that can be double-clicked . . . simple!

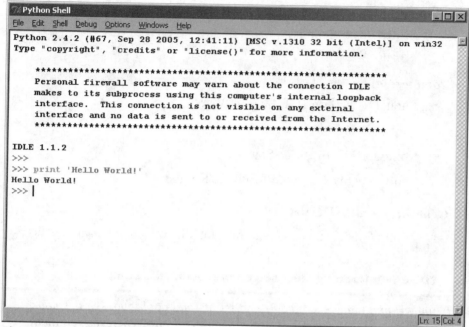

Python Shell

File   Edit   Shell   Debug   Options   Windows   Help

```
Python 2.4.2 (#67, Sep 28 2005, 12:41:11) [MSC v.1310 32 bit (Intel)] on win32
Type "copyright", "credits" or "license()" for more information.

    ************************************************************
    Personal firewall software may warn about the connection IDLE
    makes to its subprocess using this computer's internal loopback
    interface.   This connection is not visible on any external
    interface and no data is sent to or received from the Internet.
    ************************************************************

IDLE 1.1.2
>>>
>>> print 'Hello World!'
Hello World!
>>> |
```

Ln: 15 Col: 4

Figure 1–5   Starting IDLE in Windows

1.5.4 Other IDEs and Execution Environments

Many software professionals actually prefer to code in their favorite text editor such as vi(m) or emacs. In addition to these and the IDEs mentioned in the previous section, there are good number of Open Source and commercial IDEs as well. Here is a short list:

Open Source
- IDLE (comes with Python distribution)

     http://python.org/idle/

- PythonWin + Win32 Extensions

     http://starship.python.net/crew/skippy/win32

- IPython (enhanced Interactive Python)

     http://ipython.scipy.org

- IDE Studio (IDLE+more)

     http://starship.python.net/crew/mike/Idle

- Eclipse

    http://pydev.sf.net
    http://eclipse.org/

Commercial

- WingIDE Python IDE by WingWare

    http://wingware.com/

- Komodo IDE by ActiveState

    http://activestate.com/Products/Komodo

General overall IDE list

    http://wiki.python.org/moin/IntegratedDevelopmentEnvironments

CORE TIP: Running the code examples in this book

You will find many example Python scripts and applications in this book, which can be downloaded from the book's Web site. When you run them, however, bear in mind that they were designed to execute either from the command line (DOS command window or Unix shell) or from an IDE. If you are using a Win32 system and double-click on a Python program, a DOS window opens up but closes when the script completes, so you may miss all of the output. If you encounter this situation, just open up a DOS window normally and run it from the command line or execute the script in an IDE instead. Alternatively, you can add a `raw_input()` *line at the bottom, which keeps the window alive until you press the RETURN key.*

1.6 Python Documentation

Python documentation can be found in numerous places. The fastest way to get to it is by viewing the online docs at the Python Web page. If you are not online and use a Win32 system, an offline compressed help file is located at `C:\Python2x\Doc\Python2x.chm`. It uses an Internet Explorer (IE) interface so that you are actually using a Web browser to view the docs. Other offline options include Adobe Portable Document Format (PDF) or PostScript (PS) files in Letter and A4 sizes. Finally, if you download the Python distribution, you will get the LaTeX source.

At the book's Web site, we created a page with a grid that has links to the docs for most versions of Python. Just visit http://corepython.com and click on "Documentation" to the left.

1.7 Comparing Python

Python has been compared with many languages. One reason is that it provides many features found in other languages. Another reason is that Python itself is derived from many other languages, including ABC, Modula-3, C, C++, Algol-68, SmallTalk, and Unix shell and other scripting languages, to name a few. Python is a virtual "greatest hits": van Rossum combined the features he admired most in the other languages he had studied and brought them together for our programming sanity.

However, more often than not, since Python is an interpreted language, you will find that most of the comparisons are with Perl, Java, Tcl, and JavaScript. Perl is another scripting language that goes well beyond the realm of the standard shell scripts. Like Python, Perl gives you the power of a full programming language as well as system call access.

Perl's greatest strength is in its string pattern matching ability, providing an extremely powerful regular expression matching engine. This has pushed Perl to become the de facto language for string text stream filtering, recognition, and extraction, and it is still the most popular language for developing Internet applications through Web servers' Common Gateway Interface (CGI). Python's regular expression engine is based significantly on Perl's.

However, Perl's obscure and overly symbolic syntax is much more difficult to decipher, resulting in a steep learning curve that inhibits the beginner, frustrating those for whom grasping concepts is impeded by semantics. This, coupled with Perl's "feature" of providing many ways of accomplishing the same task, introduces inconsistency and factionization of developers. Finally, all too often the reference book is required reading to decipher a Perl script that was written just a couple of months back.

Python is often compared to Java because of their similar OO nature and syntax. Java's syntax, although much simpler than C++'s, can still be fairly cumbersome, especially if you want to perform just a small task. Python's simplicity offers a much more rapid development environment than using just pure Java. One major evolution in Python's relationship with Java is the development of Jython, a Python interpreter written completely in Java. It is now possible to run Python programs with only the presence of a Java VM (virtual machine). We will mention more of

Jython's advantages briefly in the following section, but for now we can tell you that in the Jython scripting environment, you can manipulate Java objects, Java can interact with Python objects, and you have access to your normal Java class libraries as if Java has always been part of the Python environment.

Python is now often compared to Ruby as well, due to the popularity of the Rails project. As we mentioned above, Python is a wider mix of multiple programming paradigms. It is not purely OO like Ruby and does not have Smalltalk-like blocks, perhaps Ruby's most distinguishable feature. Python does have a byte-code interpreter, where Ruby does not. Python is perhaps more readable, as Ruby can really be thought of as more of an OO Perl. With regard to Rails, Python has several own Web application frameworks, such as Django and Turbogears, to name two.

Tcl is another scripting language that shares similarities shares Python. Tcl is one of the first truly easy-to-use scripting languages to provide the programmer extensibility as well as system call access. Tcl is still popular today and perhaps somewhat more restrictive (due to its limited types) than Python, but it shares Python's ability to extend past its original design. More importantly, Tcl is often used with its graphical toolkit partner, Tk, in developing graphical user interface (GUI) applications. Due to its popularity, Tk has been ported to Perl (Perl/Tk) and Python (Tkinter). Also, it can be argued that Python's classes, modules, and packages make writing large programs in Python more pleasant than writing them in Tcl.

Python has some light functional programming (FP) constructs, which likens it to languages such as Lisp or Scheme. Although Python cannot be considered a traditional functional language, it continues to borrow features from languages such as Lisp and Haskell. For instance, list comprehensions were a welcome addition from the Haskell world, and Lisp programmers will feel at home with `lambda`, `map`, `filter`, and `reduce`.

JavaScript is another OO language very similar to Python. Any proficient JavaScript programmer will have little or no difficulty learning Python. The particularly astute reader will note that JavaScript is based on a prototype system, whereas Python follows a more traditional OO system that differentiates objects and classes.

Here is a list of some Web pages that have information on comparing or transitioning between Python and other languages:

Perl

http://www2.linuxjournal.com/article/3882
http://llama.med.harvard.edu/~fgibbons/PerlPythonPhrasebook.html

http://aplawrence.com/Unixart/pythonvsperl.html
http://pleac.sf.net/pleac_python
http://www.garshol.priv.no/download/text/perl.html

Java

http://dirtsimple.org/2004/12/python-is-not-java.html
http://twistedmatrix.com/users/glyph/rant/python-vs-java.html
http://netpub.cstudies.ubc.ca/oleary/python/python_java_comparison.php

Lisp

http://strout.net/python/pythonvslisp.html
http://norvig.com/python-lisp.html

Ruby

http://blog.ianbicking.org/ruby-python-power.html
http://www.rexx.com/~oinkoink/Ruby_v_Python.html
http://dev.rubycentral.com/faq/rubyfaq-2.html

Perl, C++

http://strombergers.com/python/

Perl, Java, C++

http://furryland.org/~mikec/bench/

C++, Java, Ruby

http://dmh2000.com/cjpr

Perl, Java, PHP, Tcl

http://www-128.ibm.com/developerworks/linux/library/l-python101.html
http://www-128.ibm.com/developerworks/linux/library/l-script-survey/

C, C++, Java, Perl, Rexx, Tcl

http://www.ubka.uni-karlsruhe.de/indexer-vvv/ira/2000/5

You can access a number of other comparisons between Python and other
languages at:

http://www.python.org/doc/Comparisons.html

1.8 Other Implementations

The "standard" version of Python is C-compiled, aka CPython. There are a few other Python implementations. We will describe some here, but for more on the various Python implementations out there, check out:

http://python.org/dev/implementations.html

Java

As we mentioned in the previous section, a Python interpreter completely written in Java, called Jython, is currently available. Although there are still minor differences between the two interpreters, they are very similar and provide a comparable startup environment.

What are the advantages of Jython? Jython . . .

- Can run anywhere a Java virtual machine (JVM) can be found
- Provides access to Java packages and class libraries
- Furnishes a scripting environment for Java development
- Enables ease of testing for Java class libraries
- Offers access to Java's native exception handling ability
- Delivers JavaBeans property and introspection ability
- Encourages Python-to-Java development (and vice versa)
- Gives GUI developers access to Java AWT/Swing libraries
- Utilizes Java's native garbage collector (so CPython's was not implemented)

A full treatment of Jython is beyond the scope of this text, but there is a good amount of information online. Jython is still an ongoing development project, so keep an eye out for new features. You can get more information at the Jython Web site at:

http://jython.org

.NET/Mono

There is now a Python implementation completely in C#, called IronPython. It is targeted at the .NET and Mono environments. You can integrate an IronPython interpreter in a .NET application that can interact with .NET objects. Extensions to IronPython can be implemented in C# or VisualBasic.NET. In addition, there is another .NET/Mono language that is Python-inspired, and it is called Boo. You can find out more information about IronPython and Boo at:

http://codeplex.com/Wiki/View.aspx?ProjectName=IronPython
http://boo.codehaus.org/

Stackless

One of the limitations of CPython is that for each Python function call, it results in a C function call. (For the computer science–oriented, we are talking about stack frames here.) This implies restrictions on CPython, most notably a limitation on the total number of concurrent function calls. This can make it difficult to implement effective user-level threading libraries or highly recursive applications in Python. If this total is exceeded, then your program will crash. By using a "stackless" implementation, you are freed from this restriction and can have any number of Python stack frames for the one C stack frame. This allows you to have many function calls and supports a very large number of threads. The main stackless implementation of Python is called . . . Stackless (surprise!).

The only problem with Stackless is that it requires significant changes to the existing CPython interpreter, so it is seen as an independent fork. Another project called Greenlets that also supports microthreads is available as a standard C extension and can be used with an unmodified version of Python. You can read about both of these projects at:

http://stackless.com
http://codespeak.net/py/current/doc/greenlet.html

1.9 Exercises

1–1. *Python Installation*. Check if Python is installed on your system. If not, download and install it!

1–2. *Executing Python*. How many different ways are there to run Python? Which do you prefer and why?

1–3. *Python Standard Library*.
  (a) Find where the Python executables and standard library modules are installed on your system.
  (b) Take a look at some of the standard library files, for example, `string.py`. It will help you get acclimated to looking at Python scripts.

1–4. *Interactive Execution*. Start your Python interactive interpreter. You can invoke it by typing in its full pathname or just its name (`python` or `python.exe`) if you have installed its location in your search path. (You can use any version or implementation of Python that is convenient to you, e.g., command line, GUI/IDE, Jython, IronPython, or Stackless.) The startup screen should look like the ones depicted in this chapter. When you see the >>>, that means the interpreter is ready to accept your Python commands.

Try entering the command for the famous Hello World! program by typing **print** 'Hello World!' (and press RETURN), then exit the interpreter. On Unix systems, ^D will send the EOF signal to terminate the Python interpreter, and on DOS systems, the keypress is ^Z. Exiting from windows in graphical user environments like the Macintosh, PythonWin or IDLE on Windows, or IDLE on Unix can be accomplished by simply closing their respective windows.

1–5. *Scripting*. As a follow-up to Exercise 1–4, create "Hello World!" as a Python script that does exactly the same thing as the interactive exercise above. If you are using the Unix system, try setting up the automatic startup line so that you can run the program without invoking the Python interpreter.

1–6. *Scripting*. Create a script that displays your name, age, favorite color, and a bit about you (background, interests, hobbies, etc.) to the screen using the **print** statement.

GETTING STARTED

Chapter Topics

- Introduction
- Input/Output
- Comments
- Operators
- Variables and Assignment
- Python Types
- Indentation
- Loops and Conditionals
- Files
- Errors
- Functions
- Classes
- Modules

Chapter 2

This "quick start" section is intended to "flash" Python to you so that any constructs recognized from previous programming experience can be used for your immediate needs. The details will be spelled out in succeeding chapters, but a high-level tour is one fast and easy way to get you into Python and show you what it has to offer. The best way to follow along is to bring up the Python interpreter in front of you and try some of these examples, and at the same time you can experiment on your own.

We introduced how to start up the Python interpreter in Chapter 1 as well as in the exercises (Problems 1–4). In all interactive examples, you will see the Python primary (>>>) and secondary (...) prompts. The primary prompt is a way for the interpreter to let you know that it is expecting the next Python statement, while the secondary prompt indicates that the interpreter is waiting for additional input to complete the current statement.

You will notice two primary ways that Python "does things" for you: statements and expressions (functions, equations, etc.). Most of you already know the difference between the two, but in case you need to review, a statement is a body of control which involves using keywords. It is similar to issuing a command to the interpreter. You ask Python to do something for you, and it will do it. Statements may or may not lead to a result or output. Let us use the **print** statement for the programmer's perennial first example, Hello World:

```
>>> print 'Hello World!'
Hello World!
```

Expressions, on the other hand, do not use keywords. They can be simple equations that you use with mathematical operators, or can be functions which are called with parentheses. They may or may not take input, and they may or may not return a (meaningful) value. (Functions that do not explicitly return a value by the programmer automatically return None, Python's equivalent to NULL.) An example of a function that takes input and has a return value is the abs() function, which takes a number and returns its absolute value is:

```
>>> abs(4)
4
>>> abs(-4)
4
```

We will introduce both statements and expressions in this chapter. Let us continue with more about the **print** statement.

2.1 Program Output, the print Statement, and "Hello World!"

In some languages, such as C, displaying to the screen is accomplished with a function, e.g., printf(), while with Python and most interpreted and scripting languages, it is a statement. Many shell script languages use an echo command for program output.

CORE NOTE: Dumping variable contents in interactive interpreter

Usually when you want to see the contents of a variable, you use the **print** *statement in your code. However, from within the interactive interpreter, you can use the* **print** *statement to give you the string representation of a variable, or just dump the variable raw—this is accomplished by simply giving the name of the variable.*

In the following example, we assign a string variable, then use **print** *to display its contents. Following that, we issue just the variable name.*

```
>>> myString = 'Hello World!'
>>> print myString
Hello World!
>>> myString
'Hello World!'
```

Notice how just giving only the name reveals quotation marks around the string. The reason for this is to allow objects other than strings to be displayed in the same manner as this string—being able to display a printable string representation of any object, not just strings. The quotes are there to indicate that the object whose value you just dumped to the display is a string. Once you become more familiar with Python, you will recognize that str() is used for **print** *statements, while repr() is what the interactive interpreter calls to display your objects.*

The underscore (_) also has special meaning in the interactive interpreter: the last evaluated expression. So after the code above has executed, _ will contain the string:

```
>>> _
Hello World!
```

Python's **print** statement, paired with the string format operator (%), supports string substitution, much like the `printf()` function in C:

```
>>> print "%s is number %d!" % ("Python", 1)
Python is number 1!
```

`%s` means to substitute a string while `%d` indicates an integer should be substituted. Another popular one is `%f` for floating point numbers. We will see more examples throughout this chapter. Python is fairly flexible, though, so you could pass in a number to `%s` without suffering any consequences with more rigid languages. See Section 6.4.1 for more information on the string format operator.

The **print** statement also allows its output directed to a file. This feature was added way back in Python 2.0. The >> symbols are used to redirect the output, as in this example with standard error:

2.0

```
import sys
print >> sys.stderr, 'Fatal error: invalid input!'
```

Here is the same example with a logfile:

```
logfile = open('/tmp/mylog.txt', 'a')
print >> logfile, 'Fatal error: invalid input!'
logfile.close()
```

2.2 Program Input and the `raw_input()` Built-in Function

The easiest way to obtain user input from the command line is with the `raw_input()` built-in function. It reads from standard input and assigns the string value to the variable you designate. You can use the `int()` built-in function to convert any numeric input string to an integer representation.

```
>>> user = raw_input('Enter login name: ')
Enter login name: root
>>> print 'Your login is:', user
Your login is: root
```

The earlier example was strictly for text input. A numeric string input (with conversion to a real integer) example follows below:

```
>>> num = raw_input('Now enter a number: ')
Now enter a number: 1024
>>> print 'Doubling your number: %d' % (int(num) * 2)
Doubling your number: 2048
```

The `int()` function converts the string `num` to an integer so that the mathematical operation can be performed. See Section 6.5.3 for more information in the `raw_input()` built-in function.

CORE NOTE: Ask for help in the interactive interpreter

If you are learning Python and need help on a new function you are not familiar with, it is easy to get that help just by calling the `help()` *built-in function and passing in the name of the function you want help with:*

```
>>> help(raw_input)
Help on built-in function raw_input in module __builtin__:

raw_input(...)
    raw_input([prompt]) -> string

Read a string from standard input. The trailing newline is stripped.
If the user hits EOF (Unix: Ctl-D, Windows: Ctl-Z+Return), raise
EOFError. On Unix, GNU readline is used if enabled. The prompt string,
if given, is printed without a trailing newline before reading.'
```

CORE STYLE: Keep user interaction outside of functions

It's very tempting for beginners to put **print** *statements and* `raw_input()` *functions wherever they need to display information to or get information from a user. However, we would like to suggest that functions should be kept "clean," meaning they should silently be used purely to take parameters and provide return values. Get all the values needed from the user, send them all to the function, retrieve the return value, and then display the results to the user. This will enable you to use the same function elsewhere without having to worry about customized output. The exception to this rule is if you create functions specifically to obtain input from the user or display output.*
More importantly, it is good practice to separate functions into two categories: those that do things (i.e., interact with the user or set variables) and those that calculate things (usually returning results). It is surely not bad practice to put a **print** *statement in a function if that was its purpose.*

2.3 Comments

As with most scripting and Unix-shell languages, the hash or pound (#) sign signals that a comment begins from the # and continues until the end of the line.

```
>>> # one comment
... print 'Hello World!'   # another comment
Hello World!
```

There are special comments called documentation strings, or "doc strings" for short. You can add a "comment" at the beginning of a module, class, or function string that serves as a doc string, a feature familiar to Java programmers:

```
def foo():
    "This is a doc string."
    return True
```

Unlike regular comments, however, doc strings can be accessed at runtime and be used to automatically generate documentation.

2.4 Operators

The standard mathematical operators that you are familiar with work the same way in Python as in most other languages.

```
+        -        *        /        //        %        **
```

Addition, subtraction, multiplication, division, and modulus (remainder) are all part of the standard set of operators. Python has two division operators, a single slash character for classic division and a double-slash for "floor" division (rounds down to nearest whole number). Classic division means that if the operands are both integers, it will perform floor division, while for floating point numbers, it represents true division. If true division is enabled, then the division operator will always perform that operation, regardless of operand types. You can read more about classic, true, and floor division in Chapter 5, "Numbers."

There is also an exponentiation operator, the double star/asterisk (**). Although we are emphasizing the mathematical nature of these operators, please note that some of these operators are overloaded for use with other data types as well, for example, strings and lists. Let us look at an example:

```
>>> print -2 * 4 + 3 ** 2
1
```

As you can see, the operator precedence is what you expect: + and - are at the bottom, followed by *, /, //, and %; then comes the unary + and -, and finally, we have ** at the top. ((3 ** 2) is calculated first, followed by (-2 * 4), then both results are summed together.)

Python also provides the standard comparison operators, which return a Boolean value indicating the truthfulness of the expression:

```
<        <=        >        >=        ==        !=        <>
```

Trying out some of the comparison operators we get:

```
>>> 2 < 4
True
>>> 2 == 4
False
>>> 2 > 4
False
>>> 6.2 <= 6
False
>>> 6.2 <= 6.2
True
>>> 6.2 <= 6.20001
True
```

Python currently supports two "not equal" comparison operators, != and <>. These are the C-style and ABC/Pascal-style notations. The latter is slowly being phased out, so we recommend against its use.

Python also provides the expression conjunction operators:

and   or   not

We can use these operations to chain together arbitrary expressions and logically combine the Boolean results:

```
>>> 2 < 4 and 2 == 4
False
>>> 2 > 4 or 2 < 4
True
>>> not 6.2 <= 6
True
>>> 3 < 4 < 5
True
```

The last example is an expression that may be invalid in other languages, but in Python it is really a short way of saying:

```
>>> 3 < 4 and 4 < 5
```

You can find out more about Python operators in Section 4.5 of the text.

CORE STYLE: Use parentheses for clarification

Parentheses are a good idea in many cases, such as when the outcome is altered if they are not there, if the code is difficult to read without them, or in situations that might be confusing without them. They are typically not required in Python, but remember that readability counts. Anyone maintaining your code will thank you, and you will thank you later.

2.5 Variables and Assignment

Rules for variables in Python are the same as they are in most other high-level languages inspired by (or more likely, written in) C. They are simply identifier names with an alphabetic first character—"alphabetic" meaning upper- or lowercase letters, including the underscore (_). Any additional characters may be alphanumeric or underscore. Python is case-sensitive, meaning that the identifier "cAsE" is different from "CaSe."

Python is dynamically typed, meaning that no pre-declaration of a variable or its type is necessary. The type (and value) are initialized on assignment. Assignments are performed using the equal sign.

```
>>> counter = 0
>>> miles = 1000.0
>>> name = 'Bob'
>>> counter = counter + 1
>>> kilometers = 1.609 * miles
>>> print '%f miles is the same as %f km' % (miles, kilometers)
1000.000000 miles is the same as 1609.000000 km
```

We have presented five examples of variable assignment. The first is an integer assignment followed by one each for floating point numbers, one for strings, an increment statement for integers, and finally, a floating point operation and assignment.

Python also supports *augmented assignment*, statements that both refer to and assign values to variables. You can take the following expression . . .

```
n = n * 10
```

. . . and use this shortcut instead:

```
n *= 10
```

Python does not support increment and decrement operators like the ones in C: n++ or --n. Because + and -- are also unary operators, Python will interpret --n as -(-n) == n, and the same is true for ++n.

2.6 Numbers

Python supports five basic numerical types, three of which are integer types.

- **int** (signed integers)
  - **long** (long integers)
  - **bool** (Boolean values)
- **float** (floating point real numbers)
- **complex** (complex numbers)

Here are some examples:

int	0101	84	−237	0x80	017	−680	−0X92
long	29979062458L	−84140l	0xDECADEDEADBEEFBADFEEDDEAL				
bool	True		False				
float	3.14159		4.2E-10		-90.	6.022e23	−1.609E−19
complex	6.23+1.5j		−1.23-875J		0+1j	9.80665-8.31441J	−.0224+0j

Numeric types of interest are the Python long and complex types. Python long integers should not be confused with C `long`s. Python longs have a capacity that surpasses any C `long`. You are limited only by the amount of (virtual) memory in your system as far as range is concerned. If you are familiar with Java, a Python long is similar to numbers of the `BigInteger` class type.

Moving forward, ints and longs are in the process of becoming unified into a single integer type. Beginning in version 2.3, overflow errors are no longer reported—the result is automagically converted to a long. In a future version of Python, the distinction will be seamless because the trailing "L" will no longer be used or required.

Boolean values are a special case of integer. Although represented by the constants `True` and `False`, if put in a numeric context such as addition with other numbers, `True` is treated as the integer with value 1, and `False` has a value of 0.

Complex numbers (numbers that involve the square root of −1, so-called "imaginary" numbers) are not supported in many languages and perhaps are implemented only as classes in others.

There is also a sixth numeric type, decimal, for decimal floating numbers, but it is not a built-in type. You must import the `decimal` module to use these types of numbers. They were added to Python (version 2.4) because of a need for more accuracy. For example, the number 1.1 cannot be accurately representing with binary floating point numbers (floats) because it has a repeating fraction in binary. Because of this, numbers like 1.1 look like this as a float:

```
>>> 1.1
1.1000000000000001
```

```
>>> print decimal.Decimal('1.1')
1.1
```

All numeric types are covered in Chapter 5.

2.7 Strings

Strings in Python are identified as a contiguous set of characters in between quotation marks. Python allows for either pairs of single or double quotes. Triple quotes (three consecutive single or double quotes) can be used to escape special characters. Subsets of strings can be taken using the index ([ ]) and slice ([:]) operators, which work with indexes starting at 0 in the beginning of the string and working their way from −1 at the end. The plus (+) sign is the string concatenation operator, and the asterisk (*) is the repetition operator. Here are some examples of strings and string usage:

```
>>> pystr = 'Python'
>>> iscool = 'is cool!'
>>> pystr[0]
'P'
>>> pystr[2:5]
'tho'
>>> iscool[:2]
'is'
>>> iscool[3:]
'cool!'
>>> iscool[-1]
'!'
>>> pystr + iscool
'Pythonis cool!'
>>> pystr + ' ' + iscool
'Python is cool!'
>>> pystr * 2
'PythonPython'
>>> '-' * 20
'--------------------'
>>> pystr = '''python
... is cool'''
>>> pystr
'python\nis cool'
>>> print pystr
python
is cool
>>>
```

You can learn more about strings in Chapter 6.

2.8 Lists and Tuples

Lists and tuples can be thought of as generic "arrays" with which to hold an arbitrary number of arbitrary Python objects. The items are ordered and accessed via index offsets, similar to arrays, except that lists and tuples can store different types of objects.

There are a few main differences between lists and tuples. Lists are enclosed in brackets ([ ]) and their elements and size can be changed. Tuples are enclosed in parentheses (( )) and cannot be updated (although their contents may be). Tuples can be thought of for now as "read-only" lists. Subsets can be taken with the slice operator ([] and [:]) in the same manner as strings.

```
>>> aList = [1, 2, 3, 4]
>>> aList
[1, 2, 3, 4]
>>> aList[0]
1
>>> aList[2:]
[3, 4]
>>> aList[:3]
[1, 2, 3]
>>> aList[1] = 5
>>> aList
[1, 5, 3, 4]
```

Slice access to a tuple is similar, except it cannot be modified:

```
>>> aTuple = ('robots', 77, 93, 'try')
>>> aTuple
('robots', 77, 93, 'try')
>>> aTuple[:3]
('robots', 77, 93)
>>> aTuple[1] = 5
Traceback (innermost last):
  File "<stdin>", line 1, in ?
TypeError: object doesn't support item assignment
```

You can find out a lot more about lists and tuples along with strings in Chapter 6.

2.9 Dictionaries

Dictionaries (or "dicts" for short) are Python's mapping type and work like associative arrays or hashes found in Perl; they are made up of key-value pairs. Keys can be almost any Python type, but are usually numbers or strings.

Values, on the other hand, can be any arbitrary Python object. Dicts are enclosed by curly braces ({ }).

```
>>> aDict = {'host': 'earth'}     # create dict
>>> aDict['port'] = 80            # add to dict
>>> aDict
{'host': 'earth', 'port': 80}
>>> aDict.keys()
['host', 'port']
>>> aDict['host']
'earth'
>>> for key in aDict:
...    print key, aDict[key]
...
host earth
port 80
```

Dictionaries are covered in Chapter 7.

2.10 Code Blocks Use Indentation

Code blocks are identified by indentation rather than using symbols like curly braces. Without extra symbols, programs are easier to read. Also, indentation clearly identifies which block of code a statement belongs to. Of course, code blocks can consist of single statements, too.

When one is new to Python, indentation may comes as a surprise. Humans generally prefer to avoid change, so perhaps after many years of coding with brace delimitation, the first impression of using pure indentation may not be completely positive. However, recall that two of Python's features are that it is simplistic in nature and easy to read. If you have a strong dislike of indentation as a delimitation ***, we invite you to revisit this notion half a year from now. More than likely, you will have discovered that life without braces is not as bad as you had originally thought.

2.11 if Statement

The standard **if** conditional statement follows this syntax:

```
if expression:
    if_suite
```

If the *expression* is non-zero or True, then the statement *if_suite* is executed; otherwise, execution continues on the first statement after. *Suite* is the term used in Python to refer to a sub-block of code and can consist of single or multiple statements. You will notice that parentheses are not required in **if** statements as they are in other languages.

```
if x < .0:
    print '"x" must be atleast 0!'
```

Python supports an **else** statement that is used with **if** in the following manner:

```
if expression:
    if_suite
else:
    else_suite
```

Python has an "else-if" spelled as **elif** with the following syntax:

```
if expression1:
    if_suite
elif expression2:
    elif_suite
else:
    else_suite
```

At the time of this writing, there has been some discussion pertaining to a switch or case statement, but nothing concrete. It is possible that we will see such an animal in a future version of the language. This may also seem strange and/or distracting at first, but a set of **if-elif-else** statements are not as "ugly" because of Python's clean syntax. If you really want to circumvent a set of chained **if-elif-else** statements, another elegant workaround is using a **for** loop (see Section 2.13) to iterate through your list of possible "cases."

You can learn more about **if**, **elif**, and **else** statements in the conditional section of Chapter 8.

2.12 while Loop

The standard **while** conditional loop statement is similar to the **if**. Again, as with every code sub-block, indentation (and dedentation) are used to delimit blocks of code as well as to indicate which block of code statements belong to:

```
while expression:
    while_suite
```

The statement *while_suite* is executed continuously in a loop until the expression becomes zero or false; execution then continues on the first succeeding statement. Like `if` statements, parentheses are not required with Python `while` statements.

```
>>> counter = 0
>>> while counter < 3:
...         print 'loop #%d' % (counter)
...         counter += 1

loop #0
loop #1
loop #2
```

Loops such as **while** and **for** (see below) are covered in the loops section of Chapter 8.

2.13 for Loop and the range() Built-in Function

The **for** loop in Python is more like a `foreach` iterative-type loop in a shell scripting language than a traditional `for` conditional loop that works like a counter. Python's **for** takes an *iterable* (such as a sequence or iterator) and traverses each element once.

```
>>> print 'I like to use the Internet for:'
I like to use the Internet for:
>>> for item in ['e-mail', 'net-surfing', 'homework',
'chat']:
...         print item
...
e-mail
net-surfing
homework
chat
```

Our output in the previous example may look more presentable if we display the items on the same line rather than on separate lines. **print** statements by default automatically add a NEWLINE character at the end of every line. This can be suppressed by terminating the **print** statement with a comma (,).

```
print 'I like to use the Internet for:'
for item in ['e-mail', 'net-surfing', 'homework', 'chat']:
    print item,
print
```

The code required further modification to include an additional **print** statement with no arguments to flush our line of output with a terminating

NEWLINE; otherwise, the prompt will show up on the same line immediately after the last piece of data output. Here is the output with the modified code:

```
I like to use the Internet for:
e-mail net-surfing homework chat
```

Elements in **print** statements separated by commas will automatically include a delimiting space between them as they are displayed.

Providing a string format gives the programmer the most control because it dictates the exact output layout, without having to worry about the spaces generated by commas. It also allows all the data to be grouped together in one place—the tuple or dictionary on the right-hand side of the format operator.

```
>>> who = 'knights'
>>> what = 'Ni!'
>>> print 'We are the', who, 'who say', what, what, what, what
We are the knights who say Ni! Ni! Ni! Ni!
>>> print 'We are the %s who say %s' % \
...      (who, ((what + ' ') * 4))
We are the knights who say Ni! Ni! Ni! Ni!
```

Using the string format operator also allows us to do some quick string manipulation before the output, as you can see in the previous example.

We conclude our introduction to loops by showing you how we can make Python's **for** statement act more like a traditional loop, in other words, a numerical counting loop. Because we cannot change the behavior of a **for** loop (iterates over a sequence), we can manipulate our sequence so that it is a list of numbers. That way, even though we are still iterating over a sequence, it will at least appear to perform the number counting and incrementing that we envisioned.

```
>>> for eachNum in [0, 1, 2]:
...      print eachNum
...
0
1
2
```

Within our loop, eachNum contains the integer value that we are displaying and can use it in any numerical calculation we wish. Because our range of numbers may differ, Python provides the range() built-in function to generate such a list for us. It does exactly what we want, taking a range of numbers and generating a list.

```
>>> for eachNum in range(3):
...      print eachNum
...
```

```
0
1
2
```

For strings, it is easy to iterate over each character:

```
>>> foo = 'abc'
>>> for c in foo:
...     print c
...
a
b
c
```

The `range()` function has been often seen with `len()` for indexing into a string. Here, we can display both elements and their corresponding index value:

```
>>> foo = 'abc'
>>> for i in range(len(foo)):
...     print foo[i], '(%d)' % i
...
a (0)
b (1)
c (2)
```

However, these loops were seen as restrictive—you either index by each element or by its index, but never both. This led to the `enumerate()` function (introduced in Python 2.3) that does give both:

```
>>> for i, ch in enumerate(foo):
...     print ch, '(%d)' % i
...
a (0)
b (1)
c (2)
```

2.14 List Comprehensions

These are just fancy terms to indicate how you can programmatically use a **for** loop to put together an entire list on a single line:

```
>>> squared = [x ** 2 for x in range(4)]
>>> for i in squared:
...     print i

0
1
4
9
```

List comprehensions can do even fancier things like being selective of what to include in the new list:

```
>>> sqdEvens = [x ** 2 for x in range(8) if not x % 2]
>>>
>>> for i in sqdEvens:
...     print i

0
4
16
36
```

2.15 Files and the `open()` and `file()` Built-in Functions

File access is one of the more important aspects of a language once you are comfortable with the syntax; there is nothing like the power of persistent storage to get some real work done.

How to Open a File

```
handle = open(file_name, access_mode = 'r')
```

The *file_name* variable contains the string name of the file we wish to open, and *access_mode* is either `'r'` for read, `'w'` for write, or `'a'` for append. Other flags that can be used in the *access_mode* string include the `'+'` for dual read-write access and the `'b'` for binary access. If the mode is not provided, a default of read-only (`'r'`) is used to open the file.

If `open()` is successful, a file object will be returned as the handle (*handle*). All succeeding access to this file must go through its file handle. Once a file object is returned, we then have access to the other functionality through its methods such as `readlines()` and `close()`. Methods are *attributes* of file objects and must be accessed via the dotted attribute notation (see the following Core Note).

CORE NOTE: What are attributes?

Attributes are items associated with a piece of data. Attributes can be simple data values or executable objects such as functions and methods. What kind of objects have attributes? Many. Classes, modules, files, and complex numbers just some of the Python objects that have attributes.

How do I access object attributes? With the dotted attribute notation, *that is, by putting together the object and attribute names, separated by a dot or period:* `object.attribute`.

Here is some code that prompts the user for the name of a text file, then opens the file and displays its contents to the screen:

```
filename = raw_input('Enter file name: ')
fobj = open(filename, 'r')
for eachLine in fobj:
    print eachLine,
fobj.close()
```

Rather than looping to read and display one line at a time, our code does something a little different. We read all lines in one fell swoop, close the file, and *then* iterate through the lines of the file. One advantage to coding this way is that it permits the file access to complete more quickly. The output and file access do not have to alternate back and forth between reading a line and printing a line. It is cleaner and separates two somewhat unrelated tasks. The caveat here is the file size. The code above is reasonable for files with reasonable sizes. Very large data files may take up too much memory, in which case you would have to revert back to reading one line at a time. (A good example can be found in the next section.)

The other interesting statement in our code is that we are again using the comma at the end of the **print** statement to suppress the printing of the NEWLINE character. Why? Because each text line of the file already contains NEWLINEs at the end of every line. If we did not suppress the NEWLINE from being added by **print**, our display would be double-spaced.

The `file()` built-in function was recently added to Python. It is identical to `open()`, but is named in such a way to indicate that is a factory function (producing file objects), similar to how `int()` produces integers and `dict()` results in dictionary objects. In Chapter 9, we cover file objects, their built-in methods attributes, and how to access your local file system. Please refer to Chapter 9 for all the details.

2.16 Errors and Exceptions

Syntax errors are detected on compilation, but Python also allows for the detection of errors during program execution. When an error is detected, the Python interpreter *raises* (aka throws, generates, triggers) an exception. Armed with the information that Python's exception reporting can generate at runtime, programmers can quickly debug their applications as well as fine-tune their software to take a specific course of action if an anticipated error occurs.

To add error detection or exception handling to your code, just "wrap" it with a **try-except** statement. The suite following the **try** statement will be the code you want to manage. The code that comes after the **except** will be the code that executes if the exception you are anticipating occurs:

```
try:
    filename = raw_input('Enter file name: ')
    fobj = open(filename, 'r')
    for eachLine in fobj:
        print eachLine,
    fobj.close()
except IOError, e:
    print 'file open error:', e
```

Programmers can explicitly raise an exception with the **raise** command. You can learn more about exceptions as well as see a complete list of Python exceptions in Chapter 10.

2.17 Functions

Like many other languages, functions in Python are called using the functional operator (( )), functions must be declared before they can be called. You do not need to declare function (return) types or explicitly return values (None, Python's NULL object is returned by default if one is not given.)

Python can be considered "call by reference." This means that any changes to these parameters within the function affect the original objects in the calling function. However, the caveat is that in Python, it is really dependent on the object type being passed. If that object allows updating, then it behaves as you would expect from "call by reference," but if that object's value cannot be changed, then it will behave like "call by value."

How to Declare Functions

```
def function_name([arguments]):
    "optional documentation string"
    function_suite
```

The syntax for declaring a function consists of the **def** keyword followed by the function name and any arguments that the function may take. Function arguments such as *arguments* above are optional, which is why they are enclosed in brackets above. (Do not physically put brackets in your code!) The statement terminates with a colon (the same way that an **if** or **while** statement is terminated), and a code suite representing the function body follows. Here is one short example:

```
def addMe2Me(x):
    'apply + operation to argument'
    return (x + x)
```

This function, presumably meaning "add me to me" takes an object, adds its current value to itself and returns the sum. While the results are fairly obvious with numerical arguments, we point out that the plus sign works for almost all types. In other words, most of the standard types support the + operator, whether it be numeric addition or sequence concatenation.

How to Call Functions

```
>>> addMe2Me(4.25)
8.5
>>>
>>> addMe2Me(10)
20
>>>
>>> addMe2Me('Python')
'PythonPython'
>>>
>>> addMe2Me([-1, 'abc'])
[-1, 'abc', -1, 'abc']
```

Calling functions in Python is similar to function invocations in many other high-level languages, by giving the name of the function followed by the functional operator, a pair of parentheses. Any optional parameters go between the parentheses, which are required even if there are no arguments. Observe how the + operator works with non-numeric types.

Default Arguments

Functions may have arguments that have default values. If present, arguments will take on the appearance of assignment in the function declaration, but in actuality, it is just the syntax for default arguments and indicates that if a value is not provided for the parameter, it will take on the assigned value as a default.

```
>>> def foo(debug=True):
...     'determine if in debug mode with default argument'
...     if debug:
...         print 'in debug mode'
...     print 'done'
...
>>> foo()
in debug mode
done
>>> foo(False)
done
```

In the example above, the debug parameter has a default value of `True`. When we do not pass in an argument to the function `foo()`, debug automatically takes on a value of `True`. On our second call to `foo()`, we deliberately send an argument of `False`, so that the default argument is not used.

Functions have many more features than we could describe in this introductory section. Please refer to Chapter 11 for more details.

2.18 Classes

Classes are a core part of object-oriented programming and serve as a "container" for related data and logic. They provide a "blueprint" for creating "real" objects, called *instances*. Because Python does not require you to program in an object-oriented way (like Java does), classes are not required learning at this time. However, we will present some examples here for those who are interested in getting a sneak peek.

How to Declare Classes

```
class ClassName(base_class[es]):
    "optional documentation string"
    static_member_declarations
    method_declarations
```

Classes are declared using the **class** keyword. A base or parent class is optional; if you do not have one, just use *object* as the base class. This header line is followed by an optional documentation string, static member declarations, and any method declarations.

```
class FooClass(object):
    """my very first class: FooClass"""
    version = 0.1            # class (data) attribute
```

```
def __init__(self, nm='John Doe'):
    """constructor"""
    self.name = nm          # class instance (data) attribute
    print 'Created a class instance for', nm
def showname(self):
    """display instance attribute and class name"""
    print 'Your name is', self.name
    print 'My name is', self.__class__.__name__
def showver(self):
    """display class(static) attribute"""
    print self.version     # references FooClass.version
def addMe2Me(self, x):      # does not use 'self'
    """apply + operation to argument"""
    return x + x
```

In the above class, we declared one static data type variable `version` shared among all instances and four methods, `__init__()`, `showname()`, `showver()`, and the familiar `addMe2Me()`. The `show*()` methods do not really do much but output the data they were created to output. The `__init__()` method has a special name, as do all those whose names begin and end with a double underscore (`__`).

The `__init__()` method is a function provided by default that is called when a class instance is created, similar to a constructor and called after the object has been instantiated. `__init__()` can be thought of as a constructor, but unlike constructors in other languages, it does not create an instance—it is really just the first method that is called after your object has been created.

Its purpose is to perform any other type of "start up" necessary for the instance to take on a life of its own. By creating our own `__init__()` method, we override the default method (which does not do anything) so that we can do customization and other "extra things" when our instance is created. In our case, we initialize a class instance attribute or member called `name`. This variable is associated only with class instances and is not part of the actual class itself. `__init__()` also features a default argument, introduced in the previous section. You will no doubt also notice the one argument which is part of every method, `self`.

What is `self`? It is basically an instance's handle to itself, the instance on which a method was called. Other OO languages often use an identifier called `this`.

How to Create Class Instances

```
>>> foo1 = FooClass()
Created a class instance for John Doe
```

The string that is displayed is a result of a call to the __init__() method which we did not explicitly have to make. When an instance is created, __init__() is automatically called, whether we provided our own or the interpreter used the default one.

Creating instances looks just like calling a function and has the exact same syntax. They are both known as "callables." Class instantiation uses the same functional operator as invoking a function or method.

Now that we have successfully created our first class instance, we can make some method calls, too:

```
>>> foo1.showname()
Your name is John Doe
My name is __main__.FooClass
>>>
>>> foo1.showver()
0.1
>>> print foo1.addMe2Me(5)
10
>>> print foo1.addMe2Me('xyz')
xyzxyz
```

The result of each function call is as we expected. One interesting piece of data is the class name. In the showname() method, we displayed the self.__class__.__name__ variable which, for an instance, represents the name of the class from which it has been instantiated. (self.__class__ refers to the actual class.) In our example, we did not pass in a name to create our instance, so the 'John Doe' default argument was used. In our next example, we do not use it.

```
>>> foo2 = FooClass('Jane Smith')
Created a class instance for Jane Smith
>>> foo2.showname()
Your name is Jane Smith
My name is FooClass
```

There is plenty more on Python classes and instances in Chapter 13.

2.19 Modules

A module is a logical way to physically organize and distinguish related pieces of Python code into individual files. A module can contain executable code, functions, classes, or any and all of the above.

When you create a Python source file, the name of the module is the same as the file except without the trailing `.py` extension. Once a module is created, you may import that module for use from another module using the **import** statement.

How to Import a Module

```
import module_name
```

How to Call a Module Function or Access a Module Variable

Once imported, a module's attributes (functions and variables) can be accessed using the familiar dotted attribute notation:

```
module.function()
module.variable
```

We will now present our Hello World! example again, but using the output functions inside the `sys` module.

```
>>> import sys
>>> sys.stdout.write('Hello World!\n')
Hello World!
>>> sys.platform
'win32'
>>> sys.version
'2.4.2 (#67, Sep 28 2005, 10:51:12) [MSC v.1310 32 bit
(Intel)]'
```

This code behaves just like our original Hello World! using the **print** statement. The only difference is that the standard output `write()` method is called, and the NEWLINE character needs to be stated explicitly because, unlike the **print** statement, `write()` does not do that for you.

You can find out more information on modules and importing in Chapter 12.

We will cover all of the above topics in much greater detail throughout the text, but hopefully we have provided enough of a "quick dip in the pool" to facilitate your needs if your primary goal is to get started working with Python as quickly as possible without too much serious reading.

CORE NOTE: What is a "PEP"?

You will find references throughout the book to PEP. A PEP is a Python Enhancement Proposal, and this is the way new features are introduced to future versions of Python. They are usually advanced reading from the beginner's point of view, but they provide a full description of a new feature, the rationale or motivation behind it, a new syntax if that is necessary, technical implementation details, backwards-compatibility information, etc. Agreement has to be made between the Python development community, the PEP authors and implementors, and finally, the creator of Python itself, Guido van Rossum, adoringly referred to as the BDFL (Benevolent Dictator for Life), before any new feature is integrated. PEP 1 introduces the PEP, its purpose and guidelines. You can find all of the PEPs in PEP 0, the PEP index, at: http://python.org/dev/peps.

2.20 Useful Functions

In this chapter, we have seen some useful built-in functions. We summarize them in Table 2.1 and present a few other useful ones (note that these may not be the full syntax, only what we feel would be useful for you now).

Table 2.1 Useful Built-In Functions for New Python Programmers

Function	Description
dir([*obj*])	Display attributes of *obj*ect or the names of global variables if no parameter given
help([*obj*])	Display *obj*ect's documentation string in a pretty-printed format or enters interactive help if no parameter given
int(*obj*)	Convert *obj*ect to an integer
len(*obj*)	Return length of *obj*ect
open(*fn, mode*)	Open file *fn* with *mode* ('r' = read, 'w' = write)
range([[*start,*]*stop*[,*step*]])	Return a list of integers that begin at *start* up to but not including *stop* in increments of *step*; *start* defaults to 0, and *step* defaults to 1
raw_input(*str*)	Wait for text input from the user, optional prompt *string* can be provided
str(*obj*)	Convert *obj*ect to a string
type(*obj*)	Return type of *obj*ect (a type object itself!)

2.21 Exercises

2–1. *Variables, **print**, and the String Format Operator.* Start the interactive interpreter. Assign values to some variables (strings, numbers, etc.) and display them within the interpreter by typing their names. Also try doing the same thing with the **print** statement. What is the difference between giving just a variable name versus using it in conjunction with **print**? Also try using the string format operator (%) to become familiar with it.

2–2. *Program Output.* Take a look at the following Python script:

```
#!/usr/bin/env python
1 + 2 * 4
```

(a) What do you think this script does?
(b) What do you think this script will output?
(c) Type the code in as a script program and execute it. Did it do what you expected? Why or why not?
(d) How does execution differ if you are running this code from within the interactive interpreter? Try it and write down the results.
(e) How can you improve the output of the script version so that it does what you expect/want?

2–3. *Numbers and Operators.* Enter the interpreter. Use Python to add, subtract, multiply, and divide two numbers (of any type). Then use the modulus operator to determine the remainder when dividing one number by another, and finally, raise one number to the power of another by using the exponentiation operator.

2–4. *User Input with* `raw_input()`.
(a) Create a small script to use `raw_input()` built-in function to take a string input from the user, then display to the user what he/she just typed in.
(b) Add another piece of similar code, but have the input be numeric. Convert the value to a number (using either `int()` or any of the other numeric conversion functions), and display the value back to the user. (Note that if your version of Python is older than 1.5, you will need to use the `string.ato*()` functions to perform the conversion.)

2–5. *Loops and Numbers*. Create some loops using both **while** and **for**.

    (a) Write a loop that counts from 0 to 10 using a **while** loop. (Make sure your solution really *does* count from 0 to 10, not 0 to 9 or 1 to 10.)

    (b) Do the same loop as in part (a), but use a **for** loop and the range() built-in function.

2–6. *Conditionals*. Detect whether a number is positive, negative, or zero. Try using fixed values at first, then update your program to accept numeric input from the user.

2–7. *Loops and Strings*. Take a user input string and display string, one character at a time. As in your above solution, perform this task with a **while** loop first, then with a **for** loop.

2–8. *Loops and Operators*. Create a fixed list or tuple of five numbers and output their sum. Then update your program so that this set of numbers comes from user input. As with the problems above, implement your solution twice, once using **while** and again with **for**.

2–9. *More Loops and Operators*. Create a fixed list or tuple of five numbers and determine their average. The most difficult part of this exercise is the division to obtain the average. You will discover that integer division truncates and that you must use floating point division to obtain a more accurate result. The float() built-in function may help you there.

2–10. *User Input with Loops and Conditionals*. Use raw_input() to prompt for a number between 1 and 100. If the input matches criteria, indicate so on the screen and exit. Otherwise, display an error and reprompt the user until the correct input is received.

2–11. *Menu-Driven Text Applications*. Take your solutions to any number of the previous five problems and upgrade your program to present a menu-driven text-based application that presents the user with a set of choices, e.g., (1) sum of five numbers, (2) average of five numbers, . . . (X) Quit. The user makes a selection, which is then executed. The program exits when the user chooses the "quit" option. The great advantage of a program like this is that it allows the user to run as many iterations of your solutions without necessarily having to restart the same program over and over again. (It is also good for the developer who is usually the first user and tester of their applications!)

2–12. *The* `dir()` *Built-In Function.*

    (a) Start up the Python interpreter. Run the `dir()` built-in function by simply typing `dir()` at the prompt. What do you see? Print the value of each element in the list you see. Write down the output for each and what you think each is.

    (b) You may be asking, so what does `dir()` do? We have already seen that adding the pair of parentheses after `dir` causes the function to run. Try typing just the name `dir` at the prompt. What information does the interpreter give you? What do you think it means?

    (c) The `type()` built-in function takes any Python object and returns its type. Try running it on `dir` by entering `type(dir)` into the interpreter. What do you get?

    (d) For the final part of this exercise, let us take a quick look at Python documentation strings. We can access the documentation for the `dir()` function by appending `.__doc__` after its name. So from the interpreter, display the document string for `dir()` by typing the following at the prompt: **print** `dir.__doc__`. Many of the built-in functions, methods, modules, and module attributes have a documentation string associated with them. We invite you to put in your own as you write your code; it may help another user down the road.

2–13. *Finding Out More About the* `sys` *Module with* `dir()`.

    (a) Start the Python interpreter again. Run the `dir()` command as in the previous exercise. Now import the `sys` module by typing **import** `sys` at the prompt. Run the `dir()` command again to verify that the `sys` module now shows up. Now run the `dir()` command on the `sys` module by typing `dir(sys)`. Now you see all the attributes of the `sys` module.

    (b) Display the `version` and `platform` variables of the `sys` module. Be sure to prepend the names with `sys` to indicate that they are attributes of `sys`. The version variable contains information regarding the version of the Python interpreter you are using, and the platform attribute contains the name of the computer system that Python believes you are running on.

(c) Finally, call the `sys.exit()` function. This is another way to quit the Python interpreter in case the keystrokes described above in problem 1–4 do not get you out of Python.

2–14. *Operator Precedence and Grouping with Parentheses.* Rewrite the mathematical expression of the **print** statement in Section 2.4, but try to group pairs of operands correctly, using parentheses.

2–15. *Elementary Sorting.*

(a) Have the user enter three numeric values and store them in three different variables. Without using lists or sorting algorithms, manually sort these three numbers from smallest to largest.

(b) How would you change your solution in part (a) to sort from largest to smallest?

2–16. *Files.* Type in and/or run the file display code in Section 2.15. Verify that it works on your system and try different input files as well.

PYTHON BASICS

Chapter Topics

- Statements and Syntax
- Variable Assignment
- Identifiers and Keywords
- Basic Style Guidelines
- Memory Management
- First Python Programs

Chapter 3

Our next goal is to go through the basic Python syntax, describe some general style guidelines, then brief you on identifiers, variables, and keywords. We will also discuss how memory space for variables is allocated and deallocated. Finally, we will be exposed to a much larger example Python program—taking the plunge, as it were. No need to worry, there are plenty of life preservers around that allow for swimming rather than the alternative.

3.1 Statements and Syntax

Some rules and certain symbols are used with regard to statements in Python:

- Hash mark (#) indicates Python comments
- NEWLINE (\n) is the standard line separator (one statement per line)
- Backslash (\ ) continues a line
- Semicolon (;) joins two statements on a line
- Colon (:) separates a header line from its suite
- Statements (code blocks) grouped as suites
- Suites delimited via indentation
- Python files organized as modules

3.1.1 Comments (#)

First things first: Although Python is one of the easiest languages to read, it does not preclude the programmer from proper and adequate usage and placement of comments in the code. Like many of its Unix scripting brethren, Python comment statements begin with the pound sign or hash symbol (#). A comment can begin anywhere on a line. All characters following the # to the end of the line are ignored by the interpreter. Use them wisely and judiciously.

3.1.2 Continuation (\ )

Python statements are, in general, delimited by NEWLINEs, meaning one statement per line. Single statements can be broken up into multiple lines by use of the backslash. The backslash symbol (\ ) can be placed before a NEWLINE to continue the current statement onto the next line.

```
# check conditions
if (weather_is_hot == 1) and \
   (shark_warnings == 0):
       send_goto_beach_mesg_to_pager()
```

There are two exceptions where lines can be continued without back-slashes. A single statement can take up more than one line when enclosing operators are used, i.e., parentheses, square brackets, or braces, and when NEWLINEs are contained in strings enclosed in triple quotes.

```
# display a string with triple quotes
print '''hi there, this is a long message for you
that goes over multiple lines... you will find
out soon that triple quotes in Python allows
this kind of fun! it is like a day on the beach!'''

# set some variables
go_surf, get_a_tan_while, boat_size, toll_money = (1,
   'windsurfing', 40.0, -2.00)
```

Given a choice between using the backslash and grouping components you can break up with a NEWLINE, i.e., with parentheses, we recommend the latter as it is more readable.

3.1.3 Multiple Statement Groups as Suites (:)

Groups of individual statements making up a single code block are called "suites" in Python (as we introduced in Chapter 2). *Compound* or *complex statements*, such as `if`, `while`, `def`, and `class`, are those that require a header line and a suite. Header lines begin the statement (with the keyword) and terminate with a colon (:) and are followed by one or more lines that make up the suite. We will refer to the combination of a header line and a suite as a *clause*.

3.1.4 Suites Delimited via Indentation

As we introduced in Section 2.10, Python employs indentation as a means of delimiting blocks of code. Code at inner levels are indented via spaces or tabs. Indentation requires exact indentation; in other words, all the lines of code in a suite must be indented at the exact same level (e.g., same number of spaces). Indented lines starting at different positions or column numbers are not allowed; each line would be considered part of another suite and would more than likely result in syntax errors.

CORE STYLE: Indent with four spaces and avoid using tabs

As someone who is perhaps new to block delimitation using whitespace, a first obvious question might be: How many spaces should I use? We think that two is too short, and six to eight is too many, so we suggest four spaces for everyone. Also, because tabs vary in the number of spaces depending on your system, we recommend not using tabs if there is any hint of cross-platform development. Both of these style guidelines are also supported by Guido van Rossum, the creator of Python, and documented in the Python Style Guide. You will find the same suggestions in our style guide in Section 3.4.

A new code block is recognized when the amount of indentation has increased, an d its termination is signaled by a "dedentation," or a reduction of indentation matching a previous level's. Code that is not indented, i.e., the highest level of code, is considered the "main" portion of the script.

The decision to create code blocks in Python using indentation was based on the belief that grouping code in this manner is more elegant and contributes to the ease of reading to which we alluded earlier. It also helps avoid "dangling-else"-type problems, including ungrouped single statement clauses (those where a C `if` statement does not use braces at all, but has two indented statements following). The second statement will execute regardless of the conditional, leading to more programmer confusion until the light bulb finally blinks on.

Finally, no "holy brace wars" can occur when using indentation. In C (also C++ and Java), starting braces may be placed on the same line as the header statement, or may start the very next line, or may be indented on the next line. Some like it one way, some prefer the other, etc. You get the picture.

3.1.5 Multiple Statements on a Single Line (;)

The semicolon (;) allows multiple statements on a single line given that neither statement starts a new code block. Here is a sample snip using the semicolon:

```
import sys; x = 'foo'; sys.stdout.write(x + '\n')
```

We caution the reader to be wary of chaining multiple statements on individual lines as it makes code much less readable, thus less "Pythonic."

3.1.6 Modules

Each Python script is considered a *module*. Modules have a physical presence as disk files. When a module gets large enough or has diverse enough functionality, it may make sense to move some of the code out to another module. Code that resides in modules may belong to an application (i.e., a script that is directly executed), or may be executable code in a library-type module that may be "imported" from another module for invocation. As we mentioned in the last chapter, modules can contain blocks of code to run, class declarations, function declarations, or any combination of all of those.

3.2 Variable Assignment

This section focuses on variable assignment. We will discuss which identifiers make valid variables in Section 3.3.

Assignment Operator

The equal sign (=) is the main Python assignment operator. (The others are augmented assignment operator [see next section].)

```
anInt = -12
aString = 'cart'
aFloat = -3.1415 * (5.0 ** 2)
anotherString = 'shop' + 'ping'
aList = [3.14e10, '2nd elmt of a list', 8.82-4.371j]
```

Be aware now that assignment does not explicitly assign a value to a variable, although it may appear that way from your experience with other programming languages. In Python, objects are referenced, so on assignment, a reference (not a value) to an object is what is being assigned, whether the object was just created or was a pre-existing object. If this is not 100 percent clear now, do not worry about it. We will revisit this topic later on in the chapter, but just keep it in mind for now.

Also, if you are familiar with C, you know that assignments are treated as expressions. This is not the case in Python, where assignments do not have inherent values. Statements such as the following are invalid in Python:

```
>>> x = 1
>>> y = (x = x + 1)   # assignments not expressions!
  File "<stdin>", line 1
    y = (x = x + 1)
           ^
SyntaxError: invalid syntax
```

Chaining together assignments is okay, though (more on this later):

```
>>> y = x = x + 1
>>> x, y
(2, 2)
```

Augmented Assignment

Beginning in Python 2.0, the equal sign can be combined with an arithmetic operation and the resulting value reassigned to the existing variable. Known as *augmented assignment*, statements such as . . .

```
x = x + 1
```

. . . can now be written as . . .

```
x += 1
```

2.0

Augmented assignment refers to the use of operators, which imply both an arithmetic operation as well as an assignment. You will recognize the following symbols if you come from a C/ C++ or Java background:

+=	-=	*=	/=	%=	**=
<<=	>>=	&=	^=	|=	

Other than the obvious syntactical change, the most significant difference is that the first object (A in our example) is examined only once. Mutable objects will be modified in place, whereas immutable objects will have the same effect as A = A + B (with a new object allocated) except that A is only evaluated once, as we have mentioned before.

```
>>> m = 12
>>> m %= 7
>>> m
5
>>> m **= 2
>>> m
25
>>> aList = [123, 'xyz']
>>> aList += [45.6e7]
>>> aList
[123, 'xyz', 456000000.0]
```

Python does not support pre-/post-increment nor pre-/post-decrement operators such as x++ or --x.

Multiple Assignment

```
>>> x = y = z = 1
>>> x
1
>>> y
1
>>> z
1
```

In the above example, an integer object (with the value 1) is created, and x, y, and z are all assigned the same reference to that object. This is the process of assigning a single object to multiple variables. It is also possible in Python to assign multiple objects to multiple variables.

"Multuple" Assignment

Another way of assigning multiple variables is using what we shall call the "multuple" assignment. This is not an official Python term, but we use "multuple" here because when assigning variables this way, the objects on both sides of the equal sign are tuples, a Python standard type we introduced in Section 2.8.

```
>>> x, y, z = 1, 2, 'a string'
>>> x
1
>>> y
2
>>> z
'a string'
```

In the above example, two integer objects (with values 1 and 2) and one string object are assigned to x, y, and z respectively. Parentheses are normally used to denote tuples, and although they are optional, we recommend them anywhere they make the code easier to read:

```
>>> (x, y, z) = (1, 2, 'a string')
```

If you have ever needed to swap values in other languages like C, you will be reminded that a temporary variable, i.e., tmp, is required to hold one value while the other is being exchanged:

```
/* swapping variables in C */
tmp = x;
x = y;
y = tmp;
```

In the above C code fragment, the values of the variables x and y are being exchanged. The tmp variable is needed to hold the value of one of the variables while the other is being copied into it. After that step, the original value kept in the temporary variable can be assigned to the second variable.

One interesting side effect of Python's "multuple" assignment is that we no longer need a temporary variable to swap the values of two variables.

```
# swapping variables in Python
>>> x, y = 1, 2
>>> x
1
>>> y
2
>>> x, y = y, x
>>> x
2
>>> y
1
```

Obviously, Python performs evaluation before making assignments.

3.3 Identifiers

Identifiers are the set of valid strings that are allowed as names in a computer language. From this all-encompassing list, we segregate out those that are *keywords*, names that form a construct of the language. Such identifiers are reserved words that may not be used for any other purpose, or else a syntax error (SyntaxError exception) will occur.

Python also has an additional set of identifiers known as *built-ins*, and although they are not reserved words, use of these special names is not recommended. (Also see Section 3.3.3.)

3.3.1 Valid Python Identifiers

The rules for Python identifier strings are like most other high-level programming languages that come from the C world:

- First character must be a letter or underscore (_)
- Any additional characters can be alphanumeric or underscore
- Case-sensitive

No identifiers can begin with a number, and no symbols other than the underscore are ever allowed. The easiest way to deal with underscores is to consider them as alphabetic characters. *Case-sensitivity* means that identifier foo is different from Foo, and both of those are different from FOO.

3.3.2 Keywords

Python's keywords are listed in Table 3.1. Generally, the keywords in any language should remain relatively stable, but should things ever change (as Python is a growing and evolving language), a list of keywords as well as an iskeyword() function are available in the keyword module.

Table 3.1 Python Keywords[a]

`and`	`as`[b]	`assert`[c]	`break`
`class`	`continue`	`def`	`del`
`elif`	`else`	`except`	`exec`
`finally`	`for`	`from`	`global`
`if`	`import`	`in`	`is`
`lambda`	`not`	`or`	`pass`
`print`	`raise`	`return`	`try`
`while`	`with`[b]	`yield`[d]	None[e]

a.   **access** keyword obsoleted as of Python 1.4.

b.   New in Python 2.6.

c.   New in Python 1.5.

d.   New in Python 2.3.

e.   Not a keyword but made a constant in Python 2.4.

3.3.3 Built-ins

In addition to keywords, Python has a set of "built-in" names available at any level of Python code that are either set and/or used by the interpreter. Although not keywords, built-ins should be treated as "reserved for the system" and not used for any other purpose. However, some circumstances may call for *overriding* (aka redefining, replacing) them. Python does not support overloading of identifiers, so only one name "binding" may exist at any given time.

We can also tell advanced readers that built-ins are members of the `__builtins__` module, which is automatically imported by the interpreter before your program begins or before you are given the `>>>` prompt in the interactive interpreter. Treat them like global variables that are available at any level of Python code.

3.3.4 Special Underscore Identifiers

Python designates (even more) special variables with underscores both prefixed and suffixed. We will also discover later that some are quite useful to the programmer while others are unknown or useless. Here is a summary of the special underscore usage in Python:

- `_xxx`   Do not import with `'from `*`module`*` import *'`
- `__xxx__`   System-defined name
- `__xxx`   Request private name mangling in classes

CORE STYLE: Avoid using underscores to begin variable names

Because of the underscore usage for special interpreter and built-in identifiers, we recommend that the programmer avoid beginning variable names with the underscore. Generally, a variable named _xxx is considered "private" and should not be used outside that module or class. It is good practice to use _xxx to denote when a variable is private. Since variables named __xxx__ often mean special things to Python, you should avoid naming normal variables this way.

3.4 Basic Style Guidelines

Comments

You do not need to be reminded that comments are useful both to you and those who come after you. This is especially true for code that has been untouched by man (or woman) for a time (that means several months in software development time). Comments should not be absent, nor should there be novellas. Keep the comments explanatory, clear, short, and concise, but get them *in* there. In the end, it saves time and energy for everyone. Above all, make sure they stay accurate!

Documentation

Python also provides a mechanism whereby documentation strings can be retrieved dynamically through the __doc__ special variable. The first unassigned string in a module, class declaration, or function declaration can be accessed using the attribute *obj*.__doc__ where *obj* is the module, class, or function name. This works during runtime too!

Indentation

Since indentation plays a major role, you will have to decide on a spacing style that is easy to read as well as the least confusing. Common sense also plays a role in choosing how many spaces or columns to indent.

1 or 2	Probably not enough; difficult to determine which block of code statements belong to
8 to 10	May be too many; code that has many embedded levels will wrap around, causing the source to be difficult to read

Four spaces is very popular, not to mention being the preferred choice of Python's creator. Five and six are not bad, but text editors usually do *not* use these settings, so they are not as commonly used. Three and seven are borderline cases.

As far as tabs go, bear in mind that different text editors have different concepts of what tabs are. It is advised not to use tabs if your code will live and run on different systems or be accessed with different text editors.

Choosing Identifier Names

The concept of good judgment also applies in choosing logical identifier names. Decide on short yet meaningful identifiers for variables. Although variable length is no longer an issue with programming languages of today, it is still a good idea to keep name sizes reasonable length. The same applies for naming your modules (Python files).

Python Style Guide(s)

Guido van Rossum wrote up a Python Style Guide ages ago. It has since been replaced by no fewer than three PEPs: 7 (Style Guide for C Code), 8 (Style Guide for Python Code), and 257 (DocString Conventions). These PEPs are archived, maintained, and updated regularly.

Over time, you will hear the term "Pythonic," which describes the Python way of writing code, organizing logic, and object behavior. Over more time, you will come to understand what that means. There is also another PEP, PEP 20, which lists the Zen of Python, starting you on your journey to discover what Pythonic really means. If you are not online and need to see this list, then use **import** this from your interpreter. Here are some links:

> www.python.org/doc/essays/styleguide.html
> www.python.org/dev/peps/pep-0007/
> www.python.org/dev/peps/pep-0008/
> www.python.org/dev/peps/pep-0020/
> www.python.org/dev/peps/pep-0257/

3.4.1 Module Structure and Layout

Modules are simply physical ways of logically organizing all your Python code. Within each file, you should set up a consistent and easy-to-read structure. One such layout is the following:

```
# (1) startup line (Unix)
# (2) module documentation
# (3) module imports
# (4) variable declarations
# (5) class declarations
# (6) function declarations
# (7) "main" body
```

Figure 3–1 illustrates the internal structure of a typical module.

(1) Startup line
> Generally used only in Unix environments, the startup line allows for script execution by name only (invoking the interpreter is not required).

(2) Module documentation
> Summary of a module's functionality and significant global variables; accessible externally as *module*.__doc__.

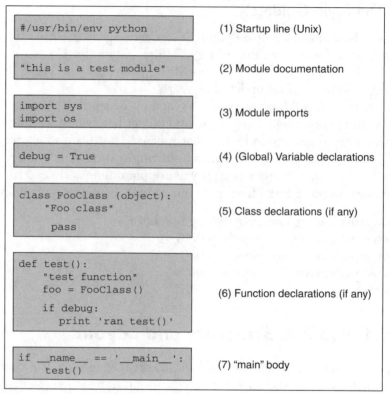

Figure 3-1 Typical Python file structure

(3) Module imports

Import all the modules necessary for all the code in current module; modules are imported once (when this module is loaded); imports within functions are not invoked until those functions are called.

(4) Variable declarations

Declare here (global) variables that are used by multiple functions in this module. We favor the use of local variables over globals, for good programming style mostly, and to a lesser extent, for improved performance and less memory usage.

(5) Class declarations

Any classes should be declared here. A class is defined when this module is imported and the **class** statement executed. Documentation variable is *class.__doc__*.

(6) Function declarations

> Functions that are declared here are accessible externally as `module.function()`; function is defined when this module is imported and the **def** statement executed. Documentation variable is `function.__doc__`.

(7) "main" body

> All code at this level is executed, whether this module is imported or started as a script; generally does not include much functional code, but rather gives direction depending on mode of execution.

CORE STYLE: "main" calls `main()`

The main body of code tends to contain lines such as the ones you see above, which check the __name__ variable and take appropriate action (see Core Note on the following page). Code in the main body typically executes the class, function, and variable declarations, then checks __name__ to see whether it should invoke another function (often called `main()`), which performs the primary duties of this module. The main body usually does no more than that. (Our example above uses `test()` rather than `main()` to avoid confusion until you read this Core Style sidebar.)

Regardless of the name, we want to emphasize that this is a great place to put a test suite in your code. As we explain in Section 3.4.2, most Python modules are created for import use only, and calling such a module directly should invoke a regression test of the code in such a module.

Most projects tend to consist of a single application and import any required modules. Thus it is important to bear in mind that most modules are created solely to be imported rather than to execute as scripts. We are more likely to create a Python library-style module whose sole purpose is to be imported by another module. After all, only one of the modules—the one that houses the main application—will be executed, either by a user from the command line, by a batch or timed mechanism such as a Unix `cron` job, via a Web server call, or through a GUI callback.

With that fact in hand, we should also remember that all modules have the ability to execute code. All Python statements in the highest level of code— that is, the lines that are not indented—will be executed on import, whether desired or not. Because of this "feature," safer code is written such that everything is in a function except for the code that should be executed on an import of a module. Again, usually only the main application module has the bulk of the executable code at its highest level. All other imported modules will have very little on the outside, and everything in functions or classes. (See Core Note that follows for more information.)

CORE NOTE: __name__ indicates how module was loaded

Because the "main" code is executed whether a module is imported or executed directly, we often need to know how this module was loaded to guide the execution path. An application may wish to import the module of another application, perhaps to access useful code which will otherwise have to be duplicated (not the OO thing to do). However, in this case, you only want access to this other application's code, not necessarily to run it. So the big question is, "Is there a way for Python to detect at runtime whether this module was imported or executed directly?" The answer is . . . (drum roll . . .) yes! The __name__ system variable is the ticket.

- *__name__ contains module name if imported*
- *__name__ contains ' __main__ ' if executed directly*

3.4.2 Create Tests in the Main Body

For good programmers and engineers, providing a test suite or harness for our entire application is the goal. Python simplifies this task particularly well for modules created solely for import. For these modules, you know that they would never be executed directly. Wouldn't it be nice if they were invoked to run code that puts that module through the test grinder? Would this be difficult to set up? Not really.

The test software should run only when this file is executed directly, i.e., not when it is imported from another module, which is the usual case. Above and in the Core Note, we described how we can determine whether a module was imported or executed directly. We can take advantage of this mechanism by using the __name__ variable. If this module was called as a script, plug the test code right in there, perhaps as part of main() or test() (or whatever you decide to call your "second-level" piece of code) function, which is called only if this module is executed directly.

The "tester" application for our code should be kept current along with any new test criteria and results, and it should run as often as the code is updated. These steps will help improve the robustness of our code, not to mention validating and verifying any new features or updates.

Tests in the main body are an easy way to provide quick coverage of your code. The Python standard library also provides the unittest module, sometimes referred to as PyUnit, as a testing framework. Use of `unittest` is beyond the scope of this book, but it is something to consider when you need serious regression testing of a large system of components.

3.5 Memory Management

So far you have seen a large number of Python code samples. We are going to cover a few more details about variables and memory management in this section, including:

- Variables not declared ahead of time
- Variable types not declared
- No memory management on programmers' part
- Variable names can be "recycled"
- **del** statement allows for explicit "deallocation"

3.5.1 Variable Declarations (or Lack Thereof)

In most compiled languages, variables must be declared before they are used. In fact, C is even more restrictive: variables have to be declared at the beginning of a code block and before any statements are given. Other languages, like C++ and Java, allow "on-the-fly" declarations, i.e., those which occur in the middle of a body of code—but these name and type declarations are still required before the variables can be used. In Python, there are no explicit variable declarations. Variables are "declared" on first assignment. Like most languages, however, variables cannot be accessed until they are (created and) assigned:

```
>>> a
Traceback (innermost last):
  File "<stdin>", line 1, in ?
NameError: a
```

Once a variable has been assigned, you can access it by using its name:

```
>>> x = 4
>>> y = 'this is a string'
>>> x
4
>>> y
'this is a string'
```

3.5.2 Dynamic Typing

Another observation, in addition to lack of variable declaration, is the lack of type specification. In Python, the type and memory space for an object are determined and allocated at runtime. Although code is byte-compiled, Python is still an interpreted language. On creation—that is, on assignment—the interpreter creates an object whose type is dictated by the syntax that is used for the operand on the right-hand side of an assignment. After the object is created, a reference to that object is assigned to the variable on the left-hand side of the assignment.

3.5.3 Memory Allocation

As responsible programmers, we are aware that when allocating memory space for variables, we are borrowing system resources, and eventually, we will have to return that which we borrowed back to the system. Python simplifies application writing because the complexities of memory management have been pushed down to the interpreter. The belief is that you should be using Python to solve problems with and not have to worry about lower-level issues that are not directly related to your solution.

3.5.4 Reference Counting

To keep track of objects in memory, Python uses the simple technique of *reference counting*. This means that internally, Python keeps track of all objects in use and how many interested parties there are for any particular object. You can think of it as simple as card-counting while playing the card game blackjack or 21. An internal tracking variable, called a *reference counter*, keeps track of how many references are being made to each object, called a *refcount* for short.

When an object is created, a reference is made to that object, and when it is no longer needed, i.e., when an object's refcount goes down to zero, it is garbage-collected. (This is not 100 percent true, but pretend it is for now.)

Incrementing the Reference Count

The refcount for an object is initially set to 1 when an object is created and (its reference) assigned.

New references to objects, also called *aliases*, occur when additional variables are assigned to the same object, passed as arguments to invoke other bodies of code such as functions, methods, or class instantiation, or assigned as members of a sequence or mapping.

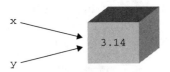

Figure 3-2 An object with two references

Let us say we make the following declarations:

```
x = 3.14
y = x
```

The statement x = 3.14 allocates a floating point number (float) object and assigns a reference x to it. x is the first reference, hence setting that object's refcount to one. The statement y = x creates an alias y, which "points to" the same integer object as x (see Figure 3-2). A new object is *not* created for y.

Instead, the only thing that happens is that the reference count for this object is incremented by one (to 2). This is one way in which an object's refcount goes up. Other ways it can increment include the object being passed into a function call, and when the object is added to a container object such as a list.

In summary, an object's refcount is increased when

- It (the object) is created

    ```
    x = 3.14
    ```

- Additional aliases for it are created

    ```
    y = x
    ```

- It is passed to a function (new local reference)

    ```
    foobar(x)
    ```

- It becomes part of a container object

    ```
    myList = [123, x, 'xyz']
    ```

Now let us look at how reference counts go down.

Decrementing the Reference Count

When references to an object "go away," the refcount is decreased. The most obvious case is when a reference goes out of scope. This occurs most often when the function in which a reference is made completes. The local (automatic) variable is gone, and an object's reference counter is decremented.

A reference also goes away when a variable is reassigned to another object. For example:

```
foo = 'xyz'
bar = foo
foo = 123
```

The reference count for string object "xyz" is one when it is created and assigned to foo. It is then incremented when bar is added as an alias. However, when foo is reassigned to the integer 123, the reference count to "xyz" is decremented by one.

Other ways in which an object's reference count goes down include explicit removal of a reference using the **del** statement (see next section), when an object is removed from a container (or if the reference count to that container itself goes to zero).

In summary, an object's refcount is decreased when:

- A local reference goes out of scope, i.e., when foobar() (see previous example) terminates
- Aliases for that object are explicitly destroyed

  del y   # or **del** x

- An alias is reassigned to another object (taking on a new reference)

  ```
  x = 123
  ```

- It is explicitly removed from a container object

  ```
  myList.remove(x)
  ```

- The container itself is deallocated

  del myList   # or goes out-of-scope

See Section 11.8 for more information on variable scope.

del Statement

The **del** statement removes a single reference to an object. Its syntax is:

  del *obj1*[, *obj2*[,... *objN*]]

For example, executing **del** y in the example above has two results:

- Removes name y from current namespace
- Lowers reference count to object x (by one)

Further still, executing **del** x will remove the final reference to the object, decrementing the reference counter to zero and causing the object to become "inaccessible" or "unreachable." It is at this point that the object becomes a candidate for garbage collection. Note that any tracing or debugging facility may keep additional references to an object, delaying or postponing that object from being garbage-collected.

3.5.5 Garbage Collection

Memory that is no longer being used is reclaimed by the system using a mechanism known as *garbage collection*. The interpreter keeps track of reference counts as above, but it is up to the garbage collector to deallocate the memory. The garbage collector is a separate piece of code that looks for objects with reference counts of zero. It is also responsible to check for objects with a reference count greater than zero that need to be deallocated. Certain situations lead to *cycles*.

A cyclic reference is where you have (at least two) objects that refer to each other, and even if all other references fall by the wayside, these references still exist, meaning that reference counting alone is not good enough.

Python's garbage collector is actually a combination of reference counting and the periodic invocation of a cyclic garbage collector. When an object's refcount reaches zero, the interpreter pauses to deallocate it and all objects that were reachable only from that object. In addition to this reference counting, the garbage collector also notices if a large number of objects have been allocated (and not deallocated though reference counting). In such cases, the interpreter will pause to try to clear out any unreferenced cycles.

3.6 First Python Programs

Now that we are familiar with the syntax, style, variable assignment, and memory allocation, it is time to look at slightly more complex code. You may or may not be familiar with all of the constructs of Python that we're going to show, but we believe that Python is so simple and elegant that you should be able to figure out what each piece of code does.

We are going to introduce two related scripts that manipulate text files. The first, makeTextFile.py, creates text files. It prompts the user for each line of text and writes the results to a file. The other, readTextFile.py, reads and displays the contents of a text file to the screen.

Take a look at both now, and see if you can figure out how each works.

Example 3.1 File Create (`makeTextFile.py`)

This application prompts the user for a (nonexistent) filename, then has the user enter each line of that file (one at a time). Finally, it writes the entire text file to disk.

```python
1   #!/usr/bin/env python
2
3   'makeTextFile.py -- create text file'
4
5   import os
6   ls = os.linesep
7
8   # get filename
9   while True:
10
11      if os.path.exists(fname):
12          print "ERROR: '%s' already exists" % fname
13      else:
14          break
15
16  # get file content (text) lines
17  all = []
18  print "\nEnter lines ('.' by itself to quit).\n"
19
20  # loop until user terminates input
21  while True:
22      entry = raw_input('> ')
23      if entry == '.':
24          break
25      else:
26          all.append(entry)
27
28  # write lines to file with proper line-ending
29  fobj = open(fname, 'w')
30  fobj.writelines(['%s%s' % (x, ls) for x in all])
31  fobj.close()
32  print 'DONE!'
```

Lines 1–3

The Unix startup line is followed by the module documentation string. Keep your documentation string simple yet descriptive enough to be useful. Ours is a bit short, but so is this script. (We invite the reader to take a look at the documentation string at the commencement of the `cgi` module in the standard library for a seriously lengthy example of module documentation.)

Lines 5–6

We import the operating system (os) module next, and in line 6, we create a new local alias for the linesep attribute of that module. By doing this, we can shorten the name of the variable and also speed up access to it.

CORE TIP: Use local variables to substitute for module attributes

Names like os.linesep require the interpreter to do two lookups: (1) lookup os to find that it is a module, and (2) look up the linesep attribute of that module. Because modules are also global variables, we pay another penalty. If you use an attribute like this often in a function, we recommend you alias it to a single local variable. Lookups are much faster—local variables are always searched first before globals, and we don't have attribute lookups either. This is one of the tricks in making your programs faster: replace often-used (and name-lengthy) module attributes with local references. Your code runs faster and has less clutter with a shorter name.

In our code snippet, we do not have a function to show you an example of using a local alias. Instead, we have a global alias, which is halfway there. At least we do not have to perform two lookups to get to the object.

Lines 8–14

If it is not apparent already, this is an "infinite loop," meaning we are presented with a body of code that will repeat and run forever unless we exit the loop—look for a **break** statement somewhere! The **while** True conditional causes this to happen because **while** statements execute whenever its conditional expression evaluates to Boolean true, and True is Boolean true.

Lines 10–14 prompt the user for an unused filename, meaning that the filename entered should not be the name of an already existing file. The raw_input() built-in function takes an argument to use as the prompt to the user. The resulting string entered by the user is the return value of raw_input(), which in this case gets assigned to fname.

If the user is unlucky enough to pick a name already in use, we notify the user and return the user to the prompt to enter another (file)name. Note that os.path.exists() is a helper function in the os.path (sub)module, which helps us make this determination. Only when a file with such a name does not exist, meaning that os.path.exists() returns False, do we break out of this loop and continue.

Lines 16–26

This is the part of our application that gives the user some instruction and prompts them for the contents of our text file, one line at a time. The `all` list will hold each line—we initialize it on line 17. Line 21 begins another infinite loop, which prompts the user for each line of the text file and only terminates when they enter a period '.' on a line by itself. The **if-else** statement on lines 23–26 look for that sentinel and break out of the loop if it is seen (line 24); otherwise it adds another line to our total (line 26).

Lines 28–32

Now that we have the entire contents in memory, we need to dump it to the text file. Line 29 opens the file for write, and line 30 writes each line to the file. Every file requires a line terminator (or termination character[s]). The construct on line 30, called a list comprehension, does the following: for every line in our file, append it with the appropriate line terminator for our platform. `'%s%s'` puts a line next to the termination character(s), and the grouping (x, ls) represents each line x of all lines and the terminator—for Unix, it is `'\n'`, DOS and Win32, `'\r\n'`, etc. By using os.linesep, we do not need to have code to check which operating system this program is running on in order to determine which line terminating character(s) to use.

The file object's `writelines()` method then takes the resulting list of lines (now with terminators) and writes it to the file. The file is then closed in line 31, and we are *done*!

Not too bad, right? Now let us look at how to view the file we just created! For this, we have your second Python program, readTextFile.py. As you will see, it is much shorter than makeTextfile.py. The complexity of file creation is almost always greater than the reading of it. The only new and interesting part for you is the appearance of an exception handler.

Lines 1–3

These are the Unix startup line and module documentation string as usual.

Lines 5–7

Unlike makeTextFile.py where we kept pegging the user for names until they he or she chooses an unused filename, we don't care in this example.

Example 3.2 File Read and Display (`readTextFile.py`)

```
1   #!/usr/bin/env python
2
3   'readTextFile.py -- read and display text file'
4
5   # get filename
6   fname = raw_input('Enter filename: ')
7   print
8
9   # attempt to open file for reading
10  try:
11      fobj = open(fname, 'r')
12  except IOError, e:
13      print "*** file open error:", e
14  else:
15      # display contents to the screen
16      for eachLine in fobj:
17          print eachLine,
18      fobj.close()
```

In other words, we are performing the validation elsewhere (if at all). Line 7 just displays a new line to separate the prompting of the filename and the contents of the file.

Lines 9–18

This next Python construct (other than the comment) represents the rest of the script. This is a **try-except-else** statement. The **try** clause is a block of code that we want to monitor for errors. In our code (lines 10–11), we are attempting to open the file with the name the user entered.

The **except** clause is where we decide what type of errors we're looking out for and what to do if such errors occur. In this case (lines 12–13), we are checking to see if the file open() failed—this is usually an IOError type of error.

Finally, lines 14–18 represent the **else** clause of a **try-except**—the code that is executed if no errors occurred in the **try** block. In our case, we display each line of the file to the screen. Note that because we are not removing the trailing whitespace (line termination) characters from each line, we have to suppress the NEWLINE that the **print** statement automatically generates—this is done by adding a trailing comma to the end of the **print** statement. We then close the file (line 18), which ends the program.

One final note regarding the use of os.path.exists() and an exception handler: The author is generally in favor of the former, when there is an existing function that can be used to detect error conditions—and even more simply, where the function is Boolean and gives you a "yes" or "no" answer. (Note that there is probably already an exception handler in such a function.) Why do you have to reinvent the wheel when there's already code just for that purpose?

An exception handler is best applied when there *isn't* such a convenient function, where you the programmer must recognize an "out of the ordinary" error condition and respond appropriately. In our case, we were able to dodge an exception because we check to see if a file exists, but there are many other situations that may cause a file open to fail, such as improper permissions, the connection to a network drive is out, etc. For safety's sake, you may end up with "checker" functions like `os.path.exists()` in addition to an exception handler, which may be able to take care of a situation where no such function is available.

You will find more examples of file system functions in Chapter 9 and more about exception handling in Chapter 10.

3.7 Related Modules/Developer Tools

The Python Style Guide (PEP 8), Python Quick Reference Guide, and the Python FAQ make for great reading as developer "tools." In addition, there are some modules that may help you become a more proficient Python programmer:

- Debugger: `pdb`
- Logger: `logging`
- Profilers: `profile`, `hotshot`, `cProfile`

The debugging module `pdb` allows you to set (conditional) breakpoints, single-step through lines of code, and check out stack frames. It also lets you perform post-mortem debugging.

2.2-2.5

The `logging` module, which was added in Python 2.3, defines functions and classes that help you implement a flexible logging system for your application. There are five levels of logging you can use: critical, error, warning, info, and debug.

Python has had a history of profilers, mostly because they were implemented at different times by different people with different needs. The original Python `profile` module was written in pure Python and measured the time spent in functions, the total time as well as the time spent per call, either only the time spent in particular functions or including subsequent (sub)functions calls from there. It is the oldest and the slowest of the three profilers but still gives useful profiling information.

The `hotshot` module was added in Python 2.2 and was intended to replace `profile` because it fixes various errors that `profile` was prone to and has improved performance due to being implemented in C. Note that `hotshot` focuses on reducing profiling overhead during execution but could take longer to deliver results. A critical bug in the timing code was fixed in Python 2.5.

The `cProfile` module, which was added in Python 2.5, was meant to replace the `hotshot` and `profile` modules. The one significant flaw identified by the authors of `cProfile` is that it takes a long time to load results from the log file, does not support detailed child function statistics, and some results appear inaccurate. It is also implemented in C.

3.8 Exercises

3–1. *Identifiers.* Why are variable name and type declarations not used in Python?

3–2. *Identifiers.* Why are function type declarations not used in Python?

3–3. *Identifiers.* Why should we avoid beginning and ending variable names with double underscores?

3–4. *Statements.* Can multiple Python statements be written on a single line?

3–5. *Statements.* Can a single Python statement be written over multiple lines?

3–6. *Variable Assignment.*

(a) Given the assignment x, y, z = 1, 2, 3, what do x, y, and z contain?

(b) What do x, y, and z contain after executing: z, x, y = y, z, x?

3–7. *Identifiers.* Which of the following are valid Python identifiers? If not, why not? Of the invalid ones, which are keywords?

int32	40XL	$aving$	printf	print
_print	this	self	__name__	0x40L
bool	true	big-daddy	2hot2touch	type
thisIsn'tAVar	thisIsAVar	R_U_Ready	Int	True
if	do	counter-1	access	_

The remaining problems deal with the `makeTextFile.py` and `readTex-tFile.py` programs.

3–8. *Python Code*. Copy the scripts to your file system and customize (tweak, improve) them. Modifications can include adding your own comments, changing the prompts ('>' is pretty boring), etc. Get comfortable looking at and editing Python code.

3–9. *Porting*. If you have Python installed on different types of computers, check to see if there are any differences in the `os.linesep` characters. Write down the type/OS and what `linesep` is.

3–10. *Exceptions*. Replace the call to `os.path.exists()` in `makeTextFile.py` with an exception handler as seen in `readTextFile.py`. On the flip side, replace the exception handler in `readTextFile.py` with a call to `os.path.exists()`.

3–11. *String Formatting*. Rather than suppressing the NEWLINE character generated by the **print** statement in `readText-File.py`, change your code so that you strip each line of its whitespace before displaying it. In this case, you can remove the trailing comma from the **print** statement. Hint: Use the string `strip()` method.

3–12. *Merging Source Files*. Combine both programs into one—call it anything you like, perhaps `readNwriteTextFiles.py`. Let the user choose whether to create or display a text file.

3–13. **Adding Features*. Take your `readNwriteTextFiles.py` solution from the previous problem and add a major feature to it: Allow the user to edit an existing text file. You can do this any way you wish, whether you let the user edit line by line or the entire document at once. Note that the latter is much more difficult as you may need help from a GUI toolkit or a screen-based text editing module such as curses. Give users the option to apply the changes (saving the file) or discard them (leaving the original file intact), and also ensure the original file is preserved in case the program exits abnormally during operation.

PYTHON OBJECTS

Chapter Topics

Chapter 4

We will now begin our journey to the core part of the language. First we will introduce what Python objects are, then discuss the most commonly used built-in types. We then discuss the standard type operators and built-in functions (BIFs), followed by an insightful discussion of the different ways to categorize the standard types to gain a better understanding of how they work. Finally, we will conclude by describing some types that Python does *not* have (mostly as a benefit for those of you with experience in another high-level language).

4.1 Python Objects

Python uses the object model abstraction for data storage. Any construct that contains any type of value is an object. Although Python is classified as an "object-oriented programming (OOP) language," OOP is not required to create perfectly working Python applications. You can certainly write a useful Python script without the use of classes and instances. However, Python's object syntax and architecture encourage or "provoke" this type of behavior. Let us now take a closer look at what a Python object is.

All Python objects have the following three characteristics: an *identity*, a *type*, and a *value*.

IDENTITY	Unique identifier that differentiates an object from all others. Any object's identifier can be obtained using the id() built-in function (BIF). This value is as close as you will get to a "memory address" in Python (probably much to the relief of some of you). Even better is that you rarely, if ever, access this value, much less care what it is at all.
TYPE	An object's type indicates what kind of values an object can hold, what operations can be applied to such objects, and what behavioral rules these objects are subject to. You can use the type() BIF to reveal the type of a Python object. Since types are also objects in Python (did we mention that Python was object-oriented?), type() actually returns an object to you rather than a simple literal.
VALUE	Data item that is represented by an object.

All three are assigned on object creation and are read-only with one exception, the value. (For new-style types and classes, it may possible to change the type of an object, but this is not recommended for the beginner.) If an object supports updates, its value can be changed; otherwise, it is also read-only. Whether an object's value can be changed is known as an object's *mutability*, which we will investigate later on in Section 4.7. These characteristics exist as long as the object does and are reclaimed when an object is deallocated.

Python supports a set of basic (built-in) data types, as well as some auxiliary types that may come into play if your application requires them. Most applications generally use the standard types and create and instantiate classes for all specialized data storage.

4.1.1 Object Attributes

Certain Python objects have attributes, data values or executable code such as methods, associated with them. Attributes are accessed in the dotted attribute notation, which includes the name of the associated object, and were introduced in the Core Note in Section 2.14. The most familiar attributes are functions and methods, but some Python types have data attributes associated with them. Objects with data attributes include (but are not limited to): classes, class instances, modules, complex numbers, and files.

4.2 Standard Types

- Numbers (separate subtypes; three are integer types)
  - Integer
    - Boolean
    - Long integer
  - Floating point real number
  - Complex number
- String
- List
- Tuple
- Dictionary

We will also refer to standard types as "primitive data types" in this text because these types represent the primitive data types that Python provides. We will go over each one in detail in Chapters 5, 6, and 7.

4.3 Other Built-in Types

- Type
- Null object (None)
- File
- Set/Frozenset
- Function/Method
- Module
- Class

These are some of the other types you will interact with as you develop as a Python programmer. We will also cover all of these in other chapters of this book with the exception of the type and None types, which we will discuss here.

4.3.1 Type Objects and the type Type Object

It may seem unusual to regard types themselves as objects since we are attempting to just describe all of Python's types to you in this chapter. However, if you keep in mind that an object's set of inherent behaviors and characteristics (such as supported operators and built-in methods) must be defined somewhere, an object's type is a logical place for this information. The amount of information necessary to describe a type cannot fit into a single string; therefore types cannot simply be strings, nor should this information be stored with the data, so we are back to types as objects.

We will formally introduce the `type()` BIF below, but for now, we want to let you know that you can find out the type of an object by calling `type()` with that object:

```
>>> type(42)
<type 'int'>
```

Let us look at this example more carefully. It does not look tricky by any means, but examine the return value of the call. We get the seemingly innocent output of `<type 'int'>`, but what you need to realize is that this is not just a simple string telling you that 42 is an integer. What you see as `<type 'int'>` is actually a type object. It just so happens that the string representation chosen by its implementors has a string inside it to let you know that it is an `int` type object.

Now you may ask yourself, so then what is the type of any type object? Well, let us find out:

```
>>> type(type(42))
<type 'type'>
```

Yes, the type of all type objects is `type`. The `type` type object is also the mother of all types and is the default metaclass for all standard Python classes. It is perfectly fine if you do not understand this now. This will make sense as we learn more about classes and types.

With the unification of types and classes in Python 2.2, type objects are playing a more significant role in both object-oriented programming as well as day-to-day object usage. Classes are now types, and instances are now objects of their respective types.

4.3.2 None, *Python's Null Object*

Python has a special type known as the Null object or `NoneType`. It has only one value, `None`. The type of `None` is `NoneType`. It does not have any operators or BIFs. If you are familiar with C, the closest analogy to the `None` *type* is `void`, while the `None` *value* is similar to the C value of `NULL`. (Other similar objects and values include Perl's `undef` and Java's `void` type and `null` value.)

None has no (useful) attributes and *always* evaluates to having a Boolean False value.

CORE NOTE: Boolean values

All standard type objects can be tested for truth value and compared to objects of the same type. Objects have inherent True *or* False *values. Objects take a* False *value when they are empty, any numeric representation of zero, or the Null object* None.

The following are defined as having false *values in Python:*
- None
- False *(Boolean)*
- *Any numeric zero:*
- 0 *(integer)*
- 0.0 *(float)*
- 0L *(long integer)*
- 0.0+0.0j *(complex)*
- " " *(empty string)*
- [] *(empty list)*
- () *(empty tuple)*
- {} *(empty dictionary)*

Any value for an object other than those above is considered to have a true *value, i.e., non-empty, non-zero, etc. User-created class instances have a* false *value when their nonzero (__nonzero__()) or length (__len__()) special methods, if defined, return a zero value.*

4.4 Internal Types

- Code
- Frame
- Traceback
- Slice
- Ellipsis
- Xrange

We will briefly introduce these internal types here. The general application programmer would typically not interact with these objects directly, but we include them here for completeness. Please refer to the source code or Python internal and online documentation for more information.

In case you were wondering about exceptions, they are now implemented as classes. In older versions of Python, exceptions were implemented as strings.

4.4.1 Code Objects

Code objects are executable pieces of Python source that are byte-compiled, usually as return values from calling the `compile()` BIF. Such objects are appropriate for execution by either **exec** or by the `eval()` BIF. All this will be discussed in greater detail in Chapter 14.

Code objects themselves do not contain any information regarding their execution environment, but they are at the heart of every user-defined function, all of which *do* contain some execution context. (The actual byte-compiled code as a code object is one attribute belonging to a function.) Along with the code object, a function's attributes also consist of the administrative support that a function requires, including its name, documentation string, default arguments, and global namespace.

4.4.2 Frame Objects

These are objects representing execution stack frames in Python. Frame objects contain all the information the Python interpreter needs to know during a runtime execution environment. Some of its attributes include a link to the previous stack frame, the code object (see above) that is being executed, dictionaries for the local and global namespaces, and the current instruction. Each function call results in a new frame object, and for each frame object, a C stack frame is created as well. One place where you can access a frame object is in a traceback object (see the following section).

4.4.3 Traceback Objects

When you make an error in Python, an exception is raised. If exceptions are not caught or "handled," the interpreter exits with some diagnostic information similar to the output shown below:

```
Traceback (innermost last):
   File "<stdin>", line N?, in ???
ErrorName: error reason
```

The traceback object is just a data item that holds the stack trace information for an exception and is created when an exception occurs. If a handler is provided for an exception, this handler is given access to the traceback object.

4.4.4 Slice Objects

Slice objects are created using the Python extended slice syntax. This extended syntax allows for different types of indexing. These various types of indexing include *stride indexing*, multi-dimensional indexing, and indexing using the Ellipsis type. The syntax for multi-dimensional indexing is `sequence[start1 : end1, start2 : end2]`, or using the ellipsis, `sequence [..., start1 : end1]`. Slice objects can also be generated by the `slice()` BIF.

Stride indexing for sequence types allows for a third slice element that allows for "step"-like access with a syntax of `sequence[starting_index : ending_index : stride]`.

Support for the stride element of the extended slice syntax have been in Python for a long time, but until 2.3 was only available via the C API or Jython (and previously JPython). Here is an example of stride indexing:

2.3

```
>>> foostr = 'abcde'
>>> foostr[::-1]
'edcba'
>>> foostr[::-2]
'eca'
>>> foolist = [123, 'xba', 342.23, 'abc']
>>> foolist[::-1]
['abc', 342.23, 'xba', 123]
```

4.4.5 Ellipsis Objects

Ellipsis objects are used in extended slice notations as demonstrated above. These objects are used to represent the actual ellipses in the slice syntax (. . .). Like the Null object `None`, ellipsis objects also have a single name, `Ellipsis`, and have a Boolean `True` value at all times.

4.4.6 XRange Objects

XRange objects are created by the BIF `xrange()`, a sibling of the `range()` BIF, and used when memory is limited and when `range()` generates an unusually large data set. You can find out more about `range()` and `xrange()` in Chapter 8.

For an interesting side adventure into Python types, we invite the reader to take a look at the `types` module in the standard Python library.

4.5 Standard Type Operators

4.5.1 Object Value Comparison

Comparison operators are used to determine equality of two data values between members of the same type. These comparison operators are supported for all built-in types. Comparisons yield Boolean `True` or `False` values, based on the validity of the comparison expression. (If you are using Python prior to 2.3 when the Boolean type was introduced, you will see integer values 1 for `True` and 0 for `False`.) A list of Python's value comparison operators is given in Table 4.1.

2.3

Note that comparisons performed are those that are appropriate for each data type. In other words, numeric types will be compared according to numeric value in sign and magnitude, strings will compare lexicographically, etc.

```
>>> 2 == 2
True
>>> 2.46 <= 8.33
True
>>> 5+4j >= 2-3j
True
>>> 'abc' == 'xyz'
False
>>> 'abc' > 'xyz'
False
>>> 'abc' < 'xyz'
True
>>> [3, 'abc'] == ['abc', 3]
False
>>> [3, 'abc'] == [3, 'abc']
True
```

Also, unlike many other languages, multiple comparisons can be made on the same line, evaluated in left-to-right order:

```
>>> 3 < 4 < 7              # same as ( 3 < 4 ) and ( 4 < 7 )
True
>>> 4 > 3 == 3            # same as ( 4 > 3 ) and ( 3 == 3 )
True
>>> 4 < 3 < 5 != 2 < 7
False
```

We would like to note here that comparisons are strictly between object values, meaning that the comparisons are between the data values and not the

Table 4.1 Standard Type Value Comparison Operators	
Operator	*Function*
expr1 < *expr2*	*expr1* is less than *expr2*
expr1 > *expr2*	*expr1* is greater than *expr2*
expr1 <= *expr2*	*expr1* is less than or equal to *expr2*
expr1 >= *expr2*	*expr1* is greater than or equal to *expr2*
expr1 == *expr2*	*expr1* is equal to *expr2*
expr1 != *expr2*	*expr1* is not equal to *expr2* (C-style)
expr1 <> *expr2*	*expr1* is not equal to *expr2* (ABC/Pascal-style)[a]

a. This "not equal" sign will be phased out in future version of Python. Use ! = instead.

actual data objects themselves. For the latter, we will defer to the object identity comparison operators described next.

4.5.2 Object Identity Comparison

In addition to value comparisons, Python also supports the notion of directly *comparing objects* themselves. Objects can be assigned to other variables (by reference). Because each variable points to the same (shared) data object, any change effected through one variable will change the object and hence be reflected through all references to the same object.

In order to understand this, you will have to think of variables as linking to objects now and be less concerned with the values themselves. Let us take a look at three examples.

Example 1: foo1 and foo2 reference the same object

```
foo1 = foo2 = 4.3
```

When you look at this statement from the value point of view, it appears that you are performing a multiple assignment and assigning the numeric value of 4.3 to both the foo1 and foo2 variables. This is true to a certain degree, but upon lifting the covers, you will find that a numeric object with the contents or value of 4.3 has been created. Then that object's reference is assigned to both foo1 and foo2, resulting in both foo1 and foo2 aliased to the same object. Figure 4–1 shows an object with two references.

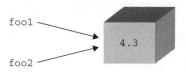

Figure 4-1   **foo1** and **foo2** reference the same object

Example 2: foo1 and foo2 reference the same object

```
foo1 = 4.3
foo2 = foo1
```

This example is very much like the first: A numeric object with value 4.3 is created, then assigned to one variable. When foo2 = foo1 occurs, foo2 is directed to the same object as foo1 since Python deals with objects by passing references. foo2 then becomes a new and additional reference for the original value. So both foo1 and foo2 now point to the same object. The same figure above applies here as well.

Example 3: foo1 and foo2 reference different objects

```
foo1 = 4.3
foo2 = 1.3 + 3.0
```

This example is different. First, a numeric object is created, then assigned to foo1. Then a second numeric object is created, and this time assigned to foo2. Although both objects are storing the exact same value, there are indeed two distinct objects in the system, with foo1 pointing to the first, and foo2 being a reference to the second. Figure 4–2 shows we now have two distinct objects even though both objects have the same value.

Why did we choose to use boxes in our diagrams? Well, a good way to visualize this concept is to imagine a box (with contents inside) as an object. When a variable is assigned an object, that creates a "label" to stick on the box, indicating a reference has been made. Each time a new reference to the same object is made, another sticker is put on the box. When references are abandoned, then a label is removed. A box can be "recycled" only when all the labels have been peeled off the box. How does the system keep track of how many labels are on a box?

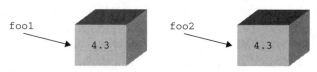

Figure 4–2   **foo1** and **foo2** reference different objects

Each object has associated with it a counter that tracks the total number of references that exist to that object. This number simply indicates how many variables are "pointing to" any particular object. This is the *reference count* that we introduced in Chapter 3, Sections 3.5.5–3.5.7. Python provides the **is** and **is not** operators to test if a pair of variables do indeed refer to the same object. Performing a check such as

```
a is b
```

is an equivalent expression to

```
id(a) == id(b)
```

The object identity comparison operators all share the same precedence level and are presented in Table 4.2.

In the example below, we create a variable, then another that points to the same object.

```
>>> a = [ 5, 'hat', -9.3]
>>> b = a
>>> a is b
True
>>> a is not b
False
>>>
>>> b = 2.5e-5
>>> b
2.5e-005
>>> a
[5, 'hat', -9.3]
>>> a is b
False
>>> a is not b
True
```

Both the **is** and **not** identifiers are Python keywords.

Table 4.2 Standard Type Object Identity Comparison Operators

Operator	Function
obj1 **is** *obj2*	*obj1* is the same object as *obj2*
obj1 **is not** *obj2*	*obj1* is not the same object as *obj2*

CORE NOTE: Interning

In the above examples with the `foo1` *and* `foo2` *objects, you will notice that we use floating point values rather than integers. The reason for this is although integers and strings are immutable objects, Python sometimes caches them to be more efficient. This would have caused the examples to appear that Python is not creating a new object when it should have. For example:*

```
>>> a = 1
>>> id(a)
8402824
>>> b = 1
>>> id(b)
8402824
>>>
>>> c = 1.0
>>> id(c)
8651220
>>> d = 1.0
>>> id(d)
8651204
```

In the above example, a *and* b *reference the same integer object, but* c *and* d *do not reference the same float object. If we were purists, we would want* a *and* b *to work just like* c *and* d *because we really did ask to create a new integer object rather than an alias, as in* b = a.

Python caches or interns only simple integers that it believes will be used frequently in any Python application. At the time of this writing, Python interns integers in the `range(-1, 100)` *but this is subject to change, so do not code your application to expect this.*

In Python 2.3, the decision was made to no longer intern strings that do not have at least one reference outside of the "interned strings table." This means that without that reference, interned strings are no longer immortal and subject to garbage collection like everything else. A BIF introduced in 1.5 to request interning of strings, `intern()`, *has now been deprecated as a result.*

4.5.3 Boolean

Expressions may be linked together or negated using the Boolean logical operators **and**, **or**, and **not**, all of which are Python keywords. These Boolean

Table 4.3 Standard Type Boolean Operators	
Operator	*Function*
not *expr*	Logical NOT of *expr* (negation)
expr1 **and** *expr2*	Logical AND of *expr1* and *expr2* (conjunction)
expr1 **or** *expr2*	Logical OR of *expr1* and *expr2* (disjunction)

operations are in highest-to-lowest order of precedence in Table 4.3. The **not** operator has the highest precedence and is immediately one level below all the comparison operators. The **and** and **or** operators follow, respectively.

```
>>> x, y = 3.1415926536, -1024
>>> x < 5.0
True
>>> not (x < 5.0)
False
>>> (x < 5.0) or (y > 2.718281828)
True
>>> (x < 5.0) and (y > 2.718281828)
False
>>> not (x is y)
True
```

Earlier, we introduced the notion that Python supports multiple comparisons within one expression. These expressions have an implicit **and** operator joining them together.

```
>>> 3 < 4 < 7       # same as "( 3 < 4 ) and ( 4 < 7 )"
True
```

4.6 Standard Type Built-in Functions

Along with generic operators, which we have just seen, Python also provides some BIFs that can be applied to all the basic object types: `cmp()`, `repr()`, `str()`, `type()`, and the single reverse or back quotes (` `` `) operator, which is functionally equivalent to `repr()`.

Table 4.4 Standard Type Built-in Functions

Function	Operation
`cmp(obj1, obj2)`	Compares *obj1* and *obj2*, returns integer *i* where: $i < 0$ if *obj1* < *obj2* $i > 0$ if *obj1* > *obj2* $i == 0$ if *obj1* == *obj2*
`repr(obj)` or `'obj'`	Returns evaluatable string representation of *obj*
`str(obj)`	Returns printable string representation of *obj*
`type(obj)`	Determines type of *obj* and return type object

4.6.1 `type()`

We now formally introduce `type()`. In Python versions earlier than 2.2, `type()` is a BIF. Since that release, it has become a "factory function." We will discuss these later on in this chapter, but for now, you may continue to think of `type()` as a BIF. The syntax for `type()` is:

```
type(object)
```

`type()` takes an object and returns its type. The return value is a `type` object.

```
>>> type(4)                         # int type
<type 'int'>
>>>
>>> type('Hello World!')            # string type
<type 'string'>
>>>
>>> type(type(4))                   # type type
<type 'type'>
```

In the examples above, we take an integer and a string and obtain their types using the `type()` BIF; in order to also verify that types themselves are types, we call `type()` on the output of a `type()` call.

Note the interesting output from the `type()` function. It does not look like a typical Python data type, i.e., a number or string, but is something enclosed by greater-than and less-than signs. This syntax is generally a clue that what you are looking at is an object. Objects may implement a printable string representation; however, this is not always the case. In these scenarios where there is no easy way to "display" an object, Python "pretty-prints" a string representation of the object. The format is usually of the form: `<object_some-thing_or_another>`. Any object displayed in this manner generally gives the object type, an object ID or location, or other pertinent information.

4.6.2 cmp ( )

The `cmp()` BIF CoMPares two objects, say, *obj1* and *obj2*, and returns a negative number (integer) if *obj1* is less than *obj2*, a positive number if *obj1* is greater than *obj2*, and zero if *obj1* is equal to *obj2*. Notice the similarity in return values as C's `strcmp()`. The comparison used is the one that applies for that type of object, whether it be a standard type or a user-created class; if the latter, `cmp()` will call the class's special `__cmp__()` method. More on these special methods in Chapter 13, on Python classes. Here are some samples of using the `cmp()` BIF with numbers and strings.

```
>>> a, b = -4, 12
>>> cmp(a,b)
-1
>>> cmp(b,a)
1
>>> b = -4
>>> cmp(a,b)
0
>>>
>>> a, b = 'abc', 'xyz'
>>> cmp(a,b)
-23
>>> cmp(b,a)
23
>>> b = 'abc'
>>> cmp(a,b)
0
```

We will look at using `cmp()` with other objects later.

4.6.3 str ( ) *and* repr ( ) *(and* `` *Operator)*

The `str()` STRing and `repr()` REPResentation BIFs or the single back or reverse quote operator (``) come in very handy if the need arises to either re-create an object through evaluation or obtain a human-readable view of the contents of objects, data values, object types, etc. To use these operations, a Python object is provided as an argument and some type of string representation of that object is returned. In the examples that follow, we take some random Python types and convert them to their string representations.

```
>>> str(4.53-2j)
'(4.53-2j)'
>>>
>>> str(1)
'1'
>>>
>>> str(2e10)
'20000000000.0'
>>>
>>> str([0, 5, 9, 9])
'[0, 5, 9, 9]'
>>>
>>> repr([0, 5, 9, 9])
'[0, 5, 9, 9]'
>>>
>>> `[0, 5, 9, 9]`
'[0, 5, 9, 9]'
```

Although all three are similar in nature and functionality, only `repr()` and `` ` `` do exactly the same thing, and using them will deliver the "official" string representation of an object that can be evaluated as a valid Python expression (using the `eval()` BIF). In contrast, `str()` has the job of delivering a "printable" string representation of an object, which may not necessarily be acceptable by `eval()`, but will look nice in a **print** statement. There is a caveat that while most return values from `repr()` can be evaluated, not all can:

```
>>> eval(`type(type)`)
  File "<stdin>", line 1
    eval(`type(type)`)
                    ^
SyntaxError: invalid syntax
```

The executive summary is that `repr()` is Python-friendly while `str()` produces human-friendly output. However, with that said, because both types of string representations coincide so often, on many occasions all three return the exact same string.

CORE NOTE: Why have both `repr()` and `` ` ``?

Occasionally in Python, you will find both an operator and a function that do exactly the same thing. One reason why both an operator and a function exist is that there are times where a function may be more useful than the operator, for example, when you are passing around executable objects like functions and where different functions may be called depending on the data item. Another example is the double-star (`**`) and `pow()` BIF, which performs "x to the y power" exponentiation for `x ** y` or `pow(x,y)`.

4.6.4 `type()` *and* `isinstance()`

Python does not support method or function overloading, so you are responsible for any "introspection" of the objects that your functions are called with. (Also see the Python FAQ 4.75.) Fortunately, we have the `type()` BIF to help us with just that, introduced earlier in Section 4.3.1.

What's in a name? Quite a lot, if it is the name of a type. It is often advantageous and/or necessary to base pending computation on the type of object that is received. Fortunately, Python provides a BIF just for that very purpose. `type()` returns the type for any Python object, not just the standard types. Using the interactive interpreter, let us take a look at some examples of what `type()` returns when we give it various objects.

```python
>>> type('')
<type 'str'>
>>>
>>> s = 'xyz'
>>> type(s)
<type 'str'>
>>>
>>> type(100)
<type 'int'>
>>> type(0+0j)
<type 'complex'>
>>> type(0L)
<type 'long'>
>>> type(0.0)
<type 'float'>
>>>
>>> type([])
<type 'list'>
>>> type(())
<type 'tuple'>
>>> type({})
<type 'dict'>
>>> type(type)
<type 'type'>
>>>
>>> class Foo: pass          # new-style class
...
>>> foo = Foo()
>>> class Bar(object): pass  # new-style class
...
>>> bar = Bar()
>>>
```

```
>>> type(Foo)
<type 'classobj'>
>>> type(foo)
<type 'instance'>
>>> type(Bar)
<type 'type'>
>>> type(bar)
<class '__main__.Bar'>
```

Types and classes were unified in Python 2.2. You will see output different from that above if you are using a version of Python older than 2.2:

```
>>> type('')
<type 'string'>
>>> type(0L)
<type 'long int'>
>>> type({})
<type 'dictionary'>
>>> type(type)
<type 'builtin_function_or_method'>
>>>
>>> type(Foo)          # assumes Foo created as in above
<type 'class'>
>>> type(foo)          # assumes foo instantiated also
<type 'instance'>
```

In addition to type(), there is another useful BIF called isinstance(). We cover it more formally in Chapter 13 (Object-Oriented Programming), but here we can introduce it to show you how you can use it to help determine the type of an object.

Example

We present a script in Example 4.1 that shows how we can use isinstance() and type() in a runtime environment. We follow with a discussion of the use of type() and how we migrated to using isinstance() instead for the bulk of the work in this example.

Running typechk.py, we get the following output:

```
-69 is a number of type: int
999999999999999999999 is a number of type: long
98.6 is a number of type: float
(-5.2+1.9j) is a number of type: complex
xxx is not a number at all!!
```

Example 4.1 Checking the Type (`typechk.py`)

The function `displayNumType()` *takes a numeric argument and uses the* `type()` *built-in to indicate its type (or "not a number," if that is the case).*

```
1   #!/usr/bin/env python
2
3   def displayNumType(num):
4       print num, 'is',
5       if isinstance(num, (int, long, float, complex)):
6           print 'a number of type:', type(num).__name__
7       else:
8           print 'not a number at all!!'
9
10  displayNumType(-69)
11  displayNumType(9999999999999999999999L)
12  displayNumType(98.6)
13  displayNumType(-5.2+1.9j)
14  displayNumType('xxx')
```

The Evolution of This Example

Original

The same function was defined quite differently in the first edition of this book:

```
def displayNumType(num):
    print num, "is",
    if type(num) == type(0):
        print 'an integer'
    elif type(num) == type(0L):
        print 'a long'
    elif type(num) == type(0.0):
        print 'a float'
    elif type(num) == type(0+0j):
        print 'a complex number'
    else:
        print 'not a number at all!!'
```

As Python evolved in its slow and simple way, so must we. Take a look at our original conditional expression:

```
if type(num) == type(0)...
```

Reducing Number of Function Calls

If we take a closer look at our code, we see a pair of calls to `type()`. As you know, we pay a small price each time a function is called, so if we can reduce that number, it will help with performance.

An alternative to comparing an object's type with a known object's type (as we did above and in the example below) is to utilize the `types` module, which we briefly mentioned earlier in the chapter. If we do that, then we can use the type object there without having to "calculate it." We can then change our code to only having one call to the `type()` function:

```
>>> import types
>>> if type(num) == types.IntType...
```

Object Value Comparison versus Object Identity Comparison

We discussed object value comparison versus object identity comparison earlier in this chapter, and if you realize one key fact, then it will become clear that our code is still not optimal in terms of performance. During runtime, there is always only one type object that represents an integer. In other words, `type(0)`, `type(42)`, `type(-100)` are always the same object: `<type 'int'>` (and this is also the same object as `types.IntType`).

If they are always the same object, then why do we have to compare their values since we already know they will be the same? We are "wasting time" extracting the values of both objects and comparing them if they are the same object, and it would be more optimal to just compare the objects themselves. Thus we have a migration of the code above to the following:

```
if type(num) is types.IntType... # or type(0)
```

Does that make sense? Object value comparison via the equal sign requires a comparison of their values, but we can bypass this check if the objects themselves are the same. If the objects are different, then we do not even need to check because that means the original variable must be of a different type (since there is only one object of each type). One call like this may not make a difference, but if there are many similar lines of code throughout your application, then it starts to add up.

Reduce the Number of Lookups

This is a minor improvement to the previous example and really only makes a difference if your application performs makes many type comparisons like our example. To actually get the integer type object, the interpreter has to look up the `types` name first, and then within that module's dictionary, find `IntType`. By using **from-import**, you can take away one lookup:

```
from types import IntType
if type(num) is IntType...
```

Convenience and Style

The unification of types and classes in 2.2 has resulted in the expected rise in the use of the `isinstance()` BIF. We formally introduce `isinstance()` in Chapter 13 (Object-Oriented Programming), but we will give you a quick preview now.

This Boolean function takes an object and one or more type objects and returns `True` if the object in question is an instance of one of the type objects. Since types and classes are now the same, `int` is now a type (object) and a class. We can use `isinstance()` with the built-in types to make our **if** statement more convenient and readable:

```
if isinstance(num, int)...
```

Using `isinstance()` along with type objects is now also the accepted style of usage when introspecting objects' types, which is how we finally arrive at our updated `typechk.py` application above. We also get the added bonus of `isinstance()` accepting a tuple of type objects to check against our object with instead of having an **if-elif-else** if we were to use only `type()`.

4.6.5 Python Type Operator and BIF Summary

A summary of operators and BIFs common to all basic Python types is given in Table 4.5. The progressing shaded groups indicate hierarchical precedence from highest-to-lowest order. Elements grouped with similar shading all have equal priority. Note that these (and most Python) operators are available as functions via the `operator` module.

Table 4.5 Standard Type Operators and Built-in Functions

Operator/Function	Description	Result[a]
String representation		
` ` ` `	String representation	str
Built-in functions		
cmp(*obj1, obj2*)	Compares two objects	int
repr(*obj*)	String representation	str
str(*obj*)	String representation	str
type(*obj*)	Determines object type	type
Value comparisons		
<	Less than	bool
>	Greater than	bool
<=	Less than or equal to	bool
>=	Greater than or equal to	bool
==	Equal to	bool
!=	Not equal to	bool
<>	Not equal to	bool
Object comparisons		
is	The same as	bool
is not	Not the same as	bool
Boolean operators		
not	Logical negation	bool
and	Logical conjunction	bool
or	Logical disjunction	bool

a.   Boolean comparisons return either True or False.

4.7   Type Factory Functions

Since Python 2.2 with the unification of types and classes, all of the built-in **2.2**
types are now classes, and with that, all of the "conversion" built-in functions
like `int()`, `type()`, `list()`, etc., are now *factory functions*. This means that
although they look and act somewhat like functions, they are actually class
names, and when you call one, you are actually instantiating an instance of
that type, like a factory producing a good.

The following familiar factory functions were formerly built-in functions:

- `int()`, `long()`, `float()`, `complex()`
- `str()`, `unicode()`, `basestring()`
- `list()`, `tuple()`
- `type()`

Other types that did not have factory functions now do. In addition, factory
functions have been added for completely new types that support the new-style
classes. The following is a list of both types of factory functions:

- `dict()`
- `bool()`
- `set()`, `frozenset()`
- `object()`
- `classmethod()`
- `staticmethod()`
- `super()`
- `property()`
- `file()`

4.8   Categorizing the Standard Types

If we were to be maximally verbose in describing the standard types, we
would probably call them something like Python's "basic built-in data object
primitive types."

- "Basic," indicating that these are the standard or core types that
  Python provides
- "Built-in," due to the fact that these types come by default in
  Python
- "Data," because they are used for general data storage
- "Object," because objects are the default abstraction for data
  and functionality

- "Primitive," because these types provide the lowest-level granularity of data storage
- "Types," because that's what they are: data types!

However, this description does not really give you an idea of how each type works or what functionality applies to them. Indeed, some of them share certain characteristics, such as how they function, and others share commonality with regard to how their data values are accessed. We should also be interested in whether the data that some of these types hold can be updated and what kind of storage they provide.

There are three different models we have come up with to help categorize the standard types, with each model showing us the interrelationships between the types. These models help us obtain a better understanding of how the types are related, as well as how they work.

4.8.1 Storage Model

The first way we can categorize the types is by how many objects can be stored in an object of this type. Python's types, as well as types from most other languages, can hold either single or multiple values. A type which holds a single literal object we will call *atomic* or *scalar* storage, and those which can hold multiple objects we will refer to as *container* storage. (Container objects are also referred to as *composite* or *compound* objects in the documentation, but some of these refer to objects other than types, such as class instances.) Container types bring up the additional issue of whether different types of objects can be stored. All of Python's container types can hold objects of different types. Table 4.6 categorizes Python's types by storage model.

Although strings may seem like a container type since they "contain" characters (and usually more than one character), they are not considered as such

Table 4.6 Types Categorized by the Storage Model

Storage Model Category	Python Types That Fit Category
Scalar/atom	Numbers (all numeric types), strings (all are literals)
Container	Lists, tuples, dictionaries

because Python does not have a character type (see Section 4.8). Thus strings are self-contained literals.

4.8.2 Update Model

Another way of categorizing the standard types is by asking the question, "Once created, can objects be changed, or can their values be updated?" When we introduced Python types early on, we indicated that certain types allow their values to be updated and others do not. *Mutable* objects are those whose values can be changed, and *immutable* objects are those whose values cannot be changed. Table 4.7 illustrates which types support updates and which do not.

Now after looking at the table, a thought that must immediately come to mind is, "Wait a minute! What do you mean that numbers and strings are immutable? I've done things like the following":

```
x = 'Python numbers and strings'
x = 'are immutable?!? What gives?'
i = 0
i = i + 1
```

"They sure as heck don't look immutable to me!" That is true to some degree, but looks can be deceiving. What is really happening behind the scenes is that the original objects are actually being replaced in the above examples. Yes, that is right. Read that again.

Rather than referring to the original objects, new objects with the new values were allocated and (re)assigned to the original variable names, and the old objects were garbage-collected. One can confirm this by using the id() BIF to compare object identities before and after such assignments.

Table 4.7 Types Categorized by the Update Model

Update Model Category	*Python Types That Fit Category*
Mutable	Lists, dictionaries
Immutable	Numbers, strings, tuples

If we added calls to id() in our example above, we may be able to see that the objects are being changed, as below:

```
>>> x = 'Python numbers and strings'
>>> print id(x)
16191392
>>> x = 'are immutable?!? What gives?'
>>> print id(x)
16191232
>>> i = 0
>>> print id(i)
7749552
>>> i = i + 1
>>> print id(i)
7749600
```

Your mileage will vary with regard to the object IDs as they will differ between executions. On the flip side, lists can be modified without replacing the original object, as illustrated in the code below:

```
>>> aList = ['ammonia', 83, 85, 'lady']
>>> aList
['ammonia', 83, 85, 'lady']
>>>
>>> aList[2]
85
>>>
>>> id(aList)
135443480
>>>
>>> aList[2] = aList[2] + 1
>>> aList[3] = 'stereo'
>>> aList
['ammonia', 83, 86, 'stereo']
>>>
>>> id(aList)
135443480
>>>
>>> aList.append('gaudy')
>>> aList.append(aList[2] + 1)
>>> aList
['ammonia', 83, 86, 'stereo', 'gaudy', 87]
>>>
>>> id(aList)
135443480
```

Notice how for each change, the ID for the list remained the same.

4.8.3 Access Model

Although the previous two models of categorizing the types are useful when being introduced to Python, they are not the primary models for differentiating the types. For that purpose, we use the access model. By this, we mean, how do we access the values of our stored data? There are three categories under the access model: *direct*, *sequence*, and *mapping*. The different access models and which types fall into each respective category are given in Table 4.8.

Direct types indicate single-element, non-container types. All numeric types fit into this category.

Sequence types are those whose elements are sequentially accessible via index values starting at 0. Accessed items can be either single elements or in groups, better known as slices. Types that fall into this category include strings, lists, and tuples. As we mentioned before, Python does not support a character type, so, although strings are literals, they are a sequence type because of the ability to access substrings sequentially.

Mapping types are similar to the indexing properties of sequences, except instead of indexing on a sequential numeric offset, elements (values) are unordered and accessed with a key, thus making mapping types a set of hashed key-value pairs.

We will use this primary model in the next chapter by presenting each access model type and what all types in that category have in common (such as operators and BIFs), then discussing each Python standard type that fits into those categories. Any operators, BIFs, and methods unique to a specific type will be highlighted in their respective sections.

So why this side trip to view the same data types from differing perspectives? Well, first of all, why categorize at all? Because of the high-level data structures that Python provides, we need to differentiate the "primitive" types from those that provide more functionality. Another reason is to be clear on what the expected behavior of a type should be. For example, if we minimize the number of times we ask ourselves, "What are the differences

Table 4.8 Types Categorized by the Access Model

Access Model Category	Types That Fit Category
Direct	Numbers
Sequence	Strings, lists, tuples
Mapping	Dictionaries

Table 4.9 Categorizing the Standard Types

Data Type	Storage Model	Update Model	Access Model
Numbers	Scalar	Immutable	Direct
Strings	Scalar	Immutable	Sequence
Lists	Container	Mutable	Sequence
Tuples	Container	Immutable	Sequence
Dictionaries	Container	Mutable	Mapping

between lists and tuples again?" or "What types are immutable and which are not?" then we have done our job. And finally, certain categories have general characteristics that apply to all types in a certain category. A good craftsman (and craftswoman) should know what is available in his or her toolboxes.

The second part of our inquiry asks, "Why all these different models or perspectives"? It seems that there is no one way of classifying all of the data types. They all have crossed relationships with each other, and we feel it best to expose the different sets of relationships shared by all the types. We also want to show how each type is unique in its own right. No two types map the same across all categories. (Of course, all numeric subtypes do, so we are categorizing them together.) Finally, we believe that understanding all these relationships will ultimately play an important implicit role during development. The more you know about each type, the more you are apt to use the correct ones in the parts of your application where they are the most appropriate, and where you can maximize performance.

We summarize by presenting a cross-reference chart (see Table 4.9) that shows all the standard types, the three different models we use for categorization, and where each type fits into these models.

4.9 Unsupported Types

Before we explore each standard type, we conclude this chapter by giving a list of types that are not supported by Python.

`char` or `byte`

Python does not have a char or byte type to hold either single character or 8-bit integers. Use strings of length one for characters and integers for 8-bit numbers.

pointer

Since Python manages memory for you, there is no need to access pointer addresses. The closest to an address that you can get in Python is by looking at an object's identity using the `id()` BIF. Since you have no control over this value, it's a moot point. However, under Python's covers, everything is a pointer.

int **versus** short **versus** long

Python's plain integers are the universal "standard" integer type, obviating the need for three different integer types, e.g., C's `int`, `short`, and `long`. For the record, Python's integers are implemented as C `long`s. Also, since there is a close relationship between Python's `int` and `long` types, users have even fewer things to worry about. You only need to use a single type, the Python integer. Even when the size of an integer is exceed, for example, multiplying two very large numbers, Python automatically gives you a long back instead of overflowing with an error.

float **versus** double

C has both a single precision `float` type and double-precision `double` type. Python's `float` type is actually a C `double`. Python does not support a single-precision floating point type because its benefits are outweighed by the overhead required to support two types of floating point types. For those wanting more accuracy and willing to give up a wider range of numbers, Python has a decimal floating point number too, but you have to import the `decimal` module to use the `Decimal` type. Floats are always estimations. Decimals are exact and arbitrary precision. Decimals make sense concerning things like money where the values are exact. Floats make sense for things that are estimates anyway, such as weights, lengths, and other measurements.

4.10 Exercises

4–1. *Python Objects*. What three attributes are associated with *all* Python objects? Briefly describe each one.

4–2. *Types*. What does immutable mean? Which Python types are mutable and which are not?

4–3. *Types*. Which Python types are sequences, and how do they differ from mapping types?

4–4.   *type().* What does the `type()` built-in function do? What kind of object does `type()` return?

4–5.   *str() and repr().* What are the differences between the `str()` and `repr()` built-in functions? Which is equivalent to the backquote (`` ` ``) operator?

4–6.   *Object Equality.* What do you think is the difference between the expressions `type(a) == type(b)` and `type(a) is type(b)`? Why is the latter preferred? What does `isinstance()` have to do it all of this?

4–7.   *dir() Built-in Function.* In several exercises in Chapter 2, we experimented with a built-in function called `dir()`, which takes an object and reveals its attributes. Do the same thing for the `types` module. Write down the list of the types that you are familiar with, including all you know about each of these types; then create a separate list of those you are not familiar with. As you learn Python, deplete the "unknown" list so that all of them can be moved to the "familiar with" list.

4–8.   *Lists and Tuples.* How are lists and tuples similar? Different?

4–9.   **Interning.* Given the following assignments:

```
a = 10
b = 10
c = 100
d = 100
e = 10.0
f = 10.0
```

What is the output of each of the following and why?

(a) `a is b`

(b) `c is d`

(c) `e is f`

NUMBERS

Chapter Topics

- Introduction to Numbers
- Integers
  - Boolean
  - Standard Integers
  - Long Integers
- Floating Point Real Numbers
- Complex Numbers
- Operators
- Built-in Functions
- Other Numeric Types
- Related Modules

Chapter 5

In this chapter, we will focus on Python's numeric types. We will cover each type in detail, then present the various operators and built-in functions that can be used with numbers. We conclude this chapter by introducing some of the standard library modules that deal with numbers.

5.1 Introduction to Numbers

Numbers provide literal or scalar storage and direct access. A number is also an immutable type, meaning that changing or updating its value results in a newly allocated object. This activity is, of course, transparent to both the programmer and the user, so it should not change the way the application is developed.

Python has several numeric types: "plain" integers, long integers, Boolean, double-precision floating point real numbers, decimal floating point numbers, and complex numbers.

How to Create and Assign Numbers (Number Objects)

Creating numbers is as simple as assigning a value to a variable:

```
anInt = 1
aLong = -9999999999999999L
aFloat = 3.14159265358979323846426433832795
aComplex = 1.23+4.56J
```

How to Update Numbers

You can "update" an existing number by (re)assigning a variable to another number. The new value can be related to its previous value or to a completely different number altogether. We put quotes around *update* because you are not really changing the value of the original variable. Because numbers are immutable, you are just making a new number and reassigning the reference. Do not be fooled by what you were taught about how variables contain values that allow you to update them. Python's object model is more specific than that.

When we learned programming, we were taught that variables act like boxes that hold values. In Python, variables act like pointers that point to boxes. For immutable types, you do not change the contents of the box, you just point your pointer at a new box. Every time you assign another number to a variable, you are creating a new object and assigning it. (This is true for all immutable types, not just numbers.)

```
anInt += 1
aFloat = 2.718281828
```

How to Remove Numbers

Under normal circumstances, you do not really "remove" a number; you just stop using it! If you really want to delete a reference to a number object, just use the **del** statement (introduced in Section 3.5.6). You can no longer use the variable name, once removed, unless you assign it to a new object; otherwise, you will cause a NameError exception to occur.

```
del anInt
del aLong, aFloat, aComplex
```

Okay, now that you have a good idea of how to create and update numbers, let us take a look at Python's four numeric types.

5.2 Integers

Python has several types of integers. There is the Boolean type with two possible values. There are the regular or plain integers: generic vanilla integers recognized on most systems today. Python also has a long integer size; however, these far exceed the size provided by C longs. We will take a look at these types of integers, followed by a description of operators and built-in functions applicable only to Python integer types.

2.3

5.2.1 Boolean

The Boolean type was introduced in Python 2.3. Objects of this type have two possible values, Boolean `True` and `False`. We will explore Boolean objects toward the end of this chapter in Section 5.7.1.

5.2.2 Standard (Regular or Plain) Integers

Python's "plain" integers are the universal numeric type. Most machines (32-bit) running Python will provide a range of -2^{31} to $2^{31}-1$, that is $-2,147,483,648$ to $2,147,483,647$. If Python is compiled on a 64-bit system with a 64-bit compiler, then the integers for that system will be 64-bit. Here are some examples of Python integers:

```
0101    84    -237    0x80    017    -680    -0X92
```

Python integers are implemented as (signed) `longs` in C. Integers are normally represented in base 10 decimal format, but they can also be specified in base 8 or base 16 representation. Octal values have a "0" prefix, and hexadecimal values have either "0x" or "0X" prefixes.

5.2.3 Long Integers

The first thing we need to say about Python long integers (or `longs` for short) is *not* to get them confused with longs in C or other compiled languages—these values are typically restricted to 32- or 64-bit sizes, whereas Python longs are limited only by the amount of (virtual) memory in your machine. In other words, they can be very L-O-N-G longs.

Longs are a superset of integers and are useful when your application requires integers that exceed the range of plain integers, meaning less than -2^{31} or greater than $2^{31}-1$. Use of longs is denoted by the letter "L", uppercase (`L`) or lowercase (`l`), appended to the integer's numeric value. Values can be expressed in decimal, octal, or hexadecimal. The following are examples of longs:

```
16384L      -0x4E8L  017L  -21474836481  052144364L

2997924581  0xDECADEDEADBEEFBADFEEDDEAL  -5432101234L
```

CORE STYLE: Use uppercase "L" with long integers

Although Python supports a case-insensitive "L" to denote longs, we recommend that you use only the uppercase "L" to avoid confusion with the number one (1). Python will display only longs with a capital "L." As integers and longs are slowly being unified, you will only see the "L" with evaluatable string representations (`repr()`) of longs. Printable string representations (`str()`) will not have the "L."

```
>>> aLong = 9999999991
>>> aLong
999999999L
>>> print aLong
999999999
```

5.2.4 Unification of Integers and Long Integers

Both integer types are in the process of being unified into a single integer type. Prior to Python 2.2, plain integer operations resulted in overflow (i.e., greater than the 2^{32} range of numbers described above), but in 2.2 or after, there are no longer such errors.

Python 2.1

```
>>> 9999 ** 8
Traceback (most recent call last):
  File "<stdin>", line 1, in ?
OverflowError: integer exponentiation
```

Python 2.2

```
>>> 9999 ** 8
99920027994400699944002799920001L
```

Removing the error was the first phase. The next step involved bit-shifting; it used to be possible to left-shift bits out of the picture (resulting in 0):

```
>>> 2 << 32
0
```

In 2.3 such an operation gives a warning, but in 2.4 the warning is gone, and the operation results in a real (long) value:

Python 2.3

```
>>> 2 << 32
__main__:1: FutureWarning: x<<y losing bits or changing
sign will return a long in Python 2.4
and up
0
```

Python 2.4

```
>>> 2 << 32
8589934592L
```

Sooner or later (probably later), there will no longer be a long type (at least not at the user level). Things will all happen quietly under the covers. Of course, those with C access will be able to enjoy both types as before, meaning, however, that your C code will still need to be able to distinguish between the different Python integer types. You can read more about the unification of integers and longs in PEP 237.

5.3 Double Precision Floating Point Numbers

Floats in Python are implemented as C doubles, double precision floating point real numbers, values that can be represented in straightforward decimal or scientific notations. These 8-byte (64-bit) values conform to the IEEE 754 definition (52M/11E/1S) where 52 bits are allocated to the mantissa, 11 bits to the exponent (this gives you about $\pm 10^{308.25}$ in range), and the final bit to the sign. That all sounds fine and dandy; however, the actual degree of precision you will receive (along with the range and overflow handling) depends completely on the architecture of the machine as well as the implementation of the compiler that built your Python interpreter.

Floating point values are denoted by a decimal point (.) in the appropriate place and an optional "e" suffix representing scientific notation. We can use either lowercase (e) or uppercase (E). Positive (+) or negative (–) signs between the "e" and the exponent indicate the sign of the exponent. Absence of such a sign indicates a positive exponent. Here are some floating point values:

```
0.0        -777.       1.6        -5.555567119 96e3 * 1.0
4.3e25     9.384e-23  -2.172818   float(12)    1.000000001
3.1416     4.2E-10    -90.        6.022e23     -1.609E-19
```

5.4 Complex Numbers

A long time ago, mathematicians were absorbed by the following equation:

$$x^2 = -1$$

The reason for this is that any real number (positive or negative) multiplied by itself results in a positive number. How can you multiply any number with itself to get a negative number? No such real number exists. So in the eighteenth century, mathematicians invented something called an *imaginary number i* (or *j*, depending on what math book you are reading) such that:

$$j = \sqrt{-1}$$

Basically a new branch of mathematics was created around this special number (or concept), and now imaginary numbers are used in numerical and mathematical applications. Combining a real number with an imaginary number forms a single entity known as a *complex number*. A complex number is any ordered pair of floating point real numbers (x, y) denoted by x + yj where x is the real part and y is the imaginary part of a complex number.

It turns out that complex numbers are used a lot in everyday math, engineering, electronics, etc. Because it became clear that many researchers were reinventing this wheel quite often, complex numbers became a real Python data type long ago in version 1.4.

Here are some facts about Python's support of complex numbers:

- Imaginary numbers by themselves are not supported in Python (they are paired with a real part of 0.0 to make a complex number)
- Complex numbers are made up of real and imaginary parts
- Syntax for a complex number: `real+imagj`
- Both real and imaginary components are floating point values
- Imaginary part is suffixed with letter "J" lowercase (`j`) or uppercase (`J`)

The following are examples of complex numbers:

```
64.375+1j    4.23-8.5j    0.23-8.55j    1.23e-045+6.7e+089j
6.23+1.5j    -1.23-875J  0+1j   9.80665-8.31441J    -.0224+0j
```

5.4.1 Complex Number Built-in Attributes

Complex numbers are one example of objects with data attributes (Section 4.1.1). The data attributes are the real and imaginary components of the complex

Table 5.1 Complex Number Attributes	
Attribute	*Description*
`num.real`	Real component of complex number *num*
`num.imag`	Imaginary component of complex number *num*
`num.conjugate()`	Returns complex conjugate of *num*

number object they belong to. Complex numbers also have a method attribute that can be invoked, returning the complex conjugate of the object.

```
>>> aComplex = -8.333-1.47j
>>> aComplex
(-8.333-1.47j)
>>> aComplex.real
-8.333
>>> aComplex.imag
-1.47
>>> aComplex.conjugate()
(-8.333+1.47j)
```

Table 5.1 describes the attributes of complex numbers.

5.5 Operators

Numeric types support a wide variety of operators, ranging from the standard type of operators to operators created specifically for numbers, and even some that apply to integer types only.

5.5.1 Mixed-Mode Operations

It may be hard to remember, but when you added a pair of numbers in the past, what was important was that you got your numbers correct. Addition using the plus (+) sign was always the same. In programming languages, this may not be as straightforward because there are different types of numbers.

When you add a pair of integers, the + represents integer addition, and when you add a pair of floating point numbers, the + represents double-precision floating point addition, and so on. Our little description extends even to non-numeric types in Python. For example, the + operator for strings represents concatenation, not addition, but it uses the same operator! The point is that for each data type that supports the + operator, there are different pieces of functionality to "make it all work," embodying the concept of *overloading*.

Now, we cannot add a number and a string, but Python does support mixed mode operations strictly between numeric types. When adding an integer and a float, a choice has to be made as to whether integer or floating point addition is used. There is no hybrid operation. Python solves this problem using something called *numeric coercion*. This is the process whereby one of the operands is converted to the same type as the other before the operation. Python performs this coercion by following some basic rules.

To begin with, if both numbers are the same type, no conversion is necessary. When both types are different, a search takes place to see whether one number can be converted to the other's type. If so, the operation occurs and both numbers are returned, one having been converted. There are rules that must be followed since certain conversions are impossible, such as turning a float into an integer, or converting a complex number to any non-complex number type.

Coercions that are possible, however, include turning an integer into a float (just add ".0") or converting any non-complex type to a complex number (just add a zero imaginary component, e.g., "0j"). The rules of coercion follow from these two examples: integers move toward float, and all move toward complex. The Python Language Reference Guide describes the `coerce()` operation in the following manner.

- If either argument is a complex number, the other is converted to complex;
- Otherwise, if either argument is a floating point number, the other is converted to floating point;
- Otherwise, if either argument is a long, the other is converted to long;
- Otherwise, both must be plain integers and no conversion is necessary (in the upcoming diagram, this describes the rightmost arrow).

The flowchart shown in Figure 5–1 illustrates these coercion rules.

Automatic numeric coercion makes life easier for the programmer because he or she does not have to worry about adding coercion code to his or her application. If explicit coercion is desired, Python does provide the `coerce()` built-in function (described later in Section 5.6.2).

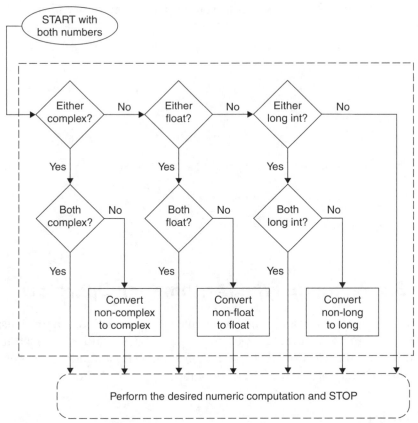

Figure 5–1 Numeric coercion

The following is an example showing you Python's automatic coercion. In order to add the numbers (one integer, one float), both need to be converted to the same type. Since float is the superset, the integer is coerced to a float before the operation happens, leaving the result as a float:

```
>>> 1 + 4.5
5.5
```

5.5.2 Standard Type Operators

The standard type operators discussed in Chapter 4 all work as advertised for numeric types. Mixed-mode operations, described above, are those which involve two numbers of different types. The values are internally converted to the same type before the operation is applied.

Here are some examples of the standard type operators in action with numbers:

```
>>> 5.2 == 5.2
True
>>> -719 >= 833
False
>>> 5+4e >= 2-3e
True
>>> 2 < 5 < 9          # same as ( 2 < 5 ) and ( 5 < 9 )
True
>>> 77 > 66 == 66      # same as ( 77 > 66 ) and ( 66 == 66 )
True
>>> 0. < -90.4 < 55.3e2 != 3 < 181
False
>>> (-1 < 1) or (1 < -1)
True
```

5.5.3 Numeric Type (Arithmetic) Operators

2.2

Python supports unary operators for no change and negation, + and –, respectively; and binary arithmetic operators +, –, *, /, %, and **, for addition, subtraction, multiplication, division, modulo, and exponentiation, respectively. In addition, there is a new division operator, //, as of Python 2.2.

Division

Those of you coming from the C world are intimately familiar with *classic division*—that is, for integer operands, *floor division* is performed, while for floating point numbers, real or *true division* is the operation. However, for those who are learning programming for the first time, or for those who rely on accurate calculations, code must be tweaked in a way to obtain the desired results. This includes casting or converting all values to floats before performing the division.

The decision has been made to change the division operator in some future version of Python from classic to true division and add another operator to perform floor division. We now summarize the various division types and show you what Python currently does, and what it will do in the future.

Classic Division

When presented with integer operands, classic division truncates the fraction, returning an integer (floor division). Given a pair of floating-point operands, it returns the actual floating-point quotient (true division). This functionality is standard among many programming languages, including Python. Example:

```
>>> 1 / 2                # perform integer result (floor)
0
>>> 1.0 / 2.0            # returns actual quotient
0.5
```

True Division

This is where division always returns the actual quotient, regardless of the type of the operands. In a future version of Python, this will be the algorithm of the division operator. For now, to take advantage of true division, one must give the **from** __future__ **import** division directive. Once that happens, the division operator (/) performs only true division:

```
>>> from __future__ import division
>>>
>>> 1 / 2                # returns real quotient
0.5
>>> 1.0 / 2.0            # returns real quotient
0.5
```

Floor Division

A new division operator (//) has been created that carries out floor division: it always truncates the fraction and rounds it to the next smallest whole number toward the left on the number line, regardless of the operands' numeric types. This operator works starting in 2.2 and does not require the __future__ directive above.

```
>>> 1 // 2               # floors result, returns integer
0
>>> 1.0 // 2.0           # floors result, returns float
0.0
>>> -1 // 2              # move left on number line
-1
```

There were strong arguments for as well as against this change, with the former from those who want or need true division versus those who either do not want to change their code or feel that altering the division operation from classic division is wrong.

This change was made because of the feeling that perhaps Python's division operator has been flawed from the beginning, especially because Python is a strong choice as a first programming language for people who aren't used to floor division. One of van Rossum's use cases is featured in his "What's New in Python 2.2" talk:

```
def velocity(distance, totalTime):
    rate = distance / totalTime
```

As you can tell, this function may or may not work correctly and is solely dependent on at least one argument being a floating point value. As mentioned above, the only way to ensure the correct value is to cast both to floats, i.e., `rate = float(distance) / float(totalTime)`. With the upcoming change to true division, code like the above can be left as is, and those who truly desire floor division can use the new double-slash (`//`) operator.

Yes, code breakage is a concern, and the Python team has created a set of scripts that will help you convert your code to using the new style of division. Also, for those who feel strongly either way and only want to run Python with a specific type of division, check out the `-Qdivision_style` option to the interpreter. An option of `-Qnew` will always perform true division while `-Qold` (currently the default) runs classic division. You can also help your users transition to new division by using `-Qwarn` or `-Qwarnall`.

More information about this big change can be found in PEP 238. You can also dig through the 2001 `comp.lang.python` archives for the heated debates if you are interested in the drama. Table 5.2 summarizes the division operators in the various releases of Python and the differences in operation when you import new division functionality.

Modulus

Integer modulo is straightforward integer division remainder, while for float, it is the difference of the dividend and the product of the divisor and the

Table 5.2 Division Operator Functionality

Operator	2.1.x and Older	2.2 and Newer (No Import)	2.2 and Newer (Import of division)
/	classic	classic	true
//	n/a	floor	floor

quotient of the quantity dividend divided by the divisor rounded down to the closest integer, i.e., `x - (math.floor(x/y) * y)`, or

$$x - \left\lfloor \frac{x}{y} \right\rfloor \times y$$

For complex number modulo, take only the real component of the division result, i.e., `x - (math.floor((x/y).real) * y)`.

Exponentiation

The exponentiation operator has a peculiar precedence rule in its relationship with the unary operators: it binds more tightly than unary operators to its left, but less tightly than unary operators to its right. Due to this characteristic, you will find the ** operator twice in the numeric operator charts in this text. Here are some examples:

```
>>> 3 ** 2
9
>>> -3 ** 2          # ** binds tighter than - to its left
-9
>>> (-3) ** 2        # group to cause - to bind first
9
>>> 4.0 ** -1.0   # ** binds looser than - to its right
0.25
```

In the second case, it performs 3 to the power of 2 (3-squared) before it applies the unary negation. We need to use the parentheses around the "−3" to prevent this from happening. In the final example, we see that the unary operator binds more tightly because the operation is 1 over quantity 4 to the first power $\frac{1}{4^1}$ or $\frac{1}{4}$. Note that 1 / 4 as an integer operation results in an integer 0, so integers are not allowed to be raised to a negative power (it is a floating point operation anyway), as we will show here:

```
>>> 4 ** -1
Traceback (innermost last):
  File "<stdin>", line 1, in ?
ValueError: integer to the negative power
```

Summary

Table 5.3 summarizes all arithmetic operators, in shaded hierarchical order from highest-to-lowest priority. All the operators listed here rank higher in priority than the bitwise operators for integers found in Section 5.5.4.

Table 5.3 Numeric Type Arithmetic Operators

Arithmetic Operator	Function
expr1 ** expr2	expr1 raised to the power of expr2[a]
+expr	(unary) expr sign unchanged
-expr	(unary) negation of expr
expr1 ** expr2	expr1 raised to the power of expr2[a]
expr1 * expr2	expr1 times expr2
expr1 / expr2	expr1 divided by expr2 (classic or true division)
expr1 // expr2	expr1 divided by expr2 (floor division [only])
expr1 % expr2	expr1 modulo expr2
expr1 + expr2	expr1 plus expr2
expr1 - expr2	expr1 minus expr2

a.   ** binds tighter than unary operators to its left and looser than unary operators to its right.

Here are a few more examples of Python's numeric operators:

```
>>> -442 - 77
-519
>>>
>>> 4 ** 3
64
>>>
>>> 4.2 ** 3.2
98.7183139527
>>> 8 / 3
2
>>> 8.0 / 3.0
2.66666666667
>>> 8 % 3
2
>>> (60. - 32.) * ( 5. / 9. )
15.5555555556
>>> 14 * 0x04
56
>>> 0170 / 4
```

```
30
>>> 0x80 + 0777
639
>>> 45L * 22L
990L
>>> 16399L + 0xA94E8L
709879L
>>> -2147483648L - 52147483648L
-54294967296L
>>> 64.375+1j + 4.23-8.5j
(68.605-7.5j)
>>> 0+1j ** 2                    # same as 0+(1j**2)
(-1+0j)
>>> 1+1j ** 2                    # same as 1+(1j**2)
0j
>>> (1+1j) ** 2
2j
```

Note how the exponentiation operator is still higher in priority than the binding addition operator that delimits the real and imaginary components of a complex number. Regarding the last example above, we grouped the components of the complex number together to obtain the desired result.

5.5.4 *Bit Operators (Integer-Only)

Python integers may be manipulated bitwise and the standard bit operations are supported: inversion, bitwise AND, OR, and exclusive OR (aka XOR), and left and right shifting. Here are some facts regarding the bit operators:

- Negative numbers are treated as their 2's complement value.
- Left and right shifts of N bits are equivalent to multiplication and division by (2 ** N) without overflow checking.
- For longs, the bit operators use a "modified" form of 2's complement, acting as if the sign bit were extended infinitely to the left.

The bit inversion operator (~) has the same precedence as the arithmetic unary operators, the highest of all bit operators. The bit shift operators (<< and >>) come next, having a precedence one level below that of the standard plus and minus operators, and finally we have the bitwise AND, XOR, and OR operators (&, ^, |), respectively. All of the bitwise operators are presented in the order of descending priority in Table 5.4.

Table 5.4 Integer Type Bitwise Operators	
Bitwise Operator	*Function*
~num	(unary) invert the bits of num, yielding -(num + 1)
num1 << num2	num1 left shifted by num2 bits
num1 >> num2	num1 right shifted by num2 bits
num1 & num2	num1 bitwise AND with num2
num1 ^ num2	num1 bitwise XOR (exclusive OR) with num2
num1	num2	num1 bitwise OR with num2

Here we present some examples using the bit operators using 30 (011110), 45 (101101), and 60 (111100):

```
>>> 30 & 45
12
>>> 30 | 45
63
>>> 45 & 60
44
>>> 45 | 60
61
>>> ~30
-31
>>> ~45
-46
>>> 45 << 1
90
>>> 60 >> 2
15
>>> 30 ^ 45
51
```

5.6 Built-in and Factory Functions

5.6.1 Standard Type Functions

In the last chapter, we introduced the cmp(), str(), and type() built-in functions that apply for all standard types. For numbers, these functions will compare two numbers, convert numbers into strings, and tell you a number's type, respectively. Here are some examples of using these functions:

```
>>> cmp(-6, 2)
-1
>>> cmp(-4.333333, -2.718281828)
-1
>>> cmp(0xFF, 255)
0
>>> str(0xFF)
'255'
>>> str(55.3e2)
'5530.0'
>>> type(0xFF)
<type 'int'>
>>> type(98765432109876543210L)
<type 'long'>
>>> type(2-1j)
<type 'complex'>
```

5.6.2 Numeric Type Functions

Python currently supports different sets of built-in functions for numeric types. Some convert from one numeric type to another while others are more operational, performing some type of calculation on their numeric arguments.

Conversion Factory Functions

The int(), long(), float(), and complex() functions are used to convert from any numeric type to another. Starting in Python 1.5, these functions will also take strings and return the numerical value represented by the string. Beginning in 1.6, int() and long() accepted a base parameter (see below) for proper string conversions—it does not work for numeric type conversion.

A fifth function, bool(), was added in Python 2.2. At that time, it was used to normalize Boolean values to their integer equivalents of one and zero for true and false values. The Boolean type was added in Python 2.3, so true and false now had constant values of True and False (instead of one and zero). For more information on the Boolean type, see Section 5.7.1.

2.2-2.3

In addition, because of the unification of types and classes in Python 2.2, all of these built-in functions were converted into factory functions. Factory functions, introduced in Chapter 4, just means that these objects are now classes, and when you "call" them, you are just creating an instance of that class.

They will still behave in a similar way to the new Python user so it is probably something you do not have to worry about.

The following are some examples of using these functions:

```
>>> int(4.25555)
4
>>> long(42)
42L
>>> float(4)
4.0
>>> complex(4)
(4+0j)
>>>
>>> complex(2.4, -8)
(2.4-8j)
>>>
>>> complex(2.3e-10, 45.3e4)
(2.3e-10+453000j)
```

Table 5.5 summarizes the numeric type factory functions.

Table 5.5 Numeric Type Factory Functions[a]

Class (Factory Function)	Operation
`bool(obj)` [b]	Returns the Boolean value of *obj*, e.g., the value of executing *obj*.__nonzero__()
`int(obj, base=10)`	Returns integer representation of string or number *obj*; similar to `string.atoi()`; optional *base* argument introduced in 1.6
`long(obj, base=10)`	Returns long representation of string or number *obj*; similar to `string.atol()`; optional *base* argument introduced in 1.6
`float(obj)`	Returns floating point representation of string or number *obj*; similar to `string.atof()`
`complex(str)` **or** `complex(real, imag=0.0)`	Returns complex number representation of *str*, or builds one given *real* (and perhaps *imaginary*) component(s)

a. Prior to Python 2.3, these were all built-in functions.
b. New in Python 2.2 as built-in function, converted to factory function in 2.3.

Operational

Python has five operational built-in functions for numeric types: abs(), coerce(), divmod(), pow(), and round(). We will take a look at each and present some usage examples.

abs() returns the absolute value of the given argument. If the argument is a complex number, then math.sqrt(num.real^2 + num.imag^2) is returned. Here are some examples of using the abs() built-in function:

```
>>> abs(-1)
1
>>> abs(10.)
10.0
>>> abs(1.2-2.1j)
2.41867732449
>>> abs(0.23 - 0.78)
0.55
```

The coerce() function, although it technically is a numeric type conversion function, does not convert to a specific type and acts more like an operator, hence our placement of it in our operational built-ins section. In Section 5.5.1, we discussed numeric coercion and how Python performs that operation. The coerce() function is a way for the programmer to explicitly coerce a pair of numbers rather than letting the interpreter do it. This feature is particularly useful when defining operations for newly created numeric class types. coerce() just returns a tuple containing the converted pair of numbers. Here are some examples:

```
>>> coerce(1, 2)
(1, 2)
>>>
>>> coerce(1.3, 134L)
(1.3, 134.0)
>>>
>>> coerce(1, 134L)
(1L, 134L)
>>>
>>> coerce(1j, 134L)
(1j, (134+0j))
>>>
>>> coerce(1.23-41j, 134L)
((1.23-41j), (134+0j))
```

The `divmod()` built-in function combines division and modulus operations into a single function call that returns the pair (quotient, remainder) as a tuple. The values returned are the same as those given for the classic division and modulus operators for integer types. For floats, the quotient returned is `math.floor(`*num1*/*num2*`)` and for complex numbers, the quotient is `math.floor((`*num1*/*num2*`).real)`.

```
>>> divmod(10,3)
(3, 1)
>>> divmod(3,10)
(0, 3)
>>> divmod(10,2.5)
(4.0, 0.0)
>>> divmod(2.5,10)
(0.0, 2.5)
>>> divmod(2+1j, 0.5-1j)
(0j, (2+1j))
```

Both `pow()` and the double star (`**`) operator perform exponentiation; however, there are differences other than the fact that one is an operator and the other is a built-in function.

The `**` operator did not appear until Python 1.5, and the `pow()` built-in takes an optional third parameter, a modulus argument. If provided, `pow()` will perform the exponentiation first, then return the result modulo the third argument. This feature is used for cryptographic applications and has better performance than `pow(x,y) % z` since the latter performs the calculations in Python rather than in C-like `pow(x, y, z)`.

```
>>> pow(2,5)
32
>>>
>>> pow(5,2)
25
>>> pow(3.141592,2)
9.86960029446
>>>
>>> pow(1+1j, 3)
(-2+2j)
```

The `round()` built-in function has a syntax of `round(`*flt*,*ndig*=0`)`. It normally rounds a floating point number to the nearest integral number and returns that result (still) as a float. When the optional *ndig* option is given, `round()` will round the argument to the specific number of decimal places.

```
>>> round(3)
3.0
>>> round(3.45)
3.0
>>> round(3.4999999)
3.0
>>> round(3.4999999, 1)
3.5
>>> import math
>>> for eachNum in range(10):
...             print round(math.pi, eachNum)
...
3.0
3.1
3.14
3.142
3.1416
3.14159
3.141593
3.1415927
3.14159265
3.141592654
3.1415926536
>>> round(-3.5)
-4.0
>>> round(-3.4)
-3.0
>>> round(-3.49)
-3.0
>>> round(-3.49, 1)
-3.5
```

Note that the rounding performed by round() moves away from zero on the number line, i.e., round(.5) goes to 1 and round(-.5) goes to −1. Also, with functions like int(), round(), and math.floor(), all may seem like they are doing the same thing; it is possible to get them all confused. Here is how you can differentiate among these:

- int() chops off the decimal point and everything after (aka truncation).
- floor() rounds you to the next smaller integer, i.e., the next integer moving in a negative direction (toward the left on the number line).
- round() (rounded zero digits) rounds you to the nearest integer period.

Here is the output for four different values, positive and negative, and the results of running these three functions on eight different numbers. (We reconverted the result from `int()` back to a float so that you can visualize the results more clearly when compared to the output of the other two functions.)

```
>>> import math
>>> for eachNum in (.2, .7, 1.2, 1.7, -.2, -.7, -1.2, -1.7):
...        print "int(%.1f)\t%+.1f" % (eachNum, float(int(each-
Num)))
...        print "floor(%.1f)\t%+.1f" % (eachNum,
...        math.floor(eachNum))
...        print "round(%.1f)\t%+.1f" % (eachNum, round(eachNum))
...        print '-' * 20
...
int(0.2)       +0.0
floor(0.2)     +0.0
round(0.2)     +0.0
--------------------
int(0.7)       +0.0
floor(0.7)     +0.0
round(0.7)     +1.0
--------------------
int(1.2)       +1.0
floor(1.2)     +1.0
round(1.2)     +1.0
--------------------
int(1.7)       +1.0
floor(1.7)     +1.0
round(1.7)     +2.0
--------------------
int(-0.2)      +0.0
floor(-0.2)    -1.0
round(-0.2)    +0.0
--------------------
int(-0.7)      +0.0
floor(-0.7)    -1.0
round(-0.7)    -1.0
--------------------
int(-1.2)      -1.0
floor(-1.2)    -2.0
round(-1.2)    -1.0
--------------------
int(-1.7)      -1.0
floor(-1.7)    -2.0
round(-1.7)    -2.0
```

Table 5.6 summarizes the operational functions for numeric types.

Table 5.6 Numeric Type Operational Built-in Functions[a]	
Function	*Operation*
`abs(`*num*`)`	Returns the absolute value of *num*
`coerce(`*num1,* *num2*`)`	Converts *num1* and *num2* to the same numeric type and returns the converted pair as a tuple
`divmod(`*num1,* *num2*`)`	Division-modulo combination returns (*num1* / *num2*, *num1* % *num2*) as a tuple; for floats and complex, the quotient is rounded down (complex uses only real component of quotient)
`pow(`*num1,* *num2,* *mod*`=1)`	Raises *num1* to *num2* power, quantity modulo *mod* if provided
`round(`*flt,* *ndig*`=0)`	(Floats only) takes a float *flt* and rounds it to *ndig* digits, defaulting to zero if not provided

a. Except for `round()`, which applies only to floats.

5.6.3 Integer-Only Functions

In addition to the built-in functions for all numeric types, Python supports a few that are specific only to integers (plain and long). These functions fall into two categories, base presentation with `hex()` and `oct()`, and ASCII conversion featuring `chr()` and `ord()`.

Base Representation

As we have seen before, Python integers automatically support octal and hexadecimal representations in addition to the decimal standard. Also, Python has two built-in functions that return string representations of an integer's octal or hexadecimal equivalent. These are the `oct()` and `hex()` built-in functions, respectively. They both take an integer (in any representation) object and return a string with the corresponding value. The following are some examples of their usage:

```
>>> hex(255)
'0xff'
>>> hex(230948231)
'0x1606627L'
>>> hex(65535*2)
'0x1fffe'
>>>
>>> oct(255)
'0377'
>>> oct(230948231)
'0130063047L'
>>> oct(65535*2)
'0377776'
```

ASCII Conversion

Python also provides functions to go back and forth between ASCII (American Standard Code for Information Interchange) characters and their ordinal integer values. Each character is mapped to a unique number in a table numbered from 0 to 255. This number does not change for all computers using the ASCII table, providing consistency and expected program behavior across different systems. chr() takes a single-byte integer value and returns a one-character string with the equivalent ASCII character. ord() does the opposite, taking a single ASCII character in the form of a string of length one and returns the corresponding ASCII value as an integer:

```
>>> ord('a')
97
>>> ord('A')
65
>>> ord('0')
48

>>> chr(97)
'a'
>>> chr(65L)
'A'
>>> chr(48)
'0'
```

Table 5.7 shows all built-in functions for integer types.

Function	Operation
hex(*num*)	Converts *num* to hexadecimal and returns as string
oct(*num*)	Converts *num* to octal and returns as string
chr(*num*)	Takes ASCII value *num* and returns ASCII character as string; 0 <= *num* <= 255 only
ord(*chr*)	Takes ASCII or Unicode *chr* (string of length 1) and returns corresponding ordinal ASCII value or Unicode code point, respectively
unichr(*num*)	Takes a Unicode code point value num and returns its Unicode character as a Unicode string; valid range depends on whether your Python was built as UCS-2 or UCS-4

Table 5.7 Integer Type Built-in Functions

5.7 Other Numeric Types

5.7.1 Boolean "Numbers"

Boolean types were added to Python starting in version 2.3. Although Boolean values are spelled "True" and "False," they are actually an integer subclass and will behave like integer values one and zero, respectively, if used in a numeric context. Here are some of the major concepts surrounding Boolean types:

2.3

- They have a constant value of either `True` or `False`.

- Booleans are subclassed from integers but cannot themselves be further derived.

- Objects that do not have a __nonzero__() method default to `True`.

- Recall that Python objects typically have a Boolean `False` value for any numeric zero or empty set.

- Also, if used in an arithmetic context, Boolean values `True` and `False` will take on their numeric equivalents of 1 and 0, respectively.

- Most of the standard library and built-in Boolean functions that previously returned integers will now return Booleans.

- Neither `True` nor `False` are keywords yet but will be in a future version.

All Python objects have an inherent `True` or `False` value. To see what they are for the built-in types, review the Core Note sidebar in Section 4.3.2. Here are some examples using Boolean values:

```
# intro
>>> bool(1)
True
>>> bool(True)
True
>>> bool(0)
False
>>> bool('1')
True
>>> bool('0')
True
>>> bool([])
False
>>> bool ( (1,) )
True

# using Booleans numerically
>>> foo = 42
>>> bar = foo < 100
>>> bar
True
>>> print bar + 100
101
>>> print '%s' % bar
True
>>> print '%d' % bar
1

# no __nonzero__()
>>> class C: pass
>>> c = C()
>>>
>>> bool(c)
True
>>> bool(C)
True
```

```
# __nonzero__() overridden to return False
>>> class C:
...      def __nonzero__(self):
...          return False
...
>>> c = C()
>>> bool(c)
False
>>> bool(C)
True

# OH NO!! (do not attempt)
>>> True, False = False, True
>>> bool(True)
False
>>> bool(False)
True
```

You can read more about Booleans in the Python documentation and
PEP 285.

5.7.2 Decimal Floating Point Numbers

Decimal floating point numbers became a feature of Python in version 2.4 (see
PEP 327), mainly because statements like the following drive many (scientific
and financial application) programmers insane (or at least enrage them):

```
>>> 0.1
0.1000000000000001
```

Why is this? The reason is that most implementations of doubles in C are
done as a 64-bit IEEE 754 number where 52 bits are allocated for the mantissa. So floating point values can only be specified to 52 bits of precision, and
in situations where you have a(n endlessly) repeating fraction, expansions of
such values in binary format are snipped after 52 bits, resulting in rounding
errors like the above. The value .1 is represented by $0.11001100110011 \ldots *$
2^{-3} because its closest binary approximation is $.0001100110011 \ldots$, or $1/16 +$
$1/32 + 1/256 + \cdots$

As you can see, the fractions will continue to repeat and lead to the rounding error when the repetition cannot "be continued." If we were to do the
same thing using a decimal number, it looks much "better" to the human eye
because they have exact and arbitrary precision. Note in the below that you
cannot mix and match decimals and floating point numbers. You can create
decimals from strings, integers, or other decimals. You must also import the
`decimal` module to use the `Decimal` number class.

```
>>> from decimal import Decimal
>>> dec = Decimal(.1)
Traceback (most recent call last):
  File "<stdin>", line 1, in ?
  File "/usr/local/lib/python2.4/decimal.py", line 523, in __new__
    raise TypeError("Cannot convert float to Decimal.  " +
TypeError: Cannot convert float to Decimal.  First convert the float to
a string
>>> dec = Decimal('.1')
>>> dec
Decimal("0.1")
>>> print dec
0.1
>>> dec + 1.0
Traceback (most recent call last):
  File "<stdin>", line 1, in ?
  File "/usr/local/lib/python2.4/decimal.py", line 906, in __add__
    other = _convert_other(other)
  File "/usr/local/lib/python2.4/decimal.py", line 2863, in
_convert_other
    raise TypeError, "You can interact Decimal only with int, long or
Decimal data types."
TypeError: You can interact Decimal only with int, long or Decimal data
types.
>>>
>>> dec + Decimal('1.0')
Decimal("1.1")
>>> print dec + Decimal('1.0')
1.1
```

You can read more about decimal numbers in the PEP as well as the Python documentation, but suffice it to say that they share pretty much the same numeric operators as the standard Python number types. Since it is a specialized numeric type, we will not include decimals in the remainder of this chapter.

5.8 Related Modules

There are a number of modules in the Python standard library that add on to the functionality of the operators and built-in functions for numeric types. Table 5.8 lists the key modules for use with numeric types. Refer to the literature or online documentation for more information on these modules.

For advanced numerical and scientific mathematics applications, there are well-known third-party packages Numeric (NumPy) and SciPy, which may be of interest to you. More information on those two packages can be found at:

http://numeric.scipy.org/
http://scipy.org/

Table 5.8 Numeric Type Related Modules

Module	Contents
decimal	Decimal floating point class Decimal
array	Efficient arrays of numeric values (characters, ints, floats, etc.)
math/cmath	Standard C library mathematical functions; most functions available in math are implemented for complex numbers in the cmath module
operator	Numeric operators available as function calls, i.e., operator.sub(*m*, *n*) is equivalent to the difference (*m* - *n*) for numbers *m* and *n*
random	Various pseudo-random number generators (obsoletes rand and whrandom)

CORE MODULE: random

The random *module is the general-purpose place to go if you are looking for random numbers. This module comes with various pseudo-random number generators and comes seeded with the current timestamp so it is ready to go as soon as it has loaded. Here are some of the most commonly used functions in the* random *module:*

randint()	*Takes two integer values and returns a random integer between those values inclusive*
randrange()	*Takes the same input as* range() *and returns a random integer that falls within that range*
uniform()	*Does almost the same thing as* randint(), *but returns a float and is inclusive only of the smaller number (exclusive of the larger number)*
random()	*Works just like* uniform() *except that the smaller number is fixed at 0.0, and the larger number is fixed at 1.0*
choice()	*Given a sequence (see Chapter 6), randomly selects and returns a sequence item*

We have now come to the conclusion of our tour of all of Python's numeric types. A summary of operators and built-in functions for numeric types is given in Table 5.9.

Table 5.9 Operators and Built-in Functions for All Numeric Types

Operator/ Built-in	Description	Int	Long	Float	Complex	Result[a]
abs()	Absolute value	•	•	•	•	*number*[a]
chr()	Character	•	•			str
coerce()	Numeric coercion	•	•	•	•	tuple
complex()	Complex factory function	•	•	•	•	complex
divmod()	Division/modulo	•	•	•	•	tuple
float()	Float factory function	•	•	•	•	float
hex()	Hexadecimal string	•	•			str
int()	Int factory function	•	•	•	•	int
long()	Long factory function	•	•	•	•	long
oct()	Octal string	•	•			str
ord()	Ordinal			(str)		int
pow()	Exponentiation	•	•	•	•	*number*
round()	Float rounding			•		float
**[b]	Exponentiation	•	•	•	•	*number*
+[c]	No change	•	•	•	•	*number*
-[c]	Negation	•	•	•	•	*number*
~[c]	Bit inversion	•	•			int/long
**[b]	Exponentiation	•	•	•	•	*number*
*	Multiplication	•	•	•	•	*number*
/	Classic or true division	•	•	•	•	*number*
//	Floor division	•	•	•	•	*number*
%	Modulo/remainder	•	•	•	•	*number*

Table 5.9 Operators and Built-in Functions for All Numeric Types (continued)

Operator/ Built-in	Description	Int	Long	Float	Complex	Result[a]
+	Addition	•	•	•	•	*number*
–	Subtraction	•	•	•	•	*number*
<<	Bit left shift	•	•			int/long
>>	Bit right shift	•	•			int/long
&	Bitwise AND	•	•			int/long
^	Bitwise XOR	•	•			int/long
|	Bitwise OR	•ᵛ	•ʷ			int/long

a. A result of "number" indicates any of the four numeric types, perhaps the same as the operands.
b. ** has a unique relationship with unary operators; see Section 5.5.3 and Table 5.2.
c. Unary operator.

5.9 Exercises

The exercises in this chapter may first be implemented as applications. Once full functionality and correctness have been verified, we recommend that the reader convert his or her code to functions that can be used in future exercises. On a related note, one style suggestion is not to use **print** statements in functions that return a calculation. The caller can perform any output desired with the return value. This keeps the code adaptable and reusable.

    5–1. *Integers.* Name the differences between Python's regular and long integers.

    5–2. *Operators.*

        (a) Create a function to calculate and return the product of two numbers.

        (b) The code which calls this function should display the result.

5–3. *Standard Type Operators.* Take test score input from the user and output letter grades according to the following grade scale/curve:

A: 90–100

B: 80–89

C: 70–79

D: 60–69

F: <60

5–4. *Modulus.* Determine whether a given year is a leap year, using the following formula: a leap year is one that is divisible by four, but not by one hundred, unless it is also divisible by four hundred. For example, 1992, 1996, and 2000 are leap years, but 1967 and 1900 are not. The next leap year falling on a century is 2400.

5–5. *Modulus.* Calculate the number of basic American coins given a value less than 1 dollar. A penny is worth 1 cent, a nickel is worth 5 cents, a dime is worth 10 cents, and a quarter is worth 25 cents. It takes 100 cents to make 1 dollar. So given an amount less than 1 dollar (if using floats, convert to integers for this exercise), calculate the number of each type of coin necessary to achieve the amount, maximizing the number of larger denomination coins. For example, given $0.76, or 76 cents, the correct output would be "3 quarters and 1 penny." Output such as "76 pennies" and "2 quarters, 2 dimes, 1 nickel, and 1 penny" are not acceptable.

5–6. *Arithmetic.* Create a calculator application. Write code that will take two numbers and an operator in the format: N1 OP N2, where N1 and N2 are floating point or integer values, and OP is one of the following: +, -, *, /, %, **, representing addition, subtraction, multiplication, division, modulus/remainder, and exponentiation, respectively, and displays the result of carrying out that operation on the input operands. Hint: You may use the string `split()` method, but you cannot use the `exal()` built-in function.

5–7. *Sales Tax.* Take a monetary amount (i.e., floating point dollar amount [or whatever currency you use]), and determine a new amount figuring all the sales taxes you must pay where you live.

5–8. *Geometry.* Calculate the area and volume of:

(a) squares and cubes

(b) circles and spheres

5–9. *Style*. Answer the following numeric format questions:

(a) Why does 17 + 32 give you 49, but 017 + 32 give you 47 and 017 + 032 give you 41, as indicated in the examples below?

```
>>> 17 + 32
49
>>> 017+ 32
47
>>> 017 + 032
41
```

(b) Why do we get 134L and not 1342 in the example below?

```
>>> 561 + 781
134L
```

5–10. *Conversion*. Create a pair of functions to convert Fahrenheit to Celsius temperature values. C = (F - 32) * (5 / 9) should help you get started. We recommend you try true division with this exercise, otherwise take whatever steps are necessary to ensure accurate results.

5–11. *Modulus*.

(a) Using loops and numeric operators, output all even numbers from 0 to 20.

(b) Same as part (a), but output all odd numbers up to 20.

(c) From parts (a) and (b), what is an easy way to tell the difference between even and odd numbers?

(d) Using part (c), write some code to determine if one number divides another. In your solution, ask the user for both numbers and have your function answer "yes" or "no" as to whether one number divides another by returning True or False, respectively.

5–12. *Limits*. Determine the largest and smallest ints, floats, and complex numbers that your system can handle.

5–13. *Conversion*. Write a function that will take a time period measured in hours and minutes and return the total time in minutes only.

5–14. *Bank Account Interest*. Create a function to take an interest percentage rate for a bank account, say, a Certificate of Deposit (CD). Calculate and return the Annual Percentage Yield (APY) if the account balance was compounded daily.

5–15. *GCD and LCM*. Determine the greatest common divisor and least common multiple of a pair of integers.

5–16. *Home Finance*. Take an opening balance and a monthly payment. Using a loop, determine remaining balances for succeeding months, including the final payment. "Payment 0"
should just be the opening balance and schedule monthly
payment amount. The output should be in a schedule format
similar to the following (the numbers used in this example
are for illustrative purposes only):

```
Enter opening balance:100.00
Enter monthly payment: 16.13

          Amount    Remaining
Pymt#      Paid      Balance
-----     ------    ---------
  0       $ 0.00    $100.00
  1       $16.13    $ 83.87
  2       $16.13    $ 67.74
  3       $16.13    $ 51.61
  4       $16.13    $ 35.48
  5       $16.13    $ 19.35
  6       $16.13    $  3.22
  7       $ 3.22    $  0.00
```

5–17. *Random Numbers*. Read up on the `random` module and do
the following problem: Generate a list of a random number
$(1 < N <= 100)$ of random numbers $(0 <= n <= 2^{31} -1)$.
Then randomly select a set of these numbers $(1 <= N <= 100)$,
sort them, and display this subset.

SEQUENCES: STRINGS, LISTS, AND TUPLES

Chapter Topics

- Introduction to Sequences
- Strings
- Lists
- Tuples

Chapter 6

The next family of Python types we will be exploring are those whose items are ordered sequentially and accessible via index offsets into its set of elements. This group, known as *sequences*, includes the following types: strings (regular and unicode), lists, and tuples.

We call these sequences because they are made up of sequences of "items" making up the entire data structure. For example, a string consists of a sequence of characters (even though Python does not have an explicit character type), so the first character of a string `"Hello"` is `'H'`, the second character is `'e'`, and so on. Likewise, lists and tuples are sequences of various Python objects.

We will first introduce all operators and built-in functions (BIFs) that apply to all sequences, then cover each type individually. For each sequence type, we will detail the following:

- Introduction
- Operators
- Built-in functions
- Built-in methods (*if applicable*)
- Special features (*if applicable*)
- Related modules (*if applicable*)

We will conclude this chapter with a reference chart that summarizes all of the operators and functions applicable to all sequences. Let us begin by taking a high-level overview.

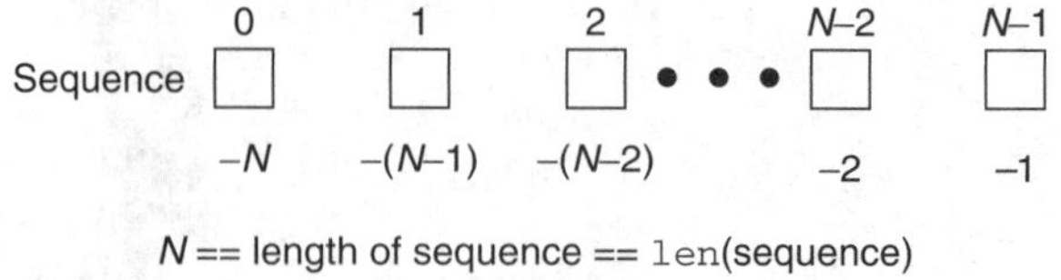

$N ==$ length of sequence $==$ len(sequence)

Figure 6–1   How sequence elements are stored and accessed

6.1 Sequences

Sequence types all share the same access model: ordered set with sequentially indexed offsets to get to each element. Multiple elements may be selected by using the slice operators, which we will explore in this chapter. The numbering scheme used starts from zero (0) and ends with one less than the length of the sequence—the reason for this is because we began at 0. Figure 6–1 illustrates how sequence items are stored.

6.1.1 Standard Type Operators

The standard type operators (see Section 4.5) generally work with all sequence types. Of course, one must comparisons with a grain of salt when dealing with objects of mixed types, but the remaining operations will work as advertised.

6.1.2 Sequence Type Operators

A list of all the operators applicable to all sequence types is given in Table 6.1. The operators appear in hierarchical order from highest to lowest with the levels alternating between shaded and not.

Membership (in, not in)

Membership test operators are used to determine whether an element is *in* or is a member of a sequence. For strings, this test is whether a character is in a string, and for lists and tuples, it is whether an object is an element of those sequences. The **in** and **not in** operators are Boolean in nature; they return True if the membership is confirmed and False otherwise.

The syntax for using the membership operators is as follows:

obj [**not**] **in** *sequence*

Table 6.1 Sequence Type Operators	
Sequence Operator	*Function*
`seq[ind]`	Element located at index *ind* of *seq*
`seq[ind1:ind2]`	Elements from *ind1* up to but not including *ind2* of *seq*
`seq * expr`	*seq* repeated *expr* times
`seq1 + seq2`	Concatenates sequences *seq1* and *seq2*
`obj` **in** `seq`	Tests if *obj* is a member of sequence *seq*
`obj` **not in** `seq`	Tests if *obj* is not a member of sequence *seq*

Concatenation (+)

This operation allows us to take one sequence and join it with another sequence of the same type. The syntax for using the concatenation operator is as follows:

```
sequence1 + sequence2
```

The resulting expression is a new sequence that contains the combined contents of sequences *sequence1* and *sequence2*. Note, however, that although this appears to be the simplest way conceptually to merge the contents of two sequences together, it is not the fastest or most efficient.

For strings, it is less memory-intensive to hold all of the substrings in a list or iterable and use one final `join()` string method call to merge them together. Similarly for lists, it is recommend that readers use the `extend()` list method instead of concatenating two or more lists together. Concatenation comes in handy when you need to merge two sequences together on the fly and cannot rely on mutable object built-in methods that do not have a return value (or more accurately, a return value of None). There is an example of this case in the section below on slicing.

Repetition (*)

The repetition operator is useful when consecutive copies of sequence elements are desired. The syntax for using the repetition operator is as follows:

```
sequence * copies_int
```

The number of copies, *copies_int*, must be an integer (prior to 1.6, long integers were not allowed). As with the concatenation operator, the object returned is newly allocated to hold the contents of the multiply replicated objects.

Slices ([ ], [:], [: :])

To put it simply: *sequences* are data structures that hold objects in an ordered manner. You can get access to individual elements with an index and pair of brackets, or a consecutive group of elements with the brackets and colons giving the indices of the elements you want starting from one index and going up to but not including the ending index.

Now we are going to explain exactly what we just said in full detail. Sequences are structured data types whose elements are placed sequentially in an ordered manner. This format allows for individual element access by index offset or by an index range of indices to select groups of sequential elements in a sequence. This type of access is called *slicing*, and the slicing operators allow us to perform such access.

The syntax for accessing an individual element is:

   sequence[index]

sequence is the name of the sequence and *index* is the offset into the sequence where the desired element is located. Index values can be positive, ranging from 0 to the maximum index (which is length of the sequence less one). Using the `len()` function (which we will formally introduce in the next section), this gives an index with the range 0 <= *index* <= `len(`*sequence*`)`-1.

Alternatively, negative indexes can be used, ranging from –1 to the negative length of the sequence, `-len(`*sequence*`)`, i.e., `-len(`*sequence*`)` <= *index* <= -1. The difference between the positive and negative indexes is that positive indexes start from the beginning of the sequences and negative indexes work backward from the end.

Attempting to retrieve a sequence element with an index outside of the length of the sequence results in an `IndexError` exception:

```
>>> names = ('Faye', 'Leanna', 'Daylen')
>>> print names[4]
Traceback (most recent call last):
  File "<stdin>", line 1, in ?
IndexError: tuple index out of range
```

Because Python is object oriented, you can also directly access an element of a sequence (without first having to assign it to a variable) like this:

```
>>> print ('Faye', 'Leanna', 'Daylen')[1]
Leanna
```

This comes in handy especially in cases where you have called a function and know that you are going to get back a sequence as a return value but are only interested in one or more elements and not the whole thing. So how do we select multiple elements?

Accessing a group of elements is similar to accessing just a single item. Starting and ending indexes may be given, separated by a colon (:). The syntax for accessing a group of elements is:

```
sequence[starting_index:ending_index]
```

Using this syntax, we can obtain a "slice" of elements in *sequence* from the *starting_index* up to but not including the element at the *ending_index* index. Both *starting_index* and *ending_index* are optional, and if not provided, or if None is used as an index, the slice will go from the beginning of the sequence or until the end of the sequence, respectively.

In Figures 6–2 to 6–6, we take an entire sequence (of soccer players) of length 5, and explore how to take various slices of such a sequence.

Figure 6–2 Entire sequence: *sequence* or *sequence*[:]

Figure 6-3   Sequence slice: *sequence*[0:3] or *sequence*[:3]

Extended Slicing with Stride Indices

The final slice syntax for sequences, known as *extended slicing*, involves a third index known as a *stride*. You can think of a stride index like a "step" value as the third element of a call to the range() built-in function or a **for** loop in languages like C/C++, Perl, PHP, and Java.

Extended slice syntax with stride indices has actually been around for a long time, built into the Python virtual machine but accessible only via extensions. This syntax was even made available in Jython (and its predecessor JPython)

Figure 6-4   Sequence slice: *sequence*[2:5] or *sequence*[2:]

Figure 6–5 Sequence slice: `sequence[1:3]`

long before version 2.3 of the C interpreter gave everyone else access to it.
Here are a few examples:

```
>>> s = 'abcdefgh'
>>> s[::-1]               # think of it as 'reverse'
'hgfedcba'
>>> s[::2]                # think of it as skipping by 2
'aceg'
```

2.3

Figure 6–6 Sequence slice: `sequence[3]`

More on Slice Indexing

The slice index syntax is more flexible than the single element index. The starting and ending indices can exceed the length of the string. In other words, the starting index can start off well left of 0, that is, an index of −100 does not exist, but does not produce an error. Similarly, an index of 100 as an ending index of a sequence with fewer than 100 elements is also okay, as shown here:

```
>>> ('Faye', 'Leanna', 'Daylen')[-100:100]
('Faye', 'Leanna', 'Daylen')
```

Here is another problem: we want to take a string and display it in a loop. Each time through we would like to chop off the last character. Here is a snippet of code that does what we want:

```
>>> s = 'abcde'
>>> i = -1
>>> for i in range(-1, -len(s), -1):
...     print s[:i]
...
abcd
abc
ab
a
```

However, what if we wanted to display the entire string at the first iteration? Is there a way we can do it without adding an additional **print** s before our loop? What if we wanted to programmatically specify no index, meaning all the way to the end? There is no real way to do that with an index as we are using negative indices in our example, and -1 is the "smallest" index. We cannot use 0, as that would be interpreted as the first element and would not display anything:

```
>>> s[:0]
''
```

Our solution is another tip: using None as an index has the same effect as a missing index, so you can get the same functionality programmatically, i.e., when you are using a variable to index through a sequence but also want to be able to access the first or last elements:

```
>>> s = 'abcde'
>>> for i in [None] + range(-1, -len(s), -1):
...     print s[:i]
...
abcde
abcd
abc
ab
a
```

So it works the way we want now. Before parting ways for now, we wanted to point out that this is one of the places where we could have created a list `[None]` and used the `extend()` method to add the `range()` output, or create a list with the `range()` elements and inserted `None` at the beginning, but we are (horribly) trying to save several lines of code here. Mutable object built-in methods like `extend()` do not have a return value, so we could not have used:

```
>>> for i in [None].extend(range(-1, -len(s), -1)):
...     print s[:i]
...
Traceback (most recent call last):
  File "<stdin>", line 1, in ?
TypeError: iteration over non-sequence
```

The reason for the error is that `[None].extend(...)` returns `None`, which is neither a sequence nor an iterable. The only way we could do it without adding extra lines of code is with the list concatenation above.

6.1.3 Built-in Functions (BIFs)

Before we look at sequence type BIFs, we wanted to let you know that you will be seeing the term *iterable* mixed in with sequence. The reason for this is that iterables are more generalized and include data types like sequences, iterators, or any object supporting iteration.

Because Python's **for** loops can iterate over any iterable type, it will seem like iterating over a pure sequence, even if it isn't one. Also, many of Python's BIFs that previously only accepted sequences as arguments have been upgraded to take iterators and iterator-like objects as well, hence the basket term, "iterable."

We will discuss in detail in this chapter BIFs that have a strong tie to sequences. We will discuss BIFs that apply more specifically to iteration in loops in Chapter 8, "Conditionals and Loops."

Conversion/Casting

The `list()`, `str()`, and `tuple()` BIFs are used to convert from any sequence type to another. You can also think of them as *casting* if coming over from another language, but there really is no conversion or casting going on. These "converters" are really factory functions (introduced in Chapter 4) that take an object and (shallow) copy its contents into a newly generated object of the desired type. Table 6.2 lists the sequence type conversion functions.

Table 6.2 Sequence Type *Conversion* Factory Functions

Function	*Operation*
list(*iter*)	Converts *iter*able to a list
str(*obj*)	Converts *obj* to string (a printable string representation)
unicode(*obj*)	Converts *obj* to a Unicode string (using default encoding)
basestring()	Abstract factory function serves only as parent class of str and unicode, so cannot be called/instantiated (see Section 6.2)
tuple(*iter*)	Converts *iter*able to a tuple

Again, we use the term "convert" loosely. But why doesn't Python just convert our argument object into another type? Recall from Chapter 4 that once Python objects are created, we cannot change their identity or their type. If you pass a list to list(), a (shallow) copy of the list's objects will be made and inserted into the new list. This is also similar to how the concatenation and repetition operators that we have seen previously do their work.

A shallow copy is where only references are copied...no new objects are made! If you also want copies of the objects (including recursively if you have container objects in containers), you will need to learn about deep copies. More information on shallow and deep copies is available toward the end of this chapter.

The str() function is most popular when converting an object into something printable and works with other types of objects, not just sequences. The same thing applies for the Unicode version of str(), unicode(). The list() and tuple() functions are useful to convert from one to another (lists to tuples and vice versa). However, although those functions are applicable for strings as well since strings are sequences, using tuple() and list() to turn strings into tuples or lists (of characters) is not common practice.

Operational

Python provides the following operational BIFs for sequence types (see Table 6.3 below). Note that len(), reversed(), and sum() can only accept sequences while the rest can take iterables. Alternatively, max() and min() can also take a list of arguments

Table 6.3 Sequence Type *Operational* Built-in Functions

Function	*Operation*
enumerate(*iter*) [a]	Takes an *iter*able and returns an enumerate object (also an iterator) which generates 2-tuple elements (index, item) of *iter* (PEP 279)
len(*seq*)	Returns length (number of items) of *seq*
max(*iter, key=None*) or max(*arg0, arg1..., key=None*) [b]	Returns "largest" element in *iter* or returns "largest" of (*arg0, arg1,* ...); if *key* is present, it should be a callback to pass to the sort() method for testing
min(*iter, key=None*) or min(*arg0, arg1.... key=None*) [b]	Returns "smallest" element in *iter;* returns "smallest" of (*arg0, arg1,* ...); if *key* is present, it should be a callback to pass to the sort() method for testing
reversed(*seq*) [c]	Takes *sequence* and returns an iterator that traverses that sequence in reverse order (PEP 322)
sorted(*iter, func=None, key=None, reverse=False*) [c]	Takes an iterable *iter* and returns a sorted list; optional arguments *func, key,* and *reverse* are the same as for the list.sort() built-in method
sum(*seq, init=0*) [a]	Returns the sum of the numbers of *seq* and optional *ini*tial value; it is equivalent to reduce (operator.add, *seq, init*)
zip([*it0, it1,...* *itN*]) [d]	Returns a list of tuples whose elements are members of each iterable passed into it, i.e., [(*it0*[0], *it1*[0],... *itN*[0]), (*it0*[1], *it1*[1],... *itN*[1]),... (*it0*[n], *it1*[n],... *itN*[n])], where n is the minimum cardinality of all of the iterables

a. New in Python 2.3.
b. *key* argument new in Python 2.5.
c. New in Python 2.4.
d. New in Python 2.0; more flexibility added in Python 2.4.

We will provide some examples of using these functions with each sequence type in their respective sections.

6.2 Strings

Strings are among the most popular types in Python. We can create them simply by enclosing characters in quotes. Python treats single quotes the same as double quotes. This contrasts with most other shell-type scripting languages, which use single quotes for literal strings and double quotes to allow escaping of characters. Python uses the "raw string" operator to create literal quotes, so no differentiation is necessary. Other languages such as C use single quotes for characters and double quotes for strings. Python does not have a character type; this is probably another reason why single and double quotes are treated the same.

Nearly every Python application uses strings in one form or another. Strings are a literal or scalar type, meaning they are treated by the interpreter as a singular value and are not containers that hold other Python objects. Strings are immutable, meaning that changing an element of a string requires creating a new string. Strings are made up of individual characters, and such elements of strings may be accessed sequentially via slicing.

2.2   With the unification of types and classes in 2.2, there are now actually *three* types of strings in Python. Both regular string (`str`) and Unicode string (`unicode`) types are actually subclassed from an abstract class called `basestring`. This class cannot be instantiated, and if you try to use the factory function to make one, you get this:

```
>>> basestring('foo')
Traceback (most recent call last):
  File "<stdin>", line 1, in <module>
TypeError: The basestring type cannot be instantiated
```

How to Create and Assign Strings

Creating strings is as simple as using a scalar value or having the `str()` factory function make one and assigning it to a variable:

```
>>> aString = 'Hello World!'      # using single quotes
>>> anotherString = "Python is cool!" # double quotes
>>> print aString                 # print, no quotes!
Hello World!
>>> anotherString                 # no print, quotes!
'Python is cool!'
```

```
>>> s = str(range(4))            # turn list to string
>>> s
'[0, 1, 2, 3]'
```

How to Access Values (Characters and Substrings) in Strings

Python does not support a character type; these are treated as strings of length one, thus also considered a substring. To access substrings, use the square brackets for slicing along with the index or indices to obtain your substring:

```
>>> aString = 'Hello World!'
>>> aString[0]
'H'
>>> aString[1:5]
'ello'
>>> aString[6:]
'World!'
```

How to Update Strings

You can "update" an existing string by (re)assigning a variable to another string. The new value can be related to its previous value or to a completely different string altogether.

```
>>> aString = aString[:6] + 'Python!'
>>> aString
'Hello Python!'
>>> aString = 'different string altogether'
>>> aString
'different string altogether'
```

Like numbers, strings are not mutable, so you cannot change an existing string without creating a new one from scratch. That means that you cannot update individual characters or substrings in a string. However, as you can see above, there is nothing wrong with piecing together parts of your old string into a new string.

How to Remove Characters and Strings

To repeat what we just said, strings are immutable, so you cannot remove individual characters from an existing string. What you can do, however, is to empty the string, or to put together another string that drops the pieces you were not interested in.

Let us say you want to remove one letter from "Hello World!"... the (lower-case) letter "l," for example:

```
>>> aString = 'Hello World!'
>>> aString = aString[:3] + aString[4:]
>>> aString
'Helo World!'
```

To clear or remove a string, you assign an empty string or use the **del** statement, respectively:

```
>>> aString = ''
>>> aString
' '
>>> del aString
```

In most applications, strings do not need to be explicitly deleted. Rather, the code defining the string eventually terminates, and the string is eventually deallocated.

6.3 Strings and Operators

6.3.1 Standard Type Operators

In Chapter 4, we introduced a number of operators that apply to most objects, including the standard types. We will take a look at how some of those apply to strings. For a brief introduction, here are a few examples using strings:

```
>>> str1 = 'abc'
>>> str2 = 'lmn'
>>> str3 = 'xyz'
>>> str1 < str2
True
>>> str2 != str3
True
>>> str1 < str3 and str2 == 'xyz'
False
```

When using the value comparison operators, strings are compared lexicographically (ASCII value order).

6.3.2 Sequence Operators

Slices ([ ] and [:])

Earlier in Section 6.1.1, we examined how we can access individual or a group of elements from a sequence. We will apply that knowledge to strings in this section. In particular, we will look at:

- Counting forward
- Counting backward
- Default/missing indexes

For the following examples, we use the single string `'abcd'`. Provided in the figure is a list of positive and negative indexes that indicate the position in which each character is located within the string itself.

0	1	2	3
a	b	c	d

−4 −3 −2 −1

Using the length operator, we can confirm that its length is 4:

```
>>> aString = 'abcd'
>>> len(aString)
4
```

When counting forward, indexes start at 0 to the left and end at one less than the length of the string (because we started from zero). In our example, the final index of our string is:

```
final_index     = len(aString) - 1
                = 4 - 1
                = 3
```

We can access any substring within this range. The slice operator with a single argument will give us a single character, and the slice operator with a range, i.e., using a colon (:), will give us multiple consecutive characters. Again, for any ranges [*start*:*end*], we will get all characters starting at offset *start* up to, but not including, the character at *end*. In other words, for all characters x in the range [*start*:*end*], *start* <= x < *end*.

```
>>> aString[0]
'a'
>>> aString[1:3]
'bc'
>>> aString[2:4]
'cd'
>>> aString[4]
Traceback (innermost last):
  File "<stdin>", line 1, in ?
IndexError: string index out of range
```

Any index outside our valid index range (in our example, 0 to 3) results in an error. Above, our access of `aString[2:4]` was valid because that returns characters at indexes 2 and 3, i.e., `'c'` and `'d'`, but a direct access to the character at index 4 was invalid.

When counting backward, we start at index –1 and move toward the beginning of the string, ending at negative value of the length of the string. The final index (the first character) is located at:

```
final_index    = -len(aString)
               = -4
>>> aString[-1]
'd'
>>> aString[-3:-1]
'bc'
>>> aString[-4]
'a'
```

When either a starting or an ending index is missing, they default to the beginning or end of the string, respectively.

```
>>> aString[2:]
'cd'
>>> aString[1:]
'bcd'
>>> aString[:-1]
'abc'
>>> aString[:]
'abcd'
```

Notice how the omission of both indices gives us a copy of the entire string.

Membership (`in`, `not in`)

The membership question asks whether a (sub)string appears in a(nother) string. `True` is returned if that character appears in the string and `False` otherwise. Note that the membership operation is not used to determine if a substring is within a string. Such functionality can be accomplished by using the string methods or string module functions `find()` or `index()` (and their brethren `rfind()` and `rindex()`).

Below are a few more examples of strings and the membership operators. Note that prior to Python 2.3, the **in** (and **not in**) operators for strings only allowed a single character check, such as the second example below (is 'n' a substring of 'abcd'). In 2.3, this was opened up to all strings, not just characters.

```
>>> 'bc' in 'abcd'
True
>>> 'n' in 'abcd'
False
>>> 'nm' not in 'abcd'
True
```

In Example 6.1, we will be using the following predefined strings found in the `string` module:

```
>>> import string
>>> string.uppercase
'ABCDEFGHIJKLMNOPQRSTUVWXYZ'
>>> string.lowercase
'abcdefghijklmnopqrstuvwxyz'
>>> string.letters
'abcdefghijklmnopqrstuvwxyzABCDEFGHIJKLMNOPQRSTUVWXYZ'
>>> string.digits
'0123456789'
```

Example 6.1 is a small script called `idcheck.py` which checks for valid Python identifiers. As we now know, Python identifiers must start with an alphabetic character. Any succeeding characters may be alphanumeric.

Example 6.1 ID Check (`idcheck.py`)

Tests for identifier validity. First symbol must be alphabetic and remaining symbols must be alphanumeric. This tester program only checks identifiers that are at least two characters in length.

```
1   #!usr/bin/env python
2
3   import string
4
5   alphas = string.letters + '_'
6   nums = string.digits
7
8   print 'Welcome to the Identifier Checker v1.0'
9   print 'Testees must be at least 2 chars long.'
10  myInput = raw_input('Identifier to test? ')
11
12  if len(myInput) > 1:
13
14      if myInput[0] not in alphas:
15          print '''invalid: first symbol must be
16              alphabetic'''
17      else:
18          for otherChar in myInput[1:]:
19
20              if otherChar not in alphas + nums:
21                  print '''invalid: remaining
22                      symbols must be alphanumeric'''
23                  break
24          else:
25              print "okay as an identifier"
```

The example also shows use of the string concatenation operator (+) introduced later in this section.

Running this script several times produces the following output:

```
$ python idcheck.py
Welcome to the Identifier Checker v1.0
Testees must be at least 2 chars long.
Identifier to test? counter
okay as an identifier
$
$ python idcheck.py
Welcome to the Identifier Checker v1.0
Testees must be at least 2 chars long.
Identifier to test? 3d_effects
invalid: first symbol must be alphabetic
```

Let us take apart the application line by line.

Lines 3–6

Import the `string` module and use some of the predefined strings to put together valid alphabetic and numeric identifier strings that we will test against.

Lines 8–12

Print the salutation and prompt for user input. The **if** statement on line 12 filters out all identifiers or candidates shorter than two characters in length.

Lines 14–16

Check to see if the first symbol is alphabetic. If it is not, display the output indicating the result and perform no further processing.

Lines 17–18

Otherwise, loop to check the other characters, starting from the second symbol to the end of the string.

Lines 20–23

Check to see if each remaining symbol is alphanumeric. Note how we use the concatenation operator (see below) to create the set of valid characters. As soon as we find an invalid character, display the result and perform no further processing by exiting the loop with **break**.

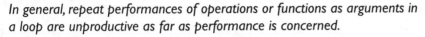

In general, repeat performances of operations or functions as arguments in a loop are unproductive as far as performance is concerned.

```
while i < len(myString):
        print 'character %d is:', myString[i]
```

The loop above wastes valuable time recalculating the length of string myString. *This function call occurs for each loop iteration. If we simply save this value once, we can rewrite our loop so that it is more productive.*

```
length = len(myString)
while i < length:
      print 'character %d is:', myString[i]
```

The same idea applies for this loop above in Example 6.1.

```
for otherChar in myInput[1:]:
      if otherChar not in alphas + nums:
          :
```

The **for** *loop beginning on line 18 contains an* **if** *statement that concatenates a pair of strings. These strings do not change throughout the course of the application, yet this calculation must be performed for each loop iteration. If we save the new string first, we can then reference that string rather than make the same calculations over and over again:*

```
alphnums = alphas + nums
for otherChar in myInput[1:]:
        if otherChar not in alphnums:
            :
```

Lines 24–25

It may be somewhat premature to show you a **for-else** loop statement, but we are going to give it a shot anyway. (For a full treatment, see Chapter 8). The **else** statement for a **for** loop is optional and, if provided, will execute if the loop finished in completion without being "broken" out of by **break**. In our application, if all remaining symbols check out okay, then we have a valid identifier name. The result is displayed to indicate as such, completing execution.

This application is not without its flaws, however. One problem is that the identifiers tested must have length greater than 1. Our application "as is" is not reflective of the true range of Python identifiers, which may be of length 1. Another problem with our application is that it does not take into consideration Python keywords, which are reserved names that cannot be used for identifiers. We leave these two tasks as exercises for the reader (see Exercise 6–2).

Concatenation (+)

Runtime String Concatenation

We can use the concatenation operator to create new strings from existing ones. We have already seen the concatenation operator in action above in Example 6–1. Here are a few more examples:

```
>>> 'Spanish' + 'Inquisition'
'SpanishInquisition'
>>>
>>> 'Spanish' + ' ' + 'Inquisition'
'Spanish Inquisition'
>>>
>>> s = 'Spanish' + ' ' + 'Inquisition' + ' Made Easy'
>>> s
'Spanish Inquisition Made Easy'
>>>
>>> import string
>>> string.upper(s[:3] + s[20])      # archaic (see below)
'SPAM'
```

The last example illustrates using the concatenation operator to put together a pair of slices from string s, the "Spa" from "Spanish" and the "M" from "Made." The extracted slices are concatenated and then sent to the `string.upper()` function to convert the new string to all uppercase letters. String methods were added to Python back in 1.6 so such examples can be replaced with a single call to the final string method (see example below). There is really no longer a need to import the `string` module unless you are trying to access some of the older string constants which that module defines.

Note: Although easier to learn for beginners, we recommend not using string concatenation when performance counts. The reason is that for every string that is part of a concatenation, Python has to allocate new memory for all strings involved, including the result. Instead, we recommend you either use the string format operator (%), as in the examples below, or put all of the substrings in a list, and using one `join()` call to put them all together:

```
>>> '%s %s' % ('Spanish', 'Inquisition')
'Spanish Inquisition'
>>>
>>> s = ' '.join(('Spanish', 'Inquisition', 'Made Easy'))
>>> s
'Spanish Inquisition Made Easy'
>>>
>>> # no need to import string to use string.upper():
>>> ('%s%s' % (s[:3], s[20])).upper()
'SPAM'
```

Compile-Time String Concatenation

The above syntax using the addition operator performs the string concatenation at runtime, and its use is the norm. There is a less frequently used syntax that is more of a programmer convenience feature. Python's syntax allows you to create a single string from multiple string literals placed adjacent to each other in the body of your source code:

```
>>> foo = "Hello" 'world!'
>>> foo
'Helloworld!'
```

It is a convenient way to split up long strings without unnecessary backslash escapes. As you can see from the above, you can mix quotation types on the same line. Another good thing about this feature is that you can add comments too, like this example:

```
>>> f = urllib.urlopen('http://'    # protocol
... 'localhost'                     # hostname
... ':8000'                         # port
... '/cgi-bin/friends2.py')         # file
```

As you can imagine, here is what `urlopen()` really gets as input:

```
>>> 'http://' 'localhost' ':8000' '/cgi-bin/friends2.py'
'http://localhost:8000/cgi-bin/friends2.py'
```

Regular String Coercion to Unicode

When concatenating regular and Unicode strings, regular strings are converted to Unicode first before the operation occurs:

```
>>> 'Hello' + u' ' + 'World' + u'!'
u'Hello World!'
```

Repetition (*)

The repetition operator creates new strings, concatenating multiple copies of the same string to accomplish its functionality:

```
>>> 'Ni!' * 3
'Ni!Ni!Ni!'
>>>
>>> '*'*40
'****************************************'
>>>
>>> print '-' * 20, 'Hello World!', '-' * 20
-------------------- Hello World! --------------------
>>> who = 'knights'
>>> who * 2
'knightsknights'
```

```
>>> who
'knights'
```

As with any standard operator, the original variable is unmodified, as indicated in the final dump of the object above.

6.4 String-Only Operators

6.4.1 Format Operator (%)

Python features a string format operator. This operator is unique to strings and makes up for the lack of having functions from C's `printf()` family. In fact, it even uses the same symbol, the percent sign (`%`), and supports all the `printf()` formatting codes.

The syntax for using the format operator is as follows:

```
format_string % (arguments_to_convert)
```

The *format_string* on the left-hand side is what you would typically find as the first argument to `printf()`: the format string with any of the

Table 6.4 Format Operator Conversion Symbols	
Format Symbol	*Conversion*
%c	Character (integer [ASCII value] or string of length 1)
%r[a]	String conversion via `repr()` prior to formatting
%s	String conversion via `str()` prior to formatting
%d / %i	Signed decimal integer
%u[b]	Unsigned decimal integer
%o[b]	(Unsigned) octal integer
%x[b] / %X[b]	(Unsigned) hexadecimal integer (lower/UPPERcase letters)
%e / %E	Exponential notation (with lowercase 'e'/UPPERcase 'E')
%f / %F	Floating point real number (fraction truncates naturally)
%g / %G	The shorter of %e and %f/%E% and %F%
%%	Percent character (%) unescaped

a.   New in Python 2.0; likely unique only to Python.
b.   %u/%o/%x/%X of negative int will return a signed string in Python 2.4.

embedded % codes. The set of valid codes is given in Table 6.4. The *arguments_to_convert* parameter matches the remaining arguments you would send to printf(), namely the set of variables to convert and display.

Python supports two formats for the input arguments. The first is a tuple (introduced in Section 2.8, formally in 6.15), which is basically the set of arguments to convert, just like for C's printf(). The second format that Python supports is a dictionary (Chapter 7). A dictionary is basically a set of hashed key-value pairs. The keys are requested in the *format_string*, and the corresponding values are provided when the string is formatted.

Converted strings can either be used in conjunction with the **print** statement to display out to the user or saved into a new string for future processing or displaying to a graphical user interface.

Other supported symbols and functionality are listed in Table 6.5.

As with C's printf(), the asterisk symbol (*) may be used to dynamically indicate the width and precision via a value in argument tuple. Before we get to our examples, one more word of caution: long integers are more than likely too large for conversion to standard integers, so we recommend using exponential notation to get them to fit.

Table 6.5 Format Operator Auxiliary Directives

Symbol	Functionality
*	Argument specifies width or precision
−	Use left justification
+	Use a plus sign (+) for positive numbers
<sp>	Use space-padding for positive numbers
#	Add the octal leading zero ('0') or hexadecimal leading '0x' or '0X', depending on whether 'x' or 'X' were used.
0	Use zero-padding (instead of spaces) when formatting numbers
%	'%%' leaves you with a single literal '%'
(var)	Mapping variable (dictionary arguments)
m.n	*m* is the minimum total width and *n* is the number of digits to display after the decimal point (if applicable)

Here are some examples using the string format operator:

Hexadecimal Output

```
>>> "%x" % 108
'6c'
>>>
>>> "%X" % 108
'6C'
>>>
>>> "%#X" % 108
'0X6C'
>>>
>>> "%#x" % 108
'0x6c'
```

Floating Point and Exponential Notation Output

```
>>>
>>> '%f' % 1234.567890
'1234.567890'
>>>
>>> '%.2f' % 1234.567890
'1234.57'
>>>
>>> '%E' % 1234.567890
'1.234568E+03'
>>>
>>> '%e' % 1234.567890
'1.234568e+03'
>>>
>>> '%g' % 1234.567890
'1234.57'
>>>
>>> '%G' % 1234.567890
'1234.57'
>>>
>>> "%e" % (111111111111111111111111L)
'1.111111e+21'
```

Integer and String Output

```
>>> "%+d" % 4
'+4'
>>>
```

```
>>> "%+d" % -4
'-4'
>>>
>>> "we are at %d%%" % 100
'we are at 100%'
>>>
>>> 'Your host is: %s' % 'earth'
'Your host is: earth'
>>>
>>> 'Host: %s\tPort: %d' % ('mars', 80)
'Host: mars    Port: 80'
>>>
>>> num = 123
>>> 'dec: %d/oct: %#o/hex: %#X' % (num, num, num)
'dec: 123/oct: 0173/hex: 0X7B'
>>>
>>> "MM/DD/YY = %02d/%02d/%d" % (2, 15, 67)
'MM/DD/YY = 02/15/67'
>>>
>>> w, p = 'Web', 'page'
>>> 'http://xxx.yyy.zzz/%s/%s.html' % (w, p)
'http://xxx.yyy.zzz/Web/page.html'
```

The previous examples all use tuple arguments for conversion. Below, we show how to use a dictionary argument for the format operator:

```
>>> 'There are %(howmany)d %(lang)s Quotation Symbols' % \
...     {'lang': 'Python', 'howmany': 3}
'There are 3 Python Quotation Symbols'
```

Amazing Debugging Tool

The string format operator is not only a cool, easy-to-use, and familiar feature, but a great and useful debugging tool as well. Practically all Python objects have a string presentation (either evaluatable from repr() or ``, or printable from str()). The **print** statement automatically invokes the str() function for an object. This gets even better. When you are defining your own objects, there are hooks for you to create string representations of your object such that repr() and str() (and `` and **print**) return an appropriate string as output. And if worse comes to worst and neither repr() or str() is able to display an object, the Pythonic default is at least to give you something of the format:

```
<... something that is useful ...>.
```

2.4

6.4.2 String Templates: Simpler Substitution

The string format operator has been a mainstay of Python and will continue to be so. One of its drawbacks, however, is that it is not as intuitive to the new Python programmer not coming from a C/C++ background. Even for current developers using the dictionary form can accidentally leave off the type format symbol, i.e., `%(lang)` vs. the more correct `%(lang)s`. In addition to remembering to put in the correct formatting directive, the programmer must also *know* the type, i.e., is it a string, an integer, etc.

The justification of the new string templates is to do away with having to remember such details and use string substitution much like those in current shell-type scripting languages, the dollar sign ($).

The `string` module is temporarily resurrected from the dead as the new `Template` class has been added to it. `Template` objects have two methods, `substitute()` and `safe_substitute()`. The former is more strict, throwing `KeyError` exceptions for missing keys while the latter will keep the substitution string intact when there is a missing key:

```
>>> from string import Template
>>> s = Template('There are ${howmany} ${lang} Quotation Symbols')
>>>
>>> print s.substitute(lang='Python', howmany=3)
There are 3 Python Quotation Symbols
>>>
>>> print s.substitute(lang='Python')
Traceback (most recent call last):
  File "<stdin>", line 1, in ?
  File "/usr/local/lib/python2.4/string.py", line 172, in substitute
    return self.pattern.sub(convert, self.template)
  File "/usr/local/lib/python2.4/string.py", line 162, in convert
    val = mapping[named]
KeyError: 'howmany'
>>>
>>> print s.safe_substitute(lang='Python')
There are ${howmany} Python Quotation Symbols
```

The new string templates were added to Python in version 2.4. More information about them can be found in the Python Library Reference Manual and PEP 292.

6.4.3 Raw String Operator (r / R)

The purpose of raw strings, introduced back in version 1.5, is to counteract the behavior of the special escape characters that occur in strings (see the subsection below on what some of these characters are). In raw strings, all characters are taken verbatim with no translation to special or non-printed characters.

This feature makes raw strings absolutely convenient when such behavior is desired, such as when composing regular expressions (see the `re` module documentation). Regular expressions (REs) are strings that define advanced search patterns for strings and usually consist of special symbols to indicate characters, grouping and matching information, variable names, and character classes. The syntax for REs contains enough symbols already, but when you have to insert additional symbols to make special characters act like normal characters, you end up with a virtual "alphanumersymbolic" soup! Raw strings lend a helping hand by not requiring all the normal symbols needed when composing RE patterns.

The syntax for raw strings is exactly the same as for normal strings with the exception of the raw string operator, the letter "**r**," which precedes the quotation marks. The "**r**" can be lowercase (**r**) or uppercase (**R**) and must be placed immediately preceding the first quote mark.

In the first of our three examples, we really want a backslash followed by an 'n' as opposed to a NEWLINE character:

```
>>> '\n'
'\n'
>>> print '\n'

>>> r'\n'
'\\n'
>>> print r'\n'
\n
```

Next, we cannot seem to open our README file. Why not? Because the \t and \r are taken as special symbols which really are not part of our filename, but are *four* individual characters that are part of our file pathname.

```
>>> f = open('C:\windows\temp\readme.txt', 'r')

Traceback (most recent call last):
  File "<stdin>", line 1, in ?
    f = open('C:\windows\temp\readme.txt', 'r')
IOError: [Errno 2] No such file or directory: 'C:\\win-
dows\\temp\readme.txt'
>>> f = open(r'C:\windows\temp\readme.txt', 'r')
>>> f.readline()
'Table of Contents (please check timestamps for last
update!)\n'
>>> f.close()
```

Finally, we are (ironically) looking for a raw pair of characters \n and not NEWLINE. In order to find it, we are attempting to use a simple regular expression that looks for backslash-character pairs that are normally single special whitespace characters:

```
>>> import re
>>> m = re.search('\\[rtfvn]', r'Hello World!\n')
>>> if m is not None: m.group()
...
>>> m = re.search(r'\\[rtfvn]', r'Hello World!\n')
>>> if m is not None: m.group()
...
'\\n'
```

6.4.4 Unicode String Operator (u / U)

The Unicode string operator, uppercase (**U**) and lowercase (**u**), introduced with Unicode string support in Python 1.6, takes standard strings or strings with Unicode characters in them and converts them to a full Unicode string object. More details on Unicode strings are available in Section 6.7.4. In addition, Unicode support is available via string methods (Section 6.6) and the regular expression engine. Here are some examples:

```
u'abc'          U+0061 U+0062 U+0063
u'\u1234'       U+1234
u'abc\u1234\n'  U+0061 U+0062 U+0063 U+1234 U+0012
```

The Unicode operator can also accept raw Unicode strings if used in conjunction with the raw string operator discussed in the previous section. The Unicode operator must precede the raw string operator.

```
ur'Hello\nWorld!'
```

6.5 Built-in Functions

6.5.1 Standard Type Functions

```
cmp ( )
```

As with the value comparison operators, the cmp() built-in function also performs a lexicographic (ASCII value-based) comparison for strings.

```
>>> str1 = 'abc'
>>> str2 = 'lmn'
>>> str3 = 'xyz'
```

```
>>> cmp(str1, str2)
-11
>>> cmp(str3, str1)
23
>>> cmp(str2, 'lmn')
0
```

6.5.2 *Sequence Type Functions*

len()

```
>>> str1 = 'abc'
>>> len(str1)
3
>>> len('Hello World!')
12
```

The len() built-in function returns the number of characters in the string as expected.

max() and min()

```
>>> str2 = 'lmn'
>>> str3 = 'xyz'
>>> max(str2)
'n'
>>> min(str3)
'x'
```

Although more useful with other sequence types, the max() and min() built-in functions do operate as advertised, returning the greatest and least characters (lexicographic order), respectively. Here are a few more examples:

```
>>> min('ab12cd')
'1'
>>> min('AB12CD')
'1'
>>> min('ABabCDcd')
'A'
```

enumerate()

```
>>> s = 'foobar'
>>> for i, t in enumerate(s):
...     print i, t
...
```

```
0 f
1 o
2 o
3 b
4 a
5 r
```

zip()

```
>>> s, t = 'foa', 'obr'
>>> zip(s, t)
[('f', 'o'), ('o', 'b'), ('a', 'r')]
```

6.5.3 String Type Functions

raw_input()

The built-in raw_input() function prompts the user with a given string and accepts and returns a user-input string. Here is an example using raw_input():

```
>>> user_input = raw_input("Enter your name: ")
Enter your name: John Doe
>>>
>>> user_input
'John Doe'
>>>
>>> len(user_input)
8
```

Earlier, we indicated that strings in Python do not have a terminating NUL character like C strings. We added in the extra call to len() to show you that what you see is what you get.

str() and unicode()

Both str() and unicode() are factory functions, meaning that they produce new objects of their type respectively. They will take any object and create a printable or Unicode string representation of the argument object. And, along with basestring, they can also be used as arguments along with objects in isinstance() calls to verify type:

```
>>> isinstance(u'\0xAB', str)
False
```

```
>>> not isinstance('foo', unicode)
True
>>> isinstance(u'', basestring)
True
>>> not isinstance('foo', basestring)
False
```

chr(), unichr(), and ord()

chr() takes a single integer argument in range(256) (e.g., between 0 and 255) and returns the corresponding character. unichr() does the same thing but for Unicode characters. The range for unichr(), added in Python 2.0, is dependent on how your Python was compiled. If it was configured for UCS2 Unicode, then a valid value falls in range(65536) or 0x0000-0xFFFF; for UCS4, the value should be in range(1114112) or 0x000000-0x110000. If a value does not fall within the allowable range(s), a ValueError exception will be raised.

ord() is the inverse of chr() (for 8-bit ASCII strings) and unichr() (for Unicode objects)—it takes a single character (string of length 1) and returns the corresponding character with that ASCII code or Unicode code point, respectively. If the given Unicode character exceeds the size specified by your Python configuration, a TypeError exception will be thrown.

```
>>> chr(65)
'A'
>>> ord('a')
97
>>> unichr(12345)
u'\u3039'
>>> chr(12345)
Traceback (most recent call last):
  File "<stdin>", line 1, in ?
    chr(12345)
ValueError: chr() arg not in range(256)
>>> ord(u'\uffffff')
Traceback (most recent call last):
  File "<stdin>", line 1, in ?
    ord(u'\uffffff')
TypeError: ord() expected a character, but string of
length 2 found
>>> ord(u'\u2345')
9029
```

6.6 String Built-in Methods

String methods were added to Python in the 1.6 to 2.0 timeframe—they also were added to Jython. These methods replace most of the functionality in the `string` module as well as to add new functionality. Table 6.6 shows all the current methods for strings. All string methods should fully support Unicode strings. Some are applicable only to Unicode strings.

Table 6.6 String Type Built-in Methods

Method Name	Description
string.capitalize()	Capitalizes first letter of *string*
string.center(*width*)	Returns a space-padded *string* with the original *string* centered to a total of *width* columns
string.count(*str*, *beg*=0, *end*=len(*string*))	Counts how many times *str* occurs in *string*, or in a substring of *string* if starting index *beg* and ending index *end* are given
string.decode(*encoding*='UTF-8', *errors*='strict')	Returns decoded string version of string; on error, default is to raise a ValueError unless *errors* is given with 'ignore' or 'replace'
string.encode(*encoding*='UTF-8', *errors*='strict')[a]	Returns encoded string version of string; on error, default is to raise a ValueError unless *errors* is given with 'ignore' or 'replace'
string.endswith(*obj*, *beg*=0, *end*=len(*string*))[b, e]	Determines if *string* or a substring of *string* (if starting index *beg* and ending index *end* are given) ends with *obj* where *obj* is typically a string; if *obj* is a tuple, then any of the strings in that tuple; returns True if so, and False otherwise
string.expandtabs(*tabsize*=8)	Expands tabs in *string* to multiple spaces; defaults to 8 spaces per tab if *tabsize* not provided
string.find(*str*, *beg*=0 *end*=len(*string*))	Determine if *str* occurs in *string*, or in a substring of *string* if starting index *beg* and ending index *end* are given; returns index if found and −1 otherwise

Table 6.6	String Type Built-in Methods (continued)

Method Name	*Description*
string.index(*str*, *beg*=0, *end*=len(*string*))	Same as find(), but raises an exception if *str* not found
string.isalnum()[a, b, c]	Returns True if *string* has at least 1 character and all characters are alphanumeric and False otherwise
string.isalpha()[a, b, c]	Returns True if *string* has at least 1 character and all characters are alphabetic and False otherwise
string.isdecimal()[b, c, d]	Returns True if *string* contains only decimal digits and False otherwise
string.isdigit()[b, c]	Returns True if *string* contains only digits and False otherwise
string.islower()[b, c]	Returns True if *string* has at least 1 cased character and all cased characters are in lowercase and False otherwise
string.isnumeric()[b, c, d]	Returns True if *string* contains only numeric characters and False otherwise
string.isspace()[b, c]	Returns True if *string* contains only whitespace characters and False otherwise
string.istitle()[b, c]	Returns True if *string* is properly "titlecased" (see title()) and False otherwise
string.isupper()[b, c]	Returns True if *string* has at least one cased character and all cased characters are in uppercase and False otherwise
string.join(*seq*)	Merges (concatenates) the string representations of elements in sequence *seq* into a string, with separator *string*
string.ljust(*width*)	Returns a space-padded *string* with the original string left-justified to a total of *width* columns
string.lower()	Converts all uppercase letters in *string* to lowercase
string.lstrip()	Removes all leading whitespace in *string*

(*continued*)

Table 6.6 String Type Built-in Methods (continued)

Method Name	Description
string.partition(*str*)[e]	Like a combination of find() and split(), splits *string* into a 3-tuple (*string_pre_str*, *str*, *string_post_str*) on the first occurrence of *str*; if not found, *string_pre_str* == *string*
string.replace(*str1*, *str2*, *num*=*string*.count(*str1*))	Replaces all occurrences of *str1* in *string* with *str2*, or at most *num* occurrences if *num* given
string.rfind(*str*, *beg*=0, *end*=len(*string*))	Same as find(), but search backward in *string*
string.rindex(*str*, *beg*=0, *end*=len(*string*))	Same as index(), but search backward in *string*
string.rjust(*width*)	Returns a space-padded *string* with the original string right-justified to a total of *width* columns
string.rpartition(*str*)[e]	Same as partition(), but search backwards in *string*
string.rstrip()	Removes all trailing whitespace of *string*
string.split(*str*="", *num*=*string*.count(*str*))	Splits *string* according to delimiter *str* (space if not provided) and returns list of substrings; split into at most *num* substrings if given
string.splitlines(*num*=string.count('\n'))[b, c]	Splits *string* at all (or *num*) NEWLINEs and returns a list of each line with NEWLINEs removed
string.startswith(*obj*, *beg*=0, *end*=len(*string*))[b, e]	Determines if *string* or a substring of *string* (if starting index *beg* and ending index *end* are given) starts with *obj* where *obj* is typically a string; if *obj* is a tuple, then any of the strings in that tuple; returns True if so, and False otherwise
string.strip([*obj*])	Performs both lstrip() and rstrip() on *string*
string.swapcase()	Inverts case for all letters in *string*
string.title()[b, c]	Returns "titlecased" version of *string*, that is, all words begin with uppercase, and the rest are lowercase (also see istitle())

Table 6.6 String Type Built-in Methods (continued)

Method Name	Description
string.translate(str, del="")	Translates *string* according to translation table *str* (256 chars), removing those in the *del* string
string.upper()	Converts lowercase letters in *string* to uppercase
string.zfill(width)	Returns original *string* left-padded with zeros to a total of *width* characters; intended for numbers, zfill() retains any sign given (less one zero)

a.   Applicable to Unicode strings only in 1.6, but to all string types in 2.0.
b.   Not available as a `string` module function in 1.5.2.
c.   New in Jython 2.1.
d.   Applicable to Unicode strings only.
e.   New or updated in Python 2.5.

Some examples of using string methods:

```
>>> quest = 'what is your favorite color?'
>>> quest.capitalize()
'What is your favorite color?'
>>>
>>> quest.center(40)
'      what is your favorite color?       '
>>>
>>> quest.count('or')
2
>>>
>>> quest.endswith('blue')
False
>>>
>>> quest.endswith('color?')
True
>>>
>>> quest.find('or', 30)
-1
>>>
>>> quest.find('or', 22)
25
>>
>>> quest.index('or', 10)
16
```

```
>>>
>>> ':'.join(quest.split())
'what:is:your:favorite:color?'
>>> quest.replace('favorite color', 'quest')
>>>
'what is your quest?'
>>>
>>> quest.upper()
'WHAT IS YOUR FAVORITE COLOR?'
```

The most complex example shown above is the one with split() and join(). We first call split() on our string, which, without an argument, will break apart our string using spaces as the delimiter. We then take this list of words and call join() to merge our words again, but with a new delimiter, the colon. Notice that we used the split() method for our string to turn it into a list, and then, we used the join() method for ':' to merge together the contents of the list.

6.7 Special Features of Strings

6.7.1 Special or Control Characters

Like most other high-level or scripting languages, a backslash paired with another single character indicates the presence of a "special" character, usually a nonprintable character, and that this pair of characters will be substituted by the special character. These are the special characters we discussed above that will not be interpreted if the raw string operator precedes a string containing these characters.

In addition to the well-known characters such as NEWLINE (\n) and (horizontal) tab (\t), specific characters via their ASCII values may be used as well: \000 or \xXX where 000 and XX are their respective octal and hexadecimal ASCII values. Here are the base 10, 8, and 16 representations of 0, 65, and 255:

	ASCII	ASCII	ASCII
Decimal	0	65	255
Octal	\000	\101	\177
Hexadecimal	\x00	\x41	\xFF

Special characters, including the backslash-escaped ones, can be stored in Python strings just like regular characters.

Another way that strings in Python are different from those in C is that Python strings are not terminated by the NUL (\000) character (ASCII value 0). NUL characters are just like any of the other special backslash-escaped characters. In fact, not only can NUL characters appear in Python strings, but there can be any number of them in a string, not to mention that they can occur anywhere within the string. They are no more special than any of the other control characters. Table 6.7 represents a summary of the escape characters supported by most versions of Python.

As mentioned before, explicit ASCII octal or hexadecimal values can be given, as well as escaping a NEWLINE to continue a statement to the next line. All valid ASCII character values are between 0 and 255 (octal 0177, hexadecimal 0XFF).

Table 6.7 String Literal Backslash Escape Characters

/X	Oct	Dec	Hex	Char	Description
\0	000	0	0x00	NUL	Null character
\a	007	7	0x07	BEL	Bell
\b	010	8	0x08	BS	Backspace
\t	011	9	0x09	HT	Horizontal tab
\n	012	10	0x0A	LF	Linefeed/ Newline
\v	013	11	0x0B	VT	Vertical tab
\f	014	12	0x0C	FF	Form feed
\r	015	13	0x0D	CR	Carriage return
\e	033	27	0x1B	ESC	Escape
\"	042	34	0x22	"	Double quote
\'	047	39	0x27	'	Single quote/ apostrophe
\\	134	92	0x5C	\	Backslash

\OOO	Octal value OOO (range is 0000 to 0177)
\xXX	'x' plus hexadecimal value XX (range is 0X00 to 0xFF)
\	escape NEWLINE for statement continuation

One use of control characters in strings is to serve as delimiters. In database or Internet/Web processing, it is more than likely that most printable characters are allowed as data items, meaning that they would not make good delimiters.

It becomes difficult to ascertain whether or not a character is a delimiter or a data item, and by using a printable character such as a colon (:) as a delimiter, you are limiting the number of allowed characters in your data, which may not be desirable.

One popular solution is to employ seldomly used, nonprintable ASCII values as delimiters. These make the perfect delimiters, freeing up the colon and the other printable characters for more important uses.

6.7.2 Triple Quotes

Although strings can be represented by single or double quote delimitation, it is often difficult to manipulate strings containing special or nonprintable characters, especially the NEWLINE character. Python's triple quotes comes to the rescue by allowing strings to span multiple lines, including verbatim NEWLINEs, tabs, and any other special characters.

The syntax for triple quotes consists of three consecutive single or double quotes (used in pairs, naturally):

```
>>> hi = '''hi
there'''
>>> hi                    # repr()
'hi\nthere'
>>> print hi              # str()
hi
there
```

Triple quotes lets the developer avoid playing quote and escape character games, all the while bringing at least a small chunk of text closer to WYSI-WIG (what you see is what you get) format.

The most powerful use cases are when you have a large block of HTML or SQL that would be completely inconvenient to use by concanentation or wrapped with backslash escapes:

```
errHTML = '''
<HTML><HEAD><TITLE>
Friends CGI Demo</TITLE></HEAD>
```

```
<BODY><H3>ERROR</H3>
<B>%s</B><P>
<FORM><INPUT TYPE=button VALUE=Back
ONCLICK="window.history.back()"></FORM>
</BODY></HTML>
'''

cursor.execute('''
        CREATE TABLE users (
        login VARCHAR(8),
        uid INTEGER,
        prid INTEGER)
''')
```

6.7.3 String Immutability

In Section 4.7.2, we discussed how strings are immutable data types, meaning that their values cannot be changed or modified. This means that if you *do* want to update a string, either by taking a substring, concatenating another string on the end, or concatenating the string in question to the end of another string, etc., a new string object must be created for it.

This sounds more complicated than it really is. Since Python manages memory for you, you won't really notice when this occurs. Any time you modify a string or perform any operation that is contrary to immutability, Python will allocate a new string for you. In the following example, Python allocates space for the strings, `'abc'` and `'def'`. But when performing the addition operation to create the string `'abcdef'`, new space is allocated automatically for the new string.

```
>>> 'abc' + 'def'
'abcdef'
```

Assigning values to variables is no different:

```
>>> s = 'abc'
>>> s = s + 'def'
>>> s
'abcdef'
```

In the above example, it looks like we assigned the string `'abc'` to `string`, then appended the string `'def'` to `string`. To the naked eye, strings look mutable. What you cannot see, however, is the fact that a new string was created when the operation "`s + 'def'`" was performed, and that the new object was then assigned back to s. The old string of `'abc'` was deallocated.

Once again, we can use the `id()` built-in function to help show us exactly what happened. If you recall, `id()` returns the "identity" of an object. This value is as close to a "memory address" as we can get in Python.

```
>> s = 'abc'
>>>
>>> id(s)
135060856
>>>
>>> s += 'def'
>>> id(s)
135057968
```

Note how the identities are different for the string before and after the update. Another test of mutability is to try to modify individual characters or substrings of a string. We will now show how any update of a single character or a slice is not allowed:

```
>>> s
'abcdef'
>>>
>>> s[2] = 'C'
Traceback (innermost last):
  File "<stdin>", line 1, in ?
AttributeError: __setitem__
>>>
>>> s[3:6] = 'DEF'
Traceback (innermost last):
   File "<stdin>", line 1, in ?
AttributeError: __setslice__
```

Both operations result in an error. In order to perform the actions that we want, we will have to create new strings using substrings of the existing string, then assign those new strings back to `string`:

```
>>> s
'abcdef'
>>>
>>> s = '%sC%s' % (s[0:2], s[3:])
>>> s
'abCdef'
>>>
>>> s[0:3] + 'DEF'
'abCDEF'
```

So for immutable objects like strings, we make the observation that only valid expressions on the left-hand side of an assignment (to the left of the equals sign [=]) must be the variable representation of an entire object such as a string, not single characters or substrings. There is no such restriction for the expression on the right-hand side.

6.8 Unicode

Unicode string support, introduced to Python in version 1.6, is used to convert between multiple double-byte character formats and encodings, and includes as much functionality as possible to manage these strings. With the addition of string methods (see Section 6.6), Python strings and regular expressions are fully featured to handle a wide variety of applications requiring Unicode string storage, access, and manipulation. We will do our best here to give an overview of Unicode support in Python. But first, let us take a look at some basic terminology and then ask ourselves, just what *is* Unicode?

6.8.1 Terminology

Table 6.8 Unicode Terminology

Term	Meaning
ASCII	American Standard Code for Information Interchange
BMP	Basic Multilingual Plane (plane 0)
BOM	Byte Order Mark (character that denotes byte-ordering)
CJK/CJKV	Abbreviation for Chinese-Japanese-Korean (and -Vietnamese)
Code point	Similar to an ASCII value, represents any value in the Unicode codespace, e.g., within `range(1114112)` or integers from 0x000000 to 0x10FFFF.
Octet	Ordered sequence of eight bits as a single unit, aka (8-bit) byte
UCS	Universal Character Set

(continued)

Table 6.8 Unicode Terminology (continued)	
Term	*Meaning*
UCS2	Universal Character Set coded in 2 octets (also see UTF-16)
UCS4	Universal Character Set coded in 4 octets
UTF	Unicode or UCS Transformation Format
UTF-8	8-bit UTF Transformation Format (unsigned byte sequence one to four bytes in length)
UTF-16	16-bit UTF Transformation Format (unsigned byte sequence usually one 16-bit word [two bytes] in length; also see UCS2)

6.8.2 What Is Unicode?

Unicode is the miracle and the mystery that makes it possible for computers to support virtually any language on the planet. Before Unicode, there was ASCII, and ASCII was simple. Every English character was stored in the computer as a seven bit number between 32 and 126. When a user entered the letter A into a text file, the computer would write the letter A to disk as the number 65. Then when the computer opened that file it would translate that number 65 back into an A when it displayed the file contents on the screen.

ASCII files were compact and easy to read. A program could just read in each byte from a file and convert the numeric value of the byte into the corresponding letter. But ASCII only had enough numbers to represent 95 printable characters. Later software manufacturers extended ASCII to 8 bits, which provided an additional 128 characters, but 223 characters still fell far short of the thousands required to support all non-European languages.

Unicode overcomes the limitations of ASCII by using one or more bytes to represent each character. Using this system, Unicode can currently represent over 90,000 characters.

6.8.3 How Do You Use Unicode?

In the early days, Python could only handle 8-bit ASCII. Strings were simple data types. To manipulate a string, a user had to create a string and then pass it to one of the functions in the `string` module. Then in 2000, we saw the releases of Python 1.6 (and 2.0), the first time Unicode was supported in Python.

In order to make Unicode strings and ASCII strings look as similar as possible, Python strings were changed from being simple data types to real objects. ASCII strings became `StringTypes` and Unicode strings became `UnicodeTypes`. Both behave very similarly. Both have string methods that correspond to functions in the string module. The `string` module was not updated and remained ASCII only. It is now deprecated and should never be used in any Unicode-compliant code. It remains in Python just to keep legacy code from breaking.

Handling Unicode strings in Python is not that different from handling ordinary ASCII strings. Python calls hard-coded strings string literals. By default all string literals are treated as ASCII. This can be changed by adding the prefix u to a string literal. This tells Python that the text inside of the string should be treated as Unicode.

```
>>> "Hello World"    # ASCII string
>>> u"Hello World"   # Unicode string
```

The built-in functions `str()` and `chr()` were not updated to handle Unicode. They only work with regular ASCII strings. If a Unicode string is passed to `str()` it will silently convert the Unicode string to ASCII. If the Unicode string contains any characters that are not supported by ASCII, `str()` will raise an exception. Likewise, `chr()` can only work with numbers 0 to 255. If you pass it a numeric value (of a Unicode character, for example) outside of that range, it will raise an exception.

New BIFs `unicode()` and `unichr()` were added that act just like `str()` and `chr()` but work with Unicode strings. The function `unicode()` can convert any Python data type to a Unicode string and any object to a Unicode representation if that object has an `__unicode__()` method. For a review of these functions, see Sections 6.1.3 and 6.5.3.

6.8.4 *What Are Codecs?*

The acronym *codec* stands for COder/DECoder. It is a specification for encoding text as byte values and decoding those byte values into text. Unlike ASCII, which used only one byte to encode a character into a number, Unicode uses multiple bytes. Plus Unicode supports several different ways of encoding characters into bytes. Four of the best-known encodings that these codecs can convert are: ASCII, ISO 8859-1/Latin-1, UTF-8, and UTF-16.

The most popular is UTF-8, which uses one byte to encode all the characters in ASCII. This makes it easier for a programmer who has to deal with both ASCII and Unicode text since the numeric values of the ASCII characters are identical in Unicode.

For other characters, UTF-8 may use one or four bytes to represent a letter, three (mainly) for CJK/East Asian characters, and four for some rare, special use, or historic characters. This makes it more difficult for programmers who have to read and write the raw Unicode data since they cannot just read in a fixed number of bytes for each character. Luckily for us, Python hides all of the details of reading and writing the raw Unicode data for us, so we don't have to worry about the complexities of reading multibyte characters in text streams. All the other codecs are much less popular than UTF-8. In fact, I would say most Python programmers will never have to deal with them, save perhaps UTF-16.

UTF-16 is probably the next most popular codec. It is simpler to read and write its raw data since it encodes every character as a single 16-bit word represented by two bytes. Because of this, the ordering of the two bytes matters. The regular UTF-16 code requires a Byte Order Mark (BOM), or you have to specifically use UTF-16-LE or UTF-16-BE to denote explicit little endian and big endian ordering.

UTF-16 is technically also variable-length like UTF-8 is, but this is uncommon usage. (People generally do not know this or simply do not even care about the rarely used code points in other planes outside the Basic Multilingual Plane (BMP). However, its format is not a superset of ASCII and makes it backward-incompatible with ASCII. Therefore, few programs implement it since most need to support legacy ASCII text.

6.8.5 Encoding and Decoding

Unicode support for multiple codecs means additional hassle for the developer. Each time you write a string to a file, you have to specify the codec (also called an "encoding") that should be used to translate its Unicode characters to bytes. Python minimizes this hassle for us by providing a Unicode string method called `encode()` that reads the characters in the string and outputs the right bytes for the codec we specify.

So every time we write a Unicode string to disk we have to "encode" its characters as a series of bytes using a particular codec. Then the next time we read the bytes from that file, we have to "decode" the bytes into a series of Unicode characters that are stored in a Unicode string object.

Simple Example

The script below creates a Unicode string, encodes it as some bytes using the UTF-8 codec, and saves it to a file. Then it reads the bytes back in from disk and decodes them into a Unicode string. Finally, it prints the Unicode string so we can see that the program worked correctly.

Line-by-Line Explanation

Lines 1–7

The usual setup plus a doc string and some constants for the codec we are using and the name of the file we are going to store the string in.

Lines 9–19

Here we create a Unicode string literal, encode it with our codec, and write it out to disk (lines 9–13). Next, we read the data back in from the file, decode it, and display it to the screen, suppressing the **print** statement's NEW-LINE because we are using the one saved with the string (lines 15–19).

Example 6.2 Simple Unicode String Example (uniFile.py)

This simple script writes a Unicode string to disk and reads it back in for display. It encodes it into UTF-8 for writing to disk, which it must then decode in to display it.

```
1   #!/usr/bin/env python
2   '''
3   An example of reading and writing Unicode strings: Writes
4   a Unicode string to a file in utf-8 and reads it back in.
5   '''
6   CODEC = 'utf-8'
7   FILE = 'unicode.txt'
8
9   hello_out = u"Hello world\n"
10  bytes_out = hello_out.encode(CODEC)
11  f = open(FILE, "w")
12  f.write(bytes_out)
13  f.close()
14
15  f = open(FILE, "r")
16  bytes_in = f.read()
17  f.close()
18  hello_in = bytes_in.decode(CODEC)
19  print hello_in,
```

When we run the program we get the following output:

```
$ unicode_example.py
Hello World
```

We also find a file called unicode.txt on the file system that contains the same string the program printed out.

```
$ cat unicode.txt
Hello World!
```

Simple Web Example

We show a similar and simple example of using Unicode with CGI in the Web Programming chapter (Chapter 20).

6.8.6 Using Unicode in Real Life

Examples like this make it look deceptively easy to handle Unicode in your code, and it is pretty easy, as long as you follow these simple rules:

- Always prefix your string literals with u.
- Never use str()... always use unicode() instead.
- Never use the outdated string module—it blows up when you pass it any non-ASCII characters.
- Avoid unnecessary encoding and decode of Unicode strings in your program. Only call the encode() method right before you write your text to a file, database, or the network, and only call the decode() method when you are reading it back in.

These rules will prevent 90 percent of the bugs that can occur when handling Unicode text. The problem is that the other 10 percent of the bugs are beyond your control. The greatest strength of Python is the huge library of modules that exist for it. They allow Python programmers to write a program in ten lines of code that might require a hundred lines of code in another language. But the quality of Unicode support within these modules varies widely from module to module.

Most of the modules in the standard Python library are Unicode compliant. The biggest exception is the pickle module. Pickling only works with ASCII strings. If you pass it a Unicode string to unpickle, it will raise an exception. You have to convert your string to ASCII first. It is best to avoid using text-based pickles. Fortunately, the binary format is now the default and it is better to stick with it. This is especially true if you are storing your pickles in a database. It is much better to save them as a BLOB than to save them as a TEXT or VARCHAR field and then have your pickles get corrupted when someone changes your column type to Unicode.

If your program uses a bunch of third-party modules, then you will probably run into a number of frustrations as you try to get all of the programs to speak Unicode to each other. Unicode tends to be an all-or-nothing proposition. Each module in your system (and all systems your program interfaces with) has to use Unicode and the same Unicode codec. If any one of these systems does not speak Unicode, you may not be able to read and save strings properly.

As an example, suppose you are building a database-enabled Web application that reads and writes Unicode. In order to support Unicode you need the following pieces to all support Unicode:

- Database server (MySQL, PostgreSQL, SQL Server, etc.)
- Database adapter (`MySQLdb`, etc.)
- Web framework (`mod_python`, `cgi`, Zope, Plane, Django etc.)

The database server is often the easiest part. You just have to make sure that all of your tables use the UTF-8 encoding.

The database adapter can be trickier. Some database adapters support Unicode, some do not. `MySQLdb`, for instance, does not default to Unicode mode. You have to use a special keyword argument `use_unicode` in the `connect()` method to get Unicode strings in the result sets of your queries.

Enabling Unicode is very simple to do in `mod_python`. Just set the text-encoding field to `"utf-8"` on the request object and `mod_python` handles the rest. Zope and other more complex systems may require more work.

6.8.7 Real-Life Lessons Learned

Mistake #1: You have a large application to write under significant time pressure. Foreign language support was a requirement, but no specifics are made available by the product manager. You put off Unicode-compliance until the project is mostly complete … it is not going to be that much effort to add Unicode support anyway, right?

Result #1: Failure to anticipate the foreign-language needs of end-users as well as integration of Unicode support with the other foreign language–oriented applications that they used. The retrofit of the entire system would be extremely tedious and time-consuming.

Mistake #2: Using the `string` module everywhere including calling `str()` and `chr()` in many places throughout the code.

Result #2: Convert to string methods followed by global search-and-replace of `str()` and `chr()` with `unicode()` and `unichr()`. The latter breaks all pickling. The pickling format has to be changed to binary. This in turn breaks the database schema, which needs to be completely redone.

Mistake #3: Not confirming that all auxiliary systems support Unicode fully.

Result #3: Having to patch those other systems, some of which may not be under your source control. Fixing Unicode bugs everywhere leads to code instability and the distinct possibility of introducing new bugs.

Summary: Enabling full Unicode and foreign-language compliance of your application is a project on its own. It needs to be well thought out and planned carefully. All software and systems involved must be "checked off," including the list of Python standard library and/or third-party external modules that are to be used. You may even have to bring onboard an entire team with internationalization (or "I18N") experience.

6.8.8 Unicode Support in Python

`unicode()` Built-in Function

The Unicode factory function should operate in a manner similar to that of the Unicode string operator (u / U). It takes a string and returns a Unicode string.

`decode()`/`encode()` Built-in Methods

The `decode()` and `encode()` built-in methods take a string and return an equivalent decoded/encoded string. `decode()` and `encode()` work for both regular and Unicode strings. `decode()` was added to Python in 2.2.

Unicode Type

A Unicode string object is subclassed from basestring and an instance is created by using the `unicode()` factory function, or by placing a u or U in front of the quotes of a string. Raw strings are also supported. Prepend a ur or UR to your string literal.

Unicode Ordinals

The standard `ord()` built-in function should work the same way. It was enhanced recently to support Unicode objects. The `unichr()` built-in function returns a Unicode object for a character (provided it is a 32-bit value); otherwise, a `ValueError` exception is raised.

Coercion

Mixed-mode string operations require standard strings to be converted to Unicode objects.

Exceptions

`UnicodeError` is defined in the exceptions module as a subclass of `ValueError`. All exceptions related to Unicode encoding/decoding should be subclasses of `UnicodeError`. See also the string `encode()` method.

Standard Encodings

Table 6.9 presents an extremely short list of the more common encodings used in Python. For a more complete listing, please see the Python Documentation. Here is an online link:

   http://docs.python.org/lib/standard-encodings.html

RE Engine Unicode-Aware

The regular expression engine should be Unicode aware. See the `re` Code Module sidebar in Section 6.9.

Table 6.9 Common Unicode Codecs/Encodings

Codec	Description
utf-8	8-bit variable length encoding (default encoding)
utf-16	16-bit variable length encoding (little/big endian)
utf-16-le	UTF-16 but explicitly little endian
utf-16-be	UTF-16 but explicitly big endian
ascii	7-bit ASCII codepage
iso-8859-1	ISO 8859-1 (Latin-1) codepage
unicode-escape	(See Python Unicode Constructors for a definition)
raw-unicode-escape	(See Python Unicode Constructors for a definition)
native	Dump of the internal format used by Python

String Format Operator

For Python format strings: `%s` performs `str(u)` for Unicode objects embedded in Python strings, so the output will be `u.encode(<default encoding>)`. If the format string is a Unicode object, all parameters are coerced to Unicode first and then put together and formatted according to the format string. Numbers are first converted to strings and then to Unicode. Python strings are interpreted as Unicode strings using the `<default encoding>`. Unicode objects are taken as is. All other string formatters should work accordingly. Here is an example:

```
u"%s %s" % (u"abc", "abc")  ⇒ u"abc abc"
```

6.9 Related Modules

Table 6.10 lists the key related modules for strings that are part of the Python standard library.

Table 6.10 Related Modules for String Types

Module	Description
`string`	String manipulation and utility functions, i.e., Template class
`re`	Regular expressions: powerful string pattern matching
`struct`	Convert strings to/from binary data format
`c/StringIO`	String buffer object that behaves like a file
`base64`	Base 16, 32, and 64 data encoding and decoding
`codecs`	Codec registry and base classes
`crypt`	Performs one-way encryption cipher
`difflib`[a]	Various "differs" for sequences
`hashlib`[b]	API to many different secure hash and message digest algorithms
`hmac`[c]	Keyed-hashing for message authentication
`md5`[d]	RSA's MD5 message digest authentication

Table 6.10 Related Modules for String Types (continued)

Module	Description
rotor	Provides multi-platform en/decryption services
sha[d]	NIST's secure hash algorithm SHA
stringprep[e]	Prepares Unicode strings for use in Internet protocols
textwrap[e]	Text-wrapping and filling
unicodedata	Unicode database

a.   New in Python 2.1.
b.   New in Python 2.5.
c.   New in Python 2.2.
d.   Obsoleted in Python 2.5 by hashlib module.
e.   New in Python 2.3.

CORE MODULE: re

Regular expressions (REs) provide advanced pattern matching scheme for strings. Using a separate syntax that describes these patterns, you can effectively use them as "filters" when passing in the text to perform the searches on. These filters allow you to extract the matched patterns as well as perform find-and-replace or divide up strings based on the patterns that you describe.

The re *module, introduced in Python 1.5, obsoletes the original* regex *and* regsub *modules from earlier releases. It represented a major upgrade in terms of Python's support for regular expressions, adopting the complete Perl syntax for REs. In Python 1.6, a completely new engine was written (SRE), which added support for Unicode strings as well as significant performance improvements. SRE replaces the old PCRE engine, which had been under the covers of the regular expression modules.*

Some of the key functions in the re *module include:* compile()*— compiles an RE expression into a reusable RE object;* match()*— attempts to match a pattern from the beginning of a string;* search()*— searches for any matching pattern in the string; and* sub()*— performs a search-and-replace of matches. Some of these functions return match objects with which you can access saved group matches (if any were found). All of Chapter 15 is dedicated to regular expressions.*

6.10 Summary of String Highlights

Characters Delimited by Quotation Marks

You can think of a string as a Python data type that you can consider as an array or contiguous set of characters between any pair of Python quotation symbols, or quotes. The two most common quote symbols for Python are the single quote, a single forward apostrophe ('), and the double quotation mark ("). The actual string itself consists entirely of those characters in between and not the quote marks themselves.

Having the choice between two different quotation marks is advantageous because it allows one type of quote to serve as a string delimiter while the other can be used as characters within the string without the need for special escape characters. Strings enclosed in single quotes may contain double quotes as characters and vice versa.

No Separate Character Type

Strings are the only literal sequence type, a sequence of characters. However, characters are not a type, so strings are the lowest-level primitive for character storage and manipulation. Characters are simply strings of length one.

String Format Operator (%) Provides `printf()`-like Functionality

The string format operator (see Section 6.4.1) provides a flexible way to create a custom string based on variable input types. It also serves as a familiar interface to formatting data for those coming from the C/C++ world.

Triple Quotes

In Section 6.7.2, we introduced the notion of triple quotes, which are strings that can have special embedded characters like NEWLINEs and tabs. Triple-quoted strings are delimited by pairs of three single (' ' ') or double (" " ") quotation marks.

Raw Strings Takes Special Characters Verbatim

In Section 6.4.2, we introduced raw strings and discussed how they do not interpret special characters escaped with the backslash. This makes raw strings ideal for situations where strings must be taken verbatim, for example, when describing regular expressions.

Python Strings Do *Not* End with NUL or '\0'

One major problem in C is running off the end of a string into memory that does not belong to you. This occurs when strings in C are not properly terminated with the NUL or '\0' character (ASCII value of zero). Along with managing memory for you, Python also removes this little burden or annoyance. Strings in Python do not terminate with NUL, and you do not have to worry about adding them on. Strings consist entirely of the characters that were designated and nothing more.

6.11   Lists

Like strings, lists provide sequential storage through an index offset and access to single or consecutive elements through slices. However, the comparisons usually end there. Strings consist only of characters and are immutable (cannot change individual elements), while lists are flexible container objects that hold an arbitrary number of Python objects. Creating lists is simple; adding to lists is easy, too, as we see in the following examples.

The objects that you can place in a list can include standard types and objects as well as user-defined ones. Lists can contain different types of objects and are more flexible than an array of C structs or Python arrays (available through the external array module) because arrays are restricted to containing objects of a single type. Lists can be populated, empty, sorted, and reversed. Lists can be grown and shrunk. They can be taken apart and put together with other lists. Individual or multiple items can be inserted, updated, or removed at will.

Tuples share many of the same characteristics of lists and although we have a separate section on tuples, many of the examples and list functions are applicable to tuples as well. The key difference is that tuples are immutable, i.e., read-only, so any operators or functions that allow updating lists, such as using the slice operator on the left-hand side of an assignment, will not be valid for tuples.

How to Create and Assign Lists

Creating lists is as simple as assigning a value to a variable. You handcraft a list (empty or with elements) and perform the assignment. Lists are delimited by surrounding square brackets ([ ]). You can also use the factory function.

```
>>> aList = [123, 'abc', 4.56, ['inner', 'list'], 7-9j]
>>> anotherList = [None, 'something to see here']
>>> print aList
[123, 'abc', 4.56, ['inner', 'list'], (7-9j)]
>>> print anotherList
[None, 'something to see here']
>>> aListThatStartedEmpty = []
>>> print aListThatStartedEmpty
[]
>>> list('foo')
['f', 'o', 'o']
```

How to Access Values in Lists

Slicing works similar to strings; use the square bracket slice operator ([ ]) along with the index or indices.

```
>>> aList[0]
123
>>> aList[1:4]
['abc', 4.56, ['inner', 'list']]
>>> aList[:3]
[123, 'abc', 4.56]
>>> aList[3][1]
'list'
```

How to Update Lists

You can update single or multiple elements of lists by giving the slice on the left-hand side of the assignment operator, and you can add to elements in a list with the append() method:

```
>>> aList
[123, 'abc', 4.56, ['inner', 'list'], (7-9j)]
>>> aList[2]
4.56
>>> aList[2] = 'float replacer'
>>> aList
[123, 'abc', 'float replacer', ['inner', 'list'], (7-9j)]
>>>
>>> anotherList.append("hi, i'm new here")
>>> print anotherList
[None, 'something to see here', "hi, i'm new here"]
>>> aListThatStartedEmpty.append('not empty anymore')
>>> print aListThatStartedEmpty
['not empty anymore']
```

How to Remove List Elements and Lists

To remove a list element, you can use either the **del** statement if you know exactly which element(s) you are deleting or the remove() method if you do not know.

```
>>> aList
[123, 'abc', 'float replacer', ['inner', 'list'], (7-9j)]
>>> del aList[1]
>>> aList
[123, 'float replacer', ['inner', 'list'], (7-9j)]
>>> aList.remove(123)
>>> aList
['float replacer', ['inner', 'list'], (7-9j)]
```

You can also use the pop() method to remove and return a specific object from a list.

Normally, removing an entire list is not something application programmers do. Rather, they tend to let it go out of scope (i.e., program termination, function call completion, etc.) and be deallocated, but if they do want to explicitly remove an entire list, they use the **del** statement:

```
del aList
```

6.12 Operators

6.12.1 Standard Type Operators

In Chapter 4, we introduced a number of operators that apply to most objects, including the standard types. We will take a look at how some of those apply to lists.

```
>>> list1 = ['abc', 123]
>>> list2 = ['xyz', 789]
>>> list3 = ['abc', 123]
>>> list1 < list2
True
>>> list2 < list3
False
>>> list2 > list3 and list1 == list3
True
```

When using the value comparison operators, comparing numbers and strings is straightforward, but not so much for lists, however. List comparisons are somewhat tricky, but logical. The comparison operators use the same algorithm as the cmp() built-in function. The algorithm basically works like this: the elements of both lists are compared until there is a determination of a winner. For example, in our example above, the output of 'abc' versus 'xyz' is determined immediately, with 'abc' < 'xyz', resulting in list1 < list2 and list2 >= list3. Tuple comparisons are performed in the same manner as lists.

6.12.2 Sequence Type Operators

Slices ([ ] and [:])

Slicing with lists is very similar to strings, but rather than using individual characters or substrings, slices of lists pull out an object or a group of objects that are elements of the list operated on. Focusing specifically on lists, we make the following definitions:

```
>>> num_list = [43, -1.23, -2, 6.19e5]
>>> str_list = ['jack', 'jumped', 'over', 'candlestick']
>>> mixup_list = [4.0, [1, 'x'], 'beef', -1.9+6j]
```

Slicing operators obey the same rules regarding positive and negative indexes, starting and ending indexes, as well as missing indexes, which default to the beginning or to the end of a sequence.

```
>>> num_list[1]
-1.23
>>>
>>> num_list[1:]
[-1.23, -2, 619000.0]
>>>
>>> num_list[2:-1]
[-2]
>>>
>>> str_list[2]
'over'
>>> str_list[:2]
['jack', 'jumped']
>>>
>>> mixup_list
[4.0, [1, 'x'], 'beef', (-1.9+6j)]
>>> mixup_list[1]
[1, 'x']
```

Unlike strings, an element of a list might also be a sequence, implying that you can perform all the sequence operations or execute any sequence built-in functions on that element. In the example below, we show that not only can we take a slice of a slice, but we can also change it, and even to an object of a different type. You will also notice the similarity to multidimensional arrays.

```
>>> mixup_list[1][1]
'x'
>>> mixup_list[1][1] = -64.875
>>> mixup_list
[4.0, [1, -64.875], 'beef', (-1.9+6j)]
```

Here is another example using num_list:

```
>>> num_list
[43, -1.23, -2, 6.19e5]
>>>
>>> num_list[2:4] = [16.0, -49]
>>>
>>> num_list
[43, -1.23, 16.0, -49]
>>>
>>> num_list[0] = [65535L, 2e30, 76.45-1.3j]
>>>
>>> num_list
[[65535L, 2e+30, (76.45-1.3j)], -1.23, 16.0, -49]
```

Notice how, in the last example, we replaced only a single element of the list, but we replaced it with a list. So as you can tell, removing, adding, and replacing things in lists are pretty freeform. Keep in mind that in order to splice elements of a list into another list, you have to make sure that the left-hand side of the assignment operator (=) is a slice, not just a single element.

Membership (**in, not in**)

With lists (and tuples), we can check whether an object is a member of a list (or tuple).

```
>>> mixup_list
[4.0, [1, 'x'], 'beef', (-1.9+6j)]
>>>
>>> 'beef' in mixup_list
True
>>>
>>> 'x' in mixup_list
False
>>>
>>> 'x' in mixup_list[1]
True
>>> num_list
```

```
[[65535L, 2e+030, (76.45-1.3j)], -1.23, 16.0, -49]
>>>
>>> -49 in num_list
True
>>>
>>> 34 in num_list
False
>>>
>>> [65535L, 2e+030, (76.45-1.3j)] in num_list
True
```

Note how 'x' is *not* a member of mixup_list. That is because 'x' itself is not actually a member of mixup_list. Rather, it is a member of mixup_uplist[1], which itself is a list. The membership operator is applicable in the same manner for tuples.

Concatenation (+)

The concatenation operator allows us to join multiple lists together. Note in the examples below that there is a restriction of concatenating like objects. In other words, you can concatenate only objects of the same type. You cannot concatenate two different types even if both are sequences.

```
>>> num_list = [43, -1.23, -2, 6.19e5]
>>> str_list = ['jack', 'jumped', 'over', 'candlestick']
>>> mixup_list = [4.0, [1, 'x'], 'beef', -1.9+6j]
>>>
>>> num_list + mixup_list
[43, -1.23, -2, 619000.0, 4.0, [1, 'x'], 'beef', (-1.9+6j)]
>>>
>>> str_list + num_list
['jack', 'jumped', 'over', 'candlestick', 43, -1.23, -2, 619000.0]
```

As we will discover in Section 6.13, starting in Python 1.5.2, you can use the extend() method in place of the concatenation operator to append the contents of a list to another. Using extend() is advantageous over concatenation because it actually appends the elements of the new list to the original, rather than creating a new list from scratch like + does. extend() is also the method used by the augmented assignment or in-place concatenation operator (+=), which debuted in Python 2.0.

2.0

We would also like to point out that the concatenation operator *does not* facilitate adding individual elements to a list. The upcoming example illustrates a case where attempting to add a new item to the list results in failure.

```
>>> num_list + 'new item'
Traceback (innermost last):
  File "<stdin>", line 1, in ?
TypeError: illegal argument type for built-in operation
```

This example fails because we had different types to the left and right of the concatenation operator. A combination of (list + string) is not valid. Obviously, our intention was to add the 'new item' string to the list, but we did not go about it the proper way. Fortunately, we have a solution:

Use the append() list built-in method (we will formally introduce append() and all other built-in methods in Section 6.13):

```
>>> num_list.append('new item')
```

Repetition (*)

Use of the repetition operator may make more sense with strings, but as a sequence type, lists and tuples can also benefit from this operation, if needed:

```
>>> num_list * 2
[43, -1.23, -2, 619000.0, 43, -1.23, -2, 619000.0]
>>>
>>> num_list * 3
[43, -1.23, -2, 619000.0, 43, -1.23, -2, 619000.0, 43,
-1.23, -2, 619000.0]
```

Augmented assignment also works, beginning in Python 2.0:

```
>>> hr = '-'
>>> hr *= 30
>>> hr
'------------------------------'
```

6.12.3 List Type Operators and List Comprehensions

There are really no special list-only operators in Python. Lists can be used with most object and sequence operators. In addition, list objects have their own methods. One construct that lists *do* have however, are *list comprehensions*. These are a combination of using list square brackets and a **for**-loop inside, a piece of logic that dictates the contents of the list object to be created. We cover list comprehensions in Chapter 8, but we present a simple example here as well as a few more throughout the remainder of the the chapter:

```
>>> [ i * 2 for i in [8, -2, 5] ]
[16, -4, 10]
>>> [ i for i in range(8) if i % 2 == 0 ]
[0, 2, 4, 6]
```

6.13 Built-in Functions

6.13.1 Standard Type Functions

cmp ( )

In Section 4.6.1, we introduced the cmp() built-in function with examples of comparing numbers and strings. But how would cmp() work with other objects such as lists and tuples, which can contain not only numbers and strings, but other objects like lists, tuples, dictionaries, and even user-created objects?

```
>>> list1, list2 = [123, 'xyz'], [456, 'abc']
>>> cmp(list1, list2)
-1
>>>
>>> cmp(list2, list1)
1
>>> list3 = list2 + [789]
>>> list3
[456, 'abc', 789]
>>>
>>> cmp(list2, list3)
-1
```

Compares are straightforward if we are comparing two objects of the same type. For numbers and strings, the direct values are compared, which is trivial. For sequence types, comparisons are somewhat more complex, but similar in manner. Python tries its best to make a fair comparison when one cannot be made, i.e., when there is no relationship between the objects or when types do not even have compare functions, then all bets are off as far as obtaining a "logical" decision.

Before such a drastic state is arrived at, more safe-and-sane ways to determine an inequality are attempted. How does the algorithm start? As we mentioned briefly above, elements of lists are iterated over. If these elements are of the same type, the standard compare for that type is performed. As soon as an inequality is determined in an element compare, that result becomes the result of the list compare. Again, these element compares are for elements of the same type. As we explained earlier, when the objects are different, performing an accurate or true comparison becomes a risky proposition.

When we compare list1 with list2, both lists are iterated over. The first true comparison takes place between the first elements of both lists, i.e., 123 vs. 456. Since 123 < 456, list1 is deemed "smaller."

If both values are the same, then iteration through the sequences continues until either a mismatch is found, or the end of the shorter sequence is reached. In the latter case, the sequence with more elements is deemed "greater." That is the reason why we arrived above at `list2 < list3`. Tuples are compared using the same algorithm. We leave this section with a summary of the algorithm highlights:

1. Compare elements of both lists.
2. If elements are of the same type, perform the compare and return the result.
3. If elements are different types, check to see if they are numbers.
   a. If numbers, perform numeric coercion if necessary and compare.
   b. If either element is a number, then the other element is "larger" (numbers are "smallest").
   c. Otherwise, types are sorted alphabetically by name.
4. If we reach the end of one of the lists, the longer list is "larger."
5. If we exhaust both lists and share the same data, the result is a tie, meaning that 0 is returned.

6.13.2 Sequence Type Functions

len()

For strings, `len()` gives the total length of the string, as in the number of characters. For lists (and tuples), it will not surprise you that `len()` returns the number of elements in the list (or tuple). Container objects found within count as a single item. Our examples below use some of the lists already defined above in previous sections.

```
>>> len(num_list)
4
>>>
>>> len(num_list*2)
8
```

max() and min()

`max()` and `min()` did not have a significant amount of usage for strings since all they did was to find the "largest" and "smallest" characters (lexicographically) in the string. For lists (and tuples), their functionality is more defined. Given a list of like objects, i.e., numbers or strings only, `max()` and `min()` could come in quite handy. Again, the quality of return values diminishes as mixed objects come into play. However, more often than not, you will be using these functions in a situation where they will provide the results you are seeking. We present a few examples using some of our earlier-defined lists.

```
>>> max(str_list)
'park'
>>> max(num_list)
[65535L, 2e+30, (76.45-1.3j)]
>>> min(str_list)
'candlestick'
>>> min(num_list)
-49
```

sorted() and reversed()

```
>>> s = ['They', 'stamp', 'them', 'when', "they're", 'small']
>>> for t in reversed(s):
...   print t,
...
small they're when them stamp They
>>> sorted(s)
['They', 'small', 'stamp', 'them', "they're", 'when']
```

For beginners using strings, notice how we are able to mix single and double quotes together in harmony with the contraction "they're." Also to those new to strings, this is a note reminding you that all string sorting is lexicographic and not alphabetic (the letter "T" comes before the letter "a" in the ASCII table.)

enumerate() and zip()

```
>>> albums = ['tales', 'robot', 'pyramid']
>>> for i, album in enumerate(albums):
...         print i, album
...
0 tales
1 robot
2 pyramid
>>>
>>> fn = ['ian', 'stuart', 'david']
>>> ln = ['bairnson', 'elliott', 'paton']
>>>
>>> for i, j in zip(fn, ln):
...         print ('%s %s' % (i,j)).title()
...
Ian Bairnson
Stuart Elliott
David Paton
```

sum()

```
>>> a = [6, 4, 5]
>>> reduce(operator.add, a)
15
>>> sum(a)
15

>>> sum(a, 5)
20
>>> a = [6., 4., 5.]
>>> sum(a)
15.0
```

list() and tuple()

The list() and tuple() factory functions take iterables like other sequences and make new lists and tuples, respectively, out of the (just shallow-copied) data. Although strings are also sequence types, they are not commonly used with list() and tuple(). These built-in functions are used more often to convert from one type to the other, i.e., when you have a tuple that you need to make a list (so that you can modify its elements) and vice versa.

```
>>> aList = ['tao', 93, 99, 'time']
>>> aTuple = tuple(aList)
>>> aList, aTuple
(['tao', 93, 99, 'time'], ('tao', 93, 99, 'time'))
>>> aList == aTuple
False
>>> anotherList = list(aTuple)
>>> aList == anotherList
True
>>> aList is anotherList
False
>>> [id(x) for x in aList, aTuple, anotherList]
[10903800, 11794448, 11721544]
```

As we already discussed at the beginning of the chapter, neither list() nor tuple() performs true *conversions* (see also Section 6.1.2). In other words, the list you passed to tuple() does not turn into a list, and the tuple you give to list() does not really become a list. Although the data set for both (the original and new object) is the same (hence satisfying ==), neither variable points to the same object (thus failing **is**). Also notice that, even though their values are the same, a list cannot "equal" a tuple.

6.13.3 List Type Built-in Functions

There are currently no special list-only built-in functions in Python unless you consider `range()` as one—its sole function is to take numeric input and generate a list that matches the criteria. `range()` is covered in Chapter 8. Lists can be used with most object and sequence built-in functions. In addition, list objects have their own methods.

6.14 List Type Built-in Methods

Lists in Python have *methods*. We will go over methods more formally in an introduction to object-oriented programming in Chapter 13, but for now think of methods as functions or procedures that apply only to specific objects. So the methods described in this section behave just like built-in functions except that they operate only on lists. Since these functions involve the mutability (or updating) of lists, none of them is applicable for tuples.

You may recall our earlier discussion of accessing object attributes using the dotted attribute notation: *object.attribute*. List methods are no different, using *list.method()*. We use the dotted notation to access the attribute (here it is a function), then use the function operators (**( )**) in a functional notation to invoke the methods.

We can use `dir()` on a list object to get its attributes including its methods:

```
>>> dir(list)     # or dir([])
['__add__', '__class__', '__contains__', '__delattr__',
'__delitem__', '__delslice__', '__doc__', '__eq__',
'__ge__', '__getattribute__', '__getitem__',
'__getslice__', '__gt__', '__hash__', '__iadd__',
'__imul__', '__init__', '__iter__', '__le__', '__len__',
'__lt__', '__mul__', '__ne__', '__new__', '__reduce__',
'__reduce_ex__', '__repr__', '__reversed__', '__rmul__',
'__setattr__', '__setitem__', '__setslice__', '__str__',
'append', 'count', 'extend', 'index', 'insert', 'pop',
'remove', 'reverse', 'sort']
```

Table 6.11 shows all the methods currently available for lists. Some examples of using various list methods are shown later.

Table 6.11 List Type Built-in Methods

List Method	Operation
`list.append(obj)`	Adds *obj* to the end of *list*
`list.count(obj)`	Returns count of how many times *obj* occurs in *list*
`list.extend(seq)` [a]	Appends contents of *seq* to *list*
`list.index(obj, i=0, j=len(list))`	Returns lowest index *k* where `list[k]` == *obj* and *i* <= *k* < *j*; otherwise `ValueError` raised
`list.insert(index, obj)`	Inserts *obj* into *list* at offset *index*
`list.pop(index=-1)` [a]	Removes and returns *obj* at given or last *index* from *list*
`list.remove(obj)`	Removes object *obj* from *list*
`list.reverse()`	Reverses objects of *list* in place
`list.sort(func=None, key=None, reverse=False)` [b]	Sorts list members with optional comparison *func*tion; *key* is a callback when extracting elements for sorting, and if *reverse* flag is `True`, then list is sorted in reverse order

a. New in Python 1.5.2.
b. Support for key and reverse added in Python 2.4.

```
>>> music_media = [45]
>>> music_media
[45]
>>>
>>> music_media.insert(0, 'compact disc')
>>> music_media
['compact disc', 45]
>>>
>>> music_media.append('long playing record')
>>> music_media
['compact disc', 45, 'long playing record']
>>>
>>> music_media.insert(2, '8-track tape')
>>> music_media
['compact disc', 45, '8-track tape', 'long playing record']
```

In the preceding example, we initiated a list with a single element, then checked the list as we either inserted elements within the list, or appended new items at the end. Let's now determine if elements are in a list and how to find out the location of where items are in a list. We do this by using the **in** operator and index() method.

```
>>> 'cassette' in music_media
False
>>> 'compact disc' in music_media
True
>>> music_media.index(45)
1
>>> music_media.index('8-track tape')
2
>>> music_media.index('cassette')
Traceback (innermost last):
  File "<interactive input>", line 0, in ?
ValueError: list.index(x): x not in list
```

Oops! What happened in that last example? Well, it looks like using index() to check if items are in a list is not a good idea, because we get an error. It would be safer to check using the membership operator **in** (or **not in**) first, and then using index() to find the element's location. We can put the last few calls to index() in a single **for** loop like this:

```
for eachMediaType in (45, '8-track tape', 'cassette'):
    if eachMediaType in music_media:
        print music_media.index(eachMediaType)
```

This solution helps us avoid the error we encountered above because index() is not called unless the object was found in the list. We will find out later how we can take charge if the error occurs, instead of bombing out as we did above.

We will now test drive sort() and reverse(), methods that will sort and reverse the elements of a list, respectively.

```
>>> music_media
['compact disc', 45, '8-track tape', 'long playing record']
>>> music_media.sort()
>>> music_media
[45, '8-track tape', 'compact disc', 'long playing record']
>>> music_media.reverse()
>>> music_media
['long playing record', 'compact disc', '8-track tape', 45]
```

CORE NOTE: Mutable object methods that alter the object *have no return value!*

One very obvious place where new Python programmers get caught is when using methods that you think should return a value. The most obvious one is sort():

```
>>> music_media.sort()          # where is the output?!?
>>>
```

The caveat about mutable object methods like sort(), extend(), *and* reverse() *is that these will perform their operation on a list in place, meaning that the contents of the existing list will be changed, but return* None! *Yes, it does fly in the face of string methods that do return values:*

```
>>> 'leanna, silly girl!'.upper()
'LEANNA, SILLY GIRL!'
```

Recall that strings are immutable—methods of immutable objects cannot modify them, so they do have to return a new object. If returning an object is a necessity for you, then we recommend that you look at the reversed() *and* sorted() *built-in functions introduced in Python 2.4.*

These work just like the list methods only they can be used in expressions because they do return objects. However, obviously the original list object is left as is, and you are getting a new object back.

Going back to the sort() method, the default sorting algorithm employed by the sort() method is a derivative of MergeSort (modestly named "timsort"), which is O(lg(n!)). We defer all other explanation to the build files where you can get all the details—source code: Objects/listobject.c and algorithm description: Objects/listsort.txt.

The extend() method will take the contents of one list and append its elements to another list:

```
>>> new_media = ['24/96 digital audio disc', 'DVD Audio
disc', 'Super Audio CD']
>>> music_media.extend(new_media)
>>> music_media
['long playing record', 'compact disc', '8-track tape',
45, '24/96 digital audio disc', 'DVD Audio disc', 'Super
Audio CD']
```

The argument to `extend()` can be any iterable, starting with 2.2. Prior to that, it had to be a sequence object, and prior to 1.6, it had to be a list. With an iterable (instead of a sequence), you can do more interesting things like:

```
>>> motd = []
>>> motd.append('MSG OF THE DAY')
>>> f = open('/etc/motd', 'r')
>>> motd.extend(f)
>>> f.close()
>>> motd
['MSG OF THE DAY', 'Welcome to Darwin!\n']
```

`pop()`, introduced in 1.5.2, will either return the last or requested item from a list and return it to the caller. We will see the `pop()` method in Section 6.15.1 as well as in the Exercises.

6.15 Special Features of Lists

6.15.1 Creating Other Data Structures Using Lists

Because of their container and mutable features, lists are fairly flexible and it is not very difficult to build other kinds of data structures using lists. Two that we can come up with rather quickly are stacks and queues.

Stack

A stack is a last-in-first-out (LIFO) data structure that works similarly to a cafeteria dining plate spring-loading mechanism. Consider the plates as objects. The first object off the stack is the last one you put in. Every new object gets "stacked" on top of the newest objects. To "push" an item on a stack is the terminology used to mean you are adding onto a stack. Likewise, to remove an element, you "pop" it off the stack. Example 6.3 shows a menu-driven program that implements a simple stack used to store strings.

Line-by-Line Explanation

Lines 1–3

In addition to the Unix startup line, we take this opportunity to clear the stack (a list).

Example 6.3 Using Lists as a Stack (`stack.py`)

This simple script uses lists as a stack to store and retrieve strings entered through this menu-driven text application using only the `append()` *and* `pop()` *list methods.*

```
1   #!/usr/bin/env python
2
3   stack = []
4
5   def pushit():
6       stack.append(raw_input('Enter new string: ').strip())
7
8   def popit():
9       if len(stack) == 0:
10          print 'Cannot pop from an empty stack!'
11      else:
12          print 'Removed [', 'stack.pop()', ']'
13
14  def viewstack():
15      print stack          # calls str() internally
16
17  CMDs = {'u': pushit, 'o': popit, 'v': viewstack}
18
19  def showmenu():
20      pr = """
21  p(U)sh
22  p(O)p
23  (V)iew
24  (Q)uit
25
26  Enter choice: """
27
28      while True:
29          while True:
30              try:
31                  choice = raw_input(pr).strip()[0].lower()
32              except (EOFError,KeyboardInterrupt,IndexError):
33                  choice = 'q'
34
35              print '\nYou picked: [%s]' % choice
36              if choice not in 'uovq':
37                  print 'Invalid option, try again'
38              else:
39                  break
40
41          if choice == 'q':
42              break
43          CMDs[choice]()
44
45  if __name__ == '__main__':
46      showmenu()
```

Lines 5–6

The `pushit()` function adds an element (a string prompted from the user) to the stack.

Lines 8–12

The `popit()` function removes an element from the stack (the more recent one). An error occurs when trying to remove an element from an empty stack. In this case, a warning is sent back to the user. When an object is popped from the stack, the user sees which element was removed. We use single backquotes or backticks (` ) to symbolize the `repr()` command, showing the string complete with quotes, not just the contents of the string.

Lines 14–15

The `viewstack()` function displays the current contents of the stack.

Line 17

Although we cover dictionaries formally in the next chapter, we wanted to give you a really small example of one here, a command vector (CMDs). The contents of the dictionary are the three "action" functions defined above, and they are accessed through the letter that the user must type to execute that command. For example, to push a string onto the stack, the user must enter `'u'`, so `'u'` is how access the `pushit()` from the dictionary. The chosen function is then executed on line 43.

Lines 19–43

The entire menu-driven application is controlled from the `showmenu()` function. Here, the user is prompted with the menu options. Once the user makes a valid choice, the proper function is called. We have not covered exceptions and **try-except** statement in detail yet, but basically that section of the code allows a user to type ^D (EOF, which generates an `EOFError`) or ^C (interrupt to quit, which generates a `KeyboardInterrupt` error), both of which will be processed by our script in the same manner as if the user had typed the `'q'` to quit the application. This is one place where the exception-handling feature of Python comes in extremely handy. The outer **while** loop lets the user continue to execute commands until they quit the application while the inner one prompts the user until they enter a valid command option.

Lines 45–46

This part of the code starts up the program if invoked directly. If this script were imported as a module, only the functions and variables would have been defined, but the menu would not show up. For more information regarding line 45 and the __name__ variable, see Section 3.4.1.

Here is a sample execution of our script:

```
$ stack.py
p(U)sh
p(O)p
(V)iew
(Q)uit

Enter choice: u

You picked: [u]
Enter new string: Python

p(U)sh
p(O)p
(V)iew
(Q)uit

Enter choice: u

You picked: [u]
Enter new string: is

p(U)sh
p(O)p
(V)iew
(Q)uit

Enter choice: u

You picked: [u]
Enter new string: cool!

p(U)sh
p(O)p
(V)iew
(Q)uit

Enter choice: v

You picked: [v]
['Python', 'is', 'cool!']

p(U)sh
p(O)p
(V)iew
(Q)uit
```

```
Enter choice: o

You picked: [o]
Removed [ 'cool!' ]

p(U)sh
p(O)p
(V)iew
(Q)uit

Enter choice: o

You picked: [o]
Removed [ 'is' ]

p(U)sh
p(O)p
(V)iew
(Q)uit

Enter choice: o

You picked: [o]
Removed [ 'Python' ]

p(U)sh
p(O)p
(V)iew
(Q)uit

Enter choice: o

You picked: [o]
Cannot pop from an empty stack!

p(U)sh
p(O)p
(V)iew
(Q)uit

Enter choice: ^D

You picked: [q]
```

Queue

A queue is a first-in-first-out (FIFO) data structure, which works like a single-file supermarket or bank teller line. The first person in line is the first one served (and hopefully the first one to exit). New elements join by being "enqueued" at the end of the line, and elements are removed from the front by being "dequeued." The following code shows how, with a little modification from our stack script, we can implement a simple queue using lists.

Example 6.4 Using Lists as a Queue (queue.py)

This simple script uses lists as a queue to store and retrieve strings entered through this menu-driven text application, using only the append() *and* pop() *list methods.*

```
1   #!/usr/bin/env python
2
3   queue = []
4
5   def enQ():
6       queue.append(raw_input('Enter new string: ').strip())
7
8   def deQ():
9       if len(queue) == 0:
10          print 'Cannot pop from an empty queue!'
11      else:
12          print 'Removed [', `queue.pop(0)`, ']'
13
14  def viewQ():
15      print queue            # calls str() internally
16
17  CMDs = {'e': enQ, 'd': deQ, 'v': viewQ}
18
19  def showmenu():
20      pr = """
21  (E)nqueue
22  (D)equeue
23  (V)iew
24  (Q)uit
25
26  Enter choice: """
27
28      while True:
29          while True:
30              try:
31                  choice = raw_input(pr).strip()[0].lower()
32              except (EOFError,KeyboardInterrupt,IndexError):
33                  choice = 'q'
34
35              print '\nYou picked: [%s]' % choice
36              if choice not in 'devq':
37                  print 'Invalid option, try again'
38              else:
39                  break
40
41          if choice == 'q':
42              break
43          CMDs[choice]()
44
45  if __name__ == '__main__':
46      showmenu()
```

Line-by-Line Explanation

Because of the similarities of this script with the `stack.py` script, we will describe in detail only the lines which have changed significantly:

Lines 1–7

The usual setup plus some constants for the rest of the script to use.

Lines 5–6

The `enQ()` function works exactly like `pushit()`, only the name has been changed.

Lines 8–12

The key difference between the two scripts lies here. The `deQ()` function, rather than taking the most recent item as `popit()` did, takes the oldest item on the list, the first element.

Lines 17, 21–24, 36

The `options` have been changed, so we need to reflect that in the prompt string and our validator.

We present some output here as well:

```
$ queue.py
(E)nqueue
(D)equeue
(V)iew
(Q)uit

Enter choice: e

You picked: [e]
Enter new queue element: Bring out

(E)nqueue
(D)equeue
(V)iew
(Q)uit

Enter choice: e

You picked: [e]
Enter new queue element: your dead!
```

```
(E)nqueue
(D)equeue
(V)iew
(Q)uit

Enter choice: v

You picked: [v]
['Bring out', 'your dead!']

(E)nqueue
(D)equeue
(V)iew
(Q)uit

Enter choice: d

You picked: [d]
Removed [ 'Bring out' ]

(E)nqueue
(D)equeue
(V)iew
(Q)uit

Enter choice: d

You picked: [d]
    Removed [ 'your dead!' ]

(E)nqueue
(D)equeue
(V)iew
(Q)uit

Enter choice: d

You picked: [d]
Cannot dequeue from empty queue!

(E)nqueue
(D)equeue
(V)iew
(Q)uit

Enter choice: ^D
You picked: [q]
```

6.16 Tuples

Tuples are another container type extremely similar in nature to lists. The only visible difference between tuples and lists is that tuples use parentheses and lists use square brackets. Functionally, there is a more significant difference, and that is the fact that tuples are immutable. Because of this, tuples can do something that lists cannot do . . . be a dictionary key. Tuples are also the default when dealing with a group of objects.

Our usual *modus operandi* is to present the operators and built-in functions for the more general objects, followed by those for sequences and conclude with those applicable only for tuples, but because tuples share so many characteristics with lists, we would be duplicating much of our description from the previous section. Rather than providing much repeated information, we will differentiate tuples from lists as they apply to each set of operators and functionality, then discuss immutability and other features unique to tuples.

How to Create and Assign Tuples

Creating and assigning tuples are practically identical to creating and assigning lists, with the exception of empty tuples—these require a trailing comma (,) enclosed in the tuple delimiting parentheses (( )) to prevent them from being confused with the natural grouping operation of parentheses. Do not forget the factory function!

```
>>> aTuple = (123, 'abc', 4.56, ['inner', 'tuple'], 7-9j)
>>> anotherTuple = (None, 'something to see here')
>>> print aTuple
(123, 'abc', 4.56, ['inner', 'tuple'], (7-9j))
>>> print anotherTuple
(None, 'something to see here')
>>> emptiestPossibleTuple = (None,)
>>> print emptiestPossibleTuple
(None,)
>>> tuple('bar')
('b', 'a', 'r')
```

How to Access Values in Tuples

Slicing works similarly to lists. Use the square bracket slice operator ([ ]) along with the index or indices.

```
>>> aTuple[1:4]
('abc', 4.56, ['inner', 'tuple'])
```

```
>>> aTuple[:3]
(123, 'abc', 4.56)
>>> aTuple[3][1]
'tuple'
```

How to Update Tuples

Like numbers and strings, tuples are immutable, which means you cannot update them or change values of tuple elements. In Sections 6.2 and 6.3.2, we were able to take portions of an existing string to create a new string. The same applies for tuples.

```
>>> aTuple = aTuple[0], aTuple[1], aTuple[-1]
>>> aTuple
(123, 'abc', (7-9j))
>>> tup1 = (12, 34.56)
>>> tup2 = ('abc', 'xyz')
>>> tup3 = tup1 + tup2
>>> tup3
(12, 34.56, 'abc', 'xyz')
```

How to Remove Tuple Elements and Tuples

Removing individual tuple elements is not possible. There is, of course, nothing wrong with putting together another tuple with the undesired elements discarded.

To explicitly remove an entire tuple, just use the **del** statement to reduce an object's reference count. It will be deallocated when that count is zero. Keep in mind that most of the time one will just let an object go out of scope rather than using **del**, a rare occurrence in everyday Python programming.

```
del aTuple
```

6.17 Tuple Operators and Built-in Functions

6.17.1 Standard and Sequence Type Operators and Built-in Functions

Object and sequence operators and built-in functions act the exact same way toward tuples as they do with lists. You can still take slices of tuples, concatenate and make multiple copies of tuples, validate membership, and compare tuples.

Creation, Repetition, Concatenation

```
>>> t = (['xyz', 123], 23, -103.4)
>>> t
(['xyz', 123], 23, -103.4)
>>> t * 2
(['xyz', 123], 23, -103.4, ['xyz', 123], 23, -103.4)
>>> t = t + ('free', 'easy')
>>> t
(['xyz', 123], 23, -103.4, 'free', 'easy')
```

Membership, Slicing

```
>>> 23 in t
True
>>> 123 in t
False
>>> t[0][1]
123
>>> t[1:]
(23, -103.4, 'free', 'easy')
```

Built-in Functions

```
>>> str(t)
(['xyz', 123], 23, -103.4, 'free', 'easy')
>>> len(t)
5
>>> max(t)
'free'
>>> min(t)
-103.4
>>> cmp(t, (['xyz', 123], 23, -103.4, 'free', 'easy'))
0
>>> list(t)
[['xyz', 123], 23, -103.4, 'free', 'easy']
```

Operators

```
>>> (4, 2) < (3, 5)
False
>>> (2, 4) < (3, -1)
True
>>> (2, 4) == (3, -1)
False
>>> (2, 4) == (2, 4)
True
```

6.17.2 Tuple Type Operators and Built-in Functions and Methods

Like lists, tuples have no operators or built-in functions for themselves. All of the list methods described in the previous section were related to a list object's mutability, i.e., sorting, replacing, appending, etc. Since tuples are immutable, those methods are rendered superfluous, thus unimplemented.

6.18 Special Features of Tuples

6.18.1 How Are Tuples Affected by Immutability?

Okay, we have been throwing around this word "immutable" in many parts of the text. Aside from its computer science definition and implications, what is the bottom line as far as applications are concerned? What are all the consequences of an immutable data type?

Of the three standard types that are immutable—numbers, strings, and tuples—tuples are the most affected. A data type that is immutable simply means that once an object is defined, its value cannot be updated, unless, of course, a completely new object is allocated. The impact on numbers and strings is not as great since they are scalar types, and when the sole value they represent is changed, that is the intended effect, and access occurs as desired. The story is different with tuples, however.

Because tuples are a container type, it is often desired to change single or multiple elements of that container. Unfortunately, this is not possible. Slice operators cannot show up on the left-hand side of an assignment. Recall this is no different for strings, and that slice access is used for read access only.

Immutability does not necessarily mean bad news. One bright spot is that if we pass in data to an API with which we are not familiar, we can be certain that our data will not be changed by the function called. Also, if we receive a tuple as a return argument from a function that we would like to manipulate, we can use the `list()` built-in function to turn it into a mutable list.

6.18.2 Tuples Are Not Quite So "Immutable"

Although tuples are defined as immutable, this does not take away from their flexibility. Tuples are not quite as immutable as we made them out to be. What do we mean by that? Tuples have certain behavioral characteristics that make them seem not as immutable as we had first advertised.

For example, we can join strings together to form a larger string. Similarly, there is nothing wrong with putting tuples together to form a larger tuple, so concatenation works. This process does not involve changing the smaller individual tuples in any way. All we are doing is joining their elements together. Some examples are presented here:

```
>>> s = 'first'
>>> s = s + ' second'
>>> s
'first second'
>>>
>>> t = ('third', 'fourth')
>>> t
('third', 'fourth')
>>>
>>> t = t + ('fifth', 'sixth')
>>> t
('third', 'fourth', 'fifth', 'sixth')
```

The same concept applies for repetition. Repetition is just concatenation of multiple copies of the same elements. In addition, we mentioned in the previous section that one can turn a tuple into a mutable list with a simple function call. Our final feature may surprise you the most. You can "modify" certain tuple elements. Whoa. What does that mean?

Although tuple objects themselves are immutable, this fact does not preclude tuples from containing mutable objects that *can* be changed.

```
>>> t = (['xyz', 123], 23, -103.4)
>>> t
(['xyz', 123], 23, -103.4)
>>> t[0][1]
123
>>> t[0][1] = ['abc', 'def']
>>> t
(['xyz', ['abc', 'def']], 23, -103.4)
```

In the above example, although t is a tuple, we managed to "change" it by replacing an item in the first tuple element (a list). We replaced t[0][1], formerly an integer, with a list ['abc', 'def']. Although we modified only a mutable object, in some ways, we also "modified" our tuple.

6.18.3 Default Collection Type

Any set of multiple objects, comma-separated, written without identifying symbols, i.e., brackets for lists, parentheses for tuples, etc., defaults to tuples, as indicated in these short examples:

```
>>> 'abc', -4.24e93, 18+6.6j, 'xyz'
('abc', -4.24e+093, (18+6.6j), 'xyz')
>>>
>>> x, y = 1, 2
>>> x, y
(1, 2)
```

Any function returning multiple objects (also no enclosing symbols) is a tuple. Note that enclosing symbols change a set of multiple objects returned to a single container object. For example:

```
def foo1():
    :
    return obj1, obj2, obj3
def foo2():
    :
    return [obj1, obj2, obj3]
def foo3():
    :
    return (obj1, obj2, obj3)
```

In the above examples, foo1() calls for the return of three objects, which come back as a tuple of three objects, foo2() returns a single object, a list containing three objects, and foo3() returns the same thing as foo1(). The only difference is that the tuple grouping is explicit.

Explicit grouping of parentheses for expressions or tuple creation is always recommended to avoid unpleasant side effects:

```
>>> 4, 2 < 3, 5     # int, comparison, int
(4, True, 5)
>>> (4, 2) < (3, 5) # tuple comparison
False
```

In the first example, the less than (<) operator took precedence over the comma delimiter intended for the tuples on each side of the less than sign. The result of the evaluation of 2 < 3 became the second element of a tuple. Properly enclosing the tuples enables the desired result.

6.18.4 Single-Element Tuples

Ever try to create a tuple with a single element? You tried it with lists, and it worked, but then you tried and tried with tuples, but you cannot seem to do it.

```
>>> ['abc']
['abc']
```

```
>>> type(['abc'])     # a list
<type 'list'>
>>>
>>> ('xyz')
'xyz'
>>> type(('xyz'))     # a string, not a tuple
<type 'str'>
```

It probably does not help your case that the parentheses are also over-loaded as the expression grouping operator. Parentheses around a single ele-ment take on that binding role rather than serving as a delimiter for tuples. The workaround is to place a trailing comma (,) after the first element to indicate that this is a tuple and not a grouping.

```
>>> ('xyz',)
('xyz',)
```

6.18.5 Dictionary Keys

Immutable objects have values that cannot be changed. That means that they will always hash to the same value. That is the requirement for an object being a valid dictionary key. As we will find out in the next chapter, keys must be hashable objects, and tuples meet that criteria. Lists are not eligible.

CORE NOTE: Lists versus Tuples

One of the questions in the Python FAQ asks, "Why are there separate tuple and list data types?" That question can also be rephrased as, "Do we really need two similar sequence types?" One reason why having lists and tuples is a good thing occurs in situations where having one is more advantageous than having the other.

One case in favor of an immutable data type is if you were manipulating sensitive data and were passing a mutable object to an unknown function (perhaps an API that you didn't even write!). As the engineer developing your piece of the software, you would definitely feel a lot more secure if you knew that the function you were calling could not alter the data.

An argument for a mutable data type is where you are managing dynamic data sets. You need to be able to create them on the fly, slowly or arbitrarily adding to them, or from time to time, deleting individual elements. This is definitely a case where the data type must be mutable. The good news is that with the list() *and* tuple() *built-in conversion functions, you can convert from one type to the other relatively painlessly.*

list() *and* tuple() *are functions that allow you to create a tuple from a list and vice versa. When you have a tuple and want a list because you need to update its objects, the* list() *function suddenly becomes your best buddy. When you have a list and want to pass it into a function, perhaps an API, and you do not want anyone to mess with the data, the* tuple() *function comes in quite useful.*

6.19 Related Modules

Table 6.12 lists the key related modules for sequence types. This list includes the array module to which we briefly alluded earlier. These are similar to lists except for the restriction that all elements must be of the same type. The copy module (see optional Section 6.20 below) performs shallow and deep

Table 6.12 Related Modules for Sequence Types

Module	*Contents*
array	Features the array restricted mutable sequence type, which requires all of its elements to be of the same type
copy	Provides functionality to perform shallow and deep copies of objects (see 6.20 below for more information)
operator	Contains sequence operators available as function calls, e.g., operator.concat(m, n) is equivalent to the concatenation (m + n) for sequences m and n
re	Perl-style regular expression search (and match); see Chapter 15
StringIO/ cStringIO	Treats long strings just like a file object, i.e., read(), seek(), etc.; C-compiled version is faster but cannot be subclassed
textwrap[a]	Utility functions for wrapping/filling text fields; also has a class
types	Contains type objects for all supported Python types
collections[b]	High-performance container data types

a.   New in Python 2.3.
b.   New in Python 2.4.

copies of objects. The `operator` module, in addition to the functional equivalents to numeric operators, also contains the same four sequence types. The `types` module is a reference of type objects representing all types that Python supports, including sequence types. Finally, the `UserList` module contains a full class implementation of a list object. Because Python types cannot be subclassed, this module allows users to obtain a class that is list-like in nature, and to derive new classes or functionality. If you are unfamiliar with object-oriented programming, we highly recommend reading Chapter 13.

6.20 *Copying Python Objects and Shallow and Deep Copies

Earlier in Section 3.5, we described how object assignments are simply object references. This means that when you create an object, then assign that object to another variable, Python does not copy the object. Instead, it copies only a *reference* to the object.

For example, let us say that you want to create a generic profile for a young couple; call it `person`. Then you copy this object for both of them. In the example below, we show two ways of copying an object, one uses slices and the other a factory function. To show we have three unrelated objects, we use the `id()` built-in function to show you each object's identity. (We can also use the **is** operator to do the same thing.)

```
>>> person = ['name', ['savings', 100.00]]
>>> hubby = person[:]        # slice copy
>>> wifey = list(person)     # fac func copy
>>> [id(x) for x in person, hubby, wifey]
[11826320, 12223552, 11850936]
```

Individual savings accounts are created for them with initial $100 deposits. The names are changed to customize each person's object. But when the husband withdraws $50.00, his actions affected his wife's account even though separate copies were made. (Of course, this is assuming that we want them to have separate accounts and not a single, joint account.) Why is that?

```
>>> hubby[0] = 'joe'
>>> wifey[0] = 'jane'
>>> hubby, wifey
(['joe', ['savings', 100.0]], ['jane', ['savings', 100.0]])
>>> hubby[1][1] = 50.00
>>> hubby, wifey
(['joe', ['savings', 50.0]], ['jane', ['savings', 50.0]])
```

The reason is that we have only made a *shallow copy*. A shallow copy of an object is defined to be a newly created object of the same type as the original object whose contents are references to the elements in the original object. In other words, the copied object itself is new, but the contents are not. Shallow copies of sequence objects are the default type of copy and can be made in any number of ways: (1) taking a complete slice `[:]`, (2) using a factory function, e.g., `list()`, `dict()`, etc., or (3) using the `copy()` function of the `copy` module.

Your next question should be: When the wife's name is assigned, how come it did not affect the husband's name? Shouldn't they both have the name `'jane'` now? The reason why it worked and we don't have duplicate names is because of the two objects in each of their lists, the first is immutable (a string) and the second is mutable (a list). Because of this, when shallow copies are made, the string is explicitly copied and a new (string) object created while the list only has its reference copied, not its members. So changing the names is not an issue but altering any part of their banking information is. Here, let us take a look at the object IDs for the elements of each list. Note that the banking object is exactly the same and the reason why changes to one affects the other. Note how, after we change their names, that the new name strings replace the original `'name'` string:

BEFORE:

```
>>> [id(x) for x in hubby]
[9919616, 11826320]
>>> [id(x) for x in wifey]
[9919616, 11826320]
```

AFTER:

```
>>> [id(x) for x in hubby]
[12092832, 11826320]
>>> [id(x) for x in wifey]
[12191712, 11826320]
```

If the intention was to create a joint account for the couple, then we have a great solution, but if we want separate accounts, we need to change something. In order to obtain a full or *deep copy* of the object—creating a new container but containing references to completely new copies (references) of the element in the original object—we need to use the `copy.deepcopy()` function. Let us redo the entire example but using deep copies instead:

```
>>> person = ['name', ['savings', 100.00]]
>>> hubby = person
```

```
>>> import copy
>>> wifey = copy.deepcopy(person)
>>> [id(x) for x in person, hubby, wifey]
[12242056, 12242056, 12224232]
>>> hubby[0] = 'joe'
>>> wifey[0] = 'jane'
>>> hubby, wifey
(['joe', ['savings', 100.0]], ['jane', ['savings', 100.0]])
>>> hubby[1][1] = 50.00
>>> hubby, wifey
(['joe', ['savings', 50.0]], ['jane', ['savings', 100.0]])
```

Now it is just the way we want it. For kickers, let us confirm that all four objects are different:

```
>>> [id(x) for x in hubby]
[12191712, 11826280]
>>> [id(x) for x in wifey]
[12114080, 12224792]
```

There are a few more caveats to object copying. The first is that non-container types (i.e., numbers, strings, and other "atomic" objects like code, type, and xrange objects) are not copied. Shallow copies of sequences are all done using complete slices. Finally, deep copies of tuples are not made if they contain only atomic objects. If we changed the banking information to a tuple, we would get only a shallow copy even though we asked for a deep copy:

```
>>> person = ['name', ('savings', 100.00)]
>>> newPerson = copy.deepcopy(person)
>>> [id(x) for x in person, newPerson]
[12225352, 12226112]
>>> [id(x) for x in person]
[9919616, 11800088]
>>> [id(x) for x in newPerson]
[9919616, 11800088]
```

CORE MODULE: copy

The shallow and deep copy operations that we just described are found in the copy *module. There are really only two functions to use from this module:* copy() *creates shallow copy, and* deepcopy() *creates a deep copy.*

6.21 Summary of Sequences

Sequence types provide various mechanisms for ordered storage of data. Strings are a general medium for carrying data, whether it be displayed to a user, stored on a disk, transmitted across the network, or be a singular container for multiple sources of information. Lists and tuples provide container storage that allows for simple manipulation and access of multiple objects, whether they be Python data types or user-defined objects. Individual or groups of elements may be accessed as slices via sequentially ordered index offsets. Together, these data types provide flexible and easy-to-use storage tools in your Python development environment. We conclude this chapter with a summary of operators, built-in functions and methods for sequence types given in Table 6.13.

Table 6.13 Sequence Type Operators, Built-in Functions and Methods

Operator, Built-in Function or Method	String	List	Tuple
[] (list creation)		•	
()			•
" "	•		
append()		•	
capitalize()	•		
center()	•		
chr()	•		
cmp()	•	•	•
count()	•	•	
decode()	•		
encode()	•		
endswith()	•		

(continued)

Table 6.13 Sequence Type Operators, Built-in Functions and Methods (continued)

Operator, Built-in Function or Method	*String*	*List*	*Tuple*
expandtabs()	•		
extend()		•	
find()	•		
hex()	•		
index()	•	•	
insert()		•	
isdecimal()	•		
isdigit()	•		
islower()	•		
isnumeric()	•		
isspace()	•		
istitle()	•		
isupper()	•		
join()	•		
len()	•	•	•
list()	•	•	•
ljust()	•		
lower()	•		
lstrip()	•		
max()	•	•	•
min()	•	•	•
oct()	•		
ord()	•		

Table 6.13 Sequence Type Operators, Built-in Functions and Methods (continued)			
Operator, Built-in Function or Method	*String*	*List*	*Tuple*
pop()		•	
raw_input()	•		
remove()		•	
replace()	•		
repr()	•	•	•
reverse()		•	
rfind()	•		
rindex()	•		
rjust()	•		
rstrip()	•		
sort()		•	
split()	•		
splitlines()	•		
startswith()	•		
str()	•	•	•
strip()	•		
swapcase()	•		
split()	•		
title()	•		
tuple()	•	•	•
type()	•	•	•

(*continued*)

Table 6.13 Sequence Type Operators, Built-in Functions and Methods (continued)			
Operator, Built-in Function or Method	**String**	**List**	**Tuple**
upper()	•		
zfill()	•		
. (attributes)	•	•	
[ ] (slice)	•	•	•
[:]	•	•	•
*	•	•	•
%	•		
+	•	•	•
in	•	•	•
not in	•	•	•

6.22 Exercises

6–1. *Strings.* Are there any string methods or functions in the string module that will help me determine if a string is part of a larger string?

6–2. *String Identifiers.* Modify the idcheck.py script in Example 6–1 such that it will determine the validity of identifiers of length 1 as well as be able to detect if an identifier is a keyword. For the latter part of the exercise, you may use the keyword module (specifically the keyword.kwlist list) to aid in your cause.

6–3. *Sorting.*

(a) Enter a list of numbers and sort the values in largest-to-smallest order.

(b) Do the same thing, but for strings and in reverse alphabetical (largest-to-smallest lexicographic) order.

6–4. *Arithmetic*. Update your solution to the test score exercise in the previous chapter such that the test scores are entered into a list. Your code should also be able to come up with an average score. See Exercises 2–9 and 5–3.

6–5. *Strings*.
(a) Update your solution to Exercise 2–7 so that you display a string one character at a time forward *and* backward.
(b) Determine if two strings match (without using comparison operators or the cmp() built-in function) by scanning each string. Extra credit: Add case-insensitivity to your solution.
(c) Determine if a string is palindromic (the same backward as it is forward). Extra credit: Add code to suppress symbols and whitespace if you want to process anything other than strict palindromes.
(d) Take a string and append a backward copy of that string, making a palindrome.

6–6. *Strings*. Create the equivalent to string.strip(): Take a string and remove all leading and trailing whitespace. (Use of string.*strip() defeats the purpose of this exercise.)

6–7. *Debugging*. Take a look at the code we present in Example 6.4 (buggy.py).
(a) Study the code and describe what this program does. Add a comment to every place you see a comment sign (#). Run the program.
(b) This problem has a big bug in it. It fails on inputs of 6, 12, 20, 30, etc., not to mention any even number in general. What is wrong with this program?
(c) Fix the bug in (b).

6–8. *Lists*. Given an integer value, return a string with the equivalent English text of each digit. For example, an input of 89 results in "eight-nine" being returned. Extra credit: Return English text with proper usage, i.e., "eighty-nine." For this part of the exercise, restrict values to be between 0 and 1,000.

6–9. *Conversion*. Create a sister function to your solution for Exercise 5–13 to take the total number of minutes and return the same time interval in hours and minutes, maximizing on the total number of hours.

6–10. *Strings*. Create a function that will return another string similar to the input string, but with its case inverted. For example, input of "Mr. Ed" will result in "mR. eD" as the output string.

Example 6.4 Buggy Program (buggy.py)

This is the program listing for Exercise 6–7. You will determine what this program does, add comments where you see "#"s, determine what is wrong with it, and provide a fix for it.

```
1   #!/usr/bin/env python
2
3   #
4   num_str = raw_input('Enter a number: ')
5
6   #
7   num_num = int(num_str)
8
9   #
10  fac_list = range(1, num_num+1)
11  print "BEFORE:", 'fac_list'
12
13  #
14  i = 0
15
16  #
17  while i < len(fac_list):
18
19      #
20      if num_num % fac_list[i] == 0:
21          del fac_list[i]
22
23      #
24      i = i + 1
25
26  #
27  print "AFTER:", 'fac_list'
```

6–11. *Conversion.*

(a) Create a program that will convert from an integer to an Internet Protocol (IP) address in the four-octet format of WWW.XXX.YYY.ZZZ.

(b) Update your program to be able to do the vice versa of the above.

6–12. *Strings.*

(a) Create a function called findchr(), with the following declaration:

def findchr(*string, char*)

findchr() will look for character char in *string* and return the index of the first occurrence of *char*, or -1 if that *char* is not part of *string*. You cannot use `string.*find()` or `string.*index()` functions or methods.

(b) Create another function called `rfindchr()` that will find the last occurrence of a character in a string. Naturally this works similarly to `findchr()`, but it starts its search from the end of the input string.

(c) Create a third function called `subchr()` with the following declaration:

```
def subchr(string, origchar, newchar)
```

`subchr()` is similar to `findchr()` except that whenever *origchar* is found, it is replaced by *newchar*. The modified string is the return value.

6–13. *Strings*. The `string` module contains three functions, `atoi()`, `atol()`, and `atof()`, that convert strings to integers, long integers, and floating point numbers, respectively. As of Python 1.5, the Python built-in functions `int()`, `long()`, and `float()` can also perform the same tasks, in addition to `complex()`, which can turn a string into a complex number. (Prior to 1.5, however, those built-in functions converted only between numeric types.)

An `atoc()` was never implemented in the `string` module, so that is your task here. `atoc()` takes a single string as input, a string representation of a complex number, e.g., '-1.23e+4-5.67j', and returns the equivalent complex number object with the given value. You cannot use `eval()`, but `complex()` is available. However, you can only use `complex()` with the following restricted syntax: `complex(real, imag)` where `real` and `imag` are floating point values.

6–14. *Random Numbers*. Design a "rock, paper, scissors" game, sometimes called "Rochambeau," a game you may have played as a kid. Here are the rules. At the same time, using specified hand motions, both you and your opponent have to pick from one of the following: rock, paper, or scissors. The winner is determined by these rules, which form somewhat of a fun paradox:

(a) the paper covers the rock,

(b) the rock breaks the scissors,

(c) the scissors cut the paper. In your computerized version, the user enters his/her guess, the computer randomly chooses, and your program should indicate a winner or draw/tie. Note: The most algorithmic solutions use the fewest number of **if** statements.

6–15. *Conversion.*

(a) Given a pair of dates in some recognizable standard format such as MM/DD/YY or DD/MM/YY, determine the total number of days that fall between both dates.

(b) Given a person's birth date, determine the total number of days that person has been alive, including all leap days.

(c) Armed with the same information from (b) above, determine the number of days remaining until that person's next birthday.

6–16. *Matrices.* Process the addition and multiplication of a pair of M by N matrices.

6–17. *Methods.* Implement a function called myPop(), which is similar to the list pop() method. Take a list as input, remove the last object from the list and return it.

6–18. In the zip() example of Section 6.12.2, what does zip(fn, ln) return?

6–19. *Multi-Column Output.* Given any number of items in a sequence or other container, display them in equally-distributed number of columns. Let the caller provide the data and the output format. For example, if you pass in a list of 100 items destined for three columns, display the data in the requested format. In this case, two columns would have 33 items while the last would have 34. You can also let the user choose horizontal or vertical sorting.

MAPPING AND SET TYPES

Chapter Topics

- Mapping Type: Dictionaries
  - Operators
  - Built-in Functions
  - Built-in Methods
  - Dictionary Keys
- Set Types
  - Operators
  - Built-in Functions
  - Built-in Methods
- Related Modules

Chapter 7

In this chapter, we take a look at Python's mapping and set types. As in earlier chapters, an introduction is followed by a discussion of the applicable operators and factory and built-in functions (BIFs) and methods. We then go into more specific usage of each data type.

7.1 Mapping Type: Dictionaries

Dictionaries are the sole mapping type in Python. Mapping objects have a one-to-many correspondence between *hashable* values (*keys*) and the objects they represent (*values*). They are similar to Perl hashes and can be generally considered as *mutable hash tables*. A dictionary object itself is mutable and is yet another container type that can store any number of Python objects, including other container types. What makes dictionaries different from sequence type containers like lists and tuples is the way the data are stored and accessed.

Sequence types use numeric keys only (numbered sequentially as indexed offsets from the beginning of the sequence). Mapping types may use most other object types as keys; strings are the most common. Unlike sequence type keys, mapping keys are often, if not directly, associated with the data value that is stored. But because we are no longer using "sequentially ordered" keys with mapping types, we are left with an unordered collection of data. As it turns out, this does not hinder our use because mapping types do not require a numeric value to index into a container to obtain the desired item. With a key, you are "mapped" directly to your value, hence the term "mapping type." The reason why they are commonly referred to as hash tables is because that is the exact type of object that dictionaries are. Dictionaries are one of Python's most powerful data types.

CORE NOTE: What are hash tables and how do they relate to dictionaries?

Sequence types use sequentially ordered numeric keys as index offsets to store your data in an array format. The index number usually has nothing to do with the data value that is being stored. There should also be a way to store data based on another associated value such as a string. We do this all the time in everyday living. You file people's phone numbers in your address book based on last name, you add events to your calendar or appointment book based on date and time, etc. For each of these examples, an associated value to a data item was your key.

Hash tables are a data structure that does exactly what we described. They store each piece of data, called a value, *based on an associated data item, called a* key. *Together, these are known as* key-value *pairs. The hash table algorithm takes your key, performs an operation on it, called a* hash function, *and based on the result of the calculation, chooses where in the data structure to store your value. Where any one particular value is stored depends on what its key is. Because of this randomness, there is no ordering of the values in the hash table. You have an unordered collection of data.*

The only kind of ordering you can obtain is by taking either a dictionary's set of keys or values. The keys() *or* values() *method returns lists, which are sortable. You can also call* items() *to get a list of keys and values as tuple pairs and sort that. Dictionaries themselves have no implicit ordering because they are hashes.*

Hash tables generally provide good performance because lookups occur fairly quickly once you have a key.

Python dictionaries are implemented as resizeable hash tables. If you are familiar with Perl, then we can say that dictionaries are similar to Perl's associative arrays or hashes.

We will now take a closer look at Python dictionaries. The syntax of a dictionary entry is *key:value*. Also, dictionary entries are enclosed in braces ({ }).

How to Create and Assign Dictionaries

Creating dictionaries simply involves assigning a dictionary to a variable, regardless of whether the dictionary has elements or not:

```
>>> dict1 = {}
>>> dict2 = {'name': 'earth', 'port': 80}
>>> dict1, dict2
({}, {'port': 80, 'name': 'earth'})
```

In Python versions 2.2 and newer, dictionaries may also be created using the factory function `dict()`. We discuss more examples later when we take a closer look at `dict()`, but here's a sneak peek for now:

2.2

```
>>> fdict = dict((['x', 1], ['y', 2]))
>>> fdict
{'y': 2, 'x': 1}
```

In Python versions 2.3 and newer, dictionaries may also be created using a very convenient built-in method for creating a "default" dictionary whose elements all have the same value (defaulting to None if not given), `fromkeys()`:

2.3

```
>>> ddict = {}.fromkeys(('x', 'y'), -1)
>>> ddict
{'y': -1, 'x': -1}
>>>
>>> edict = {}.fromkeys(('foo', 'bar'))
>>> edict
{'foo': None, 'bar': None}
```

How to Access Values in Dictionaries

To traverse a dictionary (normally by key), you only need to cycle through its keys, like this:

```
>>> dict2 = {'name': 'earth', 'port': 80}
>>>
>>>> for key in dict2.keys():
...     print 'key=%s, value=%s' % (key, dict2[key])
...
key=name, value=earth
key=port, value=80
```

Beginning with Python 2.2, you no longer need to use the `keys()` method to extract a list of keys to loop over. Iterators were created to simplify accessing of sequence-like objects such as dictionaries and files. Using just the

2.2

dictionary name itself will cause an iterator over that dictionary to be used in a **for** loop:

```
>>> dict2 = {'name': 'earth', 'port': 80}
>>>
>>>> for key in dict2:
...         print 'key=%s, value=%s' % (key, dict2[key])
...
key=name, value=earth
key=port, value=80
```

To access individual dictionary elements, you use the familiar square brackets along with the key to obtain its value:

```
>>> dict2['name']
'earth'
>>>
>>> print 'host %s is running on port %d' % \
...   (dict2['name'], dict2['port'])
host earth is running on port 80
```

Dictionary `dict1` defined above is empty while `dict2` has two data items. The keys in `dict2` are `'name'` and `'port'`, and their associated value items are `'earth'` and `80`, respectively. Access to the value is through the key, as you can see from the explicit access to the `'name'` key.

If we attempt to access a data item with a key that is not part of the dictionary, we get an error:

```
>>> dict2['server']
Traceback (innermost last):
  File "<stdin>", line 1, in ?
KeyError: server
```

In this example, we tried to access a value with the key `'server'` which, as you know from the code above, does not exist. The best way to check if a dictionary has a specific key is to use the dictionary's `has_key()` method, or better yet, the **in** or **not in** operators starting with version 2.2. The `has_key()` method will be obsoleted in future versions of Python, so it is best to just use **in** or **not in**.

2.2

We will introduce all of a dictionary's methods below. The Boolean `has_key()` and the **in** and **not in** operators are Boolean, returning `True` if a dictionary has that key and `False` otherwise. (In Python versions preceding Boolean constants [older than 2.3], the values returned are 1 and 0, respectively.)

```
>>> 'server' in dict2 # or dict2.has_key('server')
False
>>> 'name' in dict # or dict2.has_key('name')
True
```

```
>>> dict2['name']
'earth'
```

Here is another dictionary example mixing the use of numbers and strings as keys:

```
>>> dict3 = {}
>>> dict3[1] = 'abc'
>>> dict3['1'] = 3.14159
>>> dict3[3.2] = 'xyz'
>>> dict3
{3.2: 'xyz', 1: 'abc', '1': 3.14159}
```

Rather than adding each key-value pair individually, we could have also entered all the data for dict3 at the same time:

```
dict3 = {3.2: 'xyz', 1: 'abc', '1': 3.14159}
```

Creating the dictionary with a set key-value pair can be accomplished if all the data items are known in advance (obviously). The goal of the examples using dict3 is to illustrate the variety of keys that you can use. If we were to pose the question of whether a key for a particular value should be allowed to change, you would probably say, "No." Right?

Not allowing keys to change during execution makes sense if you think of it this way: Let us say that you created a dictionary element with a key and value. Somehow during execution of your program, the key changed, perhaps due to an altered variable. When you went to retrieve that data value again with the original key, you got a KeyError (since the key changed), and you had no idea how to obtain your value now because the key had somehow been altered. For this reason, keys must be hashable, so numbers and strings are fine, but lists and other dictionaries are not. (See Section 7.5.2 for why keys must be hashable.)

How to Update Dictionaries

You can update a dictionary by adding a new entry or element (i.e., a key-value pair), modifying an existing entry, or deleting an existing entry (see below for more details on removing an entry).

```
>>> dict2['name'] = 'venus'  # update existing entry
>>> dict2['port'] = 6969     # update existing entry
>>> dict2['arch'] = 'sunos5' # add new entry
>>>
>>> print 'host %(name)s is running on port %(port)d' %
dict2
host venus is running on port 6969
```

If the key does exist, then its previous value will be overridden by its new value. The **print** statement above illustrates an alternative way of using the string format operator (%), specific to dictionaries. Using the dictionary argument, you can shorten the `print` request somewhat because naming of the dictionary occurs only once, as opposed to occurring for each element using a tuple argument.

You may also add the contents of an entire dictionary to another dictionary by using the `update()` built-in method. We will introduce this method in Section 7.4.

How to Remove Dictionary Elements and Dictionaries

Removing an entire dictionary is not a typical operation. Generally, you either remove individual dictionary elements or clear the entire contents of a dictionary. However, if you really want to "remove" an entire dictionary, use the **del** statement (introduced in Section 3.5.5). Here are some deletion examples for dictionaries and dictionary elements:

```
del dict2['name']      # remove entry with key 'name'
dict2.clear()          # remove all entries in dict1
del dict2              # delete entire dictionary
dict2.pop('name')      # remove & return entry w/key
```

CORE TIP: Avoid using built-in object names as identifiers for variables!

For those of you who began traveling in the Python universe before version 2.3, you may have once used dict *as an identifier for a dictionary. However, because* dict() *is now a type and factory function, overriding it may cause you headaches and potential bugs. The interpreter will allow such overriding—hey, it thinks you seem smart and look like you know what you are doing! So be careful. Do* NOT *use variables named after built-in types like:* dict, list, file, bool, str, input, *or* len!

7.2 Mapping Type Operators

Dictionaries will work with all of the standard type operators but do not support operations such as concatenation and repetition. Those operations, although they make sense for sequence types, do not translate to mapping types. In the next two subsections, we introduce you to the operators you can use with dictionaries.

7.2.1 Standard Type Operators

The standard type operators were introduced in Chapter 4. Here are some basic examples using some of those operators:

```
>>> dict4 = {'abc': 123}
>>> dict5 = {'abc': 456}
>>> dict6 = {'abc': 123, 98.6: 37}
>>> dict7 = {'xyz': 123}
>>> dict4 < dict5
True
>>> (dict4 < dict6) and (dict4 < dict7)
True
>>> (dict5 < dict6) and (dict5 < dict7)
True
>>> dict6 < dict7
False
```

How are all these comparisons performed? Like lists and tuples, the process is a bit more complex than it is for numbers and strings. The algorithm is detailed in Section 7.3.1.

7.2.2 Mapping Type Operators

Dictionary Key-Lookup Operator ([ ])

The only operator specific to dictionaries is the key-lookup operator, which works very similarly to the single element slice operator for sequence types.

For sequence types, an index offset is the sole argument or subscript to access a single element of a sequence. For a dictionary, lookups are by key, so that is the argument rather than an index. The key-lookup operator is used for both assigning values to and retrieving values from a dictionary:

```
d[k] = v     # set value 'v' in dictionary with key 'k'
d[k]         # lookup value in dictionary with key 'k'
```

(Key) Membership (**in**, **not in**)

Beginning with Python 2.2, programmers can use the **in** and **not in** operators to check key membership instead of the has_key() method:

```
2.2
```

```
>>> 'name' in dict2
True
>>> 'phone' in dict2
False
```

7.3 Mapping Type Built-in and Factory Functions

7.3.1 *Standard Type Functions* [type(), str(), *and* cmp()]

The type() factory function, when applied to a dict, returns, as you might expect, the dict type, "<type 'dict'>". The str() factory function will produce a printable string representation of a dictionary. These are fairly straightforward.

In each of the last three chapters, we showed how the cmp() BIF worked with numbers, strings, lists, and tuples. So how about dictionaries? Comparisons of dictionaries are based on an algorithm that starts with sizes first, then keys, and finally values. However, using cmp() on dictionaries isn't usually very useful.

The next subsection goes into further detail about the algorithm used to compare dictionaries, but this is advanced reading, and definitely optional since comparing dictionaries is not very useful or very common.

*Dictionary Comparison Algorithm

In the following example, we create two dictionaries and compare them, then slowly modify the dictionaries to show how these changes affect their comparisons:

```
>>> dict1 = {}
>>> dict2 = {'host': 'earth', 'port': 80}
>>> cmp(dict1, dict2)
-1
>>> dict1['host'] = 'earth'
>>> cmp(dict1, dict2)
-1
```

In the first comparison, dict1 is deemed smaller because dict2 has more elements (2 items vs. 0 items). After adding one element to dict1, it is still smaller (2 vs. 1), even if the item added is also in dict2.

```
>>> dict1['port'] = 8080
>>> cmp(dict1, dict2)
1
>>> dict1['port'] = 80
>>> cmp(dict1, dict2)
0
```

After we add the second element to dict1, both dictionaries have the same size, so their keys are then compared. At this juncture, both sets of keys match, so comparison proceeds to checking their values. The values for the `'host'` keys are the same, but when we get to the `'port'` key, dict2 is deemed larger because its value is greater than that of dict1's `'port'` key (8080 vs. 80). When resetting dict2's `'port'` key to the same value as dict1's `'port'` key, then both dictionaries form equals: They have the same size, their keys match, and so do their values, hence the reason that 0 is returned by `cmp()`.

```
>>> dict1['prot'] = 'tcp'
>>> cmp(dict1, dict2)
1
>>> dict2['prot'] = 'udp'
>>> cmp(dict1, dict2)
-1
```

As soon as an element is added to one of the dictionaries, it immediately becomes the "larger one," as in this case with dict1. Adding another key-value pair to dict2 can tip the scales again, as both dictionaries' sizes match and comparison progresses to checking keys and values.

```
>>> cdict = {'fruits':1}
>>> ddict = {'fruits':1}
>>> cmp(cdict, ddict)
0
>>> cdict['oranges'] = 0
>>> ddict['apples'] = 0
>>> cmp(cdict, ddict)
14
```

Our final example reminds as that `cmp()` may return values other than −1, 0, or 1. The algorithm pursues comparisons in the following order.

(1) Compare Dictionary Sizes

If the dictionary lengths are different, then for `cmp(dict1, dict2)`, `cmp()` will return a positive number if *dict1* is longer and a negative number if *dict2* is longer. In other words, the dictionary with more keys is greater, i.e.,

```
len(dict1) > len(dict2) ⇒ dict1 > dict2
```

(2) Compare Dictionary Keys

If both dictionaries are the same size, then their keys are compared; the order in which the keys are checked is the same order as returned by the `keys()` method. (It is important to note here that keys that are the same will map to the same locations in the hash table. This keeps key-checking consistent.) At the point where keys from both do not match, they are directly compared and `cmp()` will return a positive number if the first differing key for *dict1* is greater than the first differing key of *dict2*.

(3) Compare Dictionary Values

If both dictionary lengths are the same and the keys match exactly, the values for each key in both dictionaries are compared. Once the first key with non-matching values is found, those values are compared directly. Then `cmp()` will return a positive number if, using the same key, the value in *dict1* is greater than the value in *dict2*.

(4) Exact Match

If we have reached this point, i.e., the dictionaries have the same length, the same keys, and the same values for each key, then the dictionaries are an exact match and 0 is returned.

Figure 7–1 illustrates the dictionary compare algorithm we just outlined.

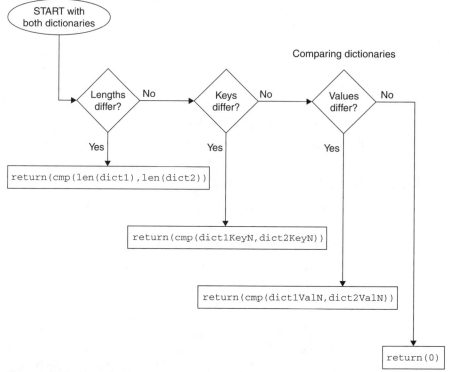

Figure 7–1 How dictionaries are compared

7.3.2 Mapping Type Related Functions

```
dict()
```

The `dict()` factory function is used for creating dictionaries. If no argument is provided, then an empty dictionary is created. The fun happens when a container object is passed in as an argument to `dict()`.

If the argument is an iterable, i.e., a sequence, an iterator, or an object that supports iteration, then each element of the iterable must come in pairs. For each pair, the first element will be a new key in the dictionary with the second item as its value. Taking a cue from the official Python documentation for `dict()`:

```
>>> dict(zip(('x', 'y'), (1, 2)))
{'y': 2, 'x': 1}
>>> dict([['x', 1], ['y', 2]])
{'y': 2, 'x': 1}
>>> dict([('xy'[i-1], i) for i in range(1,3)])
{'y': 2, 'x': 1}
```

If it is a(nother) mapping object, i.e., a dictionary, then `dict()` will just create a new dictionary and copy the contents of the existing one. The new dictionary is actually a shallow copy of the original one and the same results can be accomplished by using a dictionary's `copy()` built-in method. Because creating a new dictionary from an existing one using `dict()` is measurably slower than using `copy()`, we recommend using the latter.

Starting in Python 2.3, it is possible to call `dict()` with an existing dictionary or keyword argument dictionary (** function operator, covered in Chapter 11):

```
>>> dict(x=1, y=2)
{'y': 2, 'x': 1}
>>> dict8 = dict(x=1, y=2)
>>> dict8
{'y': 2, 'x': 1}
>>> dict9 = dict(**dict8)
>>> dict9
{'y': 2, 'x': 1}
```

We remind viewers that the `dict9` example is only an exercise in understanding the calling semantics of `dict()` and not a realistic example. It would be wiser (and better performance-wise) to execute something more along the lines of:

```
>>> dict9 = dict8.copy()
>>> dict9
{'y': 2, 'x': 1}
```

len()

The len() BIF is flexible. It works with sequences, mapping types, and sets (as we will find out later on in this chapter). For a dictionary, it returns the total number of items, that is, key-value pairs:

```
>>> dict2 = {'name': 'earth', 'port': 80}
>>> dict2
{'port': 80, 'name': 'earth'}
>>> len(dict2)
2
```

We mentioned earlier that dictionary items are unordered. We can see that above, when referencing dict2, the items are listed in reverse order from which they were entered into the dictionary.

hash()

The hash() BIF is not really meant to be used for dictionaries per se, but it can be used to determine whether an object is fit to be a dictionary key (or not). Given an object as its argument, hash() returns the hash value of that object. The object can only be a dictionary key if it is *hashable* (meaning this function returns a[n integer] value without errors or raising an exception). Numeric values that are equal (when pitted against each other using a comparison operator) hash to the same value (even if their types differ). A TypeError will occur if an unhashable type is given as the argument to hash() (and consequently if an attempt is made to use such an object as the key when assigning a value to a dictionary):

```
>>> hash([])
Traceback (innermost last):
  File "<stdin>", line 1, in ?
TypeError: list objects are unhashable
>>>
>>> dict2[{}] = 'foo'
Traceback (most recent call last):
  File "<stdin>", line 1, in ?
TypeError: dict objects are unhashable
```

In Table 7.1, we summarize these three mapping type related functions.

Table 7.1 Mapping Type Related Functions

Function	Operation
dict([container])	Factory function for creating a dictionary populated with items from container, if provided; if not, an empty dict is created
len(mapping)	Returns the length of mapping (number of key-value pairs)
hash(obj)	Returns hash value of obj

7.4 Mapping Type Built-in Methods

Dictionaries have an abundance of methods to help you get the job done, as indicated in Table 7.2.

Below, we showcase some of the more common dictionary methods. We have already seen has_key() and its replacements **in** and **not in** at work above. Attempting to access a nonexistent key will result in an exception (KeyError) as we saw in Section 7.1.

Basic dictionary methods focus on their keys and values. These are keys(), which returns a list of the dictionary's keys, values(), which returns a list of the dictionary's values, and items(), which returns a list of (key, value) tuple pairs. These are useful when you wish to iterate through a dictionary's keys or values, albeit in no particular order.

```
>>> dict2.keys()
['port', 'name']
>>>
>>> dict2.values()
[80, 'earth']
>>>
>>> dict2.items()
[('port', 80), ('name', 'earth')]
>>>
>>> for eachKey in dict2.keys():
...     print 'dict2 key', eachKey, 'has value', dict2[eachKey]
...
dict2 key port has value 80
dict2 key name has value earth
```

The keys() method is fairly useful when used in conjunction with a **for** loop to retrieve a dictionary's values as it returns a list of a dictionary's keys.

Table 7.2 Dictionary Type Methods

Method Name	Operation
dict.clear[a]()	Removes all elements of *dict*
dict.clear[a]()	Returns a (shallow[b]) copy of *dict*
dict.fromkeys[c] (*seq*, *val*=None)	Creates and returns a new dictionary with the elements of *seq* as the keys and *val* as the initial value (defaults to None if not given) for all keys
dict.get(*key*, *default*=None)[a]	For key *key*, returns value or *default* if *key* not in *dict* (note that *default*'s default is None)
dict.has_key(*key*)	Returns True if *key* is in *dict*, False otherwise; partially deprecated by the **in** and **not in** operators in 2.2 but still provides a functional interface
dict.items()	Returns a list of the (key, value) tuple pairs of *dict*
dict.keys()	Returns a list of the keys of *dict*
dict.iter*[d]()	iteritems(), iterkeys(), itervalues() are all methods that behave the same as their non-iterator counterparts but return an iterator instead of a list
dict.pop[c](*key* [, *default*])	Similar to get() but removes and returns *dict*[*key*] if key present and raises KeyError if key not in *dict* and *default* not given
dict.setdefault (*key*, default=None)[e]	Similar to get(), but sets *dict*[*key*]=*default* if key is not already in *dict*
dict.update(*dict2*)[a]	Add the key-value pairs of *dict2* to *dict*
dict.values()	Returns a list of the values of *dict*

a. New in Python 1.5.
b. More information regarding shallow and deep copies can be found in Section 6.19.
c. New in Python 2.3.
d. New in Python 2.2.
e. New in Python 2.0.

However, because its items (as with any keys of a hash table) are unordered, imposing some type of order is usually desired.

In Python versions prior to 2.4, you would have to call a dictionary's keys() method to get the list of its keys, then call that list's sort() method to get a sorted list to iterate over. Now a built-in function named sorted(), made especially for iterators, exists, which returns a sorted iterator:

2.4

```
>>> for eachKey in sorted(dict2):
...         print 'dict2 key', eachKey, 'has value',
dict2[eachKey]
...
dict2 key name has value earth
dict2 key port has value 80
```

The update() method can be used to add the contents of one directory to another. Any existing entries with duplicate keys will be overridden by the new incoming entries. Nonexistent ones will be added. All entries in a dictionary can be removed with the clear() method.

```
>>> dict2= {'host':'earth', 'port':80}
>>> dict3= {'host':'venus', 'server':'http'}
>>> dict2.update(dict3)
>>> dict2
{'server': 'http', 'port': 80, 'host': 'venus'}
>>> dict3.clear()
>>> dict3
{}
```

The copy() method simply returns a copy of a dictionary. Note that this is a shallow copy only. Again, see Section 6.19 regarding shallow and deep copies. Finally, the get() method is similar to using the key-lookup operator ([ ]), but allows you to provide a default value returned if a key does not exist. If a key does not exist and a default value is not given, then None is returned. This is a more flexible option than just using key-lookup because you do not have to worry about an exception being raised if a key does not exist.

```
>>> dict4 = dict2.copy()
>>> dict4
{'server': 'http', 'port': 80, 'host': 'venus'}
>>> dict4.get('host')
'venus'
>>> dict4.get('xxx')
>>> type(dict4.get('xxx'))
<type 'None'>
>>> dict4.get('xxx', 'no such key')
'no such key'
```

2.0

The built-in method, setdefault(), added in version 2.0, has the sole purpose of making code shorter by collapsing a common idiom: you want to check if a dictionary has a key. If it does, you want its value. If the dictionary does not have the key you are seeking, you want to set a default value and then return it. That is precisely what `setdefault()` does:

```
>>> myDict = {'host': 'earth', 'port': 80}
>>> myDict.keys()
['host', 'port']
>>> myDict.items()
[('host', 'earth'), ('port', 80)]
>>> myDict.setdefault('port', 8080)
80
>>> myDict.setdefault('prot', 'tcp')
'tcp'
>>> myDict.items()
[('prot', 'tcp'), ('host', 'earth'), ('port', 80)]
```

Earlier, we took a brief look at the `fromkeys()` method, but here are a few more examples:

```
>>> {}.fromkeys('xyz')
{'y': None, 'x': None, 'z': None}
>>>
>>> {}.fromkeys(('love', 'honor'), True)
{'love': True, 'honor': True}
```

Currently, the `keys()`, `items()`, and `values()` methods return lists. This can be unwieldy if such data collections are large, and the main reason why `iteritems()`, `iterkeys()`, and `itervalues()` were added to Python in 2.2. They function just like their list counterparts only they return iterators, which by lazier evaluation, are more memory-friendly. In future versions of Python, even more flexible and powerful objects will be returned, tentatively called *views*. Views are collection interfaces which give you access to container objects. For example, you may be able to delete a key from a view, which would then alter the corresponding dictionary accordingly.

7.5 Dictionary Keys

Dictionary values have no restrictions. They can be any arbitrary Python object, i.e., from standard objects to user-defined objects. However, the same cannot be said of keys.

7.5.1 More Than One Entry per Key Not Allowed

One rule is that you are constrained to having only one entry per key. In other words, multiple values per the same key are not allowed. (Container objects such as lists, tuples, and other dictionaries are fine.) When key *collisions* are detected (meaning duplicate keys encountered during assignment), the last (most recent) assignment wins.

```
>>> dict1 = {' foo':789, 'foo': 'xyz'}
>>> dict1
{'foo': 'xyz'}
>>>
>>> dict1['foo'] = 123
>>> dict1
{'foo': 123}
```

Rather than producing an error, Python does not check for key collisions because that would involve taking up memory for each key-value pair assigned. In the above example where the key 'foo' is given twice on the same line, Python applies the key-value pairs from left to right. The value 789 may have been set at first, but is quickly replaced by the string 'xyz'. When assigning a value to a nonexistent key, the key is created for the dictionary and value added, but if the key does exist (a collision), then its current value is replaced. In the above example, the value for the key 'foo' is replaced twice; in the final assignment, 'xyz' is replaced by 123.

7.5.2 Keys Must Be Hashable

As we mentioned earlier in Section 7.1, most Python objects can serve as keys; however they have to be hashable objects—mutable types such as lists and dictionaries are disallowed because they cannot be hashed.

All immutable types are hashable, so they can definitely be used as keys. One caveat is numbers: Numbers of the same value represent the same key. In other words, the integer 1 and the float 1.0 hash to the same value, meaning that they are identical as keys.

Also, there are some mutable objects that are (barely) hashable, so they are eligible as keys, but there are very few of them. One example would be a class that has implemented the __hash__() special method. In the end, an immutable value is used anyway as __hash__() must return an integer.

Why must keys be hashable? The hash function used by the interpreter to calculate where to store your data is based on the value of your key. If the key was a mutable object, its value could be changed. If a key changes, the hash function will map to a different place to store the data. If that was the case, then the hash function could never reliably store or retrieve the associated value. Hashable keys were chosen for the very fact that their values cannot change. (This question can also be found in the Python FAQ.)

We know that numbers and strings are allowed as keys, but what about tuples? We know they are immutable, but in Section 6.17.2, we hinted that they might not be as immutable as they could be. The clearest example of that was when we modified a list object that was one of our tuple elements. To allow tuples as valid keys, one more restriction must be enacted: Tuples are valid keys only if they only contain immutable arguments like numbers and strings.

We conclude this chapter on dictionaries by presenting a program (userpw.py as in Example 7.1) that manages usernames and passwords in a mock login entry database system. This script accepts new users given that

Example 7.1 Dictionary Example (userpw.py)

This application manages a set of users who join the system with a login name and a password. Once established, existing users can return as long as they remember their login and password. New users cannot create an entry with someone else's login name.

```python
1   #!/usr/bin/env python
2
3   db = {}
4
5   def newuser():
6       prompt = 'login desired: '
7       while True:
8           name = raw_input(prompt)
9           if db.has_key(name):
10              prompt = 'name taken, try another: '
11              continue
12          else:
13              break
14      pwd = raw_input('passwd: ')
15      db[name] = pwd
16
17  def olduser():
18      name = raw_input('login: ')
19      pwd = raw_input('passwd: ')
20      passwd = db.get(name)
21      if passwd == pwd:
22          print 'welcome back', name
23      else:
24          print 'login incorrect'
25
26  def showmenu():
27      prompt = """
28  (N)ew User Login
29  (E)xisting User Login
30  (Q)uit
```

Example 7.1 Dictionary Example (`userpw.py`) **(continued)**

```
31
32   Enter choice: """
33
34   done = False
35       while not done:
36
37           chosen = False
38           while not chosen:
39               try:
40                   choice =
     raw_input(prompt).strip()[0].lower()
41               except (EOFError, KeyboardInterrupt):
42                   choice = 'q'
43               print '\nYou picked: [%s]' % choice
44               if choice not in 'neq':
45                   print 'invalid option, try again'
46               else:
47                   chosen = True
48
49           if choice == 'q': done = True
50           if choice == 'n': newuser()
51           if choice == 'e': olduser()
52
53   if __name__ == '__main__':
54       showmenu()
```

they provide a login name and a password. Once an "account" has been set up, an existing user can return as long as the user gives the login and correct password. New users cannot create an entry with an existing login name.

Line-by-Line Explanation

Lines 1–3

After the Unix-startup line, we initialize the program with an empty user database. Because we are not storing the data anywhere, a new user database is created every time this program is executed.

Lines 5–15

The `newuser()` function is the code that serves new users. It checks to see if a name has already been taken, and once a new name is verified, the user is prompted for his or her password (no encryption exists in our simple program), and his or her password is stored in the dictionary with his or her user name as the key.

Lines 17–24

The olduser() function handles returning users. If a user returns with the correct login and password, a welcome message is issued. Otherwise, the user is notified of an invalid login and returned to the menu. We do not want an infinite loop here to prompt for the correct password because the user may have inadvertently entered the incorrect menu option.

Lines 26–51

The real controller of this script is the showmenu() function. The user is presented with a friendly menu. The prompt string is given using triple quotes because it takes place over multiple lines and is easier to manage on multiple lines than on a single line with embedded '\n' symbols. Once the menu is displayed, it waits for valid input from the user and chooses which mode of operation to follow based on the menu choice. The **try-except** statements we describe here are the same as for the stack.py and queue.py examples from the last chapter (see Section 6.14.1).

Lines 53–54

This is the familiar code that will only call showmenu() to start the application if the script was involved directly (not imported). Here is a sample execution of our script:

```
$ userpw.py

(N)ew User Login
(E)xisting User Login
(Q)uit

Enter choice: n

You picked: [n]
login desired: king arthur
passwd: grail

(N)ew User Login
(E)xisting User Login
(Q)uit

Enter choice: e

You picked: [e]
login: sir knight
```

```
passwd: flesh wound
login incorrect

(N)ew User Login
(E)xisting User Login
(Q)uit

Enter choice: e

You picked: [e]
login: king arthur
passwd: grail
welcome back king arthur

(N)ew User Login
(E)xisting User Login
(Q)uit

Enter choice: ^D
You picked: [q]
```

7.6 Set Types

In mathematics, a set is any collection of distinct items, and its members are often referred to as set elements. Python captures this essence in its set type objects. A set object is an unordered collection of hashable values. Yes, set members would make great dictionary keys. Mathematical sets translate to Python set objects quite effectively and testing for set membership and operations such as union and intersection work in Python as expected.

Like other container types, sets support membership testing via **in** and **not in** operators, cardinality using the `len()` BIF, and iteration over the set membership using for loops. However, since sets are unordered, you do not index into or slice them, and there are no keys used to access a value.

There are two different types of sets available, mutable (`set`) and immutable (`frozenset`). As you can imagine, you are allowed to add and remove elements from the mutable form but not the immutable. Note that mutable sets are not hashable and thus cannot be used as either a dictionary key or as an element of another set. The reverse is true for frozen sets, i.e., they have a hash value and can be used as a dictionary key or a member of a set.

Sets became available in Python 2.3 via the `sets` module and accessed via the `ImmutableSet` and `Set` classes. However, it was decided that having

2.3-2.4

them as built-in types was a better idea, so these classes were then ported to C along with some improvements and integrated into Python 2.4. You can read more about those improvements as well as set types in general in PEP 218 at http://python.org/peps/pep-0218.html.

Although sets are now an official Python type, they have often been seen in many Python applications (as user-defined classes), a wheel that has been reinvented many times over, similar to complex numbers (which eventually became a Python type way back in 1.4). Until current versions of Python, most users have tried to shoehorn set functionality into standard Python types like lists and dictionaries as proxies to a real set type (even if they were not the perfect data structure for their applications). Now users have more options, including a "real" set type.

Before we go into detail regarding Python set objects, we have to mentally translate the mathematical symbols to Python (see Table 7.3) so that we are clear on terminology and functionality.

Table 7.3 Set Operation and Relation Symbols

Mathematical Symbol	Python Symbol	Description
∈	**in**	Is a member of
∉	**not in**	Is not a member of
=	==	Is equal to
≠	!=	Is not equal to
⊂	<	Is a (strict) subset of
⊆	<=	Is a subset of (includes improper subsets)
⊃	>	Is a (strict) superset of
⊇	>=	Is a superset of (includes improper supersets)
∩	&	Intersection
∪			Union
− or \	−	Difference or relative complement
Δ	^	Symmetric difference

How to Create and Assign Set Types

There is no special syntax for sets like there is for lists ([ ]) and dictionaries ({ }) for example. Lists and dictionaries can also be created with their corresponding factory functions list() and dict(), and that is also the only way sets can be created, using *their* factory functions set() and frozenset():

```
>>> s = set('cheeseshop')
>>> s
set(['c', 'e', 'h', 'o', 'p', 's'])
>>> t = frozenset('bookshop')
>>> t
frozenset(['b', 'h', 'k', 'o', 'p', 's'])
>>> type(s)
<type 'set'>
>>> type(t)
<type 'frozenset'>
>>> len(s)
6
>>> len(s) == len(t)
True
>>> s == t
False
```

How to Access Values in Sets

You are either going to iterate through set members or check if an item is a member (or not) of a set:

```
>>> 'k' in s
False
>>> 'k' in t
True
>>> 'c' not in t
True

>>> for i in s:
...     print i
...
c
e
h
o
p
s
```

How to Update Sets

You can add and remove members to and from a set using various built-in methods and operators:

```
>>> s.add('z')
>>> s
set(['c', 'e', 'h', 'o', 'p', 's', 'z'])
>>> s.update('pypi')
>>> s
set(['c', 'e', 'i', 'h', 'o', 'p', 's', 'y', 'z'])
>>> s.remove('z')
>>> s
set(['c', 'e', 'i', 'h', 'o', 'p', 's', 'y'])
>>> s -= set('pypi')
>>> s
set(['c', 'e', 'h', 'o', 's'])
```

As mentioned before, only mutable sets can be updated. Any attempt at such operations on immutable sets is met with an exception:

```
>>> t.add('z')
Traceback (most recent call last):
  File "<stdin>", line 1, in ?
AttributeError: 'frozenset' object has no attribute 'add'
```

How to Remove Set Members and Sets

We saw how to remove set members above. As far as removing sets themselves, like any Python object, you can let them go out of scope or explicitly remove them from the current namespace with **del**. If the reference count goes to zero, then it is tagged for garbage collection.

```
>>> del s
>>>
```

7.7 Set Type Operators

7.7.1 Standard Type Operators (all set types)

Membership (`in`, `not in`)

As for sequences, Python's in and not in operators are used to determine whether an element is (or is not) a member of a set.

```
>>> s = set('cheeseshop')
>>> t = frozenset('bookshop')
```

```
>>> 'k' in s
False
>>> 'k' in t
True
>>> 'c' not in t
True
```

Set Equality/Inequality

Equality (or inequality) may be checked between the same or different set types. Two sets are equal if and only if every member of each set is a member of the other. You can also say that each set must be a(n improper) subset of the other, e.g., both expressions s <= t and s >= t are true, or (s <= t **and** s >= t) **is** True. Equality (or inequality) is independent of set type or ordering of members when the sets were created—it is all based on the set membership.

```
>>> s == t
False
>>> s != t
True
>>> u = frozenset(s)
>>> s == u
True
>>> set('posh') == set('shop')
True
```

Subset Of/Superset Of

Sets use the Python comparison operators to check whether sets are subsets or supersets of other sets. The "less than" symbols (<, <=) are used for subsets while the "greater than" symbols (>, >=) are used for supersets.

Less-than and greater-than imply strictness, meaning that the two sets being compared cannot be equal to each other. The equal sign allows for less strict improper subsets and supersets.

Sets support both proper (<) and improper (<=) subsets as well as proper (>) and improper (>=) supersets. A set is "less than" another set if and only if the first set is a proper subset of the second set (is a subset but not equal), and a set is "greater than" another set if and only if the first set is a proper superset of the second set (is a superset but not equal).

```
>>> set('shop') < set('cheeseshop')
True
>>> set('bookshop') >= set('shop')
True
```

7.7.2 Set Type Operators (All Set Types)

Union (|)

The union operation is practically equivalent to the OR (or inclusive disjunction) of sets. The union of two sets is another set where each element is a member of at least one of the sets, i.e., a member of one set *or* the other. The union symbol has a method equivalent, `union()`.

```
>>> s | t
set(['c', 'b', 'e', 'h', 'k', 'o', 'p', 's'])
```

Intersection (&)

You can think of the intersection operation as the AND (or conjunction) of sets. The intersection of two sets is another set where each element must be a member of at both sets, i.e., a member of one set *and* the other. The intersection symbol has a method equivalent, `intersection()`.

```
>>> s & t
set(['h', 's', 'o', 'p']
```

Difference/Relative Complement (−)

The difference, or relative complement, between two sets is another set where each element is in one set but not the other. The difference symbol has a method equivalent, `difference()`.

```
>>> s - t
set(['c', 'e'])
```

Symmetric Difference (^)

Similar to the other Boolean set operations, symmetric difference is the XOR (or exclusive disjunction) of sets. The symmetric difference between two sets is another set where each element is a member of one set but not the other. The symmetric difference symbol has a method equivalent, `symmetric_difference()`.

```
>>> s ^ t
set(['k', 'b', 'e', 'c'])
```

Mixed Set Type Operations

In the above examples, s is a set while t is a frozenset. Note that each of the resulting sets from using the set operators above result in sets. However note that the resulting type is different when the operands are reversed:

```
>>> t | s
frozenset(['c', 'b', 'e', 'h', 'k', 'o', 'p', 's'])
>>> t ^ s
frozenset(['c', 'b', 'e', 'k'])
>>> t - s
frozenset(['k', 'b'])
```

If both types are sets or frozensets, then the type of the result is the same type as each of the operands, but if operations are performed on mixed types (set and frozenset, and vice versa), the type of the resulting set is the same type as the left operand, which we can verify in the above.

And no, the plus sign is not an operator for the set types:

```
>>> v = s + t
Traceback (most recent call last):
  File "<stdin>", line 1, in ?
TypeError: unsupported operand type(s) for +: 'set' and
'set'
>>> v = s | t
>>> v
set(['c', 'b', 'e', 'h', 'k', 'o', 'p', 's'])
>>> len(v)
8
>>> s < v
True
```

7.7.3 Set Type Operators (Mutable Sets Only)

(Union) Update (|=)

The update operation adds (possibly multiple) members from another set to the existing set. The method equivalent is `update()`.

```
>>> s = set('cheeseshop')
>>> u = frozenset(s)
>>> s |= set('pypi')
>>> s
set(['c', 'e', 'i', 'h', 'o', 'p', 's', 'y'])
```

Retention/Intersection Update (&=)

The retention (or intersection update) operation keeps only the existing set members that are also elements of the other set. The method equivalent is `intersection_update()`.

```
>>> s = set(u)
>>> s &= set('shop')
>>> s
set(['h', 's', 'o', 'p'])
```

Difference Update (−=)

The difference update operation returns a set whose elements are members of the original set after removing elements that are (also) members of the other set. The method equivalent is `difference_update()`.

```
>>> s = set(u)
>>> s -= set('shop')
>>> s
set(['c', 'e'])
```

Symmetric Difference Update (^=)

The symmetric difference update operation returns a set whose members are either elements of the original or other set but not both. The method equivalent is `symmetric_difference_update()`.

```
>>> s = set(u)
>>> t = frozenset('bookshop')
>>> s ^= t
>>> s
set(['c', 'b', 'e', 'k'])
```

7.8 Built-in Functions

7.8.1 Standard Type Functions

len()

The `len()` BIF for sets returns cardinality (or the number of elements) of the set passed in as the argument.

```
>>> s = set(u)
>>> s
set(['p', 'c', 'e', 'h', 's', 'o'])
>>> len(s)
6
```

7.8.2 Set Type Factory Functions

set() *and* frozenset()

The set() and frozenset() factory functions generate mutable and immutable sets, respectively. If no argument is provided, then an empty set is created. If one is provided, it must be an iterable, i.e., a sequence, an iterator, or an object that supports iteration such as a file or a dictionary.

```
>>> set()
set([])
>>> set([])
set([])
>>> set(())
set([])
>>> set('shop')
set(['h', 's', 'o', 'p'])
>>>
>>> frozenset(['foo', 'bar'])
frozenset(['foo', 'bar'])
>>>
>>> f = open('numbers', 'w')
>>> for i in range(5):
...     f.write('%d\n' % i)
...
>>> f.close()
>>> f = open('numbers', 'r')
>>> set(f)
set(['0\n', '3\n', '1\n', '4\n', '2\n'])
>>> f.close()
```

7.9 Set Type Built-in Methods

7.9.1 Methods (All Set Types)

We have seen the operator equivalents to most of the built-in methods, summarized in Table 7.4.

The one method without an operator equivalent is copy(). Like the dictionary method of the same name, it is faster to create a copy of the object using copy() than it is using a factory function like set(), frozenset(), or dict().

Table 7.4 Set Type Methods	
Method Name	*Operation*
`s.issubset(t)`	Returns `True` if every member of *s* is in *t*, `False` otherwise
`s.issuperset(t)`	Returns `True` if every member of *t* is in *s*, `False` otherwise
`s.union(t)`	Returns a new set with the members of *s* or *t*
`s.intersection(t)`	Returns a new set with members of *s* and *t*
`s.difference(t)`	Returns a new set with members of *s* but not *t*
`s.symmetric_difference(t)`	Returns a new set with members of *s* or *t* but not both
`s.copy()`	Returns a new set that is a (shallow) copy of *s*

7.9.2 Methods (Mutable Sets Only)

Table 7.5 summarizes all of the built-in methods that only apply to mutable sets, and similar to the methods above, we have already seen most of their operator equivalents.

The new methods here are `add()`, `remove()`, `discard()`, `pop()`, and `clear()`. For the methods that take an object, the argument must be hashable.

7.9.3 Using Operators versus Built-in Methods

As you can see, there are many built-in methods that have near-equivalents when using operators. By "near-equivalent," we mean that there is one major difference: when using the operators, both operands must be sets while for the methods, objects can be iterables too. Why was it implemented this way? The official Python documentation states that "[this] precludes error-prone constructions like `set('abc')` [and] `'cbs'` in favor of the more readable `set('abc').intersection('cbs')`."

Table 7.5 Mutable Set Type Methods	

Method Name	*Operation*
`s.update(t)`	Updates *s* with elements added from *t*; in other words, *s* now has members of either *s* or *t*
`s.intersection_update(t)`	Updates *s* with members of both *s* and *t*
`s.difference_update(t)`	Updates *s* with members of *s* without elements of *t*
`s.symmetric_difference_update(t)`	Updates *s* with members of *s* or *t* but not both
`s.add(obj)`	Adds object *obj* to set *s*
`s.remove(obj)`	Removes object *obj* from set *s*; KeyError raised if *obj* is not an element of *s* (*obj* **not in** *s*)
`s.discard(obj)`	Removes object *obj* if *obj* is an element of *s* (*obj* **in** *s*)
`s.pop()`	Removes and returns an arbitrary object of *s*
`s.clear()`	Removes all elements from *s*

7.10 Operator, Function/Method Summary Table for Set Types

In Table 7.6, we summarize all of the set type operators, functions, and methods.

7.11 Related Modules

The `sets` module became available in 2.3 and may be useful if you wish to subclass the `Set` or `ImmutableSet` classes. Although set types were integrated into Python 2.4, there are currently no plans to deprecate the module.

Table 7.6 Set Type Operators, Functions, and Methods

Function/Method Name	*Operator Equivalent*	*Description*
All Set Types		
`len(s)`		Set cardinality: number of elements in s
`set([obj])`		Mutable set factory function; if *obj* given, it must be iterable, new set elements taken from *obj*; if not, creates an empty set
`frozenset ([obj])`		Immutable set factory function; operates the same as `set()` except returns immutable set
	obj **in** *s*	Membership test: is *obj* an element of *s*?
	obj **not in** *s*	Non-membership test: is *obj* not an element of *s*?
	s == *t*	Equality test: do *s* and *t* have exactly the same elements?
	s != *t*	Inequality test: opposite of ==
	s < *t*	(Strict) subset test; *s* != *t* and all elements of *s* are members of *t*
`s.issubset(t)`	*s* <= *t*	Subset test (allows improper subsets): all elements of s are members of *t*
	s > *t*	(Strict) superset test: *s* != *t* and all elements of *t* are members of *s*
`s.issuperset(t)`	*s* >= *t*	Superset test (allows improper supersets): all elements of *t* are members of *s*
`s.union(t)`	*s* | *t*	Union operation: elements in *s* or *t*
`s.intersec-tion(t)`	*s* & *t*	Intersection operation: elements in *s* and *t*
`s.difference(t)`	*s* - *t*	Difference operation: elements in *s* that are not elements of *t*
`s.symmetric_ difference(t)`	*s* ^ *t*	Symmetric difference operation: elements of either *s* or *t* but not both
`s.copy()`		Copy operation: return (shallow) copy of *s*

Table 7.6 Set Type Operators, Functions, and Methods (continued)		
Function/Method Name	*Operator Equivalent*	*Description*
Mutable Sets Only		
`s.update(t)`	`s |= t`	(Union) update operation: members of *t* added to *s*
`s.intersection_update(t)`	`s &= t`	Intersection update operation: *s* only contains members of the original *s* and *t*
`s.difference_update(t)`	`s -= t`	Difference update operation: *s* only contains original members who are not in *t*
`s.symmetric_difference_update(t)`	`s ^= t`	Symmetric difference update operation: *s* only contains members of *s* or *t* but not both
`s.add(obj)`		Add operation: add *obj* to *s*
`s.remove(obj)`		Remove operation: remove *obj* from *s*; `KeyError` raised if *obj* not in *s*
`s.discard(obj)`		Discard operation: friendlier version of `remove()`—remove *obj* from *s* if *obj* in *s*
`s.pop()`		Pop operation: remove and return an arbitrary element of *s*
`s.clear()`		Clear operation: remove all elements of *s*

Some general online references for sets which you may find useful include:

http://en.wikipedia.org/wiki/Set
http://www.geocities.com/basicmathsets/set.html
http://www.math.uah.edu/stat/foundations/Sets.xhtml

7.12 Exercises

7–1. *Dictionary Methods.* What dictionary method would we use to combine two dictionaries together?

7–2. *Dictionary Keys.* We know that dictionary values can be arbitrary Python objects, but what about the keys? Try using different types of objects as the key other than numbers or strings. What worked for you and what didn't? As for the failures, why do you think they didn't succeed?

7–3. *Dictionary and List Methods.*

(a) Create a dictionary and display its keys alphabetically.

(b) Now display both the keys and values sorted in alphabetical order by the key.

(c) Same as part (b), but sorted in alphabetical order by the value. (Note: This has no practical purpose in dictionaries or hash tables in general because most access and ordering [if any] is based on the keys. This is merely an exercise.)

7–4. *Creating Dictionaries.* Given a pair of identically sized lists, say, `[1, 2, 3,...]`, and `['abc', 'def', 'ghi',...]`, process all that list data into a single dictionary that looks like: `{1: 'abc', 2: 'def', 3: 'ghi',...}`.

7–5. `userpw2.py`. The following problems deal with the program in Example 7.1, a manager of a database of name-password key-value pairs.

(a) Update the script so that a timestamp (see the `time` module) is also kept with the password indicating date and time of last login. This interface should prompt for login and password and indicate a successful or failed login as before, but if successful, it should update the last login timestamp. If the login occurs within four hours of the last login, tell the user, "You already logged in at: <*last_login_timestamp*>."

(b) Add an "administration" menu to include the following two menu options: (1) remove a user and (2) display a list of all users in the system and their passwords

(c) The passwords are currently not encrypted. Add password-encryption if so desired (see the `crypt`, `rotor`, or other cryptographic modules).

(d) *Add a GUI interface, i.e., Tkinter, on top of this application.

(e) Allow usernames to be case-insensitive.

(f) Restrict usernames by not allowing symbols or whitespace.

(g) Merge the "new user" and "old user" options together. If a new user tries to log in with a nonexistent username, prompt if they are new and if so, do the proper setup. Otherwise, they are an existing user so log in as normal.

7–6. *Lists and Dictionaries*. Create a crude stock portfolio database system. There should be at least four data columns: stock ticker symbol, number of shares, purchase price, and current price—you can add more if you wish, such as percentage gain(loss), 52-week high/low, beta, etc.

Have the user input values for each column to create a single row. Each row should be created as list. Another all-encompassing list will hold all these rows. Once the data is entered, prompt the user for one column to use as the sort metric. Extract the data values of that column into a dictionary as keys, with their corresponding values being the row that contains that key. Be mindful that the sort metric must have non-coincidental keys or else you will lose a row because dictionaries are not allowed to have more than one value with the same key. You may also choose to have additional calculated output, such as percentage gain/loss, current portfolio values, etc.

7–7. *Inverting Dictionaries*. Take a dictionary as input and return one as output, but the values are now the keys and vice versa.

7–8. *Human Resources*. Create a simple name and employee number dictionary application. Have the user enter a list of names and employee numbers. Your interface should allow a sorted output (sorted by name) that displays employee names followed by their employee numbers. Extra credit: Come up with an additional feature that allows for output to be sorted by employee numbers.

7–9. *Translations.*

(a) Create a character translator (that works similar to the Unix `tr` command). This function, which we will call `tr()`, takes three strings as arguments: source, destination, and base strings, and has the following declaration:

```
def tr(srcstr, dststr, string)
```

`srcstr` contains the set of characters you want "translated," `dststr` contains the set of characters to translate to, and `string` is the string to perform the translation on. For example, if `srcstr == 'abc'`, `dststr == 'mno'`, and `string == 'abcdef'`, then `tr()` would output `'mnodef'`. Note that `len(srcstr) == len(dststr)`. For this exercise, you can use the `chr()` and `ord()` BIFs, but they are not necessary to arrive at a solution.

(b) Add a new flag argument to this function to perform case-insensitive translations.

(c) Update your solution so that it can process character deletions. Any extra characters in `srcstr` that are beyond those that could be mapped to characters in `dststr` should be filtered. In other words, these characters are mapped to no characters in `dststr`, and are thus filtered from the modified string that is returned. For example, if `srcstr == 'abcdef'`, `dststr == 'mno'`, and `string == 'abcdefghi'`, then `tr()` would output `'mnoghi'`. Note now that `len(srcstr) >= len(dststr)`.

7–10. *Encryption*. Using your solution to the previous problem, and create a "rot13" translator. "rot13" is an old and fairly simplistic encryption routine whereby each letter of the alphabet is rotated 13 characters. Letters in the first half of the alphabet will be rotated to the equivalent letter in the second half and vice versa, retaining case. For example, a goes to n and X goes to K. Obviously, numbers and symbols are immune from translation.

(b) Add an application on top of your solution to prompt the user for strings to encrypt (and decrypt on reapplication of the algorithm), as in the following examples:

```
% rot13.py
Enter string to rot13: This is a short sentence.
Your string to en/decrypt was: [This is a short
sentence.].
The rot13 string is: [Guvf vf n fubeg fragrapr.].
%
% rot13.py
Enter string to rot13: Guvf vf n fubeg fragrapr.
Your string to en/decrypt was: [Guvf vf n fubeg
fragrapr.].
The rot13 string is: [This is a short sentence.].
```

7–11. *Definitions*. What constitutes valid dictionary keys? Give examples of valid and invalid dictionary keys.

7–12. *Definitions*. (a) What is a set in the mathematical sense? (b) What is a set type as it relates to Python?

7–13. *Random Numbers*. The next problems use a customization of Exercise 5–17: use `randint()` or `randrange()` in the `random` module to generate a set of numbers: generate between 1 to 10 random numbers numbered randomly between 0 and 9 (inclusive). These values constitute a set A (A can be mutable or otherwise). Create another random set B in a similar manner. Display A | B and A & B each time sets A and B are generated.

7–14. *User Validation*. Alter the previous problem where instead of displaying A | B and A & B, ask the user to input solutions to A | B and A & B, and let the user know if his or her solution was right or wrong. If it is not correct, give the user the ability to correct and revalidate his or her answers. Display the correct results if three incorrect answers are submitted. Extra credit: Use your knowledge of sets to generate potential subsets and ask the user whether they are indeed subsets (or not), and provide corrections and answers as necessary as in the main part of this problem.

7–15. *Set Calculator*. This exercise is inspired by Exercise 12.2 in the free online Java textbook located at http://math.hws.edu/ javanotes. Create an application that allows users to input a pair of sets, A and B, and allow users to give an operation symbol, i.e., in, not in, &, |, ^, <, <=, >, >=, ==, !=, etc. (For sets, you define the input syntax—they do not have to be enclosed in brackets as the Java example.) Parse the entire input string and execute the operation on the input sets as requested by the user. Your solution should require fewer lines of Python than the one in Java.

CONDITIONALS AND LOOPS

Chapter Topics

- **if** Statement
- **else** Statement
- **elif** Statement
- Conditional Expressions
- **while** Statement
- **for** Statement
- **break** Statement
- **continue** Statement
- **pass** Statement
- **else** Statement ... Take Two
- Iterators
- List Comprehensions
- Generator Expressions

Chapter 8

The primary focus of this chapter are Python's conditional and looping statements, and all their related components. We will take a close look at **if**, **while**, **for**, and their friends **else**, **elif**, **break**, **continue**, and **pass**.

8.1 `if` Statement

The **if** statement for Python will seem amazingly familiar. It is made up of three main components: the keyword itself, an expression that is tested for its truth value, and a code suite to execute if the expression evaluates to non-zero or true. The syntax for an **if** statement is:

```
if expression:
    expr_true_suite
```

The suite of the **if** clause, `expr_true_suite`, will be executed only if the above conditional expression results in a Boolean true value. Otherwise, execution resumes at the next statement following the suite.

8.1.1 Multiple Conditional Expressions

The Boolean operators **and**, **or**, and **not** can be used to provide multiple conditional expressions or perform negation of expressions in the same **if** statement.

```
if not warn and (system_load >= 10):
    print "WARNING: losing resources"
    warn += 1
```

8.1.2 Single Statement Suites

If the suite of a compound statement, i.e., **if** clause, **while** or **for** loop, consists only of a single line, it may go on the same line as the header statement:

```
if make_hard_copy: send_data_to_printer()
```

Single line statements such as the above are valid syntax-wise; however, although it may be convenient, it may make your code more difficult to read, so we recommend you indent the suite on the next line. Another good reason is that if you must add another line to the suite, you have to move that line down anyway.

8.2 else Statement

Like other languages, Python features an **else** statement that can be paired with an **if** statement. The **else** statement identifies a block of code to be executed if the conditional expression of the **if** statement resolves to a false Boolean value. The syntax is what you expect:

```
if expression:
    expr_true_suite
else:
    expr_false_suite
```

Now we have the obligatory usage example:

```
if passwd == user.passwd:
    ret_str = "password accepted"
    id = user.id
    valid = True
else:
    ret_str = "invalid password entered... try again!"
    valid = False
```

8.2.1 "Dangling else" Avoidance

Python's design of using indentation rather than braces for code block delimitation not only helps to enforce code correctness, but it even aids implicitly in avoiding potential problems in code that *is* syntactically correct. One of those such problems is the (in)famous "dangling else" problem, a semantic optical illusion.

We present some C code here to illustrate our example (which is also illuminated by K&R and other programming texts):

```c
/* dangling-else in C */
if (balance > 0.00)
    if (((balance - amt) > min_bal) && (atm_cashout() == 1))
        printf("Here's your cash; please take all bills.\n");
else
    printf("Your balance is zero or negative.\n");
```

The question is, which **if** does the **else** belong to? In the C language, the rule is that the **else** stays with the closest **if**. In our example above, although indented for the outer **if** statement, the **else** statement really belongs to the inner **if** statement because the C compiler ignores superfluous whitespace. As a result, if you have a positive balance but it is below the minimum, you will get the horrid (and erroneous) message that your balance is either zero or negative.

Although solving this problem may be easy due to the simplistic nature of the example, any larger sections of code embedded within this framework may be a hair-pulling experience to root out. Python puts up guardrails not necessarily to prevent you from driving off the cliff, but to steer you away from danger. The same example in Python will result in one of the following choices (one of which is correct):

```python
if balance > 0.00:
    if balance - amt > min_bal and atm_cashout():
        print "Here's your cash; please take all bills."
else:
    print 'Your balance is zero or negative.'
```

or

```python
if balance > 0.00:
    if balance - amt > min_bal and atm_cashout():
        print "Here's your cash; please take all bills."
    else:
        print 'Your balance is zero or negative.'
```

Python's use of indentation forces the proper alignment of code, giving the programmer the ability to make a conscious decision as to which **if** an **else** statement belongs to. By limiting your choices and thus reducing ambiguities, Python encourages you to develop correct code the first time. It is impossible to create a dangling else problem in Python. Also, since parentheses are not required, Python code is easier to read.

8.3 `elif` (aka `else-if`) Statement

elif is the Python `else-if` statement. It allows one to check multiple expressions for truth value and execute a block of code as soon as one of the conditions evaluates to true. Like the **else**, the **elif** statement is optional. However, unlike **else**, for which there can be at most one statement, there can be an arbitrary number of **elif** statements following an **if**.

```
if expression1:
    expr1_true_suite
elif expression2:
    expr2_true_suite
            :
elif expressionN:
    exprN_true_suite
else:
    none_of_the_above_suite
```

Proxy for `switch/case` Statement?

At some time in the future, Python may support the `switch` or `case` statement, but you can simulate it with various Python constructs. But even a good number of **if-elif** statements are not that difficult to read in Python:

```
if user.cmd == 'create':
    action = "create item"

elif user.cmd == 'delete':
    action = 'delete item'

elif user.cmd == 'update':
    action = 'update item'

else:
    action = 'invalid choice... try again!'
```

Although the above statements do work, you can simplify them with a sequence and the membership operator:

```
if user.cmd in ('create', 'delete', 'update'):
    action = '%s item' % user.cmd
else:
    action = 'invalid choice... try again!'
```

We can create an even more elegant solution using Python dictionaries, which we learned about in Chapter 7, "Mapping and Set Types."

```
msgs = {'create': 'create item',
    'delete': 'delete item',
    'update': 'update item'}
default = 'invalid choice... try again!'
action = msgs.get(user.cmd, default)
```

One well-known benefit of using mapping types such as dictionaries is that the searching is very fast compared to a sequential lookup as in the above **if-elif-else** statements or using a **for** loop, both of which have to scan the elements one at a time.

8.4 Conditional Expressions (aka "the Ternary Operator")

If you are coming from the C/C++ or Java world, it is difficult to ignore or get over the fact that Python has not had a conditional or ternary operator (C ? X : Y) for the longest time. (C is the conditional expression; X represents the resultant expression if C is True and Y if C is False.) van Rossum Guido has resisted adding such a feature to Python because of his belief in keeping code simple and not giving programmers easy ways to obfuscate their code.

2.5

However, after more than a decade, he has given in, mostly because of the error-prone ways in which people have tried to simulate it using **and** and **or**, many times incorrectly. According to the FAQ, the one way of getting it right is (C **and** [X] **or** [Y])[0]. The only problem was that the community could not agree on the syntax. (You really have to take a look at PEP 308 to see all the different proposals.) This is one of the areas of Python in which people have expressed strong feelings.

The final decision came down to van Rossum Guido choosing the most favored (and his most favorite) of all the choices, then applying it to various modules in the standard library. According to the PEP, "this review approximates a sampling of real-world use cases, across a variety of applications, written by a number of programmers with diverse backgrounds." And this is the syntax that was finally chosen for integration into Python 2.5: X **if** C **else** Y.

The main motivation for even having a ternary operator is to allow the setting of a value based on a conditional all on a single line, as opposed to the standard way of using an **if-else** statement, as in this min() example using numbers x and y:

```
>>> x, y = 4, 3
>>> if x < y:
...     smaller = x
... else:
...     smaller = y
...
>>> smaller
3
```

In versions prior to 2.5, Python programmers at best could do this:

```
>>> smaller = (x < y and [x] or [y])[0]
>>> smaller
3
```

In versions 2.5 and newer, this can be further simplified to:

```
>>> smaller = x if x < y else y
>>> smaller
3
```

8.5 `while` Statement

Python's **while** is the first looping statement we will look at in this chapter. In fact, it is a conditional looping statement. In comparison with an **if** statement where a true expression will result in a single execution of the **if** clause suite, the suite in a **while** clause will be executed continuously in a loop until that condition is no longer satisfied.

8.5.1 General Syntax

Here is the syntax for a **while** loop:

```
while expression:
    suite_to_repeat
```

The *suite_to_repeat* clause of the **while** loop will be executed continuously in a loop until *expression* evaluates to Boolean `False`. This type of looping mechanism is often used in a counting situation, such as the example in the next subsection.

8.5.2 Counting Loops

```
count = 0
while (count < 9):
    print 'the index is:', count
    count += 1
```

The suite here, consisting of the **print** and increment statements, is executed repeatedly until `count` is no longer less than 9. With each iteration, the current value of the index `count` is displayed and then bumped up by 1. If we take this snippet of code to the Python interpreter, entering the source and seeing the resulting execution would look something like:

```
>>> count = 0
>>> while (count < 9):
...         print 'the index is:', count
...         count += 1
...
the index is: 0
the index is: 1
the index is: 2
the index is: 3
the index is: 4
the index is: 5
the index is: 6
the index is: 7
the index is: 8
```

8.5.3 Infinite Loops

One must use caution when using **while** loops because of the possibility that the condition never resolves to a false value. In such cases, we would have a loop that never ends on our hands. These "infinite" loops are not necessarily bad things—many communications "servers" that are part of client/server systems work exactly in that fashion. It all depends on whether or not the loop was meant to run forever, and if not, whether the loop has the possibility of terminating; in other words, will the expression ever be able to evaluate to false?

```
while True:
    handle, indata = wait_for_client_connect()
    outdata = process_request(indata)
    ack_result_to_client(handle, outdata)
```

For example, the piece of code above was set deliberately to never end because `True` is not going to somehow change to `False`. The main point of this server code is to sit and wait for clients to connect, presumably over a network link. These clients send requests which the server understands and processes.

After the request has been serviced, a return value or data is returned to the client who may either drop the connection altogether or send another request. As far as the server is concerned, it has performed its duty to this one client and returns to the top of the loop to wait for the next client to come along. You will find out more about client/server computing in Chapter 16, "Network Programming" and Chapter 17, "Internet Client Programming."

8.6 for Statement

The other looping mechanism in Python comes to us in the form of the **for** statement. It represents the single most powerful looping construct in Python. It can loop over sequence members, it is used in list comprehensions and generator expressions, and it knows how to call an iterator's `next()` method and gracefully ends by catching `StopIteration` exceptions (all under the covers). If you are new to Python, we will tell you now that you will be using **for** statements a lot.

Unlike the traditional conditional looping **for** statement found in mainstream languages like C/C++, Fortran, or Java, Python's **for** is more akin to a shell or scripting language's iterative **foreach** loop.

8.6.1 General Syntax

The **for** loop traverses through individual elements of an iterable (like a sequence or iterator) and terminates when all the items are exhausted. Here is its syntax:

```
for iter_var in iterable:
    suite_to_repeat
```

With each loop, the *iter_var* iteration variable is set to the current element of the iterable (sequence, iterator, or object that supports iteration), presumably for use in *suite_to_repeat*.

8.6.2 Used with Sequence Types

In this section, we will see how the **for** loop works with the different sequence types. The examples will include string, list, and tuple types.

```
>>> for eachLetter in 'Names':
...         print 'current letter:', eachLetter
...
current letter: N
current letter: a
current letter: m
current letter: e
current letter: s
```

When iterating over a string, the iteration variable will always consist of only single characters (strings of length 1). Such constructs may not necessarily be useful. When seeking characters in a string, more often than not, the programmer will either use **in** to test for membership, or one of the string module functions or string methods to check for substrings.

One place where seeing individual characters does come in handy is during the debugging of sequences in a **for** loop in an application where you are expecting strings or entire objects to show up in your **print** statements. If you see individual characters, this is usually a sign that you received a single string rather than a sequence of objects.

There are three basic ways of iterating over a sequence:

Iterating by Sequence Item

```
>>> nameList = ['Walter', "Nicole", 'Steven', 'Henry']
>>> for eachName in nameList:
...         print eachName, "Lim"
...
Walter Lim
Nicole Lim
Steven Lim
Henry Lim
```

In the above example, a list is iterated over, and for each iteration, the eachName variable contains the list element that we are on for that particular iteration of the loop.

Iterating by Sequence Index

An alternative way of iterating through each item is by index offset into the sequence itself:

```
>>> nameList = ['Cathy', "Terry", 'Joe', 'Heather',
'Lucy']
>>> for nameIndex in range(len(nameList)):
...     print "Liu,", nameList[nameIndex]
...
Liu, Cathy
Liu, Terry
Liu, Joe
Liu, Heather
Liu, Lucy
```

Rather than iterating through the elements themselves, we are iterating through the indices of the list.

We employ the assistance of the `len()` built-in function, which provides the total number of elements in the tuple as well as the `range()` built-in function (which we will discuss in more detail below) to give us the actual sequence to iterate over.

```
>>> len(nameList)
5
>>> range(len(nameList))
[0, 1, 2, 3, 4]
```

Using `range()`, we obtain a list of the indexes that `nameIndex` iterates over; and using the slice/subscript operator (`[ ]`), we can obtain the corresponding sequence element.

Those of you who are performance pundits will no doubt recognize that iteration by sequence item wins over iterating via index. If not, this is something to think about. (See Exercise 8–13.)

Iterating with Item *and* Index

2.3

The best of both worlds comes from using the `enumerate()` built-in function, which was added to Python in version 2.3. Enough said . . . here is some code:

```
>>> nameList = ['Donn', 'Shirley', 'Ben', 'Janice',
...     'David', 'Yen', 'Wendy']
>>> for i, eachLee in enumerate(nameList):
...     print "%d %s Lee" % (i+1, eachLee)
...
1 Donn Lee
2 Shirley Lee
```

```
3 Ben Lee
4 Janice Lee
5 David Lee
6 Yen Lee
7 Wendy Lee
```

8.6.3 Used with Iterator Types

Using **for** loops with iterators is identical to using them with sequences. The only difference is that the **for** statement must do a little bit of extra work on your behalf. An iterator does not represent a set of items to loop over.

Instead, iterator objects have a next() method, which is called to get subsequent items. When the set of items has been exhausted, the iterator raises the StopIteration exception to signal that it has finished. Calling next() and catching StopIteration is built-in to the **for** statement.

When you are using a **for** loop with an iterator, the code is nearly identical to that of looping over sequence items. In fact, for most cases, you cannot tell that you are iterating over a sequence or an iterator, hence the reason why you will see us refer to iterating over an iterable, which could mean a sequence, an iterator, or any object that supports iteration, e.g., has a next() method.

8.6.4 range() Built-in Function

We mentioned above during our introduction to Python's **for** loop that it is an iterative looping mechanism. Python also provides a tool that will let us use the **for** statement in a traditional pseudo-conditional setting, i.e., when counting from one number to another and quitting once the final number has been reached or some condition is no longer satisfied.

The built-in function range() can turn your foreach-like **for** loop back into one that you are more familiar with, i.e., counting from 0 to 10, or counting from 10 to 100 in increments of 5.

range() Full Syntax

Python presents two different ways to use range(). The full syntax requires that two or all three integer arguments are present:

```
range(start, end, step=1)
```

range() will then return a list where for any k, $start <= k < end$ and k iterates from start to end in increments of step. step cannot be 0, or an error condition will occur.

```
>>> range(2, 19, 3)
[2, 5, 8, 11, 14, 17]
```

If *step* is omitted and only two arguments given, step takes a default value of 1.

```
>>> range(3, 7)
[3, 4, 5, 6]
```

Let's take a look at an example used in the interpreter environment:

```
>>> for eachVal in range(2, 19, 3):
...         print "value is:", eachVal
...
value is: 2
value is: 5
value is: 8
value is: 11
value is: 14
value is: 17
```

Our **for** loop now "counts" from 2 to 19, incrementing by steps of 3. If you are familiar with C, then you will notice the direct correlation between the arguments of range() and those of the variables in the C **for** loop:

```
/* equivalent loop in C */
for (eachVal = 2; eachVal < 19; eachVal += 3) {
    printf("value is: %d\n", eachVal);
}
```

Although it seems like a conditional loop now (checking if eachVal < 19), reality tells us that range() takes our conditions and generates a list that meets our criteria, which in turn is used by the same Python **for** statement.

range() Abbreviated Syntax

range() also has two abbreviated syntax formats:

```
range(end)

range(start, end)
```

We saw the shortest syntax earlier in Chapter 2. Given only a single value, *start* defaults to 0, *step* defaults to 1, and range() returns a list of numbers from zero up to the argument *end*:

```
>>> range(5)
[0, 1, 2, 3, 4]
```

Given two values, this midsized version of range() is exactly the same as the long version of range() taking two parameters with step defaulting to

1. We will now take this to the Python interpreter and plug in **for** and **print** statements to arrive at:

```
>>> for count in range(2, 5):
...     print count
...
2
3
4
```

CORE NOTE: Why not just one syntax for `range()`?

Now that you know both syntaxes for `range()`, *one nagging question you may have is, why not just combine the two into a single one that looks like this?*

```
range(start=0, end, step=1) # invalid
```

This syntax will work for a single argument or all three, but not two. It is illegal because the presence of `step` *requires* `start` *to be given. In other words, you cannot provide* `end` *and* `step` *in a two-argument version because they will be (mis)interpreted as* `start` *and* `end`.

8.6.5 *xrange() Built-in Function*

`xrange()` is similar to `range()` except that if you have a really large range list, `xrange()` may come in handier because it does not have to make a complete copy of the list in memory. This built-in was made for exclusive use in **for** loops. It does not make sense outside a **for** loop. Also, as you can imagine, the performance will not be as good because the entire list is *not* in memory. In future versions of Python, `range()` will eventually become like `xrange()`, returing an iterable object (not a list nor an iterator though)—it will be similar to views as discussed in the previous chapter.

8.6.6 *Sequence-Related Built-in Functions*

```
sorted(), reversed(), enumerate(), zip()
```

Below are some examples of using these loop-oriented sequence-related functions. The reason why they are "sequence-related" is that half of them (sorted() and zip()) return a real sequence (list), while the other two (reversed() and enumerate()) return iterators (sequence-like).

```
>>> albums = ('Poe', 'Gaudi', 'Freud', 'Poe2')
>>> years = (1976, 1987, 1990, 2003)
>>> for album in sorted(albums):
...       print album,
...
Freud Gaudi Poe Poe2
>>>
>>> for album in reversed(albums):
...       print album,
...
Poe2 Freud Gaudi Poe
>>>
>>> for i, album in enumerate(albums):
...       print i, album
...
0 Poe
1 Gaudi
2 Freud
3 Poe2
>>>
>>> for album, yr in zip(albums, years):
...       print yr, album
...
1976 Poe
1987 Gaudi
1990 Freud
2003 Poe2
```

Now that we have covered all the loops Python has to offer, let us take a look at the peripheral commands that typically go together with loops. These include statements to abandon the loop (**break**) and to immediately begin the next iteration (**continue**).

8.7 break Statement

The **break** statement in Python terminates the current loop and resumes execution at the next statement, just like the traditional **break** found in C. The most common use for **break** is when some external condition is triggered (usually by testing with an **if** statement), requiring a hasty exit from a loop. The **break** statement can be used in both **while** and **for** loops.

```
count = num / 2
while count > 0:
```

```
if num % count == 0:
    print count, 'is the largest factor of', num
    break
count -= 1
```

The task of this piece of code is to find the largest divisor of a given number num. We iterate through all possible numbers that could possibly be factors of num, using the count variable and decrementing for every value that does *not* divide num. The first number that evenly divides num is the largest factor, and once that number is found, we no longer need to continue and use **break** to terminate the loop.

```
phone2remove = '555-1212'
for eachPhone in phoneList:
    if eachPhone == phone2remove:
        print "found", phone2remove, '... deleting'
        deleteFromPhoneDB(phone2remove)
        break
```

The **break** statement here is used to interrupt the iteration of the list. The goal is to find a target element in the list, and, if found, to remove it from the database and break out of the loop.

8.8 continue Statement

CORE NOTE: continue **statements**

*Whether in Python, C, Java, or any other structured language that features the **continue** statement, there is a misconception among some beginning programmers that the traditional **continue** statement "immediately starts the next iteration of a loop." While this may seem to be the apparent action, we would like to clarify this somewhat invalid supposition. Rather than beginning the next iteration of the loop when a **continue** statement is encountered, a **continue** statement terminates or discards the remaining statements in the current loop iteration and goes back to the top. If we are in a conditional loop, the conditional expression is checked for validity before beginning the next iteration of the loop. Once confirmed, then the next iteration begins. Likewise, if the loop were iterative, a determination must be made as to whether there are any more arguments to iterate over. Only when that validation has completed successfully can we begin the next iteration.*

The **continue** statement in Python is not unlike the traditional **continue** found in other high-level languages. The **continue** statement can be used in both **while** and **for** loops. The **while** loop is conditional, and the **for** loop is iterative, so using **continue** is subject to the same requirements (as high-lighted in the Core Note above) before the next iteration of the loop can begin. Otherwise, the loop will terminate normally.

```
valid = False
count = 3
while count > 0:
    input = raw_input("enter password")
    # check for valid passwd
    for eachPasswd in passwdList:
        if input == eachPasswd:
            valid = True
            break
    if not valid:        # (or valid == 0)
        print "invalid input"
        count -= 1
        continue
    else:
        break
```

In this combined example using **while**, **for**, **if**, **break**, and **continue**, we are looking at validating user input. The user is given three opportunities to enter the correct password; otherwise, the valid variable remains a false value of 0, which presumably will result in appropriate action being taken soon after.

8.9 pass Statement

One Python statement not found in C is the **pass** statement. Because Python does not use curly braces to delimit blocks of code, there are places where code is syntactically required. We do not have the equivalent empty braces or single semicolon the way C does to indicate "do nothing." If you use a Python state-ment that expects a sub-block of code or suite, and one is not present, you will get a syntax error condition. For this reason, we have **pass**, a statement that does absolutely nothing—it is a true NOP, to steal the "No OPeration" assembly code jargon. Style- and development-wise, **pass** is also useful in places where your code will eventually go, but has not been written yet (in stubs, for example):

```
def foo_func():
    pass
```

or

```
if user_choice == 'do_calc':
    pass
else:
    pass
```

This code structure is helpful during the development or debugging stages because you want the structure to be there while the code is being created, but you do not want it to interfere with the other parts of the code that have been completed already. In places where you want nothing to execute, **pass** is a good tool to have in the box.

Another popular place is with exception handling, which we will take a look at in Chapter 10; this is where you can track an error if it occurs, but take no action if it is not fatal (you just want to keep a record of the event or perform an operation under the covers if an error occurs).

8.10 else Statement . . . Take Two

In C (as well as in most other languages), you will *not* find an **else** statement outside the realm of conditional statements, yet Python bucks the trend again by offering these in **while** and **for** loops. How do they work? When used with loops, an **else** clause will be executed only if a loop finishes to completion, meaning they were not abandoned by **break**.

One popular example of **else** usage in a **while** statement is in finding the largest factor of a number. We have implemented a function that performs this task, using the **else** statement with our **while** loop. The showMaxFactor() function in Example 8.1 (maxFact.py) utilizes the **else** statement as part of a **while** loop.

Example 8.1 while-else Loop Example (maxFact.py)

This program displays the largest factors for numbers between 10 and 20. If the number is prime, the script will indicate that as well.

```
1   #!/usr/bin/env python
2
3   def showMaxFactor(num):
4       count = num / 2
5       while count > 1:
6           if num % count == 0:
7               print 'largest factor of %d is %d' % \
8                   (num, count)
9               break
10          count -= 1
11      else:
12          print num, "is prime"
13
14  for eachNum in range(10, 21):
15      showMaxFactor(eachNum)
```

The loop beginning on line 3 in showMaxFactor() counts down from half the amount (starts checking if two divides the number, which would give the largest factor). The loop decrements each time (line 10) through until a divisor is found (lines 6–9). If a divisor has not been found by the time the loop decrements to 1, then the original number must be prime. The **else** clause on lines 11–12 takes care of this case. The main part of the program on lines 14–15 fires off the requests to showMaxFactor() with the numeric argument.

Running our program results in the following output:

```
largest factor of 10 is 5
11 is prime
largest factor of 12 is 6
13 is prime
largest factor of 14 is 7
largest factor of 15 is 5
largest factor of 16 is 8
17 is prime
largest factor of 18 is 9
19 is prime
largest factor of 20 is 10
```

Likewise, a **for** loop can have a post-processing **else**. It operates exactly the same way as for a **while** loop. As long as the **for** loop exits normally (not via **break**), the **else** clause will be executed. We saw such an example in Section 8.5.3.

Table 8.1 summarizes with which conditional or looping statements auxiliary statements can be used.

Table 8.1 Auxiliary Statements to Loops and Conditionals

Auxiliary Statements	Loops and Conditionals		
	if	while	for
elif	•		
else	•	•	•
break		•	•
continue		•	•
pass[a]	•	•	•

a.　**pass** is valid anywhere a suite (single or multiple statements) is required (also includes **elif**, **else**, **class**, **def**, **try**, **except**, **finally**).

8.11 Iterators and the `iter()` Function

8.11.1 What Are Iterators?

Iterators were added to Python in version 2.2 to give sequence-like objects a sequence-like interface. We formally introduced sequences back in Chapter 6. They are just data structures that you can "iterate" over by using their index starting at 0 and continuing till the final item of the sequence. Because you can do this "counting," iterating over sequences is trivial. Iteration support in Python works seamlessly with sequences but now also allows programmers to iterate through non-sequence types, including user-defined objects.

2.2

Iterators come in handy when you are iterating over something that is not a sequence but exhibits behavior that makes it *seem* like a sequence, for example, keys of a dictionary, lines of a file, etc. When you use loops to iterate over an object item, you will not be able to easily tell whether it is an iterator or a sequence. The best part is that you do not have to care because Python makes it seem like a sequence.

8.11.2 Why Iterators?

The defining PEP (234) cites that iterators:

- Provide an extensible iterator interface.
- Bring performance enhancements to list iteration.
- Allow for big performance improvements in dictionary iteration.
- Allow for the creation of a true iteration interface as opposed to overriding methods originally meant for random element access.
- Be backward-compatible with all existing user-defined classes and extension objects that emulate sequences and mappings.
- Result in more concise and readable code that iterates over non-sequence collections (mappings and files, for instance).

8.11.3 How Do You Iterate?

Basically, instead of an index to count sequentially, an iterator is any item that has a `next()` method. When the next item is desired, either you or a looping mechanism like **for** will call the iterators `next()` method to get the next value. Once the items have been exhausted, a StopIteration exception is raised, not to indicate an error, but to let folks know that we are done.

Iterators do have some restrictions, however. For example, you cannot move backward, go back to the beginning, or copy an iterator. If you want to iterate over the same objects again (or simultaneously), you have to create another iterator object. It isn't all that bad, however, as there are various tools to help you with using iterators.

There is a reversed() built-in function that returns an iterator that traverses an iterable in reverse order. The enumerate() BIF also returns an iterator. Two new BIFs, any() and all(), made their debut in Python 2.5— they will return True if any or all items traversed across an iterator have a Boolean True value, respectively. We saw earlier in the chapter how you can use it in a **for** loop to iterate over both the index and the item of an iterable. There is also an entire module called itertools that contains various iterators you may find useful.

8.11.4 Using Iterators with . . .

Sequences

As mentioned before, iterating through Python sequence types is as expected:

```
>>> myTuple = (123, 'xyz', 45.67)
>>> i = iter(myTuple)
>>> i.next()
123
>>> i.next()
'xyz'
>>> i.next()
45.67
>>> i.next()
Traceback (most recent call last):
  File "", line 1, in ?
StopIteration
```

If this had been an actual program, we would have enclosed the code inside a **try-except** block. Sequences now automatically produce their own iterators, so a **for** loop:

```
for i in seq:
    do_something_to(i)
```

under the covers now really behaves like this:

```
fetch = iter(seq)
while True:
    try:
        i = fetch.next()
    except StopIteration:
        break
    do_something_to(i)
```

However, your code does not need to change because the **for** loop itself calls the iterator's next() method (as well as monitors for StopIteration).

Dictionaries

Dictionaries and files are two other Python data types that received the iteration makeover. A dictionary's iterator traverses its keys. The idiom **for** eachKey **in** myDict.keys() can be shortened to **for** eachKey **in** myDict as shown here:

```
>>> legends = { ('Poe', 'author'): (1809, 1849, 1976),
...    ('Gaudi', 'architect'): (1852, 1906, 1987),
...    ('Freud', 'psychoanalyst'): (1856, 1939, 1990)
... }
...
>>> for eachLegend in legends:
...     print 'Name: %s\tOccupation: %s' % eachLegend
...     print '  Birth: %s\tDeath: %s\tAlbum: %s\n' \
...     % legends[eachLegend]
...
Name: Freud     Occupation: psychoanalyst
  Birth: 1856   Death: 1939     Album: 1990

Name: Poe       Occupation: author
  Birth: 1809   Death: 1849     Album: 1976

Name: Gaudi     Occupation: architect
  Birth: 1852   Death: 1906     Album: 1987
```

In addition, three new built-in dictionary methods have been introduced to define the iteration: myDict.iterkeys() (iterate through the keys), myDict.itervalues() (iterate through the values), and myDict.iter-items() (iterate through key/value pairs). Note that the **in** operator has been modified to check a dictionary's keys. This means the Boolean expression myDict.has_key(anyKey) can be simplified as anyKey **in** myDict.

Files

File objects produce an iterator that calls the `readline()` method. Thus, they loop through all lines of a text file, allowing the programmer to replace essentially **for** `eachLine` **in** `myFile.readlines()` with the more simplistic **for** `eachLine` **in** `myFile`:

```
>>> myFile = open('config-win.txt')
>>> for eachLine in myFile:
...     print eachLine,    # comma suppresses extra \n
...
[EditorWindow]
font-name: courier new
font-size: 10
>>> myFile.close()
```

8.11.5 Mutable Objects and Iterators

Remember that interfering with mutable objects while you are iterating them is not a good idea. This was a problem before iterators appeared. One popular example of this is to loop through a list and remove items from it if certain criteria are met (or not):

```
for eachURL in allURLs:
    if not eachURL.startswith('http://'):
        allURLs.remove(eachURL)          # YIKES!!
```

All sequences are immutable except lists, so the danger occurs only there. A sequence's iterator only keeps track of the Nth element you are on, so if you change elements around during iteration, those updates will be reflected as you traverse through the items. If you run out, then `StopIteration` will be raised.

When iterating through keys of a dictionary, you must not modify the dictionary. Using a dictionary's `keys()` method is okay because `keys()` returns a list that is independent of the dictionary. But iterators are tied much more intimately with the actual object and will not let us play that game anymore:

```
>>> myDict = {'a': 1, 'b': 2, 'c': 3, 'd': 4}
>>> for eachKey in myDict:
...     print eachKey, myDict[eachKey]
...     del myDict[eachKey]
...
a 1
Traceback (most recent call last):
  File "", line 1, in ?
RuntimeError: dictionary changed size during iteration
```

This will help prevent buggy code. For full details on iterators, see PEP 234.

8.11.6 How to Create an Iterator

You can take an item and call `iter()` on it to turn it into an iterator. Its syntax is one of the following:

```
iter(obj)
iter(func, sentinel)
```

If you call `iter()` with one object, it will check if it is just a sequence, for which the solution is simple: It will just iterate through it by (integer) index from 0 to the end. Another way to create an iterator is with a class. As we will see in Chapter 13, a class that implements the `__iter__()` and `next()` methods can be used as an iterator.

If you call `iter()` with two arguments, it will repeatedly call *func* to obtain the next value of iteration until that value is equal to *sentinel*.

8.12 List Comprehensions

List comprehensions (or "list comps" for short) come to us from the functional programming language Haskell. They are an extremely valuable, simple, and flexible utility tool that helps us create lists on the fly. They were added to Python in version 2.0.

2.0

Up ahead in Functions (Chapter 11), we will be discussing long-time Python functional programming features like **lambda**, `map()`, and `filter()`. They have been around in Python for quite a while, but with list comprehensions, they have simplified their use to only requiring a list comp instead. `map()` is a function that applies an operation to list members, and `filter()` filters out list members based on a conditional expression. Finally, **lambda** allows you to create one-line function objects on the fly. It is not important that you learn them now, but you will see examples of them in this section because we are discussing the merits of list comps. Let us take a look at the simpler list comprehension syntax first:

```
[expr for iter_var in iterable]
```

The core of this statement is the **for** loop, which iterates over each item of *iterable*. The prefixed *expr* is applied for each member of the sequence, and the resulting values comprise the list that the expression yields. The iteration variable need not be part of the expression.

Here is a sneak preview of some code from Chapter 11. It has a **lambda** function that squares the members of a sequence:

```
>>> map(lambda x: x ** 2, range(6))
[0, 1, 4, 9, 16, 25]
```

We can replace this code with the following list comprehension statement:

```
>>> [x ** 2 for x in range(6)]
[0, 1, 4, 9, 16, 25]
```

In the new statement, only one function call (range()) is made (as opposed to three—range(), map(), and the **lambda** function). You may also use parentheses around the expression if [(x ** 2) for x in range(6)] is easier for you to read. This syntax for list comprehensions can be a substitute for and is more efficient than using the map() built-in function along with **lambda**.

List comprehensions also support an extended syntax with the **if** statement:

```
[expr for iter_var in iterable if cond_expr]
```

This syntax will filter or "capture" sequence members only if they meet the condition provided for in the cond_expr conditional expression during iteration.

Recall the following odd() function below, which determines whether a numeric argument is odd or even (returning 1 for odd numbers and 0 for even numbers):

```
def odd(n):
    return n % 2
```

We were able to take the core operation from this function, and use it with filter() and **lambda** to obtain the set of odd numbers from a sequence:

```
>>> seq = [11, 10, 9, 9, 10, 10, 9, 8, 23, 9, 7, 18, 12, 11, 12]
>>> filter(lambda x: x % 2, seq)
[11, 9, 9, 9, 23, 9, 7, 11]
```

As in the previous example, we can bypass the use of filter() and **lambda** to obtain the desired set of numbers with list comprehensions:

```
>>> [x for x in seq if x % 2]
[11, 9, 9, 9, 23, 9, 7, 11]
```

Let us end this section with a few more practical examples.

Matrix Example

Do you want to iterate through a matrix of three rows and five columns? It is as easy as:

```
>>> [(x+1,y+1) for x in range(3) for y in range(5)]
[(1, 1), (1, 2), (1, 3), (1, 4), (1, 5), (2, 1), (2, 2), (2,
3), (2, 4), (2, 5), (3, 1), (3, 2), (3, 3), (3, 4), (3, 5)]
```

Disk File Example

Now let us say we have the following data file and want to count the total number of non-whitespace characters in the file `hhga.txt`:

```
And the Lord spake, saying, "First shalt thou take out the
Holy Pin. Then shalt thou count to three, no more, no less.
Three shall be the number thou shalt count, and the number of
the counting shall be three. Four shalt thou not count, nei-
ther count thou two, excepting that thou then proceed to
three. Five is right out. Once the number three, being the
third number, be reached, then lobbest thou thy Holy Hand
Grenade of Antioch towards thy foe, who, being naughty in My
sight, shall snuff it."
```

We know that we can iterate through each line with for line in data, but more than that, we can also go and split each line up into words, and we can sum up the number of words to get a total like this:

```
>>> f = open('hhga.txt', 'r')
>>> len([word for line in f for word in line.split()])
91
```

Let us get a quick total file size:

```
import os
>>> os.stat('hhga.txt').st_size
499L
```

Assuming that there is at least one whitespace character in the file, we know that there are fewer than 499 *non*-whitespace characters in the file. We can sum up the length of each word to arrive at our total:

```
>>> f.seek(0)
>>> sum([len(word) for line in f for word in line.split()])
408
```

Note we have to rewind back to the beginning of the file each time through because the iterator exhausts it. But wow, a non-obfuscated one-liner now does something that used to take many lines of code to accomplish!

As you can see, list comps support multiple nested **for** loops and more than one **if** clause. The full syntax can be found in the official documentation. You can also read more about list comprehensions in PEP 202.

8.13 Generator Expressions

Generator expressions extend naturally from list comprehensions ("list comps"). When list comps came into being in Python 2.0, they revolutionized the language by giving users an extremely flexible and expressive way to designate the contents of a list on a single line. Ask any long-time Python user what new features have changed the way they program Python, and list comps should be near the top of the list.

Another significant feature that was added to Python in version 2.2 was the generator. A generator is a specialized function that allows you to return a value and "pause" the execution of that code and resume it at a later time. We will discuss generators in Chapter 11.

The one weakness of list comps is that all of the data have to be made available in order to create the entire list. This can have negative consequences if an iterator with a large dataset is involved. Generator expressions resolve this issue by combining the syntax and flexibility of list comps with the power of generators.

Introduced in Python 2.4, generator expressions are similar to list comprehensions in that the basic syntax is nearly identical; however, instead of building a list with values, they return a generator that "yields" after processing each item. Because of this, generator expressions are much more memory efficient by performing "lazy evaluation." Take a look at how similar they appear to list comps:

LIST COMPREHENSION:

```
[expr for iter_var in iterable if cond_expr]
```

GENERATOR EXPRESSION:

```
(expr for iter_var in iterable if cond_expr)
```

Generator expressions do not make list comps obsolete. They are just a more memory-friendly construct, and on top of that, are a great use case of generators. We now present a set of generator expression examples, including a long-winded one at the end showing you how Python code has changed over the years.

Disk File Example

In the previous section on list comprehensions, we took a look at finding the total number of non-whitespace characters in a text file. In the final snippet of code, we showed you how to perform that in one line of code using a list comprehension. If that file became unwieldy due to size, it would become fairly unfriendly memory-wise because we would have to put together a very long list of word lengths.

Instead of creating that large list, we can use a generator expression to perform the summing. Instead of building up this long list, it will calculate individual lengths and feed it to the `sum()` function, which takes not just lists but also iterables like generator expressions. We can then shorten our example above to be even more optimal (code- and execution-wise):

```
>>> sum(len(word) for line in data for word in line.split())
408
```

All we did was remove the enclosing list comprehension square brackets: Two bytes shorter and it saves memory . . . very environmentally friendly!

Cross-Product Pairs Example

Generator expressions are like list comprehensions in that they are lazy, which is their main benefit. They are also great ways of dealing with other lists and generators, like `rows` and `cols` here:

```
rows = [1, 2, 3, 17]

def cols():        # example of simple generator
    yield 56
    yield 2
    yield 1
```

We do not need to create a new list. We can piece together things on the fly. Let us create a generator expression for `rows` and `cols`:

```
x_product_pairs = ((i, j) for i in rows for j in cols())
```

Now we can loop through `x_product_pairs`, and it will loop through `rows` and `cols` lazily:

```
>>> for pair in x_product_pairs:
...     print pair
...
(1, 56)
(1, 2)
(1, 1)
(2, 56)
(2, 2)
(2, 1)
(3, 56)
(3, 2)
(3, 1)
```

```
(17, 56)
(17, 2)
(17, 1)
```

Refactoring Example

Let us look at some evolutionary code via an example that finds the longest line in a file. In the old days, the following was acceptable for reading a file:

```
f = open('/etc/motd', 'r')
longest = 0
while True:
    linelen = len(f.readline().strip())
    if not linelen: break
    if linelen > longest:
        longest = linelen
f.close()
return longest
```

Actually, this is not *that* old. If it were really old Python code, the Boolean constant `True` would be the integer one, and instead of using the string `strip()` method, you would be using the `string` module:

```
import string
       :
len(string.strip(f.readline()))
```

Since that time, we realized that we could release the (file) resource sooner if we read all the lines at once. If this was a log file used by many processes, then it behooves us not to hold onto a (write) file handle for an extended period of time. Yes, our example is for read, but you get the idea. So the preferred way of reading in lines from a file changed slightly to reflect this preference:

```
f = open('/etc/motd', 'r')
longest = 0
allLines = f.readlines()
f.close()
for line in allLines:
    linelen = len(line.strip())
    if linelen > longest:
        longest = linelen
return longest
```

List comps allow us to simplify our code a little bit more and give us the ability to do more processing before we get our set of lines. In the next snippet, in addition to reading in the lines from the file, we call the string `strip()` method immediately instead of waiting until later.

```
f = open('/etc/motd', 'r')
longest = 0
allLines = [x.strip() for x in f.readlines()]
f.close()
for line in allLines:
    linelen = len(line)
    if linelen > longest:
        longest = linelen
return longest
```

Still, both examples above have a problem when dealing with a large file as `readlines()` reads in all its lines. When iterators came around, and files became their own iterators, `readlines()` no longer needed to be called. While we are at it, why can't we just make our data set the set of line *lengths* (instead of lines)? That way, we can use the `max()` built-in function to get the longest string length:

```
f = open('/etc/motd', 'r')
allLineLens = [len(x.strip()) for x in f]
f.close()
return max(allLineLens)
```

The only problem here is that even though you are iterating over `f` line by line, the list comprehension itself needs all lines of the file read into memory in order to generate the list. Let us simplify our code even more: we will replace the list comp with a generator expression and move it inside the call to `max()` so that all of the complexity is on a single line:

```
f = open('/etc/motd', 'r')
longest = max(len(x.strip()) for x in f)
f.close()
return longest
```

One more refactoring, which we are not as much fans of, is dropping the file mode (defaulting to read) and letting Python clean up the open file. It is not as bad as if it were a file open for write, however, but it does work:

```
return max(len(x.strip()) for x in open('/etc/motd'))
```

We have come a long way, baby. Note that even a one-liner is not obfuscated enough in Python to make it difficult to read. Generator expressions were added in Python 2.4, and you can read more about them in PEP 289.

8.14 Related Modules

Iterators were introduced in Python 2.2, and the `itertools` module was added in the next release (2.3) to aid developers who had discovered how useful iterators were but wanted some helper tools to aid in their development. The interesting thing is that if you read the documentation for the various utilities in itertools, you will discover generators. So there is a relationship between iterators and generators. You can read more about this relationship in Chapter 11, "Functions."

8.15 Exercises

8–1. *Conditionals*. Study the following code:

```
# statement A
if x > 0:
    # statement B
    pass

elif x < 0:
    # statement C
    pass

else:
    # statement D
    pass

# statement E
```

(a) Which of the statements above (A, B, C, D, E) will be executed if x < 0?

(b) Which of the statements above will be executed if x == 0?

(c) Which of the statements above will be executed if x > 0?

8–2. *Loops*. Write a program to have the user input three (3) numbers: (**f**)rom, (**t**)o, and (**i**)ncrement. Count from **f** to **t** in increments of **i**, *inclusive* of **f** and **t**. For example, if the input is **f** == 2, **t** == 26, and **i** == 4, the program would output: 2, 6, 10, 14, 18, 22, 26.

8–3. *range()*. What argument(s) could we give to the `range()` built-in function if we wanted the following lists to be generated?

(a) [0, 1, 2, 3, 4, 5, 6, 7, 8, 9]

(b) [3, 6, 9, 12, 15, 18]

(c) [-20, 200, 420, 640, 860]

8–4. *Prime Numbers*. We presented some code in this chapter to determine a number's largest factor or if it is prime. Turn this code into a Boolean function called isprime() such that the input is a single value, and the result returned is True if the number is prime and False otherwise.

8–5. *Factors*. Write a function called getfactors() that takes a single integer as an argument and returns a list of all its factors, including 1 and itself.

8–6. *Prime Factorization*. Take your solutions for isprime() and getfactors() in the previous problems and create a function that takes an integer as input and returns a list of its prime factors. This process, known as *prime factorization*, should output a list of factors such that if multiplied together, they will result in the original number. Note that there could be repeats in the list. So if you gave an input of 20, the output would be [2, 2, 5].

8–7. *Perfect Numbers*. A perfect number is one whose factors (except itself) sum to itself. For example, the factors of 6 are 1, 2, 3, and 6. Since $1 + 2 + 3$ is 6, it (6) is considered a perfect number. Write a function called isperfect() which takes a single integer input and outputs 1 if the number is perfect and 0 otherwise.

8–8. *Factorial*. The factorial of a number is defined as the product of all values from one to that number. A shorthand for N factorial is N! where N! == factorial(N) == $1 * 2 * 3 * \ldots * (N-2) * (N-1) * N$. So 4! == $1 * 2 * 3 * 4$. Write a routine such that given N, the value N! is returned.

8–9. *Fibonacci Numbers*. The Fibonacci number sequence is 1, 1, 2, 3, 5, 8, 13, 21, etc. In other words, the next value of the sequence is the sum of the previous two values in the sequence. Write a routine that, given N, displays the value of the Nth Fibonacci number. For example, the first Fibonacci number is 1, the 6th is 8, and so on.

8–10. *Text Processing*. Determine the total number of vowels, consonants, and words (separated by spaces) in a text sentence. Ignore special cases for vowels and consonants such as "h," "y," "qu," etc. Extra credit: create code to handle those special case.

8–11. *Text Processing*. Write a program to ask the user to input a list of names, in the format "Last Name, First Name," i.e., last name, comma, first name. Write a function that manages the input so that when/if the user types the names in the wrong order, i.e., "First Name Last Name," the error is corrected, and the user is notified. This function should also keep track of the number of input mistakes. When the user is done, sort the list, and display the sorted names in "Last Name, First Name" order.

EXAMPLE input and output (you don't have to do it this way exactly):

```
% nametrack.py
Enter total number of names: 5

Please enter name 0: Smith, Joe
Please enter name 1: Mary Wong
>> Wrong format... should be Last, First.
>> You have done this 1 time(s) already. Fixing input...
Please enter name 2: Hamilton, Gerald
Please enter name 3: Royce, Linda
Please enter name 4: Winston Salem
>> Wrong format... should be Last, First.
>> You have done this 2 time(s) already. Fixing input...

The sorted list (by last name) is:
    Hamilton, Gerald
    Royce, Linda
    Salem, Winston
    Smith, Joe
    Wong, Mary
```

8–12. *(Integer) Bit Operators.* Write a program that takes begin and end values and prints out a decimal, binary, octal, hexadecimal chart like the one shown below. If any of the characters are printable ASCII characters, then print those, too. If none is, you may omit the ASCII column header.

```
SAMPLE OUTPUT 1
---------------
Enter begin value: 9
Enter end value: 18
DEC        BIN        OCT        HEX
-----------------------------------
   9       01001      11         9
  10       01010      12         a
  11       01011      13         b
  12       01100      14         c
  13       01101      15         d
  14       01110      16         e
  15       01111      17         f
  16       10000      20         10
  17       10001      21         11
  18       10010      22         12
```

```
SAMPLE OUTPUT 2
---------------
Enter begin value: 26
Enter end value: 41
DEC     BIN       OCT     HEX     ASCII
----------------------------------------
 26     011010     32     1a
 27     011011     33     1b
 28     011100     34     1c
 29     011101     35     1d
 30     011110     36     1e
 31     011111     37     1f
 32     100000     40     20
 33     100001     41     21       !
 34     100010     42     22       "
 35     100011     43     23       #
 36     100100     44     24       $
 37     100101     45     25       %
 38     100110     46     26       &
 39     100111     47     27       '
 40     101000     50     28       (
 41     101001     51     29       )
```

8–13. *Performance.* In Section 8.5.2, we examined two basic ways
of iterating over a sequence: (1) by sequence item, and (2) via
sequence index. We pointed out at the end that the latter
does not perform as well over the long haul (on my system
here, a test suite shows performance is nearly twice as bad
[83% worse]). Why do you think that is?

FILES AND INPUT/OUTPUT

Chapter Topics

- File Objects
  - File Built-in Functions
  - File Built-in Methods
  - File Built-in Attributes
- Standard Files
- Command-Line Arguments
- File System
- File Execution
- Persistent Storage
- Related Modules

Chapter 9

This chapter is intended to give you an in-depth introduction to the use of files and related input/output capabilities of Python. We introduce the file object (its built-in function, and built-in methods and attributes), review the standard files, discuss accessing the file system, hint at file execution, and briefly mention persistent storage and modules in the standard library related to "file-mania."

9.1 File Objects

File objects can be used to access not only normal disk files, but also any other type of "file" that uses that abstraction. Once the proper "hooks" are installed, you can access other objects with file-style interfaces in the same manner you would access normal files.

You will find many cases where you are dealing with "file-like" objects as you continue to develop your Python experience. Some examples include "opening a URL" for reading a Web page in real-time and launching a command in a separate process and communicating to and from it like a pair of simultaneously open files, one for write and the other for read.

The open() built-in function (see below) returns a file object that is then used for all succeeding operations on the file in question. There are a large number of other functions that return a file or file-like object. One primary reason for this abstraction is that many input/output data structures prefer to adhere to a common interface. It provides consistency in behavior as well as implementation. Operating systems like Unix even feature files as an underlying and architectural interface for communication. Remember, files are simply a contiguous sequence of bytes. Anywhere data need to be sent usually involves a byte stream of some sort, whether the stream occurs as individual bytes or blocks of data.

9.2 File Built-in Functions [`open()` and `file()`]

As the key to opening file doors, the `open()` [and `file()`] built-in function provides a general interface to initiate the file input/output (I/O) process. The `open()` BIF returns a file object on a successful opening of the file or else results in an error situation. When a failure occurs, Python generates or *raises* an `IOError` exception—we will cover errors and exceptions in the next chapter. The basic syntax of the `open()` built-in function is:

```
file_object = open(file_name, access_mode='r', buffering=-1)
```

The *file_name* is a string containing the name of the file to open. It can be a relative or absolute/full pathname. The *access_mode* optional variable is also a string, consisting of a set of flags indicating which mode to open the file with. Generally, files are opened with the modes `'r,'` `'w,'` or `'a,'` representing read, write, and append, respectively. A `'U'` mode also exists for universal NEWLINE support (see below).

Any file opened with mode `'r'` or `'U'` must exist. Any file opened with `'w'` will be truncated first if it exists, and then the file is (re)created. Any file opened with `'a'` will be opened for append. All writes to files opened with `'a'` will be from end-of-file, even if you seek elsewhere during access. If the file does not exist, it will be created, making it the same as if you opened the file in `'w'` mode. If you are a C programmer, these are the same file open modes used for the C library function `fopen()`.

There are other modes supported by `fopen()` that will work with Python's `open()`. These include the `'+'` for read-write access and `'b'` for binary access. One note regarding the binary flag: `'b'` is antiquated on all Unix systems that are POSIX-compliant (including Linux) because they treat all files as binary files, including text files. Here is an entry from the

Linux manual page for `fopen()`, from which the Python `open()` function is derived:

> The mode string can also include the letter "b" either as a last character or as a character between the characters in any of the two-character strings described above. This is strictly for compatibility with ANSI C3.159-1989 ("ANSI C") and has no effect; the "b" is ignored on all POSIX conforming systems, including Linux. (Other systems may treat text files and binary files differently, and adding the "b" may be a good idea if you do I/O to a binary file and expect that your program may be ported to non-Unix environments.)

You will find a complete list of file access modes, including the use of `'b'` if you choose to use it, in Table 9.1. If *access_mode* is not given, it defaults automatically to `'r.'`

The other optional argument, *buffering*, is used to indicate the type of buffering that should be performed when accessing the file. A value of 0 means

Table 9.1   Access Modes for File Objects

File Mode	Operation
r	Open for read
rU or U[a]	Open for read with universal NEWLINE support (PEP 278)
w	Open for write (truncate if necessary)
a	Open for append (always works from EOF, create if necessary)
r+	Open for read and write
w+	Open for read and write (see w above)
a+	Open for read and write (see a above)
rb	Open for binary read
wb	Open for binary write (see w above)
ab	Open for binary append (see a above)
rb+	Open for binary read and write (see r+ above)
wb+	Open for binary read and write (see w+ above)
ab+	Open for binary read and write (see a+ above)

a.   New in Python 2.5.

no buffering should occur, a value of 1 signals line buffering, and any value greater than 1 indicates buffered I/O with the given value as the buffer size. The lack of or a negative value indicates that the system default buffering scheme should be used, which is line buffering for any teletype or tty-like device and normal buffering for everything else. Under normal circumstances, a *buffering* value is not given, thus using the system default.

Here are some examples for opening files:

```
fp = open('/etc/motd')          #open file for read
fp = open('test', 'w')          #open file for write
fp = open('data', 'r+')         #open file for read/write
fp = open(r'c:\io.sys', 'rb')   #open binary file for read
```

9.2.1 The `file()` Factory Function

2.2

The `file()` built-in function came into being in Python 2.2, during the types and classes unification. At this time, many built-in types that did not have associated built-in functions were given factory functions to create instances of those objects, i.e., `dict()`, `bool()`, `file()`, etc., to go along with those that did, i.e., `list()`, `str()`, etc.

Both `open()` and `file()` do exactly the same thing and one can be used in place of the other. Anywhere you see references to `open()`, you can mentally substitute `file()` without any side effects whatsoever.

For foreseeable versions of Python, both `open()` and `file()` will exist side by side, performing the exact same thing. Generally, the accepted style is that you use `open()` for reading/writing files, while `file()` is best used when you want to show that you are dealing with file objects, i.e., **if** `instance(f, file)`.

9.2.2 Universal NEWLINE Support (UNS)

In an upcoming Core Note sidebar, we describe how certain attributes of the `os` module can help you navigate files across different platforms, all of which terminate lines with different endings, i.e., `\n`, `\r`, or `\r\n`. Well, the Python interpreter has to do the same thing, too—the most critical place is when importing modules. Wouldn't it be nicer if you just wanted Python to treat all files the same way?

2.3

That is the whole point of the UNS, introduced in Python 2.3, spurred by PEP 278. When you use the `'U'` flag to open a file, all line separators (or terminators) will be returned by Python via any file input method, i.e., `read*()`, as a NEWLINE character (`\n`) regardless of what the line-endings are. (The `'rU'` mode is also supported to correlate with the `'rb'` option.) This feature will also support files that have multiple types of line-endings. A `file.newlines` attribute tracks the types of line separation characters "seen."

If the file has just been opened and no line-endings seen, `file.newlines` is `None`. After the first line, it is set to the terminator of the first line, and if one more type of line-ending is seen, then `file.newlines` becomes a tuple containing each type seen. Note that UNS only applies to reading text files. There is no equivalent handling of file output.

UNS is turned on by default when Python is built. If you do not wish to have this feature, you can disable it by using the `--without-universal-newlines` switch when running Python's `configure` script. If you must manage the line-endings yourself, then check out the Core Note and use those `os` module attributes!

9.3   File Built-in Methods

Once `open()` has completed successfully and returned a file object, all subsequent access to the file transpires with that "handle." File methods come in four different categories: input, output, movement within a file, which we will call "intra-file motion," and miscellaneous. A summary of all file methods can be found in Table 9.3. We will now discuss each category.

9.3.1   Input

The `read()` method is used to read bytes directly into a string, reading at most the number of bytes indicated. If no *size* is given (the default value is set to integer –1) or *size* is negative, the file will be read to the end. It will be phased out and eventually removed in a future version of Python.

The `readline()` method reads one line of the open file (reads all bytes until a line-terminating character like NEWLINE is encountered). The line, including termination character(s), is returned as a string. Like `read()`, there is also an optional *size* option, which, if not provided, defaults to -1, meaning read until the line-ending characters (or EOF) are found. If present, it is possible that an incomplete line is returned if it exceeds *size* bytes.

The `readlines()` method does not return a string like the other two input methods. Instead, it reads all (remaining) lines and returns them as a list of strings. Its optional argument, *sizhint*, is a hint on the maximum size desired in bytes. If provided and greater than zero, approximately *sizhint* bytes in whole lines are read (perhaps slightly more to round up to the next buffer size) and returned as a list.

In Python 2.1, a new type of object was used to efficiently iterate over a set of lines from a file: the xreadlines object (found in the xreadlines module). Calling *file*.xreadlines() was equivalent to xreadlines.xreadlines(*file*). Instead of reading all the lines in at once, xreadlines() reads in chunks at a time, and thus were optimal for use with **for** loops in a memory-conscious way. However, with the introduction of iterators and the new file iteration in Python 2.3, it was no longer necessary to have an xreadlines() method because it is the same as using iter(*file*), or in a **for** loop, is replaced by **for** eachLine **in** *file*. Easy come, easy go.

2.1-2.3

Another odd bird is the readinto() method, which reads the given number of bytes into a writable buffer object, the same type of object returned by the unsupported buffer() built-in function. (Since buffer() is not supported, neither is readinto().)

9.3.2 Output

The write() built-in method has the opposite functionality as read() and readline(). It takes a string that can consist of one or more lines of text data or a block of bytes and writes the data to the file.

The writelines() method operates on a list just like readlines(), but takes a list of strings and writes them out to a file. Line termination characters are not inserted between each line, so if desired, they must be added to the end of each line before writelines() is called.

Note that there is no "writeline()" method since it would be equivalent to calling write() with a single line string terminated with a NEWLINE character.

CORE NOTE: Line separators are preserved

When reading lines in from a file using file input methods like read() *or* readlines(), *Python does not remove the line termination characters. It is up to the programmer. For example, the following code is fairly common to see in Python code:*

```
f = open('myFile', 'r')
data = [line.strip() for line in f.readlines()]
f.close()
```

Similarly, output methods like write() *or* writelines() *do not add line terminators for the programmer... you have to do it yourself before writing the data to the file.*

9.3.3 Intra-file Motion

The seek() method (analogous to the fseek() function in C) moves the file pointer to different positions within the file. The offset in bytes is given along with a *relative offset* location, whence. A value of 0, the default, indicates distance from the beginning of a file (note that a position measured from the beginning of a file is also known as the *absolute offset*), a value of 1 indicates movement from the current location in the file, and a value of 2 indicates that the offset is from the end of the file. If you have used fseek() as a C programmer, the values 0, 1, and 2 correspond directly to the constants SEEK_SET, SEEK_CUR, and SEEK_END, respectively. Use of the seek() method comes into play when opening a file for read and write access.

tell() is a complementary method to seek(); it tells you the current location of the file—in bytes from the beginning of the file.

9.3.4 File Iteration

Going through a file line by line is simple:

```
for eachLine in f:
        :
```

Inside this loop, you are welcome to do whatever you need to with eachLine, representing a single line of the text file (which includes the trailing line separators).

Before Python 2.2, the best way to read in lines from a file was using *file*.readlines() to read in all the data, giving the programmer the ability to free up the file resource as quickly as possible. If that was not a concern, then programmers could call *file*.readline() to read in one line at a time. For a brief time, *file*.xreadlines() was the most efficient way to read in a file.

Things all changed in 2.2 when Python introduced iterators and file iteration. In file iteration, file objects became their own iterators, meaning that users could now iterate through lines of a file using a **for** loop without having to call read*() methods. Alternatively, the iterator next method, *file*.next() could be called as well to read in the next line in the file. Like all other iterators, Python will raise StopIteration when no more lines are available.

So remember, if you see this type of code, this is the "old way of doing it," and you can safely remove the call to readline().

```
for eachLine in f.readline():
        :
```

2.2

File iteration is more efficient, and the resulting Python code is easier to write (and read). Those of you new to Python now are getting all the great new features and do not have to worry about the past.

9.3.5 Others

The `close()` method completes access to a file by closing it. The Python garbage collection routine will also close a file when the file object reference has decreased to zero. One way this can happen is when only one reference exists to a file, say, `fp = open(...)`, and `fp` is reassigned to another file object before the original file is explicitly closed. Good programming style suggests closing the file before reassignment to another file object. It is possible to lose output data that is buffered if you do not explicitly close a file.

The `fileno()` method passes back the file descriptor to the open file. This is an integer argument that can be used in lower-level operations such as those featured in the `os` module, i.e., `os.read()`.

Rather than waiting for the (contents of the) output buffer to be written to disk, calling the `flush()` method will cause the contents of the internal buffer to be written (or flushed) to the file immediately. `isatty()` is a Boolean built-in method that returns `True` if the file is a tty-like device and `False` otherwise. The `truncate()` method truncates the file to the size at the current file position or the given *size* in bytes.

9.3.6 File Method Miscellany

We will now reprise our first file example from Chapter 2:

```
filename = raw_input('Enter file name: ')
f = open(filename, 'r')
allLines = f.readlines()
f.close()
for eachLine in allLines:
    print eachLine,   # suppress print's NEWLINE
```

We originally described how this program differs from most standard file access in that all the lines are read ahead of time before any display to the screen occurs. Obviously, this is not advantageous if the file is large. In that case, it may be a good idea to go back to the tried-and-true way of reading and displaying one line at a time using a file iterator:

```
filename = raw_input('Enter file name: ')
f = open(filename, 'r')
for eachLine in f:
    print eachLine,
f.close()
```

CORE NOTE: Line separators and other file system inconsistencies

One of the inconsistencies of operating systems is the line separator character that their file systems support. On POSIX (Unix family or Mac OS X) systems, the line separator is the NEWLINE (\n) character. For old MacOS, it is the RETURN (\r), and DOS and Win32 systems use both (\r\n). Check your operating system to determine what your line separator(s) are.

Other differences include the file pathname separator (POSIX uses "/", DOS and Windows use "\", and the old MacOS uses ":"), the separator used to delimit a set of file pathnames, and the denotations for the current and parent directories.

These inconsistencies generally add an irritating level of annoyance when creating applications that run on all three platforms (and more if more architectures and operating systems are supported). Fortunately, the designers of the os *module in Python have thought of this for us. The* os *module has five attributes that you may find useful. They are listed in Table 9.2.*

Table 9.2 os **Module Attributes to Aid in Multi-platform Development**

os *Module Attribute*	*Description*
linesep	String used to separate lines in a file
sep	String used to separate file pathname components
pathsep	String used to delimit a set of file pathnames
curdir	String name for current working directory
pardir	String name for parent (of current working directory)

Regardless of your platform, these variables will be set to the correct values when you import the os *module: One less headache to worry about.*

We would also like to remind you that the comma placed at the end of the **print** statement is to suppress the NEWLINE character that **print** normally adds at the end of output. The reason for this is because every line from the text file already contains a NEWLINE. readline() and `readlines()` do not strip off any whitespace characters in your line (see exercises.) If we omitted the comma, then your text file display would be doublespaced one NEWLINE which is part of the input and another added by the **print** statement.

File objects also have a `truncate()` method, which takes one optional argument, `size`. If it is given, then the file will be truncated to, at most, `size` bytes. If you call `truncate()` without passing in a size, it will default to the current location in the file. For example, if you just opened the file and call `truncate()`, your file will be effectively deleted, truncated to zero bytes because upon opening a file, the "read head" is on byte 0, which is what `tell()` returns.

Before moving on to the next section, we will show two more examples, the first highlighting output to files (rather than input), and the second performing both file input and output as well as using the `seek()` and `tell()` methods for file positioning.

```
filename = raw_input('Enter file name: ')
fobj = open(filename, 'w')
while True:
    aLine = raw_input("Enter a line ('.' to quit): ")
    if aLine != ".":
        fobj.write('%s%s' % (aLine, os.linesep))
    else:
        break
fobj.close()
```

Here we ask the user for one line at a time, and send them out to the file. Our call to the `write()` method must contain a NEWLINE because `raw_input()` does not preserve it from the user input. Because it may not be easy to generate an end-of-file character from the keyboard, the program uses the period (.) as its end-of-file character, which, when entered by the user, will terminate input and close the file.

The second example opens a file for read and write, creating the file from scratch (after perhaps truncating an already existing file). After writing data to the file, we move around within the file using `seek()`. We also use the `tell()` method to show our movement.

```
>>> f = open('/tmp/x', 'w+')
>>> f.tell()
0
>>> f.write('test line 1\n')    # add 12-char string [0-11]
>>> f.tell()
12
>>> f.write('test line 2\n')    # add 12-char string [12-23]
>>> f.tell()                    # tell us current file location (end))
24
```

```
>>> f.seek(-12, 1)          # move back 12 bytes
>>> f.tell()                # to beginning of line 2
12
>>> f.readline()
'test line 2\012'
>>> f.seek(0, 0)            # move back to beginning
>>> f.readline()
'test line 1\012'
>>> f.tell()                # back to line 2 again
12
>>> f.readline()
'test line 2\012'
>>> f.tell()                # at the end again
24
>>> f.close()               # close file
```

Table 9.3 lists all the built-in methods for file objects.

Table 9.3 Methods for File Objects

File Object Method	Operation
file.close()	Closes *file*
file.fileno()	Returns integer file descriptor (FD) for *file*
file.flush()	Flushes internal buffer for *file*
file.isatty()	Returns True if *file* is a tty-like device and False otherwise
file.next[a]()	Returns the next line in the file [similar to *file*.readline()] or raises StopIteration if no more lines are available
file.read(*size*=-1)	Reads *size* bytes of file, or all remaining bytes if *size* not given or is negative, as a string and return it
file.readinto[b](*buf*, *size*)	Reads *size* bytes from *file* into buffer *buf* (unsupported)
file.readline(*size*=-1)	Reads and returns one line from *file* (includes line-ending characters), either one full line or a maximum of *size* characters

(continued)

Table 9.3 Methods for File Objects (continued)	
File Object Method	*Operation*
`file.readlines(sizhint=0)`	Reads and returns all lines from `file` as a list (includes all line termination characters); if `sizhint` given and > 0, whole lines are returned consisting of approximately `sizhint` bytes (could be rounded up to next buffer's worth)
`file.xreadlines`[c]`()`	Meant for iteration, returns lines in `file` read as chunks in a more efficient way than `readlines()`
`file.seek(off, whence=0)`	Moves to a location within `file`, `off` bytes offset from `whence` (0 == beginning of file, 1 == current location, or 2 == end of file)
`file.tell()`	Returns current location within `file`
`file.truncate (size=file.tell())`	Truncates `file` to at most `size` bytes, the default being the current file location
`file.write(str)`	Writes string `str` to `file`
`file.writelines(seq)`	Writes `seq` of strings to `file`; `seq` should be an iterable producing strings; prior to 2.2, it was just a list of strings

a.   New in Python 2.2.
b.   New in Python 1.5.2 but unsupported.
c.   New in Python 2.1 but deprecated in Python 2.3.

9.4 File Built-in Attributes

File objects also have data attributes in addition to methods. These attributes hold auxiliary data related to the file object they belong to, such as the file name (`file.name`), the mode with which the file was opened (`file.mode`), whether the file is closed (`file.closed`), and a flag indicating whether an additional space character needs to be displayed before successive data items when using the **print** statement (`file.softspace`). Table 9.4 lists these attributes along with a brief description of each.

Table 9.4 Attributes for File Objects	

File Object Attribute	Description
file.closed	True if *file* is closed and False otherwise
file.encoding[a]	Encoding that this file uses—when Unicode strings are written to file, they will be converted to byte strings using *file*.encoding; a value of None indicates that the system default encoding for converting Unicode strings should be used
file.mode	Access mode with which *file* was opened
file.name	Name of *file*
file.newlines[a]	None if no line separators have been read, a string consisting of one type of line separator, or a tuple containing all types of line termination characters read so far
file.softspace	0 if space explicitly required with print, 1 otherwise; rarely used by the programmer—generally for internal use only

a. New in Python 2.3.

9.5 Standard Files

There are generally three standard files that are made available to you when your program starts. These are standard input (usually the keyboard), standard output (buffered output to the monitor or display), and standard error (unbuffered output to the screen). (The "buffered" or "unbuffered" output refers to that third argument to open()). These files are named stdin, stdout, and stderr and take their names from the C language. When we say these files are "available to you when your program starts," that means that these files are pre-opened for you, and access to these files may commence once you have their file handles.

Python makes these file handles available to you from the sys module. Once you import sys, you have access to these files as sys.stdin, sys.stdout, and sys.stderr. The **print** statement normally outputs to sys.stdout while the raw_input() built-in function receives its input from sys.stdin.

Just remember that since sys.* are files, you have to manage the line separation characters. The **print** statement has the built-in feature of automatically adding one to the end of a string to output.

9.6 Command-Line Arguments

The sys module also provides access to any *command-line arguments* via sys.argv. Command-line arguments are those arguments given to the program in addition to the script name on invocation. Historically, of course, these arguments are so named because they are given on the command line along with the program name in a text-based environment like a Unix- or DOS-shell. However, in an IDE or GUI environment, this would not be the case. Most IDEs provide a separate window with which to enter your "command-line arguments." These, in turn, will be passed into the program as if you started your application from the command line.

Those of you familiar with C programming may ask, "Where is argc?" The names "argc" and "argv" stand for "argument count" and "argument vector," respectively. The argv variable contains an array of strings consisting of each argument from the command line while the argc variable contains the number of arguments entered. In Python, the value for argc is simply the number of items in the sys.argv list, and the first element of the list, sys.argv[0], is always the program name. Summary:

- sys.argv *is the list of command-line arguments*
- len(sys.argv) *is the number of command-line arguments* (*aka* argc)

Let us create a small test program called argv.py with the following lines:

```
import sys

print 'you entered', len(sys.argv), 'arguments...'
print 'they were:', str(sys.argv)
```

Here is an example invocation and output of this script:

```
$ argv.py 76 tales 85 hawk
you entered 5 arguments...
they were: ['argv.py', '76', 'tales', '85', 'hawk']
```

Are command-line arguments useful? Commands on Unix-based systems are typically programs that take input, perform some function, and send output as a stream of data. These data are usually sent as input directly to the next program, which does some other type of function or calculation and sends the new output to another program, and so on. Rather than saving the output of each program and potentially taking up a good amount of disk space, the output is usually "piped" into the next program as *its* input.

This is accomplished by providing data on the command line or through standard input. When a program displays or sends output to the standard output file, the result would be displayed on the screen—unless that program is also "piped" to another program, in which case that standard output file is really the standard input file of the next program. I assume you get the drift by now!

Command-line arguments allow a programmer or administrator to start a program perhaps with different behavioral characteristics. Much of the time, this execution takes place in the middle of the night and runs as a batch job without human interaction. Command-line arguments and program options enable this type of functionality. As long as there are computers sitting idle at night and plenty of work to be done, there will always be a need to run programs in the background on our very expensive "calculators."

Python has two modules to help process command-line arguments. The first (and original), `getopt` is easier but less sophisticated, while `optparse`, introduced in Python 2.3, is more powerful library and is much more object-oriented than its predecessor. If you are just getting started, we recommend `getopt`, but once you outgrow its feature set, then check out `optparse`.

2.3

9.7 File System

Access to your file system occurs mostly through the Python `os` module. This module serves as the primary interface to your operating system facilities and services from Python. The `os` module is actually a front-end to the real module that is loaded, a module that is clearly operating system–dependent. This "real" module may be one of the following: `posix` (Unix-based, i.e., Linux, MacOS X, *BSD, Solaris, etc.), `nt` (Win32), `mac` (old MacOS), `dos` (DOS), `os2` (OS/2), etc. You should never import those modules directly. Just import `os` and the appropriate module will be loaded, keeping all the underlying work hidden from sight. Depending on what your system supports, you may not have access to some of the attributes, which may be available in other operating system modules.

In addition to managing processes and the process execution environment, the `os` module performs most of the major file system operations that the application developer may wish to take advantage of. These features include removing and renaming files, traversing the directory tree, and managing file accessibility. Table 9.5 lists some of the more common file or directory operations available to you from the os module.

A second module that performs specific pathname operations is also available. The os.path module is accessible through the os module. Included with this module are functions to manage and manipulate file pathname components, obtain file or directory information, and make file path inquiries. Table 9.6 outlines some of the more common functions in os.path.

These two modules allow for consistent access to the file system regardless of platform or operating system. The program in Example 9.1 (ospathex.py) test drives some of these functions from the os and os.path modules.

Table 9.5 os Module File/Directory Access Functions

Function	Description
File Processing	
mkfifo()/mknod()[a]	Create named pipe/create filesystem node
remove()/unlink()	Delete file
rename()/renames()[b]	Rename file
*stat[c]()	Return file statistics
symlink()	Create symbolic link
utime()	Update timestamp
tmpfile()	Create and open ('w+b') new temporary file
walk()[a]	Generate filenames in a directory tree
Directories/Folders	
chdir()/fchdir()[a]	Change working directory/via a file descriptor
chroot()[d]	Change root directory of current process
listdir()	List files in directory

Table 9.5 os Module File/Directory Access Functions (continued)

Function	Description
Directories/Folders	
getcwd()/getcwdu()[a]	Return current working directory/same but in Unicode
mkdir()/makedirs()	Create directory(ies)
rmdir()/removedirs()	Remove directory(ies)
Access/Permissions	
access()	Verify permission modes
chmod()	Change permission modes
chown()/lchown()[a]	Change owner and group ID/same, but do not follow links
umask()	Set default permission modes
File Descriptor Operations	
open()	Low-level operating system open [for files, use the standard open() built-in functions
read()/write()	Read/write data to a file descriptor
dup()/dup2()	Duplicate file descriptor/same but to another FD
Device Numbers	
makedev()[a]	Generate raw device number from major and minor device numbers
major()[a]/minor()[a]	Extract major/minor device number from raw device number

a.   New in Python 2.3.
b.   New in Python 1.5.2.
c.   Includes stat(), lstat(), xstat().
d.   New in Python 2.2.

Table 9.6 `os.path` Module Pathname Access Functions

Function	Description
Separation	
`basename()`	Remove directory path and return leaf name
`dirname()`	Remove leaf name and return directory path
`join()`	Join separate components into single pathname
`split()`	Return (*dirname()*, *basename()*) tuple
`splitdrive()`	Return (*drivename*, *pathname*) tuple
`splitext()`	Return (*filename*, *extension*) tuple
Information	
`getatime()`	Return last file access time
`getctime()`	Return file creation time
`getmtime()`	Return last file modification time
`getsize()`	Return file size (in bytes)
Inquiry	
`exists()`	Does pathname (file or directory) exist?
`isabs()`	Is pathname absolute?
`isdir()`	Does pathname exist and is a directory?
`isfile()`	Does pathname exist and is a file?
`islink()`	Does pathname exist and is a symbolic link?
`ismount()`	Does pathname exist and is a mount point?
`samefile()`	Do both pathnames point to the same file?

Example 9.1   **os** & **os.path** Modules Example (`ospathex.py`)

This code exercises some of the functionality found in the os *and* os.path *modules. It creates a test file, populates a small amount of data in it, renames the file, and dumps its contents. Other auxiliary file operations are performed as well, mostly pertaining to directory tree traversal and file pathname manipulation.*

```
1   #!/usr/bin/env python
2
3   import os
4   for tmpdir in ('/tmp', r'c:\temp'):
5       if os.path.isdir(tmpdir):
6           break
7   else:
8       print 'no temp directory available'
9       tmpdir = ''
10
11  if tmpdir:
12      os.chdir(tmpdir)
13      cwd = os.getcwd()
14      print '*** current temporary directory'
15      print cwd
16
17      print '*** creating example directory...'
18      os.mkdir('example')
19      os.chdir('example')
20      cwd = os.getcwd()
21      print '*** new working directory:'
22      print cwd
23      print '*** original directory listing:'
24      print os.listdir(cwd)
25
26      print '*** creating test file...'
27      fobj = open('test', 'w')
28      fobj.write('foo\n')
29      fobj.write('bar\n')
30      fobj.close()
31      print '*** updated directory listing:'
32      print os.listdir(cwd)
33
34      print "*** renaming 'test' to 'filetest.txt'"
35      os.rename('test', 'filetest.txt')
36      print '*** updated directory listing:'
37      print os.listdir(cwd)
38
39      path = os.path.join(cwd, os.listdir (cwd)[0])
40      print '*** full file pathname'
41      print path
```

Example 9.1   os & os.path Modules Example (ospathex.py) (continued)

```
42      print '*** (pathname, basename) =='
43      print os.path.split(path)
44      print '*** (filename, extension) =='
45      print os.path.splitext(os.path.basename(path))
46
47      print '*** displaying file contents:'
48      fobj = open(path)
49      for eachLine in fobj:
50          print eachLine,
51      fobj.close()
52
53      print '*** deleting test file'
54      os.remove(path)
55      print '*** updated directory listing:'
56      print os.listdir(cwd)
57      os.chdir(os.pardir)
58      print '*** deleting test directory'
59      os.rmdir('example')
60      print '*** DONE'
```

The os.path submodule to os focuses more on file pathnames. Some of the more commonly used attributes are found in Table 9.6.

Running this program on a Unix platform, we get the following output:

```
$ ospathex.py
*** current temporary directory
/tmp
*** creating example directory...
*** new working directory:
/tmp/example
*** original directory listing:
[]
*** creating test file...
*** updated directory listing:
['test']
*** renaming 'test' to 'filetest.txt'
*** updated directory listing:
['filetest.txt']
*** full file pathname:
/tmp/example/filetest.txt
*** (pathname, basename) ==
('/tmp/example', 'filetest.txt')
```

```
*** (filename, extension) ==
('filetest', '.txt')
*** displaying file contents:
foo
bar
*** deleting test file
*** updated directory listing:
[]
*** deleting test directory
*** DONE
```

Running this example from a DOS window results in very similar execution:

```
C:\>python ospathex.py
*** current temporary directory
c:\windows\temp
*** creating example directory...
*** new working directory:
c:\windows\temp\example
*** original directory listing:
[]
*** creating test file...
*** updated directory listing:
['test']
*** renaming 'test' to 'filetest.txt'
*** updated directory listing:
['filetest.txt']
*** full file pathname:
c:\windows\temp\example\filetest.txt
*** (pathname, basename) ==
('c:\\windows\\temp\\example', 'filetest.txt')
*** (filename, extension) ==
('filetest', '.txt')
*** displaying file contents:
foo
bar
*** deleting test file
*** updated directory listing:
[]
*** deleting test directory
*** DONE
```

Rather than providing a line-by-line explanation here, we will leave it to the reader as an exercise. However, we will walk through a similar interactive example (including errors) to give you a feel for what it is like to execute this script one step at a time. We will break into the code every now and then to describe the code we just encountered.

```
>>> import os
>>> os.path.isdir('/tmp')
True
>>> os.chdir('/tmp')
>>> cwd = os.getcwd()
>>> cwd
'/tmp'
```

This first block of code consists of importing the os module (which also grabs the os.path module). We verify that '/tmp' is a valid directory and change to that temporary directory to do our work. When we arrive, we call the getcwd() method to tell us where we are.

```
>>> os.mkdir('example')
>>> os.chdir('example')
>>> cwd = os.getcwd()
>>> cwd
'/tmp/example'
>>>
>>> os.listdir() # oops, forgot name
Traceback (innermost last):
  File "<stdin>", line 1, in ?
TypeError: function requires at least one argument
>>>
>>> os.listdir(cwd) # that's better :)
[]
```

Next, we create a subdirectory in our temporary directory, after which we will use the listdir() method to confirm that the directory is indeed empty (since we just created it). The problem with our first call to listdir() was that we forgot to give the name of the directory we want to list. That problem is quickly remedied on the next line of input.

```
>>> fobj = open('test', 'w')
>>> fobj.write('foo\n')
>>> fobj.write('bar\n')
>>> fobj.close()
>>> os.listdir(cwd)
['test']
```

We then create a test file with two lines and verify that the file has been created by listing the directory again afterward.

```
>>> os.rename('test', 'filetest.txt')
>>> os.listdir(cwd)
['filetest.txt']
```

```
>>>
>>> path = os.path.join(cwd, os.listdir(cwd)[0])
>>> path
'/tmp/example/filetest.txt'
>>>
>>> os.path.isfile(path)
True
>>> os.path.isdir(path)
False
>>>
>>> os.path.split(path)
('/tmp/example', 'filetest.txt')
>>>
>>> os.path.splitext(os.path.basename(path))
('filetest', '.ext')
```

This section is no doubt an exercise of os.path functionality, testing join(), isfile(), isdir() which we have seen earlier, split(), basename(), and splitext(). We also call the rename() function from os. Next, we display the file, and finally, we delete the temporary files and directories:

```
>>> fobj = open(path)
>>> for eachLine in fobj:
...        print eachLine,
...
foo
bar
>>> fobj.close()
>>> os.remove(path)
>>> os.listdir(cwd)
[]
>>> os.chdir(os.pardir)
>>> os.rmdir('example')
```

CORE MODULE(S): os **(and** os.path**)**

As you can tell from our lengthy discussion above, the os *and* os.path *modules provide different ways to access the file system on your computer. Although our study in this chapter is restricted to file access only, the* os *module can do much more. It lets you manage your process environment, contains provisions for low-level file access, allows you to create and manage new processes, and even enables your running Python program to "talk" directly to another running program. You may find yourself a common user of this module in no time. Read more about the* os *module in Chapter 14.*

9.8 File Execution

Whether we want to simply run an operating system command, invoke a binary executable, or another type of script (perhaps a shell script, Perl, or Tcl/Tk), this involves executing another file somewhere else on the system. Even running other Python code may call for starting up another Python interpreter, although that may not always be the case. In any regard, we will defer this subject to Chapter 14, "Execution Environment." Please proceed there if you are interested in how to start other programs, perhaps even communicating with them, and for general information regarding Python's execution environment.

9.9 Persistent Storage Modules

In many of the exercises in this text, user input is required. After many iterations, it may be somewhat frustrating being required to enter the same data repeatedly. The same may occur if you are entering a significant amount of data for use in the future. This is where it becomes useful to have persistent storage, or a way to archive your data so that you may access them at a later time instead of having to re-enter all of that information. When simple disk files are no longer acceptable and full relational database management systems (RDBMSs) are overkill, simple persistent storage fills the gap. The majority of the persistent storage modules deals with storing strings of data, but there are ways to archive Python objects as well.

9.9.1 `pickle` *and* `marshal` *Modules*

Python provides a variety of modules that implement minimal persistent storage. One set of modules (`marshal` and `pickle`) allows for pickling of Python objects. Pickling is the process whereby objects more complex than primitive types can be converted to a binary set of bytes that can be stored or transmitted across the network, then be converted back to their original object forms. Pickling is also known as flattening, serializing, or marshalling. Another set of modules (`dbhash/bsddb`, `dbm`, `gdbm`, `dumbdbm`) and their "manager" (`anydbm`) can provide persistent storage of Python strings only. The last module (`shelve`) can do both.

As we mentioned before, both `marshal` and `pickle` can flatten Python objects. These modules do not provide "persistent storage" per se, since they do not provide a namespace for the objects, nor can they provide concurrent write access to persistent objects. What they can do, however, is to pickle Python objects to allow them to be stored or transmitted. Storage, of course, is sequential in nature (you store or transmit objects one after another). The difference between marshal and pickle is that marshal can handle only simple Python objects (numbers, sequences, mapping, and code) while pickle can transform recursive objects, objects that are multi-referenced from different places, and user-defined classes and instances. The pickle module is also available in a turbo version called cPickle, which implements all functionality in C.

9.9.2 DBM-style Modules

The *db* series of modules writes data in the traditional DBM format. There are a large number of different implementations: dbhash/bsddb, dbm, gdbm, and dumbdbm. If you are particular about any specific DBM module, feel free to use your favorite, but if you are not sure or do not care, the generic anydbm module detects which DBM-compatible modules are installed on your system and uses the "best" one at its disposal. The dumbdbm module is the most limited one, and is the default used if none of the other packages is available. These modules do provide a namespace for your objects, using objects that behave similar to a combination of a dictionary object and a file object. The one limitation of these systems is that they can store only strings. In other words, they do not serialize Python objects.

9.9.3 shelve Module

Finally, we have a somewhat more complete solution, the shelve module. The shelve module uses the anydbm module to find a suitable DBM module, then uses cPickle to perform the pickling process. The shelve module permits concurrent read access to the database file, but not shared read/write access. This is about as close to persistent storage as you will find in the Python standard library. There may be other external extension modules that implement "true" persistent storage. The diagram in Figure 9–1 shows the relationship between the pickling modules and the persistent storage modules, and how the shelve object appears to be the best of both worlds.

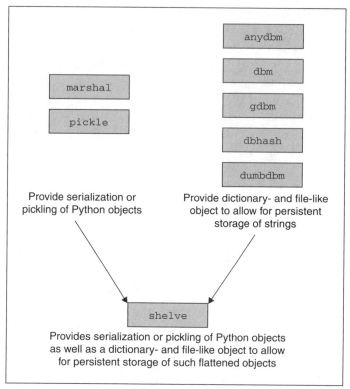

Figure 9–1 Python modules for serialization and persistency

CORE MODULE: `pickle` **and** `cPickle`

The `pickle` *module allows you to store Python objects directly to a file without having to convert them to strings or to necessarily write them out as binary files using low-level file access. Instead, the* `pickle` *module creates a Python-only binary version that allows you to cleanly read and write objects in their entirety without having to worry about all the file details. All you need is a valid file handle, and you are ready to read or write objects from or to disk.*

The two main functions in the `pickle` *module are* `dump()` *and* `load()`. *The* `dump()` *function takes a file handle and a data object and saves the object in a format it understands to the given file. When a pickled object is loaded from disk using* `load()`, *it knows exactly how to restore that object to its original configuration before it was saved to disk. We recommend you take a look at* `pickle` *and its "smarter" brother,* `shelve`, *which gives you dictionary-like functionality so there is even less file overhead on your part.*

`cPickle` *is the faster C-compiled version of* `pickle`.

9.10 Related Modules

There are plenty of other modules related to files and input/output, all of which work on most of the major platforms. Table 9.7 lists some of the file-related modules.

Table 9.7 Related File Modules

Module(s)	Contents
base64	Encoding/decoding of binary strings to/from text strings
binascii	Encoding/decoding of binary and ASCII-encoded binary strings
bz2[a]	Allows access to BZ2 compressed files
csv[a]	Allows access to comma-separated value files
filecmp[b]	Compares directories and files
fileinput	Iterates over lines of multiple input text files
getopt/optparse[a]	Provides command-line argument parsing/manipulation
glob/fnmatch	Provides Unix-style wildcard character matching
gzip/zlib	Reads and writes GNU zip (gzip) files (needs zlib module for compression)
shutil	Offers high-level file access functionality
c/StringIO	Implements file-like interface on top of string objects
tarfile[a]	Reads and writes TAR archive files, even compressed ones
tempfile	Generates temporary file names or files
uu	uuencode and uudecode files
zipfile[c]	Tools and utilities to read and write ZIP archive files

a. New in Python 2.3.
b. New in Python 2.0.
c. New in Python 1.6.

The `fileinput` module iterates over a set of input files and reads their contents one line at a time, allowing you to iterate over each line, much like the way the Perl (< >) operator works without any provided arguments. File names that are not explicitly given will be assumed to be provided from the command-line.

The `glob` and `fnmatch` modules allow for file name pattern-matching in the good old-fashioned Unix shell-style, for example, using the asterisk (*) wildcard character for all string matches and the (?) for matching single characters.

Core Tip: Tilde (~) expansion via `os.path.expanduser()`

Although the `glob` and `fnmatch` allow for Unix-style pattern-matching, they do not enable the expansion of the tilde (home directory) character, ~. This is handled by the `os.path.expanduser()` function. You pass in a path containing a tilde, and it returns the equivalent absolute file path. Here are two examples, in a Unix-based environment and in Win32:

```
>>> os.path.expanduser('~/py')
'/home/wesley/py'

>>> os.path.expanduser('~/py')
'C:\\Documents and Settings\\wesley/py'
```

In addition, Unix-flavored systems also support the "~user" notation indicating the home directory for a specific user. Also, note that the Win32 version does not change forward slashes to the DOS backslashes in a directory path.

The `gzip` and `zlib` modules provide direct file access to the `zlib` compression library. The `gzip` module, written on top of the `zlib` module, allows for standard file access, but provides for automatic `gzip`-compatible compression and decompression. `bz2` is like `gzip` but for bzipped files.

The `zipfile` module introduced in 1.6 allows the programmer to create, modify, and read `zip` archive files. (The `tarfile` module serves as an equivalent for TAR archive files.) In 2.3, Python was given the ability to import modules archived in zip files as well. See Section 12.5.7 for more information.

The `shutil` module furnishes high-level file access, performing such functions as copying files, copying file permissions, and recursive directory tree copying, to name a few.

The `tempfile` module can be used to generate temporary filenames and files.

In our earlier chapter on strings, we described the `StringIO` module (and its C-compiled companion `cStringIO`), and how it overlays a file interface on top of string objects. This interface includes all of the standard methods available to regular file objects.

The modules we mentioned in the Persistent Storage section above (Section 9.9) include examples of a hybrid file- and dictionary-like object.

Some other Python modules that generate file-like objects include network and file socket objects (`socket` module), the `popen*()` file objects that connect your application to other running processes (`os` and `popen2` modules), the `fdopen()` file object used in low-level file access (`os` module), and opening a network connection to an Internet Web server via its Uniform Resource Locator (URL) address (`urllib` module). Please be aware that not all standard file methods may be implemented for these objects. Likewise, they may provide functionality in addition to what is available for regular files.

Refer to the documentation for more details on these file access-related modules. In addition, you can find out more about `file()`/`open()`, files, file objects, and UNS at:

> http://docs.python.org/lib/built-in-funcs.html
> http://docs.python.org/lib/bltin-file-objects.html
> http://www.python.org/doc/2.3/whatsnew/node7.html
> http://www.python.org/doc/peps/pep-0278/

9.11 Exercises

9–1. *File Filtering.* Display all lines of a file, except those that *start* with a pound sign (#), the comment character for Python, Perl, Tcl, and most other scripting languages.

Extra credit: Also strip out comments that begin after the first character.

9–2. *File Access.* Prompt for a number N and file F, and display the first N lines of F.

9–3. *File Information.* Prompt for a filename and display the number of lines in that text file.

9–4. *File Access.* Write a "pager" program. Your solution should prompt for a filename, and display the text file 25 lines at a time, pausing each time to ask the user to "press a key to continue."

9–5. *Test Scores.* Update your solution to the test scores problems (Exercises 5–3 and 6–4) by allowing a set of test scores be loaded from a file. We leave the file format to your discretion.

9–6. *File Comparison.* Write a program to compare two text files. If they are different, give the line and column numbers in the files where the first difference occurs.

9–7. *Parsing Files.* Win32 users: Create a program that parses a Windows `.ini` file. POSIX users: Create a program that parses the `/etc/services` file. All other platforms: Create a program that parses a system file with some kind of structure to it.

9–8. *Module Introspection*. Extract module attribute information. Prompt the user for a module name (or accept it from the command line). Then, using `dir()` and other built-in functions, extract all its attributes, and display their names, types, and values.

9–9. *"PythonDoc."* Go to the directory where your Python standard library modules are located. Examine each `.py` file and determine whether a `__doc__` string is available for that module. If so, format it properly and catalog it. When your program has completed, it should present a nice list of those modules that have documentation strings and what they are. There should be a trailing list showing which modules do not have documentation strings (the shame list). Extra credit: Extract documentation for all classes and functions within the standard library modules.

9–10. *Home Finances*. Create a home finance manager. Your solution should be able to manage savings, checking, money market, certificate of deposit (CD), and similar accounts. Provide a menu-based interface to each account as well as operations such as deposits, withdrawals, debits, and credits. An option should be given to a user to remove transactions as well. The data should be stored to file when the user quits the application (but randomly during execution for backup purposes).

9–11. *Web site Addresses*.

(a) Write a URL bookmark manager. Create a text-driven menu-based application that allows the user to add, update, or delete entries. Entries include a site name, Web site URL address, and perhaps a one-line description (optional). Allow search functionality so that a search "word" looks through both names and URLs for possible matches. Store the data to a disk file when the user quits the application, and load up the data when the user restarts.

(b) Upgrade your solution to part (a) by providing output of the bookmarks to a legible and syntactically correct HTML file (`.htm` or `.html`) so that users can then point their browsers to this output file and be presented with a list of their bookmarks. Another feature to implement is allowing the creation of "folders" to allow grouping of related bookmarks. Extra credit: Read the literature on regular expressions and the Python `re` module. Add regular expression validation of URLs that users enter into their databases.

9–12. *Users and Passwords.*

Do Exercise 7–5, which keeps track of usernames and passwords. Update your code to support a "last login time" (7–5a). See the documentation for the time module to obtain timestamps for when users "log in" to the system.

Also, create the concept of an "administrative" user that can dump a list of all the users, their passwords (you can add encryption on top of the passwords if you wish [7–5c]), and their last login times (7–5b).

(a) The data should be stored to disk, one line at a time, with fields delimited by colons (:), e.g., "`joe:boohoo: 953176591.145`", for each user. The number of lines in the file will be the number of users that are part of your system.

(b) Further update your example such that instead of writing out one line at a time, you pickle the entire data object and write that out instead. Read the documentation on the `pickle` module to find out how to flatten or serialize your object, as well as how to perform I/O using picked objects. With the addition of this new code, your solution should take up fewer lines than your solution in part (a).

(c) Replace your login database and explicit use of `pickle` by converting your code to use `shelve` files. Your resulting source file should actually take up fewer lines than your solution to part (b) because some of the maintenance work is gone.

9–13. *Command-Line Arguments.*

(a) What are they, and why might they be useful?

(b) Write code to display the command-line arguments which were entered.

9–14. *Logging Results.* Convert your calculator program (Exercise 5–6) to take input from the command line, i.e.,

```
$ calc.py 1 + 2
```

Output the result only. Also, write each expression and result to a disk file. Issuing a command of...

```
$ calc.py print
```

. . . will cause the entire contents of the "register tape" to be dumped to the screen and file reset/truncated. Here is an example session:

```
$ calc.py 1 + 2
3
```

```
$ calc.py 3 ^ 3
27
$ calc.py print
1 + 2
3
3 ^ 3
27
$ calc.py print
$
```

Extra credit: Also strip out comments that begin after the first character.

9–15. *Copying Files.* Prompt for two filenames (or better yet, use command-line arguments). The contents of the first file should be copied to the second file.

9–16. *Text Processing.* You are tired of seeing lines on your e-mail wrap because people type lines that are too long for your mail reader application. Create a program to scan a text file for all lines longer than 80 characters. For each of the offending lines, find the closest word before 80 characters and break the line there, inserting the remaining text to the next line (and pushing the previous next line down one). When you are done, there should be no lines longer than 80 characters.

9–17. *Text Processing.* Create a crude and elementary text file editor. Your solution is menu-driven, with the following options:
    (1) create file [prompt for filename and any number of lines of input],
    (2) display file [dump its contents to the screen],
    (3) edit file (prompt for line to edit and allow user to make changes),
    (4) save file, and
    (5) quit.

9–18. *Searching Files.* Obtain a byte value (0–255) and a filename. Display the number of times that byte appears in the file.

9–19. *Generating Files.* Create a sister program to the previous problem. Create a binary data file with random bytes, but one particular byte will appear in that file a set number of times. Obtain the following three values:
    (1) a byte value (0–255),
    (2) the number of times that byte should appear in the data file, and
    (3) the total number of bytes that make up the data file.
    Your job is to create that file, randomly scatter the requested byte across the file, ensure that there are no duplicates, the

file contains exactly the number of occurrences that byte was requested for, and that the resulting data file is exactly the size requested.

9–20. *Compressed Files*. Write a short piece of code that will compress and decompress gzipped or bzipped files. Confirm your solution works by using the command-line `gzip` or `bzip2` programs or a GUI program like PowerArchiver, StuffIt, and/or WinZip.

9–21. *ZIP Archive Files*. Create a program that can extract files from or add files to, and perhaps creating, a ZIP archive file.

9–22. *ZIP Archive Files*. The `unzip -l` command to dump the contents of ZIP archive is boring. Create a Python script called `lszip.py` that gives additional information such as: the compressed file size, the compressed percentage of each file (by comparing the original and compressed file sizes), and a full `time.ctime()` timestamp instead of the unzip output (of just the date and HH:MM). Hint: The `date_time` attribute of an archived file does not contain enough information to feed to `time.mktime()`... it is up to you!

9–23. *TAR Archive Files*. Repeat the previous problem for TAR archive files. One difference between these two types of files is that ZIP files are generally compressed, but TAR files are not and usually require the support of `gzip` or `bzip2`. Add either type of compression support. Extra credit: Support both `gzip` and `bzip2`.

9–24. *File Transfer Between Archive Files*. Take your solutions from the previous two problems and write a program that moves files between ZIP (`.zip`) and TAR/gzip (`.tgz`/`.tar.gz`) or TAR/bzip2 (`.tbz`/`.tar.bz2`) archive files. The files may preexist; create them if necessary.

9–25. *Universal Extractor*. Create an application that will take any number of files in an archived and/or compression format, i.e., .zip, .tgz, .tar.gz, .gz, .bz2, .tar.bz2, .tbz, and a target directory. The program will uncompress the standalone files to the target while all archived files will be extracted into subdirectories named the same as the archive file without the file extension. For example, if the target directory was `incoming`, and the input files were `header.txt.gz` and `data.tgz`, `header.txt` will be extracted to `incoming` while the files in `data.tgz` will be pulled out into `incoming/data`.

ERRORS AND EXCEPTIONS

Chapter Topics

- What Are Exceptions?
- Exceptions in Python
- Detecting and Handling Exceptions
- Context Management
- Raising Exceptions
- Assertions
- Standard Exceptions
- Creating Exceptions
- Why Exceptions?
- Related Modules

Chapter 10

Errors are an everyday occurrence in the life of a programmer. In days hopefully long since past, errors were either fatal to the program (or perhaps the machine) or produced garbage output that was not recognized as valid input by other computers or programs or by the humans who submitted the job to be run. Any time an error occurred, execution was halted until the error was corrected and code was re-executed. Over time, demand surged for a "softer" way of dealing with errors other than termination. Programs evolved such that not every error was malignant, and when they did happen, more diagnostic information was provided by either the compiler or the program during runtime to aid the programmer in solving the problem as quickly as possible. However, errors are errors, and any resolution usually took place after the program or compilation process was halted. There was never really anything a piece of code could do but exit and perhaps leave some crumbs hinting at a possible cause—until *exceptions* and *exception handling* came along.

Although we have yet to cover classes and object-oriented programming in Python, many of the concepts presented here involve classes and class instances.[1] We conclude the chapter with an optional section on how to create your own exception classes.

---

1. As of Python 1.5, all standard exceptions are implemented as classes. If new to classes, instances, and other object-oriented terminology, the reader should see Chapter 13 for clarification.

This chapter begins by exposing the reader to exceptions, exception handling, and how they are supported in Python. We also describe how programmers can generate exceptions within their code. Finally, we reveal how programmers can create their own exception classes.

10.1 What Are Exceptions?

10.1.1 Errors

Before we get into detail about what exceptions are, let us review what errors are. In the context of software, errors are either syntactical or logical in nature. Syntax errors indicate errors with the construct of the software and cannot be executed by the interpreter or compiled correctly. These errors must be repaired before execution can occur.

Once programs are semantically correct, the only errors that remain are logical. Logical errors can either be caused by lack of or invalid input, or, in other cases, by the inability of the logic to generate, calculate, or otherwise produce the desired results based on the input. These errors are sometimes known as domain and range failures, respectively.

When errors are detected by Python, the interpreter indicates that it has reached a point where continuing to execute in the current flow is no longer possible. This is where exceptions come into the picture.

10.1.2 Exceptions

Exceptions can best be described as action that is taken outside of the normal flow of control because of errors. This action comes in two distinct phases: The first is the error that causes an exception to occur, and the second is the detection (and possible resolution) phase.

The first phase takes place when an *exception condition* (sometimes referred to as *exceptional condition*) occurs. Upon detection of an error and recognition of the exception condition, the interpreter performs an operation called *raising* an exception. Raising is also known as triggering, throwing, or generating, and is the process whereby the interpreter makes it known to the current control flow that something is wrong. Python also supports the ability of the programmer to raise exceptions. Whether triggered by the Python interpreter or the programmer, exceptions signal that an error has occurred. The current flow of execution is interrupted to process this error and take appropriate action, which happens to be the second phase.

The second phase is where exception handling takes place. Once an exception is raised, a variety of actions can be invoked in response to that exception. These can range anywhere from ignoring the error, to logging the error but otherwise taking no action, performing some corrective measures and aborting the program, or alleviating the problem to allow for resumption of execution. Any of these actions represents a *continuation*, or an alternative branch of control. The key is that the programmer can dictate how the program operates when an error occurs.

As you may have already concluded, errors during runtime are primarily caused by external reasons, such as poor input, a failure of some sort, etc. These causes are not under the direct control of the programmer, who can anticipate only a few of the errors and code the most general remedies.

Languages like Python, which support the raising and—more importantly—the handling of exceptions, empower the developer by placing them in a more direct line of control when errors occur. The programmer not only has the ability to detect errors, but also to take more concrete and remedial actions when they occur. Due to the ability to manage errors during runtime, application robustness is increased.

Exceptions and exception handling are not new concepts. They are also present in Ada, Modula-3, C++, Eiffel, and Java. The origins of exceptions probably come from operating systems code that handles exceptions such as system errors and hardware interruptions. Exception handling as a software tool made its debut in the mid-1960s with PL/1 being the first major programming language that featured exceptions. Like some of the other languages supporting exception handling, Python is endowed with the concepts of a "try" block and "catching" exceptions and, in addition, provides for more "disciplined" handling of exceptions. By this we mean that you can create different handlers for different exceptions, as opposed to a general "catch-all" code where you may be able to detect the exception that occurred in a post-mortem fashion.

10.2 Exceptions in Python

As you were going through some of the examples in the previous chapters, you no doubt noticed what happens when your program "crashes" or terminates due to unresolved errors. A "traceback" notice appears along with a notice containing as much diagnostic information as the interpreter can give you, including the error name, reason, and perhaps even the line number near or exactly where the error occurred. All errors have a similar format, regardless of whether running within the Python interpreter or standard script execution, providing a consistent error interface. All errors, whether they be syntactical or logical, result from behavior incompatible with the Python interpreter and cause exceptions to be raised.

Let us take a look at some exceptions now.

NameError: *attempt to access an undeclared variable*

```
>>> foo
Traceback (innermost last):
  File "<stdin>", line 1, in ?
NameError: name 'foo' is not defined
```

NameError indicates access to an uninitialized variable. The offending identifier was not found in the Python interpreter's symbol table. We will be discussing *namespaces* in the next two chapters, but as an introduction, regard them as "address books" linking names to objects. Any object that is accessible should be listed in a namespace. Accessing a variable entails a search by the interpreter, and if the name requested is not found in any of the namespaces, a NameError exception will be generated.

ZeroDivisionError: *division by any numeric zero*

```
>>> 1/0
Traceback (innermost last):
  File "<stdin>", line 1, in ?
ZeroDivisionError: integer division or modulo by zero
```

Our example above used floats, but in general, any numeric division-by-zero will result in a ZeroDivisionError exception.

SyntaxError: *Python interpreter syntax error*

```
>>> for
  File "<string>", line 1
    for
       ^
SyntaxError: invalid syntax
```

SyntaxError exceptions are the only ones that do not occur at runtime. They indicate an improperly constructed piece of Python code which cannot execute until corrected. These errors are generated at compile-time, when the interpreter loads and attempts to convert your script to Python bytecode. These may also occur as a result of importing a faulty module.

IndexError: *request for an out-of-range index for sequence*

```
>>> aList = []
>>> aList[0]
Traceback (innermost last):
  File "<stdin>", line 1, in ?
IndexError: list index out of range
```

IndexError is raised when attempting to access an index that is outside the valid range of a sequence.

KeyError: *request for a non-existent dictionary key*

```
>>> aDict = {'host': 'earth', 'port': 80}
>>> print aDict['server']
Traceback (innermost last):
  File "<stdin>", line 1, in ?
KeyError: server
```

Mapping types such as dictionaries depend on keys to access data values. Such values are not retrieved if an incorrect/nonexistent key is requested. In this case, a KeyError is raised to indicate such an incident has occurred.

IOError: *input/output error*

```
>>> f = open("blah")
Traceback (innermost last):
  File "<stdin>", line 1, in ?
IOError: [Errno 2] No such file or directory: 'blah'
```

Attempting to open a nonexistent disk file is one example of an operating system input/output (I/O) error. Any type of I/O error raises an IOError exception.

AttributeError: *attempt to access an unknown object attribute*

```
>>> class myClass(object):
...         pass
...
>>> myInst = myClass()
>>> myInst.bar = 'spam'
>>> myInst.bar
'spam'
>>> myInst.foo
Traceback (innermost last):
  File "<stdin>", line 1, in ?
AttributeError: foo
```

In our example, we stored a value in `myInst.bar`, the `bar` attribute of instance `myInst`. Once an attribute has been defined, we can access it using the familiar dotted-attribute notation, but if it has not, as in our case with the `foo` (non-)attribute, an `AttributeError` occurs.

10.3   Detecting and Handling Exceptions

Exceptions can be detected by incorporating them as part of a **try** statement. Any code suite of a **try** statement will be monitored for exceptions.

There are two main forms of the **try** statement: **try-except** and **try-finally**. These statements are mutually exclusive, meaning that you pick only one of them. A **try** statement can be accompanied by one or more **except** clauses, exactly one **finally** clause, or a hybrid **try-except-finally** combination.

try-except statements allow one to detect and handle exceptions. There is even an optional **else** clause for situations where code needs to run only when no exceptions are detected. Meanwhile, **try-finally** statements allow only for detection and processing of any obligatory cleanup (whether or not exceptions occur), but otherwise have no facility in dealing with exceptions. The combination, as you might imagine, does both.

10.3.1   try-except *Statement*

The **try-except** statement (and more complicated versions of this statement) allows you to define a section of code to monitor for exceptions and also provides the mechanism to execute handlers for exceptions.

The syntax for the most general **try-except** statement is given below. It consists of the keywords along with the **try** and **except** blocks (*try_suite* and *except_suite*) as well as optionally saving the *reason* of failure:

```
try:
    try_suite        # watch for exceptions here
except Exception[, reason]:
    except_suite     # exception-handling code
```

Let us give one example, then explain how things work. We will use our `IOError` example from above. We can make our code more robust by adding a **try-except** "wrapper" around the code:

```
>>> try:
...     f = open('blah', 'r')
... except IOError, e:
...     print 'could not open file:', e
...
could not open file: [Errno 2] No such file or directory
```

As you can see, our code now runs seemingly without errors. In actuality, the same IOError still occurred when we attempted to open the nonexistent file. The difference? We added code to both detect and handle the error. When the IOError exception was raised, all we told the interpreter to do was to output a diagnostic message. The program continues and does not "bomb out" as our earlier example—a minor illustration of the power of exception handling. So what is really happening codewise?

During runtime, the interpreter attempts to execute all the code within the **try** statement. If an exception does not occur when the code block has completed, execution resumes past the **except** statement. When the specified exception named on the **except** statement does occur, we save the reason, and control flow immediately continues in the handler (all remaining code in the **try** clause is skipped) where we display our error message along with the cause of the error.

In our example above, we are catching only IOError exceptions. Any other exception will not be caught with the handler we specified. If, for example, you want to catch an OSError, you have to add a handler for that particular exception. We will elaborate on the **try-except** syntax more as we progress further in this chapter.

CORE NOTE: Skipping code, continuation, and upward propagation

The remaining code in the **try** *suite from the point of the exception is never reached (hence never executed). Once an exception is raised, the race is on to decide on the continuing flow of control. The remaining code is skipped, and the search for a handler begins. If one is found, the program continues in the handler.*

If the search is exhausted without finding an appropriate handler, the exception is then propagated to the caller's level for handling, meaning the stack frame immediately preceding the current one. If there is no handler at the next higher level, the exception is yet again propagated to its caller. If the top level is reached without an appropriate handler, the exception is considered unhandled, *and the Python interpreter will display the traceback and exit.*

10.3.2 Wrapping a Built-in Function

We will now present an interactive example—starting with the bare necessity of detecting an error, then building continuously on what we have to further improve the robustness of our code. The premise is in detecting errors while trying to convert a numeric string to a proper (numeric object) representation of its value.

The `float()` built-in function has a primary purpose of converting any numeric type to a float. In Python 1.5, `float()` was given the added feature of being able to convert a number given in string representation to an actual float value, obsoleting the use of the `atof()` function of the `string` module. Readers with older versions of Python may still use `string.atof()`, replacing `float()`, in the examples we use here.

```
>>> float(12345)
12345.0
>>> float('12345')
12345.0
>>> float('123.45e67')
1.2345e+069
```

Unfortunately, `float()` is not very forgiving when it comes to bad input:

```
>>> float('foo')
Traceback (innermost last):
  File "<stdin>", line 1, in ?
    float('foo')
ValueError: invalid literal for float(): foo
>>>
>>> float(['this is', 1, 'list'])
Traceback (innermost last):
  File "<stdin>", line 1, in ?
    float(['this is', 1, 'list'])
TypeError: float() argument must be a string or a number
```

Notice in the errors above that `float()` does not take too kindly to strings that do not represent numbers or non-strings. Specifically, if the correct argument type was given (string type) but that type contained an invalid value, the exception raised would be `ValueError` because it was the value that was improper, not the type. In contrast, a list is a bad argument altogether, not even being of the correct type; hence, `TypeError` was thrown.

Our exercise is to call `float()` "safely," or in a more "safe manner," meaning that we want to ignore error situations because they do not apply to our task of converting numeric string values to floating point numbers, yet are not severe enough errors that we feel the interpreter should abandon execution. To accomplish this, we will create a "wrapper" function, and, with the help of **try-except**, create the environment that we envisioned. We shall call it `safe_float()`. In our first iteration, we will scan and ignore only `ValueErrors`, because they are the more likely culprit.

`TypeErrors` rarely happen since somehow a non-string must be given to `float()`.

```
def safe_float(obj):
    try:
        return float(obj)
    except ValueError:
        pass
```

The first step we take is to just "stop the bleeding." In this case, we make the error go away by just "swallowing it." In other words, the error will be detected, but since we have nothing in the **except** suite (except the **pass** statement, which does nothing but serve as a syntactical placeholder for where code is supposed to go), no handling takes place. We just ignore the error.

One obvious problem with this solution is that we did not explicitly return anything to the function caller in the error situation. Even though None is returned (when a function does not return any value explicitly, i.e., completing execution without encountering a **return** *object* statement), we give little or no hint that anything wrong took place. The very least we should do is to explicitly return None so that our function returns a value in both cases and makes our code somewhat easier to understand:

```
def safe_float(obj):
    try:
        retval = float(obj)
    except ValueError:
        retval = None
    return retval
```

Bear in mind that with our change above, nothing about our code changed except that we used one more local variable. In designing a well-written application programmer interface (API), you may have kept the return value more flexible. Perhaps you documented that if a proper argument was passed to `safe_float()`, then indeed, a floating point number would be returned, but in the case of an error, you chose to return a string indicating the problem with the input value. We modify our code one more time to reflect this change:

```
def safe_float(obj):
    try:
        retval = float(obj)
    except ValueError:
        retval = 'could not convert non-number to float'
    return retval
```

The only thing we changed in the example was to return an error string as opposed to just `None`. We should take our function out for a test drive to see how well it works so far:

```
>>> safe_float('12.34')
12.34
>>> safe_float('bad input')
'could not convert non-number to float'
```

We made a good start—now we can detect invalid string input, but we are still vulnerable to invalid *objects* being passed in:

```
>>> safe_float({'a': 'Dict'})
Traceback (innermost last):
  File "<stdin>", line 3, in ?
    retval = float(obj)
TypeError: float() argument must be a string or a number
```

We will address this final shortcoming momentarily, but before we further modify our example, we would like to highlight the flexibility of the **try-except** syntax, especially the **except** statement, which comes in a few more flavors.

10.3.3 try *Statement with Multiple* **excepts**

Earlier in this chapter, we introduced the following general syntax for **except**:

```
except Exception[, reason]:
    suite_for_exception_Exception
```

The **except** statement in such formats specifically detects exceptions named *Exception*. You can chain multiple **except** statements together to handle different types of exceptions with the same **try**:

```
except Exception1[, reason1]:
    suite_for_exception_Exception1
except Exception2[, reason2]:
    suite_for_exception_Exception2
        :
```

This same **try** clause is attempted, and if there is no error, execution continues, passing all the **except** clauses. However, if an exception *does* occur, the interpreter will look through your list of handlers attempting to match the exception with one of your handlers (**except** clauses). If one is found, execution proceeds to *that* **except** suite.

Our `safe_float()` function has some brains now to detect specific exceptions. Even smarter code would handle each appropriately. To do that, we have to have separate **except** statements, one for each exception type. That is no problem as Python allows except statements can be chained together. We will now create separate messages for each error type, providing even more detail to the user as to the cause of his or her problem:

```
def safe_float(obj):
    try:
        retval = float(obj)
    except ValueError:
        retval = 'could not convert non-number to float'
    except TypeError:
        retval = 'object type cannot be converted to float'
    return retval
```

Running the code above with erroneous input, we get the following:

```
>>> safe_float('xyz')
'could not convert non-number to float'
>>> safe_float(())
'argument must be a string'
>>> safe_float(200L)
200.0
>>> safe_float(45.67000)
45.67
```

10.3.4 except *Statement with Multiple Exceptions*

We can also use the same **except** clause to handle multiple exceptions. **except** statements that process more than one exception require that the set of exceptions be contained in a tuple:

```
except (Exception1, Exception2)[, reason]:
    suite_for_Exception1_and_Exception2
```

The above syntax example illustrates how two exceptions can be handled by the same code. In general, any number of exceptions can follow an **except** statement as long as they are all properly enclosed in a tuple:

```
except (Exc1[, Exc2[, ... ExcN]])[, reason]:
    suite_for_exceptions_Exc1_to_ExcN
```

If for some reason, perhaps due to memory constraints or dictated as part of the design that all exceptions for our `safe_float()` function must be handled by the same code, we can now accommodate that requirement:

```
def safe_float(obj):
    try:
        retval = float(obj)
    except (ValueError, TypeError):
        retval = 'argument must be a number or numeric string'
    return retval
```

Now there is only the single error string returned on erroneous input:

```
>>> safe_float('Spanish Inquisition')
'argument must be a number or numeric string'
>>> safe_float([])
'argument must be a number or numeric string'
>>> safe_float('1.6')
1.6
>>> safe_float(1.6)
1.6
>>> safe_float(932)
932.0
```

10.3.5 Catching All Exceptions

Using the code we saw in the previous section, we are able to catch any number of specific exceptions and handle them. What about cases where we want to catch *all* exceptions? The short answer is yes, we can definitely do it. The code for doing it was significantly improved in 1.5 when exceptions became classes. Because of this, we now have an exception hierarchy to follow.

If we go all the way up the exception tree, we find `Exception` at the top, so our code will look like this:

```
try:
    :
except Exception, e:
    # error occurred, log 'e', etc.
```

Less preferred is the bare **except** clause:

```
try:
    :
except:
    # error occurred, etc.
```

This syntax is not as "Pythonic" as the other. Although this code catches the most exceptions, it does not promote good Python coding style. One of the chief reasons is that it does not take into account the potential root causes of problems that may generate exceptions. Rather than investigating and discovering what types of errors may occur and how they may be prevented from happening, we have a catch-all that may not do the right thing.

We are not naming any specific exceptions to catch—it does not give us any information about the possible errors that could happen in our `try` block. Another thing is that by catching all errors, you may be silently dropping important errors that really should be sent to the caller to properly take care of them. Finally, we do not have the opportunity to save the reason for the exception. Yes, you can get it through `sys.exc_ info()`, but then you would have to import `sys` and execute that function—both of which can be avoided, especially if all we wanted was the instance telling us why the exception occurred. It is a distinct possibility that the bare exception clause will be deprecated in a future release of Python. (See also Core Style note).

One aspect of catching all exceptions that you need to be aware of is that there are several exceptions that are not due to an error condition. These two exceptions are `SystemExit` and `KeyboardInterrupt`. `SystemExit` is for when the current Python application wants to quit, and `KeyboardInterrupt` is when a user presses CTRL-C (^C) to terminate Python. These will be caught by both code snippets above when we really want to pass them upward. A typical workaround code pattern will look like this:

```
try:
    :
except (KeyboardInterupt, SystemExit):
    # user wants to quit
    raise                   # reraise back to caller
except Exception:
    # handle real errors
```

A few things regarding exceptions did change in Python 2.5. Exceptions were moved to new-style classes, a new "mother of all exception" classes named `BaseException` was installed, and the exception hierarchy was switched around (very slightly) to get rid of that idiom of having to create two handlers. Both `KeyboardInterrupt` and `SystemExit` have been pulled out from being children of `Exception` to being its peers:

```
- BaseException
  |- KeyboardInterrupt
  |- SystemExit
  |- Exception

     |- (all other current built-in exceptions)
```

2.5

You can find the entire exception hierarchy (before and after these changes) in Table 10.2.

The end result is that now you do not have to write the extra handler for those two exceptions if you have a handler for just `Exception`. This code will suffice:

```
try:
    :
except Exception, e:
    # handle real errors
```

If you really want to catch all errors, you can still do that too, but use
BaseException instead:

```
try:
    :
except BaseException, e:
    # handle all errors
```

And of course, there is the less preferred bare **except**.

CORE STYLE: Do not handle and ignore all errors

The **try-except** statement has been included in Python to provide a
powerful mechanism for programmers to track down potential errors and
perhaps to provide logic within the code to handle situations where it may
not otherwise be possible, for example, in C. The main idea is to minimize
the number of errors and still maintain program correctness. As with all
tools, they must be used properly.

One incorrect use of **try-except** is to serve as a giant bandage over
large pieces of code. By that we mean putting large blocks, if not your entire
source code, within a **try** and/or have a large generic **except** to "filter"
any fatal errors by ignoring them:

```
# this is really bad code
try:
    large_block_of_code    # bandage of large piece of code
except Exception:          # same as except:
    pass                   # blind eye ignoring all errors
```

Obviously, errors cannot be avoided, and the job of **try-except** is to
provide a mechanism whereby an acceptable problem can be remedied or
properly dealt with, and not be used as a filter. The construct above will
hide many errors, but this type of usage promotes a poor engineering
practice that we certainly cannot endorse.

Bottom line: Avoid using **try-except** around a large block of code with a
pass just to hide errors. Instead, either handle specific exceptions and
ignore them (**pass**), or handle all errors and take a specific action. Do not
do both (handle all errors, ignore all errors).

10.3.6 "Exceptional Arguments"

No, the title of this section has nothing to do with having a major fight.
Instead, we are referring to the fact that an exception may have an *argument*

or *reason* passed along to the exception handler when they are raised. When an exception is raised, parameters are generally provided as an additional aid for the exception handler. Although reasons for exceptions are optional, the standard built-in exceptions do provide at least one argument, an error string indicating the cause of the exception.

Exception parameters can be ignored in the handler, but the Python provides syntax for saving this value. We have already seen it in the syntax above: to access any provided exception reason, you must reserve a variable to hold the argument. This argument is given on the **except** header line and follows the exception type you are handling. The different syntaxes for the **except** statement can be extended to the following:

```
# single exception
except Exception[, reason]:
    suite_for_Exception_with_Argument

# multiple exceptions
except (Exception1, Exception2, ..., ExceptionN)[, reason]:
    suite_for_Exception1_to_ExceptionN_with_Argument
```

reason is a class instance containing diagnostic information from the code raising the exception. The exception arguments themselves go into a tuple that is stored as an attribute of the class instance, an instance of the exception class from which it was instantiated. In the first alternate syntax above, *reason* is an instance of the `Exception` class.

For most standard built-in exceptions, that is, exceptions derived from `StandardError`, the tuple consists of a single string indicating the cause of the error. The actual exception name serves as a satisfactory clue, but the error string enhances the meaning even more. Operating system or other environment type errors, i.e., `IOError`, will also include an operating system error number that precedes the error string in the tuple.

Whether a *reason* contains just a string or a combination of an error number and a string, calling `str(reason)` should present a human-readable cause of an error. However, do not lose sight that *reason* is really a class instance—you are only getting the error information via that class's special method `__str__()`. We have a complete treatment of special methods as we explore object-oriented programming in Chapter 13.

The only caveat is that not all exceptions raised in third-party or otherwise external modules adhere to this standard protocol of error string or error number and error string. We recommend you follow such a standard when raising your own exceptions (see Core Style note).

CORE STYLE: Follow exception argument protocol

When you raise built-in exceptions in your own code, try to follow the protocol established by the existing Python code as far as the error information that is part of the tuple passed as the exception argument. In other words, if you raise a ValueError, *provide the same argument information as when the interpreter raises a* ValueError *exception, and so on. This helps keep the code consistent and will prevent other applications that use your module from breaking.*

The example below is when an invalid object is passed to the float() built-in function, resulting in a TypeError exception:

```
>>> try:
...     float(['float() does not', 'like lists', 2])
... except TypeError, diag:# capture diagnostic info
...     pass
...
>>> type(diag)
<class 'exceptions.TypeError'>
>>>
>>> print diag
float() argument must be a string or a number
```

The first thing we did was cause an exception to be raised from within the **try** statement. Then we passed cleanly through by ignoring but saving the error information. Calling the type() built-in function, we were able to confirm that our exception was indeed an instance of the TypeError exception class. Finally, we displayed the error by calling print with our diagnostic exception argument.

To obtain more information regarding the exception, we can use the special __class__ instance attribute, which identifies which class an instance was instantiated from. Class objects also have attributes, such as a documentation string and a string name that further illuminate the error type:

```
>>> diag                       # exception instance object
<exceptions.TypeError instance at 8121378>
>>> diag.__class__             # exception class object
<class exceptions.TypeError at 80f6d50>
>>> diag.__class__.__doc__     # exception class documentation string
'Inappropriate argument type.'
>>> diag.__class__.__name__    # exception class name
'TypeError'
```

As we will discover in Chapter 13—Classes and OOP—the special instance attribute __class__ exists for all class instances, and the __doc__ class attribute is available for all classes that define their documentation strings.

We will now update our safe_float() one more time to include the exception argument, which is passed from the interpreter from within float() when exceptions are generated. In our last modification to safe_float(), we merged both the handlers for the `ValueError` and `TypeError` exceptions into one because we had to satisfy some requirement. The problem, if any, with this solution is that no clue is given as to which exception was raised or what caused the error. The only thing returned is an error string that indicated some form of invalid argument. Now that we have the exception argument, this no longer has to be the case.

Because each exception will generate its own exception argument, if we chose to return this string rather than a generic one we made up, it would provide a better clue as to the source of the problem. In the following code snippet, we replace our single error string with the string representation of the exception argument.

```
def safe_float(object):
   try:
       retval = float(object)
   except (ValueError, TypeError), diag:
       retval = str(diag)
   return retval
```

Upon running our new code, we obtain the following (different) messages when providing improper input to `safe_float()`, even if both exceptions are managed by the same handler:

```
>>> safe_float('xyz')
'invalid literal for float(): xyz'
>>> safe_float({})
'object can't be converted to float'
```

10.3.7 Using Our Wrapped Function in an Application

We will now feature `safe_float()` in a mini application that takes a credit card transaction data file (`carddata.txt`) and reads in all transactions, including explanatory strings. Here are the contents of our example `carddata.txt` file:

```
% cat carddata.txt
# carddata.txt
previous balance
25
debits
21.64
541.24
25
credits
-25
-541.24
finance charge/late fees
7.30
5
```

Our program, `cardrun.py`, is given in Example 10.1.

Example 10.1 Credit Card Transactions (`cardrun.py`)

We use `safe_float()` to process a set of credit card transactions given in a file and read in as strings. A log file tracks the processing.

```python
1   #!/usr/bin/env python
2
3   def safe_float(obj):
4       'safe version of float()'
5       try:
6           retval = float(obj)
7       except (ValueError, TypeError), diag:
8           retval = str(diag)
9       return retval
10
11  def main():
12      'handles all the data processing'
13      log = open('cardlog.txt', 'w')
14      try:
15          ccfile = open('carddata.txt', 'r')
16      except IOError, e:
17          log.write('no txns this month\n')
18          log.close()
19          return
20
21      txns = ccfile.readlines()
22      ccfile.close()
23      total = 0.00
24      log.write('account log:\n')
25
26      for eachTxn in txns:
27          result = safe_float(eachTxn)
28          if isinstance(result, float):
29              total += result
30              log.write('data... processed\n')
31          else:
32              log.write('ignored: %s' % result)
33      print '$%.2f (new balance)' % (total)
34      log.close()
35
36  if __name__ == '__main__':
37      main()
```

Line-by-Line Explanation

Lines 3–9

This chunk of code contains the body of our `safe_float()` function.

Lines 11–34

The core part of our application performs three major tasks: (1) read the credit card data file, (2) process the input, and (3) display the result. Lines 14–22 perform the extraction of data from the file. You will notice that there is a **try-except** statement surrounding the file open.

A log file of the processing is also kept. In our example, we are assuming the log file can be opened for write without any problems. You will find that our progress is kept by the log. If the credit card data file cannot be accessed, we will assume there are no transactions for the month (lines 16–19).

The data are then read into the `txns` (transactions) list where it is iterated over in lines 26–32. After every call to `safe_float()`, we check the result type using the `isinstance()` built-in function. In our example, we check to see if `safe_float()` returns a string or float. Any string indicates an error situation with a string that could not be converted to a number, while all other values are floats that can be added to the running subtotal. The final new balance is then displayed as the final line of the `main()` function.

Lines 36–37

These lines represent the general "start only if not imported" functionality.

Upon running our program, we get the following output:

```
$ cardrun.py
$58.94 (new balance)
```

Taking a peek at the resulting log file (`cardlog.txt`), we see that it contains the following log entries after `cardrun.py` processed the transactions found in `carddata.txt`:

```
$ cat cardl og.txt
account log:
ignored: invalid literal for float(): # carddata.txt
ignored: invalid literal for float(): previous balance
data... processed
ignored: invalid literal for float(): debits
data... processed
data... processed
data... processed
ignored: invalid literal for float(): credits
data... processed
```

```
data... processed
ignored: invalid literal for float(): finance charge/
late fees
data... processed
data... processed
```

10.3.8 `else` Clause

We have seen the **else** statement with other Python constructs such as conditionals and loops. With respect to **try-except** statements, its functionality is not that much different from anything else you have seen: The **else** clause executes if no exceptions were detected in the preceding **try** suite.

All code within the **try** suite must have completed successfully (i.e., concluded with no exceptions raised) before any code in the **else** suite begins execution. Here is a short example in Python pseudocode:

```
import 3rd_party_module

log = open('logfile.txt', 'w')

try:
    3rd_party_module.function()
except:
    log.write("*** caught exception in module\n")
else:
    log.write("*** no exceptions caught\n")

log.close()
```

In the preceding example, we import an external module and test it for errors. A log file is used to determine whether there were defects in the third-party module code. Depending on whether an exception occurred during execution of the external function, we write differing messages to the log.

10.3.9 `finally` Clause

A **finally** clause is one where its suite or block of code is executed regardless of whether an exception occurred or whether it was caught (or not). You may use a **finally** clause with **try** by itself or with **try-except** (with or without an **else** clause). The standalone **try-finally** is covered in the next section, so we will just focus on the latter here.

Starting in Python 2.5, you can use the **finally** clause (again) with **try-except** or **try-except-else**. We say "again" because believe it or not, it is not a new feature. This was a feature available in Python back in the early days but was removed in Python 0.9.6 (April 1992). At the time, it helped simplify

2.5

the bytecode generation process and was easier to explain, and van Rossum believed that a unified **try-except(-else)-finally** would not be very popular anyway. How things change well over a decade later!

Here is what the syntax would look like with **try-except-else-finally**:

```
try:
    A
except MyException:
    B
else:
    C
finally:
    D
```

The equivalent in Python 0.9.6 through 2.4.x. is the longer:

```
try:
    try:
        A
    except MyException:
        B
    else:
        C
finally:
    D
```

Of course, in either case, you can have more than one **except** clause, however the syntax requires at least one except clause and both the **else** and **finally** clauses are optional. A, B, C, and D are suites (code blocks). The suites will execute in that order as necessary. (Note the only flows possible are A-C-D [normal] and A-B-D [exception].) The **finally** block will be executed whether exceptions occur in A, B, and/or C. Code written with the older idiom will continue to run, so there are no backward-compatibility problems.

10.3.10 try-finally *Statement*

An alternative is to use **finally** alone with **try**. The **try-finally** statement differs from its **try-except** brethren in that it is not used to handle exceptions. Instead it is used to maintain consistent behavior regardless of whether or not exceptions occur. We know that the **finally** suite executes regardless of an exception being triggered within the **try** suite.

```
try:
    try_suite
finally:
    finally_suite  # executes regardless
```

When an exception does occur within the **try** suite, execution jumps immediately to the **finally** suite. When all the code in the **finally** suite completes, the exception is reraised for handling at the next higher layer. Thus it is common to see a **try-finally** nested as part of a **try-except** suite.

One place where we can add a **try-finally** statement is by improving our code in cardrun.py so that we catch any problems that may arise from reading the data from the carddata.txt file. In the current code in Example 10.1, we do not detect errors during the read phase (using readlines()):

```
try:
    ccfile = open('carddata.txt')
except IOError:
    log.write('no txns this month\n')

txns = ccfile.readlines()
ccfile.close()
```

It is possible for readlines() to fail for any number of reasons, one of which is if carddata.txt was a file on the network (or a floppy) that became inaccessible. Regardless, we should improve this piece of code so that the entire input of data is enclosed in the **try** clause:

```
try:
    ccfile = open('carddata.txt', 'r')
    txns = ccfile.readlines()
    ccfile.close()
except IOError:
    log.write('no txns this month\n')
```

All we did was to move the readlines() and close() method calls to the try suite. Although our code is more robust now, there is still room for improvement. Notice what happens if there was an error of some sort. If the open succeeds, but for some reason the readlines() call does not, the exception will continue with the **except** clause. No attempt is made to close the file. Wouldn't it be nice if we closed the file regardless of whether an error occurred or not? We can make it a reality using **try-finally**:

```
try:
    try:
        ccfile = open('carddata.txt', 'r')
        txns = ccfile.readlines()
    except IOError:
        log.write('no txns this month\n')
finally:
    ccfile.close()
```

This code snippet will attempt to open the file and read in the data. If an error occurs during this step, it is logged, and then the file is properly closed. If no errors occur, the file is still closed. (The same functionality can be achieved using the unified **try-except-finally** statement above.) An alternative implementation involves switching the **try-except** and **try-finally** clauses:

```
try:
    try:
        ccfile = open('carddata.txt', 'r')
        txns = ccfile.readlines()
    finally:
        ccfile.close()
except IOError:
    log.write('no txns this month\n')
```

The code works virtually the same with some differences. The most obvious one is that the closing of the file happens before the exception handler writes out the error to the log. This is because **finally** automatically reraises the exception.

One argument for doing it this way is that if an exception happens within the **finally** block, you are able to create another handler at the same outer level as the one we have, so in essence, be able to handle errors in both the original **try** block as well as the **finally** block. The only thing you lose when you do this is that if the **finally** block does raise an exception, you have lost context of the original exception unless you have saved it somewhere.

An argument against having the **finally** inside the **except** is that in many cases, the exception handler needs to perform some cleanup tasks as well, and if you release those resources with a **finally** block that comes before the exception handler, you have lost the ability to do so. In other words, the **finally** block is not as "final" as one would think.

One final note: If the code in the **finally** suite raises another exception, or is aborted due to a **return**, **break**, or **continue** statement, the original exception is lost and cannot be reraised.

10.3.11 try-except-else-finally: *aka the Kitchen Sink*

We can combine all the varying syntaxes that we have seen so far in this chapter to highlight all the different ways you can handle exceptions:

```
try:
    try_suite

except Exception1:
    suite_for_Exception1

except (Exception2, Exception3, Exception4):
    suite_for_Exceptions_2_3_and_4

except Exception5, Argument5:
    suite_for_Exception5_plus_argument

except (Exception6, Exception7), Argument67:
    suite_for_Exceptions6_and_7_plus_argument

except:
    suite_for_all_other_exceptions

else:
    no_exceptions_detected_suite

finally:
    always_execute_suite
```

Recall from above that using a **finally** clause combined with **try-except** or **try-except-else** is "new" as of Python 2.5. The most important thing to take away from this section regarding the syntax is that you must have at least one **except** clause; both the **else** and **finally** clauses are optional.

10.4 Context Management

10.4.1 *with Statement*

The unification of **try-except** and **try-finally** as described above makes programs more "Pythonic," meaning, among many other characteristics, simpler to write and easier to read. Python already does a great job at hiding things under the covers so all you have to do is worry about how to solve the problem you have. (Can you imagine porting a complex Python application into C++ or Java?!?)

Another example of hiding lower layers of abstraction is the **with** statement, made official as of Python 2.6. (It was introduced in 2.5 as a preview and to serve warnings for those applications using with as an identifier that it will become a keyword in 2.6. To use this feature in 2.5, you must import it with **from** __future__ **import** with_statement.)

2.5-2.6

Like **try-except-finally**, the **with** statement, has a purpose of simplifying code that features the common idiom of using the **try-except** and **try-finally** pairs in tandem. The specific use that the **with** statement targets is when **try-except** and **try-finally** are used together in order to achieve the sole allocation of a shared resource for execution, then releasing it once the job is done. Examples include files (data, logs, database, etc.), threading resources and synchronization primitives, database connections, etc.

However, instead of just shortening the code and making it easier to use like **try-except-finally**, the **with** statement's goal is to remove the **try**, **except**, and **finally** keywords and the allocation and release code from the picture altogether. The basic syntax of the **with** statement looks like this:

```
with context_expr [as var]:
    with_suite
```

It looks quite simple, but making it work requires some work under the covers. The reason is it not as simple as it looks is because you cannot use the **with** statement merely with any expression in Python. It only works with objects that support what is called the *context management protocol*. This simply means that only objects that are built with "context management" can be used with a **with** statement. We will describe what that means soon.

Now, like any new video game hardware, when this feature was released, some folks out there took the time to develop new games for it so that you can play when you open the box. Similarly, there were already some Python objects that support the protocol. Here is a short list of the first set:

- `file`
- `decimal.Context`
- `thread.LockType`
- `threading.Lock`
- `threading.RLock`
- `threading.Condition`
- `threading.Semaphore`
- `threading.BoundedSemaphore`

Since files are first on the list and the simplest example, here is a code snippet of what it looks like to use a **with** statement:

```
with open('/etc/passwd', 'r') as f:
    for eachLine in f:
        # ...do stuff with eachLine or f...
```

What this code snippet will do is... well, this *is* Python, so you can probably already guess. It will do some preliminary work, such as attempt to open the file, and if all goes well, assign the file object to f. Then it iterates over each line in the file and does whatever processing you need to do. Once the file has been exhausted, it is closed. If an exception occurs either at the beginning, middle, or end of the block, then some cleanup code must be done, but the file will still be closed automatically.

Now, because a lot of the details have been pushed down and away from you, there are really two levels of processing that need to occur: First, the stuff at the user level—as in, the things you need to take care of as the user of the object—and second, at the object level. Since this object supports the context management protocol, it has to do some "context management."

10.4.2 *Context Management Protocol

Unless you will be designing objects for users of the **with** statement, i.e., programmers who will be using your objects to design their applications with, most Python programmers are going to be just users of the **with** statement and can skip this optional section.

We are not going into a full and deep discussion about context management here, but we will explain the types of objects and the functionality that are necessary to be protocol-compliant and thus be eligible to be used with the **with** statement.

Previously, we described a little of how the protocol works in our example with the file object. Let us elaborate some more here.

Context Expression (*context_expr*), Context Manager

When the **with** statement is executed, the context expression is evaluated to obtain what is called a *context manager*. The job of the context manager is to provide a *context object*. It does this by invoking its required __context__() special method. The return value of this method is the context object that will be used for this particular execution of the with_suite. One side note is that a context object itself can be its own manager, so *context_expr* can really be either a real context manager or a context object serving as its own manager. In the latter case, the context object also has a __context__() method, which returns self, as expected.

Context Object, *with_suite*

Once we have a context object, its __enter__() special method is invoked.
This does all the preliminary stuff before the *with_suite* executes. You will
notice in the syntax above that there is an optional **as** *var* piece following
context_expr on the **with** statement line. If *var* is provided, it is assigned
the return value of __enter__(). If not, the return value is thrown away. So
for our file object example, its context object's __enter__() returns the file
object so it can be assigned to f.

Now the *with_suite* executes. When execution of *with_suite* terminates, whether "naturally" or via exception, the context object's __exit__()
special method is called. __exit__() takes three arguments. If *with_suite*
terminates normally, all three parameters passed in are None. If an exception
occurred, then the three arguments are the same three values returned when
calling the sys.exc_info() function (see section 10.12): type (exception
class), value (this exception's instance), and traceback, the corresponding
traceback object.

It is up to you to decide how you want to handle the exception here in
__exit__(). The usual thing to do after you are done is not to return any-
thing from __exit__() or return None or some other Boolean False
object. This will cause the exception to be reraised back to your user for handling. If you want to explicitly silence the exception, then return any object
that has a Boolean True value. If an exception did not occur or you returned
True after handling an exception, the program will continue on the next
statement after the **with** clause.

Since context management makes the most sense for shared resources,
you can imagine that the __enter__() and __exit__() methods will
primarily be used for doing the lower-level work required to allocate and
release resources, i.e., database connections, lock allocation, semaphore
decrement, state management, opening/closing of files, exception handling, etc.

To help you with writing context managers for objects, there is the contextlib module, which contains useful functions/decorators with which
you can apply over your functions or objects and not have to worry about
implementing a class or separate __context__(), __enter__(),
__exit__() special methods.

For more information or more examples of context management,
check out the official Python documentation on the **with** statement and
contextlib module, class special methods (related to **with** and contexts),
PEP 343, and the "What's New in Python 2.5" document.

10.5 *Exceptions as Strings

Prior to Python 1.5, standard exceptions were implemented as strings. However, this became limiting in that it did not allow for exceptions to have relationships to each other. With the advent of exception classes, this is no longer the case. As of 1.5, all standard exceptions are now classes. It is still possible for programmers to generate their own exceptions as strings, but we recommend using exception classes from now on.

For backward compatibility, it is possible to revert to string-based exceptions. Starting the Python interpreter with the command-line option -X will provide you with the standard exceptions as strings. This feature will be obsolete beginning with Python 1.6.

2.5-2.6 Python 2.5 begins the process of deprecating string exceptions from Python forever. In 2.5, raise of string exceptions generates a warning. In 2.6, the catching of string exceptions results in a warning. Since they are rarely used and are being deprecated, we will no longer consider string exceptions within the scope of this book and have removed it. (You may find the original text in prior editions of this book.) The only point of relevance and the final thought is a caution: You may use an external or third-party module, which may still have string exceptions. String exceptions are a bad idea anyway. One reader vividly recalls seeing Linux RPM exceptions with spelling errors in the exception text.

10.6 Raising Exceptions

The interpreter was responsible for raising all of the exceptions we have seen so far. These exist as a result of encountering an error during execution. A programmer writing an API may also wish to throw an exception on erroneous input, for example, so Python provides a mechanism for the programmer to explicitly generate an exception: the **raise** statement.

10.6.1 raise *Statement*

Syntax and Common Usage

The **raise** statement is quite flexible with the arguments it supports, translating to a large number of different formats supported syntactically. The general syntax for **raise** is:

```
raise [SomeException [, args [, traceback]]]
```

The first argument, *SomeException*, is the name of the exception to raise. If present, it must either be a string, class, or instance (more below). *SomeException* must be given if any of the other arguments (*args* or *traceback*) are present. A list of all Python standard exceptions is given in Table 10.2.

The second expression contains optional `args` (aka parameters, values) for the exception. This value is either a single object or a tuple of objects. When exceptions are detected, the exception arguments are always returned as a tuple. If `args` is a tuple, then that tuple represents the same set of exception arguments that are given to the handler. If `args` is a single object, then the tuple will consist solely of this one object (i.e., a tuple with one element). In most cases, the single argument consists of a string indicating the cause of the error. When a tuple is given, it usually equates to an error string, an error number, and perhaps an error location, such as a file, etc.

The final argument, `traceback`, is also optional (and rarely used in practice), and, if present, is the traceback object used for the exception—normally a traceback object is newly created when an exception is raised. This third argument is useful if you want to reraise an exception (perhaps to point to the previous location from the current). Arguments that are absent are represented by the value `None`.

The most common syntax used is when *SomeException* is a class. No additional parameters are ever required, but in this case, if they are given, they can be a single object argument, a tuple of arguments, or an exception class instance. If the argument is an instance, then it can be an instance of the given class or a derived class (subclassed from a pre-existing exception class). No additional arguments (i.e., exception arguments) are permitted if the argument is an instance.

More Exotic/Less Common Usage

What happens if the argument is an instance? No problems arise if `instance` is an instance of the given exception class. However, if `instance` is *not* an instance of the class or an instance of a subclass of the class, then a new instance of the exception class will be created with exception arguments copied from the given instance. If `instance` is an instance of a subclass of the exception class, then the new exception will be instantiated from the subclass, not the original exception class.

If the additional parameter to the **raise** statement used with an exception class is not an instance—instead, it is a singleton or tuple—then the class is instantiated and `args` is used as the argument list to the exception. If the second parameter is not present or `None`, then the argument list is empty.

If *SomeException* is an instance, then we do not need to instantiate anything. In this case, additional parameters must not be given or must be `None`.

The exception type is the class that instance belongs to; in other words, this is equivalent to raising the class with this instance, i.e., **raise** instance.__class__, instance.

Use of string exceptions is deprecated in favor of exception classes, but if SomeException is a string, then it raises the exception identified by string, with any optional parameters (args) as arguments.

Finally, the **raise** statement by itself *without any parameters* is a new construct, introduced in Python 1.5, and causes the last exception raised in the current code block to be reraised. If no exception was previously raised, a TypeError exception will occur, because there was no previous exception to reraise.

Due to the many different valid syntax formats for **raise** (i.e., SomeException can be either a class, instance, or a string), we provide Table 10.1 to illuminate all the different ways which **raise** can be used.

Table 10.1 Using the **raise** Statement

raise *syntax*	*Description*
raise exclass	Raise an exception, creating an instance of exclass (without any exception arguments)
raise exclass()	Same as above since classes are now exceptions; invoking the class name with the function call operator instantiates an instance of exclass, also with no arguments
raise exclass, args	Same as above, but also providing exception arguments args, which can be a single argument or a tuple
raise exclass(args)	Same as above
raise exclass, args, tb	Same as above, but provides traceback object tb to use
raise exclass, instance	Raise exception using instance (normally an instance of exclass); if instance is an instance of a *subclass* of exclass, then the new exception will be of the subclass type (not of exclass); if instance is *not* an instance of exclass *or* an instance of a *subclass* of exclass, then a new instance of exclass will be created with exception arguments copied from instance

Table 10.1 Using the **raise** Statement (continued)	

raise *syntax*	*Description*
raise *instance*	Raise exception using `instance`: the exception type is the class that instantiated `instance`; equivalent to **raise** `instance.__class__`, `instance` (same as above)
raise *string*	(*Archaic*) Raises `string` exception
raise *string, args*	Same as above, but raises exception with `args`
raise *string, args, tb*	Same as above, but provides traceback object `tb` to use
raise	(*New in 1.5*) Reraises previously raised exception; if no exception was previously raised, a `TypeError` is raised

10.7 Assertions

Assertions are diagnostic predicates that must evaluate to Boolean `True`; otherwise, an exception is raised to indicate that the expression is false. These work similarly to the assert macros, which are part of the C language preprocessor, but in Python these are runtime constructs (as opposed to precompile directives).

If you are new to the concept of assertions, no problem. The easiest way to think of an assertion is to liken it to a **raise-if** statement (or to be more accurate, a **raise-if-not** statement). An expression is tested, and if the result comes up false, an exception is raised.

Assertions are carried out by the **assert** statement, introduced back in version 1.5.

10.7.1 assert Statement

The **assert** statement evaluates a Python expression, taking no action if the assertion succeeds (similar to a **pass** statement), but otherwise raising an `AssertionError` exception. The syntax for **assert** is:

```
assert expression[, arguments]
```

Here are some examples of the use of the **assert** statement:

```
assert 1 == 1
assert 2 + 2 == 2 * 2
assert len(['my list', 12]) < 10
assert range(3) == [0, 1, 2]
```

AssertionError exceptions can be caught and handled like any other exception using the **try-except** statement, but if not handled, they will terminate the program and produce a traceback similar to the following:

```
>>> assert 1 == 0
Traceback (innermost last):
  File "<stdin>", line 1, in ?
AssertionError
```

As with the **raise** statement we investigated in the previous section, we can provide an exception argument to our **assert** command:

```
>>> assert 1 == 0, 'One does not equal zero silly!'
Traceback (innermost last):
  File "<stdin>", line 1, in ?
AssertionError: One does not equal zero silly!
```

Here is how we would use a **try-except** statement to catch an AssertionError exception:

```
try:
    assert 1 == 0, 'One does not equal zero silly!'
except AssertionError, args:
    print '%s: %s' % (args.__class__.__name__, args)
```

Executing the above code from the command line would result in the following output:

```
AssertionError: One does not equal zero silly!
```

To give you a better idea of how **assert** works, imagine how the **assert** statement may be implemented in Python if written as a function. It would probably look something like this:

```
def assert(expr, args=None):
    if __debug__ and not expr:
        raise AssertionError, args
```

The first **if** statement confirms the appropriate syntax for the assert, meaning that expr should be an expression. We compare the type of expr to a real expression to verify. The second part of the function evaluates the expression and raises AssertionError, if necessary. The built-in variable __debug__ is 1 under normal circumstances, 0 when optimization is requested (command-line option -O).

10.8 Standard Exceptions

Table 10.2 lists all of Python's current set of standard exceptions. All exceptions are loaded into the interpreter as built-ins so they are ready before your script starts or by the time you receive the interpreter prompt, if running interactively.

Table 10.2 Python Built-In Exceptions

Exception Name	*Description*
BaseException[a]	Root class for all exceptions
SystemExit[b]	Request termination of Python interpreter
KeyboardInterrupt[c]	User interrupted execution (usually by typing ^C)
Exception[d]	Root class for regular exceptions
StopIteration[e]	Iteration has no further values
GeneratorExit[a]	Exception sent to generator to tell it to quit
SystemExit[h]	Request termination of Python interpreter
StandardError[g]	Base class for all standard built-in exceptions
ArithmeticError[d]	Base class for all numeric calculation errors
FloatingPointError[d]	Error in floating point calculation
OverflowError	Calculation exceeded maximum limit for numerical type
ZeroDivisionError	Division (or modulus) by zero error (all numeric types)
AssertionError[d]	Failure of **assert** statement
AttributeError	No such object attribute

(continued)

Table 10.2 Python Built-In Exceptions (continued)

Exception Name	Description
EOFError	End-of-file marker reached without input from built-in
EnvironmentError[d]	Base class for operating system environment errors
IOError	Failure of input/output operation
OSError[d]	Operating system error
WindowsError[h]	MS Windows system call failure
ImportError	Failure to import module or object
KeyboardInterrupt[f]	User interrupted execution (usually by typing ^C)
LookupError[d]	Base class for invalid data lookup errors
IndexError	No such index in sequence
KeyError	No such key in mapping
MemoryError	Out-of-memory error (non-fatal to Python interpreter)
NameError	Undeclared/uninitialized object (non-attribute)
UnboundLocalError[h]	Access of an uninitialized local variable
ReferenceError[e]	Weak reference tried to access a garbage-collected object
RuntimeError	Generic default error during execution
NotImplementedError[d]	Unimplemented method
SyntaxError	Error in Python syntax
IndentationError[g]	Improper indentation
TabError[g]	Improper mixture of tabs and spaces
SystemError	Generic interpreter system error

Table 10.2 Python Built-In Exceptions (continued)

Exception Name	Description
TypeError	Invalid operation for type
ValueError	Invalid argument given
UnicodeError[h]	Unicode-related error
UnicodeDecodeError[i]	Unicode error during decoding
UnicodeEncodeError[i]	Unicode error during encoding
UnicodeTranslateError[f]	Unicode error during translation
Warning[j]	Root class for all warnings
DeprecationWarning[j]	Warning about deprecated features
FutureWarning[i]	Warning about constructs that will change semantically in the future
OverflowWarning[k]	Old warning for auto-long upgrade
PendingDeprecation Warning[i]	Warning about features that will be deprecated in the future
RuntimeWarning[j]	Warning about dubious runtime behavior
SyntaxWarning[j]	Warning about dubious syntax
UserWarning[j]	Warning generated by user code

a. New in Python 2.5.
b. Prior to Python 2.5, SystemExit subclassed Exception.
c. Prior to Python 2.5, KeyboardInterrupt subclassed StandardError.
d. New in Python 1.5, when class-based exceptions replaced strings.
e. New in Python 2.2.
f. New in Python 1.6.
g. New in Python 2.0.
h. New in Python 1.6.
i. New in Python 2.3.
j. New in Python 2.1.
k. New in Python 2.2 but removed in Python 2.4.

All standard/built-in exceptions are derived from the root class `BaseException`. There are currently three immediate subclasses of `BaseException`: `SystemExit`, `KeyboardInterrupt`, and `Exception`. All other built-in exceptions are subclasses of `Exceptions`. Every level of indentation of an exception listed in Table 10.2 indicates one level of exception class derivation.

2.5-2.9 As of Python 2.5, all exceptions are new-style classes and are ultimately subclassed from `BaseException`. At this release, `SystemExit` and `KeyboardInterrupt` were taken out of the hierarchy for `Exception` and moved up to being under `BaseException`. This is to allow statements like **except** `Exception` to catch all errors and not program exit conditions.

From Python 1.5 through Python 2.4.x, exceptions were classic classes, and prior to that, they were strings. String-based exceptions are no longer acceptable constructs and are officially deprecated beginning with 2.5, where you will not be able to *raise* string exceptions. In 2.6, you cannot *catch* them.

There is also a requirement that all new exceptions be ultimately subclassed from `BaseException` so that all exceptions will have a common interface. This will transition will begin with Python 2.7 and continue through the remainder of the 2.x releases.

10.9 *Creating Exceptions

Although the set of standard exceptions is fairly wide-ranging, it may be advantageous to create your own exceptions. One situation is where you would like additional information from what a standard or module-specific exception provides. We will present two examples, both related to `IOError`.

`IOError` is a generic exception used for input/output problems, which may arise from invalid file access or other forms of communication. Suppose we wanted to be more specific in terms of identifying the source of the problem. For example, for file errors, we want to have a `FileError` exception that behaves like `IOError`, but with a name that has more meaning when performing file operations.

Another exception we will look at is related to network programming with sockets. The exception generated by the `socket` module is called `socket.error` and is not a built-in exception. It is subclassed from the generic `Exception` exception. However, the exception arguments from `socket.error` closely resemble those of `IOError` exceptions, so we are going to define a new exception called `NetworkError`, which subclasses from `IOError` but contains at least the information provided by `socket.error`.

Like classes and object-oriented programming, we have not formally covered network programming at this stage, but skip ahead to Chapter 16 if you need to.

We now present a module called myexc.py with our newly customized exceptions FileError and NetworkError. The code is in Example 10.2.

Example 10.2 Creating Exceptions (myexc.py)

This module defines two new exceptions, FileError and NetworkError, as well as reimplements more diagnostic versions of open() [myopen()] and socket.connect() [myconnect()]. Also included is a test function [test()] that is run if this module is executed directly.

```
1   #!/usr/bin/env python
2
3   import os, socket, errno, types, tempfile
4
5   class NetworkError(IOError):
6       pass
7
8   class FileError(IOError):
9       pass
10
11  def updArgs(args, newarg=None):
12      if isinstance(args, IOError):
13          myargs = []
14          myargs.extend([arg for arg in args])
15      else:
16          myargs = list(args)
17
18      if newarg:
19          myargs.append(newarg)
20
21      return tuple(myargs)
22
23  def fileArgs(file, mode, args):
24      if args[0] == errno.EACCES and \
25              'access' in dir(os):
26          perms = ''
27          permd = { 'r': os.R_OK, 'w': os.W_OK,
28              'x': os.X_OK}
29          pkeys = permd.keys()
30          pkeys.sort()
31          pkeys.reverse()
32
```

(continued)

Example 10.2 Creating Exceptions (`myexc.py`) (continued)

```
33              for eachPerm in 'rwx':
34                  if os.access(file, permd[eachPerm]):
35                      perms += eachPerm
36                  else:
37                      perms += '-'
38
39          if isinstance(args, IOError):
40              myargs = []
41              myargs.extend([arg for arg in args])
42          else:
43              myargs = list(args)
44
45          myargs[1] = "'%s' %s (perms: '%s')" % \
46              (mode, myargs[1], perms)
47
48          myargs.append(args.filename)
49
50      else:
51          myargs = args
52
53      return tuple(myargs)
54
55  def myconnect(sock, host, port):
56      try:
57          sock.connect((host, port))
58
59      except socket.error, args:
60          myargs = updArgs(args)     # conv inst2tuple
61          if len(myargs) == 1:       # no #s on some errs
62              myargs = (errno.ENXIO, myargs[0])
63
64          raise NetworkError, \
65              updArgs(myargs, host + ':' + str(port))
66
67  def myopen(file, mode='r'):
68      try:
69          fo = open(file, mode)
70      except IOError, args:
71          raise FileError, fileArgs(file, mode, args)
72
73      return fo
74
75  def testfile():
76
77      file = mktemp()
78      f = open(file, 'w')
79      f.close()
80
```

Example 10.2 Creating Exceptions (`myexc.py`) (continued)

```
81          for eachTest in ((0, 'r'), (0100, 'r'),
82                  (0400, 'w'), (0500, 'w')):
83              try:
84                  os.chmod(file, eachTest[0])
85                  f = myopen(file, eachTest[1])
86
87              except FileError, args:
88                  print "%s: %s" % \
89                      (args.__class__.__name__, args)
90              else:
91                  print file, "opened ok... perm ignored"
92                  f.close()
93
94          os.chmod(file, 0777)# enable all perms
95          os.unlink(file)
96
97  def testnet():
98      s = socket.socket(socket.AF_INET,
99          socket.SOCK_STREAM)
100
101      for eachHost in ('deli', 'www'):
102          try:
103              myconnect(s, 'deli', 8080)
104          except NetworkError, args:
105              print "%s: %s" % \
106                  (args.__class__.__name__, args)
107
108  if __name__ == '__main__':
109      testfile()
110      testnet()
```

Lines 1–3

The Unix startup script and importation of the `socket`, `os`, `errno`, `types`, and `tempfile` modules help us start this module.

Lines 5–9

Believe it or not, these five lines make up our new exceptions. Not just one, but both of them. Unless new functionality is going to be introduced, creating a new exception is just a matter of subclassing from an already existing exception. In our case, that would be `IOError`. `EnvironmentError`, from which `IOError` is derived, would also work, but we wanted to convey that our exceptions were definitely I/O-related.

We chose `IOError` because it provides two arguments, an error number and an error string. File-related [uses `open()`] `IOError` exceptions even support a third argument that is not part of the main set of exception arguments, and that would be the filename. Special handling is done for this third argument, which lives outside the main tuple pair and has the name `filename`.

Lines 11–21

The entire purpose of the `updArgs()` function is to "update" the exception arguments. What we mean here is that the original exception is going to provide us a set of arguments. We want to take these arguments and make them part of our new exception, perhaps embellishing or adding a third argument (which is not added if nothing is given—`None` is a default argument, which we will study in the next chapter). Our goal is to provide the more informative details to the user so that if and when errors occur, the problems can be tracked down as quickly as possible.

Lines 23–53

The `fileArgs()` function is used only by `myopen()` (see below). In particular, we are seeking error `EACCES`, which represents "permission denied." We pass all other `IOError` exceptions along without modification (lines 54–55). If you are curious about `ENXIO`, `EACCES`, and other system error numbers, you can hunt them down by starting at file `/usr/include/sys/errno.h` on a Unix system, or `C:\Msdev\include\Errno.h` if you are using Visual C++ on Windows.

In line 27, we are also checking to make sure that the machine we are using supports the `os.access()` function, which helps you check what kind of file permissions you have for any particular file. We do not proceed unless we receive both a permission error as well as the ability to check what kind of permissions we have. If all checks out, we set up a dictionary to help us build a string indicating the permissions we have on our file.

The Unix file system uses explicit file permissions for the user, group (more than one user can belong to a group), and other (any user other than the owner or someone in the same group as the owner) in read, write, and execute ('r', 'w', 'x') order. Windows supports some of these permissions.

Now it is time to build the permission string. If the file has a permission, its corresponding letter shows up in the string, otherwise a dash (-) appears. For example, a string of "rw-" means that you have read and write access to it. If the string reads "r-x", you have only read and execute access; "---" means no permission at all.

After the permission string has been constructed, we create a temporary argument list. We then alter the error string to contain the permission string, something that standard `IOError` exception does not provide. "Permission denied" sometimes seems silly if the system does not tell you what permissions you have to correct the problem. The reason, of course, is security. When intruders do not have permission to access something, the last thing you want them to see is what the file permissions are, hence the dilemma. However, our example here is merely an exercise, so we allow for the temporary "breach of security." The point is to verify whether or not the `os.chmod()` functions call affected file permissions the way they are supposed to.

The final thing we do is to add the filename to our argument list and return the set of arguments as a tuple.

Lines 55–65

Our new `myconnect()` function simply wraps the standard socket method `connect()` to provide an `IOError`-type exception if the network connection fails. Unlike the general `socket.error` exception, we also provide the hostname and port number as an added value to the programmer.

For those new to network programming, a hostname and port number pair are analogous to an area code and telephone number when you are trying to contact someone. In this case, we are trying to contact a program running on the remote host, presumably a server of some sort; therefore, we require the host's name and the port number that the server is listening on.

When a failure occurs, the error number and error string are quite helpful, but it would be even more helpful to have the exact host-port combination as well, since this pair may be dynamically generated or retrieved from some database or name service. That is the value-add we are bestowing on our version of `connect()`. Another issue arises when a host cannot be found. There is no direct error number given to us by the `socket.error` exception, so to make it conform to the `IOError` protocol of providing an error number-error string pair, we find the closest error number that matches. We choose `ENXIO`.

Lines 67–73

Like its sibling `myconnect()`, `myopen()` also wraps around an existing piece of code. Here, we have the `open()` function. Our handler catches only `IOError` exceptions. All others will pass through and on up to the next level (when no handler is found for them). Once an `IOError` is caught, we raise our own error and customized arguments as returned from `fileArgs()`.

Lines 75–95

We shall perform the file testing first, here using the `testfile()` function. In order to begin, we need to create a test file that we can manipulate by changing its permissions to generate permission errors. The `tempfile` module contains code to create temporary file names or temporary files themselves. We just need the name for now and use our new `myopen()` function to create an empty file. Note that if an error occurred here, there would be no handler, and our program would terminate fatally—the test program should not continue if we cannot even *create* a test file.

Our test uses four different permission configurations. A zero means no permissions at all, 0100 means execute-only, 0400 indicates read-only, and 0500 means read- and execute-only (0400 + 0100). In all cases, we will attempt to open a file with an invalid mode. The `os.chmod()` function is responsible for updating a file's permission modes. (Note: These permissions all have a leading zero in front, indicating that they are octal [base 8] numbers.)

If an error occurs, we want to display diagnostic information similar to the way the Python interpreter performs the same task when uncaught exceptions occur, and that is giving the exception name followed by its arguments. The `__class__` special variable represents the class object from which an instance was created. Rather than displaying the entire class name here (`myexc.FileError`), we use the class object's `__name__` variable to just display the class name (`FileError`), which is also what you see from the interpreter in an unhandled error situation. Then the arguments that we arduously put together in our wrapper functions follow.

If the file opened successfully, that means the permissions were ignored for some reason. We indicate this with a diagnostic message and close the file. Once all tests have been completed, we enable all permissions for the file and remove it with the `os.unlink()` function. (`os.remove()` is equivalent to `os.unlink()`.)

Lines 97–106

The next section of code (`testnet()`) tests our `NetworkError` exception. A socket is a communication endpoint with which to establish contact with another host. We create such an object, then use it in an attempt to connect to a host with no server to accept our connect request and a host not on our network.

Lines 108–110

We want to execute our `test*()` functions only when invoking this script directly, and that is what the code here does. Most of the scripts given in this text utilize the same format.

Running this script on a Unix-flavored box, we get the following output:

```
$myexc.py
FileError: [Errno 13] 'r' Permission denied (perms: '---'):
 '/usr/tmp/@18908.1'
FileError: [Errno 13] 'r' Permission denied (perms: '--x'):
 '/usr/tmp/@18908.1'
FileError: [Errno 13] 'w' Permission denied (perms: 'r--'):
 '/usr/tmp/@18908.1'
FileError: [Errno 13] 'w' Permission denied (perms: 'r-x'):
 '/usr/tmp/@18908.1'
NetworkError: [Errno 146] Connection refused: 'deli:8080'
NetworkError: [Errno 6] host not found: 'www:8080'
```

The results are slightly different on a Win32 machine:

```
D:\python> python myexc.py
C:\WINDOWS\TEMP\~-195619-1 opened ok... perms ignored
C:\WINDOWS\TEMP\~-195619-1 opened ok... perms ignored
FileError: [Errno 13] 'w' Permission denied (perms: 'r-x'):
 'C:\\WINDOWS\\TEMP\\~-195619-1'
FileError: [Errno 13] 'w' Permission denied (perms: 'r-x'):
 'C:\\WINDOWS\\TEMP\\~-195619-1'
NetworkError: [Errno 10061] winsock error: 'deli:8080'
NetworkError: [Errno 6] host not found: 'www:8080'
```

You will notice that Windows does not support read permissions on files, which is the reason why the first two file open attempts succeeded. Your mileage may vary (YMMV) on your own machine and operating system.

10.10 Why Exceptions (Now)?

There is no doubt that errors will be around as long as software is around. The difference in today's fast-paced computing world is that our execution environments have changed, and so has our need to adapt error-handling to accurately reflect the operating context of the software that we develop. Modern-day applications generally run as self-contained graphical user interfaces (GUIs) or in a client/server architecture such as the Web.

The ability to handle errors at the application level has become even more important recently in that users are no longer the only ones directly running applications. As the Internet and online electronic commerce become more pervasive, Web servers will be the primary users of application software. This means that applications cannot just fail or crash outright anymore, because if they do, system errors translate to browser errors, and these in turn lead to frustrated users. Losing eyeballs means losing advertising revenue and potentially significant amounts of irrecoverable business.

If errors do occur, they are generally attributed to some invalid user input. The execution environment must be robust enough to handle the application-level error and be able to produce a user-level error message. This must translate to a "non-error" as far as the Web server is concerned because the application must complete successfully, even if all it does is return an error message to present to the user as a valid Hypertext Markup Language (HTML) Web page displaying the error.

If you are not familiar with what I am talking about, does a plain Web browser screen with the big black words saying, "Internal Server Error" sound familiar? How about a fatal error that brings up a pop-up that declares "Document contains no data"? As a user, do either of these phrases mean anything to you? No, of course not (unless you are an Internet software engineer), and to the average user, they are an endless source of confusion and frustration. These errors are a result of a failure in the execution of an application. The application either returns invalid Hypertext Transfer Protocol (HTTP) data or terminates fatally, resulting in the Web server throwing its hands up into the air, saying, "I give up!"

This type of faulty execution should not be allowed, if at all possible. As systems become more complex and involve more apprentice users, additional care should be taken to ensure a smooth user application experience. Even in the face of an error situation, an application should terminate successfully, as to not affect its execution environment in a catastrophic way. Python's exception handling promotes mature and correct programming.

10.11 Why Exceptions at All?

If the above section was not motivation enough, imagine what Python programming might be like without program-level exception handling. The first thing that comes to mind is the loss of control client programmers have over their code. For example, if you created an interactive application that allocates and utilizes a large number of resources, if a user hit ^C or other keyboard interrupt, the application would not have the opportunity to perform cleanup, resulting in perhaps loss of data or data corruption. There is also no mechanism to take alternative action such as prompting the users to confirm whether they really want to quit or if they hit the Control key accidentally.

Another drawback would be that functions would have to be rewritten to return a "special" value in the face of an error situation, for example, None. The engineer would be responsible for checking each and every return value from a function call. This may be cumbersome because you may have to check return values, which may not be of the same type as the object you are expecting if no errors occurred. And what if your function wants to return None as a valid data value? Then you would have to come up with another return value, perhaps a negative number. We probably do not need to remind you that negative numbers may be valid in a Python context, such as an index into a sequence. As a programmer of application programmer interfaces (APIs), you would then have to document every single return error your users may encounter based on the input received. Also, it is difficult (and tedious) to propagate errors (and reasons) of multiple layers of code.

There is no simple propagation like the way exceptions do it. Because error data needs to be transmitted upwards in the call hierarchy, it is possible to misinterpret the errors along the way. A totally unrelated error may be stated as the cause when in fact it had nothing to do with the original problem to begin with. We lose the bottling-up and safekeeping of the original error that exceptions provide as they are passed from layer to layer, not to mention completely losing track of the data we were originally concerned about! Exceptions simplify not only the code, but the entire error management scheme, which should not play such a significant role in application development. And with Python's exception handling capabilities, it does not have to.

10.12 Exceptions and the sys Module

An alternative way of obtaining exception information is by accessing the exc_info() function in the sys module. This function provides a 3-tuple of information, more than what we can achieve by simply using only the exception argument. Let us see what we get using sys.exc_info():

```
>>> try:
...     float('abc123')
... except:
...     import sys
...     exc_tuple = sys.exc_info()
...
>>> print exc_tuple
(<class exceptions.ValueError at f9838>, <exceptions.
ValueError instance at 122fa8>,
<traceback object at 10de18>)
>>>
```

```
>>> for eachItem in exc_tuple:
...     print eachItem
...
exceptions.ValueError
invalid literal for float(): abc123
<traceback object at 10de18>
```

What we get from `sys.exc_info()` in a tuple are:

- `exc_type`: exception class object
- `exc_value`: (this) exception class instance object
- `exc_traceback`: traceback object

The first two items we are familiar with: the actual exception class and this particular exception's instance (which is the same as the exception argument which we discussed in the previous section). The third item, a traceback object, is new. This object provides the execution context of where the exception occurred. It contains information such as the execution frame of the code that was running and the line number where the exception occurred.

In older versions of Python, these three values were available in the `sys` module as `sys.exc_type`, `sys.exc_value`, and `sys.exc_traceback`. Unfortunately, these three are global variables and not thread-safe. We recommend using `sys.exc_info()` instead. All three will be phased out and eventually removed in a future version of Python.

10.13 Related Modules

Table 10.3 lists some of the modules related to this chapter.

Table 10.3 Exception-Related Standard Library Modules

Module	*Description*
`exceptions`	Built-in exceptions (never need to import this module)
`contextlib`[a]	Context object utilities for use with the **with** statement
`sys`	Contains various exception-related objects and functions (see `sys.ex*`)

a. New in Python 2.5.

10.14 Exercises

10–1. *Raising Exceptions.* Which of the following can *raise* exceptions during program execution? Note that this question does not ask what may *cause* exceptions.
(a) The user (of your program)
(b) The interpreter
(c) The program(er)
(d) All of the above
(e) Only (b) and (c)
(f) Only (a) and (c)

10–2. *Raising Exceptions.* Referring to the list in the problem above, which could raise exceptions while running within the interactive interpreter?

10–3. *Keywords.* Name the keyword(s) which is (are) used to raise exceptions.

10–4. *Keywords.* What is the difference between **try-except** and **try-finally**?

10–5. *Exceptions.* Name the exception that would result from executing the following pieces of Python code from within the interactive interpreter (refer back to Table 10.2 for a list of all built-in exceptions):

(a)
```
>>> if 3 < 4 then: print '3 IS less than 4!'
```

(b)
```
>>> aList = ['Hello', 'World!', 'Anyone',
'Home?']
    >>> print 'the last string in aList is:', aList
    [len(aList)]
```

(c)
```
>>> x
```

(d)
```
>>> x = 4 % 0
```

(e)
```
>>> import math
>>> i = math.sqrt(-1)
```

10–6. *Improving open().* Create a wrapper for the open() function. When a program opens a file successfully, a file handle will be returned. If the file open fails, rather than generating an error, return None to the callers so that they can open files without an exception handler.

10–7. *Exceptions.* What is the difference between Python pseudocode snippets (a) and (b)? Answer in the context of statements A and B, which are part of both pieces of code. (Thanks to Guido for this teaser!)

(a)
```
try:
    statement_A
except ...:
    . . .
else:
    statement_B
```

(b)
```
try:
    statement_A
    statement_B
except ...:
    . . .
```

10–8. *Improving* `raw_input()`. At the beginning of this chapter, we presented a "safe" version of the `float()` built-in function to detect and handle two different types of exceptions that `float()` generates. Likewise, the `raw_input()` function can generate two different exceptions, either `EOFError` or `KeyboardInterrupt` on end-of-file (EOF) or cancelled input, respectively. Create a wrapper function, perhaps `safe_input()`; rather than raising an exception if the user entered EOF (^D in Unix or ^Z in DOS) or attempted to break out using ^C, have your function return `None` that the calling function can check for.

10–9. *Improving* `math.sqrt()`. The `math` module contains many functions and some constants for performing various mathematics-related operations. Unfortunately, this module does not recognize or operate on complex numbers, which is the reason why the `cmath` module was developed. Create a function, perhaps `safe_sqrt()`, which wraps `math.sqrt()`, but is smart enough to handle a negative parameter and return a complex number with the correct value back to the caller.

FUNCTIONS AND FUNCTIONAL PROGRAMMING

Chapter Topics

- What Are Functions?
- Calling Functions
- Creating Functions
- Passing Functions
- Formal Arguments
- Variable-Length Arguments
- Functional Programming
- Variable Scope
- Recursion
- Generators

Chapter 11

We were introduced to functions in Chapter 2, and we have seen them created and called throughout the text. In this chapter, we will look beyond the basics and give you a full treatment of all the other features associated with functions. In addition to the expected behavior, functions in Python support a variety of invocation styles and argument types, including some functional programming interfaces. We conclude this chapter with a look at Python's scoping and take an optional side trip into the world of recursion.

11.1 What Are Functions?

Functions are the structured or procedural programming way of organizing the logic in your programs. Large blocks of code can be neatly segregated into manageable chunks, and space is saved by putting oft-repeated code in functions as opposed to multiple copies everywhere—this also helps with consistency because changing the single copy means you do not have to hunt for and make changes to multiple copies of duplicated code. The basics of functions in Python are not much different from those of other languages with which you may be familiar. After a bit of review here in the early part of this chapter, we will focus on what else Python brings to the table.

Functions can appear in different ways . . . here is a sampling profile of how you will see functions created, used, or otherwise referenced:

declaration/definition	`def foo(): print 'bar'`
function object/reference	`foo`
function call/invocation	`foo()`

11.1.1 Functions versus Procedures

Functions are often compared to procedures. Both are entities that can be invoked, but the traditional function or "black box," perhaps taking some or no input parameters, performs some amount of processing, and concludes by sending back a return value to the caller. Some functions are Boolean in nature, returning a "yes" or "no" answer, or, more appropriately, a non-zero or zero value, respectively. Procedures are simply special cases, functions that do not return a value. As you will see below, Python procedures are implied functions because the interpreter implicitly returns a default value of `None`.

11.1.2 Return Values and Function Types

Functions may return a value back to their callers and those that are more procedural in nature do not explicitly return anything at all. Languages that treat procedures as functions usually have a special type or value name for functions that "return nothing." These functions default to a return type of `"void"` in C, meaning no value returned. In Python, the equivalent return object type is `None`.

The `hello()` function acts as a procedure in the code below, returning no value. If the return value is saved, you will see that its value is `None`:

```
>>> def hello():
...     print 'hello world'
>>>
>>> res = hello()
hello world
>>> res
>>> print res
None
>>> type(res)
<type 'None'>
```

Also, like most other languages, you may return only one value/object from a function in Python. One difference is that in returning a container type, it will seem as if you can actually return more than a single object. In other words, you cannot leave the grocery store with multiple items, but you can throw them all in a single shopping bag, which you walk out of the store with, perfectly legal.

```
def foo():
    return ['xyz', 1000000, -98.6]

def bar():
    return 'abc', [42, 'python'], "Guido"
```

The `foo()` function returns a list, and the `bar()` function returns a tuple. Because of the tuple's syntax of not requiring the enclosing parentheses, it creates the perfect illusion of returning multiple items. If we were to properly enclose the tuple items, the definition of `bar()` would look like this:

```
def bar():
    return ('abc', [4-2j, 'python'], "Guido")
```

As far as return values are concerned, tuples can be saved in a number of ways. The following three ways of saving the return values are equivalent:

```
>>> aTuple = bar()
>>> x, y, z = bar()
>>> (a, b, c) = bar()
>>>
>>> aTuple
('abc', [(4-2j), 'python'], 'Guido')
>>> x, y, z
('abc', [(4-2j), 'python'], 'Guido')
>>> (a, b, c)
('abc', [(4-2j), 'python'], 'Guido')
```

In the assignments for x, y, z, and a, b, c, each variable will receive its corresponding return value in the order the values are returned. The `aTuple` assignment takes the entire implied tuple returned from the function. Recall that a tuple can be "unpacked" into individual variables or not at all and its reference assigned directly to a single variable. (Refer back to Section 6.18.3 for a review.)

In short, when no items are explicitly returned or if `None` is returned, then Python returns `None`. If the function returns exactly one object, then that is the object that Python returns and the type of that object stays the same. If the function returns multiple objects, Python gathers them all together and returns them in a tuple. Yes, we claim that Python is more flexible than languages like C where only one return value is allowed, but in all honesty, Python follows the same tradition. The programmer is just given the impression that he or she can return more than one object.

Table 11.1 Return Values and Types	
Stated Number of Objects to Return	Type of Object That Python Returns
0	None
1	object
>1	tuple

Table 11.1 summarizes the number of items "returned" from a function, and the object that Python actually returns.

Many languages that support functions maintain the notion that a function's type is the type of its return value. In Python, no direct type correlation can be made since Python is dynamically typed and functions can return values of different types. Because overloading is not a feature, the programmer can use the `type()` built-in function as a proxy for multiple declarations with different *signatures* (multiple prototypes of the same overloaded function that differ based on its arguments).

11.2 Calling Functions

11.2.1 Function Operator

Functions are called using the same pair of parentheses that you are used to. In fact, some consider (( )) to be a two-character operator, the function operator. As you are probably aware, any input parameters or arguments must be placed between these calling parentheses. Parentheses are also used as part of function declarations to define those arguments. Although we have yet to formally study classes and object-oriented programming, you will discover that the function operator is also used in Python for class instantiation.

11.2.2 Keyword Arguments

The concept of keyword arguments applies only to function invocation. The idea here is for the caller to identify the arguments by parameter name in a function call. This specification allows for arguments to be missing or out-of-order because the interpreter is able to use the provided keywords to match values to parameters.

For a simple example, imagine a function `foo()`, which has the following pseudocode definition:

```
def foo(x):
    foo_suite  # presumably does some processing with 'x'
```

Standard calls to `foo()`: `foo(42)`   `foo('bar')`   `foo(y)`
Keyword calls to `foo()`:   `foo(x=42)`   `foo(x='bar')` `foo(x=y)`

For a more realistic example, let us assume you have a function called `net_conn()` and you know that it takes two parameters, say, `host` and `port`:

```
def net_conn(host, port):
        net_conn_suite
```

Naturally, we can call the function, giving the proper arguments in the correct positional order in which they were declared:

```
net_conn('kappa', 8080)
```

The `host` parameter gets the string `'kappa'` and `port` gets integer 8080. Keyword arguments allow out-of-order parameters, but you must provide the name of the parameter as a "keyword" to have your arguments match up to their corresponding argument names, as in the following:

```
net_conn(port=8080, host='chino')
```

Keyword arguments may also be used when arguments are allowed to be "missing." These are related to functions that have default arguments, which we will introduce in the next section.

11.2.3 Default Arguments

Default arguments are those that are declared with default values. Parameters that are not passed on a function call are thus allowed and are assigned the default value. We will cover default arguments more formally in Section 11.5.2.

11.2.4 Grouped Arguments

Python also allows the programmer to execute a function without explicitly specifying individual arguments in the call as long as you have grouped the arguments in either a tuple (non-keyword arguments) or a dictionary (keyword arguments), both of which we will explore in this chapter. Basically, you can put all the arguments in either a tuple or a dictionary (or both), and just call a function with those buckets of arguments and not have to explicitly put them in the function call:

```
func(*tuple_grp_nonkw_args, **dict_grp_kw_args)
```

The `tuple_grp_nonkw_args` are the group of non-keyword arguments as a tuple, and the `dict_grp_kw_args` are a dictionary of keyword arguments. As we already mentioned, we will cover all of these in this chapter, but just be aware of this feature that allows you to stick arguments in tuples and/or dictionaries and be able to call functions without explicitly stating each one by itself in the function call.

In fact, you can give formal arguments, too! These include the standard positional parameters as well as keyword argument, so the full syntax allowed in Python for making a function call is:

```
func(positional_args, keyword_args,
    *tuple_grp_nonkw_args, **dict_grp_kw_args)
```

All arguments in this syntax are optional—everything is dependent on the individual function call as far as which parameters to pass to the function. This syntax has effectively deprecated the `apply()` built-in function. (Prior to Python 1.6, such argument objects could only be passed to `apply()` with the function object for invocation.)

Example

In our math game in Example 11.1 (`easyMath.py`), we will use the current function calling convention to generate a two-item argument list to send to the appropriate arithmetic function. (We will also show where `apply()` would have come in if it had been used.)

The `easyMath.py` application is basically an arithmetic math quiz game for children where an arithmetic operation—addition or subtraction— is randomly chosen. We use the functional equivalents of these operators, `add()` and `sub()`, both found in the `operator` module. We then generate the list of arguments (two, since these are binary operators/ operations). Then random numbers are chosen as the operands. Since we do not want to support negative numbers in this more elementary edition of this application, we sort our list of two numbers in largest-to-smallest order, then call the corresponding function with this argument list and the randomly chosen arithmetic operator to obtain the correct solution to the posed problem.

Example 11.1 Arithmetic Game (easyMath.py)

Randomly chooses numbers and an arithmetic function, displays the question, and verifies the results. Shows answer after three wrong tries and does not continue until the user enters the correct answer.

```python
1   #!/usr/bin/env python
2
3   from operator import add, sub
4   from random import randint, choice
5
6   ops = {'+': add, '-': sub}
7   MAXTRIES = 2
8
9   def doprob():
10      op = choice('+-')
11      nums = [randint(1,10) for i in range(2)]
12      nums.sort(reverse=True)
13      ans = ops[op](*nums)
14      pr = '%d %s %d = ' % (nums[0], op, nums[1])
15      oops = 0
16      while True:
17          try:
18              if int(raw_input(pr)) == ans:
19                  print 'correct'
20                  break
21              if oops == MAXTRIES:
22                  print 'answer\n%s%d'%(pr, ans)
23              else:
24                  print 'incorrect... try again'
25                  oops += 1
26          except (KeyboardInterrupt, \
27                  EOFError, ValueError):
28              print 'invalid input... try again'
29
30  def main():
31      while True:
32          doprob()
33          try:
34              opt = raw_input('Again? [y]').lower()
35              if opt and opt[0] == 'n':
36                  break
37          except (KeyboardInterrupt, EOFError):
38              break
39
40  if __name__ == '__main__':
41      main()
```

Line-by-Line Explanation

Lines 1–4

Our code begins with the usual Unix startup line followed by various imports of the functions that we will be using from the `operator` and random module.

Lines 6–7

The global variables we use in this application are a set of operations and their corresponding functions, and a value indicating how many times (three: 0, 1, 2) we allow the user to enter an incorrect answer before we reveal the solution. The function dictionary uses the operator's symbol to index into the dictionary, pulling out the appropriate arithmetic function.

Lines 9–28

The `doprob()` function is the core engine of the application. It randomly picks an operation and generates the two operands, sorting them from largest-to-smallest order in order to avoid negative numbers for subtraction problems. It then invokes the math function with the values, calculating the correct solution. The user is then prompted with the equation and given three opportunities to enter the correct answer.

Line 10 uses the `random.choice()` function. Its job is to take a sequence—a string of operation symbols in our case—and randomly choose one item and return it.

Line 11 uses a list comprehension to randomly choose two numbers for our exercise. This example is simple enough such that we could have just called `randint()` twice to get our operands, i.e., `nums = [randint (1,10)`, `randint(1,10)]`, but we wanted to use a list comprehension so that you could see another example of its use as well as in case we wanted to upgrade this problem to take on more than just two numbers, similar to the reason why instead of cutting and pasting the same piece of code, we put it into a **for** loop.

Line 12 will only work in Python 2.4 and newer because that is when the reverse flag was added to the `list.sort()` method (as well as the new `sorted()` built-in function). If you are using an earlier Python version, you need to either:

- Add an inverse comparison function to get a reverse sort, i.e., **lambda** x, y: cmp(y, x), or
- Call `nums.sort()` followed by `nums.reverse()`

Don't be afraid of **lambda** if you have not seen it before. We will cover it in this chapter, but for now, you can think of it as a one-line anonymous function.

Line 13 is where `apply()` would have been used if you are using Python before 1.6. This call to the appropriate operation function would have been coded as `apply(ops[op], nums)` instead of `ops[op](*nums)`.

Lines 16–28 represent the controlling loop handling valid and invalid user input. The **while** loop is "infinite," running until either the correct answer is given or the number of allowed attempts is exhausted, three in our case. It allows the program to accept erroneous input such as non-numbers, or various keyboard control characters. Once the user exceeds the maximum number of tries, the answer is presented, and the user is "forced" to enter the correct value, not proceeding until that has been done.

Lines 30–41

The main driver of the application is `main()`, called from the top level if the script is invoked directly. If imported, the importing function either manages the execution by calling `doprob()`, or calls `main()` for program control. `main()` simply calls `doprob()` to engage the user in the main functionality of the script and prompts the user to quit or to try another problem.

Since the values and operators are chosen randomly, each execution of `easyMath.py` should be different. Here is what we got today (oh, and your answers may vary as well!):

```
$ easyMath.py
7 - 2 = 5
correct
Again? [y]
7 * 6 = 42
correct
Again? [y]
7 * 3 = 20
incorrect... try again
7 * 3 = 22
incorrect... try again
7 * 3 = 23
sorry... the answer is
7 * 3 = 21
7 * 3 = 21
correct
Again? [y]
7 - 5 = 2
correct
Again? [y] n
```

11.3 Creating Functions

11.3.1 def Statement

Functions are created using the **def** statement, with a syntax like the following:

```
def function_name(arguments):
    "function_documentation_string"
    function_body_suite
```

The header line consists of the **def** keyword, the function name, and a set of arguments (if any). The remainder of the **def** clause consists of an optional but highly recommended documentation string and the required function body suite. We have seen many function declarations throughout this text, and here is another:

```
def helloSomeone(who):
    'returns a salutory string customized with the input'
    return "Hello " + str(who)
```

11.3.2 Declaration versus Definition

Some programming languages differentiate between function declarations and function definitions. A function declaration consists of providing the parser with the function name, and the names (and traditionally the types) of its arguments, without necessarily giving any lines of code for the function, which is usually referred to as the function definition.

In languages where there is a distinction, it is usually because the function definition may belong in a physically different location in the code from the function declaration. Python does not make a distinction between the two, as a function clause is made up of a declarative header line immediately followed by its defining suite.

11.3.3 Forward References

Like some other high-level languages, Python does not permit you to reference or call a function before it has been declared. We can try a few examples to illustrate this:

```
def foo():
    print 'in foo()'
    bar()
```

If we were to call `foo()` here, it would fail because `bar()` has not been declared yet:

```
>>> foo()
in foo()
Traceback (innermost last):
  File "<stdin>", line 1, in ?
  File "<stdin>", line 3, in foo
NameError: bar
```

We will now define `bar()`, placing its declaration before `foo()`'s declaration:

```
def bar():
    print 'in bar()'

def foo():
    print 'in foo()'
    bar()
```

Now we can safely call `foo()` with no problems:

```
>>> foo()
in foo()
in bar()
```

In fact, we can even declare `foo()` before `bar()`:

```
def foo():
    print 'in foo()'
    bar()

def bar():
    print 'in bar()'
```

Amazingly enough, this code still works fine with no forward referencing problems:

```
>>> foo()
in foo()
in bar()
```

This piece of code is fine because even though a call to `bar()` (from `foo()`) appears before `bar()`'s definition, `foo()` *itself* is not called before `bar()` is declared. In other words, we declared `foo()`, then `bar()`, and *then* called `foo()`, but by that time, `bar()` existed already, so the call succeeds.

Notice that the output of `foo()` succeeded before the error came about. `NameError` is the exception that is always raised when any uninitialized identifiers are accessed.

11.3.4 Function Attributes

We will briefly discuss namespaces later on in this chapter, especially their relationship to variable scope. There will be a more in-depth treatment of namespaces in the next chapter; however, here we want to point out a basic feature of Python namespaces.

You get a free one with every Python module, class, and function. You can have a variable named x in modules foo and bar, but can use them in your current application upon importing both modules. So even though the same variable name is used in both modules, you are safe because the dotted-attribute notation implies a separate namespace for both, i.e., there is no naming conflict in this snippet of code:

```
import foo, bar
print foo.x + bar.x
```

Function attributes are another area of Python to use the dotted-attribute notation and have a namespace. (More on namespaces later on in this chapter as well as Chapter 12 on Python modules.)

2.1

```
def foo():
    'foo() -- properly created doc string'

def bar():
    pass

bar.__doc__ = 'Oops, forgot the doc str above'
bar.version = 0.1
```

In foo() above, we create our documentation string as normal, e.g., the first unassigned string after the function declaration. When declaring bar(), we left everything out and just used the dotted-attribute notation to add its doc string as well as another attribute. We can then access the attributes freely. Below is an example with the interactive interpreter. (As you may already be aware, using the built-in function help() gives more of a pretty-printing format than just using the vanilla print of the __doc__ attribute, but you can use either one you wish.)

```
>>> help(foo)
Help on function foo in module __main__:

foo()
    foo() -- properly created doc string
>>> print bar.version

0.1
```

```
>>> print foo.__doc__
foo() -- properly created doc string
>>> print bar.__doc__
Oops, forgot the doc str above
```

Notice how we can define the documentation string outside of the function declaration. Yet we can still access it at runtime just like normal. One thing that you cannot do, however, is get access to the attributes in the function declaration. In other words, there is no such thing as a "self" inside a function declaration so that you can make an assignment like __dict__['version'] = 0.1. The reason for this is because the function object has not even been created yet, but afterward you have the function object and can add to its dictionary in the way we described above . . . another free namespace!

Function attributes were added to Python in 2.1, and you can read more about them in PEP 232.

11.3.5 *Inner or Nested Functions*

It is perfectly legitimate to create function (object)s inside other functions. That is the definition of an *inner* or *nested function*. Because Python now supports statically nested scoping (introduced in 2.1 but standard as of 2.2), inner functions are actually useful now. It made no sense for older versions of Python, which only supported the global and one local scope. So how does one create a nested function?

The (obvious) way to create an inner function is to define a function from within an outer function's definition (using the **def** keyword), as in:

```
def foo():
    def bar():
        print 'bar() called'

    print 'foo() called'
    bar()

foo()
bar()
```

If we stick this code in a module, say inner.py, and run it, we get the following output:

```
foo() called
bar() called
Traceback (most recent call last):
  File "inner.py", line 11, in ?
    bar()
NameError: name 'bar' is not defined
```

One interesting aspect of inner functions is that they are wholly contained inside the outer function's *scope* (the places where you can access an object; more on scope later on in this chapter). If there are no outside references to bar(), it cannot be called from anywhere else except inside the outer function, hence the reason for the exception you see at the end of execution in the above code snippet.

Another way of creating a function object while inside a(nother) function is by using the **lambda** statement. We will cover this later on in section 11.7.1.

Inner functions turn into something special called *closures* if the definition of an inner function contains a reference to an object defined in an outer function. (It can even be beyond the immediately enclosing outer function too.) We will learn more about closures coming up in Section 11.8.4. In the next section, we will introduce decorators, but the example application also includes a preview of a closure.

11.3.6 *Function (and Method) Decorators

The main motivation behind *decorators* came from Python object-oriented programming (OOP). Decorators are just "overlays" on top of function calls. These overlays are just additional calls that are applied when a function or method is declared.

The syntax for decorators uses a leading "at-sign" (@) followed by the decorator function name and optional arguments. The line following the decorator declaration is the function being decorated, along with *its* optional arguments. It looks something like this:

```
@decorator(dec_opt_args)
def func2Bdecorated(func_opt_args):
    :
```

So how (and why) did this syntax come into being? What was the inspiration behind decorators? Well, when static and class methods were added to Python in 2.2, the idiom required to realize them was clumsy, confusing, and makes code less readable, i.e.,

```
class MyClass(object):
    def staticFoo():
        :
    staticFoo = staticmethod(staticFoo)
        :
```

(It was clearly stated for that release that this was not the final syntax anyway.) Within this class declaration, we define a method named static-Foo(). Now since this is intended to become a static method, we leave out the self argument, which is required for standard class methods, as you will see in Chapter 12. The staticmethod() built-in function is then used to "convert" the function into a static method, but note how "sloppy" it looks with **def** staticFoo() followed by staticFoo = staticmethod (staticFoo). With decorators, you can now replace that piece of code with the following:

```
class MyClass(object):
    @staticmethod
    def staticFoo():
        :
```

Furthermore, decorators can be "stacked" like function calls, so here is a more general example with multiple decorators:

```
@deco2
@deco1
def func(arg1, arg2, ...): pass
```

This is equivalent to creating a *composite* function:

```
def func(arg1, arg2, ...): pass
func = deco2(deco1(func))
```

Function composition in math is defined like this: (g • f)(x) = g(f(x)). For consistency in Python:

```
@g
@f
def foo():
    :
```

. . . is the same as foo = g(f(foo)).

Decorators With and Without Arguments

Yes the syntax is slightly mind-bending at first, but once you are comfortable with it, the only twist on top of that is when you use decorators with arguments. Without arguments, a decorator like:

```
@deco
def foo(): pass
```

. . . is pretty straightforward:

```
foo = deco(foo)
```

Function composition without arguments (as seen above) follows. However, a decorator decomaker() *with* arguments:

```
@decomaker(deco_args)
def foo(): pass
```

. . . needs to itself return a decorator that takes the function as an argument. In other words, decomaker() does something with *deco_args* and returns a function object that is a decorator that takes foo as its argument. To put it simply:

```
foo = decomaker(deco_args)(foo)
```

Here is an example featuring multiple decorators in which one takes an argument:

```
@deco1(deco_arg)
@deco2
def func(): pass
```

This is equivalent to:

```
func = deco1(deco_arg)(deco2(func))
```

We hope that if you understand these examples here, things will become much clearer. We present a more useful yet still simple script below where the decorator does not take an argument. Example 11.8 is an intermediate script with a decorator that *does* take an argument.

So What *Are* Decorators?

We know that decorators are really functions now. We also know that they take function objects. But what will they do with those functions? Generally, when you wrap a function, you eventually *call* it. The nice thing is that we can do that whenever it is appropriate for our wrapper. We can run some preliminary code before executing the function or some cleanup code afterward, like postmortem analysis. It is up to the programmer. So when you see a decorator function, be prepared to find some code in it, and somewhere embedded within its definition, a call or at least *some* reference, to the target function.

This feature essentially introduces the concept that Java developers call AOP, or aspect-oriented programming. You can place code in your decorators for concerns that cut across your application. For example, you can use decorators to:

- Introduce logging
- Insert timing logic (aka *instrumentation*) for monitoring performance
- Add transactional capabilities to functions

The ability to support decorators is very important for creating enterprise applications in Python. You will see that the bullet points above correspond quite closely to our example below as well as Example 11.2.

Decorator Example

We have an extremely simple example below, but it should get you started in really understanding how decorators work. This example "decorates" a (useless) function by displaying the time that it was executed. It is a "timestamp decoration" similar to the timestamp server that we discuss in Chapter 16.

Example 11.2 Example of Using a Function Decorator (deco.py)

This demonstration of a decorator (and closures) shows that it is merely a "wrapper" with which to "decorate" (or overlay) a function, returning the altered function object and reassigning it to the original identifier, forever losing access to the original function object.

```
1   #!/usr/bin/env python
2
3   from time import ctime, sleep
4
5   def tsfunc(func):
6       def wrappedFunc():
7           print '[%s] %s() called' % (
8               ctime(), func.__name__)
9           return func()
10      return wrappedFunc
11
12  @tsfunc
13  def foo():
14      pass
15
16  foo()
17  sleep(4)
18
19  for i in range(2):
20      sleep(1)
21      foo()
```

Running this script, we get the following output:

```
[Sun Mar 19 22:50:28 2006] foo() called
[Sun Mar 19 22:50:33 2006] foo() called
[Sun Mar 19 22:50:34 2006] foo() called
```

Line-by-Line Explanation

Lines 5–10

Following the startup and module import lines, the `tsfunc()` function is a decorator that displays a timestamp (to standard output) of when a function is called. It defines an inner function `wrappedFunc()`, which adds the timestamp and calls the target function. The return value of the decorator is the "wrapped" function.

Lines 12–21

We define function `foo()` with an empty body (which does nothing) and decorate it with `tsfunc()`. We then call it once as a proof-of-concept, wait four seconds, then call it twice more, pausing one second before each invocation.

As a result, after it has been called once, the second time it is called should be five (4 + 1) seconds after the first call, and the third time around should only be one second after that. This corresponds perfectly to the program output seen above.

You can read more about decorators in the Python Language Reference, the "What's New in Python 2.4" document, and the defining PEP 318.

11.4 Passing Functions

The concept of function pointers is an advanced topic when learning a language such as C, but not Python where functions are like any other object. They can be referenced (accessed or aliased to other variables), passed as arguments to functions, be elements of container objects such as lists and dictionaries, etc. The one unique characteristic of functions which may set them apart from other objects is that they are callable, i.e., they can be invoked via the function operator. (There are other callables in Python. For more information, see Chapter 14.)

In the description above, we noted that functions can be aliases to other variables. Because all objects are passed by reference, functions are no different. When assigning to another variable, you are assigning the reference to the same object; and if that object is a function, then all aliases to that same object are callable:

```
>>> def foo():
...         print 'in foo()'
...
>>> bar = foo
>>> bar()
in foo()
```

When we assigned `foo` to `bar`, we are assigning the same function object to `bar`, thus we can invoke `bar()` in the same way we call `foo()`. Be sure you understand the difference between "`foo`" (reference of the function object) and "`foo()`" (invocation of the function object).

Taking our reference example a bit further, we can even pass functions in as arguments to other functions for invocation:

```
>>> def bar(argfunc):
...         argfunc()
...
>>> bar(foo)
in foo()
```

Note that it is the function object `foo` that is being passed to `bar()`. `bar()` is the function that actually calls `foo()` (which has been aliased to the local variable `argfunc` in the same way that we assigned `foo` to `bar` in the previous example). Now let us examine a more realistic example, `numconv.py`, whose code is given in Example 11.3.

Example 11.3   Passing and Calling (Built-in) Functions (`numConv.py`)

A more realistic example of passing functions as arguments and invoking them from within the function. This script simply converts a sequence of numbers to the same type using the conversion function that is passed in. In particular, the `test()` *function passes in a built-in function* `int()`, `long()`, *or* `float()` *to perform the conversion.*

```
 1   #!/usr/bin/env python
 2
 3   def convert(func, seq):
 4       'conv. sequence of numbers to same type'
 5       return [func(eachNum) for eachNum in seq]
 6
 7   myseq = (123, 45.67, -6.2e8, 999999999L)
 8   print convert(int, myseq)
 9   print convert(long, myseq)
10   print convert(float, myseq)
```

If we were to run this program, we would get the following output:

```
$ numconv.py
[123, 45, -620000000, 999999999]
[123L, 45L, -620000000L, 999999999L]
[123.0, 45.67, -620000000.0, 999999999.0]
```

11.5 Formal Arguments

A Python function's set of formal arguments consists of all parameters passed to the function on invocation for which there is an exact correspondence to those of the argument list in the function declaration. These arguments include all required arguments (passed to the function in correct positional order), keyword arguments (passed in or out of order, but which have key-words present to match their values to their proper positions in the argument list), and all arguments that have default values that may or may not be part of the function call. For all of these cases, a name is created for that value in the (newly created) local namespace and it can be accessed as soon as the function begins execution.

11.5.1 Positional Arguments

These are the standard vanilla parameters that we are all familiar with. Posi-tional arguments must be passed in the exact order in which they are defined for the functions that are called. Also, without the presence of any default arguments (see next section), the exact number of arguments passed to a function (call) must be exactly the number declared:

```
>>> def foo(who):        # defined for only 1 argument
...        print 'Hello', who
...
>>> foo()                # 0 arguments... BAD
Traceback (innermost last):
  File "<stdin>", line 1, in ?
TypeError: not enough arguments; expected 1, got 0
>>>
>>> foo('World!')        # 1 argument... WORKS
Hello World!
>>>
>>> foo('Mr.', 'World!')# 2 arguments... BAD
Traceback (innermost last):
  File "<stdin>", line 1, in ?
TypeError: too many arguments; expected 1, got 2
```

The foo() function has one positional argument. That means that any call to foo() must have exactly one argument, no more, no less. You will become extremely familiar with TypeError otherwise. Note how informative the Python errors are. As a general rule, all positional arguments for a function must be provided whenever you call it. They may be passed into the function call in position or out of position, granted that a keyword argument is provided to match it to its proper position in the argument list (review Section 11.2.2). Default arguments, however, do not have to be provided because of their nature.

11.5.2 Default Arguments

Default arguments are parameters that are defined to have a default value if one is not provided in the function call for that argument. Such definitions are given in the function declaration header line. C++ supports default arguments too and has the same syntax as Python: the argument name is followed by an "assignment" of its default value. This assignment is merely a syntactical way of indicating that this assignment will occur if no value is passed in for that argument.

The syntax for declaring variables with default values in Python is such that all positional arguments must come before any default arguments:

```
def func(posargs, defarg1=dval1, defarg2=dval2,...):
    "function_documentation_string"
    function_body_suite
```

Each default argument is followed by an assignment statement of its default value. If no value is given during a function call, then this assignment is realized.

Why Default Arguments?

Default arguments add a wonderful level of robustness to applications because they allow for some flexibility that is not offered by the standard positional parameters. That gift comes in the form of simplicity for the applications programmer. Life is not as complicated when there are a fewer number of parameters that one needs to worry about. This is especially helpful when one is new to an API interface and does not have enough knowledge to provide more targeted values as arguments.

The concept of using default arguments is analogous to the process of installing software on your computer. How often does one choose the "default install" over the "custom install?" I would say probably almost always. It is a matter of convenience and know-how, not to mention a time-saver. And if you *are* one of those gurus who always chooses the custom install, please keep in mind that you are one of the minority.

Another advantage goes to the developers, who are given more control over the software they create for their consumers. When providing default values, they can selectively choose the "best" default value possible, thereby hoping to give the user some freedom of not having to make that choice. Over time, as the users becomes more familiar with the system or API, they may eventually be able to provide their own parameter values, no longer requiring the use of "training wheels."

Here is one example where a default argument comes in handy and has some usefulness in the growing electronic commerce industry:

```
>>> def taxMe(cost, rate=0.0825):
...     return cost + (cost * rate)
...
>>> taxMe(100)
108.25
>>>
>>> taxMe(100, 0.05)
105.0
```

In the example above, the `taxMe()` function takes the cost of an item and produces a total sale amount with sales tax added. The cost is a required parameter while the tax rate is a default argument (in our example, 8.25%). Perhaps you are an online retail merchant, with most of your customers coming from the same state or county as your business. Consumers from locations with different tax rates would like to see their purchase totals with their corresponding sales tax rates. To override the default, all you have to do is provide your argument value, such as the case with `taxMe(100, 0.05)` in the above example. By specifying a `rate` of 5%, you provided an argument as the `rate` parameter, thereby overriding or bypassing its default value of 0.0825.

All required parameters must be placed before any default arguments. Why? Simply because they are mandatory, whereas default arguments are not. Syntactically, it would be impossible for the interpreter to decide which values match which arguments if mixed modes were allowed. A `SyntaxError` is raised if the arguments are not given in the correct order:

```
>>> def taxMe2(rate=0.0825, cost):
...     return cost * (1.0 + rate)
...
SyntaxError: non-default argument follows default argument
```

Let us take a look at keyword arguments again, using our old friend `net_conn()`.

```
def net_conn(host, port):
    net_conn_suite
```

As you will recall, this is where you can provide your arguments out of order (positionally) if you name the arguments. With the above declarations, we can make the following (regular) positional or keyword argument calls:

- `net_conn('kappa', 8000)`
- `net_conn(port=8080, host='chino')`

However, if we bring default arguments into the equation, things change, although the above calls are still valid. Let us modify the declaration of `net_conn()` such that the `port` parameter has a default value of 80 and add another argument named `stype` (for server type) with a default value of `'tcp'`:

```
def net_conn(host, port=80, stype='tcp'):
    net_conn_suite
```

We have just expanded the number of ways we can call `net_conn()`. The following are all valid calls to `net_conn()`:

- `net_conn('phaze', 8000, 'udp')`   `# no def args used`
- `net_conn('kappa')`   `# both def args used`
- `net_conn('chino', stype='icmp')`   `# use port def arg`
- `net_conn(stype='udp', host='solo')`   `# use port def arg`
- `net_conn('deli', 8080)`   `# use stype def arg`
- `net_conn(port=81, host='chino')`   `# use stype def arg`

What is the one constant we see in all of the above examples? The sole required parameter, `host`. There is no default value for `host`, thus it is expected in all calls to `net_conn()`.

Keyword arguments prove useful for providing for out-of-order positional arguments, but, coupled with default arguments, they can also be used to "skip over" missing arguments as well, as evidenced from our examples above.

Default Function Object Argument Example

We will now present yet another example of where a default argument may prove beneficial. The `grabWeb.py` script, given in Example 11.4, is a simple script whose main purpose is to grab a Web page from the Internet and temporarily store it to a local file for analysis. This type of application can be used to test the integrity of a Web site's pages or to monitor the load on a server (by measuring connectability or download speed). The `process()` function can be anything we want, presenting an infinite number of uses. The one we chose for this exercise displays the first and last non-blank lines of the retrieved Web page. Although this particular example may not prove too useful in the real world, you can imagine what kinds of applications you can build on top of this code.

Example 11.4   Grabbing Web Pages (grabWeb.py)

This script downloads a Web page (defaults to local www server) and displays the first and last non-blank lines of the HTML file. Flexibility is added due to both default arguments of the download() *function, which will allow overriding with different URLs or specification of a different processing function.*

```python
1   #!/usr/bin/env python
2
3   from urllib import urlretrieve
4
5   def firstNonBlank(lines):
6       for eachLine in lines:
7           if not eachLine.strip():
8               continue
9           else:
10              return eachLine
11
12  def firstLast(webpage):
13      f = open(webpage)
14      lines = f.readlines()
15      f.close()
16      print firstNonBlank(lines),
17      lines.reverse()
18      print firstNonBlank(lines),
19
20  def download(url='http://www',
21          process=firstLast):
22      try:
23          retval = urlretrieve(url)[0]
24      except IOError:
25          retval = None
26      if retval:              # do some processing
27          process(retval)
28
29  if __name__ == '__main__':
30      download()
```

Running this script in our environment gives the following output, although your mileage will definitely vary since you will be viewing a completely different Web page altogether.

```
$ grabWeb.py
<!DOCTYPE HTML PUBLIC "-//W3C//DTD HTML 3.2 Final//EN">
</HTML>
```

11.6 Variable-Length Arguments

There may be situations where your function is required to process an unknown number of arguments. These are called *variable-length argument lists*. Variable-length arguments are not named explicitly in function declarations because the number of arguments is unknown before runtime (and even during execution, the number of arguments may be different on successive calls), an obvious difference from formal arguments (positional and default), which *are* named in function declarations. Python supports variable-length arguments in two ways because function calls provide for both keyword and non-keyword argument types.

In Section 11.2.4, we looked at how you can use the * and ** characters in function calls to specify grouped sets of arguments, non-keyword and keyword arguments. In this section, we will see the same symbols again, but this time in function declarations, to signify the receipt of such arguments when functions are called. This syntax allows functions to accept more than just the declared formal arguments as defined in the function declaration.

11.6.1 Non-keyword Variable Arguments (Tuple)

When a function is invoked, all formal (required and default) arguments are assigned to their corresponding local variables as given in the function declaration. The remaining non-keyword variable arguments are inserted in order into a tuple for access. Perhaps you are familiar with "varargs" in C (i.e., `va_list`, `va_arg`, and the ellipsis [`...`]). Python provides equivalent support—iterating over the tuple elements is the same as using `va_arg` in C. For those who are *not* familiar with C or varargs, they just represent the syntax for accepting a variable (not fixed) number of arguments passed in a function call.

The variable-length argument tuple must follow all positional and default parameters, and the general syntax for functions with tuple or non-keyword variable arguments is as follows:

```
def function_name([formal_args,] *vargs_tuple):
    "function_documentation_string"
    function_body_suite
```

The asterisk operator (*) is placed in front of the variable that will hold all remaining arguments once all the formal parameters if have been exhausted. The tuple is empty if there are no additional arguments given.

As we saw earlier, a `TypeError` exception is generated whenever an incorrect number of arguments is given in the function invocation. By adding a variable argument list variable at the end, we can handle the situation when more than enough arguments are passed to the function because all the extra (non-keyword) ones will be added to the variable argument tuple. (Extra keyword arguments require a keyword variable argument parameter [see the next section].)

As expected, all formal arguments must precede informal arguments for the same reason that positional arguments must come before keyword arguments.

```
def tupleVarArgs(arg1, arg2='defaultB', *theRest):
    'display regular args and non-keyword variable args'
    print 'formal arg 1:', arg1
    print 'formal arg 2:', arg1
    for eachXtrArg in theRest:
        print 'another arg:', eachXtrArg
```

We will now invoke this function to show how variable argument tuples work:

```
>>> tupleVarArgs('abc')
formal arg 1: abc
formal arg 2: defaultB
>>>
>>> tupleVarArgs(23, 4.56)
formal arg 1: 23
formal arg 2: 4.56
>>>
>>> tupleVarArgs('abc', 123, 'xyz', 456.789)
formal arg 1: abc
formal arg 2: 123
another arg: xyz
another arg: 456.789
```

11.6.2 Keyword Variable Arguments (Dictionary)

In the case where we have a variable number or extra set of keyword arguments, these are placed into a dictionary where the "keyworded" argument variable names are the keys, and the arguments are their corresponding values. Why must it be a dictionary? Because a pair of items is given for every argument—the name of the argument and its value—it is a natural fit to use a dictionary to hold these arguments. Here is the syntax of function definitions that use the variable argument dictionary for extra keyword arguments:

```
def function_name([formal_args,][*vargst,] **vargsd):
    function_documentation_string
    function_body_suite
```

To differentiate keyword variable arguments from non-keyword informal arguments, a double asterisk (**) is used. The ** is overloaded so as not to be confused with exponentiation. The keyword variable argument dictionary should be the last parameter of the function definition prepended with the '**'. We now present an example of how to use such a dictionary:

```
def dictVarArgs(arg1, arg2='defaultB', **theRest):
    'display 2 regular args and keyword variable args'
    print 'formal arg1:', arg1
    print 'formal arg2:', arg2
    for eachXtrArg in theRest.keys():
        print 'Xtra arg %s: %s' % \
            (eachXtrArg, str(theRest[eachXtrArg]))
```

Executing this code in the interpreter, we get the following output:

```
>>> dictVarArgs(1220, 740.0, c='grail')
formal arg1: 1220
formal arg2: 740.0
Xtra arg c: grail
>>>
>>> dictVarArgs(arg2='tales', c=123, d='poe', arg1='mystery')
formal arg1: mystery
formal arg2: tales
Xtra arg c: 123
Xtra arg d: poe
>>>
>>> dictVarArgs('one', d=10, e='zoo', men=('freud', 'gaudi'))
formal arg1: one
formal arg2: defaultB
Xtra arg men: ('freud', 'gaudi')
Xtra arg d: 10
Xtra arg e: zoo
```

Both keyword and non-keyword variable arguments may be used in the same function as long as the keyword dictionary is last and is preceded by the non-keyword tuple, as in the following example:

```
def newfoo(arg1, arg2, *nkw, **kw):
    display regular args and all variable args'
    print 'arg1 is:', arg1
    print 'arg2 is:', arg2
    for eachNKW in nkw:
        print 'additional non-keyword arg:', eachNKW
    for eachKW in kw.keys():
        print "additional keyword arg '%s': %s" % \
            (eachKW, kw[eachKW])
```

Calling our function within the interpreter, we get the following output:

```
>>> newfoo('wolf', 3, 'projects', freud=90, gamble=96)
arg1 is: wolf
arg2 is: 3
additional non-keyword arg: projects
additional keyword arg 'freud': 90
additional keyword arg 'gamble': 96
```

11.6.3 Calling Functions with Variable Argument Objects

Above in Section 11.2.4, we introduced the use of * and ** to specify sets of arguments in a function call. Here we will show you more examples of that syntax, with a slight bias toward functions accepting variable arguments.

We will now use our friend `newfoo()`, defined in the previous section, to test the new calling syntax. Our first call to `newfoo()` will use the old-style method of listing all arguments individually, even the variable arguments that follow all the formal arguments:

```
>>> newfoo(10, 20, 30, 40, foo=50, bar=60)
arg1 is: 10
arg2 is: 20
additional non-keyword arg: 30
additional non-keyword arg: 40
additional keyword arg 'foo': 50
additional keyword arg 'bar': 60
```

We will now make a similar call; however, instead of listing the variable arguments individually, we will put the non-keyword arguments in a tuple and the keyword arguments in a dictionary to make the call:

```
>>> newfoo(2, 4, *(6, 8), **{'foo': 10, 'bar': 12})
arg1 is: 2
arg2 is: 4
additional non-keyword arg: 6
additional non-keyword arg: 8
additional keyword arg 'foo': 10
additional keyword arg 'bar': 12
```

Finally, we will make another call but build our tuple and dictionary outside of the function invocation:

```
>>> aTuple = (6, 7, 8)
>>> aDict = {'z': 9}
>>> newfoo(1, 2, 3, x=4, y=5, *aTuple, **aDict)
```

```
arg1 is: 1
arg2 is: 2
additional non-keyword arg: 3
additional non-keyword arg: 6
additional non-keyword arg: 7
additional non-keyword arg: 8
additional keyword arg 'z': 9
additional keyword arg 'x': 4
additional keyword arg 'y': 5
```

Notice how our tuple and dictionary arguments make only a subset of the final tuple and dictionary received within the function call. The additional non-keyword value '3' and keyword pairs for 'x' and 'y' were also included in the final argument lists even though they were not part of the '*' and '**' variable argument parameters.

Prior to 1.6, variable objects could only be passed to apply() with the function object for invocation. This current calling syntax effectively obsoletes the use of apply(). Below is an example of using these symbols to call any function object with any type of parameter set.

Functional Programming Example

Another useful application of functional programming comes in terms of debugging or performance measurement. You are working on functions that need to be fully tested or run through regressions every night, or that need to be timed over many iterations for potential improvements. All you need to do is to create a diagnostic function that sets up the test environment, then calls the function in question. Because this system should be flexible, you want to allow the testee function to be passed in as an argument. So a pair of such functions, timeit() and testit(), would probably be useful to the software developer today.

We will now present the source code to one such example of a testit() function (see Example 11.5). We will leave a timeit() function as an exercise for the reader (see Exercise 11.12).

This module provides an execution test environment for functions. The testit() function takes a function and arguments, then invokes that function with the given arguments under the watch of an exception handler. If the function completes successfully, a True return value packaged with the return value of the function is sent back to the caller. Any failure causes False to be returned along with the reason for the exception. (Exception is the root class for all runtime exceptions; review Chapter 10 for details.)

Example 11.5 Testing Functions (`testit.py`)

`testit()` *invokes a given function with its arguments, returning* `True` *packaged with the return value of the function on success or* `False` *with the cause of failure.*

```python
1   #!/usr/bin/env python
2
3   def testit(func, *nkwargs, **kwargs):
4
5       try:
6           retval = func(*nkwargs, **kwargs)
7           result = (True, retval)
8       except Exception, diag:
9           result = (False, str(diag))
10      return result
11
12  def test():
13      funcs = (int, long, float)
14      vals = (1234, 12.34, '1234', '12.34')
15
16      for eachFunc in funcs:
17          print '-' * 20
18          for eachVal in vals:
19              retval = testit(eachFunc,
20                              eachVal)
21              if retval[0]:
22                  print '%s(%s) =' % \
23          (eachFunc.__name__, `eachVal`), retval[1]
24              else:
25                  print '%s(%s) = FAILED:' % \
26          (eachFunc.__name__, `eachVal`), retval[1]
27
28  if __name__ == '__main__':
29      test()
```

The unit tester function `test()` runs a set of numeric conversion functions on an input set of four numbers. There are two failure cases in this test set to confirm such functionality. Here is the output of running the script:

```
$ testit.py
--------------------
int(1234) = 1234
int(12.34) = 12
int('1234') = 1234
int('12.34') = FAILED: invalid literal for int(): 12.34
--------------------
long(1234) = 1234L
```

```
long(12.34) = 12L
long('1234') = 1234L
long('12.34') = FAILED: invalid literal for long(): 12.34
--------------------
float(1234) = 1234.0
float(12.34) = 12.34
float('1234') = 1234.0
float('12.34') = 12.34
```

11.7 Functional Programming

Python is not and will probably not ever claim to be a functional programming language, but it does support a number of valuable functional programming constructs. There are also some that behave like functional programming mechanisms but may not be traditionally considered as such. What Python *does* provide comes in the form of four built-in functions and lambda expressions.

11.7.1 Anonymous Functions and `lambda`

Python allows one to create *anonymous functions* using the **lambda** keyword. They are "anonymous" because they are not declared in the standard manner, i.e., using the **def** statement. (Unless assigned to a local variable, such objects do not create a name in any namespace either.) However, as functions, they may also have arguments. An entire lambda "statement" represents an expression, and the body of that expression must also be given on the same line as the declaration. We now present the syntax for anonymous functions:

> **lambda** [*arg1*[, *arg2*, ... *argN*]]: *expression*

Arguments are optional, and if used, are usually part of the expression as well.

CORE NOTE: lambda **expression returns callable function object**

---

*Calling **lambda** with an appropriate expression yields a function object that can be used like any other function. They can be passed to other functions, aliased with additional references, be members of container objects, and as callable objects, be invoked (with any arguments, if necessary). When called, these objects will yield a result equivalent to the same expression if given the same arguments. They are indistinguishable from functions that return the evaluation of an equivalent expression.*

Before we look at any examples using **lambda**, we would like to review single-line statements and then show the resemblances to lambda expressions.

```
def true():
    return True
```

The above function takes no arguments and always returns `True`. Single line functions in Python may be written on the same line as the header. Given that, we can rewrite our `true()` function so that it looks something like the following:

```
def true(): return True
```

We will present the named functions in this manner for the duration of this chapter because it helps one visualize their lambda equivalents. For our `true()` function, the equivalent expression (no arguments, returns `True`) using **lambda** is:

```
lambda :True
```

Usage of the named `true()` function is fairly obvious, but not for **lambda**. Do we just use it as is, or do we need to assign it somewhere? A lambda function by itself serves no purpose, as we see here:

```
>>> lambda :True
<function <lambda> at f09ba0>
```

In the above example, we simply used **lambda** to create a function (object), but did not save it anywhere nor did we call it. The reference count for this function object is set to True on creation of the function object, but because no reference is saved, goes back down to zero and is garbage-collected. To keep the object around, we can save it into a variable and invoke it any time after. Perhaps now is a good opportunity:

```
>>> true = lambda :True
>>> true()
True
```

Assigning it looks much more useful here. Likewise, we can assign lambda expressions to a data structure such as a list or tuple where, based on some input criteria, we can choose which function to execute as well as what the arguments would be. (In the next section, we will show how to use lambda expressions with functional programming constructs.)

Let us now design a function that takes two numeric or string arguments and returns the sum for numbers or the concatenated string. We will show the standard function first, followed by its unnamed equivalent.

```
def add(x, y): return x + y  ⟺  lambda x, y: x + y
```

Default and variable arguments are permitted as well, as indicated in the following examples:

```
def usuallyAdd2(x, y=2): return x+y ⇔ lambda x, y=2: x+y
def showAllAsTuple(*z): return z      ⇔ lambda *z: z
```

Seeing is one thing, so we will now try to make you believe by showing how you can try them in the interpreter:

```
>>> a = lambda x, y=2: x + y
>>> a(3)
5
>>> a(3,5)
8
>>> a(0)
2
>>> a(0,9)
9
>>>
>>> b = lambda *z: z
>>> b(23, 'zyx')
(23, 'zyx')
>>> b(42)
(42,)
```

One final word on **lambda**: Although it appears that **lambda** is a one-line version of a function, it is not equivalent to an "inline" statement in C++, whose purpose is bypassing function stack allocation during invocation for performance reasons. A lambda expression works just like a function, creating a frame object when called.

11.7.2 Built-in Functions: apply(), filter(),map(),reduce()

In this section, we will look at the `apply()`, `filter()`, `map()`, and `reduce()` built-in functions as well as give some examples to show how they can be used. These functions provide the functional programming features found in Python. A summary of these functions is given in Table 11.2. All take a function object to somehow invoke.

As you may imagine, lambda functions fit nicely into applications using any of these functions because all of them take a function object with which to execute, and **lambda** provides a mechanism for creating functions on the fly.

Table 11.2 Functional Programming Built-in Functions

Built-in Function	Description
`apply(func[, nkw][, kw])`[a]	Calls *func* with optional arguments, *nkw* for non-keyword arguments and *kw* for keyword arguments; the return value is the return value of the function call
`filter(func, seq)`[b]	Invokes Boolean function *func* iteratively over each element of *seq*; returns a sequence for those elements for which *func* returned true
`map(func, seq1[, seq2...])`[b]	Applies function *func* to each element of given sequence(s) and provides return values in a list; if *func* is None, *func* behaves as the identity function, returning a list consisting of *n*-tuples for sets of elements of each sequence
`reduce(func, seq[, init])`	Applies binary function *func* to elements of sequence *seq*, taking a pair at a time (previous result and next sequence item), continually applying the current result with the next value to obtain the succeeding result, finally reducing our sequence to a single return value; if initial value *init* given, first compare will be of *init* and first sequence element rather than the first two sequence elements

a. Effectively deprecated in 1.6 to be phased out in future versions of Python.
b. Partially deprecated by list comprehensions introduced in Python 2.0.

*apply()

As mentioned before, the calling syntax for functions, which now allow for a tuple of variable arguments as well as a dictionary of keyword variable arguments, effectively deprecates `apply()` as of Python 1.6. The function will be phased out and eventually removed in a future version of Python. We mention it here for historical purposes as well as for those maintaining code that uses `apply()`.

filter()

The second built-in function we examine in this chapter is `filter()`. Imagine going to an orchard and leaving with a bag of apples you picked off the trees. Wouldn't it be nice if you could run the entire bag through a filter to keep just the good ones? That is the main premise of the `filter()` function.

Given a sequence of objects and a "filtering" function, run each item of the sequence through the filter, and keep only the ones that the function returns true for. The `filter()` function calls the given Boolean function for each item of the provided sequence. Each item for which `filter()` returns a non-zero (true) value is appended to a list. The object that is returned is a "filtered" sequence of the original.

If we were to code `filter()` in pure Python, it might look something like this:

```
def filter(bool_func, seq):
    filtered_seq = []
    for eachItem in seq:
        if bool_func(eachItem):
            filtered_seq.append(eachItem)
    return filtered_seq
```

One way to understand `filter()` better is by visualizing its behavior. Figure 11–1 attempts to do just that.

In Figure 11–1, we observe our original sequence at the top, items `seq[0]`, `seq[1]`, . . . `seq[N-1]` for a sequence of size N. For each call to `bool_func()`, i.e., `bool_func(seq[0])`, `bool_func(seq[1])`, etc., a return value of `False` or `True` comes back (as per the definition of a Boolean function—ensure that indeed your function does return one or the other). If `bool_func()` returns `True` for any sequence item, that element is inserted

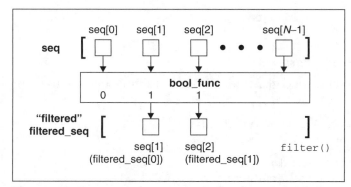

Figure 11-1 How the `filter()` built-in function works

into the return sequence. When iteration over the entire sequence has been completed, `filter()` returns the newly created sequence.

We present below a script that shows one way to use `filter()` to obtain a short list of random odd numbers. The script generates a larger set of random numbers first, then filters out all the even numbers, leaving us with the desired dataset. When we first coded this example, `oddnogen.py` looked like the following:

```
from random import randint

def odd(n):
    return n % 2

allNums = []
for eachNum in range(9):
    allNums.append(randint(1, 99))
print filter(odd, allNums)
```

This code consists of two functions: `odd()`, a Boolean function that determined if an integer was odd (true) or even (false), and `main()`, the primary driving component. The purpose of `main()` is to generate ten random numbers between 1 and 100; then `filter()` is called to remove all the even numbers. Finally, the set of odd numbers is displayed, preceded by the size of our filtered list.

Importing and running this module several times, we get the following output:

```
$ python oddnogen.py
[9, 33, 55, 65]

$ python oddnogen.py
[39, 77, 39, 71, 1]

$ python oddnogen.py
[23, 39, 9, 1, 63, 91]

$ python oddnogen.py
[41, 85, 93, 53, 3]
```

Refactoring Pass 1

We notice on second glance that `odd()` is simple enough to be replaced by a **lambda** expression:

```
from random import randint

allNums = []
for eachNum in range(9):
    allNums.append(randint(1, 99))
print filter(lambda n: n%2, allNums)
```

Refactoring Pass 2

We have already mentioned how list comprehensions can be a suitable replacement for `filter()` so here it is:

```
from random import randint

allNums = []
for eachNum in range(9):
    allNums.append(randint(1, 99))
print [n for n in allNums if n%2]
```

Refactoring Pass 3

We can further simplify our code by integrating another list comprehension to put together our final list. As you can see below, because of the flexible syntax of list comps, there is no longer a need for intermediate variables. (To make things fit, we import `randint()` with a shorter name into our code.)

```
from random import randint as ri
print [n for n in [ri(1,99) for i in range(9)] if n%2]
```

Although longer than it should be, the line of code making up the core part of this example is not as obfuscated as one might think.

map()

The `map()` built-in function is similar to `filter()` in that it can process a sequence through a function. However, unlike `filter()`, `map()` "maps" the function call to each sequence item and returns a list consisting of all the return values.

In its simplest form, `map()` takes a function and sequence, applies the function to each item of the sequence, and creates a return value list that is comprised of each application of the function. So if your mapping function is to add 2 to each number that comes in and you feed that function to `map()` along with a list of numbers, the resulting list returned is the same set of numbers as the original, but with 2 added to each number. If we were to code how this simple form of `map()` works in Python, it might look something like the code below that is illustrated in Figure 11–2.

```
def map(func, seq):
    mapped_seq = []
    for eachItem in seq:
        mapped_seq.append(func(eachItem))
    return mapped_seq
```

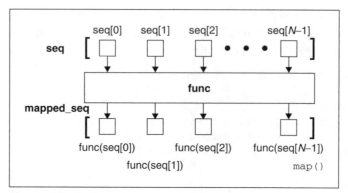

Figure 11-2 How the `map()` built-in function works

We can whip up a few quick **lambda** functions to show you how `map()` works on real data:

```
>>> map((lambda x: x+2), [0, 1, 2, 3, 4, 5])
[2, 3, 4, 5, 6, 7]
>>>
>>> map(lambda x: x**2, range(6))
[0, 1, 4, 9, 16, 25]
>>> [x+2 for x in range(6)]
[2, 3, 4, 5, 6, 7]
>>>
>>>[x**2 for x in range(6)]
[0, 1, 4, 9, 16, 25]
```

We have also discussed how map () can sometimes can be replaced by list comprehensions, so here we refactor our two examples above.

The more general form of `map()` can take more than a single sequence as its input. If this is the case, then `map()` will iterate through each sequence in parallel. On the first invocation, it will bundle the first element of each sequence into a tuple, apply the `func` function to it, and return the result as a tuple into the *mapped_seq* mapped sequence that is finally returned as a whole when `map()` has completed execution.

Figure 11–2 illustrated how `map()` works with a single sequence. If we used `map()` with *M* sequences of *N* objects each, our previous diagram would be converted to something like the diagram presented in Figure 11–3.

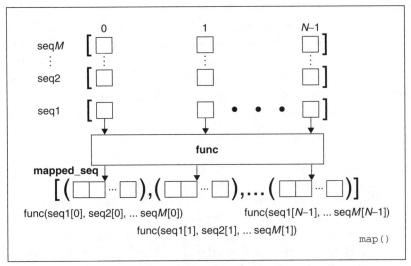

Figure 11–3 How the **map()** built-in function works with > 1 sequence

Here are several examples using map() with multiple sequences:

```
>>> map(lambda x, y: x + y, [1,3,5], [2,4,6])
[3, 7, 11]
>>>
>>> map(lambda x, y: (x+y, x-y), [1,3,5], [2,4,6])
[(3, -1), (7, -1), (11, -1)]
>>>
>>> map(None, [1,3,5], [2,4,6])
[(1, 2), (3, 4), (5, 6)]
```

The last example above uses map() and a function object of None to merge elements of unrelated sequences together. This idiom was so commonly used prior to Python 2.0 that a new built-in function, zip(), was added just to address it:

2.0

```
>>> zip([1,3,5], [2,4,6])
[(1, 2), (3, 4), (5, 6)]
```

reduce()

The final functional programming piece is reduce(), which takes a *binary function* (a function that takes two values, performs some calculation and returns one value as output), a sequence, and an optional initializer, and methodologically "reduces" the contents of that list down to a single value, hence its name. In other languages, this concept is known as *folding*.

It does this by taking the first two elements of the sequence and passing them to the binary function to obtain a single value. It then takes this value and the next item of the sequence to get yet another value, and so on until the sequence is exhausted and one final value is computed.

You may try to visualize `reduce()` as the following equivalence example:

```
reduce(func, [1, 2, 3])     ≡     func(func(1, 2), 3)
```

Some argue that the "proper functional" use of `reduce()` requires only one item to be taken at a time for `reduce()`. In our first iteration above, we took two items because we did not have a "result" from the previous values (because we did not *have* any previous values). This is where the optional initializer comes in (see the `init` variable below). If the initializer is given, then the first iteration is performed on the initializer and the first item of the sequence, and follows normally from there.

If we were to try to implement `reduce()` in pure Python, it might look something like this:

```python
def reduce(bin_func, seq, init=None):
    lseq = list(seq)        # convert to list
    if init is None:        # initializer?
        res = lseq.pop(0) #    no
    else:
        res = init          #    yes
    for item in lseq:       # reduce sequence
        res = bin_func(res, item) # apply function
    return res                         # return result
```

This may be the most difficult of the four conceptually, so we should again show you an example as well as a functional diagram (see Figure 11–4). The "hello world" of `reduce()` is its use of a simple addition function or its **lambda** equivalent seen earlier in this chapter:

- **def** mySum(x,y): **return** x+y
- **lambda** x,y: x+y

Given a list, we can get the sum of all the values by simply creating a loop, iteratively going through the list, adding the current element to a running subtotal, and being presented with the result once the loop has completed:

```python
>>> def mySum(x,y): return x+y
>>> allNums = range(5)        # [0, 1, 2, 3, 4]
>>> total = 0
```

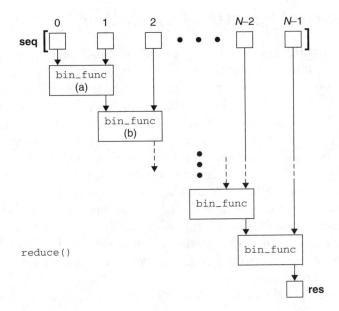

(a) The value of this result is bin_func(seq[0], seq[1])
(b) The value of this result is bin_func(bin_func(seq[0], seq[1]), seq[2]), etc.

Figure 11–4 How the reduce() built-in function works

```
>>> for eachNum in allNums:
...     total = mySum(total, eachNum)
...
>>> print 'the total is:', total
the total is: 10
```

Using **lambda** and reduce(), we can do the same thing on a single line:

```
>>> print 'the total is:', reduce((lambda x,y: x+y), range(5))
the total is: 10
```

The reduce() function performs the following mathematical operations given the input above:

$$((((0 + 1) + 2) + 3) + 4) \Rightarrow 10$$

It takes the first two elements of the list (0 and 1), calls mySum() to get 1, then calls mySum() again with that result and the next item 2, gets the result from that, pairs it with the next item 3 and calls mySum(), and finally takes the entire subtotal and calls mySum() with 4 to obtain 10, which is the final return value.

11.7.3 Partial Function Application

The notion of *currying* combines the concepts of functional programming and default and variable arguments together. A function taking N arguments that is "curried" embalms the first argument as a fixed parameter and returns another function object taking (the remaining) N-1 arguments, akin to the actions of the LISP primitive functions car and cdr, respectively. Currying can be generalized into *partial function application* (PFA), in which any number (and order) of arguments is parlayed into another function object with the remainder of the arguments to be supplied later.

In a way, this seems similar to default arguments where if arguments are not provided, they take on a "default" value. In the case of PFAs, the arguments do not have a default value for all calls to a function, only to a specific set of calls. You can have multiple partial function calls, each of which may pass in different arguments to the function, hence the reason why default arguments cannot be used.

2.5   This feature was introduced in Python 2.5 and made available to users via the functools module.

Simple Functional Example

How about creating a simple little example? Let us take two simple functions add() and mul(), both found in the operator module. These are just functional interfaces to the + and * operators that we are already familiar with, e.g., add(x, y) is the same as x + y. Say that we wanted to add one to a number or multiply another by 100 quite often in our applications.

Rather than having multiple calls like add(1, foo), add(1, bar), mul(100, foo), mul(100, bar), would it not be nice to just have existing functions that simplify the function call, i.e., add1(foo), add1(bar), mul100(foo), mul100(bar), but without having to write functions add1() and mul100()? Well, now you can with PFAs. You can create a PFA by using the partial() function found in the functional module:

```
>>> from operator import add, mul
>>> from functools import partial
>>> add1 = partial(add, 1)      # add1(x) == add(1, x)
>>> mul100 = partial(mul, 100) # mul100(x) == mul(100, x)
>>>
>>> add1(10)
11
>>> add1(1)
2
```

```
>>> mul100(10)
1000
>>> mul100(500)
50000
```

This example may or may not open your eyes to the power of PFAs, but we have to start somewhere. PFAs are best used when calling functions that take many parameters. It is also easier to use PFAs with keyword arguments, because specific arguments can be given explicitly, either as curried arguments, or those more "variable" that are passed in at runtime, and we do not have to worry about ordering. Below is an example from the Python documentation for use in applications where binary data (as strings) need to be converted to integers fairly often:

```
>>> baseTwo = partial(int, base=2)
>>> baseTwo.__doc__ = 'Convert base 2 string to an int.'
>>> baseTwo('10010')
18
```

This example uses the int() built-in function and fixes the base to 2 specifically for binary string conversion. Now instead of multiple calls to int() all with the same second parameter (of 2), e.g., int('10010', 2), we can simply use our new baseTwo() function with a single argument. Good style is also followed because it adds a documentation string to the "new (partial) function," and it is also another good use of "function attributes" (see Section 11.3.4 above). One important thing to note is that the keyword argument base is required here.

Be Wary of Keywords

If you create the partial function without the base keyword, e.g., baseTwoBAD = partial(int, 2), it would pass the arguments to int() in the wrong order because the fixed arguments are always placed to the left of the runtime arguments, meaning that baseTwoBAD(x) == int(2, x). If you call it, it would pass in 2 as the number to convert and the base as '10010', resulting in an exception:

```
>>> baseTwoBAD = partial(int, 2)
>>> baseTwoBAD('10010')
Traceback (most recent call last):
  File "<stdin>", line 1, in <module>
TypeError: an integer is required
```

With the keyword in place, the order is preserved properly since, as you know, keyword arguments always come after the formal arguments, so baseTwo(x) == int(x, base=2).

Simple GUI Class Example

PFAs also extended to all callables like classes and methods. An excellent example of using PFAs is in providing "partial-GUI templating." GUI widgets often have many parameters, such as text, length, maximum size, background and foreground colors, both active and otherwise, etc. If we wanted to "fix" some of those arguments, such as making all text labels be in white letters on a blue background, you can customize it exactly that way into a pseudo template for similar objects.

Example 11.6   Partial Function Application GUI (pfaGUI.py)

This a more useful example of partial function application, or more accurately, "partial class instantiation" in this case ... why?

```
1  #!/usr/bin/env python
2
3  from functools import partial
4  import Tkinter
5
6  root = Tkinter.Tk()
7  MyButton = partial(Tkinter.Button, root,
8      fg='white', bg='blue')
9  b1 = MyButton(text='Button 1')
10 b2 = MyButton(text='Button 2')
11 qb = MyButton(text='QUIT', bg='red',
12     command=root.quit)
13 b1.pack()
14 b2.pack()
15 qb.pack(fill=Tkinter.X, expand=True)
16 root.title('PFAs!')
17 root.mainloop()
```

In lines 7–8, we create the "partial class instantiator" (because that is what it is instead of a partial function) for Tkinter.Button, fixing the parent window argument root and both foreground and background colors. We create two buttons b1 and b2 matching this template providing only the text label as unique to each. The quit button (lines 11–12) is slightly more customized, taking on a different background color (red, which overrides the blue default) and installing a callback to close the window when it is pressed. (The other two buttons have no function when they are pressed.)

Without the `MyButton` "template," you would have to use the "full" syntax each time (because you are still not giving all the arguments as there are plenty of parameters you are not passing that have default values):

```
b1 = Tkinter.Button(root, fg='white', bg='blue', text='Button 1')
b2 = Tkinter.Button(root, fg='white', bg='blue', text='Button 2')
qb = Tkinter.Button(root, fg='white', text='QUIT', bg='red',
            command=root.quit)
```

Here is a snapshot of what this simple GUI looks like:

Why bother with so much repetition when your code can be more compact and easy to read? You can find out more about GUI programming in Chapter 18 (Section 18.3.5), where we feature a longer example of using PFAs.

From what you have seen so far, you can see that PFA takes on the flavors of templating and "style-sheeting" in terms of providing defaults in a more functional programming environment. You can read more about them in the documentation for the `functools` module documentation found in the Python Library Reference, the "What's New in Python 2.5" document, and the specifying PEP 309.

11.8 Variable Scope

The *scope* of an identifier is defined to be the portion of the program where its declaration applies, or what we refer to as "variable visibility." In other words, it is like asking yourself in which parts of a program do you have access to a specific identifier. Variables either have local or global scope.

11.8.1 Global versus Local Variables

Variables defined within a function have *local* scope, and those at the highest level in a module have *global* scope. In their famous "dragon" book on compiler theory, Aho, Sethi, and Ullman summarize it this way:

"The portion of the program to which a declaration applies is called the *scope* of that declaration. An occurrence of a name in a procedure is said to be *local* to the procedure if it is in the scope of a declaration within the procedure; otherwise, the occurrence is said to be *nonlocal*."

One characteristic of global variables is that unless deleted, they have a lifespan that lasts as long as the script that is running and whose values are accessible to all functions, whereas local variables, like the stack frame they reside in, live temporarily, only as long as the functions they are defined in are currently active. When a function call is made, its local variables come into scope as they are declared. At that time, a new local name is created for that object, and once that function has completed and the frame deallocated, that variable will go out of scope.

```
global_str = 'foo'
def foo():
    local_str = 'bar'
    return global_str + local_str
```

In the above example, `global_str` is a global variable while `local_str` is a local variable. The `foo()` function has access to both global and local variables while the main block of code has access only to global variables.

CORE NOTE: Searching for identifiers (aka variables, names, etc.)

When searching for an identifier, Python searches the local scope first. If the name is not found within the local scope, then an identifier must be found in the global scope or else a `NameError` *exception is raised.*

A variable's scope is related to the namespace in which it resides. We will cover namespaces formally in Chapter 12; suffice it to say for now that namespaces are just naming domains that map names to objects, a virtual set of what variable names are currently in use, if you will. The concept of scope relates to the namespace search order that is used to find a variable. All names in the local namespace are within the local scope when a function is executing. That is the first namespace searched when looking for a variable. If it is not found there, then perhaps a globally scoped variable with that name can be found. These variables are stored (and searched) in the global and built-in namespaces.

It is possible to "hide" or override a global variable just by creating a local one. Recall that the local namespace is searched first, being in its local scope. If the name is found, the search does not continue to search for a globally scoped variable, hence overriding any matching name in either the global or built-in namespaces.

Also, be careful when using local variables with the same names as global variables. If you use such names in a function (to access the global value) before you assign the local value, you will get an exception (`NameError` or `UnboundLocalError`), depending on which version of Python you are using.

11.8.2 global Statement

Global variable names can be overridden by local variables if they are declared within the function. Here is another example, similar to the first, but the global and local nature of the variable are not as clear.

```
def foo():
    print "\ncalling foo()..."
    bar = 200
    print "in foo(), bar is", bar
bar = 100
print "in __main__, bar is", bar
foo()
print "\nin __main__, bar is (still)", bar
```

It gave the following output:

```
in __main__, bar is 100
calling foo()...
in foo(), bar is 200
in __main__, bar is (still) 100
```

Our local `bar` pushed the global `bar` out of the local scope. To specifically reference a named global variable, one must use the **global** statement. The syntax for global is:

```
global var1[, var2[, ... varN]]]
```

Modifying the example above, we can update our code so that we use the global version of `is_this_global` rather than create a new local variable.

```
>>> is_this_global = 'xyz'
>>> def foo():
...         global is_this_global
...         this_is_local = 'abc'
...         is_this_global = 'def'
...         print this_is_local + is_this_global
...
>>> foo()
abcdef
>>> print is_this_global
def
```

11.8.3 Number of Scopes

Python syntactically supports multiple levels of functional nesting, and as of Python 2.1, matching statically nested scoping. However, in versions prior to 2.1, a maximum of two scopes was imposed: a function's local scope and the global scope. Even though more levels of functional nesting exist, you could not access more than two scopes:

```python
def foo():
    m = 3
    def bar():
        n = 4
        print m + n
    print m
    bar()
```

Although this code executes perfectly fine today . . .

```
>>> foo()
3
7
```

. . . executing it resulted in errors in Python before 2.1:

```
>>> foo()
Traceback (innermost last):
  File "<stdin>", line 1, in ?
  File "<stdin>", line 7, in foo
  File "<stdin>", line 5, in bar
NameError: m
```

The access to `foo()`'s local variable m within function `bar()` is illegal because m is declared local to `foo()`. The only scopes accessible from `bar()` are `bar()`'s local scope and the global scope. `foo()`'s local scope is *not* included in that short list of two. Note that the output for the "**print** m" statement succeeded, and it is the function call to `bar()` that fails. Fortunately with Python's current nested scoping rules, this is not a problem today.

11.8.4 Closures

With Python's statically nested scoping, it becomes useful to define inner functions as we have seen earlier. In the next section, we will focus on scope and **lambda**, but inner functions also suffered the same problem before Python 2.1 when the scoping rules changed to what they are today.

If references are made from inside an inner function to an object defined in any outer scope (but not in the global scope), the inner function then is known as a *closure*. The variables defined in the outer function but used or referred to by the inner function are called *free variables*. Closures are an important concept in functional programming languages, with Scheme and Haskell being two of them. Closures are syntactically simple (as simple as inner functions) yet still very powerful.

A closure combines an inner function's own code and scope along with the scope of an outer function. Closure lexical variables do not belong to the global namespace scope or the local one—they belong to someone else's namespace and carry an "on the road" kind of scope. (Note that they differ from objects in that those variables live in an object's namespace while closure variables live in a function's namespace and scope.) So why would you want to use closures?

Closures are useful for setting up calculations, hiding state, letting you move around function objects and scope at will. Closures come in handy in GUI or event-driven programming where a lot of APIs support callbacks. The same applies for retrieving database rows and processing the data in the exact same manner. Callbacks are just functions. Closures are functions, too, but they carry some additional scope with them. They are just functions with an extra feature . . . another scope.

You will probably feel that the use of closures draws a strong parallel to partial function application as introduced earlier in this chapter, but PFA is really more like currying than the use of closures because it is not as much as about function calling as it is about using variables defined in another scope.

Simple Closure Example

Below is a short example of using closures. We will simulate a counter and also simulate making an integer mutable by enclosing it as a single element of a list.

```
def counter(start_at=0):
    count = [start_at]
    def incr():
        count[0] += 1
        return count[0]
    return incr
```

The only thing counter() does is to accept an initial value to start counting at and assigns it as the sole member of the list count. Then an incr() inner function is defined. By using the variable count inside it, we have created a closure because it now carries with it the scope of counter(). incr() increments the running count and returns it. Then the final magic is that `counter()` returns `incr`, a (callable) function object.

If we run this interactively, we get the output below—note how similar it looks to instantiating a counter object and executing the instance:

```
>>> count = counter(5)
>>> print count()
6
>>> print count()
7
>>> count2 = counter(100)
>>> print count2()
101
>>> print count()
8
```

The one difference is that we were able to do something that previously required us to write a class, and not only that, but to have to override the `__call__()` special method of that class to make its instances callable. Here we were able to do it with a pair of functions.

Now, in many cases, a class is the right thing to use. Closures are more appropriate in cases whenever you need a callback that has to have its own scope, especially if it is something small and simple, and often, clever. As usual, if you use a closure, it is a good idea to comment your code and/or use doc strings to explain what you are doing.

*Chasing Down Closure Lexical Variables

The next two sections contain material for advanced readers . . . feel free to skip it if you wish. We will discuss how you can track down free variables with a function's `func_closure` attribute. Here is a code snippet that demonstrates it.

If we run this piece of code, we get the following output:

```
no f1 closure vars
f2 closure vars: ['<cell at 0x5ee30: int object at
    0x200377c>']
f3 closure vars: ['<cell at 0x5ee90: int object at
    0x2003770>', '<cell at 0x5ee30: int object at
    0x200377c>']
<int 'w' id=0x2003788 val=1>
<int 'x' id=0x200377c val=2>
<int 'y' id=0x2003770 val=3>
<int 'z' id=0x2003764 val=4>
```

Example 11.7   Tracking Closure Variables (`closureVars.py`)

This example shows how we can track closure variables by using a function's `func_closure` *variable.*

```
1   #!/usr/bin/env python
2
3   output = '<int %r id=%#0x val=%d>'
4   w = x = y = z = 1
5
6   def f1():
7       x = y = z = 2
8
9           def f2():
10              y = z = 3
11
12              def f3():
13                  z = 4
14                  print output % ('w', id(w), w)
15                  print output % ('x', id(x), x)
16                  print output % ('y', id(y), y)
17                  print output % ('z', id(z), z)
18
19              clo = f3.func_closure
20              if clo:
21                  print "f3 closure vars:", [str(c) for c in clo]
22              else:
23                  print "no f3 closure vars"
24              f3()
25
26          clo = f2.func_closure
27          if clo:
28              print "f2 closure vars:", [str(c) for c in clo]
29          else:
30              print "no f2 closure vars"
31          f2()
32
33  clo = f1.func_closure
34  if clo:
35      print "f1 closure vars:", [str(c) for c in clo]
36  else:
37      print "no f1 closure vars"
38  f1()
```

Line-by-Line Explanation

Lines 1–4

This script starts by creating a template to output a variable: its name, ID, and value, and then sets global variables w, x, y, and z. We define the template so that we do not have to copy the same output format string multiple times.

Lines 6–9, 26–31

The definition of the `f1()` function includes a creating local variables `x`, `y`, and `z` plus the definition of an inner function `f2()`. (Note that all local variables shadow or hide accessing their equivalently named global variables.) If `f2()` uses any variables that are defined in `f1()`'s scope, i.e., not global and not local to `f2()`, those represent free variables, and they will be tracked by `f1.func_closure`.

Lines 9–10, 19–24

Practically duplicating the code for `f1()`, these lines do the same for `f2()`, which defines locals `y` and `z` plus an inner function `f3()`. Again, note that the locals here shadow globals as well as those in intermediate localized scopes, e.g., `f1()`'s. If there are any free variables for `f3()`, they will be displayed here.

You will no doubt notice that references to free variables are stored in cell objects, or simply, *cells*. What are these guys? Cells are basically a way to keep references to free variables alive after their defining scope(s) have completed (and are no longer on the stack).

For example, let us assume that function `f3()` has been passed to some other function so that it can be called later, even after `f2()` has completed. You do not want to have `f2()`'s stack frame around because that will keep all of `f2()`'s variables alive even if we are only interested in the free variables used by `f3()`. Cells hold on to the free variables so that the rest of `f2()` can be deallocated.

Lines 12–17

This block represents the definition of `f3()`, which creates a local variable `z`. We then display `w`, `x`, `y`, `z`, all chased down from the innermost scope outward. The variable `w` cannot be found in `f3()`, `f2()`, or `f1()`, therefore, it is a global. The variable `x` is not found in `f3()` or `f2()`, so it is a closure variable from `f1()`. Similarly, `y` is a closure variable from `f2()`, and finally, `z` is local to `f3()`.

Lines 33–38

The rest of `main()` attempts to display closure variables for `f1()`, but it will never happen since there are no scopes in between the global scope and `f1()`'s—there is no scope that `f1()` can borrow from, ergo no closure can be created—so the conditional expression on line 34 will never evaluate to `True`. This code is just here for decorative purposes.

*Advanced Closures and Decorators Example

We saw a simple example of using closures and decorators in back in Section 11.3.6, `deco.py`. The following is a slightly more advanced example, to show you the real power of closures. The application "logs" function calls. The user chooses whether they want to log a function call before or after it has been invoked. If post-log is chosen, the execution time is also displayed.

Example 11.8 Logging Function Calls with Closures (`funcLog.py`)

This example shows a decorator that takes an argument that ultimately determines which closure will be used. Also featured is the power of closures.

```python
1   #!/usr/bin/env python
2
3   from time import time
4
5   def logged(when):
6       def log(f, *args, **kargs):
7           print '''Called:
8   function: %s
9   args: %r
10  kargs: %r''' % (f, args, kargs)
11
12      def pre_logged(f):
13          def wrapper(*args, **kargs):
14              log(f, *args, **kargs)
15              return f(*args, **kargs)
16          return wrapper
17
18      def post_logged(f):
19          def wrapper(*args, **kargs):
20              now = time()
21              try:
22                  return f(*args, **kargs)
23              finally:
24                  log(f, *args, **kargs)
25                  print "time delta: %s" % (time()-now)
26          return wrapper
27
28      try:
29          return {"pre": pre_logged,
30                  "post": post_logged}[when]
31      except KeyError, e:
32          raise ValueError(e), 'must be "pre" or "post"'
33
34  @logged("post")
35  def hello(name):
36      print "Hello,", name
37
38  hello("World!")
```

If you execute this script, you will get output similar to the following:

```
$ funcLog.py
Hello, World!
Called:
    function: <function hello at 0x555f0>
    args: ('World!',)
    kargs: {}
    time delta: 0.000471115112305
```

Line-by-Line Explanation

Lines 5–10, 28–32

This body of code represents the core part of the logged() function, whose responsibility it is to take the user's request as to when the function call should be logged. Should it be before the target function is called or after? logged() has three helper inner functions defined within its definition: log(), pre_logged(), and post_logged().

log() is the function that does the actual logging. It just displays to standard output the name of the function and its arguments. If you were to use this function "in the real world," you would most likely send this output to a file, a database, or perhaps standard error (sys.stderr).

The last part of logged() in lines 28–32 is actually the first lines of code in the function that are not function declarations. It reads the user's selection when, and returns one of the *logged() functions so that *it* can then be called with the target function to wrap it.

Lines 12–26

pre_logged() and post_logged() will both wrap the target function and log it in accordance with its name, e.g., post_logged() will log the function call *after* the target function has executed while pre_logged() does it before execution.

Depending on the user's selection, one of pre_logged() and post_logged() will be returned. When the decorator is called, it evaluates the decorator function first along with its argument. e.g., logged(when). Then the returned function object is called with the target function as its parameter, e.g., pre_logged(f) or post_logged(f).

Both *logged() functions include a closure named wrapper(). It calls the target function while logging it as appropriate. The functions return the wrapped function object, which then is reassigned to the original target function identifier.

Lines 34–38

The main part of this script simply decorates the `hello()` function and executes it with the modified function object. When you call `hello()` on line 38, it is not the same as the function object that was created on line 35. The decorator on line 34 wraps the original function object with the specified decoration and returns a wrapped version of `hello()`.

11.8.5 Scope and `lambda`

Python's **lambda** anonymous functions follow the same scoping rules as standard functions. A `lambda` expression defines a new scope, just like a function definition, so the scope is inaccessible to any other part of the program except for that local `lambda`/function.

Those `lambda` expressions declared local to a function are accessible only within that function; however, the expression in the **lambda** statement has the same scope access as the function. You can also think of a function and a `lambda` expression as siblings.

```
x = 10
def foo():
    y = 5
    bar = lambda :x+y
    print bar()
```

We know that this code works fine now . . .

```
>>> foo()
15
```

. . . however, we must again look to the past to see an extremely common idiom that was necessary to get code to work in older versions of Python. Before 2.1, we would get an error like what you see below because while the function and **lambda** have access to global variables, neither has access to the other's local scopes:

```
>>> foo()
Traceback (innermost last):
  File "<stdin>", line 1, in ?
  File "<stdin>", line 4, in foo
  File "<stdin>", line 3, in <lambda>
NameError: y
```

In the example above, although the lambda expression was created in the local scope of foo(), it has access to only two scopes: its local scope and the global scope (also see Section 11.8.3). The solution was to add a variable with a default argument so that we could pass in a variable from an outer local scope to an inner one. In our example above, we would change the line with the lambda to look like this:

```
bar = lambda y=y: x+y
```

With this change, it now works. The outer y's value will be passed in as an argument and hence the local y (local to the lambda function). You will see this common idiom all over Python code that you will come across; however, it still does not address the possibility of the outer y changing values, such as:

```
x = 10
def foo():
    y = 5
    bar = lambda y=y: x+y
    print bar()
    y = 8
    print bar()
```

The output is "totally wrong":

```
>>> foo()
15
15
```

The reason for this is that the value of the outer y was passed in and "set" in the **lambda**, so even though its value changed later on, the **lambda** definition did not. The only other alternative back then was to add a local variable z within the *lambda* expression that references the function local variable y.

```
x = 10
def foo():
    y = 5
    bar = lambda z:x+z
    print bar(y)
    y = 8
    print bar(y)
```

All of this was necessary in order to get the correct output:

```
>>> foo()
15
18
```

This was also not preferred as now all places that call bar() would have to be changed to pass in a variable. Beginning in 2.1, the entire thing works perfectly without any modification:

```
x = 10
def foo():
    y = 5
    bar = lambda :x+y
    print bar(y)
    y = 8
    print bar(y)
>>> foo()
15
18
```

Are you not glad that "correct" statically nested scoping was (finally) added to Python? Many of the "old-timers" certainly are. You can read more about this important change in PEP 227.

11.8.6 Variable Scope and Namespaces

From our study in this chapter, we can see that at any given time, there are either one or two active scopes—no more, no less. Either we are at the top-level of a module where we have access only to the global scope, or we are executing in a function where we have access to its local scope as well as the global scope. How do namespaces relate to scope?

From the Core Note in Section 11.8.1 we can also see that, at any given time, there are either two or three active namespaces. From within a function, the local scope encompasses the local namespace, the first place a name is searched for. If the name exists here, then checking the global scope (global and built-in namespaces) is skipped. From the global scope (outside of any function), a name lookup begins with the global namespace. If no match is found, the search proceeds to the built-in namespace.

We will now present Example 11.9, a script with mixed scope everywhere. We leave it as an exercise to the reader to determine the output of the program.

Example 11.9 Variable Scope (`scope.py`)

Local variables hide global variables, as indicated in this variable scope program. What is the output of this program? (And why?)

```
1   #!/usr/bin/env python
2   j, k = 1, 2
3
4   def proc1():
5
6       j, k = 3, 4
7       print "j == %d and k == %d" % (j, k)
8       k = 5
9
10  def proc2():
11
12      j = 6
13      proc1()
14      print "j == %d and k == %d" % (j, k)
15
16
17  k = 7
18  proc1()
19  print "j == %d and k == %d" % (j, k)
20
21  j = 8
22  proc2()
23  print "j == %d and k == %d" % (j, k)
```

Also see Section 12.3.1 for more on namespaces and variable scope.

11.9 *Recursion

A function is *recursive* if it contains a call to itself. According to Aho, Sethi, and Ullman, "[a] procedure is *recursive* if a new activation can begin before an earlier activation of the same procedure has ended." In other words, a new invocation of the same function occurs within that function before it finished.

Recursion is used extensively in language recognition as well as in mathematical applications that use recursive functions. Earlier in this text, we took a first look at the factorial function where we defined:

$$N! \equiv \text{factorial}(N) \equiv 1 * 2 * 3 \ldots * N$$

We can also look at factorial this way:

```
factorial(N) = N!
             = N * (N-1)!
             = N * (N-1) * (N-2)!
                  :
             = N * (N-1) * (N-2) ... * 3 * 2 * 1
```

We can now see that factorial is recursive because `factorial(N) = N * factorial(N-1)`. In other words, to get the value of `factorial(N)`, one needs to calculate `factorial(N-1)`. Furthermore, to find `factorial(N-1)`, one needs to computer `factorial(N-2)`, and so on.

We now present the recursive version of the factorial function:

```python
def factorial(n):
    if n == 0 or n == 1: # 0! = 1! = 1
        return 1
    else:
        return (n * factorial(n-1))
```

11.10 Generators

Earlier in Chapter 8, we discussed the usefulness behind iterators and how they give non-sequence objects a sequence-like iteration interface. They are simple to understand because they only have one method, a `next()` that is called to get the next item.

However, unless you implement a class as an iterator, iterators really do not have much "intelligence." Would it not be much more powerful to call a function that somehow "generated" the next value in the iteration and returned with something as simple as a `next()` call? That is one motivation for *generators*.

Another aspect of generators is even more powerful . . . the concept of *coroutines*. A coroutine is an independent function call that can run, be paused or suspended, and be continued or resumed where it left off. There is also communication between the caller and the (called) coroutine. For example, when a coroutine pauses, we can receive an intermediate return value from it, and when calling back into one, to be able to pass in additional or altered parameters, yet still be able to pick up where we last left it, with all state still intact.

Coroutines that are suspended yielding intermediate values and resumed multiple times are called generators, and that is exactly what Python generators do. Generators were added to Python in 2.2 and made standard in 2.3 (see PEP 255), and although powerful enough, they were significantly enhanced in Python 2.5 (see PEP 342). These enhancements bring generators even closer to being full coroutines because values (and exceptions) are allowed to

2.2-2.5

be passed back into a resumed function. Also, generators can now yield control while waiting for a generator *it* has called to yield a result instead of blocking to wait for that result to come back before the calling generator can suspend (and yield a result). Let us take a closer look at generators starting from the top.

What is a generator Python-wise? Syntactically, a generator is a function with a **yield** statement. A function or subroutine only returns once, but a generator can pause execution and yield intermediate results—that is the functionality of the **yield** statement, to return a value to the caller and to pause execution. When the next() method of a generator is invoked, it resumes right where it left off (when it yielded [a value and] control back to the caller).

When generators were added back in 2.2, because it introduced a new keyword, **yield**, for backward compatibility, you needed to import generators from the __future__ module in order to use them. This was no longer necessary when generators became standard beginning with 2.3.

11.10.1 Simple Generator Features

Generators behave in another manner similar to iterators: when a real return or end-of-function is reached and there are no more values to yield (when calling next()), a StopIteration exception is raised. Here is an example, the simplest of generators:

```
def simpleGen():
    yield 1
    yield '2 --> punch!'
```

Now that we have our generator function, let us call it to get and save a generator object (so that we can call its next() method to get successive intermediate values from it):

```
>>> myG = simpleGen()
>>> myG.next()
1
>>> myG.next()
'2 --> punch!'
>>> myG.next()
Traceback (most recent call last):
  File "", line 1, in ?
    myG.next()
StopIteration
```

Since Python's **for** loops have next() calls and a handler for StopIter-ation, it is almost always more elegant to use a **for** loop instead of manually iterating through a generator (or an iterator for that matter):

```
>>> for eachItem in simpleGen():
...     print eachItem
...
1
'2 --> punch!'
```

Of course that was a silly example: why not use a real iterator for that? More motivation comes from being able to iterate through a sequence that requires the power of a function rather than static objects already sitting in some sequence.

In the following example, we are going to create a random iterator that takes a sequence and returns a random item from that sequence:

```
from random import randint
def randGen(aList):
    while len(aList) > 0:
        yield aList.pop(randint(0, len(aList)))
```

The difference is that each item returned is also consumed from that sequence, sort of like a combination of list.pop() and random.choice():

```
>>> for item in randGen(['rock', 'paper', 'scissors']):
...     print item
...
scissors
rock
paper
```

We will see a simpler (and infinite) version of this generator as a class iterator coming up in a few chapters when we cover Object-Oriented Programming. Several chapters ago in Section 8.12, we discussed the syntax of generator expressions. The object returned from using this syntax is a generator, but serves as a short form, allowing for the simplistic syntax of a list comprehension.

These simple examples should give you an idea of how generators work, but you may be asking, "Where can I use generators in my application?" Or perhaps, you may be asking, "What are the most appropriate places for using this powerful construct?"

The "best" places to use generators are when you are iterating through a large dataset that is cumbersome to repeat or reiterate over, such as a large disk file, or a complex database query. For every row of data, you wish to perform non-elementary operations and processing, but you "do not want to lose your place" as you are cursoring or iterating over it.

You want to grab a wad of data, yield it back to the caller for processing and possible insertion into a(nother) database for example, and then you want to do a `next()` to get the next wad of data, and so forth. The state is preserved across suspends and resumptions, so you are more comfortable that you have a safe environment in which to process your data. Without generators, you application code will likely have a very long function, with a very lengthy **for** loop inside of it.

Of course, just because a language has a feature does not mean you have to use it. If there does not appear to be an obvious fit in your application, then do not add any more complexity! You will know when generators are the right thing to use when you come across an appropriate situation.

11.10.2 Enhanced Generator Features

2.5

A few enhancements were made to generators in Python 2.5, so in addition to `next()` to get the next value generated, users can now send values back into generators [`send()`], they can raise exceptions in generators [`throw()`], and request that a generator quit [`close()`].

Due to the two-way action involved with code calling `send()` to send values to a generator (and the generator **yield**ing values back out), the **yield** statement now must be an expression since you may be receiving an incoming object when resuming execution back in the generator. Below is a simple example demonstrating some of these features. Let us take our simple closure example, the counter:

```python
def counter(start_at=0):
    count = start_at
    while True:
        val = (yield count)
        if val is not None:
            count = val
        else:
            count += 1
```

This generator takes an initial value, and counts up by one for each call to continue the generator [`next()`]. Users also have the option to reset this value if they so desire by calling `send()` with the new counter value instead of calling `next()`. This generator runs forever, so if you wish to terminate it, call the `close()` method. If we run this code interactively, we get the following output:

```
>>> count = counter(5)
>>> count.next()
5
>>> count.next()
6
>>> count.send(9)
9
>>> count.next()
10
>>> count.close()
>>> count.next()
Traceback (most recent call last):
  File "<stdin>", line 1, in <module>
StopIteration
```

You can read more about generators in PEPs 255 and 342, as well as in this *Linux Journal* article introducing readers to the new features in Python 2.2:

http://www.linuxjournal.com/article/5597

11.11 Exercises

11–1. *Arguments*. Compare the following three functions:

```
def countToFour1():
    for eachNum in range(5):
        print eachNum,

def countToFour2(n):
    for eachNum in range(n, 5):
        print eachNum,

def countToFour3(n=1):
    for eachNum in range(n, 5):
        print eachNum,
```

What do you think will happen as far as output from the program, given the following input values? Enter the output into Table 11.2 below. Write in "ERROR" if you think one will occur with the given input or "NONE" if there is no output.

11–2. *Functions*. Combine your solutions for Exercise 5–2 such that you create a combination function that takes the same pair of numbers and returns both their sum and product at the same time.

Table 11.2 Output Chart for Problem 11-1

Input	countToFour1	countToFour2	countToFour3
2			
4			
5			
(nothing)			

11–3. *Functions.* In this exercise, we will be implementing the max() and min() built-in functions.

(a) Write simple functions max2() and min2() that take two items and return the larger and smaller item, respectively. They should work on arbitrary Python objects. For example, max2(4, 8) and min2(4, 8) would each return 8 and 4, respectively.

(b) Create new functions my_max() and my_min() that use your solutions in part (a) to recreate max() and min(). These functions return the largest and smallest item of non-empty sequences, respectively. They can also take a set of arguments as input. Test your solutions for numbers and strings.

11–4. *Return Values.* Create a complementary function to your solution for Exercise 5–13. Create a function that takes a total time in minutes and returns the equivalent in hours and minutes.

11–5. *Default Arguments.* Update the sales tax script you created in Exercise 5–7 such that a sales tax rate is no longer required as input to the function. Create a default argument using your local tax rate if one is not passed in on invocation.

11–6. *Variable-Length Arguments.* Write a function called printf(). There is one positional argument, a format string. The rest are variable arguments that need to be displayed to standard output based on the values in the format string, which allows the special string format operator directives such as %d, %f, etc. Hint: The solution is trivial—there is no need to implement the string operator functionality, but you do need to use the string format operator (%) explicitly.

11–7. *Functional Programming with* `map()`. Given a pair of identically sized lists, say `[1, 2, 3, ...]`, and `['abc', 'def', 'ghi', ...]`, merge both lists into a single list consisting of tuples of elements of each list so that our result looks like: `{[(1, 'abc'), (2, 'def'), (3, 'ghi'), ...}`. (Although this problem is similar in nature to a problem in Chapter 6, there is no direct correlation between their solutions.) Then create another solution using the `zip()` built-in function.

11–8. *Functional Programming with* `filter()`. Use the code you created for Exercise 5–4 to determine leap years. Update your code so that it is a function if you have not done so already. Then write some code to take a list of years and return a list of only leap years. Then convert it to using list comprehensions.

11–9. *Functional Programming with* `reduce()`. Review the code in Section 11.7.2 that illustrated how to sum up a set of numbers using `reduce()`. Modify it to create a new function called `average()` that calculates the simple average of a set of numbers.

11–10. *Functional Programming with* `filter()`. In the Unix file system, there are always two special files in each folder/directory: '.' indicates the current directory and '..' represents the parent directory. Given this knowledge, take a look at the documentation for the `os.listdir()` function and describe what this code snippet does:

```
files = filter(lambda x: x and x[0] != '.', os.
listdir(folder))
```

11–11. *Functional Programming with* `map()`. Write a program that takes a filename and "cleans" the file by removing all leading and trailing whitespace from each line. Read in the original file and write out a new one, either creating a new file or overwriting the existing one. Give your user the option to pick which of the two to perform. Convert your solution to using list comprehensions.

11–12. *Passing Functions.* Write a sister function to the `testit()` function described in this chapter. Rather than testing execution for errors, `timeit()` will take a function object (along with any arguments) and time how long it takes to execute the function. Return the following values: function return value, time elapsed. You can use `time.clock()` or `time. time()`, whichever provides you with greater accuracy. (The general consensus is to use `time.time()` on POSIX and `time.clock()` on Win32 systems.) Note: The `timeit()` function is not related to the `timeit` module (introduced in Python 2.3).

11–13. *Functional Programming with* `reduce()` *and Recursion.* In Chapter 8, we looked at N factorial or N! as the product of all numbers from 1 to N.

(a) Take a minute to write a small, simple function called `mult(x, y)` that takes x and y and returns their product.

(b) Use the `mult()` function you created in part (a) along with `reduce()` to calculate factorials.

(c) Discard the use of `mult()` completely and use a **lambda** expression instead.

(d) In this chapter, we presented a recursive solution to finding N! Use the `timeit()` function you completed in the problem above and time all three versions of your factorial function (iterative, `reduce()`, and recursive). Explain any differences in performance, anticipated and actual.

11–14. **Recursion.* We also looked at Fibonacci numbers in Chapter 8. Rewrite your previous solution for calculating Fibonacci numbers (Exercise 8–9) so that it now uses recursion.

11–15. **Recursion.* Rewrite your solution to Exercise 6–5, which prints a string backwards to use recursion. Use recursion to print a string forward *and* backward.

11–16. *Upgrading* `easyMath.py`. This script, presented as Example 11.1, served as the beginnings of a program to help young people develop their math skills. Further enhance this program by adding multiplication as a supported operation. Extra credit: Add division as well; this is more difficult as you must find valid integer divisors. Fortunately for you, there is already code to ensure the numerator is greater than the denominator so you do not need to support fractions.

11–17. *Definitions.*

(a) Describe the differences between partial function application and currying.

(b) What are the differences between partial function application and closures?

(c) Finally, how do iterators and generators differ?

11–18. *Synchronized Function Calling.* Go back and review the husband and wife situation presented in Chapter 6 (Section 6.20)
when introducing shallow and deep copies. They shared a
common account where simultaneous access to their bank
account might have adverse effects.

Create an application where calls to functions that change
the account balance must be *synchronized*. In other words,
only one process or thread can execute the function(s) at any
given time. Your first attempt may use files, but a real solution will use decorators and synchronization primitives
found in either the `threading` or `mutex` modules. You may
look ahead to Chapter 17 for more inspiration.

MODULES

Chapter Topics

- What Are Modules?
- Modules and Files
- Namespaces
- Importing Modules
- Importing Module Attributes
- Module Built-in Functions
- Packages
- Other Features of Modules

Chapter 12

This chapter focuses on Python modules and how data are imported from modules into your programming environment. We will also take a look at packages. Modules are a means to organize Python code, and packages help you organize modules. We conclude this chapter with a look at other related aspects of modules.

12.1 What Are Modules?

A *module* allows you to logically organize your Python code. When code gets to be large enough, the tendency is to break it up into organized pieces that can still interact with one another at a functioning level. These pieces generally have attributes that have some relation to one another, perhaps a single class with its member data variables and methods, or maybe a group of related, yet independently operating functions. These pieces should be shared, so Python allows a module the ability to "bring in" and use attributes from other modules to take advantage of work that has been done, maximizing code reusability. This process of associating attributes from other modules with your module is called *importing*. In a nutshell, modules are self-contained and organized pieces of Python code that can be shared.

12.2 Modules and Files

If modules represent a logical way to organize your Python code, then files are a way to physically organize modules. To that end, each file is considered an individual module, and vice versa. The filename of a module is the module name appended with the .py file extension. There are several aspects we need to discuss with regard to what the file structure means to modules. Unlike other languages in which you import classes, in Python you import modules or module attributes.

12.2.1 Module Namespaces

We will discuss namespaces in detail later in this chapter, but the basic concept of a namespace is an individual set of mappings from names to objects. As you are no doubt aware, module names play an important part in the naming of their attributes. The name of the attribute is always prepended with the module name. For example, the atoi() function in the string module is called string.atoi(). Because only one module with a given name can be loaded into the Python interpreter, there is no intersection of names from different modules; hence, each module defines its own unique namespace. If I created a function called atoi() in my own module, perhaps mymodule, its name would be mymodule.atoi(). So even if there is a name conflict for an attribute, the *fully qualified name*—referring to an object via dotted attribute notation—prevents an exact and conflicting match.

12.2.2 Search Path and Path Search

The process of importing a module requires a process called a *path search*. This is the procedure of checking "predefined areas" of the file system to look for your mymodule.py file in order to load the mymodule module. These predefined areas are no more than a set of directories that are part of your Python *search path*. To avoid the confusion between the two, think of a path search as the pursuit of a file through a set of directories, the search path.

There may be times where importing a module fails:

```
>>> import xxx
Traceback (innermost last):
  File "<interactive input>", line 1, in ?
ImportError: No module named xxx
```

When this error occurs, the interpreter is telling you it cannot access the requested module, and the likely reason is that the module you desire is not in the search path, leading to a path search failure.

A default search path is automatically defined either in the compilation or installation process. This search path may be modified in one of two places.

One is the PYTHONPATH environment variable set in the *shell* or command-line interpreter that invokes Python. The contents of this variable consist of a colon-delimited set of directory paths. If you want the interpreter to use the contents of this variable, make sure you set or update it before you start the interpreter or run a Python script.

Once the interpreter has started, you can access the path itself, which is stored in the sys module as the sys.path variable. Rather than a single string that is colon-delimited, the path has been "split" into a list of individual directory strings. Below is an example search path for a Unix machine. Your mileage will definitely vary as you go from system to system.

```
>>> sys.path
['', '/usr/local/lib/python2.x/', '/usr/local/lib/
python2.x/plat-sunos5', '/usr/local/lib/python2.x/
lib-tk', '/usr/local/lib/python2.x/lib-dynload', '/
usr/local/lib/Python2.x/site-packages',]
```

Bearing in mind that this is just a list, we can definitely take liberty with it and modify it at our leisure. If you know of a module you want to import, yet its directory is not in the search path, by all means use the list's append() method to add it to the path, like so:

```
sys.path.append('/home/wesc/py/lib')
```

Once this is accomplished, you can then load your module. As long as one of the directories in the search path contains the file, then it will be imported. Of course, this adds the directory only to the end of your search path. If you want to add it elsewhere, such as in the beginning or middle, then you have to use the insert() list method for those. In our examples above, we are updating the sys.path attribute interactively, but it will work the same way if run as a script.

Here is what it would look like if we ran into this problem interactively:

```
>>> import sys
>>> import mymodule
Traceback (innermost last):
  File "<stdin>", line 1, in ?
ImportError: No module named mymodule
>>>
>>> sys.path.append('/home/wesc/py/lib')
>>> sys.path
['', '/usr/local/lib/python2.x/', '/usr/local/lib/
python2.x/plat-sunos5', '/usr/local/lib/python2.x/
lib-tk', '/usr/local/lib/python2.x/lib-dynload', '/usr/
local/lib/python2.x/site-packages','/home/wesc/py/lib']
>>>
```

```
>>> import mymodule
>>>
```

On the flip side, you may have too many copies of a module. In the case of duplicates, the interpreter will load the first module it finds with the given name while rummaging through the search path in sequential order.

To find out what modules have been successfully imported (and loaded) as well as from where, take a look at `sys.modules`. Unlike `sys.path`, which is a list of modules, `sys.modules` is a dictionary where the keys are the module names with their physical location as the values.

12.3 Namespaces

A *namespace* is a mapping of names (identifiers) to objects. The process of adding a name to a namespace consists of *binding* the identifier to the object (and increasing the reference count to the object by one). The Python Language Reference also includes the following definitions: "changing the mapping of a name is called *rebinding* [, and] removing a name is *unbinding*."

As briefly introduced in Chapter 11, there are either two or three active namespaces at any given time during execution. These three namespaces are the local, global, and built-ins namespaces, but local name-spaces come and go during execution, hence the "two or three" we just alluded to. The names accessible from these namespaces are dependent on their *loading order*, or the order in which the namespaces are brought into the system.

The Python interpreter loads the built-ins namespace first. This consists of the names in the `__builtins__` module. Then the global namespace for the executing module is loaded, which then becomes the active namespace when the module begins execution. Thus we have our two active namespaces.

CORE NOTE: `__builtins__` **versus** `__builtin__`

The `__builtins__` module should not be confused with the `__builtin__` module. The names, of course, are so similar that it tends to lead to some confusion among new Python programmers who have gotten this far. The `__builtins__` module consists of a set of built-in names for the built-ins namespace. Most, if not all, of these names come from the `__builtin__` module, which is a module of the built-in functions, exceptions, and other attributes. In standard Python execution, `__builtins__` contains all the names from `__builtin__`. Python *used to have a restricted execution model that allowed modification of* __builtins__ *where key pieces from* __builtin__ *were left out to create a sandbox environment. However, due its security flaws and the difficulty involved with repairing it, restricted execution is no longer supported in Python (as of 2.3).*

When a function call is made during execution, the third, a local, namespace is created. We can use the globals() and locals() built-in functions to tell us which names are in which namespaces. We will discuss both functions in more detail later on in this chapter.

12.3.1 Namespaces versus Variable Scope

Okay, now that we know what namespaces are, how do they relate to variable scope again? They seem extremely similar. The truth is, you are quite correct.

Namespaces are purely mappings between names and objects, but scope dictates how, or rather where, one can access these names based on the physical location from within your code. We illustrate the relationship between namespaces and variable scope in Figure 12–1.

Notice that each of the namespaces is a self-contained unit. But looking at the namespaces from the scoping point of view, things appear different. All names within the local namespace are within my local scope. Any name outside my local scope is in my global scope.

Also keep in mind that during the execution of the program, the local namespaces and scope are transient because function calls come and go, but the global and built-ins namespaces remain.

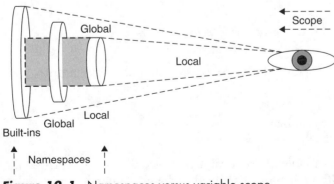

Figure 12–1   Namespaces versus variable scope

Our final thought to you in this section is, when it comes to namespaces, ask yourself the question, "Does it have it?" And for variable scope, ask, "Can I see it?"

12.3.2 Name Lookup, Scoping, and Overriding

So how do scoping rules work in relationship to namespaces? It all has to do with name lookup. When accessing an attribute, the interpreter must find it in one of the three namespaces. The search begins with the local namespace. If the attribute is not found there, then the global namespace is searched. If that is also unsuccessful, the final frontier is the built-ins namespace. If the exhaustive search fails, you get the familiar:

```
>>> foo
Traceback (innermost last):
   File "<stdin>", line 1, in ?
NameError: foo
```

Notice how the figure features the foremost-searched namespaces "shadowing" namespaces, which are searched afterward. This is to try to convey the effect of *overriding*. This shadowing effect is illustrated by the gray boxes in Figure 12-1. For example, names found in the local namespace will hide access to objects in the global or built-ins namespaces. This is the process whereby names may be taken out of scope because a more local namespace contains a name. Take a look at the following piece of code that was introduced in the previous chapter:

```
def foo():
    print "\ncalling foo()..."
    bar = 200
    print "in foo(), bar is", bar

bar = 100
print "in __main__, bar is", bar
foo()
```

When we execute this code, we get the following output:

```
in __main__, bar is 100

calling foo()...
in foo(), bar is 200
```

The bar variable in the local namespace of foo() overrode the global bar variable. Although bar exists in the global namespace, the lookup found the one in the local namespace first, hence "overriding" the global one. For more information regarding scope, see Section 11.8 of Chapter 11.

12.3.3 Namespaces for Free!

One of Python's most useful features is the ability to get a namespace almost anywhere you need a place to put things. We have seen in the previous chapter how you can just add attributes to functions at whim (using the familiar dotted-attribute notation):

```
def foo():
    pass
foo.__doc__ = 'Oops, forgot to add doc str above!'
foo.version = 0.2
```

In this chapter, we have shown how modules themselves make namespaces and how you access them in the same way:

```
mymodule.foo()
mymodule.version
```

Although we will discuss object-oriented programming (OOP) in Chapter 13, how about an example even simpler than a "Hello World!" to introduce you to Python classes?

```
class MyUltimatePythonStorageDevice(object):
    pass

bag = MyUltimatePythonStorageDevice()
bag.x = 100
bag.y = 200
bag.version = 0.1
bag.completed = False
```

You can throw just about anything you want in a namespace. This use of a class (instance) is perfectly fine, and you don't even have to know much about OOP to be able to use a class! (Note: These guys are called *instance attributes*.) Fancy names aside, the instance is just used as a namespace.

You will see just how useful they are as you delve deeper into OOP and discover what a convenience it is during runtime just to be able to store temporary (but important) values! As stated in the final tenet of the Zen of Python:

"Namespaces are one honking great idea—let's do more of those!"

(To see the complete Zen, just import the `this` module within the interactive interpreter.)

12.4 Importing Modules

12.4.1 The *import* Statement

Importing a module requires the use of the **import** statement, whose syntax is:

```
import module1
import module2[
      :
import moduleN
```

It is also possible to import multiple modules on the same line like this . . .

```
import module1[, module2[,... moduleN]]
```

. . . but the resulting code is not as readable as having multiple import statements. Also, there is no performance hit and no change in the way that the Python bytecode is generated, so by all means, use the first form, which is the preferred form.

CORE STYLE: Module ordering for import statements

It is recommended that all module imports happen at the top of Python modules. Furthermore, imports should follow this ordering:

- *Python Standard Library modules*
- *Python third party modules*
- *Application-specific modules*

Separate these groups with an empty line between the imports of these three types of modules. This helps ensure that modules are imported in a consistent manner and helps minimize the number of **import** *statements required in each of the modules. You can read more about this and other import tips in Python's Style Guide, written up as PEP 8.*

When this statement is encountered by the interpreter, the module is imported if found in the search path. Scoping rules apply, so if imported from the top level of a module, it has global scope; if imported from a function, it has local scope.

When a module is imported the first time, it is loaded and executed.

12.4.2 The `from-import` Statement

It is possible to import specific module elements into your own module. By this, we really mean importing specific names from the module into the current namespace. For this purpose, we can use the **from-import** statement, whose syntax is:

```
from module import name1[, name2[, ... nameN]]
```

12.4.3 Multi-Line Import

The multi-line import feature was added in Python 2.4 specifically for long **from-import** statements. When importing many attributes from the same module, import lines of code tend to get long and wrap, requiring a NEWLINE-escaping backslash. Here is the example *imported* (pun intended) directly from PEP 328:

2.4

```
from Tkinter import Tk, Frame, Button, Entry, Canvas, \
             Text, LEFT, DISABLED, NORMAL, RIDGE, END
```

Your other option is to have multiple **from-import** statements:

```
from Tkinter import Tk, Frame, Button, Entry, Canvas, Text
from Tkinter import LEFT, DISABLED, NORMAL, RIDGE, END
```

We are also trying to stem usage on the unfavored **from** Tkinter **import** * (see the Core Style sidebar in Section 12.5.3). Instead, programmers should be free to use Python's standard grouping mechanism (parentheses) to create a more reasonable multi-line **import** statement:

```
from Tkinter import (Tk, Frame, Button, Entry, Canvas,
             Text, LEFT, DISABLED, NORMAL, RIDGE, END)
```

You can find out more about multi-line imports in the documentation or in PEP 328.

12.4.4 Extended `Import` Statement (`as`)

2.0

There are times when you are importing either a module or module attribute with a name that you are already using in your application, or perhaps it is a name that you do not want to use. Maybe the name is too long to type everywhere, or more subjectively, perhaps it is a name that you just plain do not like.

This had been a fairly common request from Python programmers: the ability to import modules and module attributes into a program using names other than their original given names. One common workaround is to assign the module name to a variable:

```
>>> import longmodulename
>>> short = longmodulename
>>> del longmodulename
```

In the example above, rather than using `longmodulename.attribute`, you would use the `short.attribute` to access the same object. (A similar analogy can be made with importing module attributes using **from-import**, see below.) However, to do this over and over again and in multiple modules can be annoying and seem wasteful. Using extended import, you can change the locally bound name for what you are importing. Statements like . . .

```
import Tkinter
from cgi import FieldStorage
```

. . . can be replaced by . . .

```
import Tkinter as tk
from cgi import FieldStorage as form
```

2.0-2.6   This feature was added in Python 2.0. At that time, "as" was not implemented as a keyword; it finally became one in Python 2.6. For more information on extended import, see the Python Language Reference Manual and PEP 221.

12.5 Features of Module Import

12.5.1 Module "Executed" When Loaded

One effect of loading a module is that the imported module is "executed," that is, the top-level portion of the imported module is directly executed. This usually includes setting up of global variables as well as performing the class and function declarations. If there is a check for __name__ to do more on direct script invocation, that is executed, too.

Of course, this type of execution may or may not be the desired effect. If not, you will have to put as much code as possible into functions. Suffice it to say that good module programming style dictates that only function and/or class definitions should be at the top level of a module.

For more information see Section 14.1.1 and the Core Note contained therein.

A new feature was added to Python which allows you to execute an installed module as a script. (Sure, running your own script is easy [$ foo.py], but executing a module in the standard library or third party package is trickier.) You can read more about how to do this in Section 14.4.3.

12.5.2 Importing versus Loading

A module is *loaded* only once, regardless of the number of times it is *imported*. This prevents the module "execution" from happening over and over again if multiple imports occur. If your module imports the sys module, and so do five of the other modules you import, it would not be wise to load sys (or any other module) each time! So rest assured, loading happens only once, on first import.

12.5.3 Names Imported into Current Namespace

Calling **from-import** brings the name into the current namespace, meaning that you do not use the attribute/dotted notation to access the module identifier. For example, to access a variable named *var* in module *module* that was imported with:

> **from** *module* **import** *var*

we would use "*var*" by itself. There is no need to reference the module since you imported *var* into your namespace. It is also possible to import all the names from the module into the current namespace using the following **from-import** statement:

> **from** *module* **import** *

CORE STYLE: Restrict your use of "from *module* **import** *"

In practice, using **from** *module* **import** * *is considered poor style because it "pollutes" the current namespace and has the potential of overriding names in the current namespace; however, it is extremely convenient if a module has many variables that are often accessed, or if the module has a very long name.*

We recommend using this form in only two situations. The first is where the target module has many attributes that would make it inconvenient to type in the module name over and over again. Two prime examples of this are the Tkinter *(Python/Tk) and* NumPy *(Numeric Python) modules, and perhaps the* socket *module. The other place where it is acceptable to use* **from** *module* **import** * *is within the interactive interpreter, to save on the amount of typing.*

12.5.4 Names Imported into Importer's Scope

Another side effect of importing just names from modules is that those names are now part of the local namespace. A side effect is possibly hiding or overriding an existing object or built-in with the same name. Also, changes to the variable affect only the local copy and not the original in the imported module's namespace. In other words, the binding is now local rather than across namespaces.

Here we present the code to two modules: an importer, `impter.py`, and an importee, `imptee.py`. Currently, `imptr.py` uses the **from-import** statement, which creates only local bindings.

```
#############
# imptee.py #
#############
foo = 'abc'
def show():
    print 'foo from imptee:', foo


#############
# impter.py #
#############
from imptee import foo, show
show()
foo = 123
print 'foo from impter:', foo
show()
```

Upon running the importer, we discover that the importee's view of its `foo` variable has not changed even though we modified it in the importer.

```
foo from imptee: abc
foo from impter: 123
foo from imptee: abc
```

The only solution is to use import and *fully qualified* identifier names using the attribute/dotted notation.

```
#############
# impter.py #
#############
import imptee
imptee.show()
imptee.foo = 123
print 'foo from impter:', imptee.foo
imptee.show()
```

Once we make the update and change our references accordingly, we now have achieved the desired effect.

```
foo from imptee: abc
foo from impter: 123
foo from imptee: 123
```

12.5.5 Back to the __future__

Back in the days of Python 2.0, it was recognized that due to improvements, new features, and current feature enhancements, certain significant changes could not be implemented without affecting some existing functionality. To better prepare Python programmers for what was coming down the line, the __future__ directives were implemented.

By using the **from-import** statement and "importing" future functionality, users can get a taste of new features or feature changes enabling them to port their applications correctly by the time the feature becomes permanent. The syntax is:

```
from __future__ import new_feature
```

It does not make sense to import __future__ so that is disallowed. (Actually, it is allowed but does not do what you want it to do, which is enable all future features.) You have to import specific features explicitly. You can read more about __future__ directives in PEP 236.

12.5.6 Warning Framework

Similar to the __future__ directive, it is also necessary to warn users when a feature is about to be changed or deprecated so that they can take action based on the notice received. There are multiple pieces to this feature, so we will break it down into components.

The first piece is the application programmer's interface (API). Programmers have the ability to issue warnings from both Python programs (via the warnings module) as well as from C [via a call to PyErr_Warn()].

Another part of the framework is a new set of warning exception classes. Warning is subclassed directly from Exception and serves as the root of all warnings: UserWarning, DeprecationWarning, SyntaxWarning, and RuntimeWarning. These are described in further detail in Chapter 10.

The next component is the warnings filter. There are different warnings of different levels and severities, and somehow the number and type of warnings should be controllable. The warnings filter not only collects information about the warning, such as line number, cause of the warning, etc., but it also controls whether warnings are ignored, displayed—they can be custom-formatted—or turned into errors (generating an exception).

Warnings have a default output to `sys.stderr`, but there are hooks to be able to change that, for example, to log it instead of displaying it to the end-user while running Python scripts subject to issued warnings. There is also an API to manipulate warning filters.

Finally, there are the command-line arguments that control the warning filters. These come in the form of options to the Python interpreter upon startup via the `-W` option. See the Python documentation or PEP 230 for the specific switches for your version of Python. The warning framework first appeared in Python 2.1.

12.5.7 Importing Modules from ZIP Files

2.3

In version 2.3, the feature that allows the import of modules contained inside ZIP archives was added to Python. If you add a `.zip` file containing Python modules (`.py`, `.pyc`, or `.pyo` files) to your search path, i.e., `PYTHONPATH` or `sys.path`, the importer will search that archive for the module as if the ZIP file was a directory.

If a ZIP file contains just a `.py` for any imported module, Python will not attempt to modify the archive by adding the corresponding `.pyc` file, meaning that if a ZIP archive does not contain a matching `.pyc` file, import speed should be expected to be slower than if they were present.

You are also allowed to add specific (sub)directories "under" a `.zip` file, i.e., `/tmp/yolk.zip/lib/` would only import from the `lib/` subdirectory within the `yolk` archive. Although this feature is specified in PEP 273, the actual implementation uses the import hooks provided by PEP 302.

12.5.8 "New" Import Hooks

2.3

The import of modules inside ZIP archives was "the first customer" of the new import hooks specified by PEP 302. Although we use the word "new," that is relative considering that it has been difficult to create custom importers because the only way to accomplish this before was to use the other modules that were either really old or didn't simplify writing importers. Another solution is to override `__import__()`, but that is not an easy thing to do because you have to pretty much (re)implement the entire import mechanism.

The new import hooks, introduced in Python 2.3, simplify it down to writing callable import classes, and getting them "registered" (or rather, "installed") with the Python interpreter via the sys module.

There are two classes that you need: a finder and a loader. An instance of these classes takes an argument—the full name of any module or package. A finder instance will look for your module, and if it finds it, return a loader object. The finder can also take a path for finding subpackages. The loader is what eventually brings the module into memory, doing whatever it needs to do to make a real Python module object, which is eventually returned by the loader.

These instances are added to sys.path_hooks. The sys.path_importer_ cache just holds the instances so that path_hooks is traversed only once. Finally, sys.meta_path is a list of instances that should be traversed before looking at sys.path, for modules whose location you know and do not need to find. The meta-path already has the loader objects reader to execute for specific modules or packages.

12.6 Module Built-in Functions

The importation of modules has some functional support from the system. We will look at those now.

12.6.1 __import__()

The __import__() function is new as of Python 1.5, and it is the function that actually does the importing, meaning that the import statement invokes the __import__() function to do its work. The purpose of making this a function is to allow for overriding it if the user is inclined to develop his or her own importation algorithm.

The syntax of __import__() is:

```
__import__(module_name[, globals[, locals[, fromlist]]])
```

The *module_name* variable is the name of the module to import, *globals* is the dictionary of current names in the global symbol table, *locals* is the dictionary of current names in the local symbol table, and *fromlist* is a list of symbols to import the way they would be imported using the **from-import** statement.

The *globals*, *locals*, and *fromlist* arguments are optional, and if not provided, default to globals(), locals(), and [], respectively.

Calling **import** sys can be accomplished with

```
sys = __import__('sys')
```

12.6.2 globals() *and* locals()

The globals() and locals() built-in functions return dictionaries of the global and local namespaces, respectively, of the caller. From within a function, the local namespace represents all names defined for execution of that function, which is what locals() will return. globals(), of course, will return those names globally accessible to that function.

From the global namespace, however, globals() and locals() return the same dictionary because the global namespace is as local as you can get while executing there. Here is a little snippet of code that calls both functions from both namespaces:

```
def foo():
    print '\ncalling foo()...'
    aString = 'bar'
    anInt = 42
    print "foo()'s globals:", globals().keys()
    print "foo()'s locals:", locals().keys()

print "__main__'s globals:", globals().keys()
print "__main__'s locals:", locals().keys()
foo()
```

We are going to ask for the dictionary keys only because the values are of no consequence here (plus they make the lines wrap even more in this text). Executing this script, we get the following output:

```
$ namespaces.py
__main__'s globals: ['__doc__', 'foo', '__name__',
'__builtins__']
__main__'s locals: ['__doc__', 'foo', '__name__',
'__builtins__']

calling foo()...
foo()'s globals: ['__doc__', 'foo', '__name__',
'__builtins__']
foo()'s locals: ['anInt', 'aString']
```

12.6.3 reload()

The reload() built-in function performs another import on a previously imported module. The syntax of reload() is:

```
reload(module)
```

module is the actual module you want to reload. There are some criteria for using the reload() module. The first is that the module must have been imported in full (not by using **from-import**), and it must have loaded successfully. The second rule follows from the first, and that is the argument to `reload()` the module itself and not a string containing the module name, i.e., it must be something like `reload(sys)` instead of `reload('sys')`.

Also, code in a module is executed when it is imported, but only once. A second import does not re-execute the code, it just binds the module name. Thus `reload()` makes sense, as it overrides this default behavior.

12.7 Packages

A *package* is a hierarchical file directory structure that defines a single Python application environment that consists of modules and subpackages. Packages were added to Python 1.5 to aid with a variety of problems including:

- Adding hierarchical organization to flat namespace
- Allowing developers to group related modules
- Allowing distributors to ship directories vs. bunch of files
- Helping resolve conflicting module names

Along with classes and modules, packages use the familiar attribute/dotted attribute notation to access their elements. Importing modules within packages use the standard **import** and **from-import** statements.

12.7.1 Directory Structure

For our package examples, we will assume the directory structure below:

```
Phone/
    __init__.py
    common_util.py
    Voicedta/
        __init__.py
        Pots.py
        Isdn.py
    Fax/
        __init__.py
        G3.py
    Mobile/
        __init__.py
        Analog.py
        Digital.py
    Pager/
        __init__.py
        Numeric.py
```

Phone is a top-level package and Voicedta, etc., are subpackages. Import subpackages by using **import** like this:

```
import Phone.Mobile.Analog
Phone.Mobile.Analog.dial()
```

Alternatively, you can use **from-import** in a variety of ways:

The first way is importing just the top-level subpackage and referencing down the subpackage tree using the attribute/dotted notation:

```
from Phone import Mobile
Mobile.Analog.dial('555-1212')
```

Furthermore, we can go down one more subpackage for referencing:

```
from Phone.Mobile import Analog
Analog.dial('555-1212')
```

In fact, you can go all the way down in the subpackage tree structure:

```
from Phone.Mobile.Analog import dial
dial('555-1212')
```

In our above directory structure hierarchy, we observe a number of __init__.py files. These are initializer modules that are required when using **from-import** to import subpackages but they can be empty if not used. Quite often, developers forget to add _inti_.py files to their package directories, so starting in Python 2.5, this triggers an ImportWarning message.

2.5

However, it is silently ignored unless the -Wd option is given when launching the interpreter.

12.7.2 Using `from-import` with Packages

Packages also support the **from-import** all statement:

```
from package.module import *
```

However, such a statement is dependent on the operating system's filesystem for Python to determine which files to import. Thus the __all__ variable in __init__.py is required. This variable contains all the module names that should be imported when the above statement is invoked if there is such a thing. It consists of a list of module names as strings.

12.7.3 Absolute Import

As the use of packages becomes more pervasive, there have been more cases of the import of subpackages that end up clashing with (and hiding or shadowing) "real" or standard library modules (actually their names). Package modules will hide any equivalently-named standard library module because it will look inside the package first to perform a *relative import*, thus hiding access to the standard library module.

Because of this, all imports are now classified as *absolute*, meaning that names must be packages or modules accessible via the Python path (sys.path or PYTHONPATH).

2.5-2.7

The rationale behind this decision is that subpackages can still be accessed via sys.path, i.e., **import** Phone.Mobile.Analog. Prior to this change, it was legal to have just **import** Analog from modules inside the Mobile subpackage.

As a compromise, Python allows relative importing where programmers can indicate the location of a subpackage to be imported by using leader dots in front of the module or package name. For more information, please see Section 12.7.4.

The absolute import feature is the default starting in Python 2.7. (This feature, absolute_import, can be imported from __future__ starting in version 2.5.) You can read more about absolute import in PEP 328.

12.7.4 Relative Import

As described previously, the absolute import feature takes away certain privileges of the module writer of packages. With this loss of freedom in **import** statements, something must be made available to proxy for that loss. This is where a relative import comes in. The relative import feature alters the import syntax slightly to let programmers tell the importer where to find a module in a subpackage. Because the **import** statements are always absolute, relative imports only apply to **from-import** statements.

2.5-2.6

The first part of the syntax is a leader dot to indicate a relative import. From there, any additional dot represents a single level above the current from where to start looking for the modules being imported.

Let us look at our example above again. From within Analog.Mobile. Digital, i.e., the Digital.py module, we cannot simply use this syntax anymore. The following will either still work in older versions of Python, generate a warning, or will not work in more contemporary versions of Python:

```
import Analog
from Analog import dial
```

This is due to the absolute import limitation. You have to use either the absolute or relative imports. Below are some valid imports:

```
from Phone.Mobile.Analog import dial
from .Analog import dial
from ..common_util import setup
from ..Fax import G3.dial.
```

Relative imports can be used starting in Python 2.5. In Python 2.6, a deprecation warning will appear for all intra-package imports not using the relative import syntax. You can read more about relative import in the Python documentation and in PEP 328.

12.8 Other Features of Modules

12.8.1 Auto-Loaded Modules

When the Python interpreter starts up in standard mode, some modules are loaded by the interpreter for system use. The only one that affects you is the __builtin__ module, which normally gets loaded in as the __builtins__ module.

The sys.modules variable consists of a dictionary of modules that the interpreter has currently loaded (in full and successfully) into the interpreter. The module names are the keys, and the location from which they were imported are the values.

For example, in Windows, the sys.modules variable contains a large number of loaded modules, so we will shorten the list by requesting only the module names. This is accomplished by using the dictionary's keys() method:

```
>>> import sys
>>> sys.modules.keys()
['os.path', 'os', 'exceptions', '__main__', 'ntpath',
'strop', 'nt', 'sys', '__builtin__', 'site',
'signal', 'UserDict', 'string', 'stat']
```

The loaded modules for Unix are quite similar:

```
>>> import sys
>>> sys.modules.keys()
['os.path', 'os', 'readline', 'exceptions',
'__main__', 'posix', 'sys', '__builtin__', 'site',
'signal', 'UserDict', 'posixpath', 'stat']
```

12.8.2 Preventing Attribute Import

If you do not want module attributes imported when a module is imported with "**from** *module* **import** ***", prepend an underscore (_) to those attribute names (you do not want imported). This minimal level of data hiding does not apply if the entire module is imported or if you explicitly import a "hidden" attribute, e.g., **import** foo._bar.

12.8.3 Case-Insensitive Import

There are various operating systems with case-insensitive file systems. Prior to version 2.1, Python attempted to "do the right thing" when importing modules on the various supported platforms, but with the growing popularity of the MacOS X and Cygwin platforms, certain deficiencies could no longer be ignored, and support needed to be cleaned up.

2.1

The world was pretty clean-cut when it was just Unix (case-sensitive) and Win32 (case-insensitive), but these new case-insensitive systems coming online were not ported with the case-insensitive features. PEP 235, which specifies this feature, attempts to address this weakness as well as taking away some "hacks" that had existed for other systems to make importing modules more consistent.

The bottom line is that for case-insensitive imports to work properly, an environment variable named PYTHONCASEOK must be defined. Python will then import the first module name that is found (in a case-insensitive manner) that matches. Otherwise Python will perform its native case-sensitive module name matching and import the first matching one it finds.

12.8.4 Source Code Encoding

Starting in Python 2.3, it is now possible to create your Python module file in a native encoding other than 7-bit ASCII. Of course ASCII is the default, but with an additional encoding directive at the top of your Python modules, it will enable the importer to parse your modules using the specified encoding and designate natively encoded Unicode strings correctly so you do not have to worry about editing your source files in a plain ASCII text editor and have to individually "Unicode-tag" each string literal.

2.3-2.5

An example directive specifying a UTF-8 file can be declared like this:

```
#!/usr/bin/env python
# -*- coding: UTF-8 -*-
```

If you execute or import modules that contain non-ASCII Unicode string literals and do not have an encoding directive at the top, this will result in a DeprecationWarning in Python 2.3 and a syntax error starting in 2.5. You can read more about source code encoding in PEP 263.

12.8.5 Import Cycles

Working with Python in real-life situations, you discover that it is possible to have import loops. If you have ever worked on any large Python project, you are likely to have run into this situation.

Let us take a look at an example. Assume we have a very large product with a very complex command-line interface (CLI). There are a million commands for your product, and as a result, you have an overly massive handler (OMH) set. Every time a new feature is added, from one to three new commands must be added to support the new feature. This will be our omh4cli.py script:

```
from cli4vof import cli4vof

# command line interface utility function
def cli_util():
    pass

# overly massive handlers for the command line interface
def omh4cli():
       :
    cli4vof()
       :
omh4cli()
```

You can pretend that the (empty) utility function is a very popular piece of code that most handlers must use. The overly massive handlers for the command-line interface are all in the omh4cli() function. If we have to add a new command, it would be called from here.

Now, as this module grows in a boundless fashion, certain smarter engineers decide to split off their new commands into a separate module and just provide hooks in the original module to access the new stuff. Therefore, the code is easier to maintain, and if bugs were found in the new stuff, one would not have to search through a one-megabyte-plus-sized Python file.

In our case, we have an excited product manager asking us to add a "very outstanding feature" (VOF). Instead of integrating our stuff into omh4cli.py, we create a new script, cli4vof.py:

```
import omh4cli

# command-line interface for a very outstanding feature
def cli4vof():
    omh4cli.cli_util()
```

As mentioned before, the utility function is a must for every command, and because we do not want to cut and paste its code from the main handler, we import the main module and call it that way. To finish off our integration, we add a call to our handler into the main overly massive handler, omh4cli().

The problem occurs when the main handler omh4cli imports our new little module cli4vof (to get the new command function) because cli4vof imports omh4cli (to get the utility function). Our module import fails because Python is trying to import a module that was not previously fully imported the first time:

```
$ python omh4cli.py
Traceback (most recent call last):
  File "omh4cli.py", line 3, in ?
    from cli4vof import cli4vof
  File "/usr/prod/cli4vof.py", line 3, in ?
    import omh4cli
  File "/usr/prod/omh4cli.py", line 3, in ?
    from cli4vof import cli4vof
ImportError: cannot import name cli4vof
```

Notice the circular import of cli4vof in the traceback. The problem is that in order to call the utility function, cli4vof has to import omh4cli. If it did not have to do that, then omh4cli would have completed its import of cli4vof successfully and there would be no problem. The issue is that when omh4cli is attempting to import cli4vof, cli4vof is trying to import omh4cli. No one finishes an import, hence the error. This is just one example of an import cycle. There are much more complicated ones out in the real world.

The workaround for this problem is almost always to move one of the **import** statements, e.g., the offending one. You will commonly see **import** statements at the bottom of modules. As a beginning Python programmer, you are used to seeing them in the beginning, but if you ever run across **import** statements at the end of modules, you will now know why. In our case, we cannot move the import of omh4cli to the end, because if cli4vof() is called, it will not have the omh4cli name loaded yet:

```
$ python omh4cli.py
Traceback (most recent call last):
  File "omh4cli.py", line 3, in ?
    from cli4vof import cli4vof
  File "/usr/prod/cli4vof.py", line 7, in ?
    import omh4cli
  File "/usr/prod/omh4cli.py", line 13, in ?
    omh4cli()
  File "/usr/prod/omh4cli.py", line 11, in omh4cli
    cli4vof()
```

```
    File "/usr/prod/cli4vof.py", line 5, in cli4vof
      omh4cli.cli_util()
  NameError: global name 'omh4cli' is not defined
```

No, our solution here is to just move the **import** statement into the cli4vof() function declaration:

```
def cli4vof():
    import omh4cli
    omh4cli.cli_util()
```

This way, the import of the cli4vof module from omh4cli completes successfully, and on the tail end, calling the utility function is successful because the omh4cli name is imported before it is called. As far as execution goes, the only difference is that from cli4vof, the import of omh4cli is performed when cli4vof.cli4vof() is called and not when the cli4vof module is imported.

12.8.6 Module Execution

There are many ways to execute a Python module: script invocation via the command-line or shell, execfile(), module import, interpreter -m option, etc. These are out of the scope of this chapter. We refer you to Chapter 14, "Execution Environment," which covers all of these features in full detail.

12.9 Related Modules

The following are auxiliary modules that you may use when dealing with the import of Python modules. Of these listed below, modulefinder, pkgutil, and zipimport are new as of Python 2.3, and the distutils package was introduced back in version 2.0.

- imp — this module gives you access to some lower-level importer functionality.
- modulefinder — this is a module that lets you find all the modules that are used by a Python script. You can either use the ModuleFinder class or just run it as a script giving it the filename of a(nother) Python module with which to do module analysis on.
- pkgutil — this module gives those putting together Python packages for distribution a way to place package files in various

places yet maintain the abstraction of a single "package" file hierarchy. It uses `*.pkg` files in a manner similar to the way the site module uses `*.pth` files to help define the package path.

- `site` — using this module along with `*.pth` files gives you the ability to specify the order in which packages are added to your Python path, i.e., `sys.path`, `PYTHONPATH`. You do not have to import it explicitly as the importer already uses it by default— you need to use the `-S` switch when starting up Python to turn it off. Also, you can perform further arbitrary site-specific customizations by adding a sitecustomize module whose import is attempted after the path manipulations have been completed.

- `zipimport` — this module allows you to be able to import Python modules that are archived in ZIP files. Note that the functionality in this file is "automagically" called by the importer so there is no need to import this file for use in any application. We mention it here solely as a reference.

- `distutils` — this package provides support for building, installing, and distributing Python modules and packages. It also aids in building Python extensions written in C/C++. More information on `distutils` can be found in the Python documentation available at these links:

  http://docs.python.org/dist/dist.html
  http://docs.python.org/inst/inst.html

12.10 Exercises

12–1. *PathSearch versus SearchPath*. What is the difference between a path search and a search path?

12–2. *Importing Attributes*. Assume you have a function called `foo()` in your module `mymodule`.
   (a) What are the two ways of importing this function into your namespace for invocation?
   (b) What are the namespace implications when choosing one over the other?

12–3. *Importing*. What are the differences between using "**import** *module*" and "**from** *module* **import** *"?

12–4. *Namespaces versus Variable Scope*. How are namespaces and variable scopes different from each other?

12–5. *Using __import__ ().*

  (a) Use __import__() to import a module into your namespace. What is the correct syntax you finally used to get it working?

  (b) Same as above, but use __import__() to import only specific names from modules.

12–6. *Extended Import.* Create a new function called importAs(). This function will import a module into your namespace, but with a name you specify, not its original name. For example, calling newname=importAs ('mymodule') will import the module mymodule, but the module and all its elements are accessible only as newname or newname.*attr*. This is the exact functionality provided by the new extended import syntax introduced in Python 2.0.

12–7. *Import Hooks.* Study the import hooks mechanism provided for by the implementation of PEP 302. Implement your own import mechanism, which allows you to obfuscate your Python modules (encryption, bzip2, rot13, etc.) so that the interpreter can decode them properly and import them properly. You may wish to look at how it works with importing zip files (see Section 12.5.7).

2.0

OBJECT-ORIENTED PROGRAMMING

Chapter Topics

- Introduction
- Object-Oriented Programming
- Classes
- Instances
- Binding and Method Invocation
- Subclassing, Derivation, and Inheritance
- Built-in Functions
- Customizing Classes
- Privacy
- Delegation and Wrapping
- Advanced Features of New-Style Classes
- Related Modules

Chapter 13

Classes finally introduce the notion of object-oriented programming (OOP) to our picture. We will first present a high-level overview, covering all the main aspects of using classes and OOP in Python. The remainder of the chapter examines details on classes, class instances, and methods. We will also describe derivation or subclassing in Python and what its inheritance model is. Finally, Python gives programmers the ability to customize classes with special functionality, including those that overload operators and emulate Python types. We will show you how to implement some of these special methods to customize your classes so that they behave more like Python's built-in types.

With this said, however, we would like to add that there have been some exciting changes with regard to Python OOP. In version 2.2, the Python community finally saw the unification of types and classes, and with the *new-style classes* come much more advanced OOP features. New-style classes represent a superset of features from *classic* (or *old-style*) *classes*, the original class objects since Python was born.

2.2

We will first present the core features common to both types of classes, and then introduce those more advanced features found only in Python's new-style classes.

13.1 Introduction

Before we get into the nitty-gritty of OOP and classes, we begin with a high-level overview, then present some simple examples to get you warmed up. If you are new to object-oriented programming, you may wish to skim this section first, then begin the formal reading in Section 13.2. If you are already familiar with object-oriented programming and want to see how it is done in Python, finish this section and go straight to Section 13.3 for more details.

The main two entities in Python object-oriented programming are classes and class instances (see Figure 13–1).

Classes and Instances

Classes and instances are related to each other: classes provide the definition of an object, and instances are "the real McCoy," the objects specified in the class definition brought to life.

Here is an example of how to create a class:

```
class MyNewObjectType(bases):
    'define MyNewObjectType class'
    class_suite
```

The keyword is **class**, followed by the class name. What follows is the suite of code that defines the class. This usually consists of various definitions and declarations. The biggest difference between declaring new-style classes and classic classes is that all new-style classes must inherit from at least one parent class. The *bases* argument is one (single inheritance) or more (multiple inheritance) parent classes to derive from.

The "mother of all classes" is object. If you do not have any ancestor classes to inherit from, use object as your default. It must exist at the top of every class hierarchy. If you do not subclass object or a class that subclasses object, then you have defined a classic class:

```
class MyNewObjectType:
    'define MyNewObjectType classic class'
    class_suite
```

Conversely, if you do not specify a parent class, or if you subclass a base class without a parent class, you have created a classic class. Most Python classes are still classic classes. There really is no problem with using them until they become obsolete in some future version of Python. We do recommend that you use new-style classes whenever possible, but for learning purposes, either type will suffice.

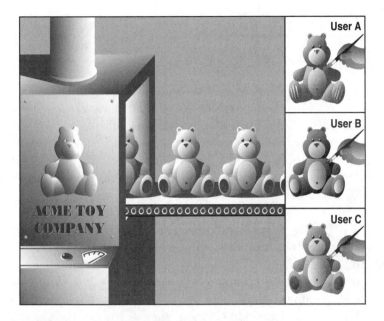

Figure 13–1 The factory manufacturing machines on the left are analogous to classes, while the toys produced are instances of their respective classes. Although each instance has the basic underlying structure, individual attributes like color or feet can be changed—these are similar to instance attributes.

The process of creating an instance is called *instantiation*, and it is carried out like this (note the conspicuous absence of a new keyword):

```
myFirstObject = MyNewObjectType()
```

The class name is given as an "invocation," using the familiar function operators (( )). You then typically assign that newly created instance to a variable. The assignment is not required syntactically, but if you do not save your instance to a variable, it will be of no use and will be automatically garbage-collected because there would no references to that instance. What you would be doing is allocating memory, then immediately deallocating it.

Classes can be as simple or as complicated as you wish them to be. At a very minimum, classes can be used as namespaces (see Chapter 11 for more on these). By this, we mean that you can store data into variables and group them in such a way that they all share the same relationship—a named relationship using the standard Python dotted-attribute notation. For example, you may have a class without any inherent attributes and merely use such a class to provide a namespace for data, giving your class characteristics similar to records in Pascal or structures in C, or, in other words, use the class simply as a container object with shared naming.

Here is an example:

```
class MyData(object):
    pass
```

Recall that the **pass** statement is used where code is required syntactically, but no operation is desired. In this case, the required code is the class suite, but we do not wish to provide one. The class we just defined has no methods or any other attributes. We will now create an instance to use the class simply as a namespace container.

```
>>> mathObj = MyData()
>>> mathObj.x = 4
>>> mathObj.y = 5
>>> mathObj.x + mathObj.y
9
>>> mathObj.x * mathObj.y
20
```

We could have used variables "x" and "y" to accomplish the same thing, but in our case, mathObj.x and mathObj.y are related by the instance name, mathObj. This is what we mean by using classes as namespace containers. mathObj.x and mathObj.y are known as *instance attributes* because they are only attributes of their instance object (mathObj), not of the class

(MyData). As we will see later on in this chapter, these attributes really are dynamic in nature: you do not need to pre-declare or pre-assign them in the constructor or anywhere else.

Methods

One way we can improve our use of classes is to add functions to them. These class functions are known by their more common name, *methods*. In Python, methods are defined as part of the class definition, but can be invoked only on an instance. In other words, the path one must take to finally be able to call a method goes like this: (1) define the class (and the methods), (2) create an instance, and finally, (3) invoke the method on that instance. Here is an example class with a method:

```
class MyDataWithMethod(object):   # define the class
    def printFoo(self):        # define the method
        print 'You invoked printFoo()!'
```

You will notice the `self` argument, which must be present in all method declarations. That argument, representing the instance object, is passed to the method implicitly by the interpreter when you invoke a method on an instance, so you, yourself, do not have to worry about passing anything in (specifically `self`, which is automatically passed in for you).

For example, if you have a method that takes two arguments, all of your calls should only pass in the second argument. Python passes in self for you as the first. If you make a mistake, do not worry about it. When an error occurs, Python will tell you that you have passed in the wrong number of arguments. You may make this mistake only once anyway... you'll certainly remember each time after that!

The requirement of the instance (`self`) in each method's signature will be something new to those of you coming from C++ or Java, so be aware of that. It is all part of Python's philosophy of being explicitly clear. In those other languages, `self` is called `"this."` You can find out more about `self` in the Core Note in Section 13.7 on page 540. Requiring the instance only applies to regular methods and not static or class methods, although the latter requires the class rather than the instance. You can find out more about static and class methods in Section 13.8 on page 542.

Now we will instantiate the class and invoke the method once we have an instance:

```
>>> myObj = MyDataWithMethod()   # create the instance
>>> myObj.printFoo()             # now invoke the method
You invoked printFoo()!
```

We conclude this introductory section by giving you a slightly more complex example of what you can do with classes (and instances) and also introducing you to the special method __init__() as well as subclassing and inheritance.

For those of you who are already familiar with object-oriented programming, __init__() is similar to the *class constructor*. If you are new to the world of OOP, a constructor is simply a special method that is typically called to create a new object. In Python, __init__() is not really the constructor. You do not call "new" to create a new object. (Python does not even have a keyword called "new" anyway.) Instead, Python creates the instance for you and then calls __init__() during instantiation to define additional behavior that should occur when a class is instantiated, i.e., setting up initial values or running some preliminary diagnostic code—basically performing any special tasks or setup after the instance is created but before the new instance is returned from the instantiation call.

(We will add **print** statements to our methods to better illustrate when certain methods are called. It is generally not typical to have input or output statements in functions unless output is a predetermined characteristic of the body of code.)

Creating a Class (Class Definition)

```
class AddrBookEntry(object):            # class definition
    'address book entry class'
    def __init__(self, nm, ph):         # define constructor
        self.name = nm                  # set name
        self.phone = ph                 # set phone#
        print 'Created instance for:', self.name
    def updatePhone(self, newph):       # define method
        self.phone = newph
        print 'Updated phone# for:', self.name
```

In the definition for the AddrBookEntry class, we define two methods: __init__() and updatePhone(). __init__() is called when instantiation occurs, that is, when AddrBookEntry() is invoked. You can think of instantiation as an implicit call to __init__() because the arguments given to AddrBookEntry() are exactly the same as those that are received by __init__() (except for self, which is passed automatically for you).

Recall that the self (instance object) argument is passed in automatically by the interpreter when the method is invoked on an instance, so in our __init__() above, the only required arguments are nm and ph, representing the name and telephone number, respectively. __init__() sets these two instance attributes on instantiation so that they are available to the programmer by the time the instance is returned from the instantiation call.

As you may have surmised, the purpose of the `updatePhone()` method is to replace an address book entry's telephone number attribute.

Creating Instances (Instantiation)

```
>>> john = AddrBookEntry('John Doe', '408-555-1212')
Created instance for: John Doe
>>> jane = AddrBookEntry('Jane Doe', '650-555-1212')
Created instance for: Jane Doe
```

These are our instantiation calls, which, in turn, invoke `__init__()`. Recall that an instance object is passed in automatically as `self`. So, in your head, you can replace `self` in methods with the name of the instance. In the first case, when object `john` is instantiated, it is `john.name` that is set, as you can confirm below.

Also, without the presence of default arguments, both parameters to `__init__()` are required as part of the instantiation.

Accessing Instance Attributes

```
>>> john
<__main__.AddrBookEntry instance at 80ee610>
>>> john.name
'John Doe'
>>> john.phone
'408-555-1212'
>>> jane.name
'Jane Doe'
>>> jane.phone
'650-555-1212'
```

Once our instance was created, we can confirm that our instance attributes were indeed set by `__init__()` during instantiation. "Dumping" the instance within the interpreter tells us what kind of object it is. (We will discover later how we can customize our class so that rather than seeing the default < . . . > Python object string, a more desired output can be customized.)

Method Invocation (via Instance)

```
>>> john.updatePhone('415-555-1212')
Updated phone# for: John Doe
>>> john.phone
'415-555-1212'
```

The `updatePhone()` method requires one argument (in addition to `self`): the new phone number. We check our instance attribute right after the call to `updatePhone()`, making sure that it did what was advertised.

Creating a Subclass

Subclassing with inheritance is a way to create and customize a new class type with all the features of an existing class but without modifying the original class definition. The new *subclass* can be customized with special functionality unique only to that new class type. Aside from its relationship to its *parent* or *base class*, a subclass has all the same features as any regular class and is instantiated in the same way as all other classes. Note below that a parent class is part of the subclass declaration:

```
class EmplAddrBookEntry(AddrBookEntry):
    'Employee Address Book Entry class'
    def __init__(self, nm, ph, id, em):
        AddrBookEntry.__init__(self, nm, ph)
        self.empid = id
        self.email = em

    def updateEmail(self, newem):
        self.email = newem
        print 'Updated e-mail address for:', self.name
```

We will now create our first subclass, `EmplAddrBookEntry`. In Python, when classes are derived, subclasses inherit the base class attributes, so in our case, we will not only define the methods `__init__()` and `update-Email()`, but `EmplAddrBookEntry` will also inherit the `updatePhone()` method from `AddrBookEntry`.

Each subclass must define its own constructor if desired, otherwise the base class constructor will be called. However, if a subclass overrides a base class constructor, the base class constructor will *not* be called automatically—such a request must be made explicitly as we have above. For our subclass, we make an initial call to the base class constructor before performing any "local" tasks, hence the call to `AddrBookEntry.__init__()` to set the name and phone number. Our subclass sets two additional instance attributes, the employee ID and e-mail address, which are set by the remaining lines of our constructor.

Note how we have to explicitly pass the `self` instance object to the base class constructor because we are not invoking that method on an instance. We are invoking that method on an instance of a subclass. Because we are not invoking it via an instance, this *unbound method* call requires us to pass an acceptable instance (`self`) to the method.

We close this section with examples of how to create an instance of the subclass, accessing its attributes and invoking its methods, including those inherited from the parent class.

Using a Subclass

```
>>> john = EmplAddrBookEntry('John Doe', '408-555-1212',
42, 'john@spam.doe')
Created instance for: John Doe
>>> john
<__main__.EmplAddrBookEntry object at 0x62030>
>>> john.name
'John Doe'
>>> john.phone
'408-555-1212'
>>> john.email
'john@spam.doe'
>>> john.updatePhone('415-555-1212')
Updated phone# for: John Doe
>>> john.phone
'415-555-1212'
>>> john.updateEmail('john@doe.spam')
Updated e-mail address for: John Doe
>>> john.email
'john@doe.spam'
```

CORE STYLE: Naming classes, attributes, and methods

Class names traditionally begin with a capital letter. This is the standard convention that will help you identify classes, especially during instantiation (which would look like a function call otherwise). In particular, data attributes should sound like data value names, and method names should indicate action toward a specific object or value. Another way to phrase this is: Use nouns for data value names and predicates (verbs plus direct objects) for methods. The data items are the objects acted upon, and the methods should indicate what action the programmer wants to perform on the object.

In the classes we defined above, we attempted to follow this guideline, with data values such as "name," "phone," and "email," and actions such as "updatePhone" and "updateEmail." This is known as "mixedCase" or "camelCase." The Python Style Guide favors using underscores over camelCase, i.e,. "update_phone," "update_email." Classes should also be well named; some of those good names include "AddrBookEntry," "RepairShop," etc.

We hope that you now have some understanding of how object-oriented programming is accomplished using Python. The remaining sections of this chapter will take you deeper into all the facets of object-oriented programming and Python classes and instances.

13.2 Object-Oriented Programming

The evolution of programming has taken us from a sequence of step-by-step instructions in a single flow of control to a more organized approach whereby blocks of code could be cordoned off into named subroutines and defined functionality. Structured or procedural programming lets us organize our programs into logical blocks, often repeated or reused. Creating applications becomes a more logical process; actions are chosen which meet the specifications, then data are created to be subjected to those actions. Deitel and Deitel refer to structured programming as "action-oriented" due to the fact that logic must be "enacted" on data that have no associated behaviors.

However, what if we *could* impose behavior on data? What if we were able to create or program a piece of data modeled after real-life entities that embody both data characteristics along with behaviors? If we were then able to access the data attributes via a set of defined interfaces (aka a set of accessor functions), such as an automated teller machine (ATM) card or a personal check to access your bank account, then we would have a system of "objects" where each could interact not only with itself, but also with other objects in a larger picture.

Object-oriented programming takes this evolutionary step by enhancing structured programming to enable a data/behavior relationship: data and logic are now described by a single abstraction with which to create these objects. Real-world problems and entities are stripped down to their bare essentials, providing an abstraction from which they can be coded similarly or into objects that can interact with objects in the system. Classes provide the definitions of such objects, and instances are realizations of such definitions. Both are vital components for object-oriented design (OOD), which simply means to build your system architected in an object-oriented fashion.

13.2.1 Relationship between OOD and OOP

Object-oriented design does not specifically require an object-oriented programming language. Indeed, OOD can be performed in purely structural languages such as C, but this requires more effort on the part of the programmer who must build data types with object qualities and characteristics. Naturally, OOP is simplified when a language has built-in OO properties that enable smoother and more rapid development of OO programs.

Conversely, an object-oriented language may not necessarily force one to write OO programs. C++ can be used simply as a "better C." Java, on the other hand, requires everything to be a class, and further dictates only one class definition per source file. In Python, however, neither classes nor OOP are required for everyday programming. Even though it is a language that is object-oriented by design and that has constructs to support OOP, Python does not restrict or require you to write OO code for your application. Rather, OOP is a powerful tool that is at your disposal when you are ready to evolve, learn, transition, or otherwise move toward OOP. The creator of Python often refers to this phenomenon as being able to "see the forest through the trees."

13.2.2 Real-World Problems

One of the most important reasons to consider working in OOD is that it provides a direct approach to modeling and solving real-world problems and situations. For example, let us attempt to model an automobile mechanic shop where you would take your car in for repair. There are two general entities we would have to create: humans who interact with and in such a "system," and a physical location for the activities that define a mechanic shop. Since there are more and different types of the former, we will describe them first, then conclude with the latter.

A class called `Person` would be created to represent all humans involved in such an activity. Instances of `Person` would include the `Customer`, the `Mechanic`, and perhaps the `Cashier`. Each of these instances would have similar as well as unique behaviors. For example, all would have the `talk()` method as a means of vocal communication as well as a `drive_car()` method. Only the `Mechanic` would have the `repair_car()` method and only the `Cashier` would have a `ring_sale()` method. The `Mechanic` will have a `repair_certification` attribute while all `Persons` would have a `drivers_license` attribute.

Finally, all of these instances would be participants in one overseeing class, called the `RepairShop`, which would have `operating_hours`, a data attribute that accesses time functionality to determine when `Customers` can bring in their vehicles and when `Employees` such as `Mechanics` and `Cashiers` show up for work. The `RepairShop` might also have a `AutoBay` class that would have instances such as `SmogZone`, `TireBrakeZone`, and perhaps one called `GeneralRepair`.

The point of our fictitious `RepairShop` is to show one example of how classes and instances plus their behaviors can be used to model a true-to-life scenario. You can probably also imagine classes such as an `Airport`, a `Restaurant`, a `ChipFabPlant`, a `Hospital`, or even a `MailOrderMusic` business, all complete with their own participants and functionality.

13.2.3 *Buzzword-Compliance

For those of you who are already familiar with all the lingo associated with OOP, here is how Python stacks up:

Abstraction/Implementation

Abstraction refers to the modeling of essential aspects, behavior, and characteristics of real-world problems and entities, providing a relevant subset as the definition of a programmatic structure that can realize such models. Abstractions not only contain the data attributes of such a model, but also define interfaces with that data. An *implementation* of such an abstraction is the realization of that data and the interfaces that go along with it. Such a realization should remain hidden from and irrelevant to the client programmer.

Encapsulation/Interfaces

Encapsulation describes the concept of data/information hiding and providing *interfaces* or accessor functions to the data attributes. Direct access to data by any client, bypassing the interfaces, goes against the principles of encapsulation, but the programmer is free to allow such access. As part of the implementation, the client should not even know how the data attributes are architected within the abstraction. In Python, all class attributes are public, but names may be "mangled" to discourage unauthorized access, but otherwise not prevented. It is up to the designer to provide the appropriate interfaces to the data so that the client programmer does not have to resort to manipulating the encapsulated data attributes.

Composition

Composition extends our description of classes, enabling multiple yet distinct classes to be combined into a larger entity to solve a real-world problem. Composition describes a singular, complex system such as a class made up of other, smaller components such as other classes, data attributes, and behaviors, all of which are combined, embodying "has-a" relationships. For example, the

RepairShop "has a" Mechanic (hopefully at least one) and also "has a" Customer (again, hopefully at least one).

These components are composed either via *association*, meaning that access to subcomponents is granted (for the RepairShop, a customer may enter and request a SmogCheck, the client programmer interfacing with components of the RepairShop), or *aggregation*, encapsulating components that are then accessed only via defined interfaces, and again, hidden from the client programmer. Continuing our example, the client programmer may be able to make a SmogCheck request on behalf of the Customer, but has no ability to interact with the SmogZone part of the RepairShop, which is accessed only via internal controls of the RepairShop when the smogCheckCar() method is called. Both forms of composition are supported in Python.

Derivation/Inheritance/Hierarchy

Derivation describes the creation of subclasses, new classes that retain all desired data and behavior of the existing class type but permit modification or other customization, all without having to modify the original class definition. *Inheritance* describes the means by which attributes of a subclass are "bequeathed from" an ancestor class. From our earlier example, a Mechanic may have more car skill attributes than a Customer, but individually, each "is a" Person, so it is valid to invoke the talk() method, which is common to all instances of Person, for either of them. *Hierarchy* describes multiple "generations" of derivation which can be depicted graphically as a "family tree," with successive subclasses having relationships with ancestor classes.

Generalization/Specialization

Generalization describes all the traits a subclass has with its parent and ancestor classes, so subclasses are considered to have an "is-a" relationship with ancestor classes because a derived object (instance) is an "example" of an ancestor class. For example, a Mechanic "is a" Person, a Car "is a" Vehicle, etc. In the family tree diagram we alluded to above, we can draw lines from subclasses to ancestors indicating "is-a" relationships. *Specialization* is the term that describes all the customization of a subclass, i.e., what attributes make it differ from its ancestor classes.

Polymorphism

The concept of *polymorphism* describes how objects can be manipulated and accessed using attributes and behaviors they have in common without regard to their specific class. Polymorphism indicates the presence of dynamic (aka late, runtime) binding, allowing for overriding and runtime type determination and verification.

Introspection/Reflection

Introspection is what gives you, the programmer, the ability to perform an activity such as "manual type checking." Also called *reflection*, this property describes how information about a particular object can be accessed by itself during runtime. Would it not be great to have the ability to take an object passed to you and be able to find out what it is capable of? This is a powerful feature that you will encounter frequently in this chapter. The `dir()` and `type()` built-in functions would have a very difficult time working if Python did not support some sort of introspection capability. Keep an eye out for these calls as well as for special attributes like __dict__, __name__, and __doc__. You may even be familiar with some of them already!

13.3 Classes

Recall that a class is a data structure that we can use to define objects that hold together data values and behavioral characteristics. Classes are entities that are the programmatic form of an abstraction for a real-world problem, and instances are realizations of such objects. One analogy is to liken classes to blueprints or molds with which to make real objects (instances). So why the term "class"? The term most likely originates from using classes to identify and categorize biological families of species to which specific creatures belong and can be derived into similar yet distinct subclasses. Many of these features apply to the concept of classes in programming.

In Python, class declarations are very similar to function declarations, a header line with the appropriate keyword followed by a suite as its definition, as indicated below:

```
def functionName(args):
    'function documentation string'
    function_suite


class ClassName(object):
    'class documentation string'
    class_suite
```

Both allow you to create functions within their declaration, closures or inner functions for functions within functions, and methods for functions defined in classes. The biggest difference is that you run functions but create objects with classes. A class is like a Python container type on steroids. In this section, we will take a close look at classes and what types of attributes they have. Just remember to keep in mind that even though classes are objects (everything in Python is an object), they are not realizations of the objects they are defining. We will look at instances in the next section, so stay tuned for that. For now, the limelight is beamed strictly on class objects.

When you create a class, you are practically creating your own kind of data type. All instances of that class are similar, but classes differ from one another (and so will instances of different classes by nature). Rather than playing with toys that came from the manufacturer and were bestowed upon you as gifts, why not design and build your own toys to play with?

Classes also allow for derivation. You can create subclasses that are classes but inherit all of the features and attributes of the "parent" class. Starting in Python 2.2, you can subclass built-in types instead of just other classes.

13.3.1 Creating Classes

Python classes are created using the **class** keyword. In the simple form of class declarations, the name of the class immediately follows the keyword:

```
class ClassName(bases):
    'class documentation string'
    class_suite
```

As outlined briefly earlier in this chapter, *bases* is the set of one or more parent classes from which to derive; and *class_suite* consists of all the component statements, defining class members, data attributes, and functions. Classes are generally defined at the top-level of a module so that instances of a class can be created anywhere in a piece of source code where the class is defined.

13.3.2 Declaration versus Definition

As with Python functions, there is no distinction between declaring and defining classes because they occur simultaneously, i.e., the definition (the class suite) immediately follows the declaration (header line with the **class** keyword) and the always recommended, but optional, documentation string. Likewise, all methods must also be defined at this time. If you are familiar with the OOP terms, Python does not support *pure virtual functions* (à la C++) or *abstract methods* (as in Java), which coerce the programmer to define a method in a subclass. As a proxy, you can simply raise the `NotImplementedError` exception in the base class method to get the same effect.

13.4 Class Attributes

What is an attribute? An attribute is a data or functional element that belongs to another object and is accessed via the familiar dotted-attribute notation. Some Python types such as complex numbers have data attributes (`real` and `imag`), while others such as lists and dictionaries have methods (functional attributes).

One interesting side note about attributes is that when you are accessing an attribute, it is also an object and may have attributes of its own which you can then access, leading to a chain of attributes, i.e., `myThing.subThing.sub-SubThing`, etc. Some familiar examples are:

- `sys.stdout.write('foo')`
- **print** `myModule.myClass.__doc__`
- `myList.extend(map(upper, open('x').readlines()))`

Class attributes are tied only to the classes in which they are defined, and since instance objects are the most commonly used objects in everyday OOP, instance data attributes are the primary data attributes you will be using. Class data attributes are useful only when a more "static" data type is required which is independent of any instances, hence the reason we are making the next section advanced, optional reading. (If you are unfamiliar with static, it just means a value that hangs around a function for each call, or a piece of data in a class that is the same across all instances. More about static data in the next subsection.)

In the succeeding subsection, we will briefly describe how methods in Python are implemented and invoked. In general, all methods in Python have the same restriction: they require an instance before they can be called.

13.4.1 Class Data Attributes

Data attributes are simply variables of the class we are defining. They can be used like any other variable in that they are set when the class is created and can be updated either by methods within the class or elsewhere in the main part of the program.

Such attributes are better known to OO programmers as *static members*, *class variables*, or *static data*. They represent data that is tied to the class object they belong to and are independent of any class instances. If you are a Java or C++ programmer, this type of data is the same as placing the `static` keyword in front of a variable declaration.

Static members are generally used only to track values associated with classes. In most circumstances, you would be using instance attributes rather than class attributes. We will compare the differences between class and instance attributes when we formally introduce instances.

Here is an example of using a class data attribute (`foo`):

```
>>> class C(object):
...        foo = 100

>>> print C.foo
100
>>> C.foo = C.foo + 1
>>> print C.foo
101
```

Note that nowhere in the code above do you see any references to class instances.

13.4.2 Methods

A method, such as the `myNoActionMethod` method of the `MyClass` class in the example below, is simply a function defined as part of a class definition (thus making methods class attributes). This means that `myNoAction-Method` applies only to objects (instances) of `MyClass` type. Note how `myNoActionMethod` is tied to its instance because invocation requires both names in the dotted attribute notation:

```
>>> class MyClass(object):
        def myNoActionMethod(self):
            pass

>>> mc = MyClass()
>>> mc.myNoActionMethod()
```

Any call to `myNoActionMethod` by itself as a function fails:

```
>>> myNoActionMethod()
Traceback (innermost last):
  File "<stdin>", line 1, in ?
    myNoActionMethod()
NameError: myNoActionMethod
```

A `NameError` exception is raised because there is no such function in the global namespace. The point is to show you that `myNoActionMethod` is a method, meaning that it belongs to the class and is not a name in the global namespace. If `myNoActionMethod` was defined as a function at the top-level, then our call would have succeeded.

We show you below that even calling the method with the class object fails.

```
>>> MyClass.myNoActionMethod()
Traceback (innermost last):
  File "<stdin>", line 1, in ?
    MyClass.myNoActionMethod()
TypeError: unbound method must be called with class
instance 1st argument
```

This `TypeError` exception may seem perplexing at first because you know that the method is an attribute of the class and so are wondering why there is a failure. We will explain this next.

Binding (Bound and Unbound Methods)

In keeping with OOP tradition, Python imposes the restriction that methods cannot be invoked without instances. An instance must be used to perform method calls. This restriction describes Python's concept of binding, where methods must be bound (to an instance) in order to be invoked directly. Unbound methods may also be called, but an instance object must be provided explicitly in order for the invocation to succeed. However, regardless of binding, methods are inherently attributes of the class they are defined in, even if they are almost always invoked via an instance. We will further explore bound and unbound methods later in Section 13.7.

13.4.3 Determining Class Attributes

There are two ways to determine what attributes a class has. The simplest way is to use the `dir()` built-in function. An alternative is to access the class dictionary attribute `__dict__`, one of a number of special attributes that is common to all classes. Let us take a look at an example:

```
>>> class MyClass(object):
...       'MyClass class definition'
...       myVersion = '1.1'            # static data
...       def showMyVersion(self):     # method
...           print MyClass.myVersion
...
```

Using the class defined above, let us use `dir()` and the special class attribute __dict__ to see this class's attributes:

```
>>> dir(MyClass)
['__class__', '__delattr__', '__dict__', '__doc__',
'__getattribute__', '__hash__', '__init__', '__module__',
'__new__', '__reduce__', '__reduce_ex__', '__repr__',
'__setattr__', '__str__', '__weakref__', 'myVersion',
'showMyVersion']

>>> MyClass.__dict__

<dictproxy object at 0x62090>

>>> print MyClass.__dict__
{'showMyVersion': <function showMyVersion at 0x59370>,
'__dict__': <attribute '__dict__' of 'MyClass' objects>,
'myVersion': '1.1', '__weakref__': <attribute
'__weakref__' of 'MyClass' objects>, '__doc__':
'MyClass class definition'}
```

There are a few more attributes added for new-style classes as well as a more robust `dir()` function. Just for comparison, here is what you would see for classic classes:

```
>>> dir(MyClass)
['__doc__', '__module__', 'showMyVersion', 'myVersion']
>>>
>>> MyClass.__dict__
{'__doc__': None, 'myVersion': 1, 'showMyVersion':
<function showMyVersion at 950ed0>, '__module__':
'__main__'}
```

As you can tell, `dir()` returns a list of (just the) names of an object's attributes while __dict__ is a dictionary whose attribute names are the keys and whose values are the data values of the corresponding attribute objects.

The output also reveals two familiar attributes of our class `MyClass`, `showMyVersion` and `myVersion`, as well as a couple of new ones. These attributes, __doc__ and __module__, are special class attributes that all classes have (in addition to __dict__). The `vars()` built-in function returns the contents of a class's __dict__ attribute when passed the class object as its argument.

13.4.4 Special Class Attributes

For any class `C`, Table 13.1 represents a list of all the special attributes of `C`:

Table 13.1 Special Class Attributes	
C.__name__	String name of class C
C.__doc__	Documentation string for class C
C.__bases__	Tuple of class C's parent classes
C.__dict__	Attributes of C
C.__module__	Module where C is defined (new in 1.5)
C.__class__	Class of which C is an instance (new-style classes only)

Using the class MyClass we just defined above, we have the following:

```
>>> MyClass.__name__
'MyClass'
>>> MyClass.__doc__
'MyClass class definition'
>>> MyClass.__bases__
(<type 'object'>,)
>>> print MyClass.__dict__
{'__doc__': None, 'myVersion': 1, 'showMyVersion':
<function showMyVersion at 950ed0>, '__module__': '__main__'}
>>> MyClass.__module__
'__main__'
>>> MyClass.__class__
<type 'type'>
```

__name__ is the string name for a given class. This may come in handy in cases where a string is desired rather than a class object. Even some built-in types have this attribute, and we will use one of them to showcase the usefulness of the __name__ string.

The type object is an example of one built-in type that has a __name__ attribute. Recall that type() returns a type object when invoked. There may be cases where we just want the string indicating the type rather than an object. We can use the __name__ attribute of the type object to obtain the string name. Here is an example:

```
>>> stype = type('What is your quest?')
>>> stype                           # stype is a type object
<type 'string'>
>>> stype.__name__                  # get type as a string
'string'
>>>
>>> type(3.14159265)                # also a type object
<type 'float'>
>>> type(3.14159265).__name__       # get type as a string
'float'
```

__doc__ is the documentation string for the class, similar to the documentation string for functions and modules, and must be the first unassigned string succeeding the header line. The documentation string is *not* inherited by derived classes, an indication that they must contain their own documentation strings.

__bases__ deals with inheritance, which we will cover later in this chapter; it contains a tuple that consists of a class's parent classes.

The aforementioned __dict__ attribute consists of a dictionary containing the data attributes of a class. When accessing a class attribute, this dictionary is searched for the attribute in question. If it is not found in __dict__, the hunt continues in the dictionary of base classes, in "depth-first search" order. The set of base classes is searched in sequential order, left-to-right in the same order as they are defined as parent classes in a class declaration. Modification of a class attribute affects only the current class's dictionary; no base class __dict__ attributes are ever modified.

Python supports class inheritance across modules. To better clarify a class's description, the __module__ was introduced in version 1.5 so that a class name is fully qualified with its module. We present the following example:

```
>>> class C(object):
...         pass
...
>>> C
<class __main__.C at 0x53f90>
>>> C.__module__
'__main__'
```

The fully qualified name of class C is "__main__.C", i.e., *source_module.class_name*. If class C was located in an imported module, such as mymod, we would see the following:

```
>>> from mymod import C
>>> C
<class mymod.C at 0x53ea0>
>>> C.__module__
'mymod'
```

In previous versions of Python without the special attribute __module__, it was much more difficult to ascertain the location of a class simply because classes did not use their fully qualified names.

Finally, because of the unification of types and classes, when you access the __class__ attribute of any class, you will find that it is indeed an instance of a type object. In other words, a class is a type now! Because classic classes do not share in this equality (a classic class is a class object, and a type is a type object), this attribute is undefined for those objects.

13.5 Instances

Whereas a class is a data structure definition type, an instance is a declaration of a variable of that type. In other words, instances are classes brought to life. Once a blueprint is provided, the next step to bring them to fruition. Instances are the objects that are used primarily during execution, and the types of all instances are the class from which they were instantiated. Prior to Python 2.2, instances were "instance types," regardless of which class they came from.

13.5.1 Instantiation: Creating Instances by Invoking Class Object

Many other OO languages provide a new keyword with which to create an instance of a class. Python's approach is much simpler. Once a class has been defined, creating an instance is no more difficult than calling a function—literally. Instantiation is realized with use of the function operator, as in the following example:

```
>>> class MyClass(object):    # define class
...       pass
>>> mc = MyClass()            # instantiate class
```

As you can see, creating instance `mc` of class `MyClass` consists of "calling" the class: `MyClass()`. The returned object is an instance of the class you called. When you "call" a class using the functional notation, the interpreter instantiates the object, and calls the closest thing Python has to a constructor (if you have written one [see the next section]) to perform any final customization such as setting instance attributes, and finally returns the instance to you.

CORE NOTE: Classes and instances before and after Python 2.2

Classes and types were unified in 2.2, making Python behave more like other object-oriented languages. Instances of any class or type are objects of those types. For example, if you ask Python to tell you, it will say that an instance `mc` *of the* `MyClass` *class is an instance of the* `MyClass` *class. Redundant yes, but the interpreter will not lie. Likewise, it will tell you that 0 is an instance of the integer type:*

```
>>> mc = MyClass()
>>> type(mc)
<class '__main__.MyClass'>
>>> type(0)
<type 'int'>
```

But if you look carefully and compare `MyClass` with `int`, you will find that both are indeed types:

```
>>> type(MyClass)
<type 'type'>
>>> type(int)
<type 'type'>
```

In contrast for those of you using classic classes and Python versions earlier than 2.2, classes are class objects and instances are instance objects. There is no further relationship between the two object types other than an instance's __class__ attribute refers to the class from which it was instantiated. Redefining `MyClass` as a classic class and running the same calls in Python 2.1 (note that `int()` has not been turned into a factory function yet ... it was still only a regular built-in function):

```
>>> type(mc)
<type 'instance'>
>>> type(0)
<type 'int'>
>>>
>>> type(MyClass)
<type 'class'>
>>> type(int)
<type 'builtin_function_or_method'>
```

To avoid any confusion, just keep in mind that when you define a class, you are not creating a new type, just a new class object; and for 2.2 and after, when you define a (new-style) class you are creating a new type.

13.5.2 __init__() "Constructor" Method

When the class is invoked, the first step in the instantiation process is to create the instance object. Once the object is available, Python checks if an __init__() *method* has been implemented. By default, no special actions are enacted on the instance without the definition of (or the overriding) of the special method __init__(). Any special action desired requires the programmer to implement __init__(), overriding its default behavior. If __init__() has not been implemented, the object is then returned and the instantiation process is complete.

However, if __init__() *has* been implemented, then that special method is invoked and the instance object passed in as the first argument (`self`), just like a standard method call. Any arguments passed to the class invocation call are passed on to __init__(). You can practically envision the call to create the instance as a call to the constructor.

In summary, (a) you do not call `new` to create an instance, and you do not define a constructor: Python creates the object for you; and (b) `__init__()`, is simply the first method that is called after the interpreter creates an instance for you in case you want to prep the object a little bit more before putting it to use.

`__init__()` is one of many special methods that can be defined for classes. Some of these special methods are predefined with inaction as their default behavior, such as `__init__()`, and must be overridden for customization while others should be implemented on an as-needed basis. We will cover many more of these special methods throughout this chapter. You will find use of `__init__()` everywhere, so we will not present an example here.

13.5.3   `__new__()` "Constructor" Method

The `__new__()` special method bears a much closer resemblance to a real constructor than `__init__()`. With the unification of types and classes in 2.2, Python users now have the ability to subclass built-in types, and so there needed to be a way to instantiate immutable objects, e.g., subclassing strings, numbers, etc.

In such cases, the interpreter calls `__new__()`, a static method, with the class and passing in the arguments made in the class instantiation call. It is the responsibility of `__new__()` to call a superclass `__new__()` to create the object (delegating upward).

The reason why we say that `__new__()` is more like a constructor than `__init__()` is that it has to return a valid instance so that the interpreter can then call `__init__()` with that instance as self. Calling a superclass `__new__()` to create the object is just like using a `new` keyword to create an object in other languages.

`__new__()` and `__init__()` are both passed the (same) arguments as in the class creation call. For an example of using `__new__()`, see Section 13.11.3.

13.5.4   `__del__()` "Destructor" Method

Likewise, there is an equivalent *destructor* special method called `__del__()`. However, due to the way Python manages garbage collection of objects (by reference counting), this function is not executed until all references to an instance object have been removed. Destructors in Python are methods that provide special processing before instances are deallocated and *are not commonly implemented* since instances are seldom deallocated explicitly. If you do override `__del__()`, be sure to call any parent class `__del__()` first so those pieces can be adequately deallocated.

Example

In the following example, we create (and override) both the __init__()
and __del__() constructor and destructor functions, respectively, then
instantiate the class and assign more aliases to the same object. The id()
built-in function is then used to confirm that all three aliases reference the
same object. The final step is to remove all the aliases by using the **del**
statement and discovering when and how many times the destructor is
called.

```
class C(P):                    # class declaration
    def __init__(self):        # "constructor"
        print 'initialized'
    def __del__(self):         # "destructor"
        P.__del__(self)        # call parent destructor
        print 'deleted'

>>> c1 = C()                   # instantiation
initialized
>>> c2 = c1                    # create additional alias
>>> c3 = c1                    # create a third alias
>>> id(c1), id(c2), id(c3)     # all refer to same object
(11938912, 11938912, 11938912)
>>> del c1                     # remove one reference
>>> del c2                     # remove another reference
>>> del c3                     # remove final reference
deleted                        # destructor finally invoked
```

Notice how, in the above example, the destructor was not called until all
references to the instance of class C were removed, e.g., when the reference
count has decreased to zero. If for some reason your __del__() method is
not being called when you are expecting it to be invoked, this means that
somehow your instance object's reference count is not zero, and there may be
some other reference to it that you are not aware of that is keeping your
object around.

Also note that the destructor is called exactly once, the first time the reference count goes to zero and the object deallocated. This makes sense
because any object in the system is allocated and deallocated only once.
Summary:

- Do not forget to call a superclass __del__() first.
- Invoking **del** x does not call x.__del__()—as you saw above,
  it just decrements the reference count of x.
- If you have a cycle or some other cause of lingering references
  to an instance, an object's __del__() may *never* be called.

- Uncaught exceptions in __del__() are *ignored* (because some variables used in __del__() may have already been deleted). Try not to do anything in __del__() not related to an instance.
- Implementing __del__() is *not* a common occurrence—only do it if you really know what you are doing.
- If you define __del__, and instance is part of a cycle, the garbage collector will *not* break the cycle—you have to do it yourself by explicitly using **del**.

CORE NOTE: Keeping track of instances

Python does not provide any internal mechanism to track how many instances of a class have been created or to keep tabs on what they are. You can explicitly add some code to the class definition and perhaps __init__() and __del__() if such functionality is desired. The best way is to keep track of the number of instances using a static member. It would be dangerous to keep track of instance objects by saving references to them, because you must manage these references properly or else your instances will never be deallocated (because of your extra reference to them)! An example follows:

```
class InstCt(object):
    count = 0                    # count is class attr

    def __init__(self):          # increment count
        InstCt.count += 1

    def __del__(self):           # decrement count
        InstCt.count -= 1

    def howMany(self):           # return count
        return InstCt.count
>>> a = InstTrack()
>>> b = InstTrack()
>>> b.howMany()
2
>>> a.howMany()
2
>>> del b
>>> a.howMany()
1
>>> del a
>>> InstTrack.count
0
```

13.6   Instance Attributes

Instances have only data attributes (methods are strictly class attributes) and are simply data values that you want to be associated with a particular instance of any class and are accessible via the familiar dotted-attribute notation. These values are independent of any other instance or of the class it was instantiated from. When an instance is deallocated, so are its attributes.

13.6.1   "Instantiating" Instance Attributes (or Creating a Better Constructor)

Instance attributes can be set any time after an instance has been created, in any piece of code that has access to the instance. However, one of the key places where such attributes are set is in the constructor, __init__().

> **CORE NOTE: Instance attributes**
>
>
>
> *Being able to create an instance attribute "on-the-fly" is one of the great features of Python classes, initially (but gently) shocking those coming from C++ or Java in which all attributes must be explicitly defined/ declared first.*
>
> *Python is not only dynamically typed but also allows for such dynamic creation of object attributes during run-time. It is a feature that once used may be difficult to live without. Of course, we should mention to the reader that one much be cautious when creating such attributes.*
>
> *One pitfall is when such attributes are created in conditional clauses: if you attempt to access such an attribute later on in your code, that attribute may not exist if the flow had not entered that conditional suite. The moral of the story is that Python gives you a new feature you were not used to before, but if you use it, you need to be more careful, too.*

Constructor First Place to Set Instance Attributes

The constructor is the earliest place that instance attributes can be set because __init__() is the first method called after instance objects have been created. There is no earlier opportunity to set instance attributes. Once __init__() has finished execution, the instance object is returned, completing the instantiation process.

Default Arguments Provide Default Instance Setup

One can also use __init__() along with default arguments to provide an effective way of preparing an instance for use in the real world. In many situations, the default values represent the most common cases for setting up instance attributes, and such use of default values precludes them from having to be given explicitly to the constructor. We also outlined some of the general benefits of default arguments in Section 11.5.2. One caveat is that default arguments should be immutable objects; mutable objects like lists and dictionaries act like static data, maintaining their contents with each method call.

Example 13.1 shows how we can use the default constructor behavior to help us calculate some sample total room costs for lodging at hotels in some of America's large metropolitan areas.

The main purpose of our code is to help someone figure out the daily hotel room rate, including any state sales and room taxes. The default is for the general area around San Francisco, which has an 8.5% sales tax and a 10% room tax. The daily room rate has no default value, thus it is required for any instance to be created.

Example 13.1 Using Default Arguments with Instantiation (hotel.py)

Class definition for a fictitious hotel room rate calculator. The __init__() constructor method initializes several instance attributes. A calcTotal() method is used to determine either a total daily room rate or the total room cost for an entire stay.

```
1  class HotelRoomCalc(object):
2      'Hotel room rate calculator'
3
4      def __init__(self, rt, sales=0.085, rm=0.1):
5          '''HotelRoomCalc default arguments:
6          sales tax == 8.5% and room tax == 10%'''
7          self.salesTax = sales
8          self.roomTax = rm
9          self.roomRate = rt
10
11     def calcTotal(self, days=1):
12         'Calculate total; default to daily rate'
13         daily = round((self.roomRate *
14             (1 + self.roomTax + self.salesTax)), 2)
15         return float(days) * daily
```

The setup work is done after instantiation by __init__() in lines 4–8, and the other core part of our code is the calcTotal() method, lines 10–14. The job of __init__() is to set the values needed to determine the total base room rate of a hotel room (not counting room service, phone calls, or other incidental items). calcTotal() is then used to either determine the total daily rate or the cost of an entire stay if the number of days is provided. The round() built-in function is used to round the calculation to the closest penny (two decimal places). Here is some sample usage of this class:

```
>>> sfo = HotelRoomCalc(299)                       # new instance
>>> sfo.calcTotal()                                # daily rate
354.32
>>> sfo.calcTotal(2)                               # 2-day rate
708.64
>>> sea = HotelRoomCalc(189, 0.086, 0.058)         # new instance
>>> sea.calcTotal()
216.22
>>> sea.calcTotal(4)
864.88
>>> wasWkDay = HotelRoomCalc(169, 0.045, 0.02)     # new instance
>>> wasWkEnd = HotelRoomCalc(119, 0.045, 0.02)     # new instance
>>> wasWkDay.calcTotal(5) + wasWkEnd.calcTotal()   # 7-day rate
1026.69
```

The first two hypothetical examples were San Francisco, which used the defaults, and then Seattle, where we provided different sales tax and room tax rates. The final example, Washington, D.C., extended the general usage by calculating a hypothetical longer stay: a five-day weekday stay plus a special rate for one weekend day, assuming a Sunday departure to return home.

Do not forget that all the flexibility you get with functions, such as default arguments, applies to methods as well. The use of variable-length arguments is another good feature to use with instantiation (based on an application's needs, of course).

__init__() Should Return None

As you are now aware, invoking a class object with the function operator creates a class instance, which is the object returned on such an invocation, as in the following example:

```
>>> class MyClass(object):
...         pass
>>> mc = MyClass()
>>> mc
<__main__.MyClass instance at 95d390>
```

If a constructor is defined, it should not return any object because the instance object is automatically returned after the instantiation call. Correspondingly, __init__() should not return any object (or return None); otherwise, there is a conflict of interest because only the instance should be returned. Attempting to return any object other than None will result in a TypeError exception:

```
>>> class MyClass:
...        def __init__(self):
...               print 'initialized'
...               return 1
...
>>> mc = MyClass()
initialized
Traceback (innermost last):
  File "<stdin>", line 1, in ?
    mc = MyClass()
TypeError: __init__() should return None
```

13.6.2 Determining Instance Attributes

The dir() built-in function can be used to show all instance attributes in the same manner that it can reveal class attributes:

```
>>> class C(object):
...        pass
>>> c = C()
>>> c.foo = 'roger'
>>> c.bar = 'shrubber'
>>> dir(c)
['__class__', '__delattr__', '__dict__', '__doc__',
'__getattribute__', '__hash__', '__init__', '__module__',
'__new__', '__reduce__', '__reduce_ex__', '__repr__',
'__setattr__', '__str__', '__weakref__', 'bar', 'foo']
```

Similar to classes, instances also have a __dict__ special attribute (also accessible by calling vars() and passing it an instance), which is a dictionary representing its attributes:

```
>>> c.__dict__
{'foo': 'roger', 'bar': 'shrubber'}
```

13.6.3 Special Instance Attributes

Instances have only two special attributes (see Table 13.2). For any instance I:

Table 13.2 Special Instance Attributes

`I.__class__`	Class from which `I` is instantiated
`I.__dict__`	Attributes of `I`

We will now take a look at these special instance attributes using the class C and its instance c:

```
>>> class C(object):       # define class
...        pass
...
>>> c = C()                # create instance
>>> dir(c)                 # instance has no attributes
[]
>>> c.__dict__             # yep, definitely no attributes
{}
>>> c.__class__            # class that instantiated us
<class '__main__.C'>
```

As you can see, c currently has no data attributes, but we can add some and recheck the __dict__ attribute to make sure they have been added properly:

```
>>> c.foo = 1
>>> c.bar = 'SPAM'
>>> '%d can of %s please' % (c.foo, c.bar)
'1 can of SPAM please'
>>> c.__dict__
{'foo': 1, 'bar': 'SPAM'}
```

The __dict__ attribute consists of a dictionary containing the attributes of an instance. The keys are the attribute names, and the values are the attributes' corresponding data values. You will only find instance attributes in this dictionary—no class attributes or special attributes.

CORE STYLE: Modifying __dict__

Although the __dict__ attributes for both classes and instances are mutable, it is recommended that you not modify these dictionaries unless or until you know exactly what you are doing. Such modification contaminates your OOP and may have unexpected side effects. It is more acceptable to access and manipulate attributes using the familiar dotted-attribute

notation. One of the few cases where you would *modify the* __dict__
attribute directly is when you are overriding the __setattr__ *special
method. Implementing* __setattr__() *is another adventure story on its
own, full of traps and pitfalls such as infinite recursion and corrupted
instance objects—but that is another tale for another time.*

13.6.4 Built-in Type Attributes

Built-in types are classes, too… do they have the same attributes as classes?
(The same goes for instances.) We can use dir() on built-in types just like
for any other object to get a list of their attribute names:

```
>>> x = 3+0.14j
>>> x.__class__
<type 'complex'>
>>> dir(x)
['__abs__', '__add__', '__class__', '__coerce__',
 '__delattr__', '__div__', '__divmod__', '__doc__', '__eq__',
 '__float__', '__floordiv__', '__ge__', '__getattribute__',
 '__getnewargs__', '__gt__', '__hash__', '__init__',
 '__int__', '__le__', '__long__', '__lt__', '__mod__',
 '__mul__', '__ne__', '__neg__', '__new__', '__nonzero__',
 '__pos__', '__pow__', '__radd__', '__rdiv__', '__rdivmod__',
 '__reduce__', '__reduce_ex__', '__repr__', '__rfloordiv__',
 '__rmod__', '__rmul__', '__rpow__', '__rsub__',
 '__rtruediv__', '__setattr__', '__str__', '__sub__',
 '__truediv__', 'conjugate', 'imag', 'real']
>>>
>>> [type(getattr(x, i)) for i in ('conjugate', 'imag',
'real')]
[<type 'builtin_function_or_method'>, <type 'float'>,
<type 'float'>]
```

Now that we know what kind of attributes a complex number has, we
can access the data attributes and call its methods:

```
>>> x.imag
2.0
>>> x.real
1.0
>>> x.conjugate()
(1-2j)
```

Attempting to access __dict__ will fail because that attribute does not exist for built-in types:

```
>>> x.__dict__
Traceback (innermost last):
  File "<stdin>", line 1, in ?
AttributeError: __dict__
```

13.6.5 *Instance Attributes versus Class Attributes*

We first described class data attributes in Section 13.4.1. As a brief reminder, class attributes are simply data values associated with a class and not any particular instances like instance attributes are. Such values are also referred to as static members because their values stay constant, even if a class is invoked due to instantiation multiple times. No matter what, static members maintain their values independent of instances unless explicitly changed. (Comparing instance attributes to class attributes is barely like that of automatic vs. static variables, but this is just a vague analogy . . . do not read too much into it, especially if you are not familiar with auto and static variables.)

Classes and instances are both namespaces. Classes are namespaces for class attributes. Instances are namespaces for instance attributes.

There are a few aspects of class attributes and instance attributes that should be brought to light. The first is that you can access a class attribute with either the class or an instance, provided that the instance does not have an attribute with the same name.

Access to Class Attributes

Class attributes can be accessed via a class or an instance. In the example below, when class C is created with the version class attribute, naturally access is allowed using the class object, i.e., C.version. When instance c is created, access to c.version fails for the instance, and then Python initiates a search for the name version first in the instance, then the class, and then the base classes in the inheritance free. In this case, it is found in the class:

```
>>> class C(object):      # define class
...       version = 1.2    # static member
...
>>> c = C()               # instantiation
>>> C.version             # access via class
1.2
```

```
>>> c.version              # access via instance
1.2
>>> C.version += 0.1       # update (only) via class
>>> C.version              # class access
1.3
>>> c.version              # instance access, which
1.3                        # also reflected change
```

However, we can only update the value when referring to it using the class, as in the `C.version` increment statement above. Attempting to set or update the class attribute using the instance name will create an instance attribute that "shadows" access to the class attribute, effectively hiding it from scope until or unless that shadow is removed.

Use Caution When Accessing Class Attribute with Instance

Any type of assignment of a local attribute will result in the creation and assignment of an instance attribute, just like a regular Python variable. If a class attribute exists with the same name, interesting side effects can occur. (This is true for both classic and new-style classes.)

```
>>> class Foo(object):
...     x = 1.5
...
>>> foo = Foo()
>>> foo.x
1.5
>>> foo.x = 1.7        # try to update class attr
>>> foo.x              # looks good so far...
1.7
>>> Foo.x              # nope, just created a new inst attr
1.5
```

In the above code snippet, a new instance attribute named `version` is created, overriding the reference to the class attribute. However, the class attribute itself is unscathed and still exists in the class domain and can still be accessed as a class attribute, as we can see above. What would happen if we delete this new reference? To find out, we will use the **del** statement on `c.version`.

```
>>> del foo.x          # delete instance attribute
>>> foo.x              # can now access class attr again
1.5
```

So by assigning an instance attribute with the same name as a class attribute, we effectively "hide" the class attribute, but once we remove the instance attribute, we can "see" the class one again. Now let us try to update the class attribute again, but this time, we will just try an innocent increment:

```
>>> foo.x += .2        # try to increment class attr
>>> foo.x
1.7
>>> Foo.x              # nope, same thing
1.5
```

It is still a "no go." We again created a new instance attribute while leaving the original class attribute intact. (For those who have or want a deeper understanding of Python: the attribute was already in the class's dictionary [__dict__]. With the assignment, one is now added to the instance's __dict__.) The expression on the right-hand side of the assignment evaluates the original class variable, adds 0.2 to it, and assigns it to a newly created instance attribute. Note that the following is an equivalent assignment, but it may provide more clarification:

```
foo.x = Foo.x + 0.2
```

But... all of this changes if the class attribute is mutable:

```
>>> class Foo(object):
...     x = {2003: 'poe2'}
...
>>> foo = Foo()
>>> foo.x
{2003: 'poe2'}
>>> foo.x[2004] = 'valid path'
>>> foo.x
{2003: 'poe2', 2004: 'valid path'}
>>> Foo.x                    # it works!!!
{2003: 'poe2', 2004: 'valid path'}
>>> del foo.x                # no shadow so cannot delete
Traceback (most recent call last):
  File "<stdin>", line 1, in ?
    del foo.x
AttributeError: x
>>>
```

Class Attributes More Persistent

Static members, true to their name, hang around while instances (and their attributes) come and go (hence independent of instances). Also, if a new instance is created after a class attribute has been modified, the updated value will be reflected. Class attribute changes are reflected across all instances:

```
>>> class C(object):
...         spam = 100          # class attribute
...
>>> c1 = C()                    # create an instance
>>> c1.spam                     # access class attr thru inst.
100
>>> C.spam += 100               # update class attribute
>>> C.spam                      # see change in attribute
200
>>> c1.spam                     # confirm change in attribute
200
>>> c2 = C()                    # create another instance
>>> c2.spam                     # verify class attribute
200
>>> del c1                      # remove one instance
>>> C.spam += 200               # update class attribute again
>>> c2.spam                     # verify that attribute changed
400
```

CORE TIP: Use a class attribute to modify itself (not an instance attribute)

As we have seen above, it is perilous to try and modify a class attribute by using an instance attribute. The reason is because instances have their own set of attributes, and there is no clear way in Python to indicate that you want to modify the class attribute of the same name, e.g., there is no **global** *keyword like there is when setting a global inside a function (instead of a local variable of the same name). Always modify a class attribute with the class name, not an instance.*

13.7 Binding and Method Invocation

Now we need to readdress the Python concept of binding, which is associated primarily with method invocation. We will first review some facts regarding methods. First, a method is simply a function defined as part of a class. (This means that methods are class attributes and not instance attributes).

Second, methods can be called only when there is an instance of the class upon which the method was invoked. When there is an instance present, the method is considered *bound* (to that instance). Without an instance, a method is considered unbound.

And finally, the first argument in any method definition is the variable self, which represents the instance object invoking the method.

CORE NOTE: What is self?

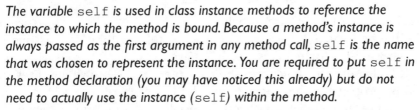

The variable self *is used in class instance methods to reference the instance to which the method is bound. Because a method's instance is always passed as the first argument in any method call,* self *is the name that was chosen to represent the instance. You are required to put* self *in the method declaration (you may have noticed this already) but do not need to actually use the instance (*self*) within the method.*

If you do not use self *in your method, you might consider creating a regular function instead, unless you have a particular reason not to. After all, your code, because it does not use the instance object in any way, "unlinks" its functionality from the class, making it seem more like a general function.*

In other object-oriented languages, self *may be named* this.

13.7.1 Invoking Bound Methods

Methods, whether bound or not, are made up of the same code. The only difference is whether there is an instance present so that the method can be invoked. In most cases, you the programmer will be calling a bound method. Let us say that you have a class MyClass and an instance of it called mc, and you want to call the MyClass.foo() method. Since you already have an instance, you can just call the method with mc.foo(). Recall that self is required to be declared as the first argument in every method declaration. Well, when you call a bound method, self never needs to be passed explicitly when you invoke it with an instance. That is your bonus for being "required" to declare self as the first argument. The only time when you have to pass it in is when you do not have an instance and need to call a method unbound.

13.7.2 Invoking Unbound Methods

Calling an unbound method happens less frequently. The main use case for calling a method belonging to a class that you do not have an instance for is the case where you are deriving a child class and override a parent method where you need to call the parent's constructor you are overriding. Let us look at an example back in the chapter introduction:

```
class EmplAddrBookEntry(AddrBookEntry):
       'Employee Address Book Entry class'
       def __init__(self, nm, ph, em):
              AddrBookEntry.__init__(self, nm, ph)
              self.empid = id
              self.email = em
```

`EmplAddrBookEntry` is a subclass of `AddrBookEntry`, and we are over-riding the constructor `__init__()`. Rather than cutting and pasting code from the parent constructor, we want to have as much code reuse as possible. This will also prevent bugs from being propagated because any fixes made would be propagated to us here in the child. This is exactly what we want—there is no need to copy lines of code. This all hinges on somehow being able to call the parent constructor, but how?

We would not have an instance of `AddrBookEntry` at runtime. What do we have? Well, we will have an instance of `EmplAddrBookEntry`, and it is so similar to `AddrBookEntry`, can't we somehow use it instead? The answer is yes!

When an `EmplAddrBookEntry` is instantiated and `__init__()` called, there is very little difference between it and an instance of `AddrBookEntry`, mainly because we have not yet had a chance to customize our `EmplAddr-BookEntry` instance to really make it different from `AddrBookEntry`.

This is the perfect place to call an unbound method. We will call the parent class constructor from the child class constructor and explicitly pass in the `self` argument as required by the (parent class) constructor (since we are without a parent class instance). The first line of `__init__()` in the child consists of a call to `__init__()` of the parent. We call it via the parent class name and pass in `self` plus its required arguments. Once that call returns, we can perform the (instance) customization that is unique to our (child) class.

13.8 Static Methods and Class Methods

2.2

Static methods and class methods were introduced in Python 2.2. They can be used with both classic classes and new-style classes. A pair of built-in functions were added to "tag," "cast," or "convert" methods declared as part of class definitions as either one of these two types of methods.

Static methods are exactly what they are if you are coming from C++ or Java. They are simply functions (no instance required) that are part of class definitions. In fact, before static methods were added to Python, users just created functions in the global namespace as a proxy for this missing feature—sometimes using a class object inside such functions to manipulate the class (or rather, class attributes). Using module functions is still far more common than using static class methods.

Recall that regular methods require an instance (`self`) as the first argument, and upon (bound) method invocation, `self` is automagically passed to the method. Well, for class methods, instead of the instance, the class is required as the first argument, and it is passed in to the method by the interpreter. The class does not need to be specifically named like `self`, but most people use `cls` as the variable name.

13.8.1 `staticmethod()` and `classmethod()` Built-in Functions

Now let us look at some examples of these types of methods using classic classes (you can also use new-style classes if you want to):

```
class TestStaticMethod:
    def foo():
        print 'calling static method foo()'

    foo = staticmethod(foo)

class TestClassMethod:
    def foo(cls):
        print 'calling class method foo()'
        print 'foo() is part of class:', cls.__name__

    foo = classmethod(foo)
```

The corresponding built-in functions are converted into their respective types and are reassigned back to the same variable name. Without the function calls, both would generate errors from the Python compiler, which is expecting regular method declarations with `self`. We can then call these functions from either the class or an instance... it makes no difference:

```
>>> tsm = TestStaticMethod()
>>> TestStaticMethod.foo()
calling static method foo()
>>> tsm.foo()
calling static method foo()
>>>
>>> tcm = TestClassMethod()
>>> TestClassMethod.foo()
calling class method foo()
foo() is part of class: TestClassMethod
>>> tcm.foo()
calling class method foo()
foo() is part of class: TestClassMethod
```

13.8.2 Using Decorators

Now, seeing code like `foo = staticmethod(foo)` can irritate some programmers. There is something unsettling about it, and many folks *were* upset with such a flimsy syntax, although van Rossum had pointed out that it was to be temporary until the semantics were worked out with the community. In Section 11.3.6 of Chapter 11, "Functions," we looked at decorators, a new feature introduced in Python 2.4. They are used in places where you want to apply a function to a function object but want to rebind the new function object to the original variable. This is a perfect place to use them to partially clean up the syntax. By using decorators, we can avoid the reassignment above:

```
class TestStaticMethod:
    @staticmethod
    def foo():
        print 'calling static method foo()'

class TestClassMethod:
    @classmethod
    def foo(cls):
        print 'calling class method foo()'
        print 'foo() is part of class:', cls.__name__
```

13.9 Composition

Once a class is defined, the goal is to use it as a model programmatically, embedding this object throughout your code, intermixing use with other data types and the logical flow of execution. There are two ways of utilizing classes in your code. The first is composition. This is where different classes are mingled with and into other classes for added functionality and code reusability. You may create instances of your class inside a larger class, containing other attributes and methods enhancing the use of the original class object. The other way is with derivation, discussed in the next section.

For example, let us imagine an enhanced design of the address book class we created at the beginning of the chapter. If, during the course of our design, we created separate classes for names, addresses, etc., we would want to integrate that work into our `AddrBookEntry` class, rather than have to redesign each of those supporting classes. We have the added advantages of time and effort saved, as well as more consistent code—when bugs are fixed in that same piece of code, that change is reflected in all the applications that reuse that code.

Such a class would perhaps contain a `Name` instance, not to mention others like `StreetAddress`, `Phone` (home, work, telefacsimile, pager, mobile, etc.), `Email` (home, work, etc.), and possibly a few `Date` instances (birthday, wedding, anniversary, etc.). Here is a simple example with some of the classes mentioned above:

```
class NewAddrBookEntry(object):    # class definition
    'new address book entry class'
    def __init__(self, nm, ph):    # define constructor
        self.name = Name(nm)       # create Name instance
        self.phone = Phone(ph)     # create Phone instance
        print 'Created instance for:', self.name
```

The `NewAddrBookEntry` class is a composition of itself and other classes. This defines a "has-a" relationship between a class and other classes it is composed of. For example, our `NewAddrBookEntry` class "has a" `Name` class instance and a `Phone` instance, too.

Creating composite objects enables such additional functionality and makes sense because the classes have nothing in common. Each class manages its own namespace and behavior. When there are more intimate relationships between objects, the concept of derivation may make more sense in your application, especially if you require like objects, with slightly different functionality.

13.10 Subclassing and Derivation

Composition works fine when classes are distinct and are a required component of larger classes, but when you desire "the same class but with some tweaking," derivation is a more logical option.

One of the more powerful aspects of OOP is the ability to take an already defined class and extend it or make modifications to it without affecting other pieces of code in the system that use the currently existing classes. OOD allows for class features to be inherited by descendant classes or subclasses. These subclasses derive the core of their attributes from base (aka ancestor, super) *classes*. In addition, this derivation may be extended for multiple generations. Classes involved in a one-level derivation (or that are adjacent vertically in a class tree diagram) have a *parent* and *child* class relationship. Those classes that derive from the same parent (or that are adjacent horizontally in a class tree diagram) have a sibling relationship. Parent and all higher-level classes are considered *ancestors*.

Using our example from the previous section, let us imagine having to create different types of address books. We are talking about more than just creating multiple instances of address books—in this case, all objects have everything in common. What if we wanted a `EmplAddrBookEntry` class whose entries would contain more work-related attributes such as employee ID and e-mail address? This would differ from a `PersonalAddrBookEntry` class, which would contain more family-oriented information such as home address, relationship, birthday, etc.

For both of these cases, we do not want to design these classes from scratch, because it would duplicate the work already accomplished to create the generic `AddressBook` class. Wouldn't it be nice to subsume all the features and characteristics of the `AddressBook` class and add specialized customization for your new, yet related, classes? This is the entire motivation and desire for class derivation.

13.10.1 Creating Subclasses

The syntax for creating a subclass looks just like that for a regular (new-style) class, a class name followed by one or more parent classes to inherit from:

```
class SubClassName (ParentClass1[, ParentClass2, ...]):
    'optional class documentation string'
    class_suite
```

If your class does not derive from any ancestor class, use `object` as the name of the parent class. The only example that differs is the declaration of a classic class that does not derive from ancestor classes—in this case, there are no parentheses:

```
class ClassicClassWithoutSuperclasses:
    pass
```

We have already seen some examples of classes and subclasses so far, but here is another simple example:

```
class Parent(object):            # define parent class
    def parentMethod(self):
        print 'calling parent method'

class Child(Parent):             # define child class
    def childMethod(self):
        print 'calling child method'
>>> p = Parent()                 # instance of parent
>>> p.parentMethod()
calling parent method
>>>
>>> c = Child()                  # instance of child
>>> c.childMethod()              # child calls its method
calling child method
>>> c.parentMethod()             # calls parent's method
calling parent method
```

13.11 Inheritance

Inheritance describes how the attributes of base classes are "bequeathed" to a derived class. A subclass inherits attributes of any of its base classes whether they be data attributes or methods.

We present an example below. P is a simple class with no attributes. C is a class with no attributes that derives from (and therefore is a subclass of) P:

```
class P(object):          # parent class
    pass
class C(P):               # child class
    pass

>>> c = C()               # instantiate child
>>> c.__class__           # child "is a" parent
<class '__main__.C'>
>>> C.__bases__           # child's parent class(es)
(<class '__main__.P'>,)
```

Because P has no attributes, nothing was inherited by C. Let us make our example more useful by giving P some attributes:

```
class P:                          # parent class
    'P class'
    def __init__(self):
        print 'created an instance of', \
            self.__class__.__name__

class C(P):                       # child class
    pass
```

We now create P with a documentation string (__doc__) and a constructor that will execute when we instantiate P, as in this interactive session:

```
>>> p = P()               # parent instance
created an instance of P
>>> p.__class__           # class that created us
<class '__main__.P'>
>>> P.__bases__           # parent's parent class(es)
(<type 'object'>,)
>>> P.__doc__             # parent's doc string
'P class'
```

The "created an instance" output comes directly from __init__(). We also display some more about the parent class P for your information. We will now instantiate C, showing you how the __init__() (constructor) method is inherited with its execution:

```
>>> c = C()                        # child instance
created an instance of C
>>> c.__class__                    # class that created us
<class '__main__.C'>
>>> C.__bases__                    # child's parent class(es)
(<class '__main__.P'>,)
>>> C.__doc__                      # child's doc string
>>>
```

C has no declared method __init__(), yet there is still output when instance c of class C is created. The reason is that C inherits __init__() from P. The __bases__ tuple now lists P as its parent class. Note that documentation strings are unique to classes, functions/methods, and modules, so a special attribute like __doc__ is not inherited by its derived classes.

13.11.1   __bases__   Class Attribute

In Section 13.4.4, we briefly introduced the __bases__ class attribute, which is a tuple containing the set of parent classes for any (sub)class. Note that we specifically state "parents" as opposed to all base classes (which includes all ancestor classes). Classes that are not derived will have an empty __bases__ attribute. Let us look at an example of how to make use of __bases__.

```
>>> class A(object): pass   # define class A
...
>>> class B(A): pass        # subclass of A
...
>>> class C(B): pass        # subclass of B (and indirectly, A)
...
>>> class D(A, B): pass     # subclass of A and B
...
>>> A.__bases__
(<type 'object'>,)
>>> C.__bases__
(<class __main__.B at 8120c90>,)
>>> D.__bases__
(<class __main__.A at 811fc90>, <class __main__.B at 8120c90>)
```

In the example above, although C is a derived class of both A (through B) and B, C's parent is B, as indicated in its declaration, so only B will show up in C.__bases__. On the other hand, D inherits from two classes, A and B. (Multiple inheritance is covered in Section 13.11.4.)

13.11.2 Overriding Methods through Inheritance

Let us create another function in P that we will override in its child class:

```
class P(object):
    def foo(self):
        print 'Hi, I am P-foo()'

>>> p = P()
>>> p.foo()
Hi, I am P-foo()
```

Now let us create the child class C, subclassed from parent P:

```
class C(P):
    def foo(self):
        print 'Hi, I am C-foo()'

>>> c = C()
>>> c.foo()
Hi, I am C-foo()
```

Although C inherits P's foo() method, it is overridden because C defines its own foo() method. One reason for overriding methods is because you may want special or different functionality in your subclass. Your next obvious question then must be, "Can I call a base class method that I overrode in my subclass?"

The answer is yes, but this is where you will have to invoke an unbound base class method, explicitly providing the instance of the subclass, as we do here:

```
>>> P.foo(c)
Hi, I am P-foo()
```

Notice that we already had an instance of P called p from above, but that is nowhere to be found in this example. We do not need an instance of P to call a method of P because we have an instance of a *subclass* of P which we can use, c. You would not typically call the parent class method this way. Instead, you would do it in the overridden method and call the base class method explicitly:

```
class C(P):
    def foo(self):
        P.foo(self)
        print 'Hi, I am C-foo()'
```

Note how we pass in `self` explicitly in this (unbound) method call. A better way to make this call would be to use the `super()` built-in method:

```
class C(P):
    def foo(self):
        super(C, self).foo()
        print 'Hi, I am C-foo()'
```

`super()` will not only find the base class method, but pass in `self` for us so we do not have to as in the previous example. Now when we call the child class method, it does exactly what you think it should do:

```
>>> c = C()
>>> c.foo()
Hi, I am P-foo()
Hi, I am C-foo()
```

CORE NOTE: Overriding __init__ does not invoke base class __init__

Similar to overriding non-special methods above, when deriving a class with a constructor __init__(), if you do not override __init__(), it will be inherited and automatically invoked. But if you do override __init__() in a subclass, the base class __init__() method is not invoked automatically when the subclass is instantiated. This may be surprising to those of you who know Java.

```
class P(object):
    def __init__(self):
        print "calling P's constructor"

class C(P):
    def __init__(self):
        print "calling C's constructor"

>>> c = C()
calling C's constructor
```

If you want the base class __init__() invoked, you need to do that explicitly in the same manner as we just described, calling the base class (unbound) method with an instance of the subclass. Updating our class C appropriately results in the following desired execution:

```
class C(P):
    def __init__(self):
        P.__init__(self)
        print "calling C's constructor"
```

```
>>> c = C()
calling P's constructor
calling C's constructor
```

In the above example, we call the base class __init__() method before the rest of the code in our own __init__() method. It is fairly common practice (if not mandatory) to initialize base classes for setup purposes, then proceed with any local setup. This rule makes sense because you want the inherited object properly initialized and "ready" by the time the code for the derived class constructor runs because it may require or set inherited attributes.

Those of you familiar with C++ would call base class constructors in a derived class constructor declaration by appending a colon to the declaration followed by calls to any base class constructors. Whether the programmer does it or not, in Java, the base class constructor always gets called (first) in derived class constructors.

Python's use of the base class name to invoke a base class method is directly comparable to Java's when using the keyword super, *and that is why the* super() *built-in function was eventually added to Python, so you could "do the correct thing" functionally:*

```
class C(P):
        def __init__(self):
            super(C, self).__init__()
            print "calling C's constructor"
```

The nice thing about using super() *is that you do not need to give any base class name explicitly… it does all the legwork for you! The importance of using* super() *is that you are not explicitly specifying the parent class. This means that if you change the class hierarchy, you only need to change one line (the* **class** *statement itself) rather than tracking through what could be a large amount of code in a class to find all mentions of what is now the old class name.*

13.11.3 Deriving Standard Types

Not being able to subclass a standard data type was one of the most significant problems of classic classes. Fortunately that was remedied back in 2.2 with the unification of types and classes and the introduction of new-style classes. Below we present two examples of subclassing a Python type, one mutable and the other not.

2.2

Immutable Type Example

Let us assume you wanted to work on a subclass of floating point numbers to be used for financial applications. Any time you get a monetary value (as a float), you always want to round evenly to two decimal places. (Yes, the Decimal class is a better solution than standard floats to accurately store floating point values, but you still need to round them [occasionally] to two digits!) The beginnings of your class can look like this:

```python
class RoundFloat(float):
    def __new__(cls, val):
        return float.__new__(cls, round(val, 2))
```

We override the __new__() special method, which customizes our object to be just a little bit different from the standard Python float: we round the original floating point number using the round() built-in function and then instantiate our float, RoundFloat. We create the actual object by calling our parent class constructor, float.__new__(). Note that all __new__() methods are class methods, and we have to explicitly pass in the class as the first argument, similar to how self is required for regular methods like __init__().

While our example is simple enough, i.e., we know we have a float, we are only subclassing from one type, etc., for general cases, it is better to use the super() built-in function to go and hunt down the appropriate superclass __new__() method to call. Below, we have modified our example with this change:

```python
class RoundFloat(float):
    def __new__(cls, val):
        return super(RoundFloat, cls).__new__(
            cls, round(val, 2))
```

This example is far from complete, so keep an eye out for getting it in better shape as we progress through this chapter. Here is some sample output:

```python
>>> RoundFloat(1.5955)
1.6
>>> RoundFloat(1.5945)
1.59
>>> RoundFloat(-1.9955)
-2.0
```

Mutable Type Example

Subclassing a mutable type is similar, and you probably do not need to use __new__() (or even __init__()) because there is typically not as much setup required. Usually the default behavior of the type you are deriving is what you want. In this simple example, we create a new dictionary type where its keys are returned sorted by the `keys()` method:

```
class SortedKeyDict(dict):
    def keys(self):
        return sorted(super(
            SortedKeyDict, self).keys())
```

Recall that a dictionary can be created with `dict()`, `dict(mapping)`, `dict(sequence_of_2_tuples)`, or `dict(**kwargs)`. Below is an example of using our new class:

```
d = SortedKeyDict((('zheng-cai', 67), ('hui-jun', 68),
    ('xin-yi', 2)))
print 'By iterator:'.ljust(12), [key for key in d]
print 'By keys():'.ljust(12), d.keys()
```

If we put all the code in a script and run it, we get the following output:

```
By iterator: ['zheng-cai', 'xin-yi', 'hui-jun']
By keys():   ['xin-yi', 'hui-jun', 'zheng-cai']
```

For our example, the iterator progresses through the keys in the hashed order while using our (overridden) `keys()` method gives the keys in lexicographically sorted order.

Always be cautious and conscious of what you are doing. What if, you say, "Your method is overly complicated with the call to `super()`," and instead, you prefer `keys()` to be simpler (and easier to understand)... like this:

```
def keys(self):
    return sorted(self.keys())
```

This is Exercise 13–19 at the end of the chapter.

13.11.4 Multiple Inheritance

Like C++, Python allows for subclassing from multiple base classes. This feature is commonly known as *multiple inheritance*. The concept is easy, but the hard work is in how to find the correct attribute when it is not defined in the current (sub)class. There are two different aspects to remember when using multiple inheritance. The first is, again, being able to find the correct attribute. Another is when you have overridden methods, all of which call parent class methods to "take care of their responsibilities" while the child class takes care of *its* own obligations. We will discuss both simultaneously but focus on the latter as we describe the *method resolution order*.

Method Resolution Order (MRO)

In Python versions before 2.2, the algorithm was simple enough: a *depth-first left-to-right* search to obtain the attribute to use with the derived class. Unlike other Python algorithms that override names as they are found, multiple inheritance takes the first name that is found.

Because of the entirely new structure of classes and types and the subclassing of built-in types, this algorithm was no longer feasible, so a new MRO algorithm had to be developed. The initial one debuting in 2.2 was a good attempt but had a flaw (see Core Note below). It was immediately replaced in 2.3, which is the current one that is in use today.

2.0-2.3

The exact resolution order is complex and is beyond the scope of this text, but you can read about it in the references given later on in this section. We can say that the new resolution method is more breadth-first than it is depth-first.

> **CORE NOTE: Python 2.2 uses a unique yet faulty MRO**
>
> *Python 2.2 was the first release using a new-style MRO that had to replace the algorithm from classic classes due to the reasons outlined above. For 2.2, the algorithm had the basic idea of following the hierarchy of each ancestor class and building a list of classes encountered, strategically removing duplicates. However, it was pointed out on the core Python developers mailing list that it fails to maintain monotonicity (order preservation), and had to be replaced by the new C3 algorithm that has been in place since 2.3.*

Let us give you an example to see how the method resolution order differs between classic and new-style classes.

Simple Attribute Lookup Example

The simple example below will highlight the differences between the old and new styles of resolution. The script consists of a pair of parent classes, a pair of child classes, and one grandchild class.

```python
class P1: #(object):               # parent class 1
    def foo(self):
        print 'called P1-foo()'

class P2: #(object):               # parent class 2
    def foo(self):
        print 'called P2-foo()'
```

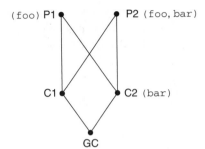

Figure 13-2 Relationships between parent, children, and grandchild classes as well as the methods they define.

```
    def bar(self):
        print 'called P2-bar()'

class C1(P1, P2):          # child 1 der. from P1, P2
    pass

class C2(P1, P2):          # child 2 der. from P1, P2
    def bar(self):
        print 'called C2-bar()'

class GC(C1, C2):          # define grandchild class
    pass                   # derived from C1 and C2
```

In Figure 13–2, we see the class relationships between the parent, children, and grandchildren classes. P1 defines foo(), P2 defines foo() and bar(), and C2 defines bar(). Let us now demonstrate the behavior of both classic and new-style classes.

Classic Classes

We are going to use classic classes first. Upon executing the above declarations in the interactive interpreter, we can confirm the resolution order that classic classes use, depth-first, left to right:

```
>>> gc = GC()
>>> gc.foo()               # GC ⇒ C1 ⇒ P1
called P1-foo()
>>> gc.bar()               # GC ⇒ C1 ⇒ P1 ⇒ P2
called P2-bar()
```

When calling foo(), it looks in the current class (GC) first. If it cannot be found, it goes up to its immediate parent, C1. The search fails there so it continues up the tree to *its* parent, P1, which is where foo() is found.

Likewise for bar(), it searches through GC, C1, and P1 before then finding it in P2. C2.bar() is never found because of the resolution order used.

Now, you may be thinking, "I would prefer to call C2's `bar()` because it is closer to me in the inheritance tree, thus more relevant." In this case, you can still use it, but you have to do it in the typical unbound fashion by invoking its fully qualified name and providing a valid instance:

```
>>> C2.bar(gc)
called C2-bar()
```

New-Style Classes

Now uncomment the (object) next to the class declarations for P1 and P2 and reexecute. The new-style method resolution gives us something different:

```
>>> gc = GC()
>>> gc.foo()              # GC ⇒ C1 ⇒ C2 ⇒ P1
called P1-foo()
>>> gc.bar()              # GC ⇒ C1 ⇒ C2
called C2-bar()
```

Instead of following the tree up each step, it looks at the siblings first, giving it more of a breadth-first flavor. When looking for `foo()`, it checks GC, followed by C1 and C2, and then finds it in P1. If P1 did not have it, it would have gone to P2. The bottom line for `foo()` is that both classic and new-style classes would have found it in P1, but they took different paths to get there.

The result for `bar()` is different, though. It searches GC and C1, and finds it next in C2 and uses it there. It does not continue up to the grandparents P1 and P2. In this case, the new-style resolution fit into the scheme better if you did prefer to call the "closest" `bar()` from GC. And of course, if you still need to call one higher up, just do it in an unbound manner as before:

```
>>> P2.bar(gc)
called P2-bar()
```

New-style classes also have an __mro__ attribute that tells you what the search order is:

```
>>> GC.__mro__
(<class '__main__.GC'>, <class '__main__.C1'>, <class
'__main__.C2'>, <class '__main__.P1'>, <class
'__main__.P2'>, <type 'object'>)
```

*MRO Problems Caused by Diamonds

The classic class method resolution never gave folks too many problems. It was simple to explain and easy to understand. Most classes were single inheritance, and multiple inheritance was usually limited to mixing two completely discrete classes together. This is where the term *mix-in* classes (or "mix-ins") comes from.

Why the Classic Classes MRO Fails

The unification of types and classes in 2.2 brought about a new "problem," and that is related to all (root) classes inheriting from `object`, the mother of all types. The diagram of a simple multiple inheritance hierarchy now formed a diamond. Taking some inspiration from Guido van Rossum's essay, let us say that you have classic classes B and C, as defined below where C overrides its constructor but B does not, and D inherits from both B and C:

```
class B:
    pass


class C:
    def __init__(self):
        print "the default constructor"


class D(B, C):
    pass
```

When we instantiate D, we get:

```
>>> d = D()
the default constructor
```

Figure 13.3 illustrates the class hierarchy for B, C, and D, as well as the problem introduced when we change the code to use new-style classes:

```
class B(object):
    pass


class C(object):
    def __init__(self):
        print "the default constructor"
```

Not much change here other than adding (object) to both class declarations, right? That is true, but as you can see in the diagram, the hierarchy is now a diamond; the real problem is in the MRO now. If we used the classic

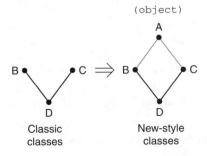

Figure 13–3 Inheritance problems are caused by the appearance of the base class required by new-style classes, forming a diamond shape in the inheritance hierarchy. An instance of D should not miss an upcall to C nor should it upcall to A twice (since both B and C derive from A). Be sure to read the "Cooperative Methods" section of Guido van Rossum's essay for further clarification.

class MRO, when instantiating D, we no longer get C.__init__()... we get object.__init__()! This is the exact reason why the MRO needed to be changed.

Although we saw that it does change the way attributes are looked up in our example above with the GC class, you do not have to worry about lots of code breaking. Classic classes will still use the old MRO while new-style classes will use its MRO. Again, if you do not need all of the features of the new-style classes, there is nothing wrong with continuing to develop using classic classes.

Summary

Classic classes have a depth-first MRO algorithm. Because new-style classes inherit from object, a new MRO had to be created because of problems ensuing from the now-diamond-shaped class hierarchy.

You can read more about new-style classes, the MROs, and more in:

- Guido van Rossum's essay on the unification of types and classes:
  http://www.python.org/download/releases/2.2.3/descrintro

- PEP 252: Making Types Look More Like Classes
  http://www.python.org/doc/peps/pep-0252

- "What's New in Python 2.2" document
  http://www.python.org/doc/2.2.3/whatsnew

- Python 2.3 Method Resolution order paper
  http://python.org/download/releases/2.3/mro/

13.12 Built-in Functions for Classes, Instances, and Other Objects

13.12.1 issubclass()

The issubclass() Boolean function determines if one class is a subclass or descendant of another class. It has the following syntax:

```
issubclass(sub, sup)
```

issubclass() returns True if the given subclass *sub* is indeed a subclass of the superclass *sup* (and False otherwise). This function allows for an "improper" subclass, meaning that a class is viewed as a subclass of itself, so the function returns True if sub is either the same class as sup or derived from sup. (A "proper" subclass is strictly a derived subclass of a class.)

Beginning with Python 2.3, the second argument of `issubclass()` can be tuple of possible parent classes for which it will return `True` if the first argument is a subclass of any of the candidate classes in the given tuple.

2.3

13.12.2 `isinstance()`

The `isinstance()` Boolean function is useful for determining if an object is an instance of a given class. It has the following syntax:

```
isinstance(obj1, obj2)
```

`isinstance()` returns `True` if *obj1* is an instance of class *obj2* or is an instance of a subclass of *obj2* (and `False` otherwise), as indicated in the following examples:

```
>>> class C1(object): pass
...
>>> class C2(object): pass
...
>>> c1 = C1()
>>> c2 = C2()
>>> isinstance(c1, C1)
True
>>> isinstance(c2, C1)
False
>>> isinstance(c1, C2)
False
>>> isinstance(c2, C2)
True
>>> isinstance(C2, c2)
Traceback (innermost last):
  File "<stdin>", line 1, in ?
    isinstance(C2, c2)
TypeError: second argument must be a class
```

Note that the second argument should be a class; otherwise, you get a `TypeError`. The only exception is if the second argument is a type object. This is allowed because you can also use `isinstance()` to check if an object *obj1* is of the type *obj2*, i.e.,

```
>>> isinstance(4, int)
True
>>> isinstance(4, str)
False
>>> isinstance('4', str)
True
```

If you are coming from Java, you may be aware of the warning against using its equivalent, `instanceof()`, due to performance reasons. A call to Python's `isinstance()` will not have the same performance hit primarily because it only needs it to perform a quick search up the class hierarchy to determine what classes it is an instance of, and even more importantly, it is written in C!

Like `issubclass()`, `isinstance()` can also take a tuple as its second argument. This feature was added in Python 2.2. It will return `True` if the first argument is an instance of any of the candidate types and classes in the given tuple. Also be sure to read more about `isinstance()` in Section 13.16.1 on page 595.

2.2

13.12.3 `hasattr()`, `getattr()`, `setattr()`, `delattr()`

The `*attr()` functions can work with all kinds of objects, not just classes and instances. However, since they are most often used with those objects, we present them here. One thing that might throw you off is that when using these functions, you pass in the object you are working on as the first argument, but the attribute name, the second argument to these functions, is the string name of the attribute. In other words, when operating with *obj.attr*, the function call will be like *attr(obj, 'attr'...)*—this will be clear in the examples that follow.

The `hasattr()` function is Boolean and its only purpose is to determine whether or not an object has a particular attribute, presumably used as a check before actually *trying* to access that attribute. The `getattr()` and `setattr()` functions retrieve and assign values to object attributes, respectively. `getattr()` will raise an `AttributeError` exception if you attempt to read an object that does not have the requested attribute, unless a third, optional default argument is given. `setattr()` will either add a new attribute to the object or replace a pre-existing one. The `delattr()` function removes an attribute from an object.

Here are some examples using all the `*attr()` BIFs:

```
>>> class myClass(object):
...      def __init__(self):
...          self.foo = 100
...
>>> myInst = myClass()
>>> hasattr(myInst, 'foo')
True
```

```
>>> getattr(myInst, 'foo')
100
>>> hasattr(myInst, 'bar')
False
>>> getattr(myInst, 'bar')
Traceback (most recent call last):
  File "<stdin>", line 1, in ?
    getattr(myInst, 'bar')
AttributeError: myClass instance has no attribute 'bar'
>>> getattr(c, 'bar', 'oops!')
'oops!'
>>> setattr(myInst, 'bar', 'my attr')
>>> dir(myInst)
['__doc__', '__module__', 'bar', 'foo']
>>> getattr(myInst, 'bar')     # same as myInst.bar
'my attr'
>>> delattr(myInst, 'foo')
>>> dir(myInst)
['__doc__', '__module__', 'bar']
>>> hasattr(myInst, 'foo')
False
```

13.12.4 dir()

We first experienced dir() in Exercises 2–12, 2–13, and 4–7. In those exercises, we used dir() to give us information about all the attributes of a module. We now know that dir() can be applied to objects as well.

In Python 2.2, dir() received a significant upgrade. Because of these changes, the voluntarily implemented __members__ and __methods__ data attributes have been deprecated. dir() provides more details than the old one. According to the documentation, "In addition to the names of instance variables and regular methods, it also shows the methods that are normally invoked through special notations, like __iadd__ (+=), __len__ (len()), __ne__ (!=)." Here are more specifics from the Python documentation:

- dir() on an instance (classic or new-style) shows the instance variables as well as the methods and class attributes defined by the instance's class and all its base classes.
- dir() on a class (classic or new-style) shows the contents of the __dict__ of the class and all its base classes. It does not show class attributes that are defined by a metaclass.
- dir() on a module shows the contents of the module's __dict__. (This is unchanged.)

- `dir()` without arguments shows the caller's local variables. (Again, unchanged.)
- There are more details; in particular, for objects that override __dict__ or __class__, these are honored, and for backwards compatibility, __members__ and __methods__ are honored if they are defined.

13.12.5 `super()`

2.2

The super() function was added in 2.2 for new-style classes. The purpose of this function is to help the programmer chase down the appropriate superclass with which the proper method can be invoked. In simple cases, the programmer will likely just call the ancestor class method in an unbound fashion. Using super() simplifies the task of search for a suitable ancestor and passes in the instance or type object on your behalf when you call it.

In Section 13.11.4, we described the method resolution order (MRO) that is used to chase down attributes in ancestor classes. For each class defined, an attribute named __mro__ is created as a tuple that lists the classes that need to be searched, in the order they are searched. Here is its syntax:

```
super(type[, obj])
```

Given *type*, super() "returns the superclass" of *type*. You may also pass in *obj*, which should be of the type *type* if you want the superclass to be bound, otherwise it will be unbound. The *obj* argument can also be a type, but it needs to be a subclass of type. In summary, when *obj* is given:

- If *obj* is an instance, then isinstance(*obj*, *type*) must be True
- If *obj* is a class or type, then issubclass(*obj*, *type*) must be True

Actually, super() is a factory function that makes a super object that uses the __mro__ attribute for a given class to find the appropriate superclass. Most notably, it searches that MRO starting from the point where the current class is found. For more details, again please see Guido van Rossum's essay on type and class unification, where he even gives a pure Python implementation of super() so you can get a better idea of how it works!

Final thought… super()'s primary use is in the lookup of a superclass attribute, e.g., super(MyClass, self).__init__(). If you are not performing such a lookup, you probably do not need to be using super().

There are various examples *how to use* `super()` scattered throughout this chapter. Also be sure to read the important notes about `super()` in Section 13.11.2, especially the Core Note in that section.

13.12.6 `vars()`

The `vars()` built-in function is similar to `dir()` except that any object given as the argument must have a `__dict__` attribute. `vars()` will return a dictionary of the attributes (keys) and values of the given object based on the values in its `__dict__` attribute. If the object provided does not have such an attribute, an `TypeError` exception is raised. If no object is provided as an argument to `vars()`, it will display the dictionary of attributes (keys) and the values of the local namespace, i.e., `locals()`. We present an example of calling `vars()` with a class instance:

```
class C(object):
    pass

>>> c = C()
>>> c.foo = 100
>>> c.bar = 'Python'
>>> c.__dict__
{'foo': 100, 'bar': 'Python'}
>>> vars(c)
{'foo': 100, 'bar': 'Python'}
```

Table 13.3 summarizes the built-in functions for classes and class instances.

Table 13.3 Built-in Functions for Classes, Instances, and Other Objects

Built-in Function	Description
`issubclass(sub, sup)`	Returns `True` if class *sub* is a subclass of class *sup*, `False` otherwise
`isinstance(obj1, obj2)`	Returns `True` if instance *obj1* is an instance of class *obj2* or is an instance of a subclass of *obj2*; will also return `True` if *obj1* is of type *obj2*; otherwise it returns `False`
`hasattr(obj, attr)`	Returns `True` if *obj* has attribute *attr* (given as a string), `False` otherwise

(continued)

Table 13.3 Built-in Functions for Classes, Instances, and Other Objects (continued)	
Built-in Function	*Description*
getattr(*obj*, *attr* [, *default*])	Retrieves attribute *attr* of *obj*; same as return *obj.attr*; if *attr* is not an attribute of *obj*, *default* returned if given; else AttributeError exception raised
setattr(*obj*, *attr*, *val*)	Sets attribute *attr* of *obj* to value val, over-riding any previously existing attribute value; otherwise, attribute is created; same as *obj.attr = val*
delattr(*obj*, *attr*)	Removes attribute *attr* (given as a string) from *obj*; same as **del** *obj.attr*
dir(*obj*=None)	Returns a list of the attributes of *obj*; if *obj* not given, dir() displays local namespace attributes, i.e., locals().keys()
super(*type*, *obj*=None)[a]	Returns a proxy object representing the super-class of *type*; if *obj* is not passed in, the super object returned is unbound; otherwise if *obj* is a type issubclass(*obj*, *type*) must be True; otherwise isinstance(*obj*, *type*) must be True
vars(*obj*=None)	Returns a dictionary of the attributes and values of *obj*; if *obj* not given, vars() displays local namespace dictionary (attributes and values), i.e., locals()

a.   New in Python 2.2; only works with new-style classes.

13.13 Customizing Classes with Special Methods

We covered two important aspects of methods in preceding sections of this chapter: first, that methods must be bound (to an instance of their corresponding class) before they can be invoked; and second, that there are two special methods which provide the functionality of constructors and destructors, namely __init__() and __del__() respectively.

In fact, __init__() and __del__() are part of a set of special methods which can be implemented. Some have the predefined default behavior of inaction while others do not and should be implemented where needed. These special methods allow for a powerful form of extending classes in Python. In particular, they allow for:

- Emulating standard types
- Overloading operators

Special methods enable classes to emulate standard types by overloading standard operators such as +, *, and even the slicing subscript and mapping operator [ ]. As with most other special reserved identifiers, these methods begin and end with a double underscore (__). Table 13.4 presents a list of all special methods and their descriptions.

Table 13.4 Special Methods for Customizing Classes

Special Method	Description
Basic Customization	
C.__init__(self[, arg1, ...])	Constructor (with any optional arguments)
C.__new__(self[, arg1, ...])[a]	Constructor (with any optional arguments); usually used for setting up subclassing of immutable data types
C.__del__(self)	Destructor
C.__str__(self)	Printable string representation; str() built-in and **print** statement
C.__repr__(self)	Evaluatable string representation; repr() built-in and ` ` operator
C.__unicode__(self)[b]	Unicode string representation; unicode() built-in
C.__call__(self, *args)	Denote callable instances
C.__nonzero__(self)	Define False value for object; bool() built-in (as of 2.2)
C.__len__(self)	"Length" (appropriate for class); len() built-in

(continued)

Table 13.4 Special Methods for Customizing Classes (continued)

Special Method	Description
Object (Value) Comparison[c]	
`C.__cmp__(self, obj)`	object comparison; `cmp()` built-in
`C.__lt__(self, obj)` and `C.__le__(self, obj)`	less than/less than or equal to; `<` and `<=` operators
`C.__gt__(self, obj)` and `C.__ge__(self, obj)`	greater than/greater than or equal to; `>` and `>=` operators
`C.__eq__(self, obj)` and `C.__ne__(self, obj)`	equal/not equal to; `==`, `!=` and `<>` operators
Attributes	
`C.__getattr__(self, attr)`	Get attribute; `getattr()` built-in; called only if attributes not found
`C.__setattr__(self, attr, val)`	Set attribute;
`C.__delattr__(self, attr)`	Delete attribute;
`C.__getattribute__(self, attr)`[a]	Get attribute; `getattr()` built-in; always called
`C.__get__(self, attr)`[a]	(descriptor) Get attribute
`C.__set__(self, attr, val)`[a]	(descriptor) Set attribute
`C.__delete__(self, attr)`[a]	(descriptor) Delete attribute
Customizing Classes / Emulating Types	
Numeric Types: Binary Operators[d]	
`C.__*add__(self, obj)`	Addition; + operator
`C.__*sub__(self, obj)`	Subtraction; – operator
`C.__*mul__(self, obj)`	Multiplication; * operator
`C.__*div__(self, obj)`	Division; / operator
`C.__*truediv__(self, obj)`[e]	True division; / operator
`C.__*floordiv__(self, obj)`[e]	Floor division; // operator
`C.__*mod__(self, obj)`	Modulo/remainder; % operator
`C.__*divmod__(self, obj)`	Division and modulo; `divmod()` built-in
`C.__*pow__(self, obj[, mod])`	Exponentiation; `pow()` built-in; ** operator
`C.__*lshift__(self, obj)`	Left shift; << operator

Table 13.4 Special Methods for Customizing Classes (continued)	
Special Method	*Description*
Customizing Classes / Emulating Types	
Numeric Types: Binary Operators[f]	
`C.__*rshift__(self, obj)`	Right shift; >> operator
`C.__*and__(self, obj)`	Bitwise AND; & operator
`C.__*or__(self, obj)`	Bitwise OR; | operator
`C.__*xor__(self, obj)`	Bitwise XOR; ^ operator
Numeric Types: Unary Operators	
`C.__neg__(self)`	Unary negation
`C.__pos__(self)`	Unary no-change
`C.__abs__(self)`	Absolute value; abs() built-in
`C.__invert__(self)`	Bit inversion; ~ operator
Numeric Types: Numeric Conversion	
`C.__complex__(self, com)`	Convert to complex; complex() built-in
`C.__int__(self)`	Convert to int; int() built-in
`C.__long__(self)`	Convert to long; long() built-in
`C.__float__(self)`	Convert to float; float() built-in
Numeric Types: Base Representation (String)	
`C.__oct__(self)`	Octal representation; oct() built-in
`C.__hex__(self)`	Hexadecimal representation; hex() built-in
Numeric Types: numeric coercion	
`C.__coerce__(self, num)`	Coerce to same numeric type; coerce() built-in
`C.__index__(self)`[g]	Coerce alternate numeric type to integer if/when necessary (e.g., for slice indexes, etc.)

(continued)

Table 13.4 Special Methods for Customizing Classes (continued)

Sequence Types[e]

C.__len__(self)	Number of items in sequence
C.__getitem__(self, ind)	Get single sequence element
C.__setitem__(self, ind, val)	Set single sequence element
C.__delitem__(self, ind)	Delete single sequence element

Special Method	*Description*
Sequence Types[e]	
C.__getslice__(self, ind1, ind2)	Get sequence slice
C.__setslice__(self, i1, i2, val)	Set sequence slice
C.__delslice__(self, ind1, ind2)	Delete sequence slice
C.__contains__(self, val)[f]	Test sequence membership; **in** keyword
C.__*add__(self, obj)	Concatenation; + operator
C.__*mul__(self, obj)	Repetition; * operator
C.__iter__(self)[e]	Create iterator class; iter() built-in
Mapping Types	
C.__len__(self)	Number of items in mapping
C.__hash__(self)	Hash function value
C.__getitem__(self, key)	Get value with given *key*
C.__setitem__(self, key, val)	Set *value* with given *key*
C.__delitem__(self, key)	Delete value with given *key*
C.__missing__(self, key)[g]	Provides default value when dictionary does not have given *key*

a.   New in Python 2.2; for use with new-style classes only.
b.   New in Python 2.3.
c.   All except cmp() new in Python 2.1.
d.   "*" either nothing (self OP obj), "r" (obj OP self), or "i" for in-place operation (new in Python 2.0), i.e., __add__, __radd__, or __iadd__.
e.   New in Python 2.2.
f.   "*" either nothing (self OP obj), "r" (obj OP self), or "i" for in-place operation (new in Python 1.6), i.e., __add__, __radd__, or __iadd__.
g.   New in Pathon 2.5.

The Basic Customization and Object (Value) Comparison special methods can be implemented for most classes and are not tied to emulation of any specific types. The latter set, also known as Rich Comparisons, was added in Python 2.1.

The Attributes group helps manage instance attributes of your class. This is also independent of emulation. There is also one more, __getattribute__(), which applies to new-style classes only, so we will describe it in an upcoming section.

2.1

The Numeric Types set of special methods can be used to emulate various numeric operations, including those of the standard (unary and binary) operators, conversion, base representation, and coercion. There are also special methods to emulate sequence and mapping types. Implementation of some of these special methods will overload operators so that they work with instances of your class type.

The additional division operators __*truediv__() and __*floordiv__() were added in Python 2.2 to support the pending change to the Python division operator—also see Section 5.5.3. Basically, if the interpreter has the new division enabled, either via a switch when starting up Python or via the import of division from __future__, the single slash division operator (/) will represent true division, meaning that it will always return a floating point value, regardless of whether floats or integers make up the operands (complex division stays the same). The double slash division operator (//) will provide the familiar floor division with which most engineers who come from the standard compiled languages like C/C++ and Java are familiar. Similarly, these methods will only work with these symbols applied to classes that implement these methods and when new division is enabled.

2.2

Numeric binary operators in the table annotated with a wildcard asterisk in their names are so denoted to indicate that there are multiple versions of those methods with slight differences in their name. The asterisk either symbolizes no additional character in the string, or a single "r" to indicate a right-hand operation. Without the "r," the operation occurs for cases that are of the format self OP obj; the presence of the "r" indicates the format obj OP self. For example, __add__(self, obj) is called for self + obj, and __radd__(self, obj) would be invoked for obj + self.

Augmented assignment, new in Python 2.0, introduces the notion of "in-place" operations. An "i" in place of the asterisk implies a combination left-hand operation plus an assignment, as in self = self OP obj. For example, __iadd__(self, obj) is called for self = self + obj.

2.0

With the arrival of new-style classes in Python 2.2, several more special methods have been added for overriding. However, as we mentioned at the beginning of the chapter, we are now focusing only on the core portion of material applicable to both classic classes as well as new-style classes,

2.2

and then later on in the chapter, we address the advanced features of new-style classes.

13.13.1 Simple Customization (`RoundFloat2`)

Our first example is totally trivial. It is based to some extent on the Round-Float class we saw earlier in the section on subclassing Python types. This example is simpler. In fact, we are not even going to subclass anything (except object of course)... we do not want to "take advantage" of all the "goodies" that come with floats. No, this time, we want to create a barebones example so that you have a better idea of how class customization works. The premise of this class is still the same as the other one: we just want a class to save a floating point number rounded to two decimal places.

```python
class RoundFloatManual(object):
    def __init__(self, val):
        assert isinstance(val, float), \
            "Value must be a float!"
        self.value = round(val, 2)
```

This class takes a single floating point value—it asserts that the type must be a float as it is passed to the constructor—and saves it as the instance attribute `value`. Let us try to execute it and create an instance of this class:

```
>>> rfm = RoundFloatManual(42)
Traceback (most recent call last):
  File "<stdin>", line 1, in ?
  File "roundFloat2.py", line 5, in __init__
    assert isinstance(val, float), \
AssertionError: Value must be a float!
>>> rfm = RoundFloatManual(4.2)
>>> rfm
<roundFloat2.RoundFloatManual object at 0x63030>
>>> print rfm
<roundFloat2.RoundFloatManual object at 0x63030>
```

As you can see, it chokes on invalid input, but provides no output if input was valid. But look what happens when we try to dump the object in the interactive interpreter. We get some information, but this is not what we were looking for. (We wanted to see the numeric value, right?) And calling **print** does not apparently help, either.

Unfortunately, neither **print** (using `str()`) nor the actual object's string representation (using `repr()`) reveals much about our object. One good idea would be to implement either __str__() or __repr__(), or both so that we can "see" what our object looks like. In other words, when you want to display your object, you actually want to see something meaningful rather than the generic Python object string (*<object* object at *id>*). Let us add a __str__() method, overriding the default behavior:

```
def __str__(self):
    return str(self.value)
```

Now we get the following:

```
>>> rfm = RoundFloatManual(5.590464)
>>> rfm
<roundFloat2.RoundFloatManual object at 0x5eff0>
>>> print rfm
5.59
>>> rfm = RoundFloatManual(5.5964)
>>> print rfm
5.6
```

We still have a few problems . . . one is that just dumping the object in the interpreter still shows the default object notation, but that is not so bad. If we wanted to fix it, we would just override __repr__(). Since our string representation is also a Python object, we can make the output of __repr__() the same as __str__().

To accomplish this, we can just copy the code from __str__() to __repr__(). This is a simple example, so it cannot really hurt us, but as a programmer, you know that is not the best thing to do. If a bug existed in __str__(), then we will copy that bug to __repr__().

The best solution is to recall that the code represented by __str__() is an object too, and like all objects, references can be made to them, so let us just make __repr__() an alias to __str__():

```
__repr__ = __str__
```

In the second example with 5.5964, we see that it rounds the value correctly to 5.6, but we still wanted two decimal places to be displayed. One more tweak, and we should be done. Here is the fix:

```
def __str__(self):
    return '%.2f' % self.value
```

And here is the resulting output with both str() and repr() output:

```
>>> rfm = RoundFloatManual(5.5964)
>>> rfm
5.60
>>> print rfm
5.60
```

Example 13.2 Basic Customization (`roundFloat2.py`)

```
1   #!/usr/bin/env python
2
3   class RoundFloatManual(object):
4       def __init__(self, val):
5           assert isinstance(val, float), \
6           "Value must be a float!"
7           self.value = round(val, 2)
8
9       def __str__(self):
10          return '%.2f' % self.value
11
12      __repr__ = __str__
```

In our original `RoundFloat` example at the beginning of this chapter, we did not have to worry about all the fine-grained object display stuff; the reason is that __str__() and __repr__() have already been defined for us as part of the float class. All we did was inherit them. Our more "manual" version required additional work from us. Do you see how useful derivation is? You do not even need to know how far up the inheritance tree the interpreter needs to go to find a declared method that you are using without guilt. We present the full code of this class in Example 13.2.

Now let us try a slightly more complex example.

13.13.2 Numeric Customization (`Time60`)

For our first realistic example, let us say we wanted to create a simple application that manipulated time as measured in hours and minutes. The class we are going to create can be used to track the time worked by an employee, the amount of time spent online by an ISP (Internet service provider) subscriber, the amount of total uptime for a database (not inclusive of downtime for backups and upgrades), the total amount of time played in a poker tournament, etc.

For our `Time60` class, we will take integers as hours and minutes as input to our constructor.

```
class Time60(object):          # ordered pair
    def __init__(self, hr, min):  # constructor
        self.hr = hr              # assign hours
        self.min = min            # assign minutes
```

Display

Also, as seen in the previous example, we want meaningful output if we display our instances, so we need to override __str__() (and __repr__() if so desired). As humans, we are used to seeing hours and minutes in colon-delimited format, e.g. "4:30," representing four and a half hours (four hours and thirty minutes):

```
def __str__(self):
    return '%d:%d' % (self.hr, self.min)
```

Using this class, we can instantiate some objects. In the example below, we are starting a timesheet to track the number of billable hours for a contractor:

```
>>> mon = Time60(10, 30)
>>> tue = Time60(11, 15)
>>>
>>> print mon, tue
10:30 11:15
```

The output is very nice, exactly what we wanted to see. What is the next step? Let us say we want our objects to interact. In particular, for our timesheet application, it is a necessity to be able to add Time60 instances together and have our objects do all meaningful operations. We would love to see something like this:

```
>>> mon + tue
21:45
```

Addition

With Python, overloading operators is simple. For the plus sign (+), we need to overload the __add__() special method, and perhaps __radd__() and __iadd__(), if applicable. More on those in a little while. Implementing __add__() does not sound too difficult—we just add the hours together followed by the minutes. Most of the complexity lies in what we do with the new totals. If we want to see "21:45," we have to realize that *that* is another Time60 object. We are not modifying mon or tue, so our method would have to create another object and fill it in with the sums we calculated.

We implement the __add__() special method in such a way that we calculate the individual sums first, then call the class constructor to return a new object:

```
def __add__(self, other):
    return self.__class__(self.hr + other.hr,
        self.min + other.min)
```

The new object is created by invoking the class as in any normal situation. The only difference is that from within the class, you typically would not invoke the class name directly. Rather, you take the __class__ attribute of self, which is the class from which self was instantiated, and invoke *that*. Because self.__class__ is the same as Time60, calling self.__class__() is the same as calling Time60().

This is the more object-oriented approach anyway. The other reason is that if we used the real class name everywhere we create a new object and later on decided to change the class name to something else, we would have to perform very careful global search-and-replace. By using self.__class__, we do not have to do anything other than change the name in the **class** directive.

With our plus sign overloading, we can now "add" Time60 objects:

```
>>> mon = Time60(10, 30)
>>> tue = Time60(11, 15)
>>> mon + tue
<time60.Time60 object at 0x62190>
>>> print mon + tue
21:45
```

Oops, we forgot to add an __repr__ alias to __str__, which is easily fixable.

One question you may have is, "What happens when I try to use an operator in an overload situation where I do not have the appropriate special methods defined?" The answer is a TypeError exception:

```
>>> mon - tue
Traceback (most recent call last):
  File "<stdin>", line 1, in ?
TypeError: unsupported operand type(s) for -: 'Time60'
and 'Time60'
```

In-Place Addition

With augmented assignment (introduced back in Python 2.0), we may also wish to override the "in-place" operators, for example, __iadd__(). This is for supporting an operation like mon += tue and having the correct result placed in mon. The only trick with overriding an __i*__() method is that it has to return self. Let us add the following bits of code to our example, fixing our repr() issue above as well as supporting augmented assignment:

```
__repr__ = __str__

def __iadd__(self, other):
    self.hr += other.hr
    self.min += other.min
    return self
```

Here is our resulting output:

```
>>> mon = Time60(10, 30)
>>> tue = Time60(11, 15)
>>> mon
10:30
>>> id(mon)
401872
>>> mon += tue
>>> id(mon)
401872
>>> mon
21:45
```

Note the use of the `id()` built-in function to confirm that before and after
the in-place addition we are indeed modifying the same object and not creating
a new one. This is a great start at a class that has a lot of potential. The complete class definition for `Time60` is given in Example 13.3.

Example 13.3 Intermediate Customization (`time60.py`)

```python
1  #!/usr/bin/env python
2
3  class Time60(object):
4      'Time60 - track hours and minutes'
5
6      def __init__(self, hr, min):
7          'Time60 constructor - takes hours and minutes'
8          self.hr = hr
9          self.min = min
10
11     def __str__(self):
12         'Time60 - string representation'
13         return '%d:%d' % (self.hr, self.min)
14
15     __repr__ = __str__
16
17     def __add__(self, other):
18         'Time60 - overloading the addition operator'
19         return self.__class__(self.hr + other.hr,
20             self.min + other.min)
21
22     def __iadd__(self, other):
23         'Time60 - overloading in-place addition'
24         self.hr += other.hr
25         self.min += other.min
26         return self
```

Example 13.4 Random Sequence Iterator (`randSeq.py`)

```
1   #!/usr/bin/env python
2
3   from random import choice
4
5   class RandSeq(object):
6       def __init__(self, seq):
7           self.data = seq
8
9       def __iter__(self):
10          return self
11
12      def next(self):
13          return choice(self.data)
```

Further Refinements

We will leave it here, but there is plenty of optimization and significant improvements that can be made to this class. For example, wouldn't it be nice if we could just feed a 2-tuple (10, 30) into our constructor rather than having to pass in two separate arguments? What about a string like "10:30"?

The answer is yes, you can, and it *is* easy to do in Python but not by overloading the constructor as the case may be with other object-oriented programming languages. Python does not allow overloading callables with multiple signatures, so the only way to make it happen is with a single constructor and performing self-introspection with the `isinstance()` and (perhaps) `type()` built-in functions.

Supporting multiple forms of input makes our application more robust and flexible. The same is true for the ability to perform other operations like subtraction. Of course these are optional and serve as icing on the cake, but what we *should* be worried about first are two moderate flaws: undesired formatting when there are fewer than ten minutes and the lack of support of *sexagesimal*[1] (base 60) operations:

```
>>> wed = Time60(12, 5)
>>> wed
12:5
>>> thu = Time60(10, 30)
>>> fri = Time60(8, 45)
>>> thu + fri
18:75
```

---

1. Latin-originated name for base 60; sometimes *hexagesimal* is used, a hybrid combining the Greek root "hexe" with the Latin "gesimal."

Displaying wed should have resulted in "12:05," and summing thu and fri should have given an output of "19:15." The fixes for these flaws and the improvements suggested just above are great practice building your class customization skills. You can get a more complete description of these upgrades in Exercise 13–20 at the end of the chapter.

Hopefully, you now have a better understanding of operator overloading, why you would want to do it, and how you can implement special methods to accomplish that task. Let's look at more complex customizations, continuing with the optional section that follows.

13.13.3 Iterators (RandSeq and AnyIter)

RandSeq

We were introduced to iterators formally in Chapter 8 but we have been using them throughout this text. They are simply a mechanism to go through items of a sequence (or sequence-like object) one at a time. In Chapter 8 we described how implementing the __iter__() and next() methods of a class can be used to create an iterator. We will demonstrate that with two examples here.

The first example is a RandSeq (short for RANDom SEQuence). We feed an initial sequence to our class, then let the user iterate (infinitely) through it via next().

The __init__() method does the aforementioned assignment. The __iter__() just returns self, which is how you declare an object is an iterator, and finally, next() is called to get successive values of iteration. The only catch with this iterator is that it never ends.

This example demonstrates some unusual things we can do with custom class iterations. One is infinite iteration. Because we read the sequence nondestructively, we never run out of elements. Each time the user calls next(), it gets the next value, but our object never raises StopIteration. If we run it, we will get output similar to the following:

```
>>> from randseq import RandSeq
>>> for eachItem in RandSeq(
...         ('rock', 'paper', 'scissors')):
...     print eachItem
...
scissors
scissors
rock
paper
paper
scissors
    :
```

Example 13.5 Any Number of Items Iterator (`anyIter.py`)

```python
1   #!/usr/bin/env python
2
3   class AnyIter(object):
4       def __init__(self, data, safe=False):
5           self.safe = safe
6           self.iter = iter(data)
7
8       def __iter__(self):
9           return self
10
11      def next(self, howmany=1):
12          retval = []
13          for eachItem in range(howmany):
14              try:
15                  retval.append(self.iter.next())
16              except StopIteration:
17                  if self.safe:
18                      break
19                  else:
20                      raise
21          return retval
```

AnyIter

In the second example, we do create an iterator object, but rather than iterating through one item at a time, we give the `next()` method an argument telling how many items to return. Here is the code for our (ANY number of items ITERator):

Like `RandSeq`, the `AnyIter` class should be fairly simple to figure out. We described the basic operation above... it works just like any other iterator except that users can request the next N items of the iterable instead of only one.

We create the object by being given an iterable and a `safe` flag. If the flag is `True`, we will return any items retrieved before exhausting the iterable, but if the flag is `False`, we will reraise the exception if the user asked for too many items. The core of any complexity lies in `next()`, specifically how it quits (lines 14–21).

In the last part of `next()`, we create a list of items to return and call the object's `next()` for each item. If we exhaust the list and get a `StopIteration` exception, we check the `safe` flag. If unsafe, we throw the exception back to the caller (**raise**); otherwise, we return whatever items we have saved up (**break** and **return**).

```
>>> a = AnyIter(range(10))
>>> i = iter(a)
>>> for j in range(1,5):
>>>     print j, ':', i.next(j)
1 : [0]
2 : [1, 2]
3 : [3, 4, 5]
4 : [6, 7, 8, 9]
```

The execution above ran fine because the iteration fit the number of items perfectly. What happens when things go awry? Let us try "unsafe" mode first, which is how we created our iterator to begin with from above:

```
>>> i = iter(a)
>>> i.next(14)
Traceback (most recent call last):
  File "<stdin>", line 1, in ?
  File "anyIter.py", line 15, in next
    retval.append(self.iter.next())
StopIteration
```

The `StopIteration` exception was raised because we exceeded our supply of items, and that exception was reraised back to the caller (line 20). If we were to recreate the iterator in "safe" mode and run it with the same example, we get back whatever the iterator could get us before running out of items:

```
>>> a = AnyIter(range(10), True)
>>> i = iter(a)
>>> i.next(14)
[0, 1, 2, 3, 4, 5, 6, 7, 8, 9]
```

13.13.4 *Multi-type Customization (`NumStr`)

Let us create another new class, `NumStr`, consisting of a number-string ordered pair, called *n* and *s*, respectively, using integers as our number type. Although the "proper" notation of an ordered pair is (n, s), we choose to represent our pair as [n :: s] just to be different. Regardless of the notation, these two data elements are inseparable as far as our model is concerned. We want to set up our new class, called `NumStr`, with the following characteristics:

Initialization

The class should be initialized with both the number and string; if either (or both) is missing, then 0 and the empty string should be used, i.e., n=0 and s=' ', as defaults.

Addition

We define the addition operator functionality as adding the numbers together and concatenating the strings; the tricky part is that the strings must be concatenated in the correct order. For example, let NumStr1 = [n1 :: s1] and NumStr2 = [n2 :: s2]. Then NumStr1 + NumStr2 is performed as [n1 + n2 :: s1 + s2] where + represents addition for numbers and concatenation for strings.

Multiplication

Similarly, we define the multiplication operator functionality as multiplying the numbers together and repeating or concatenating the strings, i.e., NumStr1 * NumStr2 = [n1 * n :: s1 * n].

False Value

This entity has a false value when the number has a numeric value of zero and the string is empty, i.e., when NumStr = [0 :: ''].

Comparisons

Comparing a pair of NumStr objects, i.e., [n1 :: s1] vs. [n2 :: s2], we find nine different combinations (i.e., n1 > n2 and s1 < s2, n1 == n2 and s1 > s2, etc.). We use the normal numeric and lexicographic compares for numbers and strings, respectively, i.e., the ordinary comparison of cmp(obj1, obj2) will return an integer less than zero if obj1 < obj2, greater than zero if obj1 > obj2, or equal to zero if the objects have the same value.

The solution for our class is to add both of these values and return the result. The interesting thing is that cmp() does not always return −1, 0, or 1 for us. It is, as described above, an integer less than, equal to, or greater than zero.

In order to correctly compare our objects, we need __cmp__() to return a value of 1 if (n1 > n2) and (s1 > s2), −1 if (n1 < n2) and (s1 < s2), and 0 if both sets of numbers and strings are the same, or if the comparisons offset each other, i.e., (n1 < n2) and (s1 > s2), or vice versa.

Example 13.6 Multi-Type Class Customization (numstr.py)

```python
1  #!/usr/bin/env python
2
3  class NumStr(object):
4
5      def __init__(self, num=0, string=''):
6          self.__num = num
7          self.__string = string
8
9      def __str__(self):          # define for str()
10         return '[%d :: %r]' % \
11             self.__num, self.__string)
12     __repr__ = __str__
13
14     def __add__(self, other):       # define for s+o
15         if isinstance(other, NumStr):
16             return self.__class__(self.__num + \
17                 other.__num, \
18                 self.__string + other.__string)
19         else:
20             raise TypeError, \
21     'Illegal argument type for built-in operation'
22
23     def __mul__(self, num):         # define for o*n
24         if isinstance(num, int):
25             return self.__class__(self.__num * num
26                 self.__string * num)
27         else:
28             raise TypeError, \
29     'Illegal argument type for built-in operation'
30
31     def __nonzero__(self):          # False if both are
32         return self.__num or len(self.__string)
33
34     def __norm_cval(self, cmpres):# normalize cmp()
35         return cmp(cmpres, 0)
36
37     def __cmp__(self, other):       # define for cmp()
38         return self.__norm_cval(
39             cmp(self.__num, other.__num)) + \
40             self.__norm_cval(
41                 cmp(self.__string, other.__string))
```

Given the above criteria, we present the code below for numstr.py, with some sample execution:

```python
>>> a = NumStr(3, 'foo')
>>> b = NumStr(3, 'goo')
>>> c = NumStr(2, 'foo')
>>> d = NumStr()
>>> e = NumStr(string='boo')
>>> f = NumStr(1)
>>> a
[3 :: 'foo']
```

```
>>> b
[3 :: 'goo']
>>> c
[2 :: 'foo']
>>> d
[0 :: '']
>>> e
[0 :: 'boo']
>>> f
[1 :: '']
>>> a < b
True
>>> b < c
False
>>> a == a
True
>>> b * 2
[6 :: 'googoo']
>>> a * 3
[9 :: 'foofoofoo']
>>> b + e
[3 :: 'gooboo']
>>> e + b
[3 :: 'boogoo']
>>> if d: 'not false'      # also bool(d)
...
>>> if e: 'not false'      # also bool(e)
...
'not false'
>>> cmp(a,b)
-1
>>> cmp(a,c)
1
>>> cmp(a,a)
0
```

Line-by-Line Explanation

Lines 1–7

The top of our script features the constructor __init__() setting up our instance initializing itself with the values passed via the class instantiator call NumStr(). If either value is missing, the attribute takes on the default false value of either zero or the empty string, depending on the argument.

One significant oddity is the use of double underscores to name our attributes. As we will find out in the next section, this is used to enforce a level, albeit elementary, of privacy. Programmers importing our module will not have straightforward access to our data elements. We are attempting to enforce one of the encapsulation properties of OO design by permitting access only through accessor functionality. If this syntax appears odd or uncomfortable to you, you can remove all double underscores from the instance attributes, and the examples will still work in the exact same manner.

All attributes that begin with a double underscore (__) are "mangled" so that these names are not as easily accessible during runtime. They are not, however, mangled in such a way so that it cannot be easily reverse-engineered. In fact, the mangling pattern is fairly well known and easy to spot. The main point is to prevent the name from being accidentally used when it is imported by an external module where conflicts may arise. The name is changed to a new identifier name containing the class name to ensure that it does not get "stepped on" unintentionally. For more information, check out Section 13.14 on privacy.

Lines 9–12

We choose the string representation of our ordered pair to be "[num :: 'str']" so it is up to __str__() to provide that representation whenever str() is applied to our instance and when the instance appears in a **print** statement. Because we want to emphasize that the second element is a string, it is more visually convincing if the users view the string surrounded by quotation marks. To that end, we use the "repr()" representation format conversion code "%r" instead of "%s." It is equivalent to calling repr() or using the single back quotation marks to give the evaluatable version of a string, which *does* have quotation marks:

```
>>> print a
[3 :: 'foo']
```

Not calling repr() on self.__string (leaving the backquotes off or using "%s") would result in the string quotations being absent:

```
return '[%d :: %s]' % (self.__num, self.__string)
```

Now calling **print** again on an instance results in:

```
>>> print a
[3 :: foo]
```

How does that look without the quotations? Not as convincing that "foo" is a string, is it? It looks more like a variable. The author is not as convinced either. (We quickly and quietly back out of that change and pretend we never even touched it.)

The first line of code after the __str__() function is the assignment of that function to another special method name, __repr__. We made a decision that an evaluatable string representation of our instance should be the same as the printable string representation. Rather than defining an entirely new function that is a duplicate of __str__(), we just create an alias, copying the reference.

When you implement __str__(), it is the code that is called by the interpreter if you ever apply the str() built-in function using that object as an argument. The same goes for __repr__() and repr().

How would our execution differ if we chose not to implement __repr__()? If the assignment is removed, only the **print** statement that calls str() will show us the contents of our object. The evaluatable string representation defaults to the Python standard of <...some_object_ information...>.

```
>>> print a            # calls str(a)
[3 :: 'foo']
>>> a                  # calls repr(a)
<NumStr.NumStr instance at 122640>
```

Lines 14–21

One feature we would like to add to our class is the addition operation, which we described earlier. One of Python's features for customizing classes is that we can overload operators to make these types of customizations more "realistic." Invoking a function such as "add(obj1, obj2)" to "add" objects obj1 and obj2 may *seem* like addition, but is it not more compelling to be able to invoke that same operation using the plus sign (+) like this? ⟹ obj1 + obj2

Overloading the plus sign requires the implementation of __add__() for self (SELF) and the other operand (OTHER). The __add__() function takes care of the Self + Other case, but we do not need to define __radd__() to handle the Other + Self because that is taken care of by the __add__() for Other. The numeric addition is not affected as much as the string concatenation because order matters.

The addition operation adds each of the two components, with the pair of results forming a new object—created as the results are passed to a call for instantiation as calling self.__class__() (again, also previously explained above). Any object other than a like type should result in a TypeError exception, which we raise in such cases.

Lines 23–29

We also overload the asterisk [by implementing __mul__()] so that both numeric multiplication and string repetition are performed, resulting in a new object, again created via instantiation. Since repetition allows only an integer to the right of the operator, we must enforce this restriction as well. We also do not define __rmul__() for the same reason.

Lines 31–32

Python objects have a Boolean value at any time. For the standard types, objects have a false value when they are either a numeric equivalent of zero or an empty sequence or mapping. For our class, we have chosen both that its numeric value must be zero *and* that the string be empty in order for any such instance to have a false value. We override the __nonzero__() method for this purpose. Other objects such as those that strictly emulate sequence or mapping types use a length of zero as a false value. In those cases, you would implement the __len__() method to effect that functionality.

Lines 34–41

__norm_cval() (short for "normalize cmp() value") is not a special method. Rather, it is a helper function to our overriding of __cmp__(); its sole purpose is to convert all positive return values of cmp() to 1, and all negative values to −1. cmp() normally returns arbitrary positive or negative values (or zero) based on the result of the comparison, but for our purposes, we need to restrict the return values to only −1, 0, and 1. Calling cmp() with integers and comparing to zero will give us the result we need, being equivalent to the following snippet of code:

```
def __norm_cval(self, cmpres):
    if cmpres < 0:
        return -1
    elif cmpres > 0:
        return 1
    else:
        return 0
```

The actual comparison of two like objects consists of comparing the numbers and the strings, and returning the sum of the comparisons.

13.14 Privacy

Attributes in Python are, by default, "public" all the time, accessible by both code within the module and modules that import the module containing the class.

Many OO languages provide some level of privacy for the data and provide only accessor functions to provide access to the values. This is known as implementation hiding and is a key component to the encapsulation of the object.

Most OO languages provide "access specifiers" to restrict access to member functions.

Double Underscore (__)

Python provides an elementary form of privacy for class elements (attributes or methods). Attributes that begin with a double underscore (__) are mangled during runtime so direct access is thwarted. In actuality, the name is prepended with an underscore followed by the class name. For example, let us take the `self.__num` attribute found in Example 13.6 (`numstr.py`). After the mangling process, the identifier used to access that data value is now `self._NumStr__num`. Adding the class name to the newly mangled result will prevent it from clashing with the same name in either ancestor or descendant classes.

Although this provides some level of privacy, the algorithm is also in the public domain and can be defeated easily. It is more of a protective mechanism for importing modules that do not have direct access to the source code or for other code within the same module.

The other purpose of this type of name-mangling is to protect __xxx variables from conflicting with derived class namespaces. If you have an __xxx attribute in a class, it will not be overridden by a child class's ___xxx attribute. (Recall that if a parent has just an xxx attribute and a child defines one, then the child's xxx overrides the parents, and the reason why you have to do `PARENT.xxx` to call the base class method of the same name.) By using __xxx, the code for the child class can safely use __xxx without worrying that it will use or affect __xxx in the parent.

Single Underscore (_)

As we discovered in Chapter 12, simple module-level privacy is provided by using a single underscore (_) character prefixing an attribute name. This prevents a module attribute from being imported with "`from` mymodule `import` `*`". This is strictly scope-based, so it will work with functions too.

With Python's new-style classes introduced in 2.2, a whole new set of features was added to give programmers a significant amount of control over how much protection is offered class and instance attributes. Although Python does not have syntax built into the language that has the flavors of `private`, `protected`, `friend`, or `protected friend`, you can customize access in the exact way that fits your needs. We cannot cover all of those possibilities but will give you an idea of the new-style we attribute access later in this chapter.

13.15 *Delegation

13.15.1 Wrapping

"Wrapping" is a term you will hear often in the Python programming world. It is a generic moniker to describe the packaging of an existing object, whether it be a data type or a piece of code, adding new, removing undesired, or otherwise modifying existing functionality to the existing object.

Before Python 2.2, the subclassing or derivation of a standard type in Python was not allowed. Even though you can do that now with the new-style classes, there is a concept that is still popular. You can always wrap any type as the core member of a class so that the new object's behavior mimics all existing behavior of the data type that you want and does not do what you do not want it to do; and perhaps it will do something a little extra. This is called "wrapping a type." In the Appendix, we will discuss how to extend Python, another form of wrapping.

Wrapping consists of defining a class whose instances have the core behavior of a standard type. In other words, it not only sings and dances now, but also walks and talks like our original type. Figure 15–4 illustrates what a type wrapped in a class looks like. The core behavior of a standard type is in the center of the figure, but it is also enhanced by new or updated functionality, and perhaps even by different methods of accessing the actual data.

Class Object (Which Behaves Like a Type)

You may also wrap classes, but this does not make as much sense because there is already a mechanism for taking an object and wrapping it in a manner as described above for a standard type. How would you take an existing class, mimic the behavior you desire, remove what you do not like, and perhaps tweak something to make the class perform differently from the original class? That process, as we discussed recently, is derivation.

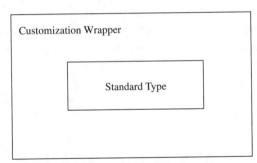

Figure 13–4 Wrapping a Type

13.15.2 Implementing Delegation

Delegation is a characteristic of wrapping that simplifies the process with regard to dictating functionality by taking advantage of pre-existing functionality to maximize code reuse.

Wrapping a type generally consists of some sort of customization to the existing type. As we mentioned before, this tweaking comes in the form of new, modified, or removed functionality compared to the original product. Everything else should remain the same, or keep its existing functionality and behavior. Delegation is the process whereby all the updated functionality is handled as part of the new class, but the existing functionality is delegated to the default attributes of the object.

The key to implementing delegation is to override the __getattr__() method with code containing a call to the built-in getattr() function. Specifically, getattr() is invoked to obtain the default object attribute (data attribute or method) and return it for access or invocation. The way the special method __getattr__() works is that when an attribute is searched for, any local ones are found first (the customized ones). If the search fails, then __getattr__() is invoked, which then calls getattr() to obtain an object's default behavior.

In other words, when an attribute is referenced, the Python interpreter will attempt to find that name in the local namespace, such as a customized method or local instance attribute. If it is not found in the local dictionary, then the class namespace is searched, just in case a class attribute was accessed. Finally, if both searches fail, the hunt begins to delegate the request to the original object, and that is when __getattr__() is invoked.

Simple Example Wrapping Any Object

Let us take a look at an example. Here we present a class that wraps nearly any object, providing such basic functionality as string representations with repr() and str(). Additional customization comes in the form of the get() method, which removes the wrapping and returns the raw object. All remaining functionality is delegated to the object's native attributes as retrieved by __getattr__() when necessary.

Here is an example of a wrapping class:

```
class WrapMe(object):
    def __init__(self, obj):
        self.__data = obj
    def get(self):
        return self.__data
```

```
    def __repr__(self):
        return 'self.__data'
    def __str__(self):
        return str(self.__data)
    def __getattr__(self, attr):
        return getattr(self.__data, attr)
```

In our first example, we will use complex numbers, because of all Python's numeric types, complex numbers are the only one with attributes: data attributes as well as its `conjugate()` built-in method. Remember that attributes can be both data attributes as well as functions or methods:

```
>>> wrappedComplex = WrapMe(3.5+4.2j)
>>> wrappedComplex                    # wrapped object: repr()
(3.5+4.2j)
>>> wrappedComplex.real               # real attribute
3.5
>>> wrappedComplex.imag               # imaginary attribute
42.2
>>> wrappedComplex.conjugate()        # conjugate() method
(3.5-4.2j)
>>> wrappedComplex.get()              # actual object
(3.5+4.2j)
```

Once we create our wrapped object type, we obtain a string representation, silently using the call to `repr()` by the interactive interpreter. We then proceed to access all three complex number attributes, none of which is defined for our class. Confirm this by looking for `real`, `imag`, and `conjugate` in our class definition . . . they are not there!

The accessing of these attributes is delegated to the object via the `getattr()` method. The final call to `get()` is not delegated because it *is* defined for our object—it returns the actual data object that we wrapped.

Our next example using our wrapping class uses a list. We will create the object, then perform multiple operations, delegating each time to list methods.

```
>>> wrappedList = WrapMe([123, 'foo', 45.67])
>>> wrappedList.append('bar')
>>> wrappedList.append(123)
>>> wrappedList
[123, 'foo', 45.67, 'bar', 123]
>>> wrappedList.index(45.67)
2
>>> wrappedList.count(123)
2
>>> wrappedList.pop()
123
>>> wrappedList
[123, 'foo', 45.67, 'bar']
```

Notice that although we are using a class instance for our examples, they exhibit behavior extremely similar to the data types they wrap. Be aware, however, that only existing attributes are delegated in this code.

Special behaviors that are not in a type's method list will not be accessible since they are not attributes. One example is the slicing operations of lists which are built-in to the type and not available as an attribute like the append() method, for example. Another way of putting it is that the slice operator ([ ]) is part of the sequence type and is not implemented through the __getitem__() special method.

```
>>> wrappedList[3]
Traceback (innermost last):
  File "<stdin>", line 1, in ?
  File "wrapme.py", line 21, in __getattr__
    return getattr(self.data, attr)
AttributeError: __getitem__
```

The AttributeError exception results from the fact that the slice operator invokes the __getitem__() method, and __getitem__() is not defined as a class instance method nor is it a method of list objects. Recall that getattr() is called only when an exhaustive search through an instance's or class's dictionaries fails to find a successful match. As you can see above, the call to getattr() is the one that fails, triggering the exception.

However, we can always cheat by accessing the real object [with our get() method] and its slicing ability instead:

```
>>> realList = wrappedList.get()
>>> realList[3]
'bar'
```

You probably have a good idea now why we implemented the get() method—just for cases like this where we need to obtain access to the original object. We can bypass assigning local variable (realList) by accessing the attribute of the object directly from the access call:

```
>>> wrappedList.get()[3]
'bar'
```

The get() method returns the object, which is then immediately indexed to obtain the sliced subset.

```
>>> f = WrapMe(open('/etc/motd'))
>>> f
<wrapMe.WrapMe object at 0x40215dac>
>>> f.get()
<open file '/etc/motd', mode 'r' at 0x40204ca0>
>>> f.readline()
```

```
'Have a lot of fun...\012'
>>> f.tell()
21
>>> f.seek(0)
>>> print f.readline(),
Have a lot of fun...
>>> f.close()
>>> f.get()
<closed file '/etc/motd', mode 'r' at 0x40204ca0>
```

Once you become familiar with an object's attributes, you begin to understand where certain pieces of information originate and are able to duplicate functionality with your newfound knowledge:

```
>>> print "<%s file %s, mode %s at %x>" % \
... (f.closed and 'closed' or 'open', 'f.name',
'f.mode', id(f.get()))
<closed file '/etc/motd', mode 'r' at 80e95e0>
```

This concludes the sampling of our simple wrapping class. We have only just begun to touch on class customization with type emulation. You will discover that you can an infinite number of enhancements make to further increase the usefulness of your code. One such enhancement is to add timestamps to objects. In the next subsection, we will add another dimension to our wrapping class: time.

Updating Our Simple Wrapping Class

Creation time, modification time, and access time are familiar attributes of files, but nothing says that you cannot add this type of information to objects. After all, certain applications may benefit from these additional pieces of information.

If you are unfamiliar with using these three pieces of chronological data, we will attempt to clarify them. The creation time (or "ctime") is the time of instantiation, the modification time (or "mtime") refers to the time that the core data was updated [accomplished by calling the new set() method], and the access time (or "atime") is the timestamp of when the data value of the object was last retrieved or an attribute was accessed.

Proceeding to updating the class we defined earlier, we create the module twrapme.py, given in Example 13.7.

How did we update the code? Well, first, you will notice the addition of three new methods: gettimeval(), gettimestr(), and set(). We also added lines of code throughout which update the appropriate timestamps based on the type of access performed.

Example 13.7 Wrapping Standard Types (`twrapme.py`)

Class definition that wraps any built-in type, adding time attributes; `get()`, `set()`, *and string representation methods; and delegating all remaining attribute access to those of the standard type.*

```
1    #!/usr/bin/env python
2
3    from time import time, ctime
4
5    class TimedWrapMe(object):
6
7        def __init__(self, obj):
8            self.__data = obj
9            self.__ctime = self.__mtime = \
10               self.__atime = time()
11
12       def get(self):
13           self.__atime = time()
14           return self.__data
15
16       def gettimeval(self, t_type):
17           if not isinstance(t_type, str) or \
18                   t_type[0] not in 'cma':
19               raise TypeError, \
20               "argument of 'c', 'm', or 'a' req'd"
21           return getattr(self, '_%s__%stime' % \
22               (self.__class__.__name__, t_type[0]))
23
24       def gettimestr(self, t_type):
25           return ctime(self.gettimeval(t_type))
26
27       def set(self, obj):
28           self.__data = obj
29           self.__mtime = self.__atime = time()
30
31       def __repr__(self):                    # repr()
32           self.__atime = time()
33           return `self.__data`
34
35       def __str__(self):                     # str()
36           self.__atime = time()
37           return str(self.__data)
38
39       def __getattr__(self, attr):           # delegate
40           self.__atime = time()
41           return getattr(self.__data, attr)
```

The `gettimeval()` method takes a single character argument, either "c," "m," or "a," for create, modify, or access time, respectively, and returns the corresponding time that is stored as a float value. `gettimestr()` simply returns a pretty-printable string version of the time as formatted by the `time.ctime()` function.

Let us take a test drive of our new module. We have already seen how delegation works, so we are going to wrap objects without attributes to highlight the new functionality we just added. In our example, we will wrap an integer, then change it to a string.

```
>>> timeWrappedObj = TimedWrapMe(932)
>>> timeWrappedObj.gettimestr('c')
'Wed Apr 26 20:47:41 2006'
>>> timeWrappedObj.gettimestr('m')
'Wed Apr 26 20:47:41 2006'
>>> timeWrappedObj.gettimestr('a')
'Wed Apr 26 20:47:41 2006'
>>> timeWrappedObj
932
>>> timeWrappedObj.gettimestr('c')
'Wed Apr 26 20:47:41 2006'
>>> timeWrappedObj.gettimestr('m')
'Wed Apr 26 20:47:41 2006'
>>> timeWrappedObj.gettimestr('a')
'Wed Apr 26 20:48:05 2006'
```

You will notice that when an object is first wrapped, the creation, modification, and last access times are all the same. Once we access the object, the access time is updated, but not the others. If we use `set()` to replace the object, the modification and last access times are updated. One final read access to our object concludes our example.

```
>>> timeWrappedObj.set('time is up!')
>>> timeWrappedObj.gettimestr('m')
'Wed Apr 26 20:48:35 2006'
>>> timeWrappedObj
'time is up!'
>>> timeWrappedObj.gettimestr('c')
'Wed Apr 26 20:47:41 2006'
>>> timeWrappedObj.gettimestr('m')
'Wed Apr 26 20:48:35 2006'
>>> timeWrappedObj.gettimestr('a')
'Wed Apr 26 20:48:46 2006'
```

Wrapping a Specific Object with Enhancements

The next example represents a class that wraps a file object. Our class will behave in the exact same manner as a regular file object with one exception: in write mode, only strings in all capital letters are written to the file.

The problem we are trying to solve here is for a case where you are writing text files whose data is to be read by an old mainframe computer. Many older style machines are restricted to uppercase letters for processing, so we want to implement a file object where all text written to the file is automatically converted to uppercase without the programmer's having to worry about it. In fact, the only noticeable difference is that rather than using the `open()` built-in function, a call is made to instantiate the `CapOpen` class. Even the parameters are exactly the same as for `open()`.

Example 13.8 represents that code, written as `capOpen.py`. Let us take a look at an example of how to use this class:

```
>>> f = CapOpen('/tmp/xxx', 'w')
>>> f.write('delegation example\n')
>>> f.write('faye is good\n')
>>> f.write('at delegating\n')
>>> f.close()
>>> f
<closed file '/tmp/xxx', mode 'w' at 12c230>
```

Example 13.8 Wrapping a File Object (`capOpen.py`)

This class extends on the example from one of the Python FAQs, providing a file-like object that customizes the `write()` *method while delegating the rest of the functionality to the file object.*

```
1  #!/usr/bin/env python
2
3  class CapOpen(object):
4      def __init__(self, fn, mode='r', buf=-1):
5          self.file = open(fn, mode, buf)
6
7      def __str__(self):
8          return str(self.file)
9
10     def __repr__(self):
11         return 'self.file'
12
13     def write(self, line):
14         self.file.write(line.upper())
15
16     def __getattr__(self, attr):
17         return getattr(self.file, attr)
```

As you can see, the only call out of the ordinary is the first one to `CapO-pen()` rather than `open()`. All other code is identical to what you would do if you were interacting with a real file object rather than a class instance that behaves like a file object. All attributes other than `write()` have been delegated to the file object. To confirm the success of our code, we load up the file and display its contents. (Note that we can use either `open()` or `CapOpen()`, but chose only `CapOpen()` because we have been working with it here in this example.)

```
>>> f = CapOpen('/tmp/xxx', 'r')
>>> for eachLine in f:
...     print eachLine,
...
DELEGATION EXAMPLE
FAYE IS GOOD
AT DELEGATING
```

13.16 Advanced Features of New-Style Classes (Python 2.2+)

2.2

13.16.1 General Features of New-Style Classes

We have already discussed some of the features tied to new-style classes. With the unification of types and classes, the most significant of these features is the ability to subclass Python data types. One side effect of this is that all of the Python "casting" or conversion built-in functions are now factory functions. When you call them, you are really instantiating an instance of the corresponding type.

The following built-in function, which have been around Python for a while, have been quietly (or perhaps not) converted to factory functions:

- `int()`, `long()`, `float()`, `complex()`
- `str()`, `unicode()`
- `list()`, `tuple()`
- `type()`

In addition, several new ones have been added to round out the posse:

- `basestring()`[1]
- `dict()`
- `bool()`
- `set()`,[2] `frozenset()`[2]
- `object()`
- `classmethod()`
- `staticmethod()`
- `super()`
- `property()`
- `file()`

These class names and factory functions have flexible usage. In addition to creating new objects of those types, they can be used as base classes when subclassing types, and they can now be used with the `isinstance()` built-in function. Using `is instance()` can help replace tired old idioms with one that requires fewer functions calls resulting in cleaner code. For example, to test if an object is an integer, we had to call `type()` twice or import the `types` module and use its attributes; but now we can just use `isinstance()` and even gain in performance:

OLD (not as good):
- **if** type(*obj*) == type(0)...
- **if** type(*obj*) == types.IntType...

BETTER:
- **if** type(*obj*) **is** type(0)...

EVEN BETTER:
- **if** isinstance(*obj*, int)...
- **if** isinstance(*obj*, (int, long))...
- **if** type(*obj*) **is** int...

Keep in mind that although `isinstance()` is flexible, it does not perform an "exact match" comparison—it will also return `True` if *obj* is an instance of the given type *or an instance of a subclass of the given type.* You will still need to use the **is** operator if you want an exact class match.

---

1. New in Python 2.3.
2. New in Python 2.4.

Please review Section 13.12.2 above for a deeper explanation of `isin-stance()` as well as its introduction in Chapter 4 and how these calls evolved along with Python.

13.16.2   `__slots__` Class Attribute

A dictionary is at the heart of all instances. The `__dict__` attribute keeps track of all instance attributes. For example, when you have an instance `inst` with an attribute `foo`, recognize that accessing it with `inst.foo` is the same as doing it with `inst.__dict__['foo']`.

This dictionary takes up a good amount of memory, and if you have a class with very few attributes but a significant number of instances of this object, then you are taking a substantial hit. To combat this, users are now able to use the `__slots__` attribute to substitute for `__dict__`.

Basically, `__slots__` is a class variable consisting of a sequence-like object representing the set of valid identifiers that make up all of an instance's attributes. This can be a list, tuple, or iterable. It can also be a single string identifying the single attribute that an instance can have. Any attempt to create an instance attribute with a name not in `__slots__` will result in an `AttributeError` exception:

```
class SlottedClass(object):
    __slots__ = ('foo', 'bar')
>>> c = SlottedClass()
>>>
>>> c.foo = 42
>>> c.xxx = "don't think so"
Traceback (most recent call last):
  File "<stdin>", line 1, in ?
AttributeError: 'SlottedClass' object has no attribute
'xxx'
```

The primary reason for this feature is the conservation of memory. A side effect is a type of security preventing users from adding instances attributes dynamically in an ad hoc manner. A class defined with a `__slots__` attribute will not have a `__dict__` (unless you add `'__dict__'` as an element of `__slots__`). For more information on `__slots__`, see the Data Model chapter of the Python (Language) Reference Manual.

13.16.3   `__getattribute__()` Special Method

Python classes have a special method named `__getattr__()`, which is called only when an attribute cannot be found in an instance's `__dict__` or its class (class's __dict__), or ancestor class (its __dict__). One place where we saw __getattr__() used was for implementing delegation.

The problem that many users encountered was that they wanted a certain function to execute for every attribute access, not just when one cannot be found. This is where __getattribute__() comes in. It works just like __getattr__() except that it is *always* called when an attribute is accessed, not just when it cannot be found.

If a class has both __getattribute__() and __getattr__() defined, the latter will not be called unless explicitly called from __getattribute__() or if __getattribute__() raises AttributeError.

Be very careful if you are going to access attributes in here... attributes of this class or an ancestor. If you cause __getattribute__() to somehow call __getattribute__() again, you will have infinite recursion. To avoid infinite recursion using this method, you should always call an ancestor class method that shares the same name in order to access any attributes it needs safely; for example, super(*obj*, self).__getattribute__(*attr*). This special method is only valid with new-style classes. As with __slots__, you can get more information on __getattribute__() by referring to the Data Model chapter of the Python (Language) Reference Manual.

13.16.4 Descriptors

Descriptors are one of the keys behind Python's new-style classes. They provide a powerful API to object attributes. You can think of a descriptor as an agent that presents object attributes. Depending on which situation you encounter when you need an attribute, you can get to it via its descriptor (if there is one for it) or in the normal way (dotted attribute notation).

If there is an agent for your object and it has a "get" attribute (really spelled __get__), it is invoked, and you get back all you need to access the object in question. The same thing applies if you are attempting to assign a value to an object with a descriptor (set) or removing an attribute (delete).

__get__(), __set__(), __delete__() Special Methods

Strictly speaking, a descriptor is really any (new-style) class that implements at least one of three special methods that serve as the *descriptor protocol*: __get__(), __set__(), and __delete__(). As mentioned just above, __get__() is used to get the value of an attribute, __set__() is used to assign a value to an attribute, and __delete__() is called when an attribute is explicitly removed using the **del** statement (or rather, its reference count decremented). Of the three, the latter is rarely implemented.

Also, not all descriptors implement the __set__() method either. These are referred to as *method descriptors*, or more accurately, *non-data descriptors*. Those that override both __get__() and __set__() are called *data descriptors*, and they are more powerful than non-data descriptors.

The signatures for __get__(), __set__(), and __delete__() look like this:

- **def** __get__(self, obj, typ=None) ⇒ value
- **def** __set__(self, obj, val) ⇒ None
- **def** __delete__(self, obj) ⇒ None

When you want to use an agent for an attribute, you install it as a class attribute, and let the agent handle all the dirty work. Anytime you try to do something to an attribute with that name, you will get the descriptor that proxies all functionality. We covered wrapping in the previous section. This is just more wrapping going on. Instead of just delegating everything to objects in your class, we are delegating slightly more complex attribute access here.

__getattribute__() Special Method (again)

Ordering matters when using descriptors, and certain aspects have precedence over others. The heart of the entire system is __getattribute__() since that special method is called for every attribute instance. It is the one that finds a class attribute or an agent to call on your behalf to access an attribute, etc.

Reviewing the signatures just above, if __get__() is called for an instance, the object is passed in and perhaps a type or class. For example, given a class X and an instance x, x.foo is translated by __getattribute__() to:

```
type(x).__dict__['foo'].__get__(x, type(x))
```

If __get__() is called for a class, then None is passed in as the object (which would be self for an instance):

```
X.__dict__['foo'].__get__(None, X)
```

Finally, if super() is called, for example given Y as a subclass of X, then super(Y, obj).foo looks in obj.__class__.__mro__ for the class right next to Y going up the tree to find class X, and then calls:

```
X.__dict__['foo'].__get__(obj, X)
```

Then it is up to *that* descriptor to return the desired object.

Precedence

The way __getattribute__() works needs to be covered, as it was implemented to behave in a very specific way. Thus it is very important to recognize this ordering:

- Class attributes
- Data descriptors
- Instance attributes
- Non-data descriptors
- Defaulting to __getattr__()

A descriptor is a class attribute, so all class attributes have the highest priority. You can even replace a descriptor by simply reassigning its original reference to other objects. They are followed closely behind by descriptors with __get__() and __set__() implemented. If you have an agent, it will do all your work for you!

Otherwise, it should just default to the local object's __dict__, meaning that it will be an instance attribute. The non-data descriptors come next. This may sound surprising because on first glance, one would think that these should be higher up in the food chain than instance attributes, but that is not the case. The purpose of non-data descriptors is only to provide a value if one is not already part of an instance, sort of how __getattr__() is only called if an attribute cannot be found in an instance's __dict__!

Speaking of __getattr__(), if no non-data descriptor is found, then __getattribute__() raises an AttributeError, and that in turn causes __getattr__() to be invoked as the last stand before AttributeError is raised to the user.

Descriptor Examples

Let us start with a very boring example... a descriptor that just discards any attempt to retrieve or set a value from and to an attribute, respectively. Actually, all of the examples here just ignore all requests, but they are incremental, and we hope that you can figure out a little more about descriptors for each one:

```
class DevNull1(object):
    def __get__(self, obj, typ=None):
        pass
    def __set__(self, obj, val):
        pass
```

We create a class that uses this descriptor and try to assign something to it as well as display its value:

```
>>> class C1(object):
...      foo = DevNull1()
...
>>> c1 = C1()
>>> c1.foo = 'bar'
>>> print 'c1.foo contains:', c1.foo
c1.foo contains: None
```

That was not too terribly exciting... how about one where the descriptor methods at least give some output to show what is going on?

```
class DevNull2(object):
    def __get__(self, obj, typ=None):
        print 'Accessing attribute... ignoring'
    def __set__(self, obj, val):
        print 'Attempt to assign %r... ignoring' % (val)
```

Now let us see this one in action:

```
>>> class C2(object):
...    foo = DevNull2()
...
>>> c2 = C2()
>>> c2.foo = 'bar'
Attempt to assign 'bar'... ignoring
>>> x = c2.foo
Accessing attribute... ignoring
>>> print 'c2.foo contains:', x
c2.foo contains: None
```

For our final example, let us add a placeholder in our descriptor class that holds some useful information about the descriptor:

```
class DevNull3(object):
    def __init__(self, name=None):
        self.name = name
    def __get__(self, obj, typ=None):
        print 'Accessing [%s]... ignoring' %
            self.name)
    def __set__(self, obj, val):
        print 'Assigning %r to [%s]... ignoring' %
            val, self.name)
```

In the output below, we show you the importance of the hierarchy mentioned above, especially where we state that a full data descriptor has precedence over an instance attribute:

```
>>> class C3(object):
...        foo = DevNull3('foo')
...
>>> c3 = C3()
>>> c3.foo = 'bar'
Assigning 'bar' to [foo]... ignoring
>>> x = c3.foo
Accessing [foo]... ignoring
>>> print 'c3.foo contains:', x
c3.foo contains: None
>>> print 'Let us try to sneak it into c3 instance...'
Let us try to sneak it into c3 instance...
>>> c3.__dict__['foo'] = 'bar'
>>> x = c3.foo
Accessing [foo]... ignoring
>>> print 'c3.foo contains:', x
c3.foo contains: None
>>> print "c3.__dict__['foo'] contains: %r" % \
          c3.__dict__['foo'], "... why?!?"
c3.__dict__['foo'] contains: 'bar' ... why?!?
```

Notice how we were able to sneak in an attribute to our instance. We were able to assign the string "bar" to c3.foo, but because the data descriptor is more important, it overrides or effectively hides our assignment.

Likewise, because instance attributes have a higher precedence than non-data attributes, you can also hide such a descriptor, just as you can hide a class attribute, by assigning an instance attribute with the same name:

```
>>> class FooFoo(object):
...        def foo(self):
...                print 'Very important foo() method.'
...
>>>
>>> bar = FooFoo()
>>> bar.foo()
Very important foo() method.
>>>
>>> bar.foo = 'It is no longer here.'
>>> bar.foo
'It is no longer here.'
>>>
>>> del bar.foo
>>> bar.foo()
Very important foo() method.
```

This was a pretty transparent example because we called it as a function, then accessed it as a string, but we could have used another function and kept the same calling mechanism, too:

```
>>> def barBar():
...         print 'foo() hidden by barBar()'
...
>>> bar.foo = barBar
>>> bar.foo()
foo() hidden by barBar()
>>>
>>> del bar.foo
>>> bar.foo()
Very important foo() method.
```

The point was to emphasize that because functions are non-data descriptors, instance attributes are ranked higher, and we can shadow any non-data descriptor simply by assigning an object to the instance (of the same name).

Our final example does a little bit more. It is a crude attempt at using the filesystem as a means of storing the contents of an attribute.

Lines 1–10

After the usual setup, we create our descriptor class with a class attribute (`saved`) that keeps track of all attributes with descriptor access. When a descriptor is created, it registers and saves the name of the attribute (passed in from the user).

Lines 12–26

When fetching an attribute, we need to ensure that users do not use it before they have even assigned a value to it. If it passes that test, then we attempt to open the pickle file to read in the saved value. An exception is raised if somehow the file cannot be opened, either because it was erased (or never created), or if it was corrupted or somehow cannot be unserialized by the `pickle` module.

Lines 28–38

Saving the attribute takes several steps: open the pickle file for write (either creating it for the first time or wiping out one that was already there), serializing the object to disk, and registering the name so users can retrieve the value. An exception is thrown if the object cannot be pickled. Note that if you are using Python 2.5 you can never merge the **try-except** and **try finally** statements (lines 30–38) together.

Example 13.9   Using a File to Store an Attribute (`descr.py`)

This class is crude but represents an interesting use of descriptors—being able to store the contents of an attribute on the filesystem.

```
1    #!/usr/bin/env python
2
3    import os
4    import pickle
5
6    class FileDescr(object):
7        saved = []
8
9        def __init__(self, name=None):
10           self.name = name
11
12       def __get__(self, obj, typ=None):
13           if self.name not in FileDescr.saved:
14               raise AttributeError, \
15                   "%r used before assignment" % self.name
16
17           try:
18               f = open(self.name, 'r')
19               val = pickle.load(f)
20               f.close()
21               return val
22           except (pickle.UnpicklingError, IOError,
23                   EOFError, AttributeError,
24                   ImportError, IndexError), e:
25               raise AttributeError, \
26                   "could not read %r: %s" % self.name
27
28       def __set__(self, obj, val):
29           f = open(self.name, 'w')
30           try:
31               try:
32                   pickle.dump(val, f)
33                   FileDescr.saved.append(self.name)
34               except (TypeError, pickle.PicklingError), e:
35                   raise AttributeError, \
36                       "could not pickle %r" % self.name
37           finally:
38               f.close()
39
40       def __delete__(self, obj):
41           try:
42               os.unlink(self.name)
43               FileDescr.saved.remove(self.name)
44           except (OSError, ValueError), e:
45               pass
```

Lines 40–45

Finally, if the attribute is explicitly deleted, the file is removed, and the name unregistered.

Here is some sample usage of this class:

```
>>> class MyFileVarClass(object):
...        foo = FileDescr('foo')
...        bar = FileDescr('bar')
...
>>> fvc = MyFileVarClass()
>>> print fvc.foo
Traceback (most recent call last):
  File "<stdin>", line 1, in ?
  File "descr.py", line 14, in __get__
    raise AttributeError, \
AttributeError: 'foo' used before assignment
>>>
>>> fvc.foo = 42
>>> fvc.bar = 'leanna'
>>>
>>> print fvc.foo, fvc.bar
42 leanna
>>>
>>> del fvc.foo
>>> print fvc.foo, fvc.bar
Traceback (most recent call last):
  File "<stdin>", line 1, in ?
  File "descr.py", line 14, in __get__
    raise AttributeError, \
AttributeError: 'foo' used before assignment
>>>
>>> fvc.foo = __builtins__
Traceback (most recent call last):
  File "<stdin>", line 1, in ?
  File "descr.py", line 35, in __set__
    raise AttributeError, \
AttributeError: could not pickle 'foo'
```

Attribute access appears normal, and the programmer cannot really tell that an object is pickled and stored to the filesystem (except in the last example where we tried to pickle a module, a no-no). We also put in a handler for cases when the pickle file gets corrupted. This is also the first descriptor where we have implemented __delete__().

One thing to keep in mind with all of our examples is that we did not use the instance obj at all. Do not confuse obj with self as the latter is the instance of the descriptor, not the instance of the original class.

Descriptor Summary

Believe it or not, you have already seen descriptors at work. Static methods, class methods, properties (see next section below), and even functions themselves are all descriptors. Think about this: functions are very generic objects in Python. There are built-in ones, user-defined ones, methods defined in classes, static methods, and class methods. Those are all examples of functions. The only difference between them is how they are called.

Functions are normally unbound. So are static methods, even though they are defined in classes. But methods need to be bound to an instance, and class methods need to be bound to a class, right? The descriptor for a function object knows all this, so depending on what type of function it is, a descriptor can "wrap up" a function object along with whatever it needs to be bound to, if applicable, and then returns that back to the caller. The way it works is that the function itself is a descriptor, and its __get__() method is what puts together the callable that it returns for you. It is quite an amazing generality, which does not break the way Python has been working all this time!

Properties and `property()` Built-in Function

Properties are a very useful and specific type of descriptor. They were meant to handle all accesses to instance attributes in a similar manner that we described for descriptors, above. When you access an instance attribute "normally," you use the dotted-attribute notation. You were updating an instance's __dict__ attribute.

With properties, although your *usage* resembles normal attribute access, the actual *implementation* of such access uses function (or method) calls. In earlier versions of Python, as seen earlier this chapter, you could use __getattr__() and __setattr__() to play with attributes in general. The problem is that all attribute access goes through those special methods (and __getattribute__()), but with properties, you can give a property specific functions to execute for getting, setting, and deleting instance attributes, so you no longer have to use those other special methods (which became quite large actually if you had many instance attributes you were trying to manage).

The `property()` built-in function can take up to four arguments. Its signature is:

```
property(fget=None, fset=None, fdel=None, doc=None)
```

Keep in mind that although normal usage of `property()` is within a class definition where the functions passed in are actually methods, `property()`

can accept functions. In fact, at the time that `property()` is called when a class is declared, those methods are unbound and thus really are functions!

Here is a simple example that creates a read-only integer attribute but hides it within the class by barely encrypting it using the bitwise XOR operator:

```
class ProtectAndHideX(object):
    def __init__(self, x):
        assert isinstance(x, int), \
            '"x" must be an integer!'
        self.__x = ~x

    def get_x(self):
        return ~self.__x

    x = property(get_x)
```

If we try it out, we see that it saves the first value we give it but does not allow us to set it again:

```
>>> inst = ProtectAndHideX('foo')
Traceback (most recent call last):
  File "<stdin>", line 1, in ?
  File "prop.py", line 5, in __init__
    assert isinstance(x, int), \
AssertionError: "x" must be an integer!
>>> inst = ProtectAndHideX(10)
>>> print 'inst.x =', inst.x
inst.x = 10
>>> inst.x = 20
Traceback (most recent call last):
  File "<stdin>", line 1, in ?
AttributeError: can't set attribute
```

Here is another example, but with a setter:

```
class HideX(object):
    def __init__(self, x):
        self.x = x

    def get_x(self):
        return ~self.__x

    def set_x(self, x):
        assert isinstance(x, int), \
            '"x" must be an integer!'
        self.__x = ~x

    x = property(get_x, set_x)
```

Here is the output of this example:

```
>>> inst = HideX(20)
>>> print inst.x
20
>>> inst.x = 30
>>> print inst.x
30
```

This property works because by the time the constructor is called to set the initial value of x, the getter already saves it as ~x to self.__x.

You can even stick in a documentation string for your attribute, as shown here in this next example:

```
from math import pi

def get_pi(dummy):
    return pi

class PI(object):
    pi = property(get_pi, doc='Constant "pi"')
```

Here we are using a function instead of a method for our property, just to show it can be done. When it is called, however, we have to keep in mind that self is going to be passed in as the first (and only) argument, so we still need to have a dummy variable to discard it. Here is the corresponding output:

```
>>> inst = PI()
>>> inst.pi
3.1415926535897931
>>> print PI.pi.__doc__
Constant "pi"
```

Can you see how properties take your functions (fget, fset, and fdel) and map them as descriptor methods __get__(), __set__(), and __delete__()? You did not have to create a descriptor class and define these callables as methods of your descriptor class. You just created functions (or methods) and gave them all to property().

One drawback to creating your descriptor methods inside your class definition is that it clutters up the class namespace. Not only that, but isn't the point of having a property to control access to an attribute? But this control does not exist if they are not forced to use the property. Our second example does not enforce this because it allows access to our property methods (since they are part of the class definition):

```
>>> inst.set_x(40)          # can we require inst.x = 40?
>>> print inst.x
40
```

A clever idiom in a recipe in the ActiveState Programmer Network Python Cookbook (http://aspn.activestate.com/ASPN/Cookbook/Python/Recipe/205183) solves both of these problems by:

- "Borrowing" a function's namespace,
- Creating the methods as inner functions intentionally named as (keyword) arguments to `property()`,
- Returning all the (function/method) names and corresponding objects in a dictionary (via `locals()`),
- Feeding it directly to `property()`, and
- Blowing away that temporary namespace

There is no method clutter in the class's namespace because the methods were defined as inner functions in someone else's namespace. The user has no access to the methods because the namespace in which they were defined was destroyed (by going out-of-scope), thus they are compelled to use the property as that is now the one and only way for them to access the attribute. Here is our modified class inspired by the recipe:

```python
class HideX(object):
    def __init__(self, x):
        self.x = x

    @property
    def x():
        def fget(self):
            return ~self.__x

        def fset(self, x):
            assert isinstance(x, int), \
                '"x" must be an integer!'
            self.__x = ~x

        return locals()
```

Our code works exactly as before, but there two big differences: (1) the namespace for the class is much smaller and consists (only) of [`'__doc__'`, `'__init__'`, `'__module__'`, `'x'`], and (2), the user can no longer use `inst.set_x(40)` to set the attribute... they have to use `init.x = 40`. We also use a function decorator (`@property`) to reassign x from a function to a property object. Since decorators were introduced in Python 2.4, those of you using 2.2.x or 2.3.x need to replace the decorator with the following assignment after the `x()` function declaration with `x = property(**x())`.

13.16.5 Metaclasses and __metaclass__

What Are Metaclasses?

Metaclasses are probably the most mind-bending feature that was added with new-style classes. Metaclasses are classes that let you define how certain classes can be constructed, basically giving you a level of control over how classes are created. (You do not even need to think at the instance level.) They have been talked about since before the days of Python 1.5 (when many minds were bent), but they are finally a reality.

Basically, you can think of a metaclass as the class of a class, or rather, a class whose instances are other classes. Believe it or not, whenever you create a class now, you are actually employing the default metaclass, which is a (or rather, *the*) type object. (If classic classes are used, the metaclasses for those are types.ClassType.) Take any class and call type() on it, and you will see what it is an instance of:

```
class C(object):
    pass

class CC:
    pass

>>> type(C)
<type 'type'>
>>>
>>> type(CC)
<type 'classobj'>
>>>
>>> import types
>>> type(CC) is types.ClassType
True
```

When Are Metaclasses Used?

Metaclasses are always used when creating classes. When executing a class definition, the interpreter has to know the correct metaclass to use. It will look for a class attribute named __metaclass__ first, and if it is there, it will use the class that is assigned to that attribute as the metaclass.

If that attribute has not been defined, it will go up and search an ancestor class for __metaclass__. All new-style classes must inherit from object or type if there are no other base classes (type (object) is type anyway).

If that is not found, it checks for a global variable named __metaclass__ and uses it if it exists. Otherwise, the class is a classic class, and types.ClassType is used as the metaclass. (Note you can do some trickery here... if you define a classic class and set __metaclass__ = type, you have parlayed it into a new-style class!)

Any time a class declaration is executed, the correct (and usually default) metaclass is determined, and that metaclass (always) passes three arguments (to its constructor): the class name, the tuple of base classes to inherit from, and the (class) attribute dictionary.

Who Are Metaclass Users?

To many, the subject of metaclasses belongs in the realm of the theoretical or pure object-oriented thinking and has no place in everyday programming. To some extent that is true; however, the most important thing to keep in mind is that the end consumers of metaclasses are programmers themselves, not application users. You can define metaclasses that "force" programmers to implement solution classes in specific ways, which can either simplify their work or make them program to a target specification.

When Are Metaclasses Created?

Metaclasses are created for the situations described just above, when you want to change the default behavior of how classes can and are created. Most Python users will not be creating or explicitly using metaclasses. The standard behavior in creating new-style or classic classes is to just take the default behavior by using the system-supplied metaclasses.

In most cases, users will not even be aware that metaclasses are providing the templated default behavior of class creation (or metaclass instantiation). Although metaclasses will not be created on a regular basis, let us take a look at a simple example below. (More examples can be found in the documents listed at the end of this subsection.)

Metaclass Example 1

The first example of metaclasses we are presenting here is (hopefully) very simple. It does not do anything at all except timestamp when a class is created using the metaclass. (As you know now, it happens when the class is created.)

Take a look at the following script. It contains print statements scattered throughout so that you can track the events as they occur:

```python
#!/usr/bin/env python

from time import ctime

print '*** Welcome to Metaclasses!'
print '\tMetaclass declaration first.'

class MetaC(type):
        def __init__(cls, name, bases, attrd):
                super(MetaC, cls).__init__(name, bases, attrd)
                print '*** Created class %r at: %s' % (
                        name, ctime())

print '\tClass "Foo" declaration next.'

class Foo(object):
        __metaclass__ = MetaC
        def __init__(self):
                print '*** Instantiated class %r at: %s' % (
                        self.__class__.__name__, ctime())

print '\tClass "Foo" instantiation next.'
f = Foo()
print '\tDONE'
```

If we run this script, we get the following output:

```
*** Welcome to Metaclasses!
    Metaclass declaration first.
    Class "Foo" declaration next.
*** Created class 'Foo' at: Tue May 16 14:25:53 2006
    Class "Foo" instantiation next.
*** Instantiated class 'Foo' at: Tue May 16 14:25:53 2006
DONE
```

Once you are comfortable with the fact that a class declaration actually causes some work to be done, then you are well under way.

Metaclass Example 2

In this second example, we are going to create a metaclass that forces programmers to supply a __str__() method in their classes so that their users can see something more useful than the generic Python object string (<object object at id>) we saw earlier in this chapter.

Our metaclass will also (strongly) suggest users override __repr__() if they have not done that either, but it is only a warning. Not implementing __str__() will result in a TypeError exception being thrown, forcing users to create a special method with that name. Here is the code for the metaclass:

```
from warnings import warn

class ReqStrSugRepr(type):

    def __init__(cls, name, bases, attrd):
        super(ReqStrSugRepr, cls).__init__(
            name, bases, attrd)

        if '__str__' not in attrd:
            raise TypeError(
    "Class requires overriding of __str__()")

        if '__repr__' not in attrd:
            warn(
    'Class suggests overriding of __repr__()\n',
                stacklevel=3)
```

We will create three example classes that use our metaclass, one that over-rides both __str__() and __repr__() special methods (Foo), one that only implements the __str__() special method (Bar), and one that implements neither (FooBar), an error situation. The full application is presented here as Example 13.10.

Running this script, we get the following output:

```
$ python meta.py
*** Defined ReqStrSugRepr (meta)class

*** Defined Foo class

sys:1: UserWarning: Class suggests overriding of
__repr__()

*** Defined Bar class

Traceback (most recent call last):
  File "meta.py", line 43, in ?
    class FooBar(object):
  File "meta.py", line 12, in __init__
    raise TypeError(
TypeError: Class requires overriding of __str__()
```

Example 13.10 Metaclass Example (`meta.py`)

*This module features a metaclass and three classes under the jurisdiction of the metaclass. After each class is created, you will see a **print** statement.*

```python
1   #!/usr/bin/env python
2
3   from warnings import warn
4
5   class ReqStrSugRepr(type):
6
7       def __init__(cls, name, bases, attrd):
8           super(ReqStrSugRepr, cls).__init__(
9               name, bases, attrd)
10
11          if '__str__' not in attrd:
12              raise TypeError(
13              "Class requires overriding of __str__()")
14
15          if '__repr__' not in attrd:
16              warn(
17              'Class suggests overriding of __repr__()\n',
18                  stacklevel=3)
19
20  print '*** Defined ReqStrSugRepr (meta)class\n'
21
22  class Foo(object):
23      __metaclass__ = ReqStrSugRepr
24
25      def __str__(self):
26          return 'Instance of class:', \
27              self.__class__.__name__
28
29      def __repr__(self):
30          return self.__class__.__name__
31
32  print '*** Defined Foo class\n'
33
34  class Bar(object):
35      __metaclass__ = ReqStrSugRepr
36
37      def __str__(self):
38          return 'Instance of class:', \
39              self.__class__.__name__
40
41  print '*** Defined Bar class\n'
42
43  class FooBar(object):
44      __metaclass__ = ReqStrSugRepr
45
46  print '*** Defined FooBar class\n'
```

Note how we got past declaring `Foo` without incident. With `Bar`, we received the warning for not implementing `__repr__()`, and `FooBar` did not pass the security check, hence the reason why the application failed to make it to the (final) **print** statement. Another important thing to note is that we did not even create any instances of the test classes... they are not even part of our picture. However, keep in mind that those classes themselves are instances of our metaclass. This is but one example of the power of metaclasses.

There are many more examples online and in the Python documentation, PEPs 252 and 253, the What's New in Python 2.2 document, and Guido van Rossum's essay entitled, "Unifying Types and Classes in Python 2.2." You can find a link to that document from the main Python release page for 2.2.3.

13.17 Related Modules and Documentation

Python has several classic classes that extend the existing functionality of the core language that we have described in this chapter. These classes were provided as a convenience before it was possible to subclass Python data types.

The `User*` modules are like precooked meals, ready to eat. We mentioned how classes have special methods that, if implemented, can customize classes so that when wrapped around a standard type, they can give instances type-like qualities.

`UserList` and `UserDict`, along with the new `UserString` (introduced in Python 1.6), represent modules that define classes that act as wrappers around list, dictionary, and string objects, respectively. The primary objective of these modules is to provide the desired functionality for you so that you do not have to implement them yourself, and to serve as base classes that are appropriate for subclassing and further customization. Python already provides an abundance of useful built-in types, but the added ability to perform "build it yourself" typing makes it an even more powerful language.

In Chapter 4, we introduced Python's standard as well as other built-in types. The `types` module is a great place to learn more about Python's types as well as those that are beyond the scope of this text. The `types` module also defines type objects that can be used to make comparisons. (Such comparisons are popular in Python because they do not support method overloading—this keeps the language simple, yet there are tools that add functionality to a part of the language where it had appeared to be lacking.)

The following piece of code checks to see if the object `data` is passed into the `foo` function as an integer or string, and does not allow any other type (raises an exception):

```
def foo(data):
    if isinstance(data, int):
        print 'you entered an integer'
    elif isinstance(data, str):
        print 'you entered a string'
    else:
        raise TypeError, 'only integers or strings!'
```

The last related module is the `operator` module. This module provides functional versions of most of Python's standard operators. There may be occasions where this type of interface proves more versatile than hard-coding use of the standard operators.

Given below is one example. As you look through the code, imagine the extra lines of code that would have been required if individual operators had been part of the implementation:

```
>>> from operator import *          # import all operators
>>> vec1 = [12, 24]
>>> vec2 = [2, 3, 4]
>>> opvec = (add, sub, mul, div)    # using +, -, *, /
>>> for eachOp in opvec:            # loop thru operators
...         for i in vec1:
...             for j in vec2:
...                 print '%s(%d, %d) = %d' % \
...                     (eachOp.__name__, i, j, eachOp(i, j))
...
add(12, 2) = 14
add(12, 3) = 15
add(12, 4) = 16
add(24, 2) = 26
add(24, 3) = 27
add(24, 4) = 28
sub(12, 2) = 10
sub(12, 3) = 9
sub(12, 4) = 8
sub(24, 2) = 22
sub(24, 3) = 21
sub(24, 4) = 20
mul(12, 2) = 24
mul(12, 3) = 36
```

```
mul(12, 4) = 48
mul(24, 2) = 48
mul(24, 3) = 72
mul(24, 4) = 96
div(12, 2) = 6
div(12, 3) = 4
div(12, 4) = 3
div(24, 2) = 12
div(24, 3) = 8
div(24, 4) = 6
```

The code snippet above defines three vectors, two containing operands and the last representing the set of operations the programmer wants to perform on each pair of available operands. The outermost loop iterates through each operation while the inner pair of loops creates every possible combination of ordered pairs from elements of each operand vector. Finally, the **print** statement simply applies the current operator with the given arguments.

A list of the modules we described above is given in Table 13.5.

There are plenty of class, and object-oriented, programming-related questions in the Python FAQ. It makes excellent supplementary material to the Python Library and Language Reference manual. For new-style classes, see PEPs 252 and 253, and the related documents from the Python 2.2 release.

Table 13.5 Class Related Modules

Module	Description
UserList	Provides a class wrapper around list objects
UserDict	Provides a class wrapper around dictionary objects
UserString[a]	Provides a class wrapper around string objects; also included is a MutableString subclass, which provides that kind of functionality, if so desired
types	Defines names for all Python object types as used by the standard Python interpreter
operator	Functional interface to the standard operators

a. New in Python 1.6.

13.18 Exercises

13–1.   *Programming.* Name some benefits of object-oriented programming over older forms of programming.

13–2.   *Functions versus Methods.* What are the differences between functions and methods?

13–3.   *Customizing Classes.* Create a class to format floating point values to monetary amounts. In this exercise, we will use United States currency, but feel free to implement your own.

Preliminary work: Create a function called `dollarize()` which takes a floating point value and returns that value as a string properly formatted with symbols and rounded to obtain a financial amount. For example: `dollarize(1234567.8901)` ⟹ '$1,234,567.89. The `dollarize()` function should allow for commas, such as 1,000,000, and dollar signs. Any negative sign should appear to the *left* of the dollar sign. Once you have completed this task, then you are ready to convert it into a useful class called `MoneyFmt`.

The `MoneyFmt` class contains a single data value, the monetary amount, and has five methods (feel free to create your own outside of this exercise). The `__init__()` constructor method initializes the data value, the `update()` method replaces the data value with a new one, the `__nonzero__()` method is Boolean, returning `True` if the data value is non-zero, the `__repr__()` method returns the amount as a float, and the `__str__()` method displays the value in the string-formatted manner that `dollarize()` does.

(a) Fill in the code to the `update()` method so that it will update the data value.

(b) Use the work you completed for `dollarize()` to fill in the code for the `__str__()` method.

(c) Fix the bug in the `__nonzero__()` method, which currently thinks that any value less than one, i.e., fifty cents ($0.50), has a false value.

(d) Extra credit: Allow the user to optionally specify an argument indicating the desire to see less-than and greater-than pairs for negative values rather than the negative sign. The default argument should use the standard negative sign.

Example 13.11 Money Formatter (moneyfmt.py)

String format class designed to "wrap" floating point values to appear as monetary amounts with the appropriate symbols.

```
1   #!/usr/bin/env python
2
3   class MoneyFmt(object):
4       def __init__(self, value=0.0): # constructor
5           self.value = float(value)
6
7       def update(self, value=None):  # allow updates
8           ###
9           ### (a) complete this function
10          ###
11
12      def __repr__(self):            # display as a float
13          return 'self.value'
14
15      def __str__(self):             # formatted display
16          val = ''
17
18          ###
19          ### (b) complete this function... do NOT
20          ###     forget about negative numbers!!
21          ###
22
23          return val
24
25      def __nonzero__(self):         # boolean test
26          ###
27          ### (c) find and fix the bug
28          ###
29
30          return int(self.value)
```

You will find the code skeleton for moneyfmt.py presented as Example 13.11. You will find a fully documented (yet incomplete) version of moneyfmt.py on the Web site. If we were to import the completed class within the interpreter, execution should behave similar to the following:

```
>>> import moneyfmt
>>>
>>> cash = moneyfmt.MoneyFmt(123.45)
>>> cash
123.45
>>> print cash
```

```
$123.45
>>>
>>> cash.update(100000.4567)
>>> cash
100000.4567
>>> print cash
$100,000.46
>>>
>>> cash.update(-0.3)
>>> cash
-0.3
>>> print cash
-$0.30
>>> repr(cash)
'-0.3'
>>> 'cash'
'-0.3'
>>> str(cash)
'-$0.30'
```

13–4. *User Registration.* Create a user database (login, password, and last login timestamp) class (see problems 7–5 and 9–12) that manages a system requiring users to log in before access to resources is allowed. This database class manages its users, loading any previously saved user information on instantiation and providing accessor functions to add or update database information. If updated, the database will save the new information to disk as part of its deallocation (see __del__()).

13–5. *Geometry.* Create a `Point` class that consists of an ordered pair (x, y) representing a point's location on the X and Y axes. X and Y coordinates are passed to the constructor on instantiation and default to the origin for any missing coordinate.

13–6. *Geometry.* Create a line/line segment class that has length and slope behaviors in addition to the main data attributes: a pair of points (see previous problem). You should override the __repr__() method (and __str__(), if you want) so that the string representing a line (or line segment) is a pair of tuples, ((x1, y1), (x2, y2)). Summary:

__repr__	Display points as pair of tuples
length	Return length of line segment—do not use "len" since that is supposed to be an integer
slope	Return slope of line segment (or None if applicable)

13–7. *Date Class*. Provide an interface to a time module where users can request dates in a few (given) date formats such as "MM/DD/YY," "MM/DD/YYYY," "DD/MM/YY," "DD/MM/YYYY," "Mon DD, YYYY," or the standard Unix date of "Day Mon DD, HH:MM:SS YYYY." Your class should maintain a single value of date and create an instance with the given time. If not given, default to the current time at execution. Additional methods:

update()　　changes the data value to reflect time given or current time as a default

display()　　takes format indicator and displays date in requested format:

```
'MDY'  ⟹ MM/DD/YY
'MDYY' ⟹ MM/DD/YYYY
'DMY'  ⟹ DD/MM/YY
'DMYY' ⟹ DD/MM/YYYY
'MODYY' ⟹ Mon DD, YYYY
```

If no format is given, default to system/ctime() format. Extra Credit: Merge the use of this class intoExercise 6–15.

13–8. *Stack Class*. A stack is a data structure with last-in-first-out (LIFO) characteristics. Think of a stack of cafeteria trays. The first one in the spring-loaded device is the last one out, and the last one in is the first one out. Your class will have the expected push() (add an item to the stack) and pop() (remove an item from the stack) methods. Add an isempty() Boolean method that returns True if the stack is empty and False otherwise, and a peek() method that returns the item at the top of the stack without popping it off.

　　Note that if you are using a list to implement your stacks, the pop() method is already available as of Python 1.5.2. Create your new class so that it contains code to detect if the pop() method is available. If so, call the built-in one; otherwise, it should execute your implementation of pop(). You should probably use a list object; if you do, do not worry about implementing any list functionality (i.e., slicing). Just make sure that your Stack class can perform both of the operations above correctly. You may subclass a real list object or come up with your own list-like object, as in Example 6.2.

13–9.   *Queue Class.* A queue is a data structure that has first-in-first-out (FIFO) characteristics. A queue is like a line where items are removed from the front and added to the rear. The class should support the following methods:

enqueue()   adds a new element to the end of a list

dequeue()   returns the first element and removes it from the list.

See the previous problem and Example 6.3 for motivation.

13–10.   *Stacks and Queues.* Write a class which defines a data structure that can behave as both a queue (FIFO) or a stack (LIFO), somewhat similar in nature to arrays in PERL. There are four methods that should be implemented:

shift()   returns the first element and removes it from the list, similar to the earlier dequeue() function

unshift()   "pushes" a new element to the front or head of the list

push()   adds a new element to the end of a list, similar to the enqueue() and push() methods from previous problems

pop()   returns the last element and removes it from the list; it works exactly the same way as pop() from before

See also Exercises 13–8 and 13–9.

13–11.   *Electronic Commerce.* You need to create the foundations of an e-commerce engine for a B2C (business-to-consumer) retailer. You need to have a class for a customer called User, a class for items in inventory called Item, and a shopping cart class called Cart. Items go in Carts, and Users can have multiple Carts. Also, multiple items can go into Carts, including more than one of any single item.

13–12.   *Chat Rooms.* You have been pretty disappointed at the current quality of chat room applications and vow to create your own, start up a new Internet company, obtain venture capital funding, integrate advertisement into your chat program, quintuple revenues in a six-month period, go public, and retire. However, none of this will happen if you do not have a pretty cool chat application.

There are three classes you will need: a `Message` class containing a message string and any additional information such as broadcast or single recipient, and a `User` class that contains all the information for a person entering your chat rooms. To really wow the VCs to get your start-up capital, you add a class `Room` that represents a more sophisticated chat system where users can create separate "rooms" within the chat area and invite others to join. Extra credit: Develop graphical user interface (GUI) applications for the users.

13–13.   *Stock Portfolio Class.* For each company, your database tracks the name, ticker symbol, purchase date, purchase price, and number of shares. Methods include: add new symbol (new purchase), remove symbol (all shares sold), and YTD or Annual Return performance for any or all symbols given a current price (and date). See also Exercise 7–6.

13–14.   *DOS.* Write a Unix interface shell for DOS machines. You present the user a command line where he or she can type in Unix commands, and you interpret them and output accordingly, i.e., the "ls" command calls "dir" to give a list of filenames in a directory, "more" uses the same command (paginating through a text file), "cat" calls "type," "cp" calls "copy," "mv" calls "ren," and "rm" invokes "del," etc.

13–15.   *Delegation.* In our final comments regarding the `CapOpen` class of Example 13.8 where we proved that our class wrote out the data successfully, we noted that we could use either `CapOpen()` or `open()` to read the file text. Why? Would anything change if we used one or the other?

13–16.   *Delegation and Functional Programming.*
   (a) Implement a `writelines()` method for the `CapOpen` class of Example 13.8. Your new function will take a list of lines and write them out converted to uppercase, similar to the way the regular `writelines()` method differs from `write()`. Note that once you are done, `writelines()` is no longer "delegated" to the file object.
   (b) Add an argument to the `writelines()` method that determines whether a NEWLINE should be added to every line of the list. This argument should default to a value of `False` for no NEWLINEs.

13–17.   *Subclassing Numeric Types*. Take your final `moneyfmt.py` script as seen in Example 13.3 as Example 13.8 and recast it so that it extends Python's float type. Be sure all operations are supported, but that it is still immutable.

13–18.   *Subclassing Sequence Types*. Create a subclass similar to your solution of the previous problem to your user registration class as seen earlier in Exercise 13–4. Allow users to change their passwords, but do not allow them to reuse the same password within a 12-month period. Extra credit: Add support for determining "similar passwords" (any algorithm is fine) and do not even allow passwords *similar* to any used within the last 12 months.

13–19.   *Subclassing Mapping Types*. As speculated for the dictionary subclass in Section 13.11.3, what if the `keys()` method were (re)written as:

```
def keys(self):
    return sorted(self.keys())
```

   (a) What happens when `keys()` is called for a method?
   (b) Why is this, and what makes our original solution work?

13–20.   *Class Customization*. Improve on the `time60.py` script as seen in Section 13.13.2, Example 13.3.
   (a) Allow "empty" instantiation: If hours and minutes are not passed in, then default to zero hours and zero minutes.
   (b) Zero-fill values to two digits because the current formatting is undesirable. In the case below, displaying `wed` should output "12:05."

```
>>> wed = Time60(12, 5)
>>> wed
12:5
```

   (c) In addition to instantiating with hours (`hr`) and minutes (`min`), also support time entered as:
   • A tuple of hours and minutes (`10, 30`)
   • A dictionary of hours and minutes (`{'hr': 10, 'min': 30}`)
   • A string representing hours and minutes (`"10:30"`)
      Extra Credit: Allow for improperly formatted strings like "`12:5`" as well.
   (d) Do we need to implement `__radd__()`? Why or why not? If not, when would or should we override it?

(e) The implementation of __repr__() is flawed and mis-
guided. We only overrode this function so that it displays
nicely in the interactive interpreter without having to use
the **print** statement. However, this breaks the charter
that repr() should always give a (valid) string representation of an evaluatable Python expression. 12:05 is not
a valid Python expression, but Time60('12:05') is.
Make it so.

(f) Add support for sexagesimal (base 60) operations. The
output for the following example should be 19:15 not
18:75:

```
>>> thu = Time60(10, 30)
>>> fri = Time60(8, 45)
>>> thu + fri
18:75
```

13–21. *Decorators and Function Call Syntax.* Toward the end of
Section 13.16.4, we used a function decorator to turn x into a
property object, but because decorators were not available
until Python 2.4, we gave an alternate syntax for older
releases:

```
X = property (**x()).
```

Exactly what happens when this assignment is executed,
and why is it equivalent to using a decorator?

EXECUTION
ENVIRONMENT

Chapter Topics

- Callable Objects
- Code Objects
- Statements and Built-in Functions
- Executing Other Programs
- Terminating Execution
- Miscellaneous Operating System Interface
- Related Modules

Chapter 14

There are multiple ways in Python to run other pieces of code outside of the currently executing program, i.e., run an operating system command or another Python script, or execute a file on disk or across the network. It all depends on what you are trying to accomplish. Some specific execution scenarios could include:

- Remain executing within our current script
- Create and manage a subprocess
- Execute an external command or program
- Execute a command that requires input
- Invoke a command across the network
- Execute a command creating output that requires processing
- Execute another Python script
- Execute a set of dynamically generated Python statements
- Import a Python module (and executing its top-level code)

There are built-ins and external modules that can provide any of the functionality described above. The programmer must decide which tool to pick from the box based on the application that requires implementation. This chapter sketches a potpourri of many of the aspects of the execution environment within Python; however, we will not discuss how to start the Python interpreter or the different command-line options. Readers seeking information on invoking or starting the Python interpreter should review Chapter 2.

Our tour of Python's execution environment consists of looking at "callable" objects and following up with a lower-level peek at code objects. We will then take a look at what Python statements and built-in functions are available to support the functionality we desire. The ability to execute other programs gives our Python script even more power, as well as being a resource-saver because certainly it is illogical to reimplement all this code, not to mention the loss of time and manpower. Python provides many mechanisms to execute programs or commands external to the current script environment, and we will run through the most common options. Next, we give a brief overview of Python's restricted execution environment, and finally, the different ways of terminating execution (other than letting a program run to completion). We begin our tour of Python's execution environment by looking at "callable" objects.

14.1 Callable Objects

A number of Python objects are what we describe as "callable," meaning any object that can be invoked with the function operator "()". The function operator is placed immediately following the name of the callable to invoke it. For example, the function "`foo`" is called with "`foo()`". You already know this. Callables may also be invoked via functional programming interfaces such as `apply()`, `filter()`, `map()`, and `reduce()`, all of which we discussed in Chapter 11. Python has four callable objects: functions, methods, classes, and some class instances. Keep in mind that any additional references or aliases of these objects are callable, too.

14.1.1 Functions

The first callable object we introduced was the function. There are three different types of function objects. The first is the Python built-in functions.

Built-in Functions (BIFs)

BIFs are functions written in C/C++, compiled into the Python interpreter, and loaded into the system as part of the first (built-in) namespace. As mentioned in previous chapters, these functions are found in the __builtin__ module and are imported into the interpreter as the __builtins__ module.

Table 14.1 Built-in Function Attributes	
BIF Attribute	*Description*
bif.__doc__	Documentation string (or None)
bif.__name__	Function name as a string
bif.__self__	Set to None (reserved for built-in methods)
bif.__module__	Name of the module where *bif* is defined (or None)

BIFs have the basic type attributes, but some of the more interesting unique ones are listed in Table 14.1.

You can list all attributes of a function by using dir():

```
>>> dir(type)
['__call__', '__class__', '__cmp__', '__delattr__', '__doc__',
 '__getattribute__', '__hash__', '__init__', '__module__',
 '__name__', '__new__', '__reduce__', '__reduce_ex__',
 '__repr__', '__self__', '__setattr__', '__str__']
```

Internally, BIFs are represented as the same type as built-in methods (BIMs), so invoking type() on a BIF or BIM results in:

```
>>> type(dir)
<type 'builtin_function_or_method'>
```

Note that this does not apply to factory functions, where type() correctly returns the type of object produced:

```
>>> type(int)
<type 'type'>
>>> type(type)
<type 'type'>
```

User-Defined Functions (UDFs)

UDFs are generally written in Python and defined at the top-level part of a module and hence are loaded as part of the global namespace (once the built-in namespace has been established). Functions may also be defined in other functions, and due to the nested scopes improvement in 2.2, we now have access to attributes in multiply-nested scopes. Hooks to attributes defined elsewhere are provided by the func_closure attribute.

Table 14.2 User-Defined Function Attributes

UDF Attribute	*Description*
*udf.*__doc__	Documentation string (also *udf.*func_doc)
*udf.*__name__	Function name as a string (also *udf.*func_name)
*udf.*func_code	Byte-compiled code object
*udf.*func_defaults	Default argument tuple
*udf.*func_globals	Global namespace dictionary; same as calling globals(x) from within function
*udf.*func_dict	Namespace for function attributes
*udf.*func_doc	(See *udf.*__doc__ above)
*udf.*func_name	(See *udf.*__name__ above)
*udf.*func_closure	Tuple of Cell objects (see the Python/C API Reference Manual) that contains references to *free variables* (those used in *udf* but defined elsewhere; see the Python [Language] Reference Manual)

Like the BIFs above, UDFs also have many attributes. The more interesting and specific ones to UDFs are listed below in Table 14.2.

Internally, user-defined functions are of the type "function," as indicated in the following example by using type():

```
>>> def foo(): pass
>>> type(foo)
<type 'function'>
```

lambda Expressions (Functions Named "<lambda>")

Lambda expressions are the same as user-defined functions with some minor differences. Although they yield function objects, lambda expressions are not created with the **def** statement and instead are created using the **lambda** keyword.

Because lambda expressions do not provide the infrastructure for naming the codes that are tied to them, lambda expressions must be called either through functional programming interfaces or have their reference be assigned to a variable, and then they can be invoked directly or again via functional programming. This variable is merely an alias and is *not* the function object's name.

Function objects created by **lambda** also share all the same attributes as user-defined functions, with the only exception resulting from the fact that they are not named; the __name__ or func_name attribute is given the string "<lambda>".

Using the type() factory function, we show that lambda expressions yield the same function objects as user-defined functions:

```
>>> lambdaFunc = lambda x: x * 2
>>> lambdaFunc(100)
200
>>> type(lambdaFunc)
<type 'function'>
```

In the example above, we assign the expression to an alias. We can also invoke type() directly on a lambda expression:

```
>>> type(lambda:1)
<type 'function'>
```

Let us take a quick look at UDF names, using lambdaFunc above and foo from the preceding subsection:

```
>>> foo.__name__
'foo'
>>> lambdaFunc.__name__
'<lambda>'
```

As we noted back in Section 11.9, programmers can also define function attributes once the function has been declared (and a function object available). All of the new attributes become part of the udf.__dict__ object. Later on in this chapter, we will discuss taking strings of Python code and executing it. There will be a combined example toward the end of the chapter highlighting function attributes and dynamic evaluation of Python code (from strings) and executing those statements.

14.1.2 Methods

In Chapter 13 we discovered methods, functions that are defined as part of a class—these are user-defined methods. Many Python data types such as lists and dictionaries also have methods, known as built-in methods. To further show this type of "ownership," methods are named with or represented alongside the object's name via the dotted-attribute notation.

Table 14.3 Built-in Method Attributes	
BIM Attribute	**Description**
`bim.__doc__`	Documentation string
`bim.__name__`	Function name as a string
`bim.__self__`	Object the method is bound to

Built-in Methods (BIMs)

We discussed in the previous section how built-in methods are similar to built-in functions. Only built-in types (BITs) have BIMs. As you can see below, the `type()` factory function gives the same output for built-in methods as it does for BIFs—note how we have to provide a built-in type (object or reference) in order to access a BIM:

```
>>> type([].append)
<type 'builtin_function_or_method'>
```

Furthermore, both BIMs and BIFs share the same attributes, too. The only exception is that now the __self__ attribute points to a Python object (for BIMs) as opposed to `None` (for BIFs):

Recall that for classes and instances, their data and method attributes can be obtained by using the `dir()` BIF with that object as the argument to `dir()`. It can also be used with BIMs:

```
>>> dir([].append)
['__call__', '__class__', '__cmp__', '__delattr__', '__doc__',
 '__getattribute__', '__hash__', '__init__', '__module__',
 '__name__', '__new__', '__reduce__', '__reduce_ex__',
 '__repr__', '__self__', '__setattr__', '__str__']
```

It does not take too long to discover, however, that using an actual object to access its methods does not prove very useful functionally, as in the last example. No reference is saved to the object, so it is immediately garbage-collected. The only thing useful you can do with this type of access is to use it to display what methods (or members) a BIT has.

User-Defined Methods (UDMs)

User-defined methods are contained in class definitions and are merely "wrappers" around standard functions, applicable only to the class they are defined for. They may also be called by subclass instances if not overridden in the subclass definition.

As explained in Chapter 13, UDMs are associated with class objects (unbound methods), but can be invoked only with class instances (bound methods). Regardless of whether they are bound or not, all UDMs are of the same type, "instance method," as seen in the following calls to `type()`:

```
>>> class C(object):              # define class
...         def foo(self): pass    # define UDM
...
>>> c = C()                       # instantiation
>>> type(C)                       # type of class
<type 'type'>
>>> type(c)                       # type of instance
<class '__main__.C'>
>>> type(C.foo)                   # type of unbound method
<type 'instancemethod'>
>>> type(c.foo)                   # type of bound method
<type 'instancemethod'>
```

UDMs have attributes as shown in Table 14.4.

Accessing the object itself will reveal whether you are referring to a bound or an unbound method. As you can also see below, a bound method reveals to which instance object a method is bound:

```
>>> C.foo                # unbound method object
<unbound method C.foo>
>>>
>>> c.foo                # bound method object
<bound method C.foo of <__main__.C object at 0x00B42DD0>
>>> c                    # instance foo()'s bound to
<__main__.C object at 0x00B42DD0>
```

Table 14.4 User-Defined Method Attributes

UDM Attribute	Description
udm.__doc__	Documentation string (same as udm.im_func.__doc__)
udm.__name__	Method name as a string (same as udm.im_func.__name__)
udm.__module__	Name of the module where udm is defined (or None)
udm.im_class	Class that method is associated with (for bound methods; if unbound, then the class that requested udm)
udm.im_func	Function object for method (see UDFs)
udm.im_self	Associated instance if bound, None if unbound

14.1.3 Classes

The callable property of classes allows instances to be created. "Invoking" a class has the effect of creating an instance, better known as instantiation. Classes have default constructors that perform no action, basically consisting of a **pass** statement. The programmer may choose to customize the instantiation process by implementing an __init__() method. Any arguments to an instantiation call are passed on to the constructor:

```
>>> class C(object):
    def __init__(self, *args):
       print 'Instantiated with these arguments:\n', args

>>> c1 = C() # invoking class to instantiate c1
Instantiated with these arguments:
()
>>> c2 = C('The number of the counting shall be', 3)
Instantiated with these arguments:
('The number of the counting shall be', 3)
```

We are already familiar with the instantiation process and how it is accomplished, so we will keep this section brief. What is new, however, is how to make *instances* callable.

14.1.4 Class Instances

Python provides the __call__() special method for classes, which allows a programmer to create objects (instances) that are callable. By default, the __call__() method is not implemented, meaning that most instances are not callable. However, if this method is overridden in a class definition, instances of such a class are made callable. Calling such instance objects is equivalent to invoking the __call__() method. Naturally, any arguments given in the instance call are passed as arguments to __call__().

You also have to keep in mind that __call__() is still a method, so the instance object itself is passed in as the first argument to __call__() as self. In other words, if foo is an instance, then foo() has the same effect as foo.__call__(foo)—the occurrence of foo as an argument—simply the reference to self that is automatically part of every method call. If __call__() has arguments, i.e., __call__(self, arg), then foo(arg) is the same as invoking foo.__call__(foo, arg). Here we present an example of a callable instance, using a similar example as in the previous section:

```
>>> class C(object):
...     def __call__(self, *args):
...         print "I'm callable!  Called with args:\n", args
...

>>> c = C()                        # instantiation
>>> c                              # our instance
<__main__.C instance at 0x00B42DD0>
>>> callable(c)                    # instance is callable
True
>>> c()                            # instance invoked
I'm callable!  Called with arguments:
()
>>> c(3)                           # invoked with 1 arg
I'm callable!  Called with arguments:
(3,)
>>> c(3, 'no more, no less')       # invoked with 2 args
I'm callable!  Called with arguments:
(3, 'no more, no less')
```

We close this subsection with a note that class instances cannot be made callable unless the __call__() method is implemented as part of the class definition.

14.2 Code Objects

Callables are a crucial part of the Python execution environment, yet they are only one element of a larger landscape. The grander picture consists of Python statements, assignments, expressions, and even modules. These other "executable objects" do not have the ability to be invoked like callables. Rather, these objects are the smaller pieces of the puzzle that make up executable blocks of code called *code objects*.

At the heart of every callable is a code object, which consists of statements, assignments, expressions, and other callables. Looking at a module means viewing one large code object that contains all the code found in the module. Then it can be dissected into statements, assignments, expressions, and callables, which recurse to another layer as they contain their own code objects.

In general, code objects can be executed as part of function or method invocations or using either the **exec** statement or eval() BIF. A bird's eye view of a Python module also reveals a single code object representing all lines of code that make up that module.

If any Python code is to be executed, that code must first be converted to byte-compiled code (aka bytecode). This is precisely what code objects are.

They do not contain any information about their execution environment, however, and that is why callables exist, to "wrap" a code object and provide that extra information.

Recall, from the previous section, the udf.func_code attribute for a UDFs? Well, guess what? That is a code object. Or how about the udm.im_func function object for UDMs? Since that is also a function object, it also has its own udm.im_func.func_code code object. So you can see that function objects are merely wrappers for code objects, and methods are wrappers for function objects. You can start anywhere and dig. When you get to the bottom, you will have arrived at a code object.

14.3 Executable Object Statements and Built-in Functions

Python provides a number of BIFs supporting callables and executable objects, including the **exec** statement. These functions let the programmer execute code objects as well as generate them using the compile() BIF. They are listed in Table 14.5.

Table 14.5 Executable Object Statements and Built-in Functions

Built-in Function or Statement	Description
callable(*obj*)	Returns True if *obj* is callable and False otherwise
compile(*string, file, type*)	Creates a code object from *string* of type *type*; *file* is where the code originates from (usually set to " ")
eval(*obj, globals*=globals(), *locals*=locals())	Evaluates *obj*, which is either an expression compiled into a code object or a string expression; global and/or local namespace may also be provided
exec *obj*	Executes *obj*, a single Python statement or set of statements, either in code object or string format; *obj* may also be a file object (opened to a valid Python script)
input(*prompt*='')	Equivalent to eval(raw_input(*prompt*=''))

14.3.1 `callable()`

`callable()` is a Boolean function that determines if an object type can be invoked via the function operator (`(` `)`). It returns `True` if the object is callable and `False` otherwise (1 and 0, respectively, for Python 2.2 and earlier). Here are some sample objects and what callable returns for each type:

```
>>> callable(dir)           # built-in function
True
>>> callable(1)             # integer
False
>>> def foo(): pass
...
>>> callable(foo)           # user-defined function
True
>>> callable('bar')         # string
False
>>> class C(object): pass
...
>>> callable(C)             # class
True
```

14.3.2 `compile()`

`compile()` is a function that allows the programmer to generate a code object on the fly, that is, during runtime. These objects can then be executed or evaluated using the **exec** statement or `eval()` BIF. It is important to bring up the point that both **exec** and `eval()` can take string representations of Python code to execute. When executing code given as strings, the process of byte-compiling such code must occur every time. The `compile()` function provides a one-time byte-code compilation of code so that the precompile does not have to take place with each invocation. Naturally, this is an advantage only if the same pieces of code are executed more than once. In these cases, it is definitely better to precompile the code.

All three arguments to `compile()` are required, with the first being a string representing the Python code to compile. The second string, although required, is usually set to the empty string. This parameter represents the file name (as a string) where this code object is located or can be found. Normal usage is for `compile()` to generate a code object from a dynamically generated string of Python code—code that obviously does not originate from an existing file.

The last argument is a string indicating the code object type. There are three possible values:

`'eval'`	Evaluatable expression [to be used with `eval()`]
`'single'`	Single executable statement [to be used with **exec**]
`'exec'`	Group of executable statements [to be used with **exec**]

Evaluatable Expression

```
>>> eval_code = compile('100 + 200', '', 'eval')
>>> eval(eval_code)
300
```

Single Executable Statement

```
>>> single_code = compile('print "Hello world!"', '', 'single')
>>> single_code
<code object ? at 120998, file "", line 0>
>>> exec single_code
Hello world!
```

Group of Executable Statements

```
>>> exec_code = compile("""
... req = input('Count how many numbers? ')
... for eachNum in range(req):
...     print eachNum
... """, '', 'exec')
>>> exec exec_code
Count how many numbers? 6
0
1
2
3
4
5
```

In the final example, we see `input()` for the first time. Since the beginning, we have been reading input from the user using `raw_input()`. The `input()` BIF is a shortcut function that we will discuss later in this chapter. We just wanted to tease you with a sneak preview.

14.3.3 `eval()`

`eval()` evaluates an expression, either as a string representation or a pre-compiled code object created via the `compile()` built-in. This is the first and most important argument to `eval()`... it is what you want to execute.

The second and third parameters, both optional, represent the objects in the global and local namespaces, respectively. If provided, *globals* must be a dictionary. If provided, *locals* can be any mapping object, e.g., one that implements the __getitem__() special method. (Before 2.4, *locals* was required to be a dictionary.) If neither of these are given, they default to objects returned by `globals()` and `locals()`, respectively. If only a *globals* dictionary is passed in, then it is also passed in as *locals*.

2.4

Okay, now let us take a look at `eval()`:

```
>>> eval('932')
932
>>> int('932')
932
```

We see that in this case, both `eval()` and `int()` yield the same result: an integer with the value 932. The paths they take are somewhat different, however. The `eval()` BIF takes the string in quotes and evaluates it as a Python expression. The `int()` BIF takes a string representation of an integer and converts it to an integer. It just so happens that the string consists exactly of the string 932, which as an expression yields the value 932, and that 932 is also the integer represented by the string "932." Things are not the same, however, when we use a pure string expression:

```
>>> eval('100 + 200')
300
>>> int('100 + 200')
Traceback (innermost last):
  File "<stdin>", line 1, in ?
ValueError: invalid literal for int(): 100 + 200
```

In this case, `eval()` takes the string and evaluates `"100 + 200"` as an expression, which, after performing integer addition, yields the value 300. The call to `int()` fails because the string argument is not a string representation of an integer—there are invalid literals in the string, namely, the spaces and "+" character.

One simple way to envision how the `eval()` function works is to imagine that the quotation marks around the expression are invisible and think, "If I were the Python interpreter, how would I view this expression?" In other words, how would the interpreter react if the same expression were entered interactively? The output after pressing the RETURN or ENTER key should be the same as what `eval()` will yield.

14.3.4 exec

Like eval(), the **exec** statement also executes either a code object or a string representing Python code. Similarly, precompiling oft-repeated code with compile() helps improve performance by not having to go through the byte-code compilation process for each invocation. The **exec** statement takes exactly one argument, as indicated here with its general syntax:

> **exec** *obj*

The executed object (*obj*) can be either a single statement or a group of statements, and either may be compiled into a code object (with "single" or "exec," respectively) or it can be just the raw string. Below is an example of multiple statements being sent to **exec** as a single string:

```
>>> exec """
... x = 0
... print 'x is currently:', x
... while x < 5:
...     x += 1
...     print 'incrementing x to:', x
... """
x is currently: 0
incrementing x to: 1
incrementing x to: 2
incrementing x to: 3
incrementing x to: 4
incrementing x to: 5
```

Finally, **exec** can also accept a valid file object to a (valid) Python file. If we take the code in the multi-line string above and create a file called xcount.py, then we could also execute the same code with the following:

```
>>> f = open('xcount.py')      # open the file
>>> exec f                     # execute the file
x is currently: 0
incrementing x to: 1
incrementing x to: 2
incrementing x to: 3
incrementing x to: 4
incrementing x to: 5
>>> exec f                     # try execution again
>>>                            # oops, it failed... why?
```

Note that once execution has completed, a successive call to **exec** fails. Well, it doesn't really *fail* . . . it just doesn't *do* anything, which may have caught you by surprise. In reality, **exec** has read all the data in the file and is sitting at the end-of-file (EOF). When **exec** is called again with the same file object, there is no more code to execute, so it does not do anything, hence the behavior seen above. How do we know that it is at EOF?

We use the file object's `tell()` method to tell us where we are in the file and then use `os.path.getsize()` to tell us how large our `xcount.py` script was. As you can see, there is an exact match:

```
>>> f.tell()                   # where are we in the file?
116
>>> f.close()                  # close the file
>>> from os.path import getsize
>>> getsize('xcount.py')       # what is the file size?
116
```

If we really want to run it again without closing and reopening the file, you can just `seek()` to the beginning of the file and call exec again. For example, let us assume that we did not call `f.close()` yet. Then we can do the following:

```
>>> f.seek(0)                  # rewind to beginning
>>> exec f
x is currently: 0
incrementing x to: 1
incrementing x to: 2
incrementing x to: 3
incrementing x to: 4
incrementing x to: 5
>>> f.close()
```

14.3.5 `input()`

The `input()` BIF is the same as the composite of `eval()` and `raw_input()`, equivalent to `eval(raw_input())`. Like `raw_input()`, `input()` has an optional parameter, which represents a string prompt to display to the user. If not provided, the string has a default value of the empty string.

Functionally, `input()` differs from `raw_input()` because `raw_input()` always returns a string containing the user's input, verbatim. `input()` performs the same task of obtaining user input; however, it takes things one step further by evaluating the input as a Python expression. This means that the data returned by input() are a Python object, the result of performing the evaluation of the input expression.

One clear example is when the user inputs a list. raw_input() returns the string representation of a list, while input() returns the actual list:

```
>>> aString = raw_input('Enter a list: ')
Enter a list: [ 123, 'xyz', 45.67 ]
>>> aString
"[ 123, 'xyz', 45.67 ]"
>>> type(aString)
<type 'str'>
```

The above was performed with raw_input(). As you can see, everything is a string. Now let us see what happens when we use input() instead:

```
>>> aList = input('Enter a list: ')
Enter a list: [ 123, 'xyz', 45.67 ]
>>> aList
[123, 'xyz', 45.67]
>>> type(aList)
<type 'list'>
```

Although the user input a string, input() evaluates that input as a Python object and returns the result of that expression.

14.3.6 Using Python to Generate and Execute Python Code at Runtime

In this section, we will look at two examples of Python scripts that take Python code as strings and execute them at runtime. The first example is more dynamic, but the second shows off function attributes at the same time.

Creating Code at Runtime and Executing It

The first example is loopmake.py script, which is a simple computer-aided software engineering (CASE) that generates and executes loops on-the-fly. It prompts the user for the various parameters (i.e., loop type (**while** or **for**), type of data to iterate over [numbers or sequences]), generates the code string, and executes it.

Example 14.1 Dynamically Generating and Executing Python Code (`loopmake.py`)

```python
1   #!/usr/bin/env python
2
3   dashes = '\n' + '-' * 50 # dashed line
4   exec_dict = {
5
6   'f': """                          # for loop
7   for %s in %s:
8       print %s
9   """,
10
11  's': """                          # sequence while loop
12  %s = 0
13  %s = %s
14  while %s < len(%s):
15      print %s[%s]
16      %s = %s + 1
17  """,
18
19  'n': """                          # counting while loop
20  %s = %d
21  while %s < %d:
22      print %s
23      %s = %s + %d
24  """
25  }
26
27  def main():
28
29      ltype = raw_input('Loop type? (For/While) ')
30      dtype = raw_input('Data type? (Number/Seq) ')
31
32      if dtype == 'n':
33          start = input('Starting value? ')
34          stop = input('Ending value (non-inclusive)? ')
35          step = input('Stepping value? ')
36          seq = str(range(start, stop, step))
37
38      else:
39          seq = raw_input('Enter sequence: ')
40
41      var = raw_input('Iterative variable name? ')
42
43      if ltype == 'f':
44          exec_str = exec_dict['f'] % (var, seq, var)
45
46      elif ltype == 'w':
47          if dtype == 's':
48              svar = raw_input('Enter sequence name? ')
49              exec_str = exec_dict['s'] % \
50      (var, svar, seq, var, svar, svar, var, var, var)
51
```

(continued)

Example 14.1   Dynamically Generating and Executing Python Code (`loopmake.py`) (continued)

```
52              elif dtype == 'n':
53                  exec_str = exec_dict['n'] % \
54          (var, start, var, stop, var, var, var, step)
55
56          print dashes
57          print 'Your custom-generated code:' + dashes
58          print exec_str + dashes
59          print 'Test execution of the code:' + dashes
60          exec exec_str
61          print dashes
62
63  if __name__ == '__main__':
64      main()
```

Here are a few example executions of this script:

```
    % loopmake.py
Loop type? (For/While) f
Data type? (Number/Sequence) n
Starting value? 0
Ending value (non-inclusive)? 4

Stepping value? 1
Iterative variable name? counter


-------------------------------------------------
The custom-generated code for you is:
-------------------------------------------------


for counter in [0, 1, 2, 3]:
    print counter


-------------------------------------------------
Test execution of the code:
-------------------------------------------------
0
1
2
3


-------------------------------------------------
% loopmake.py
Loop type? (For/While) w
Data type? (Number/Sequence) n
Starting value? 0
```

```
Ending value (non-inclusive)? 4
Stepping value? 1
Iterative variable name? counter


--------------------------------------------------
Your custom-generated code:
--------------------------------------------------


counter = 0
while counter < 4:
    print counter
    counter = counter + 1


--------------------------------------------------
Test execution of the code:
--------------------------------------------------
0
1
2
3


--------------------------------------------------


% loopmake.py
Loop type? (For/While) f
Data type? (Number/Sequence) s
Enter sequence: [932, 'grail', 3.0, 'arrrghhh']
Iterative variable name? eachItem


--------------------------------------------------
Your custom-generated code:
--------------------------------------------------


for eachItem in [932, 'grail', 3.0, 'arrrghhh']:
    print eachItem


--------------------------------------------------
Test execution of the code:
--------------------------------------------------
932
grail
3.0
arrrghhh


--------------------------------------------------
% loopmake.py
Loop type? (For/While) w
Data type? (Number/Sequence) s
```

```
Enter sequence: [932, 'grail', 3.0, 'arrrghhh']
Iterative variable name? eachIndex
Enter sequence name? myList


-----------------------------------------------------
Your custom-generated code:
-----------------------------------------------------

eachIndex = 0
myList = [932, 'grail', 3.0, 'arrrghhh']
while eachIndex < len(myList):
    print myList[eachIndex]
    eachIndex = eachIndex + 1


-----------------------------------------------------
Test execution of the code:
-----------------------------------------------------
932
grail
3.0
arrrghhh


-----------------------------------------------------
```

Line-by-Line Explanation

Lines 1–25

In this first part of the script, we are setting up two global variables. The first is a static string consisting of a line of dashes (hence the name) and the second is a dictionary of the skeleton code we will need to use for the loops we are going to generate. The keys are "f" for a **for** loop, "s" for a **while** loop iterating through a sequence, and "n" for a counting **while** loop.

Lines 27–30

Here we prompt the user for the type of loop he or she wants and what data types to use.

Lines 32–36

Numbers have been chosen; they provide the starting, stopping, and incremental values. In this section of code, we are introduced to the input() BIF for the first time. As we shall see in Section 14.3.5, input() is similar to raw_input() in that it prompts the user for string input, but unlike raw_input(), input() also evaluates the input as a Python expression, rendering a Python object even if the user typed it in as a string.

Lines 38–39
A sequence was chosen; enter the sequence here as a string.

Line 41
Get the name of the iterative loop variable that the user wants to use.

Lines 43–44
Generate the **for** loop, filling in all the customized details.

Lines 46–50
Generate a **while** loop which iterates through a sequence.

Lines 52–54
Generate a counting **while** loop.

Lines 56–61
Output the generated source code as well as the resulting output from execution of the aforementioned generated code.

Lines 63–64
Execute `main()` only if this module was invoked directly.

To keep the size of this script to a manageable size, we had to trim all the comments and error checking from the original script. You can find both the original as well as an alternate version of this script on the book's Web site.

The extended version includes extra features such as not requiring enclosing quotation marks for string input, default values for input data, and detection of invalid ranges and identifiers; it also does not permit built-in names or keywords as variable names.

Conditionally Executing Code

Our second example highlights the usefulness of function attributes introduced back in Chapter 11, "Functions", inspired by the example in PEP 232. Let us assume that you are a software QA developer encouraging your engineers to install either regression testers or regression instruction code into the main source but do not want the testing code mixed with the production code. You can tell your engineers to create a string representing the testing code. When your test framework executes, it checks to see if that function has defined a test body, and if so, (evaluates and) executes it. If not, it will skip and continue as normal.

Example 14.2 Function Attributes (`funcAttrs.py`)

Calling `sys.exit()` *causes the Python interpreter to quit. Any integer argument to* `exit()` *will be returned to the caller as the exit status, which has a default value of 0.*

```
1   #!/usr/bin/env python
2
3   def foo():
4       return True
5
6   def bar():
7       'bar() does not do much'
8       return True
9
10  foo.__doc__ = 'foo() does not do much'
11  foo.tester = '''
12  if foo():
13      print 'PASSED'
14  else:
15      print 'FAILED'
16  '''
17
18  for eachAttr in dir():
19      obj = eval(eachAttr)
20      if isinstance(obj, type(foo)):
21          if hasattr(obj, '__doc__'):
22              print '\nFunction "%s" has a doc
                 string:\n\t%s' % (eachAttr, obj.__doc__)
23          if hasattr(obj, 'tester'):
24              print 'Function "%s" has a tester... execut-
                 ing' % eachAttr
25              exec obj.tester
26          else:
27              print 'Function "%s" has no tester... skip-
                 ping' % eachAttr
28      else:
29          print '"%s" is not a function' % eachAttr
```

Lines 1–8

We define `foo()` and `bar()` in the first part of this script. Neither function does anything other than return `True`. The one difference between the two is that `foo()` has no attributes while `bar()` gets a documentation string.

Lines 10–16

Using function attributes, we add a doc string and a regression or unit tester string to `foo()`. Note that the tester string is actually comprised of real lines of Python code.

Lines 18–29

Okay, the real work happens here. We start by iterating through the current (global) namespace using the `dir()` BIF. It returns a list of the object names. Since these are all strings, we need line 19 to turn them into real Python objects.

Other than the expected system variables, i.e., `__builtins__`, we expect our functions to show up. We are only interested in functions; the code in line 20 will let us skip any non-function objects encountered. Once we know we have a function, we check to see if it has a doc string, and if so, we display it.

Lines 23–27 perform some magic. If the function has a `tester` attribute, then execute it, otherwise let the user know that no unit tester is available. The last few lines display the names of non-function objects encountered.

Upon executing the script, we get the following output:

```
$ python funcAttr.py
"__builtins__" is not a function
"__doc__" is not a function
"__file__" is not a function
"__name__" is not a function

Function "bar" has a doc string:
        bar() does not do much
Function "bar" has no tester... skipping

Function "foo" has a doc string:
        foo() does not do much
Function "foo" has a tester... executing
PASSED
```

14.4 Executing Other (Python) Programs

When we discuss the execution of other programs, we distinguish between Python programs and all other non-Python programs, which include binary executables or other scripting language source code. We will cover how to run other Python programs first, then how to use the `os` module to invoke external programs.

14.4.1 Import

During runtime, there are a number of ways to execute another Python script. As we discussed earlier, importing a module the first time will cause the code at the top level of that module to execute. This is the behavior of Python importing, whether desired or not. We remind you that the only code that belongs to the top level of a module are global variables, and class and function declarations.

CORE NOTE: All modules executed when imported

This is just a friendly reminder: As already alluded to earlier in Chapters 3 and 12, we will tell you one more time that Python modules are executed when they are imported! When you import the `foo` *module, it runs all of the top-level (not indented) Python code, i.e., "main()". If* `foo` *contains a declaration for the* `bar` *function, then* **def** `foo(...)` *is executed. Why is that again?*

Well, just think what needs to be done in order for the call `foo.bar()` *to succeed. Somehow* `bar` *has to be recognized as a valid name in the* `foo` *module (and in* `foo`'s *namespace), and second, the interpreter needs to know it is a declared function, just like any other function in your local module.*

Now that we know what we need to do, what do we do with code that we do not want executed every time our module is imported? Indent it and put it in the suite for the **if** `__name__ == '__main__'`.

These should be followed by an **if** statement that checks __name__ to determine if a script is invoked, i.e., "**if** __name__ == '__main__'". In these cases, your script can then execute the main body of code, or, if this script was meant to be imported, it can run a test suite for the code in this module.

One complication arises when the imported module itself contains **import** statements. If the modules in these **import** statements have not been loaded yet, they will be loaded and their top-level code executed, resulting in recursive import behavior. We present a simple example below. We have two modules `import1` and `import2,` both with **print** statements at their outermost level. `import1` imports `import2` so that when we import `import1` from within Python, it imports and "executes" `import2` as well.

Here are the contents of `import1.py`:

```
# import1.py
print 'loaded import1'
import import2
```

And here are the contents of `import2.py`:

```
# import2.py
print 'loaded import2'
```

Here is the output when we import `import1` from Python:

```
>>> import import1
loaded import1
loaded import2
>>>
```

Following our suggested workaround of checking the value of __name__, we can change the code in `import1.py` and `import2.py` so that this behavior does not occur.

Here is the modified version of `import1.py`:

```
# import1.py
import import2
if __name__ == '__main__':
    print 'loaded import1'
```

The following is the code for `import2.py`, changed in the same manner:

```
# import2.py
if __name__ == '__main__'
    print 'loaded import2'
```

We no longer get any output when we import `import1` from Python:

```
>>> import import1
>>>
```

Now it does not necessarily mean that this is the behavior you should code for all situations. There may be cases where you *want* to display output to confirm a module import. It all depends on your situation. Our goal is to provide pragmatic programming examples to prevent unintended side effects.

14.4.2 `execfile()`

It should seem apparent that importing a module is not the preferred method of executing a Python script from within another Python script; that is not what the importing process is. One side effect of importing a module is the execution of the top-level code.

Earlier in this chapter, we described how the **exec** statement can be used with a file object argument to read the contents of a Python script and execute it. This can be accomplished with the following code segment:

```
f = open(filename, 'r')
exec f
f.close()
```

The three lines can be replaced by a single call to `execfile()`:

```
execfile(filename)
```

Although the code above does execute a module, it does so only in its current execution environment (i.e., its global and local namespace). There may be a desire to execute a module with a different set of global and local namespaces instead of the default ones. The full syntax of `execfile()` is very similar to that of `eval()`:

```
execfile(filename, globals=globals(), locals=locals())
```

Like `eval()`, both `globals` and `locals` are optional and default to the executing environments' namespaces if not given. If only `globals` is given, then `locals` defaults to `globals`. If provided, `locals` can be any mapping object [an object defining/overriding `__getitem__()`], although before 2.4, it was required to be a dictionary. Warning: be very careful with your local namespace (in terms of modifying it). It is much safer to pass in a dummy "locals" dictionary and check for any side effects. Altering the local namespace is not guaranteed by `execfile()`! See the Python Library Reference Manual's entry for `execfile()` for more details.

14.4.3 Executing Modules as Scripts

2.4

A new command-line option (or switch) was added in Python 2.4 that allows you to directly execute a module as a script from your shell or DOS prompt. When you are writing your own modules as scripts, it is easy to execute them. From your working directory, you would just call your script on the command line:

```
$ myScript.py # or $ python myScript.py
```

This is not as easy if you are dealing with modules that are part of the standard library, installed in site-packages, or just modules in packages, especially if they also share the same name as an existing Python module. For example, let us say you wanted to run the free Web server that comes with Python so that you can create and test Web pages and CGI scripts you wrote.

You would have to type something like the following at the command line:

```
$ python /usr/local/lib/python2x/CGIHTTPServer.py
Serving HTTP on 0.0.0.0 port 8000 ...
```

That is a long line to type, and if it is a third-party, you would have to dig into `site-packages` to find exactly where it is located, etc. Can we run a module from the command line without the full pathname and let Python's import mechanism do the legwork for us?

That answer is yes. We can use the Python `-c` command-line switch:

```
$ python -c "import CGIHTTPServer; CGIHTTPServer.test()"
```

This option allows you to specify a Python statement you wish to run. So it does work, but the problem is that the `__name__` module is not `'__main__'`... it is whatever module name you are using. (You can refer back to Section 3.4.1 for a review of `__name__` if you need to.) The bottom line is that the interpreter has loaded your module by import and not as a script. Because of this, all of the code under **if** `__name__ == '__main__'` will not execute, so you have to do it manually like we did above calling the `test()` function of the module.

So what we really want is the best of both worlds—being able to execute a module in your library but as a script and not as an imported module. That is the main motivation behind the `-m` option. Now you can run a script like this:

```
$ python -m CGIHTTPServer
```

That is quite an improvement. Still, the feature was not as fully complete as some would have liked. So in Python 2.5, the `-m` switch was given even more capability. Starting with 2.5, you can use the same option to run modules inside packages or modules that need special loading, such as those inside ZIP files, a feature added in 2.3 (see Section 12.5.7 on page 396). Python 2.4 only lets you execute standard library modules. So running special modules like PyChecker (Python's "lint"), the debugger (`pdb`), or any of the profilers (note that these are modules that load and run *other* modules) was not solved with the initial `-m` solution but is fixed in 2.5.

2.3-2.5

14.5 Executing Other (Non-Python) Programs

We can also execute non-Python programs from within Python. These include binary executables, other shell scripts, etc. All that is required is a valid execution environment, i.e., permissions for file access and execution must be granted, shell scripts must be able to access their interpreter (Perl, bash, etc.), binaries must be accessible (and be of the local machine's architecture).

Finally, the programmer must bear in mind whether our Python script is required to communicate with the other program that is to be executed. Some programs require input, others return output as well as an error code upon completion (or both). Depending on the circumstances, Python provides a variety of ways to execute non-Python programs. All of the functions discussed in this section can be found in the os module. We provide a summary for you in Table 14.6 (where appropriate, we annotate those that are available only for certain platforms) as an introduction to the remainder of this section.

Table 14.6 os **Module Functions for External Program Execution (🅤** *Unix only,* **🅦** *Windows only)*

os *Module Function*	*Description*
system(*cmd*)	Execute program cmd given as string, wait for program completion, and return the exit code (on Windows, the exit code is always 0)
fork()	Create a child process that runs in parallel to the parent process [usually used with exec*()]; return twice... once for the parent and once for the child 🅤
execl(*file, arg0, arg1,...*)	Execute *file* with argument list *arg0, arg1*, etc.
execv(*file, arglist*)	Same as execl() except with argument vector (list or tuple) *arglist*
execle(*file, arg0, arg1,... env*)	Same as execl() but also providing environment variable dictionary *env*
execve(*file, arglist, env*)	Same as execle() except with argument vector *arglist*
execlp(*cmd, arg0, arg1,...*)	Same as execl() but search for full file pathname of cmd in user search path
execvp(*cmd, arglist*)	Same as execlp() except with argument vector *arglist*

Table 14.6 os Module Functions for External Program Execution (🅤 Unix only, 🅦 Windows only) (continued)

os *Module Function*	*Description*
execlpe(*cmd, arg0, arg1,... env*)	Same as execlp() but also providing environment variable dictionary *env*
execvpe(*cmd, arglist, env*)	Same as execvp() but also providing environment variable dictionary *env*
spawn*[a](mode, file, args[, env])	*spawn*() family executes path in a new process given *args* as arguments and possibly an environment variable dictionary *env*; *mode* is a magic number indicating various modes of operation
wait()	Wait for child process to complete [usually used with fork() and exec*()] 🅤
waitpid(*pid, options*)	Wait for specific child process to complete [usually used with fork() and exec*()] 🅤
popen(*cmd, mode*='r', *buffering*=-1)	Execute *cmd* string, returning a file-like object as a communication handle to the running program, defaulting to read *mode* and default system *buffering*
startfile[b](path)	Execute *path* with its associated application 🅦

a. spawn*() functions named similarly to exec*() (both families have eight members); spawnv() and spawnve() new in Python 1.5.2 and the other six spawn*() functions new in Python 1.6; also spawnlp(), spawnlpe(), spawnvp() and spawnvpe() are Unix-only.

b. New in Python 2.0.

As we get closer to the operating system layer of software, you will notice that the consistency of executing programs, even Python scripts, across platforms starts to get a little dicey. We mentioned above that the functions described in this section are in the os module. Truth is, there are multiple os modules. For example, the one for Unix-based systems (i.e., Linux, MacOS X, Solaris, *BSD, etc.) is the posix module. The one for Windows is nt (regardless of which version of Windows you are running; DOS users get the dos module), and the one for old MacOS is the mac module. Do not worry, Python will load the correct module when you call **import** os. You should never need to import a specific operating system module directly.

Before we take a look at each of these module functions, we want to point out for those of you using Python 2.4 and newer, there is a subprocess module that pretty much can substitute for all of these functions. We will show you later on in this chapter how to use some of these functions, then at the end give the equivalent using the subprocess.Popen class and subprocess.call() function.

14.5.1 os.system()

The first function on our list is system(), a rather simplistic function that takes a system command as a string name and executes it. Python execution is suspended while the command is being executed. When execution has completed, the exit status will be given as the return value from system() and Python execution resumes.

system() preserves the current standard files, including standard output, meaning that executing any program or command displaying output will be passed on to standard output. Be cautious here because certain applications such as common gateway interface (CGI) programs will cause Web browser errors if output other than valid Hypertext Markup Language (HTML) strings are sent back to the client via standard output. system() is generally used with commands producing no output, some of which include programs to compress or convert files, mount disks to the system, or any other command to perform a specific task that indicates success or failure via its exit status rather than communicating via input and/or output. The convention adopted is an exit status of 0 indicating success and non-zero for some sort of failure.

For the purpose of providing an example, we will execute two commands that *do* have program output from the interactive interpreter so that you can observe how system() works.

```
>>> import os
>>> result = os.system('cat /etc/motd')
Have a lot of fun...
>>> result
0
>>> result = os.system('uname -a')
Linux solo 2.2.13 #1 Mon Nov 8 15:08:22 CET 1999 i586 unknown
>>> result
0
```

You will notice the output of both commands as well as the exit status of their execution, which we saved in the result variable. Here is an example executing a DOS command:

```
>>> import os
>>> result = os.system('dir')

Volume in drive C has no label
Volume Serial Number is 43D1-6C8A
Directory of C:\WINDOWS\TEMP

.                <DIR>         01-08-98  8:39a .
..               <DIR>         01-08-98  8:39a ..
         0 file(s)                 0 bytes
         2 dir(s)       572,588,032 bytes free
>>> result
0
```

14.5.2 os.popen()

The popen() function is a combination of a file object and the system() function. It works in the same way as system() does, but in addition, it has the ability to establish a one-way connection to that program and then to access it like a file. If the program requires input, then you would call popen() with a mode of 'w' to "write" to that command. The data that you send to the program will then be received through its standard input. Likewise, a mode of 'r' will allow you to spawn a command, then as it writes to standard output, you can read that through your file-like handle using the familiar read*() methods of file object. And just like for files, you will be a good citizen and close() the connection when you are finished.

In one of the system() examples we used above, we called the Unix uname program to give us some information about the machine and operating system we are using. That command produced a line of output that went directly to the screen. If we wanted to read that string into a variable and perform internal manipulation or store that string to a log file, we could, using popen(). In fact, the code would look like the following:

```
>>> import os
>>> f = os.popen('uname -a')
>>> data = f.readline()
>>> f.close()
>>> print data,
Linux solo 2.2.13 #1 Mon Nov 8 15:08:22 CET 1999 i586 unknown
```

As you can see, popen() returns a file-like object; also notice that read-line(), as always, preserves the NEWLINE character found at the end of a line of input text.

14.5.3 `os.fork(), os.exec*(),` `os.wait*()`

Without a detailed introduction to operating systems theory, we present a light introduction to processes in this section. `fork()` takes your single executing flow of control known as a process and creates a "fork in the road," if you will. The interesting thing is that your system takes *both* forks—meaning that you will have two consecutive and parallel running programs (running the same code no less because both processes resume at the next line of code immediately succeeding the `fork()` call).

The original process that called `fork()` is called the *parent process*, and the new process created as a result of the call is known as the *child process*. When the child process returns, its return value is always zero; when the parent process returns, its return value is always the process identifier (aka process ID, or PID) of the child process (so the parent can keep tabs on all its children). The PIDs are the only way to tell them apart, too!

We mentioned that both processes will resume immediately after the call to `fork()`. Because the code is the same, we are looking at identical execution if no other action is taken at this time. This is usually not the intention. The main purpose for creating another process is to run another program, so we need to take divergent action as soon as parent and child return. As we stated above, the PIDs differ, so this is how we tell them apart.

The following snippet of code will look familiar to those who have experience managing processes. However, if you are new, it may be difficult to see how it works at first, but once you get it, you get it.

```
ret = os.fork()         # spawn 2 processes, both return
if ret == 0:            # child returns with PID of 0
    child_suite         # child code
else:                   # parent returns with child's PID
    parent_suite        # parent code
```

The call to `fork()` is made in the first line of code. Now both child and parent processes exist running simultaneously. The child process has its own copy of the virtual memory address space and contains an exact replica of the parent's address space—yes, both processes are nearly identical. Recall that `fork()` returns twice, meaning that both the parent and the child return. You might ask, how can you tell them apart if they both return? When the parent returns, it comes back with the PID of the child process. When the child returns, it has a return value of 0. This is how we can differentiate the two processes.

Using an **if-else** statement, we can direct code for the child to execute (i.e., the **if** clause) as well as the parent (the **else** clause). The code for the child is where we can make a call to any of the exec*() functions to run a completely different program or some function in the same program (as long as both child and parent take divergent paths of execution). The general convention is to let the children do all the dirty work while the parent either waits patiently for the child to complete its task or continues execution and checks later to see if the child finished properly.

All of the exec*() functions load a file or command and execute it with an argument list (either individually given or as part of an argument list). If applicable, an environment variable dictionary can be provided for the command. These variables are generally made available to programs to provide a more accurate description of the user's current execution environment. Some of the more well-known variables include the user name, search path, current shell, terminal type, localized language, machine type, operating system name, etc.

All versions of exec*() will replace the Python interpreter running in the current (child) process with the given file as the program to execute now. Unlike system(), there is no return to Python (since Python was replaced). An exception will be raised if exec*() fails because the program cannot execute for some reason.

The following code starts up a cute little game called "xbill" in the child process while the parent continues running the Python interpreter. Because the child process never returns, we do not have to worry about any code for the child after calling exec*(). Note that the command is also a required first argument of the argument list.

```
ret = os.fork()
if ret == 0:                    # child code
    execvp('xbill', ['xbill'])
else:                           # parent code
    os.wait()
```

In this code, you also find a call to wait(). When children processes have completed, they need their parents to clean up after them. This task, known as "reaping a child," can be accomplished with the wait*() functions. Immediately following a fork(), a parent can wait for the child to complete and do the clean-up then and there. A parent can also continue processing and reap the child later, also using one of the wait*() functions.

Regardless of which method a parent chooses, it must be performed. When a child has finished execution but has not been reaped yet, it enters a limbo state and becomes known as a *zombie* process. It is a good idea to minimize the number of zombie processes in your system because children in this state retain all the system resources allocated in their lifetimes, which do not get freed or released until they have been reaped by the parent.

A call to `wait()` suspends execution (i.e., waits) until a child process (any child process) has completed, terminating either normally or via a signal. `wait()` will then reap the child, releasing any resources. If the child has already completed, then `wait()` just performs the reaping procedure. `waitpid()` performs the same functionality as `wait()` with the additional arguments' PID to specify the process identifier of a specific child process to wait for plus options (normally zero or a set of optional flags logically OR'd together).

14.5.4 `os.spawn*()`

The `spawn*()` family of functions are similar to `fork()` and `exec*()` in that they execute a command in a new process; however, you do not need to call two separate functions to create a new process and cause it to execute a command. You only need to make one call with the `spawn*()` family. With its simplicity, you give up the ability to "track" the execution of the parent and child processes; its model is more similar to that of starting a function in a thread. Another difference is that you have to know the magic mode parameter to pass to `spawn*()`.

On some operating systems (especially embedded real-time operating systems [RTOs]), `spawn*()` is much faster than `fork()`. (Those where this is not the case usually use copy-on-write tricks.) Refer to the Python Library Reference Manual for more details (see the Process Management section of the manual on the `os` module) on the `spawn*()` functions. Various members of the `spawn*()` family were added to Python between 1.5 and 1.6 (inclusive).

14.5.5 `subprocess` *Module*

After Python 2.3 came out, work was begun on a module named `popen5`. The naming continued the tradition of all the previous `popen*()` functions that came before, but rather than continuing this ominous trend, the module was eventually named `subprocess`, with a class named `Popen` that has functionality to centralize most of the process-oriented functions we have discussed so far in this chapter. There is also a convenience function named `call()` that can easily slide into where **os.system**() lives. The subprocess module made its debut in Python 2.4. Below is an example of what it can do:

Replacing `os.system()`

Linux Example:

```
>>> from subprocess import call
>>> import os
>>> res = call(('cat', '/etc/motd'))
Linux starship 2.4.18-1-686 #4 Sat Nov 29 10:18:26 EST 2003 i686
GNU/Linux
>>> res
0
```

Win32 Example:

```
>>> res = call(('dir', r'c:\windows\temp'), shell=True)
 Volume in drive C has no label.
 Volume Serial Number is F4C9-1C38

 Directory of c:\windows\temp

03/11/2006  02:08 AM    <DIR>          .
03/11/2006  02:08 AM    <DIR>          ..
02/21/2006  08:45 PM                 851 install.log
02/21/2006  07:02 PM                 444 tmp.txt
               2 File(s)          1,295 bytes
               3 Dir(s)   55,001,104,384 bytes free
```

Replacing `os.popen()`

The syntax for creating an instance of Popen is only slightly more complex than calling the `os.popen()` function:

```
>>> from subprocess import Popen, PIPE
>>> f = Popen(('uname', '-a'), stdout=PIPE).stdout
>>> data = f.readline()
>>> f.close()
>>> print data,
Linux starship 2.4.18-1-686 #4 Sat Nov 29 10:18:26 EST 2003 i686
GNU/Linux
```

```
>>> f = Popen('who', stdout=PIPE).stdout
>>> data = [ eachLine.strip() for eachLine in f ]
>>> f.close()
>>> for eachLine in data:
...    print eachLine
...
wesc       console   Mar 11 12:44
wesc       ttyp1     Mar 11 16:29
wesc       ttyp2     Mar 11 16:40   (192.168.1.37)
wesc       ttyp3     Mar 11 16:49   (192.168.1.37)
wesc       ttyp4     Mar 11 17:51   (192.168.1.34)
```

14.5.6 Related Functions

Table 14.7 lists some of the functions (and their modules) that can perform some of the tasks described.

Table 14.7 Various Functions for File Execution

File Object Attribute	Description
os/popen2.popen2[a]()	Executes a file and open file read and write access from (stdout) and to (stdin) the newly created running program
os/popen2.popen3[a]()	Executes a file and open file read and write access from (stdout and stderr) and (stdin) to the newly created running program
os/popen2.popen4[b]()	Executes a file and open file read and write access from (stdout and stderr combined) and (stdin) to the newly created running program
commands.getoutput()	Executes a file in a subprocess, returns all output as a string Ⓤ
subprocess.call[c]()	Convenience function that creates a subprocess.Popen, waits for the command to complete, then returns the status code; like os.system() but is a more flexible alternative

a.   New to os module in Python 2.0.
b.   New (to os and popen2 modules) in Python 2.0.
c.   New in Python 2.4.

14.6 Restricted Execution

At one time in Python's history, there was the concept of restricted execution using the `rexec` and `Bastion` modules. The first allowed you to modify the built-in objects that were made available to code executing in a sandbox. The second served as an attribute filter and wrapper around your classes. However, due to a well-known vulnerability and the difficulty in fixing the security hole, these modules are no longer used or accessible; their documentation serves only those maintaining old code using these modules.

14.7 Terminating Execution

Clean execution occurs when a program runs to completion, where all statements in the top level of your module finish execution and your program exits. There may be cases where you may want to exit from Python sooner, such as a fatal error of some sort. Another case is when conditions are not sufficient to continue execution.

In Python, there are varying ways to respond to errors. One is via exceptions and exception handling. Another way is to construct a "cleaner" approach so that the main portions of code are cordoned off with **if** statements to execute only in non-error situations, thus letting error scenarios terminate "normally." However, you may also desire to exit the calling program with an error code to indicate that such an event has occurred.

14.7.1 `sys.exit()` *and* `SystemExit`

The primary way to exit a program immediately and return to the calling program is the `exit()` function found in the `sys` module. The syntax for `sys.exit()` is:

```
sys.exit(status=0)
```

When `sys.exit()` is called, a `SystemExit` exception is raised. Unless monitored (in a **try** statement with an appropriate **except** clause), this exception is generally not caught or handled, and the interpreter exits with the given status argument, which defaults to zero if not provided. `System Exit` is the only exception that is not viewed as an error. It simply indicates the desire to exit Python.

One popular place to use sys.exit() is after an error is discovered in the way a command was invoked, in particular, if the arguments are incorrect, invalid, or if there are an incorrect number of them. The following Example 14.4 (args.py) is just a test script we created to require that a certain number of arguments be given to the program before it can execute properly.

Executing this script we get the following output:

```
$ args.py
At least 2 arguments required (incl. cmd name).
usage:  args.py arg1 arg2 [arg3... ]
$ args.py XXX
At least 2 arguments required (incl. cmd name).
usage:  args.py arg1 arg2 [arg3... ]
$ args.py 123 abc
number of args entered: 3
args (incl. cmd name) were: ['args.py', '123', 'abc']
$ args.py -x -2 foo
number of args entered: 4
args (incl. cmd name) were: ['args.py', '-x', '-2',
'foo']
```

Example 14.4 Exiting Immediately (args.py)

Calling sys.exit() *causes the Python interpreter to quit. Any integer argument to* exit() *will be returned to the caller as the exit status, which has a default value of 0.*

```
1  #!/usr/bin/env python
2
3  import sys
4
5  def usage():
6      print 'At least 2 arguments (incl. cmd name).'
7      print 'usage: args.py arg1 arg2 [arg3... ]'
8      sys.exit(1)
9
10 argc = len(sys.argv)
11 if argc < 3:
12     usage()
13 print "number of args entered:", argc
14 print "args (incl. cmd name) were:", sys.argv
```

Many command-line-driven programs test the validity of the input before proceeding with the core functionality of the script. If the validation fails at any point, a call is made to a usage() function to inform the user what problem caused the error as well as a usage "hint" to aid the user so that he or she will invoke the script properly the next time.

14.7.2 `sys.exitfunc()`

sys.exitfunc() is disabled by default, but can be overridden to provide additional functionality, which takes place when sys.exit() is called and before the interpreter exits. This function will not be passed any arguments, so you should create your function to take no arguments.

If sys.exitfunc has already been overridden by a previously defined exit function, it is good practice to also execute *that* code as part of your exit function. Generally, exit functions are used to perform some type of shutdown activity, such as closing a file or network connection, and it is always a good idea to complete these maintenance tasks, such as releasing previously held system resources.

Here is an example of how to set up an exit function, being sure to execute one if one has already been set:

```
import sys

prev_exit_func = getattr(sys, 'exitfunc', None)

def my_exit_func(old_exit = prev_exit_func):
  #      :
  # perform cleanup
  #      :
  if old_exit is not None and callable(old_exit):
    old_exit()

sys.exitfunc = my_exit_func
```

We execute the old exit function after our cleanup has been performed. The getattr() call simply checks to see whether a previous exitfunc has been defined. If not, then None is assigned to prev_exit_func; otherwise, prev_exit_func becomes a new alias to the exiting function, which is then passed as a default argument to our new exit function, my_exit_func.

The call to getattr() could have been rewritten as:

```
if hasattr(sys, 'exitfunc'):
    prev_exit_func = sys.exitfunc  # getattr(sys, 'exitfunc')
else:
    prev_exit_func = None
```

14.7.3 os._exit() *Function*

The _exit() function of the os module should not be used in general practice. (It is platform-dependent and available only on certain platforms, i.e., Unix-based and Win32.) Its syntax is:

```
os._exit(status)
```

This function provides functionality opposite to that of sys.exit() and sys.exitfunc(), exiting Python immediately without performing *any* cleanup (Python or programmer-defined) at all. Unlike sys.exit(), the status argument is required. Exiting via sys.exit() is the preferred method of quitting the interpreter.

14.7.4 os.kill() *Function*

The kill() function of the os module performs the traditional Unix function of sending a signal to a process. The arguments to kill() are the process identification number (PID) and the signal you wish to send to that process. The typical signal that is sent is either SIGINT, SIGQUIT, or more drastically, SIGKILL, to cause a process to terminate.

14.8 Miscellaneous Operating System Interface

In this chapter, we have seen various ways to interact with your *operating system* (OS) via the os module. Most of the functions we looked at dealt with either files or external process execution. There are a few more that allow for more specific actions for the current user and process, and we will look at them briefly here. Most of the functions described in Table 14.8 work on POSIX systems only, unless also denoted for Windows environment.

Table 14.8 Various *os* **Module Attributes (Ⓦ** *Also available for Win32)*

os Module Attribute	Description
uname()	Obtains system information (hostname, operating system version, patch level, system architecture, etc.)
getuid()/ setuid(*uid*)	Gets/sets the real user ID of the current process
getpid()/getppid()	Gets real process ID (PID) of current/parent processⓌ
getgid()/ setgid(*gid*)	Gets/sets real group ID (GID) of current process
getsid()/setsid()	Gets session ID (SID) or create and return a new one
umask(*mask*)	Sets the current numeric umask while returning the previous one (*mask* is used for file permissions)Ⓦ
getenv(*ev*)/ putenv(*ev*, *value*), environ	Gets/sets *value* of environment variable *ev*; the attribute os.environ is a dictionary representing all current environment variablesⓌ
geteuid()/setegid()	Gets/sets effective user ID (UID) of current process
getegid()/setegid()	Gets/sets effective group ID (GID) of current process
getpgid(*pid*)/ setpgid(*pid*, *pgrp*)	Gets/sets process GID process *pid*; for get, if *pid* is 0, the process GID of the current process is returned
getlogin()	Returns login of user running current process
times()	Returns tuple of various process timesⓌ
strerror(*code*)	Returns error message corresponding to error *code*Ⓦ
getloadavg()[a]	Returns tuple of values representing the system load average during the past 1, 5, and 15 minutes

a.   New in Python 2.3.

Module	Description
atexit[a]	Registers handlers to execute when Python interpreter exits
popen2	Provides additional functionality on top of os.popen(): provides ability to communicate via standard files to the other process; use subprocess for Python 2.4 and newer)
commands	Provides additional functionality on top of os.system(): saves all program output in a string which is returned (as opposed to just dumping output to the screen); use subprocess for Python 2.4 and newer)Ⓤ
getopt	Processes options and command-line arguments in such applications
site	Processes site-specific modules or packages
platform[b]	Attributes of the underlying platform and architecture
subprocess[c]	Subprocess management (intended to replace old functions and modules such as os.system(), os.spawn*(), os.popen*(), popen2.*, commands.*)

Table 14.9 Execution Environment Related Modules

a. New in Python 2.0.
b. New in Python 2.3.
c. New in Python 2.4.

14.9 Related Modules

In Table 14.9 you will find a list of modules other than os and sys that relate to the execution environment theme of this chapter.

14.10 Exercises

14–1. *Callable Objects*. Name Python's callable objects.
exec versus eval(). What is the difference between the exec statement and the eval() *BIF?*

14–2. *input() versus raw.input()*. What is the difference between the BIFs input() and raw_input()?

14–3. *Execution Environment*. Create a Python script that runs other Python scripts.

14–4. `os.system()`. Choose a familiar system command that performs a task without requiring input and either outputs to the screen or does not output at all. Use the `os.system()` call to run that program. Extra credit: Port your solution to `subprocess.call()`.

14–5. `commands.getoutput()`. Solve the previous problem using `commands.getoutput()`.

14–6. *popen() Family.* Choose another familiar system command that takes text from standard input and manipulates or otherwise outputs the data. Use `os.popen()` to communicate with this program. Where does the output go? Try using `popen2.popen2()` instead.

14–7. *subprocess Module.* Take your solutions from the previous problem and port them to the `subprocess` module.

14–8. *Exit Function.* Design a function to be called when your program exits. Install it as `sys.exitfunc()`, run your program, and show that your exit function was indeed called.

14–9. *Shells.* Create a shell (operating system interface) program. Present a command-line interface that accepts operating system commands for execution (any platform).

   Extra credit 1: Support pipes (see the `dup()`, `dup2()`, and `pipe()` functions in the os module). This piping procedure allows the standard output of one process to be connected to the standard input of another.

   Extra credit 2: Support inverse pipes using parentheses, giving your shell a functional programming-like interface. In other words, instead of piping commands like. . .

```
ps -ef | grep root | sort -n +1
```

   . . . support a more functional style like. . .

```
sort(grep(ps -ef, root), -n, +1)
```

14–10. *fork()/exec*() versus spawn*().* What is the difference between using the `fork()`-`exec*()` pairs vs. the `spawn*()` family of functions? Do you get more with one over the other?

14–11. *Generating and Executing Python Code.* Take the `funcAttrs.py` script (Example 14.4) and use it to add testing code to functions that you have in some of your existing programs. Build a testing framework that runs your test code every time it encounters your special function attributes.

Part II

ADVANCED TOPICS

REGULAR EXPRESSIONS

Chapter Topics

- Introduction/Motivation
- Special Characters and Symbols
- Regular Expressions and Python
- `re` Module

Chapter 15

15.1 Introduction/Motivation

Manipulating text/data is a big thing. If you don't believe me, look very carefully at what computers primarily do today. Word processing, "fill-out-form" Web pages, streams of information coming from a database dump, stock quote information, news feeds—the list goes on and on. Because we may not know the exact text or data that we have programmed our machines to process, it becomes advantageous to be able to express this text or data in patterns that a machine can recognize and take action upon.

If I were running an electronic mail (e-mail) archiving company, and you were one of my customers who requested all his or her e-mail sent and received last February, for example, it would be nice if I could set a computer program to collate and forward that information to you, rather than having a human being read through your e-mail and process your request manually. You would be horrified (and infuriated) that someone would be rummaging through your messages, even if his or her eyes were *supposed* to be looking only at time-stamp. Another example request might be to look for a subject line like "ILOVEYOU" indicating a virus-infected message and remove those e-mail messages from your personal archive. So this begs the question of how we can program machines with the ability to look for patterns in text.

Regular expressions (REs) provide such an infrastructure for advanced text pattern matching, extraction, and/or search-and-replace functionality. REs are simply strings that use special symbols and characters to indicate pattern repetition or to represent multiple characters so that they can "match" a set of strings with similar characteristics described by the pattern (Figure 15–1). In other words, they enable matching of multiple strings—an RE pattern that matched only one string would be rather boring and ineffective, wouldn't you say?

Figure 15–1   You can use regular expressions, such as the one here, which recognizes valid Python identifiers. "`[A-Za-z]\w+`" means the first character should be alphabetic, i.e., either A–Z or a–z, followed by at least one (+) alphanumeric character (\w). In our filter, notice how many strings go into the filter, but the only ones to come out are the ones we asked for via the RE. One example that did not make it was "4xZ" because it starts with a number.

Python supports REs through the standard library `re` module. In this introductory subsection, we will give you a brief and concise introduction. Due to its brevity, only the most common aspects of REs used in everyday Python programming will be covered. Your experience will, of course, vary. We highly recommend reading any of the official supporting documentation as well as external texts on this interesting subject. You will never look at strings the same way again!

CORE NOTE: Searching versus matching

Throughout this chapter, you will find references to searching and matching. When we are strictly discussing regular expressions with respect to patterns in strings, we will say "matching," referring to the term pattern-matching. In Python terminology, there are two main ways to accomplish pattern-matching: searching, i.e., looking for a pattern match in any part of a string, and matching, i.e., attempting to match a pattern to an entire string (starting from the beginning). Searches are accomplished using the `search()` *function or method, and matching is done with the* `match()` *function or method. In summary, we keep the term "matching" universal when referencing patterns, and we differentiate between "searching" and "matching" in terms of how Python accomplishes pattern-matching.*

15.1.1 Your First Regular Expression

As we mentioned above, REs are strings containing text and special characters that describe a pattern with which to recognize multiple strings. We also briefly discussed a regular expression *alphabet* and for general text, the alphabet used for regular expressions is the set of all uppercase and lowercase letters plus numeric digits. Specialized alphabets are also possible, for instance, one consisting of only the characters "0" and "1". The set of all strings over this alphabet describes all binary strings, i.e., "0," "1," "00," "01," "10," "11," "100," etc.

Let us look at the most basic of regular expressions now to show you that although REs are sometimes considered an "advanced topic," they can also be rather simplistic. Using the standard alphabet for general text, we present some simple REs and the strings that their patterns describe. The following regular expressions are the most basic, "true vanilla," as it were. They simply consist of a string pattern that matches only one string, the string defined by the regular expression. We now present the REs followed by the strings that match them:

RE Pattern	String(s) Matched
foo	foo
Python	Python
abc123	abc123

The first regular expression pattern from the above chart is "foo." This pattern has no special symbols to match any other symbol other than those described, so the only string that matches this pattern is the string "foo." The same thing applies to "Python" and "abc123." The power of regular expressions comes in when special characters are used to define character sets, subgroup matching, and pattern repetition. It is these special symbols that allow an RE to match a set of strings rather than a single one.

15.2 Special Symbols and Characters

We will now introduce the most popular of the *metacharacters*, special characters and symbols, which give regular expressions their power and flexibility. You will find the most common of these symbols and characters in Table 15.1.

Table 15.1 Common Regular Expression Symbols and Special Characters

Notation	Description	Example RE
Symbols		
literal	Match literal string value *literal*	foo
re1|*re2*	Match regular expressions *re1* or *re2*	foo|bar
.	Match *any character* (except NEWLINE)	b.b
^	Match *start of string*	^Dear
$	Match *end of string*	/bin/*sh$
*	Match *0 or more* occurrences of preceding RE	[A-Za-z0-9]*
+	Match *1 or more* occurrences of preceding RE	[a-z]+\.com
?	Match *0 or 1* occurrence(s) of preceding RE	goo?
{*N*}	Match *N* occurrences of preceding RE	[0-9]{3}

Table 15.1 Common Regular Expression Symbols and Special Characters (continued)

Notation	Description	Example RE
Symbols		
{M,N}	Match from *M* to *N* occurrences of preceding RE	[0-9]{5,9}
[...]	Match any single character from *character* class	[aeiou]
[..x-y..]	Match any single character in the *range from* x to y	[0-9], [A-Za-z]
[^...]	*Do not match* any character from character class, including any ranges, if present	[^aeiou], [^A-Za-z0-9_]
(*|+|?|{})?	Apply "non-greedy" versions of above occurrence/repetition symbols (*, +, ?, {})	.*?[a-z]
(...)	Match enclosed RE and save as *subgroup*	([0-9]{3})?, f(oo|u)bar
Special Characters		
\d	Match any decimal *digit*, same as [0-9] (\D is inverse of \d: do not match any numeric digit)	data\d+.txt
\w	Match any *alphanumeric* character, same as [A-Za-z0-9_] (\W is inverse of \w)	[A-Za-z_]\w+
\s	Match *any whitespace* character, same as [\n\t\r\v\f] (\S is inverse of \s)	of\sthe
\b	Match any *word boundary* (\B is inverse of \b)	\bThe\b
\nn	Match saved *subgroup nn* (see (...) above)	price: \16
\c	Match any *special character c* verbatim (i.e., without its special meaning, literal)	\., \\, *
\A (\Z)	Match *start (end) of string* (also see ^ and $ above)	\ADear

15.2.1 Matching More Than One RE Pattern with Alternation (|)

The pipe symbol (|), a vertical bar on your keyboard, indicates an *alternation* operation, meaning that it is used to choose from one of the different regular expressions, which are separated by the pipe symbol. For example, below are some patterns that employ alternation, along with the strings they match:

RE Pattern	Strings Matched
at|home	at, home
r2d2|c3po	r2d2, c3po
bat|bet|bit	bat, bet, bit

With this one symbol, we have just increased the flexibility of our regular expressions, enabling the matching of more than just one string. Alternation is also sometimes called union or logical OR.

15.2.2 Matching Any Single Character (.)

The dot or period (.) symbol matches any single character except for NEWLINE (Python REs have a compilation flag [S or DOTALL], which can override this to include NEWLINEs.). Whether letter, number, whitespace not including "\n," printable, non-printable, or a symbol, the dot can match them all.

RE Pattern	Strings Matched
f.o	Any character between "f" and "o", e.g., fao, f9o, f#o, etc.
..	Any pair of characters
.end	Any character before the string end

Q: What if I want to match the dot or period character?

A: In order to specify a dot character explicitly, you must escape its functionality with a backslash, as in "\.".

15.2.3 Matching from the Beginning or End of Strings or Word Boundaries (^/$ /\b /\B)

There are also symbols and related special characters to specify searching for patterns at the beginning and ending of strings. To match a pattern starting from the beginning, you must use the carat symbol (^) or the special character \A (backslash-capital "A"). The latter is primarily for keyboards that do not have the carat symbol, i.e., international. Similarly, the dollar sign ($) or \z will match a pattern from the end of a string.

Patterns that use these symbols differ from most of the others we describe in this chapter since they dictate location or position. In the Core Note above, we noted that a distinction is made between "matching," attempting matches of entire strings starting at the beginning, and "searching," attempting matches from anywhere within a string. With that said, here are some examples of "edge-bound" RE search patterns:

RE Pattern	Strings Matched
`^From`	Any string that starts with `From`
`/bin/tcsh$`	Any string that ends with `/bin/tcsh`
`^Subject: hi$`	Any string consisting solely of the string `Subject: hi`

Again, if you want to match either (or both) of these characters verbatim, you must use an escaping backslash. For example, if you wanted to match any string that ended with a dollar sign, one possible RE solution would be the pattern ".*\$$".

The `\b` and `\B` special characters pertain to word boundary matches. The difference between them is that `\b` will match a pattern to a word boundary, meaning that a pattern must be at the beginning of a word, whether there are any characters in front of it (word in the middle of a string) or not (word at the beginning of a line). And likewise, `\B` will match a pattern only if it appears starting in the middle of a word (i.e., not at a word boundary). Here are some examples:

RE Pattern	Strings Matched
`the`	Any string containing `the`
`\bthe`	Any word that starts with `the`
`\bthe\b`	Matches only the word `the`
`\Bthe`	Any string that contains but does not begin with `the`

15.2.4 Creating Character Classes ([ ])

While the dot is good for allowing matches of any symbols, there may be occasions where there are specific characters you want to match. For this reason, the bracket symbols ([ ]) were invented. The regular expression will match any of the enclosed characters. Here are some examples:

RE Pattern	Strings Matched
`b[aeiu]t`	`bat`, `bet`, `bit`, `but`
`[cr][23][dp][o2]`	A string of 4 characters: first is "r" or "c," then "2" or "3," followed by "d" or "p," and finally, either "o" or "2," e.g., `c2do`, `r3p2`, `r2d2`, `c3po`, etc.

One side note regarding the RE "`[cr][23][dp][o2]`"—a more restrictive version of this RE would be required to allow only "r2d2" or "c3po" as valid strings. Because brackets merely imply "logical OR" functionality, it is not possible to use brackets to enforce such a requirement. The only solution is to use the pipe, as in "`r2d2|c3po`".

For single-character REs, though, the pipe and brackets are equivalent. For example, let's start with the regular expression "ab," which matches only the string with an "a" followed by a "b". If we wanted either a one-letter string, i.e., either "a" or a "b," we could use the RE "`[ab]`." Because "a" and "b" are individual strings, we can also choose the RE "`a|b`". However, if we wanted to match the string with the pattern "ab" followed by "cd," we cannot use the brackets because they work only for single characters. In this case, the only solution is "`ab|cd`," similar to the "`r2d2/c3po`" problem just mentioned.

15.2.5 Denoting Ranges (–) and Negation (^)

In addition to single characters, the brackets also support ranges of characters. A hyphen between a pair of symbols enclosed in brackets is used to indicate a range of characters, e.g., A–Z, a–z, or 0–9 for uppercase letters, lowercase letters, and numeric digits, respectively. This is a lexicographic range, so you are not restricted to using just alphanumeric characters. Additionally, if a caret (^) is the first character immediately inside the open left bracket, this symbolizes a directive *not* to match any of the characters in the given character set.

RE Pattern	Strings Matched
`z.[0-9]`	"z" followed by any character then followed by a single digit
`[r-u][env-y]` `[us]`	"r" "s," "t" or "u" followed by "e," "n," "v," "w," "x," or "y" followed by "u" or "s"
`[^aeiou]`	A non-vowel character (Exercise: Why do we say "non-vowels" rather than "consonants"?)
`[^\t\n]`	Not a TAB or NEWLINE
`["-a]`	In an ASCII system, all characters that fall between "" and "a," i.e., between ordinals 34 and 97

15.2.6 Multiple Occurrence/Repetition Using Closure Operators (*, +, ?, { })

We will now introduce the most common RE notations, namely, the special symbols *, +, and ?, all of which can be used to match single, multiple, or no occurrences of string patterns. The asterisk or star operator (*) will match zero or more occurrences of the RE immediately to its left (in language and compiler theory, this operation is known as the *Kleene Closure*). The plus operator (+) will match one or more occurrences of an RE (known as *Positive Closure*), and the question mark operator (?) will match exactly 0 or 1 occurrences of an RE.

There are also brace operators ({ }) with either a single value or a comma-separated pair of values. These indicate a match of exactly N occurrences (for {N}) or a range of occurrences, i.e., {M, N} will match from M to N occurrences. These symbols may also be escaped with the backslash, i.e., "*" matches the asterisk, etc.

In the table above, we notice the question mark is used more than once (overloaded), meaning either matching 0 or 1 occurrences, or its other meaning: if it follows any matching using the close operators, it will direct the regular expression engine to match as few repetitions as possible.

What does that last part mean, "as few . . . as possible?" When pattern-matching is employed using the grouping operators, the regular expression engine will try to "absorb" as many characters as possible which match the pattern. This is known as being *greedy*. The question mark tells the engine to lay off and if possible, take as few characters as possible in the current match, leaving the rest to match as many of succeeding characters of the next pattern (if applicable). We will show you a great example where non-greediness is required toward the end of the chapter. For now, let us continue to look at the closure operators:

RE Pattern	Strings Matched
`[dn]ot?`	"d" or "n," followed by an "o" and, at most, one "t" after that, i.e., do, no, dot, not
`0?[1-9]`	Any numeric digit, possibly prepended with a "0," e.g., the set of numeric representations of the months January to September, whether single- or double-digits
`[0-9]{15,16}`	Fifteen or sixteen digits, e.g., credit card numbers
`</?[^>]+>`	Strings that match all valid (and invalid) HTML tags
`[KQRBNP][a-h][1-8]-[a-h][1-8]`	Legal chess move in "long algebraic" notation (move only, no capture, check, etc.), i.e., strings which start with any of "K," "Q," "R," "B," "N," or "P" followed by a hyphenated-pair of chess board grid locations from "a1" to "h8" (and everything in between), with the first coordinate indicating the former position and the second being the new position.

15.2.7 Special Characters Representing Character Sets

We also mentioned that there are special characters that may represent character sets. Rather than using a range of "0–9," you may simply use "\d" to indicate the match of any decimal digit. Another special character "\w" can be used to denote the entire alphanumeric character class, serving as a shortcut for "A-Za-z0-9_", and "\s" for whitespace characters. Uppercase versions of these strings symbolize *non*-matches, i.e., "\D" matches any non-decimal digit (same as "[^0-9]"), etc.

Using these shortcuts, we will present a few more complex examples:

RE Pattern	Strings Matched
\w+-\d+	Alphanumeric string and number separated by a hyphen
[A-Za-z]\w*	Alphabetic first character, additional characters (if present) can be alphanumeric (almost equivalent to the set of valid Python identifiers [see exercises])
\d{3}-\d{3}-\d{4}	(American) telephone numbers with an area code prefix, as in 800-555-1212
\w+@\w+\.com	Simple e-mail addresses of the form *XXX@YYY.com*

15.2.8 Designating Groups with Parentheses (( ))

Now, perhaps we have achieved the goal of matching a string and discarding non-matches, but in some cases, we may also be more interested in the data that we did match. Not only do we want to know whether the entire string matched our criteria, but also whether we can extract any specific strings or substrings that were part of a successful match. The answer is yes. To accomplish this, surround any RE with a pair of parentheses.

A pair of parentheses (( )) can accomplish either (or both) of the below when used with regular expressions:

- Grouping regular expressions
- Matching subgroups

One good example for wanting to group regular expressions is when you have two different REs with which you want to compare a string. Another reason is to group an RE in order to use a repetition operator on the entire RE (as opposed to an individual character or character class).

One side effect of using parentheses is that the substring that matched the pattern is saved for future use. These subgroups can be recalled for the same match or search, or extracted for post-processing. You will see some examples of pulling out subgroups at the end of Section 15.3.9.

Why are matches of subgroups important? The main reason is that there are times where you want to extract the patterns you match, in addition to making a match. For example, what if we decided to match the pattern "\w+-\d+" but wanted save the alphabetic first part and the numeric second part individually? This may be desired because with any successful match, we may want to see just what those strings were that matched our RE patterns.

If we add parentheses to both subpatterns, i.e., "(\w+)-(\d+)," then we can access each of the matched subgroups individually. Subgrouping is preferred because the alternative is to write code to determine we have a match, then execute another separate routine (which we also had to create) to parse the entire match just to extract both parts. Why not let Python do it, since it is a supported feature of the re module, instead of reinventing the wheel?

RE Pattern	Strings Matched
`\d+(\.\d*)?`	Strings representing simple floating point number, that is, any number of digits followed optionally by a single decimal point and zero or more numeric digits, as in "0.004," "2," "75." etc.
`(Mr?s?\. )?[A-Z][a-z]* [ A-Za-z-]+`	First name and last name, with a restricted first name (must start with uppercase; lowercase only for remaining letters, if any), the full name prepended by an optional title of "Mr.," "Mrs.," "Ms.," or "M.," and a flexible last name, allowing for multiple words, dashes, and uppercase letters

15.3 REs and Python

Now that we know all about regular expressions, we can examine how Python currently supports regular expressions through the re module. The re module was introduced to Python in version 1.5. If you are using an older version of Python, you will have to use the now-obsolete regex and regsub modules—these older modules are more Emacs-flavored, are not as full-featured, and are in many ways incompatible with the current re module. Both modules were removed from Python in 2.5, and import either of the modules from 2.5 and above triggers Import Error exception.

2.5

However, regular expressions are still regular expressions, so most of the basic concepts from this section can be used with the old regex and regsub software. In contrast, the new re module supports the more powerful and regular Perl-style (Perl5) REs, allows multiple threads to share the same compiled RE objects, and supports named subgroups. In addition, there is a transition module called `reconvert` to help developers move from `regex/regsub` to `re`. However, be aware that although there are different flavors of regular expressions, we will primarily focus on the current incarnation for Python.

The `re` engine was rewritten in 1.6 for performance enhancements as well as adding Unicode support. The interface was not changed, hence the reason the module name was left alone. The new `re` engine—known internally as `sre`—thus replaces the existing 1.5 engine—internally called `pcre`.

15.3.1 `re` Module: Core Functions and Methods

The chart in Table 15.2 lists the more popular functions and methods from the `re` module. Many of these functions are also available as methods of compiled regular expression objects "regex objects" and RE "match objects." In this subsection, we will look at the two main functions/methods, `match()` and `search()`, as well as the `compile()` function. We will introduce several more in the next section, but for more information on all these and the others that we do not cover, we refer you to the Python documentation.

Table 15.2 Common Regular Expression Functions and Methods

Function/Method	Description
`re` Module Function Only	
`compile(pattern, flags=0)`	Compile RE `pattern` with any optional `flags` and return a regex object
`re` Module Functions and regex Object Methods	
`match(pattern, string, flags=0)`	Attempt to match RE `pattern` to `string` with optional `flags`; return match object on success, `None` on failure
`search(pattern, string, flags=0)`	Search for first occurrence of RE `pattern` within `string` with optional `flags`; return match object on success, `None` on failure
`findall(pattern, string[, flags])`[a]	Look for all (non-overlapping) occurrences of `pattern` in `string`; return a list of matches
`finditer(pattern, string[, flags])`[b]	Same as `findall()` except returns an iterator instead of a list; for each match, the iterator returns a match object

Table 15.3 Common Regular Expression Functions and Methods (continued)

Function/Method	Description
split(pattern, string, max=0)	Split *string* into a list according to RE *pattern* delimiter and return list of successful matches, splitting at most *max* times (split all occurrences is the default)
sub(pattern, repl, string, max=0)	Replace all occurrences of the RE *pattern* in *string* with *repl*, substituting all occurrences unless *max* provided (also see subn() which, in addition, returns the number of substitutions made)
Match Object Methods	
group(num=0)	Return entire match (or specific subgroup *num*)
groups()	Return all matching subgroups in a tuple (empty if there weren't any)

a. New in Python 1.5.2; *flags* parameter added in 2.4.
b. New in Python 2.2; *flags* parameter added in 2.4.

CORE NOTE: RE compilation (to compile or not to compile?)

In Chapter 14, we described how Python code is eventually compiled into bytecode, which is then executed by the interpreter. In particular, we mentioned that calling eval() *or* **exec** *with a code object rather than a string provides a significant performance improvement due to the fact that the compilation process does not have to be performed. In other words, using precompiled code objects is faster than using strings because the interpreter will have to compile it into a code object (anyway) before execution.*

The same concept applies to REs—regular expression patterns must be compiled into regex objects before any pattern matching can occur. For REs, which are compared many times during the course of execution, we highly recommend using precompilation first because, again, REs have to be compiled anyway, so doing it ahead of time is prudent for performance reasons. re.compile() *provides this functionality.*

The module functions do cache the compiled objects, though, so it's not as if every search() *and* match() *with the same RE pattern requires compilation. Still, you save the cache lookups and do not have to make function calls with the same string over and over. In Python 1.5.2, this cache held up to 20 compiled RE objects, but in 1.6, due to the additional overhead of Unicode awareness, the compilation engine is a bit slower, so the cache has been extended to 100 compiled regex objects.*

15.3.2 Compiling REs with `compile()`

Almost all of the re module functions we will be describing shortly are available as methods for regex objects. Remember, even with our recommendation, precompilation is not required. If you compile, you will use methods; if you don't, you will just use functions. The good news is that either way, the names are the same whether a function or a method. (This is the reason why there are module functions and methods that are identical, e.g., search(), match(), etc., in case you were wondering.) Since it saves one small step for most of our examples, we will use strings instead. We will throw in a few with compilation, though, just so you know how it is done.

Optional flags may be given as arguments for specialized compilation. These flags allow for case-insensitive matching, using system locale settings for matching alphanumeric characters, etc. Please refer to the documentation for more details. These flags, some of which have been briefly mentioned (i.e., DOTALL, LOCALE), may also be given to the module versions of match() and search() for a specific pattern match attempt—these flags are mostly for compilation reasons, hence the reason why they can be passed to the module versions of match() and search(), which do compile an RE pattern once. If you want to use these flags with the methods, they must already be integrated into the compiled regex objects.

In addition to the methods below, regex objects also have some data attributes, two of which include any compilation flags given as well as the regular expression pattern compiled.

15.3.3 Match Objects and the `group()` and `groups()` Methods

There is another object type in addition to the regex object when dealing with regular expressions, the *match object*. These are the objects returned on successful calls to match() or search(). Match objects have two primary methods, group() and groups().

group() will either return the entire match, or a specific subgroup, if requested. groups() will simply return a tuple consisting of only/all the subgroups. If there are no subgroups requested, then groups() returns an empty tuple while group() still returns the entire match.

Python REs also allow for named matches, which are beyond the scope of this introductory section on REs. We refer you to the complete re module documentation regarding all the more advanced details we have omitted here.

15.3.4 Matching Strings with match()

`match()` is the first `re` module function and RE object (regex object) method we will look at. The `match()` function attempts to match the pattern to the string, starting at the beginning. If the match is successful, a match object is returned, but on failure, `None` is returned. The `group()` method of a match object can be used to show the successful match. Here is an example of how to use `match()` [and `group()`]:

```
>>> m = re.match('foo', 'foo')   # pattern matches string
>>> if m is not None:            # show match if successful
...         m.group()
...
'foo'
```

The pattern "foo" matches exactly the string "foo." We can also confirm that `m` is an example of a match object from within the interactive interpreter:

```
>>> m                            # confirm match object returned
<re.MatchObject instance at 80ebf48>
```

Here is an example of a failed match where `None` is returned:

```
>>> m = re.match('foo', 'bar')# pattern does not match string
>>> if m is not None: m.group()# (1-line version of if
clause)
...
>>>
```

The match above fails, thus `None` is assigned to `m`, and no action is taken due to the way we constructed our **if** statement. For the remaining examples, we will try to leave out the **if** check for brevity, if possible, but in practice it is a good idea to have it there to prevent `AttributeError` exceptions (`None` is returned on failures, which does not have a `group()` attribute [method].)

A match will still succeed even if the string is longer than the pattern as long as the pattern matches from the beginning of the string. For example, the pattern "foo" will find a match in the string "food on the table" because it matches the pattern from the beginning:

```
>>> m = re.match('foo', 'food on the table') # match succeeds
>>> m.group()
'foo'
```

As you can see, although the string is longer than the pattern, a successful match was made from the beginning of the string. The substring "foo" represents the match, which was extracted from the larger string.

We can even sometimes bypass saving the result altogether, taking advantage of Python's object-oriented nature:

```
>>> re.match('foo', 'food on the table').group()
'foo'
```

Note from a few paragraphs above that an `AttributeError` will be generated on a non-match.

15.3.5 Looking for a Pattern within a String with search() (Searching versus Matching)

The chances are greater that the pattern you seek is somewhere in the middle of a string, rather than at the beginning. This is where `search()` comes in handy. It works exactly in the same way as match except that it searches for the first occurrence of the given RE pattern anywhere with its string argument. Again, a match object is returned on success and `None` otherwise.

We will now illustrate the difference between `match()` and `search()`. Let us try a longer string match attempt. This time, we will try to match our string "foo" to "seafood":

```
>>> m = re.match('foo', 'seafood')      # no match
>>> if m is not None: m.group()
...
>>>
```

As you can see, there is no match here. `match()` attempts to match the pattern to the string from the beginning, i.e., the "f" in the pattern is matched against the "s" in the string, which fails immediately. However, the string "foo" *does* appear (elsewhere) in "seafood," so how do we get Python to say "yes"? The answer is by using the `search()` function. Rather than attempting a *match*, `search()` looks for the first occurrence of the pattern within the string. `search()` searches strictly from left to right.

```
>>> m = re.search('foo', 'seafood')   # use search() instead
>>> if m is not None: m.group()
...
'foo'                      # search succeeds where match failed
>>>
```

We will be using the `match()` and `search()` regex object methods and the `group()` and `groups()` match object methods for the remainder of this subsection, exhibiting a broad range of examples of how to use regular expressions with Python. We will be using almost all of the special characters and symbols that are part of the regular expression syntax.

15.3.6 Matching More than One String (|)

In Section 15.2, we used the pipe in the RE "bat|bet|bit." Here is how we would use that RE with Python:

```
>>> bt = 'bat|bet|bit'          # RE pattern: bat, bet, bit
>>> m = re.match(bt, 'bat')     # 'bat' is a match
>>> if m is not None: m.group()
...
'bat'
>>> m = re.match(bt, 'blt')     # no match for 'blt'
>>> if m is not None: m.group()
...
>>> m = re.match(bt, 'He bit me!')# does not match string
>>> if m is not None: m.group()
...
>>> m = re.search(bt, 'He bit me!')# found 'bit' via search
>>> if m is not None: m.group()
...
'bit'
```

15.3.7 Matching Any Single Character (.)

In the examples below, we show that a dot cannot match a NEWLINE or a non-character, i.e., the empty string:

```
>>> anyend = '.end'
>>> m = re.match(anyend, 'bend')     # dot matches 'b'
>>> if m is not None: m.group()
...
'bend'
>>> m = re.match(anyend, 'end')      # no char to match
>>> if m is not None: m.group()
...
>>> m = re.match(anyend, '\nend')    # any char except \n
>>> if m is not None: m.group()
...
>>> m = re.search('.end', 'The end.')# matches ' ' in search
>>> if m is not None: m.group()
...
' end'
```

The following is an example of searching for a real dot (decimal point) in a regular expression where we escape its functionality with a backslash:

```
>>> patt314 = '3.14'                   # RE dot
>>> pi_patt = '3\.14'                  # literal dot (dec. point)
>>> m = re.match(pi_patt, '3.14')      # exact match
>>> if m is not None: m.group()
...
'3.14'
>>> m = re.match(patt314, '3014')      # dot matches '0'
>>> if m is not None: m.group()
...
'3014'
>>> m = re.match(patt314, '3.14')      # dot matches '.'
>>> if m is not None: m.group()
...
'3.14'
```

15.3.8 Creating Character Classes ([ ])

Earlier, we had a long discussion about "[cr][23][dp][o2]" and how it differs from "r2d2|c3po." With the examples below, we will show that "r2d2|c3po" is more restrictive than "[cr][23][dp][o2]":

```
>>> m = re.match('[cr][23][dp][o2]', 'c3po')# matches 'c3po'
>>> if m is not None: m.group()
...
'c3po'
>>> m = re.match('[cr][23][dp][o2]', 'c2do')# matches 'c2do'
>>> if m is not None: m.group()
...
'c2do'
>>> m = re.match('r2d2|c3po', 'c2do')# does not match 'c2do'
>>> if m is not None: m.group()
...
>>> m = re.match('r2d2|c3po', 'r2d2')# matches 'r2d2'
>>> if m is not None: m.group()
...
'r2d2'
```

15.3.9 Repetition, Special Characters, and Grouping

The most common aspects of REs involve the use of special characters, multiple occurrences of RE patterns, and using parentheses to group and extract submatch patterns. One particular RE we looked at related to simple e-mail addresses ("\w+@\w+\.com"). Perhaps we want to match more e-mail addresses than this RE allows. In order to support an additional hostname in front of the domain, i.e., "www.xxx.com" as opposed to accepting only "xxx.com" as the entire domain, we have to modify our existing RE. To indicate that the hostname is optional, we create a pattern that matches the hostname (followed by a dot), use the ? operator indicating zero or one copy of this pattern, and insert the optional RE into our previous RE as follows: "\w+@(\w+\.)?\w+\.com." As you can see from the examples below, either one or two names are now accepted in front of the ".com":

```
>>> patt = '\w+@(\w+\.)?\w+\.com'
>>> re.match(patt, 'nobody@xxx.com').group()
'nobody@xxx.com'
>>> re.match(patt, 'nobody@www.xxx.com').group()
'nobody@www.xxx.com'
```

Furthermore, we can even extend our example to allow any number of intermediate subdomain names with the pattern below. Take special note of our slight change from using ? to *. : "\w+@(\w+\.)*\w+\.com":

```
>>> patt = '\w+@(\w+\.)*\w+\.com'
>>> re.match(patt, 'nobody@www.xxx.yyy.zzz.com').group()
'nobody@www.xxx.yyy.zzz.com'
```

However, we must add the disclaimer that using solely alphanumeric characters does not match all the possible characters that may make up e-mail addresses. The above RE patterns would not match a domain such as "xxx-yyy.com" or other domains with "\w" characters.

Earlier, we discussed the merits of using parentheses to match and save subgroups for further processing rather than coding a separate routine to manually parse a string after an RE match had been determined. In particular, we discussed a simple RE pattern of an alphanumeric string and a number separated by a hyphen, "\w+-\d+," and how adding subgrouping to form a new RE, "(\w+)-(\d+)," would do the job. Here is how the original RE works:

```
>>> m = re.match('\w\w\w-\d\d\d', 'abc-123')
>>> if m is not None: m.group()
...
'abc-123'

>>> m = re.match('\w\w\w-\d\d\d', 'abc-xyz')
>>> if m is not None: m.group()
...
>>>
```

In the above code, we created an RE to recognize three alphanumeric characters followed by three digits. Testing this RE on "abc-123," we obtained positive results while "abc-xyz" fails. We will now modify our RE as discussed before to be able to extract the alphanumeric string and number. Note how we can now use the `group()` method to access individual subgroups or the `groups()` method to obtain a tuple of all the subgroups matched:

```
>>> m = re.match('(\w\w\w)-(\d\d\d)', 'abc-123')
>>> m.group()                     # entire match
'abc-123'
>>> m.group(1)                    # subgroup 1
'abc'
>>> m.group(2)                    # subgroup 2
'123'
>>> m.groups()                    # all subgroups
('abc', '123')
```

As you can see, `group()` is used in the normal way to show the entire match, but can also be used to grab individual subgroup matches. We can also use the `groups()` method to obtain a tuple of all the substring matches.

Here is a simpler example showing different group permutations, which will hopefully make things even more clear:

```
>>> m = re.match('ab', 'ab')       # no subgroups
>>> m.group()                      # entire match
'ab'
>>> m.groups()                     # all subgroups
()
>>>
>>> m = re.match('(ab)', 'ab')     # one subgroup
>>> m.group()                      # entire match
'ab'
>>> m.group(1)                     # subgroup 1
'ab'
>>> m.groups()                     # all subgroups
('ab',)
>>>
>>> m = re.match('(a)(b)', 'ab')   # two subgroups
>>> m.group()                      # entire match
'ab'
>>> m.group(1)                     # subgroup 1
'a'
>>> m.group(2)                     # subgroup 2
'b'
>>> m.groups()                     # all subgroups
```

```
('a', 'b')
>>>
>>> m = re.match('(a(b))', 'ab')          # two subgroups
>>> m.group()                             # entire match
'ab'
>>> m.group(1)                            # subgroup 1
'ab'
>>> m.group(2)                            # subgroup 2
'b'
>>> m.groups()                            # all subgroups
('ab', 'b')
```

15.3.10 Matching from the Beginning and End of Strings and on Word Boundaries

The following examples highlight the positional RE operators. These apply more for searching than matching because `match()` always starts at the beginning of a string.

```
>>> m = re.search('^The', 'The end.')      # match
>>> if m is not None: m.group()
...
'The'
>>> m = re.search('^The', 'end. The')      # not at beginning
>>> if m is not None: m.group()
...
>>> m = re.search(r'\bthe', 'bite the dog') # at a boundary
>>> if m is not None: m.group()
...
'the'
>>> m = re.search(r'\bthe', 'bitethe dog')  # no boundary
>>> if m is not None: m.group()
...
>>> m = re.search(r'\Bthe', 'bitethe dog')  # no boundary
>>> if m is not None: m.group()
...
'the'
```

You will notice the appearance of raw strings here. You may want to take a look at the Core Note toward the end of the chapter for clarification on why they are here. In general, it is a good idea to use raw strings with regular expressions.

There are four other `re` module functions and regex object methods we think you should be aware of: `findall()`, `sub()`, `subn()`, and `split()`.

15.3.11 Finding Every Occurrence with *findall()*

findall() is new to Python as of version 1.5.2. It looks for all non-overlapping occurrences of an RE pattern in a string. It is similar to search() in that it performs a string search, but it differs from match() and search() in that findall() always returns a list. The list will be empty if no occurrences are found but if successful, the list will consist of all matches found (grouped in left-to-right order of occurrence).

```
>>> re.findall('car', 'car')
['car']
>>> re.findall('car', 'scary')
['car']
>>> re.findall('car', 'carry the barcardi to the car')
['car', 'car', 'car']
```

Subgroup searches result in a more complex list returned, and that makes sense, because subgroups are a mechanism that allow you to extract specific patterns from within your single regular expression, such as matching an area code that is part of a complete telephone number, or a login name that is part of an entire e-mail address.

For a single successful match, each subgroup match is a single element of the resulting list returned by findall(); for multiple successful matches, each subgroup match is a single element in a tuple, and such tuples (one for each successful match) are the elements of the resulting list. This part may sound confusing at first, but if you try different examples, it will help clarify things.

15.3.12 Searching and Replacing with *sub()* [and *subn()*]

There are two functions/methods for search-and-replace functionality: sub() and subn(). They are almost identical and replace all matched occurrences of the RE pattern in a string with some sort of replacement. The replacement is usually a string, but it can also be a function that returns a replacement string. subn() is exactly the same as sub(), but it also returns the total number of substitutions made—both the newly substituted string and the substitution count are returned as a 2-tuple.

```
>>> re.sub('X', 'Mr. Smith', 'attn: X\n\nDear X,\n')
'attn: Mr. Smith\012\012Dear Mr. Smith,\012'
>>>
>>> re.subn('X', 'Mr. Smith', 'attn: X\n\nDear X,\n')
```

```
('attn: Mr. Smith\012\012Dear Mr. Smith,\012', 2)
>>>
>>> print re.sub('X', 'Mr. Smith', 'attn: X\n\nDear X,\n')
attn: Mr. Smith

Dear Mr. Smith,

>>> re.sub('[ae]', 'X', 'abcdef')
'XbcdXf'
>>> re.subn('[ae]', 'X', 'abcdef')
('XbcdXf', 2)
```

15.3.13 Splitting (on Delimiting Pattern) with split()

The re module and RE object method split() work similarly to its string counterpart, but rather than splitting on a fixed string, they split a string based on an RE pattern, adding some significant power to string splitting capabilities. If you do not want the string split for every occurrence of the pattern, you can specify the maximum number of splits by setting a value (other than zero) to the max argument.

If the delimiter given is not a regular expression that uses special symbols to match multiple patterns, then re.split() works in exactly the same manner as string.split(), as illustrated in the example below (which splits on a single colon):

```
>>> re.split(':', 'str1:str2:str3')
['str1', 'str2', 'str3']
```

But with regular expressions involved, we have an even more powerful tool. Take, for example, the output from the Unix who command, which lists all the users logged into a system:

```
% who
wesc      console    Jun 20 20:33
wesc      pts/9      Jun 22 01:38   (192.168.0.6)
wesc      pts/1      Jun 20 20:33   (:0.0)
wesc      pts/2      Jun 20 20:33   (:0.0)
wesc      pts/4      Jun 20 20:33   (:0.0)
wesc      pts/3      Jun 20 20:33   (:0.0)
wesc      pts/5      Jun 20 20:33   (:0.0)
wesc      pts/6      Jun 20 20:33   (:0.0)
wesc      pts/7      Jun 20 20:33   (:0.0)
wesc      pts/8      Jun 20 20:33   (:0.0)
```

Perhaps we want to save some user login information such as login name, teletype they logged in at, when they logged in, and from where. Using `string.split()` on the above would not be effective, since the spacing is erratic and inconsistent. The other problem is that there is a space between the month, day, and time for the login timestamps. We would probably want to keep these fields together.

You need some way to describe a pattern such as, "split on two or more spaces." This is easily done with regular expressions. In no time, we whip up the RE pattern "\s\s+," which does mean at least two whitespace characters. Let's create a program called `rewho.py` that reads the output of the `who` command, presumably saved into a file called `whodata.txt`. Our `rewho.py` script initially looks something like this:

```
import re
f = open('whodata.txt', 'r')
for eachLine in f.readlines():
        print re.split('\s\s+', eachLine)
f.close()
```

We will now execute the `who` command, saving the output into `whodata.txt`, and then call `rewho.py` and take a look at the results:

```
% who > whodata.txt
% rewho.py
['wesc', 'console', 'Jun 20 20:33\012']
['wesc', 'pts/9', 'Jun 22 01:38\011(192.168.0.6)\012']
['wesc', 'pts/1', 'Jun 20 20:33\011(:0.0)\012']
['wesc', 'pts/2', 'Jun 20 20:33\011(:0.0)\012']
['wesc', 'pts/4', 'Jun 20 20:33\011(:0.0)\012']
['wesc', 'pts/3', 'Jun 20 20:33\011(:0.0)\012']
['wesc', 'pts/5', 'Jun 20 20:33\011(:0.0)\012']
['wesc', 'pts/6', 'Jun 20 20:33\011(:0.0)\012']
['wesc', 'pts/7', 'Jun 20 20:33\011(:0.0)\012']
['wesc', 'pts/8', 'Jun 20 20:33\011(:0.0)\012']
```

It was a good first try, but not quite correct. For one thing, we did not anticipate a single TAB (ASCII \011) as part of the output (which looked like at least two spaces, right?), and perhaps we aren't really keen on saving the NEWLINE (ASCII \012), which terminates each line. We are now going to fix those problems as well as improve the overall quality of our application by making a few more changes.

First, we would rather run the `who` command from within the script, instead of doing it externally and saving the output to a `whodata.txt` file—doing this repeatedly gets tiring rather quickly. To accomplish invoking another program from within ours, we call upon the `os.popen()` command, discussed briefly in Section 14.5.2. Although `os.popen()` is available only on Unix systems, the point is to illustrate the functionality of `re.split()`, which is available on all platforms.

We get rid of the trailing NEWLINEs and add the detection of a single TAB as an additional, alternative `re.split()` delimiter. Presented in Example 15.1 is the final version of our `rewho.py` script:

Example 15.1 Split Output of Unix `who` Command (`rewho.py`)

This script calls the `who` command and parses the input by splitting up its data along various types of whitespace characters.

```
1   #!/usr/bin/env python
2
3   from os import popen
4   from re import split
5
6   f = popen('who', 'r')
7   for eachLine in f.readlines():
8     print split('\s\s+|\t', eachLine.strip())
9   f.close()
```

Running this script, we now get the following (correct) output:

```
% rewho.py
['wesc', 'console', 'Jun 20 20:33']
['wesc', 'pts/9', 'Jun 22 01:38', '(192.168.0.6)']
['wesc', 'pts/1', 'Jun 20 20:33', '(:0.0)']
['wesc', 'pts/2', 'Jun 20 20:33', '(:0.0)']
['wesc', 'pts/4', 'Jun 20 20:33', '(:0.0)']
['wesc', 'pts/3', 'Jun 20 20:33', '(:0.0)']
['wesc', 'pts/5', 'Jun 20 20:33', '(:0.0)']
['wesc', 'pts/6', 'Jun 20 20:33', '(:0.0)']
['wesc', 'pts/7', 'Jun 20 20:33', '(:0.0)']
['wesc', 'pts/8', 'Jun 20 20:33', '(:0.0)']
```

A similar exercise can be achieved in a DOS/Windows environment using the `dir` command in place of `who`.

While the subject of ASCII characters is still warm, we would like to note that there can be confusion between regular expression special characters and special ASCII symbols. We may use \n to represent an ASCII NEW-LINE character, but we may use \d meaning a regular expression match of a single numeric digit. Problems may occur if there is a symbol used by both ASCII and regular expressions, so in the Core Note on the following page, we recommend the use of Python raw strings to prevent any problems. One more caution: the "\w" and "\W" alphanumeric character sets are affected by

the L or LOCALE compilation flag and in Python 1.6 and newer, by Unicode
flags starting in 2.0 (U or UNICODE).

CORE NOTE: Use of Python raw strings

*You may have seen the use of raw strings in some of the examples above.
Regular expressions were a strong motivation for the advent of raw strings. The
reason is because of conflicts between ASCII characters and regular expression
special characters. As a special symbol, "\b" represents the ASCII character for
backspace, but "\b" is also a regular expression special symbol, meaning
"match" on a word boundary. In order for the RE compiler to see the two
characters "\b" as your string and not a (single) backspace, you need to escape
the backslash in the string by using another backslash, resulting in "\\b."*

*This can get messy, especially if you have a lot of special characters in your
string, adding to the confusion. We were introduced to raw strings back in
Chapter 6, and they can be (and are often) used to help keep REs looking
somewhat manageable. In fact, many Python programmers swear by these
and only use raw strings when defining regular expressions.*

*Here are some examples of differentiating between the backspace "\b"
and the regular expression "\b," with and without raw strings:*

```
>>> m = re.match('\bblow', 'blow') # backspace, no match
>>> if m is not None: m.group()
...
>>> m = re.match('\\bblow', 'blow') # escaped \, now it works
>>> if m is not None: m.group()
...
'blow'
>>> m = re.match(r'\bblow', 'blow') # use raw string instead
>>> if m is not None: m.group()
...
'blow'
```

*You may have recalled that we had no trouble using "\d" in our regular
expressions without using raw strings. That is because there is no ASCII
equivalent special character, so the regular expression compiler already
knew you meant a decimal digit.*

15.4 Regular Expressions Example

We will now run through an in-depth example of the different ways of using regular expressions for string manipulation. The first step is to come up with some
code that actually generates some random (but-not-so-random) data on which to
operate. In Example 15.2, we present gendata.py, a script that generates a

Example 15.2 Data Generator for RE Exercises (`gendata.py`)

Create random data for regular expressions practice and output the generated data to the screen.

```
1   #!/usr/bin/env python
2
3   from random import randint, choice
4   from string import lowercase
5   from sys import maxint
6   from time import ctime
7
8   doms = ( 'com', 'edu', 'net', 'org', 'gov' )
9
10  for i in range(randint(5, 10)):
11      dtint = randint(0, maxint-1)   # pick date
12      dtstr = ctime(dtint)           # date string
13
14      shorter = randint(4, 7)        # login shorter
15      em = ''
16      for j in range(shorter):       # generate login
17          em += choice(lowercase)
18
19      longer = randint(shorter, 12) # domain longer
20      dn = ''
21      for j in range(longer):        # create domain
22          dn += choice(lowercase)
23
24      print '%s::%s@%s.%s::%d-%d-%d' % (dtstr, em,
25          dn, choice(doms), dtint, shorter, longer)
```

data set. Although this program simply displays the generated set of strings to standard output, this output may very well be redirected to a test file.

This script generates strings with three fields, delimited by a pair of colons, or a double-colon. The first field is a random (32-bit) integer, which is converted to a date (see the accompanying Core Note). The next field is a randomly generated electronic mail (e-mail) address, and the final field is a set of integers separated by a single dash (-).

Running this code, we get the following output (your mileage will definitely vary) and store it locally as the file `redata.txt`:

```
Thu Jul 22 19:21:19 2004::izsp@dicqdhytvhv.edu::1090549279-4-11
Sun Jul 13 22:42:11 2008::zqeu@dxaibjgkniy.com::1216014131-4-11
Sat May  5 16:36:23 1990::fclihw@alwdbzpsdg.edu::641950583-6-10
Thu Feb 15 17:46:04 2007::uzifzf@dpyivihw.gov::1171590364-6-8
Thu Jun 26 19:08:59 2036::ugxfugt@jkhuqhs.net::2098145339-7-7
Tue Apr 10 01:04:45 2012::zkwaq@rpxwmtikse.com::1334045085-5-10
```

You may or may not be able to tell, but the output from this program is ripe for regular expression processing. Following our line-by-line explanation, we will implement several REs to operate on these data, as well as leave plenty for the end-of-chapter exercises.

Line-by-Line Explanation

Lines 1–6

In our example script, we require the use of multiple modules. But since we are utilizing only one or two functions from these modules, rather than importing the entire module, we choose in this case to import only specific attributes from these modules. Our decision to use **from-import** rather than **import** was based solely on this reasoning. The **from-import** lines follow the Unix startup directive on line 1.

Line 8

`doms` is simply a set of higher-level domain names from which we will randomly pick for each randomly generated e-mail address.

Lines 10–12

Each time `gendata.py` executes, between 5 and 10 lines of output are generated. (Our script uses the `random.randint()` function for all cases where we desire a random integer.) For each line, we choose a random integer from the entire possible range (0 to 2^{31} - 1 [`sys.maxint`]), then convert that integer to a date using `time.ctime()`. System time in Python and most Unix-based computers is based on the number of seconds that have elapsed since the "epoch," midnight UTC/GMT on January 1, 1970. If we choose a 32-bit integer, that represents one moment in time from the epoch to the maximum possible time, 2^{32} seconds *after* the epoch.

Lines 14–22

The login name for the fake e-mail address should be between 4 and 7 characters in length. To put it together, we randomly choose between 4 and 7 random lowercase letters, concatenating each letter to our string one at a time. The functionality of the `random.choice()` function is given a sequence, return a random element of that sequence. In our case, the sequence is the set of all 26 lowercase letters of the alphabet, `string.lowercase`.

We decided that the main domain name for the fake e-mail address should be between 4 and 12 characters in length, but at least as long as the login name. Again, we use random lowercase letters to put this name together letter by letter.

Lines 24–25

The key component of our script puts together all of the random data into the output line. The date string comes first, followed by the delimiter. We then put together the random e-mail address by concatenating the login name, the "@" symbol, the domain name, and a randomly chosen high-level domain. After the final double-colon, we put together a random integer string using the original time chosen (for the date string), followed by the lengths of the login and domain names, all separated by a single hyphen.

15.4.1 Matching a String

For the following exercises, create both permissive and restrictive versions of your REs. We recommend you test these REs in a short application that utilizes our sample `redata.txt` file above (or use your own generated data from running `gendata.py`). You will need to use it again when you do the exercises.

To test the RE before putting it into our little application, we will import the `re` module and assign one sample line from `redata.txt` to a string variable `data`. These statements are constant across both illustrated examples.

```
>>> import re
>>> data = 'Thu Feb 15 17:46:04 2007::uzifzf@dpyivihw.gov::1171590364-6-8'
```

In our first example, we will create a regular expression to extract (only) the days of the week from the timestamps from each line of the data file `redata.txt`. We will use the following RE:

"^Mon|^Tue|^Wed|^Thu|^Fri|^Sat|^Sun"

This example requires that the string start with ("^" RE operator) any of the seven strings listed. If we were to "translate" the above RE to English, it would read something like, "the string should start with "Mon," "Tue,". . . , "Sat," or "Sun.""

Alternatively, we can bypass all the carat operators with a single carat if we group the day strings like this:

"^(Mon|Tue|Wed|Thu|Fri|Sat|Sun)"

The parentheses around the set of strings mean that one of these strings must be encountered for a match to succeed. This is a "friendlier" version of the original RE we came up with, which did not have the parentheses. Using our modified RE, we can take advantage of the fact that we can access the matched string as a subgroup:

```
>>> patt = '^(Mon|Tue|Wed|Thu|Fri|Sat|Sun)'
>>> m = re.match(patt, data)
>>> m.group()                          # entire match
'Thu'
>>> m.group(1)                         # subgroup 1
'Thu'
>>> m.groups()                         # all subgroups
('Thu',)
```

This feature may not seem as revolutionary as we have made it out to be for this example, but it is definitely advantageous in the next example or anywhere you provide extra data as part of the RE to help in the string matching process, even though those characters may not be part of the string you are interested in.

Both of the above REs are the most restrictive, specifically requiring a set number of strings. This may not work well in an internationalization environment where localized days and abbreviations are used. A looser RE would be: "^\w{3}." This one requires only that a string begin with three consecutive alphanumeric characters. Again, to translate the RE into English, the carat indicates "begins with," the "\w" means any single alphanumeric character, and the "{3}" means that there should be 3 consecutive copies of the RE which the "{3}" embellishes. Again, if you want grouping, parentheses should be used, i.e., "^(\w{3})":

```
>>> patt = '^(\w{3})'
>>> m = re.match(patt, data)
>>> if m is not None: m.group()
...
'Thu'
>>> m.group(1)
'Thu'
```

Note that an RE of "^(\w){3}" is not correct. When the "{3}" was inside the parentheses, the match for three consecutive alphanumeric characters was made first, then represented as a group. But by moving the "{3}" outside, it is now equivalent to three consecutive single alphanumeric characters:

```
>>> patt = '^(\w){3}'
>>> m = re.match(patt, data)
>>> if m is not None: m.group()
...
'Thu'
>>> m.group(1)
'u'
```

The reason why only the "u" shows up when accessing subgroup 1 is that subgroup 1 was being continually replaced by the next character. In other words, m.group(1) started out as "T," then changed to "h," then finally was replaced by "u." These are three individual (and overlapping) groups of a single alphanumeric character, as opposed to a single group consisting of three consecutive alphanumeric characters.

In our next (and final) example, we will create a regular expression to extract the numeric fields found at the end of each line of `redata.txt`.

15.4.2 Search versus Match, and Greediness too

Before we create any REs, however, we realize that these integer data items are at the end of the data strings. This means that we have a choice of using either search or match. Initiating a search makes more sense because we know exactly what we are looking for (set of three integers), that what we seek is not at the beginning of the string, and that it does not make up the entire string. If we were to perform a match, we would have to create an RE to match the entire line and use subgroups to save the data we are interested in. To illustrate the differences, we will perform a search first, then do a match to show you that searching is more appropriate.

Since we are looking for three integers delimited by hyphens, we create our RE to indicate as such: "\d+-\d+-\d+". This regular expression means, "any number of digits (at least one, though) followed by a hyphen, then more digits, another hyphen, and finally, a final set of digits." We test our RE now using `search()`:

```
>>> patt = '\d+-\d+-\d+'
>>> re.search(patt, data).group()        # entire match
'1171590364-6-8'
```

A match attempt, however, would fail. Why? Because matches start at the beginning of the string, the numeric strings are at the rear. We would have to create another RE to match the entire string. We can be lazy though, by using ".+" to indicate just an arbitrary set of characters followed by what we are really interested in:

```
patt = '.+\d+-\d+-\d+'
>>> re.match(patt, data).group()        # entire match
'Thu Feb 15 17:46:04 2007::uzifzf@dpyivihw.gov::1171590364-
6-8'
```

This works great, but we really want the number fields at the end, not the entire string, so we have to use parentheses to group what we want:

```
>>> patt = '.+(\d+-\d+-\d+)'
>>> re.match(patt, data).group(1)        # subgroup 1
'4-6-8'
```

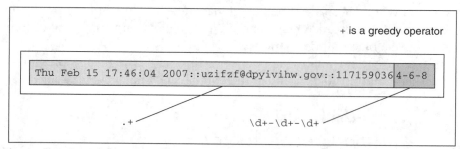

Figure 15–2   Why our match went awry: + is a greedy operator

What happened? We should have extracted "`1171590364-6-8`," not just "`4-6-8`." Where is the rest of the first integer? The problem is that regular expressions are inherently greedy. That means that with wildcard patterns, regular expressions are evaluated in left-to-right order and try to "grab" as many characters as possible which match the pattern. In our case above, the "`.+`" grabbed every single character from the beginning of the string, including most of the first integer field we wanted. The "`\d+`" needed only a single digit, so it got "4", while the "`.+`" matched everything from the beginning of the string up to that first digit: "Thu Feb 15 17:46:04 2007::uzifzf@dpyivihw.gov::117159036", as indicated below in Figure 15–2.

One solution is to use the "don't be greedy" operator, "`?`". It can be used after "`*`", "`+`", or "`?`". This directs the regular expression engine to match as few characters as possible. So if we place a "`?`" after the "`.+`", we obtain the desired result illustrated in Figure 15–3.

```
>>> patt = '.+?(\d+-\d+-\d+)'
>>> re.match(patt, data).group(1)          # subgroup 1
'1171590364-6-8'
```

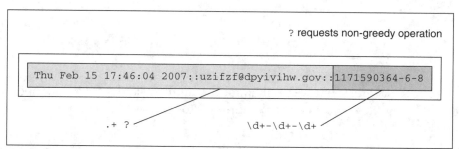

Figure 15–3   Solving the greedy problem: ? requests non-greediness

Another solution, which is actually easier, is to recognize that "::" is our field separator. You can then just use the regular string `strip('::')` method and get all the parts, then take another split on the dash with `strip('-')` to obtain the three integers you were originally seeking. Now, we did not choose this solution first because this is how we put the strings together to begin with using `gendata.py`!

One final example: let us say we want to pull out only the middle integer of the three-integer field. Here is how we would do it (using a search so we don't have to match the entire string): "`-(\d+)-`". Trying out this pattern, we get:

```
>>> patt = '-(\d+)-'
>>> m = re.search(patt, data)
>>> m.group()                    # entire match
'-6-'
>>> m.group(1)                   # subgroup 1
'6'
```

We barely touched upon the power of regular expressions, and in this limited space we have not been able to do them justice. However, we hope that we have given an informative introduction so that you can add this powerful tool to your programming skills. We suggest you refer to the documentation for more details on how to use REs with Python. For more complete immersion into the world of regular expressions, we recommend *Mastering Regular Expressions* by Jeffrey E. F. Friedl.

15.5 Exercises

Regular Expressions. Create regular expressions in Exercises 15–1 to 15–12 to:

15–1. Recognize the following strings: "bat," "bit," "but," "hat," "hit," or "hut."

15–2. Match any pair of words separated by a single space, i.e., first and last names.

15–3. Match any word and single letter separated by a comma and single space, as in last name, first initial.

15–4. Match the set of all valid Python identifiers.

15–5. Match a street address according to your local format (keep your RE general enough to match any number of street words, including the type designation). For example, American street addresses use the format: 1180 Bordeaux Drive. Make your RE general enough to support multi-word street names like: 3120 De la Cruz Boulevard.

15–6. Match simple Web domain names that begin with "www." and end with a ".com" suffix, e.g., www.yahoo.com. Extra credit if your RE also supports other high-level domain names: .edu, .net, etc., e.g., www.ucsc.edu.

15–7. Match the set of the string representations of all Python integers.

15–8. Match the set of the string representations of all Python longs.

15–9. Match the set of the string representations of all Python floats.

15–10. Match the set of the string representations of all Python complex numbers.

15–11. Match the set of all valid e-mail addresses (start with a loose RE, then try to tighten it as much as you can, yet maintain correct functionality).

15–12. Match the set of all valid Web site addresses (URLs) (start with a loose RE, then try to tighten it as much as you can, yet maintain correct functionality).

15–13. `type()`. The `type()` built-in function returns a type object, which is displayed as a Pythonic-looking string:

```
>>> type(0)
<type 'int'>
>>> type(.34)
<type 'float'>
>>> type(dir)
<type 'builtin_function_or_method'>
```

Create an RE that would extract out the actual type name from the string. Your function should take a string like this "`<type 'int'>`" and return "int". (Ditto for all other types, i.e., 'float', 'builtin_function_or_method', etc.) Note: You are implementing the value that is stored in the __name__ attribute for classes and some built-in types.

15–14. *Regular Expressions*. In Section 15.2, we gave you the RE pattern that matched the single- or double-digit string representations of the months January to September ("`0?[1-9]`"). Create the RE that represents the remaining three months in the standard calendar.

15–15. *Regular Expressions*. Also in Section 15.2, we gave you the RE pattern that matched credit card (CC) numbers ("`[0-9]{15,16}`"). However, this pattern does not allow for hyphens separating blocks of numbers. Create the RE that allows hyphens, but only in the correct locations. For example, 15-digit CC numbers have a pattern of 4-6-5, indicating four digits-hyphen-six digits-hyphen-five digits, and 16-digit CC numbers have a 4-4-4-4 pattern. Remember to "balloon" the size of the entire string correctly. Extra credit: There is a standard algorithm for determining whether a CC number is valid. Write some code not only to recognize a correctly formatted CC number, but also a valid one.

The next set of problems (15–16 through 15–27) deal specifically with the data that are generated by `gendata.py`. *Before approaching problems 15–17 and 15–18, you may wish to do 15–16 and all the regular expressions first.*

15–16. Update the code for `gendata.py` so that the data are written directly to `redata.txt` rather than output to the screen.

15–17. Determine how many times each day of the week shows up for any incarnation of `redata.txt`. (Alternatively, you can also count how many times each month of the year was chosen.)

15–18. Ensure there is no data corruption in `redata.txt` by confirming that the first integer of the integer field matches the timestamp given at the front of each output line.

Create regular expressions to:

15–19. Extract the complete timestamps from each line.

15–20. Extract the complete e-mail address from each line.

15–21. Extract only the months from the timestamps.

15–22. Extract only the years from the timestamps.

15–23. Extract only the time (HH:MM:SS) from the timestamps.

15–24. Extract only the login and domain names (both the main domain name and the high-level domain together) from the e-mail address.

15–25. Extract only the login and domain names (both the main domain name and the high-level domain) from the e-mail address.

15–26. Replace the e-mail address from each line of data with your e-mail address.

15–27. Extract the months, days, and years from the timestamps and output them in "Mon Day, Year" format, iterating over each line only once.

For problems 15–28 and 15–29, recall the regular expression introduced in Section 15.2, which matched telephone numbers but allowed for an optional area code prefix: `\d{3}-\d{3}-\d{4}`. *Update this regular expression so that:*

15–28. Area codes (the first set of three-digits and the accompanying hyphen) are optional, i.e., your RE should match both 800-555-1212 as well as just 555-1212.

15–29. Either parenthesized or hyphenated area codes are supported, not to mention optional; make your RE match 800-555-1212, 555-1212, and also (800) 555-1212.

NETWORK PROGRAMMING

Chapter Topics

- Introduction: Client/Server Architecture
- Sockets: Communication Endpoints
    - Socket Addresses
    - Connection-Oriented versus Connectionless Sockets
- Network Programming in Python
    - `socket` Module
    - Socket Object Methods
    - TCP/IP Client and Server
    - UDP/IP Client and Server
- `SocketServer` Module
- Introduction to the Twisted Framework
- Related Modules

Chapter 16

In this section, we will take a brief look at network programming using sockets. We will first present some background information on network programming, how sockets apply to Python, and then show you how to use some of Python's modules to build networked applications.

16.1 Introduction

16.1.1 What Is Client/Server Architecture?

What is client/server architecture? It means different things to different people, depending on whom you ask as well as whether you are describing a software or a hardware system. In either case, the premise is simple: The *server*, a piece of hardware or software, is providing a "service" that is needed by one or more *clients*, users of the service. Its sole purpose of existence is to wait for (client) requests, service those clients, then wait for more requests.

Clients, on the other hand, contact a (predetermined) server for a particular request, send over any necessary data, and wait for the server to reply, either completing the request or indicating the cause of failure. While the server runs indefinitely processing requests, clients make a one-time request for service, receive that service, and thus conclude their transaction. A client may make additional requests at some later time, but these are considered separate transactions.

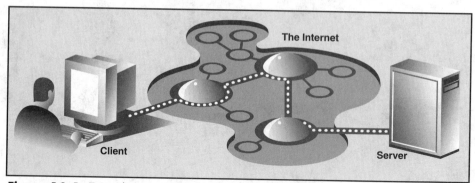

Figure 16–1 Typical conception of a client/server system on the Internet

The most common notion of "client/server" today is illustrated in Figure 16–1. A user or client computer is retrieving information from a server across the Internet. Although such a system is indeed an example of a client/server architecture, it isn't the only one. Furthermore, client/server architecture can be applied to computer hardware as well as software.

Hardware Client/Server Architecture

Print(er) servers are examples of hardware servers. They process incoming print jobs and send them to a printer (or some other printing device) attached to such a system. Such a computer is generally network-accessible and client machines would send print requests.

Another example of a hardware server is a file server. These are typically machines with large, generalized storage capacity, which is remotely accessible to clients. Client machines "mount" the disks from the server machine onto their local machine as if the disk itself were on the local machine. One of the most popular network operating systems that support file servers is Sun Microsystems' Network File System (NFS). If you are accessing a networked disk drive and cannot tell whether it is local or on the network, then the client/server system has done its job. The goal is for the user experience to be exactly the same as a local disk—the "abstraction" is normal disk access. It is up to the programmed "implementation" to make it behave in such a manner.

Software Client/Server Architecture

Software servers also run on a piece of hardware but do not have dedicated peripheral devices as hardware servers do, i.e., printers, disk drives, etc. The primary services provided by software servers include program execution, data transfer retrieval, aggregation, update, or other types of programmed or data manipulation.

One of the more common software servers today is the Web server. A corporate machine is set up with Web pages and/or Web applications, then the Web server is started. The job of such a server is to accept client requests, send back Web pages to (Web) clients, i.e., browsers on users' computers, and wait for the next client request. These servers are started with the expectation of "running forever." Although they do not achieve that goal, they go for as long as possible unless stopped by some external force, i.e., explicitly shut down or catastrophically due to hardware failure.

Database servers are another kind of software server. They take client requests for either storage or retrieval, perform that service, then wait for more business. They are also designed to run "forever."

The last type of software server we will discuss are windows servers. These servers can almost be considered hardware servers. They run on a machine with an attached display, such as a monitor of some sort. Windows clients are actually programs that require a windowing environment with which to execute. These are generally considered graphical user interface (GUI) applications. If they are executed without a window server, i.e., in a text-based environment such as a DOS window or a Unix shell, they are unable to start. Once a windows server is accessible, then things are fine.

Such an environment becomes even more interesting when networking comes into play. The usual display for a windows client is the server on the local machine, but it is possible in some networked windowing environments, such as the X Window system, to choose another machine's window server as a display. In such situations, you can be running a GUI program on one machine, but have it displayed at another!

Bank Tellers as Servers?

One way to imagine how client/server architecture works is to create in your mind the image of a bank teller who neither eats, sleeps, nor rests, serving one customer after another in a line that never seems to end (see Figure 16–2). The line may be long or it may be empty on occasion, but at any given moment, a customer may show up. Of course, such a teller was fantasy years ago, but automated teller machines (ATMs) seem to come close to such a model now.

The teller is, of course, the server that runs in an infinite loop. Each customer is a client with a need that requires servicing. Customers arrive and are serviced by the teller in a first-come-first-served manner. Once a transaction has been completed, the client goes away while the server either serves the next customer or sits and waits until one comes along.

Why is all this important? The reason is that this style of execution is how client/server architecture works in a general sense. Now that you have the

Figure 16–2 The bank teller in this diagram works "forever" serving client requests. The teller runs in an infinite loop receiving requests, servicing them, and going back to serve or wait for another client. There may be a long line of clients, or there may be none at all, but in either case, a server's work is never done.

basic idea, let us adapt it to network programming, which follows the software client/server architecture model.

16.1.2 Client/Server Network Programming

Before any servicing can be accomplished, a server must perform some preliminary setup procedures to prepare for the work that lies ahead. A communication endpoint is created which allows a server to "listen" for requests. One can liken our server to a company receptionist or switchboard operator who answers calls on the main corporate line. Once the phone number and equipment are installed and the operator arrives, the service can begin.

This process is the same in the networked world—once a communication endpoint has been established, our listening server can now enter its infinite loop to wait for clients to connect and be serviced. Of course, we must not forget to put that phone number on company letterhead, in advertisements, or some sort of press release; otherwise, no one will ever call!

On a related note, potential clients must be made aware that this server exists to handle their needs—otherwise, the server will never get a single request. Imagine creating a brand new Web site. It may be the most super-duper, awesome, amazing, useful, and coolest Web site of all, but if the Web address or Uniform Resource Locator (URL) is never broadcast or advertised in any way, no one will ever know about it, and it will never see the light of day. The same thing applies for the new telephone number of corporate headquarters. No calls will ever be received if the number is not made known to the public.

Now you have a good idea as to how the server works. You have gotten past the difficult part. The client side stuff is much more simple than on the server side. All the client has to do is to create its single communication endpoint, establish a connection to the server. The client can now make a request, which includes any necessary exchange of data. Once the request has been serviced and the client has received the result or some sort of acknowledgement, communication is terminated.

16.2 Sockets: Communication Endpoints

16.2.1 What Are Sockets?

Sockets are computer networking data structures that embody the concept of the "communication endpoint" described in the previous section. Networked applications must create sockets before any type of communication can commence. They can be likened to telephone jacks, without which engaging in communication is impossible.

Sockets originated in the 1970s from the University of California, Berkeley version of Unix, known as BSD Unix. Therefore, you will sometimes hear these sockets referred to as "Berkeley sockets" or "BSD sockets." Sockets were originally created for same-host applications where they would enable one running program (aka a process) to communicate with another running program. This is known as *interprocess communication,* or IPC. There are two types of sockets, file-based and network-oriented.

Unix sockets are the first family of sockets we are looking at and have a "family name" of AF_UNIX (aka AF_LOCAL, as specified in the POSIX1.g standard), which stands for "*address family*: UNIX." Most popular platforms, including Python, use the term "address families" and "AF" abbreviation while other perhaps older systems may refer to address families as "domains" or "protocol families" and use "PF" rather than "AF." Similarly, AF_LOCAL (standardized in 2000–2001) is supposed to replace AF_UNIX, however, for backward-compatibility, many systems use both and just make them aliases to the same constant. Python itself still uses AF_UNIX.

Because both processes run on the same machine, these sockets are file-based, meaning that their underlying infrastructure is supported by the file system. This makes sense because the file system is a shared constant between processes running on the same host.

The second type of socket is networked-based and has its own family name, AF_INET, or "address family: Internet." Another address family, AF_INET6, is used for Internet Protocol version 6 (IPv6) addressing. There are other address families, all of which are either specialized, antiquated, seldom used, or remain unimplemented. Of all address families, AF_INET is now the most widely used. Support for a special type of Linux socket was introduced in Python 2.5. The AF_NETLINK family of (connectionless [see below]) sockets allow for IPC between user- and kernel-level code using the standard BSD socket interface and is seen as an elegant and less risky solution over previous and more cumbersome solutions such as adding new system calls, /proc support, or "IOCTL"s to an operating system.

2.5

Python supports only the AF_UNIX, AF_NETLINK, and AF_INET* families. Because of our focus on network programming, we will be using AF_INET for most of the remaining part of this chapter.

16.2.2 Socket Addresses: Host-Port Pairs

If a socket is like a telephone jack, a piece of infrastructure that enables communication, then a hostname and port number are like an area code and telephone number combination. Having the hardware and ability to communicate doesn't do any good unless you know whom and where to "dial." An Internet address is comprised of a hostname and port number pair, and such an address is required for networked communication. It goes without saying that there should also be someone listening at the other end; otherwise, you get the familiar tones followed by "I'm sorry, that number is no longer in service. Please check the number and try your call again." You have probably seen one networking analogy during Web surfing, for example, "Unable to contact server. Server is not responding or is unreachable."

Valid port numbers range from 0–65535, although those less than 1024 are reserved for the system. If you are using a Unix system, the list of reserved port numbers (along with servers/protocols and socket types) is found in the /etc/services file. A list of well-known port numbers is accessible at this Web site:

http://www.iana.org/assignments/port-numbers

16.2.3 Connection-Oriented versus Connectionless

Connection-Oriented

Regardless of which address family you are using, there are two different styles of socket connections. The first type is connection-oriented. What this basically means is that a connection must be established before communication can occur, such as calling a friend using the telephone system. This type of communication is also referred to as a "virtual circuit" or "stream socket."

Connection-oriented communication offers sequenced, reliable, and unduplicated delivery of data, and without record boundaries. That basically means that each message may be broken up into multiple pieces, which are all guaranteed to arrive ("exactly once" semantics means no loss or duplication of data) at their destination, to be put back together and in order, and delivered to the waiting application.

The primary protocol that implements such connection types is the Transmission Control Protocol (better known by its acronym TCP). To create TCP sockets, one must use SOCK_STREAM as the type of socket one wants to create. The SOCK_STREAM name for a TCP socket is based on one of its denotations as stream socket. Because these sockets use the Internet Protocol (IP) to find hosts in the network, the entire system generally goes by the combined names of both protocols (TCP and IP) or TCP/IP.

Connectionless

In stark contrast to virtual circuits is the datagram type of socket, which is connectionless. This means that no connection is necessary before communication can begin. Here, there are no guarantees of sequencing, reliability, or non-duplication in the process of data delivery. Datagrams do preserve record boundaries, however, meaning that entire messages are sent rather than being broken into pieces first, like connection-oriented protocols.

Message delivery using datagrams can be compared to the postal service. Letters and packages may not arrive in the order they were sent. In fact, they might not arrive at all! To add to the complication, in the land of networking, *duplication* of messages is even possible.

So with all this negativity, why use datagrams at all? (There must be *some* advantage over using stream sockets!) Because of the guarantees provided by connection-oriented sockets, a good amount of overhead is required for their setup as well as in maintaining the virtual circuit connection. Datagrams do not have this overhead and thus are "less expensive." They usually provide better performance and may be suitable for some types of applications.

The primary protocol that implements such connection types is the User Datagram Protocol (better known by its acronym UDP). To create UDP sockets, we must use SOCK_DGRAM as the type of socket we want to create. The SOCK_DGRAM name for a UDP socket, as you can probably tell, comes from the word "datagram." Because these sockets also use the

Internet Protocol to find hosts in the network, this system also has a more general name, going by the combined names of both of these protocols (UDP and IP), or UDP/IP.

16.3 Network Programming in Python

Now that you know all about client/server architecture, sockets, and networking, let us try to bring this concept to Python. The primary module we will be using in this section is the `socket` module. Found within this module is the `socket()` function, which is used to create socket objects. Sockets also have their own set of methods, which enable socket-based network communication.

16.3.1 `socket()` Module Function

To create a socket, you must use the `socket.socket()` function, which has the general syntax:

```
socket(socket_family, socket_type, protocol=0)
```

The *socket_family* is either AF_UNIX or AF_INET, as explained earlier, and the *socket_type* is either SOCK_STREAM or SOCK_DGRAM, also explained earlier. The *protocol* is usually left out, defaulting to 0.

So to create a TCP/IP socket, you call `socket.socket()` like this:

```
tcpSock = socket.socket(socket.AF_INET, socket.SOCK_STREAM)
```

Likewise, to create a UDP/IP socket you perform:

```
udpSock = socket.socket(socket.AF_INET, socket.SOCK_DGRAM)
```

Since there are numerous `socket` module attributes, this is one of the exceptions where using "**from** *module* **import** *" is somewhat acceptable because of the number of module attributes. If we applied "**from** socket **import** *", we bring the socket attributes into our namespace, but our code is shortened considerably, i.e.,

```
tcpSock = socket(AF_INET, SOCK_STREAM)
```

Once we have a socket object, all further interaction will occur using that socket object's methods.

16.3.2 Socket Object (Built-in) Methods

In Table 16.1, we present a list of the most common socket methods. In the next subsection, we will create both TCP and UDP clients and servers, all of which use these methods. Although we are focusing on Internet sockets, these methods have similar meanings when using Unix sockets.

Table 16.1 Common Socket Object Methods

Method	Description
Server Socket Methods	
s.bind()	Bind address (hostname, port number pair) to socket
s.listen()	Set up and start TCP listener
s.accept()	Passively accept TCP client connection, waiting until connection arrives (blocking)
Client Socket Methods	
s.connect()	Actively initiate TCP server connection
s.connect_ex()	Extended version of connect() where problems are returned as error codes rather than an exception being thrown
General Socket Methods	
s.recv()	Receive TCP message
s.send()	Transmit TCP message
s.sendall()	Transmit TCP message completely
s.recvfrom()	Receive UDP message
s.sendto()	Transmit UDP message
s.getpeer-name()	Remote address connected to socket (TCP)
s.getsock-name()	Address of current socket
s.getsock-opt()	Return value of given socket option
s.setsock-opt()	Set value for given socket option
s.close()	Close socket

(continued)

Table 16.1 Common Socket Object Methods (continued)

Method	Description
Blocking-Oriented Socket Methods	
`s.setblocking()`	Set blocking or non-blocking mode of socket
`s.settimeout()`[a]	Set timeout for blocking socket operations
`s.gettimeout()`[a]	Get timeout for blocking socket operations
File-Oriented Socket Methods	
`s.fileno()`	File descriptor of socket
`s.makefile()`	Create a file object associated with socket

a. New in Python 2.3.

CORE TIP: Install clients and servers on different computers to run networked applications

In our multitude of examples in this chapter, you will often see code and output referring to host "localhost" or see an IP address of 127.0.0.1. Our examples are running the client(s) and server(s) on the same machine. We encourage the reader to change the hostnames and copy the code to different computers as it is much more fun developing and playing around with code that lets machines talk to one another across the network, and to see network programs that really do work!

16.3.3 Creating a TCP Server

We will first present some general pseudocode involved with creating a generic TCP server, then describe in general what is going on. Keep in mind that this is only one way of designing your server. Once you become comfortable with server design, you will be able to modify the pseudocode to operate the way you want it to:

```
ss = socket()            # create server socket
ss.bind()                # bind socket to address
ss.listen()              # listen for connections
inf_loop:                # server infinite loop
    cs = ss.accept()     # accept client connection
```

```
comm_loop:                      # communication loop
      cs.recv()/cs.send()  # dialog (receive/send)
   cs.close()                 # close client socket
ss.close()                    # close server socket # (opt)
```

All sockets are created using the `socket.socket()` function. Servers need to "sit on a port" and wait for requests, so they all must "bind" to a local address. Because TCP is a connection-oriented communication system, some infrastructure must be set up before a TCP server can begin operation. In particular, TCP servers must "listen" for (incoming) connections. Once this setup process is complete, a server can start its infinite loop.

A simple (single-threaded) server will then sit on an `accept()` call waiting for a connection. By default, `accept()` is blocking, meaning that execution is suspended until a connection arrives. Sockets do support a non-blocking mode; refer to the documentation or operating systems textbooks for more details on why and how you would use non-blocking sockets.

Once a connection is accepted, a separate client socket is returned [by `accept()`] for the upcoming message interchange. Using the new client socket is similar to handing off a customer call to a service representative. When a client eventually does come in, the main switchboard operator takes the incoming call and patches it through, using another line to the right person to handle their needs.

This frees up the main line, i.e., the original server socket, so that the operator can resume waiting for new calls (client requests) while the customer and the service representative he or she was connected to carry on their own conversation. Likewise, when an incoming request arrives, a new communication port is created to converse directly with that client while the main one is free to accept new client connections.

CORE TIP: Spawning threads to handle client requests

We do not implement this in our examples, but it is also fairly common to hand a client request off to a new thread or process to complete the client processing. The `SocketServer` *module, a high-level socket communication module written on top of* `socket`, *supports both threaded and spawned process handling of client requests. We refer the reader to the documentation to obtain more information about the* `SocketServer` *module as well as the exercises in Chapter 17, Multithreaded Programming.*

Once the temporary socket is created, communication can commence, and both client and server proceed to engage in a dialog of sending and receiving using this new socket until the connection is terminated. This usually happens when one of the parties either closes its connection or sends an empty string to its partner.

In our code, after a client connection is closed, the server goes back to wait for another client connection. The final line of code, where we close the server socket, is optional. It is never encountered since the server is supposed to run in an infinite loop. We leave this code in our example as a reminder to the reader that calling the close() method is recommended when implementing an intelligent exit scheme for the server, for example, a handler that detects some external condition whereby the server should be shut down. In those cases, a close() method call is warranted.

In Example 16.1, we present tsTserv.py, a TCP server program that takes the data string sent from a client and returns it timestamped (format: "[timestamp]data") back to the client. ("tsTserv" stands for *timestamp TCP server*. The other files are named in a similar manner.)

Example 16.1 TCP Timestamp Server (tsTserv.py)

Creates a TCP server that accepts messages from clients and returns them with a timestamp prefix.

```python
1    #!/usr/bin/env python
2
3    from socket import *
4    from time import ctime
5
6    HOST = ''
7    PORT = 21567
8    BUFSIZ = 1024
9    ADDR = (HOST, PORT)
10
11   tcpSerSock = socket(AF_INET, SOCK_STREAM)
12   tcpSerSock.bind(ADDR)
13   tcpSerSock.listen(5)
14
15   while True:
16       print 'waiting for connection...'
17       tcpCliSock, addr = tcpSerSock.accept()
18       print '...connected from:', addr
19
20       while True:
21           data = tcpCliSock.recv(BUFSIZ)
22           if not data:
23               break
24           tcpCliSock.send('[%s] %s' % (
25               ctime(), data))
26
27       tcpCliSock.close()
28   tcpSerSock.close()
```

Line-by-Line Explanation

Lines 1–4

After the Unix start-up line, we import `time.ctime()` and all the attributes from the `socket` module.

Lines 6–13

The HOST variable is blank, an indication to the `bind()` method that it can use any address that is available. We also choose an arbitrarily random port number, which does not appear to be used or reserved by the system. For our application, we set the buffer size to 1K. You may vary this size based on your networking capability and application needs. The argument for the `listen()` method is simply a maximum number of incoming connection requests to accept before connections are turned away or refused.

The TCP server socket (`tcpSerSock`) is allocated on line 11, followed by the calls to bind the socket to the server's address and to start the TCP listener.

Lines 15–28

Once we are inside the server's infinite loop, we (passively) wait for a connection. When one comes in, we enter the dialog loop where we wait for the client to send its message. If the message is blank, that means that the client has quit, so we would break from the dialog loop, close the client connection, and go back to wait for another client. If we did get a message from the client, then we format and return the same data but prepended with the current timestamp. The final line is never executed, but is there as a reminder to the reader that a `close()` call should be made if a handler is written to allow for a more graceful exit, as we discussed before.

16.3.4 Creating a TCP Client

Creating a client is much simpler than a server. Similar to our description of the TCP server, we will present the pseudocode with explanations first, then show you the real thing.

```
cs = socket()               # create client socket
cs.connect()                # attempt server connection
comm_loop:                  # communication loop
    cs.send()/cs.recv()     # dialog (send/receive)
cs.close()                  # close client socket
```

As we noted before, all sockets are created using `socket.socket()`. Once a client has a socket, however, it can immediately make a connection to a server by using the socket's `connect()` method. When the connection has been established, then it can participate in a dialog with the server. Once the client has completed its transaction, it may close its socket, terminating the connection.

We present the code for `tsTclnt.py` in Example 16.2; it connects to the server and prompts the user for line after line of data. The server returns this data timestamped, which is presented to the user by the client code.

Line-by-Line Explanation

Lines 1–3

After the Unix startup line, we import all the attributes from the `socket` module.

Example 16.2 TCP Timestamp Client (`tsTclnt.py`)

Creates a TCP client that prompts the user for messages to send to the server, gets them back with a timestamp prefix, and displays the results to the user.

```python
1   #!/usr/bin/env python
2
3   from socket import *
4
5   HOST = 'localhost'
6   PORT = 21567
7   BUFSIZ = 1024
8   ADDR = (HOST, PORT)
9
10  tcpCliSock = socket(AF_INET, SOCK_STREAM)
11  tcpCliSock.connect(ADDR)
12
13  while True:
14      data = raw_input('> ')
15      if not data:
16          break
17      tcpCliSock.send(data)
18      data = tcpCliSock.recv(BUFSIZ)
19      if not data:
20          break
21      print data
22
23  tcpCliSock.close()
```

Lines 5–11

The HOST and PORT variables refer to the server's hostname and port number. Since we are running our test (in this case) on the same machine, HOST contains the local hostname (change it accordingly if you are running your server on a different host). The port number PORT should be exactly the same as what you set for your server (otherwise there won't be much communication[!]). We also choose the same buffer size, 1K.

The TCP client socket (tcpCliSock) is allocated on line 10, followed by (an active) call to connect to the server.

Lines 13–23

The client also has an infinite loop, but it is not meant to run forever like the server's loop. The client loop will exit on either of two conditions: the user enters no input (lines 14–16), or the server somehow quit and our call to the recv() method fails (lines 18–20). Otherwise, in a normal situation, the user enters in some string data, which is sent to the server for processing. The newly timestamped input string is then received and displayed to the screen.

16.3.5 Executing Our TCP Server and Client(s)

Now let us run the server and client programs to see how they work. Should we run the server first or the client first? Naturally, if we ran the client first, no connection would be possible because there is no server waiting to accept the request. The server is considered a passive partner because it has to establish itself first and passively wait for a connection. A client, on the other hand, is an active partner because it actively initiates a connection. In other words:

Start the server first (before any clients try to connect).

In our example running of the client and server, we use the same machine, but there is nothing to stop us from using another host for the server. If this is the case, then just change the hostname. (It is rather exciting when you get your first networked application running the server and client from different machines!)

We now present the corresponding (input and) output from the client program, which exits with a simple RETURN (or Enter key) keystroke with no data entered:

```
$ tsTclnt.py
> hi
[Sat Jun 17 17:27:21 2006] hi
> spanish inquisition
[Sat Jun 17 17:27:37 2006] spanish inquisition
>
$
```

The server's output is mainly diagnostic:

```
$ tsTserv.py
waiting for connection...
...connected from: ('127.0.0.1', 1040)
waiting for connection...
```

The "... connected from ..." message was received when our client made its connection. The server went back to wait for new clients while we continued receiving "service." When we exited from the server, we had to break out of it, resulting in an exception. The best way to avoid such an error is to create a more graceful exit, as we have been discussing.

CORE TIP: Exit gracefully and call server `close()` method

One way to create this "friendly" exit is to put the server's `while` *loop inside the* `except` *clause of a* `try-except` *statement and monitor for* `EOFError` *or* `KeyboardInterrupt` *exceptions. Then in the* `except` *clause, you can make a call to close the server's socket.*

The interesting thing about this simple networked application is that we are not only showing how our data take a round trip from the client to the server and back to the client, but we also use the server as a sort of "time server," because the timestamp we receive is purely from the server.

16.3.6 *Creating a UDP Server*

UDP servers do not require as much setup as TCP servers because they are not connection-oriented. There is virtually no work that needs to be done other than just waiting for incoming connections.

```
ss = socket()                        # create server socket
ss.bind()                            # bind server socket
inf_loop:                            # server infinite loop
    cs = ss.recvfrom()/ss.sendto()# dialog (receive/send)
ss.close()                           # close server socket
```

As you can see from the pseudocode, there is nothing extra other than the usual create-the-socket and bind it to the local address (host/port pair). The infinite loop consists of receiving a message from a client, returning a timestamped one, then going back to wait for another message. Again, the `close()` call is optional and will not be reached due to the infinite loop, but it serves as a reminder that it should be part of the graceful or intelligent exit scheme we've been mentioning.

Example 16.3 UDP Timestamp Server (`tsUserv.py`)

Creates a UDP server that accepts messages from clients and returns them with a timestamp prefix.

```python
1  #!/usr/bin/env python
2
3  from socket import *
4  from time import ctime
5
6  HOST = ''
7  PORT = 21567
8  BUFSIZ = 1024
9  ADDR = (HOST, PORT)
10
11 udpSerSock = socket(AF_INET, SOCK_DGRAM)
12 udpSerSock.bind(ADDR)
13
14 while True:
15     print 'waiting for message...'
16     data, addr = udpSerSock.recvfrom(BUFSIZ)
17     udpSerSock.sendto('[%s] %s' % (
18         ctime(), data), addr)
19     print '...received from and returned to:', addr
20
21 udpSerSock.close()
```

One other significant different between UDP and TCP servers is that because datagram sockets are connectionless, there is no "handing off" of a client connection to a separate socket for succeeding communication. These servers just accept messages and perhaps reply.

You will find the code to `tsUserv.py` in Example 16.3, a UDP version of the TCP server seen earlier. It accepts a client message and returns it to the client timestamped.

Line-by-Line Explanation

Lines 1–4

After the Unix startup line, we import `time.ctime()` and all the attributes from the `socket` module, just like the TCP server setup.

Lines 6–12

The `HOST` and `PORT` variables are the same as before, and for all the same reasons. The call `socket()` differs only in that we are now requesting a datagram/UDP socket type, but `bind()` is invoked in the same way as in the

TCP server version. Again, because UDP is connectionless, no call to "lis-ten() for incoming connections" is made here.

Lines 14–21

Once we are inside the server's infinite loop, we (passively) wait for a message (a datagram). When one comes in, we process it (by adding a timestamp to it), then send it right back and go back to wait for another message. The socket close() method is there for show only, as indicated before.

16.3.7 Creating a UDP Client

Of the four highlighted here in this section, the UDP client is the shortest bit of code that we will look at. The pseudocode looks like this:

```
cs = socket()                    # create client socket
comm_loop:                       # communication loop
    cs.sendto()/cs.recvfrom()    # dialog (send/receive)
cs.close()                       # close client socket
```

Once a socket object is created, we enter the dialog loop of exchanging messages with the server. When communication is complete, the socket is closed.
The real client code, tsUclnt.py, is presented in Example 16.4.

Line-by-Line Explanation
Lines 1–3

After the Unix startup line, we import all the attributes from the socket module, again, just like in the TCP version of the client.

Lines 5–10

Because we are running the server on our local machine again, we use "local-host" and the same port number on the client side, not to mention the same 1K buffer. We allocate our socket object in the same way as the UDP server.

Lines 12–22

Our UDP client loop works in almost the exact manner as the TCP client. The only difference is that we do not have to establish a connection to the UDP server first; we simply send a message to it and await the reply. After the timestamped string is returned, we display it to the screen and go back for more. When the input is complete, we break out of the loop and close the socket.

Example 16.4 UDP Timestamp Client (`tsUclnt.py`)

Creates a UDP client that prompts the user for messages to send to the server, gets them back with a timestamp prefix, and displays them back to the user.

```
1   #!/usr/bin/env python
2
3   from socket import *
4
5   HOST = 'localhost'
6   PORT = 21567
7   BUFSIZ = 1024
8   ADDR = (HOST, PORT)
9
10  udpCliSock = socket(AF_INET, SOCK_DGRAM)
11
12  while True:
13      data = raw_input('> ')
14      if not data:
15          break
16      udpCliSock.sendto(data, ADDR)
17      data, ADDR = udpCliSock.recvfrom(BUFSIZ)
18      if not data:
19          break
20      print dataudpCliSock.close()
21
22  udpCliSock.close()
```

16.3.8 Executing Our UDP Server and Client(s)

The UDP client behaves the same as the TCP client:

```
$ tsUclnt.py
> hi
[Sat Jun 17 19:55:36 2006] hi
> spam! spam! spam!
[Sat Jun 17 19:55:40 2006] spam! spam! spam!
>
$
```

Likewise for the server:

```
$ tsUserv.py
waiting for message...
...received from and returned to: ('127.0.0.1', 1025)
waiting for message...
```

In fact, we output the client's information because we can be receiving messages from multiple clients and sending replies, and such output helps by telling us where messages came from. With the TCP server, we know where messages come from because each client makes a connection. Note how the messages says, "waiting for message" as opposed to "waiting for connection."

16.3.9 `socket` *Module Attributes*

In addition to the `socket.socket()` function which we are now familiar with, the `socket` module features many more attributes that are used in network application development. Some of the most popular ones are shown in Table 16.2.

For more information, we refer you to the `socket` Module documentation in the Python Library Reference.

Table 16.2 `socket` **Module Attributes**

Attribute Name	Description
Data Attributes	
`AF_UNIX, AF_INET, AF_INET6`[a]	Socket address families supported by Python
`SO_STREAM, SO_DGRAM`	Socket types (TCP = stream, UDP = datagram)
`has_ipv6`[b]	Boolean flag indicating whether IPv6 is supported
Exceptions	
`error`	Socket-related error
`herror`[a]	Host and address-related error
`gaierror`[a]	Address-related error
`timeout`[b]	Timeout expiration
Functions	
`socket()`	Create a socket object from the given address family, socket type, and protocol type (optional)
`socketpair()`[c]	Create a pair of socket objects from the given address family, socket type, and protocol type (optional)
`fromfd()`	Create a socket object from an open file descriptor

Table 16.2 `socket` Module Attributes (continued)	
Attribute Name	***Description***
Data Attributes	
`ssl()`[d]	Initiates a Secure Socket Layer connection over socket; does *not* perform certificate validation
`getaddrinfo()`[a]	Gets address information
`getfqdn()`[e]	Returns fully qualified domain name
`gethostname()`	Returns current hostname
`gethostbyname()`	Maps a hostname to its IP address
`gethostbyname_ex()`	Extended version of `gethostbyname()` returning hostname, set of alias hostnames, and list of IP addresses
`gethostbyaddr()`	Maps an IP address to DNS info; returns same 3-tuple as `gethostbyname_ex()`
`getprotobyname()`	Maps a protocol name (e.g. `'tcp'`) to a number
`getservbyname()` / `getservbyport()`	Maps a service name to a port number or vice-versa; a protocol name is optional for either function
`ntohl()`/`ntohs()`	Converts integers from network to host byte order
`htonl()`/`htons()`	Converts integers from host to network byte order
`inet_aton()` / `inet_ntoa()`	Convert IP address octet string to 32-bit packed format or vice versa (for IPv4 addresses only)
`inet_pton()` / `inet_ntop()`[b]	Convert IP address string to packed binary format or vice versa (for both IPv4 and IPv6 addresses)
`getdefaulttimeout()` / `setdefaulttimeout()`[b]	Return default socket timeout in seconds (float); set default socket timeout in seconds (float)

a.   New in Python 2.2.
b.   New in Python 2.3.
c.   New in Python 2.4.
d.   New in Python 1.6.
e.   New in Python 2.0.

16.4 *SocketServer Module

SocketServer is a higher-level module in the standard library. Its goal is to simplify a lot of the boilerplate code that is necessary to create networked clients and servers. In this module are various classes created on your behalf:

Table 16.3 SocketServer Module Classes	
Class	*Description*
BaseServer	Contains core server functionality and hooks for mix-in classes; used only for derivation so you will not create instances of this class; use TCPServer or UDPServer instead
TCPServer/ UDPServer	Basic networked synchronous TCP/UDP server
UnixStream- Server/ UnixData- gramServer	Basic file-based synchronous TCP/UDP server
ForkingMixIn/ Threading MixIn	Core forking or threading functionality; used only as mix-in classes with one of the server classes to achieve some asynchronicity; you will not instantiate this class directly
ForkingTCP- Server/Fork- ingUDPServer	Combination of ForkingMixIn and TCPServer/ UDPServer
ThreadingTCP- Server/ Thread- ingUDPServer	Combination of ThreadingMixIn and TCPServer/ UDPServer
BaseRequest- Handler	Contains core functionality for handling service requests; used only for derivation so you will not create instances of this class; use StreamRequestHandler or Datagram- RequestHandler instead
StreamRequest Handler/Data- gramRequest- Handler	Implement service handler for TCP/UDP servers

We will create a TCP client and server that duplicates the base TCP example shown earlier. You will notice the immediate similarities but should recognize how some of the dirty work is now taken care of so you do not have to worry about that boilerplate code. These represent the simplest synchronous server you can write. Please check out the exercises at the end of the chapter to turn your server into an asynchronous one.

In addition to hiding implementation details from you, another difference is that we are now writing our applications using classes. Doing things in an object-oriented way helps us organize our data and logically direct functionality to the right places. You will also notice that our applications are now "event-driven," meaning they only work when "reacting to" an occurrence of an *event* in our system.

Events include the sending and receiving of messages. In fact, you will see that our class definition only consists of an event handler for the receiving of a client message. All other functionality is taken from the `SocketServer` classes we use. GUI programming (Chapter 18) is also event-driven. You will notice the similarity immediately as the final line of our code is usually a server's infinite loop waiting for and responding to client service requests. It works almost the same as our infinite while loop in the original base TCP server we create earlier in the chapter.

In our original server loop, we block waiting for a request, then service it when something comes in, and then go back to waiting. In the server loop here, instead of building your code in the server, you define a handler that the server can just call your function when it receives an incoming request.

16.4.1   Creating a `SocketServer` *TCP Server*

In our code, we first import our server classes, then define the same host constants as before. That is followed by our request handler class, and then startup. More details follow our code snippet.

Line-by-Line Explanation

Lines 1–9

The initial stuff consists of importing the right classes from `Socket-Server`. Note that we are using the Python 2.4 multi-line import. If you are using an earlier version of Python, then you will have use the fully-qualified *module.attribute* names or put both attribute imports on the same line:

```
from SocketServer import TCPServer as TCP, StreamRequestHandler as SRH
```

2.4

Example 16.5 SocketServer Timestamp TCP Server (tsTservSS.py)

Creates a timestamp TCP server using SocketServer *classes* TCPServer *and* StreamRequestHandler.

```
1   #!/usr/bin/env python
2
3   from SocketServer import (TCPServer as TCP,
4       StreamRequestHandler as SRH)
5   from time import ctime
6
7   HOST = ''
8   PORT = 21567
9   ADDR = (HOST, PORT)
10
11  class MyRequestHandler(SRH):
12      def handle(self):
13          print '...connected from:', self.client_address
14          self.wfile.write('[%s] %s' % (ctime(),
15              self.rfile.readline()))
16
17  tcpServ = TCP(ADDR, MyRequestHandler)
18  print 'waiting for connection...'
19  tcpServ.serve_forever()
```

Lines 11–15

The bulk of the work happens here. We derive our request handler MyRequest-Handler as a subclass of SocketServer's StreamRequestHandler and override its handle() method, which is stubbed out in the Base Request class with no default action as:

```
def handle(self):
    pass
```

The handle() method is called when an incoming message is received from a client. The StreamRequestHandler class treats input and output sockets as file-like objects, so we will use readline() to get the client message and write() to send a string back to the client.

In accordance, we need additional carriage return and NEWLINE characters in both the client and server code. Actually, you will *not* see it in the code because we are just reusing those which come from the client. Other than these minor differences we have mentioned, it should look just like our earlier server.

Lines 17–19

The final bits of code create the TCP server with the given host information and request handler class. We then have our entire infinite loop waiting for and servicing client requests.

16.4.2 *Creating a* `SocketServer` *TCP Client*

Our client will naturally resemble our original client, much more so than the server, but it has to be tweaked a bit to work well with our new server.

Line-by-Line Explanation

Lines 1–8

Nothing special here . . . this is an exact replica of our original client code.

Example 16.6 `SocketServer` **Timestamp TCP Client** (`tsTclntSS.py`)

This is a timestamp TCP client that knows how to speak to the file-like `Socket Server` ***class*** `StreamRequestHandler` ***objects.***

```
1   #!/usr/bin/env python
2
3   from socket import *
4
5   HOST = 'localhost'
6   PORT = 21567
7   BUFSIZ = 1024
8   ADDR = (HOST, PORT)
9
10  while True:
11      tcpCliSock = socket(AF_INET, SOCK_STREAM)
12      tcpCliSock.connect(ADDR)
13      data = raw_input('> ')
14      if not data:
15          break
16      tcpCliSock.send('%s\r\n' % data)
17      data = tcpCliSock.recv(BUFSIZ)
18      if not data:
19          break
20      print data.strip()
21      tcpCliSock.close()
```

Lines 10–21

The default behavior of the SocketServer request handlers is to accept a connection, get the request, and close the connection. This makes it so that we cannot keep our connection throughout the execution of our application, so we need to create a new socket each time we send a message to the server.

This behavior makes the TCP server act more like a UDP server; however, this can be changed by overriding the appropriate methods in our request handler classes. We leave this as an exercise at the end of this chapter.

Other than the fact that our client is somewhat "inside-out" now (because we have to create a connection each time), the only other minor difference was previewed in the line-by-line explanation for the server code: the handler class we are using treats socket communication like a file, so we have to send line-termination characters (carriage return and NEWLINE) each way. The server just retains and reuses the ones we send here. When we get a message back from the server, we strip() them and just use the NEWLINE automatically provided by the **print** statement.

16.4.3 Executing our TCP Server and Client(s)

Here is the output of our SocketServer TCP client:

```
$ tsTclntSS.py
> 'Tis but a scratch.
[Tue Apr 18 20:55:49 2006] 'Tis but a scratch.
> Just a flesh wound.
[Tue Apr 18 20:55:56 2006] Just a flesh wound.
>
$
```

And here is the server's:

```
$ tsTservSS.py
waiting for connection...
...connected from: ('127.0.0.1', 53476)
...connected from: ('127.0.0.1', 53477)
```

The output is similar to that of our original TCP client and servers, however, you will notice that we connected to the server twice.

16.5 Introduction to the Twisted Framework

Twisted is a complete event-driven networking framework that allows you to both use and develop complete asynchronous networked applications and protocols. It is *not* part of the Python Standard library at the time of writing and must be downloaded and installed separately (see link at the end of the chapter). It provides a significant amount of support for you to build complete systems with: network protocols, threading, security and authentication, chat/IM, DBM and RDBMS database integration, Web/Internet, e-mail, command-line arguments, GUI toolkit integration, etc.

Using Twisted to implement our tiny simplistic example is like using a sledge-hammer to pound a thumbtack, but you have to get started somehow, and our application is the equivalent to the "hello world" of networked applications.

Like `SocketServer`, most of the functionality of Twisted lies in its classes. In particular for our examples, we will be using the classes found in the reactor and protocol subpackages of Twisted's Internet component.

16.5.1 Creating a Twisted Reactor TCP Server

You will find our code similar to that of the SocketServer example. Instead of a handler class, we create a protocol class and override several methods in the same manner as installing callbacks. Also, this example is asynchronous. Let us take a look at the server now.

Line-by-Line Explanation

Lines 1–6

The setup lines of code include the usual module imports, most notably the `protocol` and `reactor` subpackages of `twisted.internet` and our constant port number.

Lines 8–14

We derive the `Protocol` class and call ours `TSServProtocol` for our timestamp server. We then override `connectionMade()`, a method that is executed when a client connects to us, and `dataReceived()`, called when a client sends a piece of data across the network. The reactor passes in the data as an argument to this method so we can get access to it right away without having to extract it ourselves.

Example 16.7 Twisted Reactor Timestamp TCP Server (`tsTservTW.py`)

This is a timestamp TCP server using Twisted Internet classes.

```
1   #!/usr/bin/env python
2
3   from twisted.internet import protocol, reactor
4   from time import ctime
5
6   PORT = 21567
7
8   class TSServProtocol(protocol.Protocol):
9       def connectionMade(self):
10          clnt = self.clnt = self.transport.getPeer().host
11          print '...connected from:', clnt
12      def dataReceived(self, data):
13          self.transport.write('[%s] %s' % (
14              ctime(), data))
15
16  factory = protocol.Factory()
17  factory.protocol = TSServProtocol
18  print 'waiting for connection...'
19  reactor.listenTCP(PORT, factory)
20  reactor.run()
```

The transport instance object is how we can communicate with the client. You can see how we use it in `connectionMade()` to get the host information about who is connecting to us as well as in `dataReceived()` to return data back to the client.

Lines 16–20

In the final part of our server, we create a protocol `Factory`. It is called a "factory" so that an instance of our protocol is "manufactured" every time we get an incoming connection. We then install a TCP listener in our reactor to check for service requests and when it gets one, to create a `TSServProtocol` instance to take care of that client.

16.5.2 Creating a Twisted Reactor TCP Client

Unlike the `SocketServer` TCP client, this one will not look like all the other clients. This one is distinctly Twisted.

Example 16.8 Twisted Reactor Timestamp TCP Client (`tsTclntTW.py`)

Our familiar timestamp TCP client written from a Twisted point of view.

```python
1   #!/usr/bin/env python
2
3   from twisted.internet import protocol, reactor
4
5   HOST = 'localhost'
6   PORT = 21567
7
8   class TSClntProtocol(protocol.Protocol):
9       def sendData(self):
10          data = raw_input('> ')
11          if data:
12              print '...sending %s...' % data
13              self.transport.write(data)
14          else:
15              self.transport.loseConnection()
16
17      def connectionMade(self):
18          self.sendData()
19
20      def dataReceived(self, data):
21          print data
22          self.sendData()
23
24  class TSClntFactory(protocol.ClientFactory):
25      protocol = TSClntProtocol
26      clientConnectionLost = clientConnectionFailed = \
27          lambda self, connector, reason: reactor.stop()
28
29  reactor.connectTCP(HOST, PORT, TSClntFactory())
30  reactor.run()
```

Line-by-Line Explanation

Lines 1–6

Again, nothing really new here other than the import of Twisted components. It is very similar to all of our other clients.

Lines 8–22

Like the server, we extend `Protocol` by overriding the same methods, `connectionMade()` and `dataReceived()`. Both execute for the same reason as the server. We also add our own method for when data need to be sent and call it `sendData()`.

Since we are the client this time, we are the ones initiating a conversation with the server. Once that connection has been established, we take the first step and send a message. The server replies, and we handle it by displaying it to the screen and sending another message to the server.

This continues in a loop until we terminate the connection by giving no input when prompted. Instead of calling the `write()` method of the transport object to send another message to the server, `loseConnection()` is executed, closing the socket. When this occurs, the factory's `clientConnection-Lost()` method will be called, and our reactor is stopped, completing execution of our script. We also stop the reactor if a `clientConnection-Failed()` for some other reason.

The final part of the script is where we create a client factory and make a connection to the server and run the reactor. Note that we instantiate the client factory here instead of passing it in to the reactor like in the server. This is because we are not the server waiting for clients to talk to us, and its factory makes a new protocol object for each connection. *We* are one client, so we make a single protocol object that connects to the server whose factory makes one to talk to ours.

16.5.3 Executing Our TCP Server and Client(s)

The Twisted client displays output similar to all our other clients:

```
$ tsTclntTW.py
> Where is hope
...sending Where is hope...
[Tue Apr 18 23:53:09 2006] Where is hope
> When words fail
...sending When words fail...
[Tue Apr 18 23:53:14 2006] When words fail
>
$
```

The server is back to a single connection. Twisted maintains the connection and does not close the transport after every message:

```
$ tsTservTW.py
waiting for connection...
...connected from: 127.0.0.1
```

The "connection from" output does not have the other information because we only asked for the host/address from the `getPeer()` method of the server's transport object.

16.6 Related Modules

Table 16.4 lists some of the other Python modules that are related to network and socket programming. The `select` module is usually used in conjunction with the `socket` module when developing lower-level socket applications. It provides the `select()` function, which manages sets of socket objects. One of the most useful things it does is to take a set of sockets and listen for active connections on them. The `select()` function will block until at least one socket is ready for communication, and when that happens, it provides you with a set of which ones are ready for reading. (It can also determine which are ready for writing, although that is not as common as the former operation.)

The `async*` and `SocketServer` modules both provide higher-level functionality as far as creating servers is concerned. Written on top of the `socket` and/or `select` modules, they enable more rapid development of client/server systems because all the lower-level code is handled for you. All you have to do is to create or subclass the appropriate base classes, and you are on your way. As we mentioned earlier, `SocketServer` even provides the capability of integrating threading or new processes into the server for more parallelized processing of client requests.

Although `async*` provide the only asynchronous development support in the standard library, we have seen a third-party package that is much more contemporary and powerful than those older modules, Twisted. Although the example code we have seen in this chapter is slightly longer than the barebones scripts, Twisted provides a much more powerful and flexible framework

Table 16.4 Network/Socket Programming Related Modules

Module	Description
socket	Lower-level networking interface as discussed in this chapter
asyncore/ asynchat	Provide infrastructure to create networked applications that process clients asynchronously
select	Manages multiple socket connections in a single-threaded network server application
SocketServer	High-level module that provides server classes for networked applications, complete with forking or threading varieties

and has implemented many protocols for you already. You can find out more about Twisted at its Web site:

```
http://twistedmatrix.com
```

The topics we have covered in this chapter deal with network programming with sockets in Python and how to create custom applications using lower-level protocol suites such as TCP/IP and UDP/IP. If you want to develop higher-level Web and Internet applications, we strongly encourage you to head to Chapter 20.

16.7 Exercises

16–1.   *Sockets*. What is the difference between connection-oriented versus connectionless?

16–2.   *Client/Server Architecture*. Describe in your own words what this term means and give several examples.

16–3.   *Sockets*. Between TCP and UDP, which type of servers accept connections and hands them off to separate sockets for client communication?

16–4.   *Clients*. Update the TCP (`tsTclnt.py`) and UDP (`tsUclnt.py`) clients so that the server name is not hardcoded into the application. Allow the user to specify a hostname and port number, and only use the default values if either or both parameters are missing.

16–5.   *Internetworking and Sockets*. Implement Guido van Rossum's sample TCP client/server programs found in Section 7.2.2 of the Python Library Reference and get them to work. Set up the server, then the client. An online version of the source is also available here:

```
http://www.python.org/doc/current/lib/
    Socket_Example.html
```

You decide the server is too boring. Update the server so that it can do much more, recognizing the following commands:

date   Server will return its current date/timestamp, i.e., `time.ctime(time.time())`

os   Get OS info (`os.name`)

ls   Give a listing of the current directory (HINTS: `os.listdir()` lists a directory, `os.curdir` is the current directory.) Extra credit: Accept "`ls` *dir*" and return *dir*'s file listing.

You do not need a network to do this assignment—your machine can talk to itself. Note: After the server exits, the binding must be cleared before you can run it again. You may experience "port already bound" errors. The operating system usually clears the binding within 5 minutes, so be patient!

16–6.   *Daytime Service.* Use the `socket.getservbyname()` to determine the port number for the "daytime" service under the UDP protocol. Check the documentation for `getservbyname()` to get the exact usage syntax (i.e., `socket.getservbyname.__doc__`). Now write an application that sends a dummy message over and wait for the reply. Once you have received a reply from the server, display it to the screen.

16–7.   *Half-Duplex Chat.* Create a simple, half-duplex chat program. By "half-duplex," we mean that when a connection is made and the service starts, only one person can type. The other participant must wait to get a message before he or she is prompted to enter a message. Once a message is sent, then the sender must wait for a reply before being allowed to send another message. One participant will be on the server side, while the other will be on the client side.

16–8.   *Full-Duplex Chat.* Update your solution to the previous problem so that your chat service is now full-duplex, meaning that both parties can send and receive independently of each other.

16–9.   *Multi-User Full Duplex Chat.* Further update your solution so that your chat service is multi-user.

16–10. *Multi-User Multi-Room Full Duplex Chat.* Now make your chat service multi-user *and* multi-room.

16–11. *Web Client.* Write a TCP client that connects to port 80 of your favorite Web site (remove the "http://" and any trailing info; use only the hostname). Once a connection has been established, send the HTTP command string "GET /\n" and write all the data that the server returns to a file. (The GET command retrieves a Web page, the "/" file indicates the file to get, and the "\n" sends the command to the server.) Examine the contents of the retrieved file. What is it? How can you check to make sure the data you received is correct? (Note: You may have to give one or two NEWLINEs after the command string. One usually works.)

16–12. *Sleep Server.* Create a "sleep" server. A client will request to be "put to sleep" for a number of seconds. The server will issue the command on behalf of the client, then return a message to the client indicating success. The client should have slept or should have been idle for the exact time requested. This is a simple implementation of a "remote procedure call" where a client's request invokes commands on another machine across the network.

16–13. *Name Server.* Design and implement a name server. Such a server is responsible for maintaining a database of host-name-port number pairs, perhaps along with the string description of the service that the corresponding servers provide. Take one or more existing servers and have them "register" their service with your name server. (Note that these servers are, in this case, clients of the name server.)

Every client that starts up has no idea where the server is that it is looking for. Also as clients of the name server, these clients should send a request to the name server indicating what type of service they are seeking. The name server, in reply, returns a hostname-port number pair to this client, which then connects to the appropriate server to process its request.

Extra credit:

(1) Add caching to your name server for popular requests;

(2) Add logging capability to your name server, keeping track of which servers have registered and which services clients are requesting;

(3) Your name server should periodically "ping" the registered hosts at their respective port numbers to ensure that the service is indeed up. Repeated failures will cause a server to be delisted from the list of services.

You may implement real services for the servers that register for your name service, or just use dummy servers (which merely acknowledge a request).

16–14. *Error Checking and Graceful Shutdown.* All of our sample client/server code in this chapter is poor in terms of error-checking. We do not handle when users press ^C to exit out of a server or ^D to terminate client input, nor do we check other improper input to `raw_input()` or handle network errors. Because of this weakness, quite often we terminate an application without closing our sockets, potentially losing data. Choose a client/server pair of one of our examples, and add enough error-checking so that each application properly shuts down, i.e., closes network connections.

16–15. *Asynchronicity and* `SocketServer`. Take the example TCP server example and use either mix-in class to support an asynchronous server. To test your server, create and run multiple clients simultaneously and show output that your server is serving requests from both interleaved.

16–16. **Extending* `SocketServer` *Classes*. In the `Socket-Server` TCP server code, we had to change our client from the original base TCP client because the `SocketServer` class does not maintain the connection between requests.

(a) Subclass the `TCPServer` and `StreamRequest-Handler` classes and rearchitect the server so that it maintains and uses a single connection for each client (not one per request).

(b) Integrate your solution for the previous problem with your solution to part (a) such that multiple clients are being serviced in parallel.

INTERNET CLIENT PROGRAMMING

Chapter Topics

- Introduction
- Transferring Files
  - File Transfer Protocol (FTP)
- Network News, Usenet, and Newsgroups
  - Network News Transfer Protocol (NNTP)
- Electronic Mail
  - Simple Mail Transfer Protocol (SMTP)
  - Post Office Protocol version 3 (POP3)
- Related Modules

Chapter 17

In an earlier chapter, we took a look at low-level networking communication protocols using sockets. This type of networking is at the heart of most of the client/server protocols which exist on the Internet today. These protocols include those for transferring files (FTP, SCP, etc.), reading Usenet newsgroups (NNTP), sending e-mail (SMTP), and downloading e-mail from a server (POP3, IMAP), etc. These protocols work in a way much like the client/server examples in the earlier chapter on socket programming. The only thing that is different is that now we have taken lower-level protocols like TCP/IP and created newer, more specific protocols on top of it to implement the higher-level services we just described.

17.1 What Are Internet Clients?

Before we take a look at these protocols, we first must ask, "What is an Internet client?" To answer this question, we simplify the Internet to a place where data are exchanged, and this interchange is made up of someone offering a service and a user of such services. You will hear the term "producer-consumer" in some circles (although this phrase is generally reserved for conversations on operating systems). Servers are the producers, providing the services, and clients consume the offered services. For any one particular service, there is usually only one server (process, host, etc.) and more than one consumer. We previously examined the client/server model, and although we do not need to create Internet clients with the low-level socket operations seen earlier, the model is an accurate match.

Here, we will look specifically at three of these Internet protocols—FTP, NNTP, and POP3—and write clients for each. What you should take away afterward are being able to recognize how similar the APIs of all of these protocols are—this is done by design, as keeping interfaces consistent is a worthy cause—and most importantly, the ability to create real clients of these and other Internet protocols. And even though we are only highlighting these three specific protocols, at the end of this chapter, you should feel confident enough to write clients for just about *any* Internet protocol.

17.2 Transferring Files

17.2.1 File Transfer Internet Protocols

One of the most popular Internet activities is file exchange. It happens *all the time*. There have been many protocols to transfer files over the Internet, with some of the most popular including the File Transfer Protocol (FTP), the Unix-to-Unix Copy Protocol (UUCP), and of course, the Web's Hypertext Transfer Protocol (HTTP). We should also include the remote (Unix) file copy command rcp (and now its more secure and flexible cousins scp and rsync).

HTTP, FTP, and scp/rsync are still quite popular today. HTTP is primarily used for Web-based file download and accessing Web services. It generally doesn't require clients to have a login and/or password on the server host to obtain documents or service. The majority of all HTTP file transfer requests are for Web page retrieval (file downloads).

On the other hand, scp and rsync require a user login on the server host. Clients must be authenticated before file transfers can occur, and files can be sent (upload) or retrieved (download). Finally, we have FTP. Like scp/rsync, FTP can be used for file upload or download; and like scp/rsync, it employs the Unix multi-user concepts of usernames and passwords: FTP clients must use the login/password of existing users. However, FTP also allows anonymous logins. Let us now take a closer look at FTP.

17.2.2 File Transfer Protocol (FTP)

The File Transfer Protocol was developed by the late Jon Postel and Joyce Reynolds in the Internet Request for Comment (RFC) 959 document and published in October 1985. It is primarily used to download publicly accessible files in an anonymous fashion. It can also be used by users to transfer files between two machines, especially in cases where you're using a Unix system as for file storage or archiving and a desktop or laptop PC for work. Before the Web became popular, FTP was one of the primary methods of transferring files on the Internet, and one of the only ways to download software and/or source code.

As described previously, one must have a login/password for accessing the remote host running the FTP server. The exception is anonymous logins, which are designed for guest downloads. These permit clients who do not have accounts to download files. The server's administrator must set up an FTP server with anonymous logins in order for these to occur. In these cases, the "login" of an unregistered user is called "anonymous," and the password is generally the e-mail address of the client. This is akin to a public login and access to directories that were designed for general consumption as opposed to logging in and transferring files as a particular user. The list of available commands via the FTP protocol is also generally more restrictive than that for real users.

The protocol is diagrammed below in Figure 17–1 and works as follows:

1. Client contacts the FTP server on the remote host
2. Client logs in with username and password (or "anonymous" and e-mail address)
3. Client performs various file transfers or information requests
4. Client completes the transaction by logging out of the remote host and FTP server

Of course, this is generally how it works. Sometimes there are circumstances whereby the entire transaction is terminated before it's completed. These include being disconnected from the network if one of the two hosts crash or because of some other network connectivity issue. For inactive clients, FTP connections will generally time out after 15 minutes (900 seconds) of inactivity.

Under the covers, it is good to know that FTP uses only TCP (see earlier chapter on network programming)—it does not use UDP in any way. Also, FTP may be seen as a more "unusual" example of client/server programming because both the clients and the servers use a pair of sockets for communication: one is the control or command port (port 21), and the other is the data port (sometimes port 20).

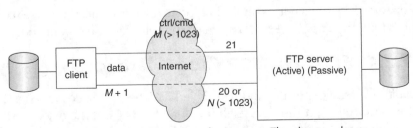

Figure 17–1 FTP Clients and Servers on the Internet. The client and server communicate using the FTP protocol on the command or control port while data is transferred using the data port.

We say "sometimes" because there are two FTP modes, Active and Passive, and the server's data port is only 20 for Active mode. After the server sets up 20 as its data port, it "actively" initiates the connection to the client's data port. For Passive mode, the server is only responsible for letting the client know where its random data port is, and the client must initiate the data connection. As you can see in this mode, the FTP server is taking a more "passive" role in setting up the data connection. Finally, there is now support for a new Extended Passive Mode to support version 6 Internet Protocol (IPv6) addresses—see RFC 2428.

Python has support for most Internet protocols, including FTP. Other supported client libraries can be found at http://docs.python.org/lib/internet.html. Now let's take a look at just how easy it is to create an Internet client with Python.

17.2.3 Python and FTP

So how do we write an FTP client using Python? What we just described in the previous section covers it pretty much. The only additional work required is to import the appropriate Python module and make the appropriate calls in Python. So let us review the protocol briefly:

1. Connect to server
2. Log in
3. Make service request(s) (and hopefully get reply[ies])
4. Quit

When using Python's FTP support, all you do is import the `ftplib` module and instantiate the `ftplib.FTP` class. All FTP activity will be accomplished using your object, i.e., logging in, transferring files, and logging out.

Here is some Python pseudocode:

```
from ftplib import FTP
f = FTP('ftp.python.org')
f.login('anonymous', 'guess@who.org')
    :
f.quit()
```

Soon we will look at a real example, but for now, let us familiarize ourselves with methods from the `ftplib.FTP` class, which you will likely use in your code.

17.2.4 `ftplib.FTP` Class Methods

We outline the most popular methods in Table 17.1. The list is not comprehensive—see the source code for the class itself for all methods—but the ones presented here are those that make up the "API" for FTP client programming in Python. In other words, you don't really need to use the others as they are either utility or administrative functions or are used by the API methods later.

Table 17.1 Methods for FTP Objects

Method	Description
`login(user='anony-mous', passwd='', acct='')`	Log in to FTP server; all arguments are optional
`pwd()`	Current working directory
`cwd(path)`	Change current working directory to `path`
`dir([path[,...[,cb]])`	Displays directory listing of `path`; optional callback `cb` passed to `retrlines()`
`nlst([path[,...])`	Like `dir()` but returns a list of filenames instead of displaying
`retrlines(cmd[, cb])`	Download text file given FTP `cmd`, e.g., "RETR filename"; optional callback `cb` for processing each line of file
`retrbinary(cmd, cb[, bs=8192[, ra]])`	Similar to `retrlines()` except for binary file; callback cb for processing each block (size `bs` defaults to 8K) downloaded *required*
`storlines(cmd, f)`	Upload text file given FTP `cmd`, e.g., "STOR filename"; open file object f required
`storbinary(cmd, f[, bs=8192])`	Similar to `storlines()` but for binary file; open file object f required, upload blocksize `bs` defaults to 8K
`rename(old, new)`	Rename remote file from `old` to `new`
`delete(path)`	Delete remote `file` located at `path`
`mkd(directory)`	Create remote `directory`
`rmd(directory)`	Remove remote `directory`
`quit()`	Close connection and quit

The methods you will most likely use in a normal FTP transaction include `login()`, `cwd()`, `dir()`, `pwd()`, `stor*()`, `retr*()`, and `quit()`. There are more FTP object methods not listed in the table which you may find useful. Please see the Python documentation for detailed information on FTP objects:

http://python.org/docs/current/lib/ftp-objects.html

17.2.5 Interactive FTP Example

An example of using FTP with Python is so simple to use that you do not even have to write a script. You can just do it all from the interactive interpreter and see the action and output in real time. This is a sample session we did years ago when there was still an FTP server running at `python.org`:

```
>>> from ftplib import FTP
>>> f = FTP('ftp.python.org')
>>> f.login('anonymous', '-help@python.org')
'230 Guest login ok, access restrictions apply.'
>>> f.dir()
total 38
drwxrwxr-x  10 1075     4127        512 May 17  2000 .
drwxrwxr-x  10 1075     4127        512 May 17  2000 ..
drwxr-xr-x   3 root     wheel       512 May 19  1998 bin
drwxr-sr-x   3 root     1400        512 Jun  9  1997 dev
drwxr-xr-x   3 root     wheel       512 May 19  1998 etc
lrwxrwxrwx   1 root     bin           7 Jun 29  1999 lib -> usr/lib
-r--r--r--   1 guido    4127         52 Mar 24  2000 motd
drwxrwsr-x   8 1122     4127        512 May 17  2000 pub
drwxr-xr-x   5 root     wheel       512 May 19  1998 usr
>>> f.retrlines('RETR motd')
Sun Microsystems Inc.   SunOS 5.6      Generic August 1997
'226 Transfer complete.
>>> f.quit()
'221 Goodbye.'
```

17.2.6 Client Program FTP Example

We mentioned previously that an example script is not even necessary since you can run one interactively and not get lost in any code. We will try anyway. For example, let us say you wanted a piece of code that goes to download the latest copy of Bugzilla from the Mozilla Web site. Example 17.1 is what we came up with. We are attempting an application here, but even so, you can probably run this one interactively, too. Our application uses the FTP library to download the file and built it with some error-checking.

It is not automated, however; it is up to you to run it whenever you want to perform the download, or if you are on a Unix-based system, you can set up a "cron" job to automate it for you. Another issue is that it will break if either the file or directory names change.

Example 17.1 FTP Download Example (`getLatestFTP.py`)

This program is used to download the latest version of a file from a Web site. You can tweak it to download your favorite application.

```python
1   #!/usr/bin/env python
2
3   import ftplib
4   import os
5   import socket
6
7   HOST = 'ftp.mozilla.org'
8   DIRN = 'pub/mozilla.org/webtools'
9   FILE = 'bugzilla-LATEST.tar.gz'
10
11  def main():
12      try:
13          f = ftplib.FTP(HOST)
14      except (socket.error, socket.gaierror), e:
15          print 'ERROR: cannot reach "%s"' % HOST
16          return
17      print '*** Connected to host "%s"' % HOST
18
19      try:
20          f.login()
21      except ftplib.error_perm:
22          print 'ERROR: cannot login anonymously'
23          f.quit()
24          return
25      print '*** Logged in as "anonymous"'
26
27      try:
28          f.cwd(DIRN)
29      except ftplib.error_perm:
30          print 'ERROR: cannot CD to "%s"' % DIRN
31          f.quit()
32          return
33      print '*** Changed to "%s" folder' % DIRN
34
35      try:
36          f.retrbinary('RETR %s' % FILE,
37                  open(FILE, 'wb').write)
38      except ftplib.error_perm:
39          print 'ERROR: cannot read file "%s"' % FILE
40          os.unlink(FILE)
41      else:
42          print '*** Downloaded "%s" to CWD' % FILE
43      f.quit()
44      return
45
46  if __name__ == '__main__':
47      main()
```

If no errors occur when we run our script, we get the following output:

```
$ getLatestFTP.py
*** Connected to host "ftp.mozilla.org"
*** Logged in as "anonymous"
*** Changed to "pub/mozilla.org/webtools" folder
*** Downloaded "bugzilla-LATEST.tar.gz" to CWD
$
```

Line-by-Line Explanation

Lines 1–9

The initial lines of code import the necessary modules (mainly to grab exception objects) and set a few constants.

Lines 11–44

The `main()` function consists of various steps of operation: create an FTP object and attempt to connect to the FTPs server (lines 12–17) and (return and) quit on any failure. We attempt to login as "anonymous" and bail if it fails (lines 19–25). The next step is to change to the distribution directory (lines 27–33), and finally, we try to download the file (lines 35–44).

On lines 35–36, we pass a callback to `retrbinary()` that should be executed for every block of binary data downloaded. This is the `write()` method of a file object we create to write out the local version of the file. We are depending on the Python interpreter to adequately close our file after the transfer is done and not to lose any of our data. Although more convenient, your author tries to not use this style as much as possible because the programmer should be responsible for freeing resources directly allocated rather than depending on other code. In this case, we should save the open file object to a variable, say `loc`, and then pass `loc.write` in the call to `ftp.retrbinary()`.

Also in this block of code, if for some reason we are not able to save the file, we remove the empty file if it is there to avoid cluttering up the file system (line 40). Finally, to avoid another pair of lines that close the FTP connection and return, we use a **try-except-else** clause (lines 35–42).

Lines 46–47

This is the usual idiom for running a standalone script.

17.2.7 Miscellaneous FTP

2.0-2.1 Python supports both Active and Passive modes. Note, however, that in Python 2.0 and before, Passive mode was off by default; in Python 2.1 and later, it is on by default.

Here is a list of typical FTP clients:

- **Command-line client program:** This is where you execute FTP transfers by running an FTP client program such as /bin/ftp, or NcFTP, which allows users to interactively participate in an FTP transaction via the command line.

- **GUI client program:** Similar to a command-line client program except it is a GUI application like WsFTP and Fetch.

- **Web browser:** In addition to using HTTP, most Web browsers (also referred to as a client) can also speak FTP. The first directive in a URL/URI is the protocol, i.e., "http://blahblah." This tells the browser to use HTTP as a means of transferring data from the given Web site. By changing the protocol, one can make a request using FTP, as in "ftp://blahblah." It looks pretty much exactly the same as an URL, which uses HTTP. (Of course, the "blahblah" can expand to the expected "host/path?attributes" after the protocol directive "ftp://". Because of the login requirement, users can add their logins and passwords (in clear text) into their URL, i.e., "ftp://user:passwd@host/path?attr1=val1&attr2=val2. . .".

- **Custom application:** A program you write that uses FTP to transfer files. It generally does not allow the user to interact with the server as the application was created for specific purposes.

All four types of clients can be creating using Python. We used ftplib above to create our custom application, but you can just as well create an interactive command-line application. On top of that, you can even bring a GUI toolkit such as Tk, wxWidgets, GTK+, Qt, MFC, and even Swing into the mix (by importing their respective Python [or Jython] interface modules) and build a full GUI application on top of your command-line client code. Finally, you can use Python's urllib module to parse and perform FTP transfers using FTP URLs. At its heart, urllib imports and uses ftplib making urllib *another* client of ftplib.

FTP is not only useful for downloading client applications to build and/or use, but it can also be helpful in your everyday job if it involves moving files between systems. For example, let us say you are an engineer or a system administrator needing to transfer files. It is an obvious choice to use the scp or rsync commands when crossing the Internet boundary or pushing files to an externally visible server. However, there is a penalty when moving extremely large logs or database files between internal machines on a secure network in that manner: security, encryption, compression/decompression, etc. If what you want to do is just build a simple FTP application that moves files for you quickly during the after-hours, using Python is a great way to do it!

You can read more about FTP in the FTP Protocol Definition/Specification (RFC 959) at ftp://ftp.isi.edu/in-notes/rfc959.txt as well as on the http://www.networksorcery.com/enp/protocol/ftp.htm Web page. Other related RFCs include 2228, 2389, 2428, 2577, 2640, and 4217. To find out more about Python's FTP support, you can start here: http://python.org/docs/current/lib/module-ftplib.html.

17.3 Network News

17.3.1 Usenet and Newsgroups

The Usenet News System is a global archival "bulletin board." There are newsgroups for just about any topic, from poems to politics, linguistics to computer languages, software to hardware, planting to cooking, finding or announcing employment opportunities, music and magic, breaking up or finding love. Newsgroups can be general and worldwide or targeted toward a specific geographic region.

The entire system is a large global network of computers that participate in sharing Usenet postings. Once a user uploads a message to his or her local Usenet computer, it will then be propagated to other adjoining Usenet computers, and then to the neighbors of *those* systems, until it's gone around the world and everyone has received the posting. Postings will live on Usenet for a finite period of time, either dictated by a Usenet system administrator or the posting itself via an expiration date/time.

Each system has a list of newsgroups that it "subscribes" to and only accepts postings of interest—not all newsgroups may be archived on a server. Usenet news service is dependent on which provider you use. Many are open to the public while others only allow access to specific users, such as paying subscribers, or students of a particular university, etc. A login and password are optional, configurable by the Usenet system administrator. The ability to post or download-only is another parameter configurable by the administrator.

17.3.2 Network News Transfer Protocol (NNTP)

The method by which users can download newsgroup postings or "articles" or perhaps post new articles is called the Network News Transfer Protocol (NNTP). It was authored by Brian Kantor (UC San Diego) and Phil Lapsley (UC Berkeley) in RFC 977, published in February 1986. The protocol has since then been updated in RFC 2980, published in October 2000.

As another example of client/server architecture, NNTP operates in a fashion similar to FTP; however, it is much simpler. Rather than having a whole set of different port numbers for logging in, data, and control, NNTP uses

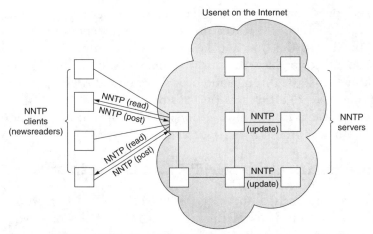

Figure 17–2 NNTP Clients and Servers on the Internet. Clients mostly read news but may also post. Articles are then distributed as servers update each other.

only one standard port for communication, 119. You give the server a request, and it responds appropriately, as shown in Figure 17–2.

17.3.3 Python and NNTP

Based on your experience with Python and FTP above, you can probably guess that there is an `nntplib` and an `nntplib.NNTP` class that you need to instantiate, and you would be right. As with FTP, all we need to do is to import that Python module and make the appropriate calls in Python. So let us review the protocol briefly:

1. Connect to server
2. Log in (if applicable)
3. Make service request(s)
4. Quit

Look somewhat familiar? It should, because it's practically a carbon copy of the FTP protocol. The only change is that the login step is optional, depending on how an NNTP server is configured.

Here is some Python pseudocode to get started:

```
from nntplib import NNTP
n = NNTP('your.nntp.server')
r,c,f,l,g = n.group('comp.lang.python')
...
n.quit()
```

Typically, once you log in, you will choose a newsgroup of interest and call the group() method. It returns the server reply, a count of the number of articles, the ID of the first and last articles, and superfluously, the group name again. Once you have this information, you will then perform some sort of action such as scroll through and browse articles, download entire postings (headers and body of article), or perhaps post an article.

Before we take a look at a real example, let's introduce some of the more popular methods of the nntplib.NNTP class.

17.3.4 *nntplib.NNTP Class Methods*

As in the previous section outlining the ftplib.FTP class methods, we will not show you all methods of nntplib.NNTP, just the ones you need in order to create an NNTP client application.

Table 17.2 Methods for NNTP Objects

Method	*Description*
group(*name*)	Select newsgroup name and return a tuple (*rsp*, *ct*, *fst*, *lst*, *group*): server response, number of articles, first and last article numbers and group name, all of which are strings (*name == group*)
xhdr(*hdr*, *artrg*, [*ofile*])	Returns list of *hdr* headers for article range *artrg* ("first-last" format) or outputs data to file *ofile*
body(*id*[, *ofile*])	Get article body given its *id*, which is either a message ID (enclosed in < . . . > or an article number (as a string); returns tuple (*rsp*, *anum*, *mid*, *data*): server response, article number (as a string), message ID (enclosed in < . . . >), and list of article lines or outputs *data* to file *ofile*
head(*id*)	Similar to body() . . . same tuple returned except lines only contain article headers
article(*id*)	Also similar to body() . . . same tuple returned except lines contain both headers and article body
stat(*id*)	Set article "pointer" to *id* (message ID or article number as above); returns tuple similar to body (*rsp*, *anum*, *mid*) but contains no data from article

Table 17.2 Methods for NNTP Objects (continued)	

Method	*Description*
next()	Used with stat(), moves article pointer to "next" article and returns similar tuple
last()	Also used with stat(), moves article pointer to "last" article and returns similar tuple
post(*ufile*)	Upload data from *ufile* file object (using *ufile*.readline()) and post to current newsgroup
quit()	Close connection and quit

As with the FTP objects table in the previous segment, there are more NNTP object methods not described here. To avoid clutter, we list only the ones we think you would most likely use. For the rest, we again refer you to the Python Library Reference.

17.3.5 Interactive NNTP Example

Here is an interactive example of how to use Python's NNTP library. It should look similar to the interactive FTP example. (The e-mail addresses have been changed for privacy reasons.)

When connecting to a group, you get a 5-tuple back from the group() method as described in Table 17.2.

```
>>> from nntplib import NNTP
>>> n = NNTP('your.nntp.server')
>>> rsp, ct, fst, lst, grp = n.group('comp.lang.python')
>>> rsp, anum, mid, data = n.article('110457')
>>> for eachLine in data:
...     print eachLine
From: "Alex Martelli" <alex@...>
Subject: Re: Rounding Question
Date: Wed, 21 Feb 2001 17:05:36 +0100

"Remco Gerlich" <remco@...> wrote:
> Jacob Kaplan-Moss <jacob@...> wrote in comp.lang.python:
>> So I've got a number between 40 and 130 that I want to round up to
>> the nearest 10.  That is:
>>
>>    40 --> 40, 41 --> 50, ..., 49 --> 50, 50 --> 50, 51 --> 60

>> Rounding like this is the same as adding 5 to the number and then
> rounding down. Rounding down is substracting the remainder if you were
> to divide by 10, for which we use the % operator in Python.
```

This will work if you use +9 in each case rather than +5 (note that he doesn't really want rounding -- he wants 41 to 'round' to 50, for ex).

Alex
```
>>> n.quit()
'205 closing connection - goodbye!'
>>>
```

17.3.6 Client Program NNTP Example

For our NNTP client example, we are going to try to be more adventurous. It will be similar to the FTP client example in that we are going to download the latest of something—this time it will be the latest article available in the Python language newsgroup, `comp.lang.python`.

Once we have it, we will display (up to) the first 20 lines in the article, and on top of that, (up to) the first 20 *meaningful* lines of the article. By that, we mean lines of real data, not quoted text (which begin with ">" or "|") or even quoted text introductions like "In article <...>, soAndSo@some.domain wrote:".

Finally, we are going to do blank lines intelligently. We will display one blank line when we see one in the article, but if there are more than one consecutive blank, we only show the first blank line of the set. Only lines with real data are counted toward the "first 20 lines," so it is possible to display a maximum of 39 lines of output, 20 real lines of data interleaved with 19 blank ones.

If no errors occur when we run our script, we may see something like this:

```
$ getLatestNNTP.py
*** Connected to host "your.nntp.server"
*** Found newsgroup "comp.lang.python"
*** Found last article (#471526):

    From: "Gerard Flanagan" <grflanagan@...>
    Subject: Re: Generate a sequence of random numbers that sum up to 1?
    Date: Sat Apr 22 10:48:20 CEST 2006
*** First (<= 20) meaningful lines:
    def partition(N=5):
        vals = sorted( random.random() for _ in range(2*N) )
        vals = [0] + vals + [1]
        for j in range(2*N+1):
            yield vals[j:j+2]
    deltas = [ x[1]-x[0] for x in partition() ]

    print deltas

    print sum(deltas)

    [0.10271966686994982, 0.13826576491042208, 0.064146913555132801,
    0.11906452454467387, 0.10501198456091299, 0.011732423830768779,
    0.11785369256442912, 0.065927165520102249, 0.098351305878176198,
    0.077786747076205365, 0.099139810689226726]
    1.0
$
```

Example 17.2 NNTP Download Example (`getFirstNNTP.py`)

This downloads and displays the first "meaningful" (up to 20) lines of the most recently available article in comp.lang.python, the Python newsgroup.

```python
1  #!/usr/bin/env python
2
3  import nntplib
4  import socket
5
6  HOST = 'your.nntp.server'
7  GRNM = 'comp.lang.python'
8  USER = 'wesley'
9  PASS = "you'llNeverGuess"
10
11 def main():
12
13     try:
14         n = nntplib.NNTP(HOST)
15         #, user=USER, password=PASS)
16     except socket.gaierror, e:
17         print 'ERROR: cannot reach host "%s"' % HOST
18         print '     ("%s")' % eval(str(e))[1]
19         return
20     except nntplib.NNTPPermanentError, e:
21         print 'ERROR: access denied on "%s"' % HOST
22         print '     ("%s")' % str(e)
23         return
24     print '*** Connected to host "%s"' % HOST
25
26     try:
27         rsp, ct, fst, lst, grp = n.group(GRNM)
28     except nntplib.NNTPTemporaryError, e:
29         print 'ERROR: cannot load group "%s"' % GRNM
30         print '     ("%s")' % str(e)
31         print '     Server may require authentication'
32         print '     Uncomment/edit login line above'
33         n.quit()
34         return
35     except nntplib.NNTPTemporaryError, e:
36         print 'ERROR: group "%s" unavailable' % GRNM
37         print '     ("%s")' % str(e)
38         n.quit()
39         return
40     print '*** Found newsgroup "%s"' % GRNM
41
42     rng = '%s-%s' % (lst, lst)
43     rsp, frm = n.xhdr('from', rng)
44     rsp, sub = n.xhdr('subject', rng)
45     rsp, dat = n.xhdr('date', rng)
46     print '''*** Found last article (#%s):
47
```

(continued)

Example 17.2 NNTP Download Example
(getFirstNNTP.py) (continued)

```
48        From: %s
49        Subject: %s
50        Date: %s
51  '''% (lst, frm[0][1], sub[0][1], dat[0][1])
52
53        rsp, anum, mid, data = n.body(lst)
54        displayFirst20(data)
55        n.quit()
56
57  def displayFirst20(data):
58      print '*** First (<= 20) meaningful lines:\n'
59      count = 0
60      lines = (line.rstrip() for line in data)
61      lastBlank = True
62      for line in lines:
63          if line:
64              lower = line.lower()
65              if (lower.startswith('>') and not \
66                  lower.startswith('>>>')) or \
67                  lower.startswith('|') or \
68                  lower.startswith('in article') or \
69                  lower.endswith('writes:') or \
70                  lower.endswith('wrote:'):
71                      continue
72          if not lastBlank or (lastBlank and line):
73              print '    %s' % line
74              if line:
75                  count += 1
76                  lastBlank = False
77              else:
78                  lastBlank = True
79          if count == 20:
80              break
81
82  if __name__ == '__main__':
83      main()
```

This output is given the original newsgroup posting, which looks like this:

```
From: "Gerard Flanagan" <grflanagan@...>
Subject: Re: Generate a sequence of random numbers that sum up to 1?
Date: Sat Apr 22 10:48:20 CEST 2006
Groups: comp.lang.python


Gerard Flanagan wrote:
> Anthony Liu wrote:
> > I am at my wit's end.
```

```
> > I want to generate a certain number of random numbers.
> >  This is easy, I can repeatedly do uniform(0, 1) for
> > example.

> > But, I want the random numbers just generated sum up
> > to 1 .

> > I am not sure how to do this.  Any idea?  Thanks.

> --------------------------------------------------------------
> import random

> def partition(start=0,stop=1,eps=5):
>     d = stop - start
>     vals = [ start + d * random.random() for _ in range(2*eps) ]
>     vals = [start] + vals + [stop]
>     vals.sort()
>     return vals

> P = partition()

> intervals = [ P[i:i+2] for i in range(len(P)-1) ]

> deltas = [ x[1] - x[0] for x in intervals ]

> print deltas

> print sum(deltas)
> --------------------------------------------------------------

def partition(N=5):
    vals = sorted( random.random() for _ in range(2*N) )
    vals = [0] + vals + [1]
    for j in range(2*N+1):
        yield vals[j:j+2]

deltas = [ x[1]-x[0] for x in partition() ]

print deltas

print sum(deltas)

[0.10271966686994982, 0.13826576491042208, 0.064146913555132801,
0.11906452454467387, 0.10501198456091299, 0.011732423830768779,
0.11785369256442912, 0.065927165520102249, 0.098351305878176198,
0.077786747076205365, 0.099139810689226726]
1.0
```

Of course, the output will always be different since articles are always being posted. No two executions will result in the same output unless your news server has not been updated with another article since you last ran the script.

Line-by-Line Explanation

Lines 1–9

This application starts with a few **import** statements and some constants, much like the FTP client example.

Lines 11–40

In the first section, we attempt to connect to the NNTP host server and bail if it tails (lines 13–24). Line 15 is commented out deliberately in case your server requires authentication (with login and password)—if so, uncomment this line and edit it in with line 14. This is followed by trying to load up the specific newsgroup. Again, it will quit if that newsgroup does not exist, is not archived by this server, or if authentication is required (lines 26–40).

Lines 42–55

In the next part we get some headers to display (lines 42–51). The ones that have the most meaning are the author, subject, and date. This data is retrieved and displayed to the user. Each call to the `xhdr()` method requires us to give the range of articles to extract the headers from. We are only interested in a single message, so the range is "X-X" where X is the last message number.

`xhdr()` returns a 2-tuple consisting of a server response (`rsp`) and a list of the headers in the range we specify. Since we are only requesting this information for one message (the last one), we just take the first element of the list (`hdr[0]`). *That* data item is a 2-tuple consisting of the article number and the data string. Since we already know the article number (because we give it in our range request), we are only interested in the second item, the data string (`hdr[0][1]`).

The last part is to download the body of the article itself (lines 53–55). It consists of a call to the `body()` method, a display the first 20 or fewer meaningful lines (as defined at the beginning of this section), a logout of the server, and complete execution.

Lines 57–80

The core piece of processing is done by the `displayFirst20()` function (lines 57–80). It takes the set of lines making up the article body and does some preprocessing like setting our counter to 0, creating a generator expression that lazily iterates through our (possibly large) set of lines making up the body, and "pretends" that we have just seen and displayed a blank line (more on this later; lines 59–61). When we strip the line of data, we only remove the trailing whitespace (rstrip()) because leading spaces may be intended lines of Python code.

One criterion we have is that we should not show any quoted text or quoted text introductions. That is what the big **if** statement is for on lines 65–71 (also include line 64). We do this checking if the line is not blank (line 63). We lowercase the line so that our comparisons are case-insensitive (line 64).

If a line begins with ">" or "|," it means it is usually a quote. We make an exception for lines that start with ">>>" since it may be an interactive interpreter line, although this does introduce a flaw that a triply-old message (one quoted three times for the fourth responder) is displayed. (One of the exercises at the end of the chapter is to remove this flaw.) Lines that begin with "in article . . .", and/or end with "writes:" or "wrote:", both with trailing colons (:), are also quoted text introductions. We skip all these with the **continue** statement.

Now to address the blank lines. We want our application to be smart. It should show blank lines as seen in the article, but it should be smart about it. If there is more than one blank line consecutively, only show the first one so the user does not see unnecessarily excessive lines, scrolling useful information off the screen. We should also not count any blank lines in our set of 20 meaningful lines. All of these requirements are taken care of in lines 72–78.

The **if** statement on line 72 says to only display the line if the last line was not blank, *or* if the last line was blank but now we have a non-blank line. In other words, if we fall through and we print the current line, it is because it is either a line with data or a blank line as long as the previous line was not blank. Now the other tricky part: if we have a non-blank line, count it and set the lastBlank flag to False since this line was not empty (lines 74–76). Otherwise, we have just seen a blank line so set the flag to True.

Now back to the business on line 61 . . . we set the lastBlank flag to True because if the first real (non-introductory or quoted) line of the body is a blank, we do not want to display it . . . we want to show the first real *data* line!

Finally, if we have seen 20 non-blank lines, then we quit and discard the remaining lines (lines 79–80). Otherwise we would have exhausted all the lines and the **for** loop terminates normally.

17.3.7 Miscellaneous NNTP

You can read more about NNTP in the NNTP Protocol Definition/ Specification (RFC 977) at ftp://ftp.isi.edu/in-notes/rfc977.txt as well as on the http://www.networksorcery.com/enp/protocol/nntp.htm Web page. Other related RFCs include 1036 and 2980. To find out more about Python's NNTP support, you can start here: http://python.org/docs/current/lib/module-nntplib.html.

17.4 Electronic Mail

Electronic mail is both archaic and modern at the same time. For those of us who have been using the Internet since the early days, e-mail seems so "old," especially compared to newer and more immediate communication mechanisms such as Web-based online chat, instant messaging (IM), and digital telephony, i.e., Voice Over Internet Protocol (VOIP), applications. The next section gives a high-level overview of how e-mail works. If you are already familiar with this and just want to move on to developing e-mail-related clients in Python, skip to the succeeding sections.

Before we take a look at the e-mail infrastructure, have you ever asked yourself what is the exact definition of an e-mail message? Well, according to RFC 2822, "[a] message consists of header fields (collectively called 'the header of the message') followed, optionally, by a body." When we think of e-mail as users, we immediately think of its contents, whether it be a real message or an unsolicited commercial advertisement (aka spam). However, the RFC states that the body itself is optional and that only the headers are required. Imagine that!

17.4.1 E-mail System Components and Protocols

Despite what you may think, electronic mail (e-mail) actually existed before the modern Internet came around. It actually started as a simple message exchange between mainframe users . . . note that there wasn't even any networking involved as they all used the same computer. Then when networking became a reality, it was possible for users on different hosts to exchange messages. This, of course, was a complicated concept as people used different computers, which used different networking protocols. It was not until the early 1980s that message exchange settled on a single de facto standard for moving e-mail around the Internet.

Before we get into the details, let's first ask ourselves, how *does* e-mail work? How does a message get from sender to recipient across the vastness of all the computers accessible on the Internet? To put it simply, there are the originating computer (the sender's message departs from here) and the destination computer (recipient's mail server). The optimal solution is if the sending machine knows exactly how to reach the receiving host because then it can make a direct connection to deliver the message. However, this is usually not the case.

The sending computer queries to find another intermediate host who can pass the message along its way to the final recipient host. Then *that* host searches for the next host who is another step closer to the destination. So in between the originating and final destination hosts are any number of machines called "hops." If you look carefully at the full e-mail headers of any message you receive, you will see a "passport" stamped with all the places your message bounced to before it finally reached you.

To get a clearer picture, let's take a look at the components of the e-mail system. The foremost component is the message transport agent (MTA). This is a server process running on a mail exchange host which is responsible for the routing, queuing, and sending of e-mail. These represent all the hosts that an e-mail message bounces from beginning at the source host all the way to the final destination host and all hops in between. Thus they are "agents" of "message transport."

In order for all this to work, MTAs need to know two things: 1) how to find out the next MTA to forward a message to, and 2) how to talk to another MTA. The first is solved by using a domain name service (DNS) lookup to find the MX (Mail eXchange) of the destination domain. This is not necessarily the final recipient, but rather, the next recipient who can eventually get the message to its final destination. Next, how do MTAs forward messages to other MTAs?

17.4.2 Sending E-mail

In order to send e-mail, your mail client must connect to an MTA, and the only language they understand is a communication protocol. The way MTAs communicate with one another is by using a message transport system (MTS). This protocol must be "known" by a pair of MTAs before they can communicate. As we described at the beginning of this section, such communication was dicey and unpredictable in the early days as there were so many different types of computer systems, each running different networking software. With the added complexity that computers were using both networked transmission as well as dial-up modem, delivery times were unpredictable. In fact, this author has had a message not show up until almost nine months after the message was originally sent! How is *that* for Internet speed? Out of this complexity rose the Simple Mail Transfer Protocol (SMTP) in 1982, one of the foundations of modern e-mail.

SMTP

SMTP was authored by the late Jonathan Postel (ISI) in RFC 821, published in August 1982. The protocol has since been updated in RFC 2821, published in April 2001. Some well-known MTAs that have implemented SMTP include:

Open Source MTAs

- Sendmail
- Postfix
- Exim
- qmail (freely distributed but not Open Source)

Commercial MTAs

- Microsoft Exchange
- Lotus Notes Domino Mail Server

Note that while they have all implemented the minimum SMTP protocol requirements as specified in RFC 2821, most of them, especially the commercial MTAs, have added even more features to their servers, which goes above and beyond the protocol definition.

SMTP is the MTS that is used by most of the MTAs on the Internet for message exchange. It is the protocol used by MTAs to transfer e-mail from (MTA) host to (MTA) host. When you send e-mail, you must connect to an outgoing SMTP server where your mail application acts as an SMTP client. Your SMTP server, therefore, is the first hop for your message.

17.4.3 Python and SMTP

Yes, there is an `smtplib` and an `smtplib.SMTP` class to instantiate. Review this familiar story:

1. Connect to server
2. Log in (if applicable)
3. Make service request(s)
4. Quit

As with NNTP, the login step is optional and only required if the server has SMTP authentication (SMTP-AUTH) enabled. SMTP-AUTH is defined in RFC 2554. And also like NNTP, speaking SMTP only requires communicating with one port on the server; this time, it's port 25.

Here is some Python pseudocode to get started:

```
from smtplib import SMTP
n = SMTP('smtp.yourdomain.com')
...
n.quit()
```

Before we take a look at a real example, let's introduce some of the more popular methods of the `smtplib.SMTP` class.

17.4.4 `smtplib.SMTP` Class Methods

As in the previous section outlining the `smtplib.SMTP` class methods, we won't show you all methods, just the ones you need in order to create an SMTP client application. For most e-mail sending applications, only two are required: `sendmail()` and `quit()`.

All arguments to `sendmail()` should conform to RFC 2822, i.e., e-mail addresses must be properly formatted, and the message body should have appropriate leading headers and contain lines that must be delimited by carriage-return and NEWLINE `\r\n` pairs.

Note that an actual message body is not required. According to RFC 2822, "[the] only required header fields are the origination date field and the originator address field(s)," i.e., "Date:" and "From:": (MAIL FROM, RCPT TO, DATA).

There are a few more methods not described here, but they are not normally required to send an e-mail message. Please see the Python documentation for information on all the SMTP object methods.

Table 17.3 Methods for SMTP Objects

Method	*Description*
`sendmail` `(from, to, msg[, mopts, ropts])`	Send *msg* from *from* to *to* (list or tuple) and optional ESMTP mail (*mopts*) and recipient (*ropts*) options
`quit()`	Close connection and quit
`login(user, passwd)`[a]	Log in to SMTP server with *user* name and *passwd*

a. SMTP-AUTH only.

17.4.5 Interactive SMTP Example

Once again, we present an interactive example:

```
>>> from smtplib import SMTP as smtp
>>> s = smtp('smtp.python.is.cool')
>>> s.set_debuglevel(1)
>>> s.sendmail('wesley@python.is.cool', ('wesley@python.is.cool',
'chun@python.is.cool'), ''' From: wesley@python.is.cool\r\nTo:
wesley@python.is.cool, chun@python.is.cool\r\nSubject: test
msg\r\n\r\nxxx\r\n.''')
send: 'ehlo myMac.local\r\n'
reply: '250-python.is.cool\r\n'
reply: '250-7BIT\r\n'
reply: '250-8BITMIME\r\n'
reply: '250-AUTH CRAM-MD5 LOGIN PLAIN\r\n'
reply: '250-DSN\r\n'
reply: '250-EXPN\r\n'
reply: '250-HELP\r\n'
reply: '250-NOOP\r\n'
reply: '250-PIPELINING\r\n'
reply: '250-SIZE 15728640\r\n'
reply: '250-STARTTLS\r\n'
reply: '250-VERS V05.00c++\r\n'
reply: '250 XMVP 2\r\n'
reply: retcode (250); Msg: python.is.cool
7BIT
8BITMIME
AUTH CRAM-MD5 LOGIN PLAIN
DSN
EXPN
HELP
NOOP
PIPELINING
SIZE 15728640
STARTTLS
VERS V05.00c++
XMVP 2
send: 'mail FROM:<wesley@python.is.cool> size=108\r\n'
reply: '250 ok\r\n'
reply: retcode (250); Msg: ok
send: 'rcpt TO:<wesley@python.is.cool>\r\n'
reply: '250 ok\r\n'
reply: retcode (250); Msg: ok
send: 'data\r\n'
reply: '354 ok\r\n'
reply: retcode (354); Msg: ok
data: (354, 'ok')
```

```
send: 'From: wesley@python.is.cool\r\nTo:
wesley@python.is.cool\r\nSubject: test
msg\r\n\r\nxxx\r\n..\r\n.\r\n'
reply: '250 ok ; id=2005122623583701300or7hhe\r\n'
reply: retcode (250); Msg: ok ; id=2005122623583701300or7hhe
data: (250, 'ok ; id=2005122623583701300or7hhe')
{}
>>> s.quit()
send: 'quit\r\n'
reply: '221 python.is.cool\r\n'
reply: retcode (221); Msg: python.is.cool
```

17.4.6 Miscellaneous SMTP

You can read more about SMTP in the SMTP Protocol Definition/Specification (RFC 2821) at ftp://ftp.isi.edu/in-notes/rfc2821.txt as well as on the http://www.networksorcery.com/enp/protocol/smtp.htm Web page. To find out more about Python's SMTP support, you can start here: http://python.org/docs/current/lib/module-smtplib.html

One of the more important aspects of e-mail which we have not discussed yet is how to properly format Internet addresses as well as e-mail messages themselves. This information is detailed in the Internet Message Format RFC, 2822, and can be downloaded at ftp://ftp.isi.edu/in-notes/rfc2822.txt.

17.4.7 Receiving E-mail

Back in the day, communicating by e-mail on the Internet was relegated to university students, researchers, and employees of private industry and commercial corporations. Desktop computers were predominantly still Unix-based workstations. Home users just dialed-up on PCs and really didn't use e-mail. When the Internet began to explode in the mid-1990s, e-mail came home to everyone.

Because it was not feasible for home users to have workstations in their dens running SMTP, a new type of system had to be devised to leave e-mail on an incoming mail host while periodically downloading mail for offline reading. Such a system consists of both a new application and a new protocol to communicate with the mail server.

The application, which runs on a home computer, is called a mail user agent (MUA). An MUA will download mail from a server, perhaps automatically deleting it in the process (or not, leaving the mail on the server to be deleted manually by the user). However, an MUA must also be able to send mail . . . in other words, it should also be able to speak SMTP to communicate directly to an MTA when sending mail. We have already seen this type of client, in the previous section when we looked at SMTP. How about downloading mail then?

17.4.8 POP and IMAP

The first protocol developed for downloading was the Post Office Protocol. As stated in the original RFC document, RFC 918 published in October 1984, "The intent of the Post Office Protocol (POP) is to allow a user's workstation to access mail from a mailbox server. It is expected that mail will be posted from the workstation to the mailbox server via the Simple Mail Transfer Protocol (SMTP)." The most recent version of POP is version 3, otherwise known as POP3. POP3, defined in RFC 1939, is still widely used today, and is the basis of our example client below.

Another protocol came a few years after POP, known as the Interactive Mail Access Protocol, or IMAP. The first version was experimental, and it was not until version 2 that its RFC was published, RFC 1064 in July 1988. The current version of IMAP in use today is IMAP4rev1, and it, too, is widely used. In fact, Microsoft Exchange, one of the predominant mail servers in the world today, uses IMAP as its download mechanism. The IMAP4rev1 protocol definition is spelled out in RFC 3501, published in March 2003. The intent of IMAP is to provide a more complete solution to the problem; however, it is more complex than POP. Further discussion of IMAP is beyond the scope of the remainder of this chapter. We refer the interested reader to the aforementioned RFC documents. The diagram in Figure 17–3 illustrates this complex system we know simply as e-mail.

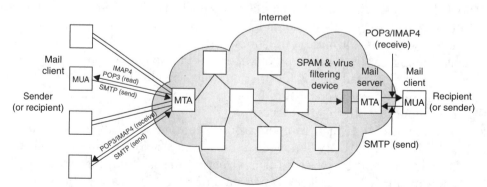

Figure 17–3 E-Mail Senders and Recipients on the Internet. Clients download and send mail via their MUAs, which talk to their corresponding MTAs. E-Mail "hops" from MTA to MTA until it reaches the correct destination.

17.4.9 Python and POP3

No surprises here: import `poplib` and instantiate the `poplib.POP3` class; the standard conversation is as expected:

1. Connect to server
2. Log in
3. Make service request(s)
4. Quit

And the expected Python pseudocode:

```
from poplib import POP3
p = POP3('pop.python.is.cool')
p.user(...)
p.pass_(...)
...
p.quit()
```

Before we take a look at a real example, let's take a look at an interactive example as well as introduce the basic methods of the `poplib.POP3` class.

17.4.10 Interactive POP3 Example

Here is an interactive example of using Python's `poplib`:

```
>>> from poplib import POP3
>>> p = POP3('pop.python.is.cool')
>>> p.user('techNstuff4U')
'+OK'
>>> p.pass_('notMyPasswd')
Traceback (most recent call last):
  File "<stdin>", line 1, in ?
  File "/usr/local/lib/python2.4/poplib.py", line 202,
in pass_
    return self._shortcmd('PASS %s' % pswd)
  File "/usr/local/lib/python2.4/poplib.py", line 165,
in _shortcmd
    return self._getresp()
  File "/usr/local/lib/python2.4/poplib.py", line 141,
in _getresp
    raise error_proto(resp)
poplib.error_proto: -ERR directory status: BAD PASSWORD
>>> p.user('techNstuff4U')
'+OK'
>>> p.pass_('youllNeverGuess')
'+OK ready'
>>> p.stat()
```

```
(102, 2023455)
>>> rsp, msg, siz = p.retr(102)
>>> rsp, siz
('+OK', 480)
>>> for eachLine in msg:
...    print eachLine
...
Date: Mon, 26 Dec 2005 23:58:38 +0000 (GMT)
Received: from c-42-32-25-43.smtp.python.is.cool
           by python.is.cool (scmrch31) with ESMTP
           id <2005122623583701300or7hhe>; Mon, 26 Dec 2005
23:58:37 +0000
From: wesley@python.is.cool
To: wesley@python.is.cool
Subject: test msg

xxx
.
>>> p.quit()
'+OK python.is.cool'
```

17.4.11 `poplib.POP3` Class Methods

The POP3 class has numerous methods to help you download and manage your inbox offline. The most widely used ones are included in Table 17.4.

Table 17.4 Methods for POP3 Objects

Method	Description
user(*login*)	Sends the *login* name to the server; awaits reply indicating the server is waiting for user's password
pass_(*passwd*)	Sends *passwd* (after user logs in with user()); an exception occurs on login/passwd failure
stat()	Returns mailbox status, a 2-tuple (*msg_ct*, *mbox_siz*): the total message count and total message size, aka octets
list([*msgnum*])	Superset of stat()... returns entire message list from server as a 3-tuple (*rsp*, *msg_list*, *rsp_siz*): server response, message list, response message size; if *msgnum* given, return data for that message only

Table 17.4 Methods for POP3 Objects (continued)	
Method	*Description*
retr(*msgnum*)	Retrieves message msgnum from server and sets its 'seen' flag; returns a 3-tuple (*rsp*, *msglines*, *msgsiz*): server response, all lines of message *msgnum*, and message size in bytes/octets
dele(*msgnum*)	Tag message number msgnum for deletion; most servers process deletes upon quit()
quit()	Logs out, commits changes (e.g., process "seen," "delete" flags, etc.), unlocks mailbox, terminates connection, and quits

When logging in, the user() method not only sends the login name to the server, but it also awaits the reply indicating the server is waiting for user's password. If pass_() fails due to authentication issues, the exception raised is poplib.error_proto. If it is successful, it gets back a positive reply, e.g., '+OK ready', and the mailbox on the server is locked until quit() is called.

For the list() method, the msg_list is of the form ['*msgnum msgsiz*',...] where *msgnum* and *msgsiz* are the message number and message sizes, respectively, of each message.

There are a few other methods not listed here. For the full details, check out the documentation for poplib in the Python Library Reference.

17.4.12 Client Program SMTP and POP3 Example

The example below shows how to use both SMTP and POP3 to create a client that both receives and downloads e-mail as well as one that uploads and sends e-mail. What we are going to do is send an e-mail message to ourselves (or some test account) via SMTP, wait for a bit—we arbitrarily chose ten seconds—and then use POP3 to download our message and assert that the messages are identical. Our operation will be a success if the program completes silently, meaning that there should be no output or any errors.

Example 17.3 SMTP and POP3 Example (myMail.py)

This script sends a test e-mail message to the destination address (via the outgoing/SMTP mail server) and retrieves it immediately from the (incoming mail/ POP) server. You must change the server names and e-mail addresses to make it work properly.

```python
1   #!/usr/bin/env python
2
3   from smtplib import SMTP
4   from poplib import POP3
5   from time import sleep
6
7   SMTPSVR = 'smtp.python.is.cool'
8   POP3SVR = 'pop.python.is.cool'
9
10  origHdrs = ['From: wesley@python.is.cool',
11      'To: wesley@python.is.cool',
12      'Subject: test msg']
13  origBody = ['xxx', 'yyy', 'zzz']
14  origMsg = '\r\n\r\n'.join(['\r\n'.join(origHdrs),
    '\r\n'.join(origBody)])
15
16  sendSvr = SMTP(SMTPSVR)
17  errs = sendSvr.sendmail('wesley@python.is.cool',
18      ('wesley@python.is.cool',), origMsg)
19  sendSvr.quit()
20  assert len(errs) == 0, errs
21  sleep(10)     # wait for mail to be delivered
22
23  recvSvr = POP3(POP3SVR)
24  recvSvr.user('wesley')
25  recvSvr.pass_('youllNeverGuess')
26  rsp, msg, siz = recvSvr.retr(recvSvr.stat()[0])
27  # strip headers and compare to orig msg
28  sep = msg.index('')
29  recvBody = msg[sep+1:]
30  assert origBody == recvBody # assert identical
```

Line-by-Line Explanation

Lines 1–8

This application starts with a few **import** statements and some constants, much like the other examples in this chapter. The constants here are the outgoing (SMTP) and incoming (POP3) mail servers.

Lines 10–14

These lines represent the preparation of the message contents. We have some mail headers followed by three lines for the message body. The From and To headers represent the message sender and recipient(s). Line 14 puts everything together into a sendable message of headers followed by a message body, all delimited by the RFC 2822-required line delimiters with a blank line separating the two sections.

Lines 16–21

We connect to the outgoing (SMTP) server and send our message. There is another pair of From and To addresses here. These are the "real" e-mail addresses, or the envelope sender and recipient(s). The recipient field should be an iterable. If a string is passed in, it will be transformed into a list of one element. For unsolicited spam e-mail, there is usually a discrepancy between the message headers and the envelope headers.

The third argument to `sendmail()` is the e-mail message itself. Once it has returned, we log out of the SMTP server and check that no errors have occurred. Then we give the servers some time to send and receive the message.

Lines 23–30

The final part of our application downloads the just-sent message and asserts that both it and the received messages are identical. A connection is made to the POP3 server with a username and password. After successful login, a `stat()` call is made to get a list of available messages. The first message is chosen (`[0]`), and `retr()` is told to download it.

We look for the blank line separating the headers and message, discard the headers, and compare the original message body with the incoming message body. If they are identical, nothing is displayed and the program ends successfully. Otherwise, an assertion is made.

Due to the numerous errors, we left out all the error-checking for this script so that it is easy on the eyes. One of the exercises at the end of the chapter is to add the error-checking.

Now you have a very good idea of how sending and receiving e-mail works in today's environment. If you wish to continue exploring this realm of programming expertise, see the next section for other e-mail-related Python modules, which will prove valuable in application development.

17.5 Related Modules

One of Python's greatest assets is the strength of its networking support in the standard library, particularly those oriented toward Internet protocols and client development. Listed below are related modules, first focusing on electronic mail followed by Internet protocols in general.

17.5.1 E-mail

Python features numerous e-mail modules and packages to help you with building an application. Some of them are listed in Table 17.5.

Table 17.5 E-Mail-Related Modules

Module/Package	Description
email	Package for processing e-mail (also supports MIME)
rfc822	RFC2822 mail header parsers
smtpd	SMTP server
base64	Base 16, 32, and 64 data encodings (RFC 3548)
mhlib	Classes for handling MH folders and messages
mailbox	Classes to support parsing mailbox file formats
mailcap	Support for handling "mailcap" files
mimetools	(deprecated) MIME message parsing tools (use email above)
mimetypes	Converts between filenames/URLs and associated MIME types
MimeWriter	(deprecated) MIME message processing (use email above)
mimify	(deprecated) Tools to MIME-process messages with (use email above)
binascii	Binary and ASCII conversion
binhex	Binhex4 encoding and decoding support

17.5.2 Other Internet Protocols

Module	Description
ftplib	FTP protocol client
gopherlib	Gopher protocol client
httplib	HTTP and HTTPS protocol client
imaplib	IMAP4 protocol client
nntplib	NNTP protocol client
poplib	POP3 protocol client
smtplib	SMTP protocol client
telnetlib	Telnet client class

Table 17.6 Internet Protocol-Related Modules

17.6 Exercises

FTP

17–1. *Simple FTP Client*. Given the FTP examples from this chapter, write a small FTP client program that goes to your favorite Web sites and downloads the latest versions of the applications you use. This may be a script that you run every few months to make sure you're using the "latest and greatest." You should probably keep some sort of table with FTP location, login, and password for your convenience.

17–2. *Simple FTP Client and Pattern-Matching*. Use your solution to the previous exercise as a starting point for creating another simple FTP client that either pushes or pulls a set of files from a remote host using patterns. For example, if you want to move a set of Python or PDF files from one host to another, allow users to enter "*.py" or "doc*.pdf" and only transfer those files whose names match.

17–3. *Smart FTP Command-Line Client*. Create a command-line FTP application similar to the vanilla Unix /bin/ftp program, however, make it a "better FTP client," meaning it should have additional useful features. You can take a look at the ncFTP application as motivation. It can be found at http://ncftp.com. For example, it has the following features: history, bookmarks (saving FTP locations with log in and password), download progress, etc. You may have to implement readline functionality for history and curses for screen control.

17–4. *FTP and Multithreading*. Create an FTP client that uses Python threads to download files. You can either upgrade your existing Smart FTP client as in the previous problem, or just write a more simple client to download files. This can be either a command-line program where you enter multiple files as arguments to the program, or a GUI where you let the user select 1+ file(s) to transfer. Extra credit: Allow patterns, i.e., *.exe. Use individual threads to download each file.

17–5. *FTP and GUI*. Take your smart FTP client developed above and add a GUI layer on top of it to form a complete FTP application. You may choose from any of the modern Python GUI toolkits.

17–6. *Subclassing*. Derive ftplib.FTP and make a new class FTP2 where you do not need to give "STOR filename" and "RETR filename" commands with all four (4) retr*() and stor*() methods . . . you only need to pass in the filename. You may choose to either override the existing methods or create new ones with a '2' suffix, i.e., retrlines2().

The file Tools/scripts/ftpmirror.py in the Python source distribution is a script that can mirror FTP sites, or portions thereof, using the ftplib module. It can be used as an extended example that applies to this module. The next five problems feature creating solutions that revolve around code like ftpmirror.py. You may use code in ftpmirror.py or implement your own solution with its code as your motivation.

17–7. *Recursion*. The ftpmirror.py script copies a remote directory recursively. Create a simpler FTP client in the spirit of ftpmirror.py but one that does *not* recurse by default. Create an "-r" option that tells the application to recursively copy subdirectories to the local filesystem.

17–8. *Pattern-Matching*. The `ftpmirror.py` script has an "`-s`" option that lets users skip files that match the given pattern, i.e., "`.exe`." Create your own simpler FTP client or update your solution to the previous exercise so that it lets the user supply a pattern and only copy those files matching that pattern. Use your solution to an earlier problem above as a starting point.

17–9. *Recursion and Pattern-Matching*. Create an FTP client that integrates both of the previous exercises.

17–10. *Recursion and ZIP files*. This problem is similar to the first recursion exercise above—instead of copying the remote files to the local filesystem, either update your existing FTP client or create a new one to download remote files and compress them into a ZIP (or TGZ or BZ2) file. This "`-z`" option allows your users to back up an FTP site in an automated manner.

17–11. *Kitchen Sink*. Implement a single, final, all-encompassing FTP application that has all the solutions to the exercises above, i.e., "`-r`", "`-s`", and "`-z`" options.

NNTP

17–12. *Introduction to NNTP*. Change Example 17.2 (`getLatestNNTP.py`) so that instead of the most recent article, it displays the first available article meaningfully.

17–13. *Improving Code*. Fix the flaw in `getLatestNNTP.py` where triple-quoted lines show up in the output. This is because we want to display Python interactive interpreter lines but not triple-quoted text. Solve this problem by checking whether the stuff that comes after the "`>>>`" is real Python code. If so, display it as a line of data; if not, do not display this quoted text. Extra credit: Use your solution to solve another minor problem: leading whitespace is not stripped from the body because it may represent indented Python code. If it really is code, display it; otherwise, it is text so `lstrip()` that before displaying.

17–14. *Finding Articles*. Create an NNTP client application that lets the user log in and choose a newsgroup of interest. Once that has been accomplished, prompt the user for keywords to search article Subject lines for. Bring up the list of articles that match the requirement and display them to the user. The user should then be allowed to choose an article to read from that list—display them and provide simple navigation like pagination, etc. If no search field is entered, bring up all current articles.

17–15.   *Searching Bodies*. Upgrade your solution to the previous problem by searching both Subject lines and article bodies. Allow for AND or OR searching of keywords. Also allow for AND or OR searching of Subject lines and article bodies, i.e., keyword(s) must be in Subject lines only, article bodies only, either, or both.

17–16.   *Threaded Newsreader*. This doesn't mean write a multi-threaded newsreader—it means organize related postings into "article threads." In other words, group related articles together, independent of when the individual articles were posted. All the articles belonging to individual threads should be listed chronologically though. Allow the user to:

(a) select individual articles (bodies) to view, then have the option to go back to the list view or to previous or next article either sequentially or related to the current thread.

(b) allow replies to threads, option to copy and quote previous article, reply to the entire newsgroup via another post. Extra credit: Allow personal reply to individual via e-mail.

(c) permanently delete threads—no future related articles should show up in the article list. For this, you will have to temporarily keep a persistent list of deleted threads so that they don't show up again. You can assume a thread is dead if no one posts an article with the same Subject line after several months.

17–17.   *GUI Newsreader*. Similar to an FTP exercise above, choose a Python GUI toolkit to implement a complete standalone GUI newsreader application.

17–18.   *Refactoring*. Like `ftpmirror.py` for FTP, there is a demo script for NNTP: `Demo/scripts/newslist.py`. Run it. This script was written a long time ago and can use a facelift. For this exercise, you are to refactor this program using features of the latest versions of Python as well as your developing skills in Python to perform the same task but run and complete in less time. This can include using list comprehensions or generator expressions, using smarter string concatenation, not calling unnecessary functions, etc.

17–19. *Caching*. Another problem with `newslist.py` is that, according to its author, "I should really keep a list of ignored empty groups and re-check them for articles on every run, but I haven't got around to it yet." Make this improvement a reality. You may use the default version as-is or your newly improved one from the previous exercise.

E-MAIL

17–20. *Identifiers*. The POP3 method `pass_()` is used to send the password to the server after giving it the login name using `login()`. Can you give any reasons why you believe this method was named with a trailing underscore, i.e., "`pass_()`", instead of just plain old "`pass()`"?

17–21. *IMAP*. Now that you are familiar with how POP works, your experience will help you with an IMAP client. Study the IMAP protocol RFC document, and use the Python `imaplib` module to help you.

The next set of exercises deal with the `myMail.py` application found in this chapter (Example 17.3).

17–22. *E-mail Headers*. In `myMail.py`, the last few lines compared the originally sent body with the body in the received e-mail. Create similar code to assert the original headers. Hint: Ignore newly added headers.

17–23. *Error Checking*. Add SMTP and POP3 error-checking.

17–24. *SMTP and IMAP*. Take our simple `myMail.py`, and added support for IMAP. Extra credit: Support both mail download protocols, letting the user choose which to use.

17–25. *E-mail Composition*. Further develop your solution to the previous problem by giving the users of your application the ability to compose and send e-mail.

17–26. *E-mail Application*. Further develop your e-mail application, turning it into something more useful by adding in mailbox management. Your application should be able to read in the current set of e-mail messages in a user's imbeds and display their Subject lines. Users should be able to select messages to view. Extra credit: Add support to view attachments via external applications.

17–27. *GUI*. Add a GUI layer on top of your solution to the previous problem to make it practically a full e-mail application.

17–28. *Elements of SPAM.* Unsolicited junk e-mail, or *spam*, is a very real and significant problem today. There are many good solutions out there, validating this market. We do not want you to (necessarily) reinvent the wheel but we would like you to get a taste of some of the elements of spam.

(a) *"mbox" format.* Before we can get started, we should convert any e-mail messages you want to work on to a common format, such as the "mbox" format. (There are others that you can use if you prefer. Once you have several (or all) work messages in mbox format, merge them all into a single file.

(b) *Headers.* Most of the clues of spam lie in the e-mail headers. (You may wish to use the email package or parse them manually yourself.) Write code that answers questions such as:

  – What e-mail client appears to have originated this message? (Check out the X-Mailer header.)
  – Is the message ID (Message-ID header) format valid?
  – Are there domain name mismatches between the From, Received, and perhaps Return-Path headers? What about domain name and IP address mismatches? Is there an X-Authentication-Warning header? If so, what does it report?

(c) *Information Servers.* Based on an IP address or domain, servers such as WHOIS, SenderBase.org, etc., may be able to help you identify the location where a piece of bulk e-mail originated. Find one or more of these services and build code to the find the country of origin, and optionally the city, network owner name, contact info, etc.

(d) *Keywords.* Certain words keep popping up in spam. You have no doubt seen them before, and in all of their variations, including using a number resembling a letter, capitalizing random letters, etc. Build a list of frequent words that you have seen definitely tied to spam, and quarantine such messages as possible spam. Extra credit: Develop an algorithm or add keyword variations to spot such trickery in messages.

(e) *Phishing*. These spam messages attempt to disguise themselves as valid e-mail from major banking institutions or well-known Internet Web sites. They contain links that lure readers to Web sites in an attempt to harvest private and extremely sensitive information such as login names, passwords, and credit card numbers. These fakers do a pretty good job of giving their fraudulent messages an accurate look-and-feel. However, they cannot hide the fact that the actual link that they direct users to does not belong to the company they are masquerading as. Many of them are obvious giveaways, i.e., horrible-looking domain names, raw IP addresses, and even IP addresses in 32-bit integer format rather than in octets. Develop code that can determine whether e-mail that looks like official communication is real or bogus.

MISCELLANEOUS

A list of various Internet protocols, including the three highlighted in this chapter, can be found at http://www.networksorcery.com/enp/topic/ipsuite.htm# Application%20layer%20protocols. A list of specific Internet protocols supported by Python (currently), can be found at http://docs.python.org/lib/internet.html

17–29. *Developing Alternate Internet Clients*. Now that you have seen four examples of how Python can help you develop Internet clients, choose another protocol with client support in a Python standard library module and write a client application for it.

17–30. *Developing New Internet Clients*. Much more difficult: find an uncommon or upcoming protocol *without* Python support and implement it. Be serious enough that you will consider writing and submitting a PEP to have your module included in the standard library distribution of a future Python release.

MULTITHREADED PROGRAMMING

Chapter Topics

- Introduction/Motivation
- Threads and Processes
- Threads and Python
- `thread` Module
- `threading` Module
- Producer–Consumer Problem and the `Queue` Module
- Related Modules

Chapter 18

In this section, we will explore the different ways you can achieve more parallelism in your code by using the multithreaded (MT) programming features found in Python. We will begin by differentiating between processes and threads in the first few of sections of this chapter. We will then introduce the notion of multithreaded programming. (Those of you already familiar with MT programming can skip directly to Section 18.3.5.) The final sections of this chapter present some examples of how to use the `threading` and `Queue` modules to accomplish MT programming with Python.

18.1 Introduction/Motivation

Before the advent of multithreaded (MT) programming, running of computer programs consisted of a single sequence of steps that were executed in synchronous order by the host's central processing unit (CPU). This style of execution was the norm whether the task itself required the sequential ordering of steps or if the entire program was actually an aggregation of multiple subtasks. What if these subtasks were independent, having no *causal* relationship (meaning that results of subtasks do not affect other subtask outcomes)? Is it not logical, then, to want to run these independent tasks all at the same time? Such parallel processing could significantly improve the performance of the overall task. This is what MT programming is all about.

MT programming is ideal for programming tasks that are asynchronous in nature, require multiple concurrent activities, and where the processing of each activity may be *nondeterministic*, i.e., random and unpredictable. Such programming tasks can be organized or partitioned into multiple streams of execution where each has a specific task to accomplish. Depending on the application, these subtasks may calculate intermediate results that could be merged into a final piece of output.

While CPU-bound tasks may be fairly straightforward to divide into subtasks and executed sequentially or in a multithreaded manner, the task of managing a single-threaded process with multiple external sources of input is not as trivial. To achieve such a programming task without multithreading, a sequential program must use one or more timers and implement a multiplexing scheme.

A sequential program will need to sample each I/O (input/output) terminal channel to check for user input; however, it is important that the program does not block when reading the I/O terminal channel because the arrival of user input is nondeterministic, and blocking would prevent processing of other I/O channels. The sequential program must use non-blocked I/O or blocked I/O with a timer (so that blocking is only temporary).

Because the sequential program is a single thread of execution, it must juggle the multiple tasks that it needs to perform, making sure that it does not spend too much time on any one task, and it must ensure that user response time is appropriately distributed. The use of a sequential program for this type of task often results in a complicated flow of control that is difficult to understand and maintain.

Using an MT program with a shared data structure such as a `Queue` (a multithreaded queue data structure discussed later in this chapter), this programming task can be organized with a few threads that have specific functions to perform:

- `UserRequestThread`: Responsible for reading client input, perhaps from an I/O channel. A number of threads would be created by the program, one for each current client, with requests being entered into the queue.
- `RequestProcessor`: A thread that is responsible for retrieving requests from the queue and processing them, providing output for yet a third thread.
- `ReplyThread`: Responsible for taking output destined for the user and either sending it back, if in a networked application, or writing data to the local file system or database.

Organizing this programming task with multiple threads reduces the complexity of the program and enables an implementation that is clean, efficient, and well organized. The logic in each thread is typically less complex because it has a specific job to do. For example, the `UserRequestThread` simply reads input from a user and places the data into a queue for further processing by another thread, etc. Each thread has its own job to do; you merely have to design each type of thread to do one thing and do it well. Use of threads for specific tasks is not unlike Henry Ford's assembly line model for manufacturing automobiles.

18.2 Threads and Processes

18.2.1 What Are Processes?

Computer *programs* are merely executables, binary (or otherwise), which reside on disk. They do not take on a life of their own until loaded into memory and invoked by the operating system. A *process* (sometimes called a *heavyweight process*) is a program in execution. Each process has its own address space, memory, a data stack, and other auxiliary data to keep track of execution. The operating system manages the execution of all processes on the system, dividing the time fairly between all processes. Processes can also *fork* or *spawn* new processes to perform other tasks, but each new process has its own memory, data stack, etc., and cannot generally share information unless interprocess communication (IPC) is employed.

18.2.2 What Are Threads?

Threads (sometimes called *lightweight processes*) are similar to processes except that they all execute within the same process, and thus all share the same context. They can be thought of as "mini-processes" running in parallel within a main process or "main thread."

A thread has a beginning, an execution sequence, and a conclusion. It has an instruction pointer that keeps track of where within its context it is currently running. It can be preempted (interrupted) and temporarily put on hold (also known as *sleeping*) while other threads are running—this is called *yielding*.

Multiple threads within a process share the same data space with the main thread and can therefore share information or communicate with one another more easily than if they were separate processes. Threads are generally executed in a concurrent fashion, and it is this parallelism and data sharing that enable the coordination of multiple tasks. Naturally, it is impossible to run truly in a concurrent manner in a single CPU system, so threads are scheduled in such a way that they run for a little bit, then yield to other threads (going to the proverbial "back of the line" to await more CPU time again). Throughout the execution of the entire process, each thread performs its own, separate tasks, and communicates the results with other threads as necessary.

Of course, such sharing is not without its dangers. If two or more threads access the same piece of data, inconsistent results may arise because of the ordering of data access. This is commonly known as a *race condition*. Fortunately, most thread libraries come with some sort of synchronization primitives that allow the thread manager to control execution and access.

Another caveat is that threads may not be given equal and fair execution time. This is because some functions block until they have completed. If not written specifically to take threads into account, this skews the amount of CPU time in favor of such greedy functions.

18.3 Python, Threads, and the Global Interpreter Lock

18.3.1 Global Interpreter Lock (GIL)

Execution of Python code is controlled by the *Python Virtual Machine* (aka the interpreter main loop). Python was designed in such a way that only one thread of control may be executing in this main loop, similar to how multiple processes in a system share a single CPU. Many programs may be in memory, but only *one* is live on the CPU at any given moment. Likewise, although multiple threads may be "running" within the Python interpreter, only one thread is being executed by the interpreter at any given time.

Access to the Python Virtual Machine is controlled by the *global interpreter lock* (GIL). This lock is what ensures that exactly one thread is running. The Python Virtual Machine executes in the following manner in an MT environment:

1. Set the GIL
2. Switch in a thread to run
3. Execute either . . .
   a. For a specified number of bytecode instructions, or
   b. If the thread voluntarily yields control (can be accomplished `time.sleep(0)`)

4. Put the thread back to sleep (switch out thread)
5. Unlock the GIL, and . . .
6. Do it all over again (lather, rinse, repeat)

When a call is made to external code, i.e., any C/C++ extension built-in function, the GIL will be locked until it has completed (since there are no Python bytecodes to count as the interval). Extension programmers do have the ability to unlock the GIL, however, so you being the Python developer shouldn't have to worry about your Python code locking up in those situations.

As an example, for any Python I/O-oriented routines (which invoke built-in operating system C code), the GIL is released before the I/O call is made, allowing other threads to run while the I/O is being performed. Code that *doesn't* have much I/O will tend to keep the processor (and GIL) for the full interval a thread is allowed before it yields. In other words, I/O-bound Python programs stand a much better chance of being able to take advantage of a multithreaded environment than CPU-bound code.

Those of you interested in the source code, the interpreter main loop, and the GIL can take a look at the `Python/ceval.c` file.

18.3.2 Exiting Threads

When a thread completes execution of the function it was created for, it exits. Threads may also quit by calling an exit function such as `thread.exit()`, or any of the standard ways of exiting a Python process, i.e., `sys.exit()` or raising the `SystemExit` exception. You cannot, however, go and "kill" a thread.

We will discuss in detail the two Python modules related to threads in the next section, but of the two, the `thread` module is the one we do *not* recommend. There are many reasons for this, but an obvious one is that when the main thread exits, all other threads die without cleanup. The other module, `threading`, ensures that the whole process stays alive until all "important" child threads have exited. (We will clarify what "important" means soon. Look for the *daemon threads* Core Tip sidebar.)

Main threads should always be good managers, though, and perform the task of knowing what needs to be executed by individual threads, what data or arguments each of the spawned threads requires, when they complete execution, and what results they provide. In so doing, those main threads can collate the individual results into a final, meaningful conclusion.

18.3.3 Accessing Threads from Python

Python supports multithreaded programming, depending on the operating system that it is running on. It is supported on most Unix-based platforms, i.e., Linux, Solaris, MacOS X, *BSD, as well as Win32 systems. Python uses POSIX-compliant threads, or "pthreads," as they are commonly known.

By default, threads are enabled when building Python from source (since Python 2.0) or the Win32 installed binary. To tell whether threads are available for your interpreter, simply attempt to import the thread module from the interactive interpreter. No errors occur when threads are available:

```
>>> import thread
>>>
```

If your Python interpreter was *not* compiled with threads enabled, the module import fails:

```
>>> import thread
Traceback (innermost last):
  File "<stdin>", line 1, in ?
ImportError: No module named thread
```

In such cases, you may have to recompile your Python interpreter to get access to threads. This usually involves invoking the configure script with the "--with-thread" option. Check the README file for your distribution to obtain specific instructions on how to compile Python with threads for your system.

18.3.4 Life Without Threads

For our first set of examples, we are going to use the time.sleep() function to show how threads work. time.sleep() takes a floating point argument and "sleeps" for the given number of seconds, meaning that execution is temporarily halted for the amount of time specified.

Let us create two "time loops," one that sleeps for 4 seconds and one that sleeps for 2 seconds, loop0() and loop1(), respectively. (We use the names "loop0" and "loop1" as a hint that we will eventually have a sequence of loops.) If we were to execute loop0() and loop1() sequentially in a one-process or single-threaded program, as onethr.py does in Example 18.1, the total execution time would be at least 6 seconds. There may or may not be a 1-second gap between the starting of loop0() and loop1(), and other execution overhead which may cause the overall time to be bumped to 7 seconds.

Example 18.1 Loops Executed by a Single Thread (`onethr.py`)

Executes two loops consecutively in a single-threaded program. One loop must complete before the other can begin. The total elapsed time is the sum of times taken by each loop.

```
1   #!/usr/bin/env python
2
3   from time import sleep, ctime
4
5   def loop0():
6       print 'start loop 0 at:', ctime()
7       sleep(4)
8       print 'loop 0 done at:', ctime()
9
10  def loop1():
11      print 'start loop 1 at:', ctime()
12      sleep(2)
13      print 'loop 1 done at:', ctime()
14
15  def main():
16      print 'starting at:', ctime()
17      loop0()
18      loop1()
19      print 'all DONE at:', ctime()
20
21  if __name__ == '__main__':
22      main()
```

We can verify this by executing `onethr.py`, which gives the following output:

```
$ onethr.py
starting at: Sun Aug 13 05:03:34 2006
start loop 0 at: Sun Aug 13 05:03:34 2006
loop 0 done at: Sun Aug 13 05:03:38 2006
start loop 1 at: Sun Aug 13 05:03:38 2006
loop 1 done at: Sun Aug 13 05:03:40 2006
all DONE at: Sun Aug 13 05:03:40 2006
```

Now, pretend that rather than sleeping, `loop0()` and `loop1()` were separate functions that performed individual and independent computations, all working to arrive at a common solution. Wouldn't it be useful to have them run in parallel to cut down on the overall running time? That is the premise behind MT that we now introduce to you.

18.3.5 Python Threading Modules

Python provides several modules to support MT programming, including the thread, threading, and Queue modules. The thread and threading modules allow the programmer to create and manage threads. The thread module provides basic thread and locking support, while threading provides higher-level, fully featured thread management. The Queue module allows the user to create a queue data structure that can be shared across multiple threads. We will take a look at these modules individually and present examples and intermediate-sized applications.

CORE TIP: Avoid use of thread module

We recommend avoiding the thread module for many reasons. The first is that the high-level threading module is more contemporary, not to mention the fact that thread support in the threading module is much improved and the use of attributes of the thread module may conflict with using the threading module. Another reason is that the lower-level thread module has few synchronization primitives (actually only one) while threading has many.

However, in the interest of learning Python and threading in general, we do present some code that uses the thread module. These pieces of code should be used for learning purposes only and will give you a much better insight as to why you would want to avoid using the thread module. These examples also show how our applications and thread programming improve as we migrate to using more appropriate tools such as those available in the threading and Queue modules.

Another reason to avoid using thread is because there is no control of when your process exits. When the main thread finishes, all threads will also die, without warning or proper cleanup. As mentioned earlier, at least threading allows the important child threads to finish first before exiting.

Use of the thread module is recommended only for experts desiring lower-level thread access. Those of you new to threads should look at the code samples to see how we can overlay threads onto our time loop application and to gain a better understanding as to how these first examples evolve to the main code samples of this chapter. Your first multithreaded application should utilize threading and perhaps other high-level thread modules, if applicable.

18.4 `thread` Module

Let's take a look at what the `thread` module has to offer. In addition to being able to spawn threads, the `thread` module also provides a basic synchronization data structure called a *lock object* (aka primitive lock, simple lock, mutual exclusion lock, mutex, binary semaphore). As we mentioned earlier, such synchronization primitives go hand in hand with thread management.

Listed in Table 18.1 are the more commonly used thread functions and `LockType` lock object methods.

The key function of the `thread` module is `start_new_thread()`. Its syntax is exactly that of the `apply()` built-in function, taking a function along with arguments and optional keyword arguments. The difference is that instead of the main thread executing the function, a new thread is spawned to invoke the function.

Let's take our `onethr.py` example and integrate threading into it. By slightly changing the call to the `loop*()` functions, we now present `mtsleep1.py` in Example 18.2.

Table 18.1   `thread` Module and Lock Objects

Function/Method	Description
`thread` Module Functions	
`start_new_thread(function, args, kwargs=None)`	Spawns a new thread and execute *function* with the given *args* and optional *kwargs*
`allocate_lock()`	Allocates `LockType` lock object
`exit()`	Instructs a thread to exit
`LockType` Lock Object Methods	
`acquire(wait=None)`	Attempts to acquire lock object
`locked()`	Returns True if lock acquired, False otherwise
`release()`	Releases lock

Example 18.2 Using the **thread** Module (`mtsleep1.py`)

The same loops from `onethr.py` *are executed, but this time using the simple multithreaded mechanism provided by the* `thread` *module. The two loops are executed concurrently (with the shorter one finishing first, obviously), and the total elapsed time is only as long as the slowest thread rather than the total time for each separately.*

```python
1   #!/usr/bin/env python
2
3   import thread
4   from time import sleep, ctime
5
6   def loop0():
7       print 'start loop 0 at:', ctime()
8       sleep(4)
9       print 'loop 0 done at:', ctime()
10
11  def loop1():
12      print 'start loop 1 at:', ctime()
13      sleep(2)
14      print 'loop 1 done at:', ctime()
15
16  def main():
17      print 'starting at:', ctime()
18      thread.start_new_thread(loop0, ())
19      thread.start_new_thread(loop1, ())
20      sleep(6)
21      print 'all DONE at:', ctime()
22
23  if __name__ == '__main__':
24      main()
```

`start_new_thread()` requires the first two arguments, so that is the reason for passing in an empty tuple even if the executing function requires no arguments.

Upon execution of this program, our output changes drastically. Rather than taking a full 6 or 7 seconds, our script now runs in 4, the length of time of our longest loop, plus any overhead.

```
$ mtsleep1.py
starting at: Sun Aug 13 05:04:50 2006
start loop 0 at: Sun Aug 13 05:04:50 2006
start loop 1 at: Sun Aug 13 05:04:50 2006
loop 1 done at: Sun Aug 13 05:04:52 2006
loop 0 done at: Sun Aug 13 05:04:54 2006
all DONE at: Sun Aug 13 05:04:56 2006
```

The pieces of code that sleep for 4 and 2 seconds now occur concurrently, contributing to the lower overall runtime. You can even see how loop 1 finishes before loop 0.

The only other major change to our application is the addition of the "sleep(6)" call. Why is this necessary? The reason is that if we did not stop the main thread from continuing, it would proceed to the next statement, displaying "all done" and exit, killing both threads running loop0() and loop1().

We did not have any code that told the main thread to wait for the child threads to complete before continuing. This is what we mean by threads requiring some sort of synchronization. In our case, we used another sleep() call as our synchronization mechanism. We used a value of 6 seconds because we know that both threads (which take 4 and 2 seconds, as you know) should have completed by the time the main thread has counted to 6.

You are probably thinking that there should be a better way of managing threads than creating that extra delay of 6 seconds in the main thread. Because of this delay, the overall runtime is no better than in our single-threaded version. Using sleep() for thread synchronization as we did is not reliable. What if our loops had independent and varying execution times? We may be exiting the main thread too early or too late. This is where locks come in.

Making yet another update to our code to include locks as well as getting rid of separate loop functions, we get mtsleep2.py, presented in Example 18.3. Running it, we see that the output is similar to mtsleep1.py. The only difference is that we did not have to wait the extra time for mtsleep1.py to conclude. By using locks, we were able to exit as soon as both threads had completed execution.

```
$ mtsleep2.py
starting at: Sun Aug 13 16:34:41 2006
start loop 0 at: Sun Aug 13 16:34:41 2006
start loop 1 at: Sun Aug 13 16:34:41 2006
loop 1 done at: Sun Aug 13 16:34:43 2006
loop 0 done at: Sun Aug 13 16:34:45 2006
all DONE at: Sun Aug 13 16:34:45 2006
```

So how did we accomplish our task with locks? Let us take a look at the source code.

Example 18.3 Using `thread` and Locks (`mtsleep2.py`)

Rather than using a call to `sleep()` *to hold up the main thread as in* `mtsleep1.py`, *the use of locks makes more sense.*

```
1   #!/usr/bin/env python
2
3   import thread
4   from time import sleep, ctime
5
6   loops = [4,2]
7
8   def loop(nloop, nsec, lock):
9       print 'start loop', nloop, 'at:', ctime()
10      sleep(nsec)
11      print 'loop', nloop, 'done at:', ctime()
12      lock.release()
13
14  def main():
15      print 'starting at:', ctime()
16      locks = []
17      nloops = range(len(loops))
18
19      for i in nloops:
20          lock = thread.allocate_lock()
21          lock.acquire()
22          locks.append(lock)
23
24      for i in nloops:
25          thread.start_new_thread(loop,
26              (i, loops[i], locks[i]))
27
28      for i in nloops:
29          while locks[i].locked(): pass
30
31      print 'all DONE at:', ctime()
32
33  if __name__ == '__main__':
34      main()
```

Line-by-Line Explanation

Lines 1–6

After the Unix startup line, we import the `thread` module and a few familiar attributes of the `time` module. Rather than hardcoding separate functions to count to 4 and 2 seconds, we will use a single `loop()` function and place these constants in a list, `loops`.

Lines 8–12

The `loop()` function will proxy for the now-removed `loop*()` functions from our earlier examples. We had to make some cosmetic changes to `loop()` so that it can now perform its duties using locks. The obvious changes are that we need to be told which loop number we are as well as how long to sleep for. The last piece of new information is the lock itself. Each thread will be allocated an acquired lock. When the `sleep()` time has concluded, we will release the corresponding lock, indicating to the main thread that this thread has completed.

Lines 14–34

The bulk of the work is done here in `main()` using three separate **for** loops. We first create a list of locks, which we obtain using the `thread.allocate_lock()` function and acquire (each lock) with the `acquire()` method. Acquiring a lock has the effect of "locking the lock." Once it is locked, we add the lock to the lock list, `locks`. The next loop actually spawns the threads, invoking the `loop()` function per thread, and for each thread, provides it with the loop number, the time to sleep for, and the acquired lock for that thread. So why didn't we start the threads in the lock acquisition loop? There are several reasons: (1) we wanted to synchronize the threads, so that "all the horses started out the gate" around the same time, and (2) locks take a little bit of time to be acquired. If your thread executes "too fast," it is possible that it completes before the lock has a chance to be acquired.

It is up to each thread to unlock its lock object when it has completed execution. The final loop just sits and spins (pausing the main thread) until both locks have been released before continuing execution. Since we are checking each lock sequentially, we may be at the mercy of all the slower loops if they are more toward the beginning of the set of loops. In such cases, the majority of the wait time may be for the first loop(s). When that lock is released, remaining locks may have already been unlocked (meaning that corresponding threads have completed execution). The result is that the main thread will fly through those lock checks without pause. Finally, you should be well aware that the final pair of lines will execute `main()` only if we are invoking this script directly.

As hinted in the earlier Core Note, we presented the `thread` module only to introduce the reader to threaded programming. Your MT application should use higher-level modules such as the `threading` module, which we will now discuss.

18.5 `threading` Module

We will now introduce the higher-level `threading` module, which gives you not only a `Thread` class but also a wide variety of synchronization mechanisms to use to your heart's content. Table 18.2 represents a list of all the objects available in the `threading` module.

In this section, we will examine how to use the `Thread` class to implement threading. Since we have already covered the basics of locking, we will not cover the locking primitives here. The `Thread()` class also contains a form of synchronization, so explicit use of locking primitives is not necessary.

Table 18.2 `threading` **Module Objects**

`threading` *Module Objects*	*Description*
`Thread`	Object that represents a single thread of execution
`Lock`	Primitive lock object (same lock object as in the `thread` module)
`RLock`	Re-entrant lock object provides ability for a single thread to (re)acquire an already-held lock (recursive locking)
`Condition`	Condition variable object causes one thread to wait until a certain "condition" has been satisfied by another thread, such as changing of state or of some data value
`Event`	General version of condition variables whereby any number of threads are waiting for some event to occur and all will awaken when the event happens
`Semaphore`	Provides a "waiting area"-like structure for threads waiting on a lock
`BoundedSemaphore`	Similar to a `Semaphore` but ensures it never exceeds its initial value
`Timer`	Similar to `Thread` except that it waits for an allotted period of time before running

CORE TIP: Daemon threads

Another reason to avoid using the `thread` *module is that it does not support the concept of* daemon (or daemonic) *threads. When the main thread exits, all child threads will be killed regardless of whether they are doing work. The concept of daemon threads comes into play here if you do not want this behavior.*

Support for daemon threads is available in the `threading` *module, and here is how they work: a daemon is typically a server that waits for client requests to service. If there is no client work to be done, the daemon just sits around idle. If you set the daemon flag for a thread, you are basically saying that it is non-critical, and it is okay for the process to exit without waiting for it to "finish." As you have seen in Chapter 16, "Network Programming" server threads run in an infinite loop and do not exit in normal situations.*

If your main thread is ready to exit and you do not care to wait for the child threads to finish, then set their daemon flag. Think of setting this flag as denoting a thread to be "not important." You do this by calling each thread's `setDaemon()` *method, e.g.,* `thread.setDae-mon(True)`, *before it begins running (*`thread.start()`.*)*

If you want to wait for child threads to finish, just leave them as-is, or ensure that their daemon flags are off by explicitly calling `thread.setDaemon (False)` *before starting them. You can check a thread's daemonic status with* `thread.isDaemon()`. *A new child thread inherits its daemonic flag from its parent. The entire Python program will stay alive until all non-daemonic threads have exited, in other words, when no active non-daemonic threads are left).*

18.5.1 Thread Class

The `Thread` class of the `threading` is your primary executive object. It has a variety of functions not available to the `thread` module, and are outlined in Table 18.3.

There are a variety of ways you can create threads using the `Thread` class. We cover three of them here, all quite similar. Pick the one you feel most comfortable with, not to mention the most appropriate for your application and future scalability (we like the final choice the best):

- Create `Thread` instance, passing in function
- Create `Thread` instance, passing in callable class instance
- Subclass `Thread` and create subclass instance

Table 18.3 Thread Object Methods

Method	Description
start()	Begin thread execution
run()	Method defining thread functionality (usually overridden by application writer in a subclass)
join(*timeout =* None)	Suspend until the started thread terminates; blocks unless *timeout* (in seconds) is given
getName()	Return name of thread
setName(*name*)	Set name of thread
isAlive()	Boolean flag indicating whether thread is still running
isDaemon()	Return daemon flag of thread
setDaemon (*daemonic*)	Set the daemon flag of thread as per the Boolean *daemonic* (must be called before thread start()ed)

Create Thread Instance, Passing in Function

In our first example, we will just instantiate Thread, passing in our function (and its arguments) in a manner similar to our previous examples. This function is what will be executed when we direct the thread to begin execution. Taking our mtsleep2.py script and tweaking it, adding the use of Thread objects, we have mtsleep3.py, shown in Example 18.4.

When we run it, we see output similar to its predecessors' output:

```
$ mtsleep3.py
starting at: Sun Aug 13 18:16:38 2006
start loop 0 at: Sun Aug 13 18:16:38 2006
start loop 1 at: Sun Aug 13 18:16:38 2006
loop 1 done at: Sun Aug 13 18:16:40 2006
loop 0 done at: Sun Aug 13 18:16:42 2006
all DONE at: Sun Aug 13 18:16:42 2006
```

So what *did* change? Gone are the locks that we had to implement when using the thread module. Instead, we create a set of Thread objects. When each Thread is instantiated, we dutifully pass in the function (target) and arguments (args) and receive a Thread instance in return. The biggest

Example 18.4 Using the `threading` Module (`mtsleep3.py`)

The `Thread` *class from the* `threading` *module has a* `join()` *method that lets the main thread wait for thread completion.*

```python
1   #!/usr/bin/env python
2
3   import threading
4   from time import sleep, ctime
5
6   loops = [4,2]
7
8   def loop(nloop, nsec):
9       print 'start loop', nloop, 'at:', ctime()
10      sleep(nsec)
11      print 'loop', nloop, 'done at:', ctime()
12
13  def main():
14      print 'starting at:', ctime()
15      threads = []
16      nloops = range(len(loops))
17
18      for i in nloops:
19          t = threading.Thread(target=loop,
20              args=(i, loops[i]))
21          threads.append(t)
22
23      for i in nloops:                # start threads
24          threads[i].start()
25
26      for i in nloops:                # wait for all
27          threads[i].join()           # threads to finish
28
29      print 'all DONE at:', ctime()
30
31  if __name__ == '__main__':
32      main()
```

difference between instantiating `Thread` [calling `Thread()`] and invoking `thread.start_new_thread()` is that the new thread does not begin execution right away. This is a useful synchronization feature, especially when you don't want the threads to start immediately.

Once all the threads have been allocated, we let them go off to the races by invoking each thread's `start()` method, but not a moment before that. And rather than having to manage a set of locks (allocating, acquiring, releasing, checking lock state, etc.), we simply call the `join()` method for each thread.

join() will wait until a thread terminates, or, if provided, a timeout occurs. Use of join() appears much cleaner than an infinite loop waiting for locks to be released (causing these locks to sometimes be known as "spin locks").

One other important aspect of join() is that it does not need to be called at all. Once threads are started, they will execute until their given function completes, whereby they will exit. If your main thread has things to do other than wait for threads to complete (such as other processing or waiting for new client requests), it should by all means do so. join() is useful only when you *want* to wait for thread completion.

Create Thread Instance, Passing in Callable Class Instance

A similar offshoot to passing in a function when creating a thread is to have a callable class and passing in an instance for execution—this is the more OO approach to MT programming. Such a callable class embodies an execution environment that is much more flexible than a function or choosing from a set of functions. You now have the power of a class object behind you, as opposed to a single function or a list/tuple of functions.

Adding our new class ThreadFunc to the code and making other slight modifications to mtsleep3.py, we get mtsleep4.py, given in Example 18.5.

If we run mtsleep4.py, we get the expected output:

```
$ mtsleep4.py
starting at: Sun Aug 13 18:49:17 2006
start loop 0 at: Sun Aug 13 18:49:17 2006
start loop 1 at: Sun Aug 13 18:49:17 2006
loop 1 done at: Sun Aug 13 18:49:19 2006
loop 0 done at: Sun Aug 13 18:49:21 2006
all DONE at: Sun Aug 13 18:49:21 2006
```

So what are the changes this time? The addition of the ThreadFunc class and a minor change to instantiate the Thread object, which also instantiates ThreadFunc, our callable class. In effect, we have a double instantiation going on here. Let's take a closer look at our ThreadFunc class.

We want to make this class general enough to use with functions other than our loop() function, so we added some new infrastructure, such as having this class hold the arguments for the function, the function itself, and also a function name string. The constructor __init__() just sets all the values.

When the Thread code calls our ThreadFunc object when a new thread is created, it will invoke the __call__() special method. Because we already have our set of arguments, we do not need to pass it to the Thread() constructor, but do have to use apply() in our code now because we have

Example 18.5   Using Callable classes (`mtsleep4.py`)

*In this example we pass in a callable class (instance) as opposed to just a function.
It presents more of an OO approach than* `mtsleep3.py`.

```python
1   #!/usr/bin/env python
2
3   import threading
4   from time import sleep, ctime
5
6   loops = [4,2]
7
8   class ThreadFunc(object):
9
10      def __init__(self, func, args, name=''):
11          self.name = name
12          self.func = func
13          self.args = args
14
15      def __call__(self):
16          apply(self.func, self.args)
17
18  def loop(nloop, nsec):
19      print 'start loop', nloop, 'at:', ctime()
20      sleep(nsec)
21      print 'loop', nloop, 'done at:', ctime()
22
23  def main():
24      print 'starting at:', ctime()
25      threads = []
26      nloops = range(len(loops))
27
28      for i in nloops:  # create all threads
29          t = threading.Thread(
30              target=ThreadFunc(loop, (i, loops[i]),
31              loop.__name__))
32          threads.append(t)
33
34      for i in nloops:  # start all threads
35          threads[i].start()
36
37      for i in nloops:  # wait for completion
38          threads[i].join()
39
40      print 'all DONE at:', ctime()
41
42  if __name__ == '__main__':
43      main()
```

an argument tuple. Those of you who have Python 1.6 and higher can use the new function invocation syntax described in Section 11.6.3 instead of using `apply()` on line 16:

```
self.res = self.func(*self.args)
```

Subclass `Thread` and Create Subclass Instance

The final introductory example involves subclassing `Thread()`, which turns out to be extremely similar to creating a callable class as in the previous example. Subclassing is a bit easier to read when you are creating your threads (lines 29–30). We will present the code for `mtsleep5.py` in Example 18.6 as well as the output obtained from its execution, and leave it as an exercise for the reader to compare `mtsleep5.py` to `mtsleep4.py`.

Here is the output for `mtsleep5.py`, again, just what we expected:

```
$ mtsleep5.py
starting at: Sun Aug 13 19:14:26 2006
start loop 0 at: Sun Aug 13 19:14:26 2006
start loop 1 at: Sun Aug 13 19:14:26 2006
loop 1 done at: Sun Aug 13 19:14:28 2006
loop 0 done at: Sun Aug 13 19:14:30 2006
all DONE at: Sun Aug 13 19:14:30 2006
```

While the reader compares the source between the `mtsleep4` and `mtsleep5` modules, we want to point out the most significant changes: (1) our `MyThread` subclass constructor must first invoke the base class constructor (line 9), and (2) the former special method `__call__()` must be called `run()` in the subclass.

We now modify our `MyThread` class with some diagnostic output and store it in a separate module called `myThread` (see Example 18.7) and import this class for the upcoming examples. Rather than simply calling `apply()` to run our functions, we also save the result to instance attribute `self.res`, and create a new method to retrieve that value, `getResult()`.

18.5.4 Fibonacci and Factorial . . . Take Two, Plus Summation

The `mtfacfib.py` script, given in Example 18.8, compares execution of the recursive Fibonacci, factorial, and summation functions. This script runs all three functions in a single-threaded manner, then performs the same task using threads to illustrate one of the advantages of having a threading environment.

Example 18.6 Subclassing `Thread` (`mtsleep5.py`)

Rather than instantiating the `Thread` class, we subclass it. This gives us more flexibility in customizing our threading objects and simplifies the thread creation call.

```python
1   #!/usr/bin/env python
2
3   import threading
4   from time import sleep, ctime
5
6   loops = (4, 2)
7
8   class MyThread(threading.Thread):
9       def __init__(self, func, args, name=''):
10          threading.Thread.__init__(self)
11          self.name = name
12          self.func = func
13          self.args = args
14
15      def run(self):
16          apply(self.func, self.args)
17
18  def loop(nloop, nsec):
19      print 'start loop', nloop, 'at:', ctime()
20      sleep(nsec)
21      print 'loop', nloop, 'done at:', ctime()
22
23  def main():
24      print 'starting at:', ctime()
25      threads = []
26      nloops = range(len(loops))
27
28      for i in nloops:
29          t = MyThread(loop, (i, loops[i]),
30              loop.__name__)
31          threads.append(t)
32
33      for i in nloops:
34          threads[i].start()
35
36      for i in nloops:
37          threads[i].join()
38
39      print 'all DONE at:', ctime()'
40
41  if __name__ == '__main__':
42      main()
```

Example 18.7 MyThread Subclass of Thread (myThread.py)

To generalize our subclass of Thread *from* mtsleep5.py, *we move the subclass to a separate module and add a* getResult() *method for callables that produce return values.*

```
1  #!/usr/bin/env python
2
3  import threading
4  from time import ctime
5
6  class MyThread(threading.Thread):
7      def __init__(self, func, args, name=''):
8          threading.Thread.__init__(self)
9          self.name = name
10         self.func = func
11         self.args = args
12
13     def getResult(self):
14         return self.res
15
16     def run(self):
17         print 'starting', self.name, 'at:', \
18             ctime()
19         self.res = apply(self.func, self.args)
20         print self.name, 'finished at:', \
21             ctime()
```

Running in single-threaded mode simply involves calling the functions one at a time and displaying the corresponding results right after the function call.

When running in multithreaded mode, we do not display the result right away. Because we want to keep our MyThread class as general as possible (being able to execute callables that do and do not produce output), we wait until the end to call the getResult() method to finally show you the return values of each function call.

Because these functions execute so quickly (well, maybe except for the Fibonacci function), you will notice that we had to add calls to sleep() to each function to slow things down so that we can see how threading may improve performance, if indeed the actual work had varying execution times—you certainly wouldn't pad your work with calls to sleep(). Anyway, here is the output:

```
$ mtfacfib.py
*** SINGLE THREAD
starting fib at: Sun Jun 18 19:52:20 2006
233
fib finished at: Sun Jun 18 19:52:24 2006
```

Example 18.8 Fibonacci, Factorial, Summation (`mtfacfib.py`)

In this MT application, we execute three separate recursive functions—first in a single-threaded fashion, followed by the alternative with multiple threads.

```python
1   #!/usr/bin/env python
2
3   from myThread import MyThread
4   from time import ctime, sleep
5
6   def fib(x):
7       sleep(0.005)
8       if x < 2: return 1
9       return (fib(x-2) + fib(x-1))
10
11  def fac(x):
12      sleep(0.1)
13      if x < 2: return 1
14      return (x * fac(x-1))
15
16  def sum(x):
17      sleep(0.1)
18      if x < 2: return 1
19      return (x + sum(x-1))
20
21  funcs = [fib, fac, sum]
22  n = 12
23
24  def main():
25      nfuncs = range(len(funcs))
26
27      print '*** SINGLE THREAD'
28      for i in nfuncs:
29          print 'starting', funcs[i].__name__, 'at:', \
30              ctime()
31          print funcs[i](n)
32          print funcs[i].__name__, 'finished at:', \
33              ctime()
34
35      print '\n*** MULTIPLE THREADS'
36      threads = []
37      for i in nfuncs:
38          t = MyThread(funcs[i], (n,),
39              funcs[i].__name__)
40          threads.append(t)
41
42      for i in nfuncs:
43          threads[i].start()
44
45      for i in nfuncs:
46          threads[i].join()
47          print threads[i].getResult()
48
49      print 'all DONE'
50
51  if __name__ == '__main__':
52      main()
```

```
starting fac at: Sun Jun 18 19:52:24 2006
479001600
fac finished at: Sun Jun 18 19:52:26 2006
starting sum at: Sun Jun 18 19:52:26 2006
78
sum finished at: Sun Jun 18 19:52:27 2006

*** MULTIPLE THREADS
starting fib at: Sun Jun 18 19:52:27 2006
starting fac at: Sun Jun 18 19:52:27 2006
starting sum at: Sun Jun 18 19:52:27 2006
fac finished at: Sun Jun 18 19:52:28 2006
sum finished at: Sun Jun 18 19:52:28 2006
fib finished at: Sun Jun 18 19:52:31 2006
233
479001600
78
all DONE
```

18.5.5 Other `Threading` Module Functions

In addition to the various synchronization and threading objects, the `Threading` module also has some supporting functions, detailed in Table 18.4.

Table 18.4 `threading` Module Functions

Function	Description
`activeCount()`	Number of currently active `Thread` objects
`currentThread()`	Returns the current `Thread` object
`enumerate()`	Returns list of all currently active `Threads`
`settrace(func)`[a]	Sets a trace *func*tion for all threads
`setprofile(func)`[a]	Sets a profile *func*tion for all threads

a.   New in Python 2.3.

18.5.6 Producer-Consumer Problem and the `Queue` Module

The final example illustrates the producer-consumer scenario where a producer of goods or services creates goods and places it in a data structure such as a queue. The amount of time between producing goods is non-deterministic, as is the consumer consuming the goods produced by the producer.

Table 18.5 Common Queue Module Attributes

Function/Method	Description
Queue *Module Function*	
queue(*size*)	Creates a Queue object of given size
Queue *Object Methods*	
qsize()	Returns queue size (approximate, since queue may be getting updated by other threads)
empty()	Returns True if queue empty, False otherwise
full()	Returns True if queue full, False otherwise
put(*item*, *block*=0)	Puts *item* in queue, if *block* given (not 0), block until room is available
get(*block*=0)	Gets *item* from queue, if *block* given (not 0), block until an item is available

We use the Queue module to provide an interthread communication mechanism that allows threads to share data with each other. In particular, we create a queue into which the producer (thread) places new goods and the consumer (thread) consumes them. To do this, we will use the following attributes from the Queue module (see Table 18.5).

Without further ado, we present the code for prodcons.py, shown in Example 18.9.

Here is the output from one execution of this script:

```
$ prodcons.py
starting writer at: Sun Jun 18 20:27:07 2006
producing object for Q... size now 1
starting reader at: Sun Jun 18 20:27:07 2006
consumed object from Q... size now 0
producing object for Q... size now 1
consumed object from Q... size now 0
producing object for Q... size now 1
producing object for Q... size now 2
producing object for Q... size now 3
consumed object from Q... size now 2
consumed object from Q... size now 1
```

```
writer finished at: Sun Jun 18 20:27:17 2006
consumed object from Q... size now 0
reader finished at: Sun Jun 18 20:27:25 2006
all DONE
```

As you can see, the producer and consumer do not necessarily alternate in execution. (Thank goodness for random numbers!) Seriously, though, real life is generally random and non-deterministic.

Line-by-Line Explanation

Lines 1–6

In this module, we will use the `Queue.Queue` object as well as our thread class `myThread.MyThread`, which we gave in Example 18.7. We will use `random.randint()` to make production and consumption somewhat varied, and also grab the usual suspects from the time module.

Lines 8–16

The `writeQ()` and `readQ()` functions each have a specific purpose, to place an object in the queue—we are using the string `'xxx'`, for example—and to consume a queued object, respectively. Notice that we are producing one object and reading one object each time.

Lines 18–26

The `writer()` is going to run as a single thread whose sole purpose is to produce an item for the queue, wait for a bit, then do it again, up to the specified number of times, chosen randomly per script execution. The `reader()` will do likewise, with the exception of consuming an item, of course.

You will notice that the random number of seconds that the writer sleeps is in general shorter than the amount of time the reader sleeps. This is to discourage the reader from trying to take items from an empty queue. By giving the writer a shorter time period of waiting, it is more likely that there will already be an object for the reader to consume by the time their turn rolls around again.

Lines 28–29

These are just setup lines to set the total number of threads that are to be spawned and executed.

Example 18.9 Producer-Consumer Problem (`prodcons.py`)

We feature an implementation of the Producer–Consumer problem using `Queue` objects and a random number of goods produced (and consumed). The producer and consumer are individually—and concurrently—executing threads.

```python
1   #!/usr/bin/env python
2
3   from random import randint
4   from time import sleep
5   from Queue import Queue
6   from myThread import MyThread
7
8   def writeQ(queue):
9       print 'producing object for Q...',
10      queue.put('xxx', 1)
11      print "size now", queue.qsize()
12
13  def readQ(queue):
14      val = queue.get(1)
15      print 'consumed object from Q... size now', \
16              queue.qsize()
17
18  def writer(queue, loops):
19      for i in range(loops):
20          writeQ(queue)
21          sleep(randint(1, 3))
22
23  def reader(queue, loops):
24      for i in range(loops):
25          readQ(queue)
26          sleep(randint(2, 5))
27
28  funcs = [writer, reader]
29  nfuncs = range(len(funcs))
30
31  def main():
32      nloops = randint(2, 5)
33      q = Queue(32)
34
35      threads = []
36      for i in nfuncs:
37          t = MyThread(funcs[i], (q, nloops),
38              funcs[i].__name__)
39          threads.append(t)
40
41      for i in nfuncs:
42          threads[i].start()
43
44      for i in nfuncs:
45          threads[i].join()
46
47      print 'all DONE'
48
49  if __name__ == '__main__':
50      main()
```

Lines 31–47

Finally, we have our `main()` function, which should look quite similar to the `main()` in all of the other scripts in this chapter. We create the appropriate threads and send them on their way, finishing up when both threads have concluded execution.

We infer from this example that a program that has multiple tasks to perform can be organized to use separate threads for each of the tasks. This can result in a much cleaner program design than a single threaded program that attempts to do all of the tasks.

In this chapter, we illustrated how a single-threaded process may limit an application's performance. In particular, programs with independent, non-deterministic, and non-causal tasks that execute sequentially can be improved by division into separate tasks executed by individual threads. Not all applications may benefit from multithreading due to overhead and the fact that the Python interpreter is a single-threaded application, but now you are more cognizant of Python's threading capabilities and can use this tool to your advantage when appropriate.

18.6 Related Modules

The table below lists some of the modules you may use when programming multithreaded applications.

Table 18.6 Threading-Related Standard Library Modules

Module	Description
thread	Basic, lower-level thread module
threading	Higher-level threading and synchronization objects
Queue	Synchronized FIFO queue for multiple threads
mutex	Mutual exclusion objects
SocketServer	TCP and UDP managers with some threading control

18.7 Exercises

18–1. *Processes versus Threads.* What are the differences between processes and threads?

18–2. *Python Threads*. Which type of multithreaded application will tend to fare better in Python, I/O-bound or CPU-bound?

18–3. *Threads*. Do you think anything significant happens if you have multiple threads on a multiple CPU system? How do you think multiple threads run on these systems?

18–4. *Threads and Files*. Update your solution to Exercise 9–19, which obtains a byte value and a file name, displaying the number of times that byte appears in the file. Let's suppose this is a really big file. Multiple readers in a file is acceptable, so create multiple threads that count in different parts of the file so that each thread is responsible for a certain part of the file. Collate the data from each thread and provide the summed-up result. Use your `timeit()` code to time both the single threaded version and your new multithreaded version and say something about the performance improvement.

18–5. *Threads, Files, and Regular Expressions*. You have a very large mailbox file—if you don't have one, put all of your e-mail messages together into a single text file. Your job is to take the regular expressions you designed in Chapter 15 that recognize e-mail addresses and Web site URLs, and use them to convert all e-mail addresses and URLs in this large file into live links so that when the new file is saved as an `.html` (or `.htm`) file, will show up in a Web browser as live and clickable. Use threads to segregate the conversion process across the large text file and collate the results into a single new `.html` file. Test the results on your Web browser to ensure the links are indeed working.

18–6. *Threads and Networking*. Your solution to the chat service application in the previous chapter (Exercises 16–7 to 16–10) may have required you to use heavyweight threads or processes as part of your solution. Convert that to be multithreaded `code`.

18–7. *Threads and Web Programming*. The `Crawler` up ahead in Example 19.1 is a single-threaded application that downloads Web pages that would benefit from MT programming. Update `crawl.py` (you could call it `mtcrawl.py`) such that independent threads are used to download pages. Be sure to use some kind of locking mechanism to prevent conflicting access to the links queue.

18–8.   *Thread Pools*. Instead of a producer thread and a consumer thread, change the code in Example 18.9, `prodcons.py`, so that you have any number of consumer threads (a *thread pool*) which can process or consume more than one item from the `Queue` at any given moment.

18–9.   *Files*. Create a set of threads to count how many lines there are in a set of (presumably large) text files. You may choose the number of threads to use. Compare the performance against a single-threaded version of this code. Hint: Review Chapter 9 (Files and I/O) exercises.

18–10. Take your solution to the previous exercise and adopt it to a task of your selection, i.e., processing a set of e-mail messages, downloading Web pages, processing RSS or Atom feeds, enhancing message processing as part of a chat server, solving a puzzle, etc.

GUI
PROGRAMMING

Chapter Topics

- Introduction
- Tkinter and Python Programming
  - `Tkinter` Module
  - Tk Widgets
- Tkinter Examples
  - Label, Button and Scale Widgets
  - An Intermediate Tk Example
- Brief Tour of Other GUIs (Tix, Pmw, wxPython, PyGTK)
- Related Modules and Other GUIs

Chapter 19

I n this chapter, we will give you a brief introduction to the subject of graphical user interface (GUI) programming. If you are somewhat new to this area or want to learn more about it, or if you want to see how it is done in Python, then this chapter is for you. We cannot show you everything about GUI application development here in this one chapter, but we will give you a very solid introduction to it. The primary GUI toolkit we will be using is Tk, Python's default GUI, and we will access Tk from its Python interface called Tkinter (short for "Tk interface").

Tk is not the "latest and greatest" nor does it have the most robust set of GUI building blocks, but it is fairly simple to use and will allow you to build GUIs that run on most platforms. We will present several simple and intermediate examples using Tkinter, followed by a few examples using other toolkits. Once you have completed this chapter, you will have the skills to build more complex applications and/or move to a more modern graphical toolkit. Python has *bindings* or *adapters* to most of the major toolkits out there, including commercial systems.

19.1 Introduction

19.1.1 What Are Tcl, Tk, and Tkinter?

Tkinter is Python's default GUI library. It is based on the Tk toolkit, originally designed for the Tool Command Language (Tcl). Due to Tk's popularity, it has been ported to a variety of other scripting languages, including Perl (Perl/Tk), Ruby (Ruby/Tk), and Python (Tkinter). With the GUI development portability and flexibility of Tk, along with the simplicity of scripting language integrated with the power of systems language, you are given the tools to rapidly design and implement a wide variety of commercial-quality GUI applications.

If you are new to GUI programming, you will be pleasantly surprised at how easy it is. You will also find that Python, along with Tkinter, provides a fast and exciting way to build applications that are fun (and perhaps useful) and that would have taken much longer if you had had to program directly in C/C++ with the native windowing system's libraries. Once you have designed the application and the look and feel that goes along with your program, you will use basic building blocks known as *widgets* to piece together the desired components, and finally, to attach functionality to "make it real."

If you are an old hand at using Tk, either with Tcl or Perl, you will find Python a refreshing way to program GUIs. On top of that, it provides an even faster rapid prototyping system for building them. Remember that you also have Python's system accessibility, networking functionality, XML, numerical and visual processing, database access, and all the other standard library and third-party extension modules.

Once you get Tkinter up on your system, it will take less than 15 minutes to get your first GUI application running.

19.1.2 Getting Tkinter Installed and Working

Like threading, Tkinter is not necessarily turned on by default on your system. You can tell whether Tkinter is available for your Python interpreter by attempting to import the `Tkinter` module. If Tkinter is available, then no errors occur:

```
>>> import Tkinter
>>>
```

If your Python interpreter was *not* compiled with Tkinter enabled, the module import fails:

```
>>> import Tkinter
Traceback (innermost last):
   File "<stdin>", line 1, in ?
   File "/usr/lib/python1.5/lib-tk/Tkinter.py", line 8, in ?
     import _tkinter # If this fails your Python may not
be configured for Tk
ImportError: No module named _tkinter
```

You may have to recompile your Python interpreter to get access to Tkinter. This usually involves editing the `Modules/Setup` file and enabling all the correct settings to compile your Python interpreter with hooks to Tkinter or choosing to have Tk installed on your system. Check the `README` file for your Python distribution for specific instructions on getting Tkinter to compile on your system. Be sure, after your compilation, that you start the *new* Python interpreter you just created; otherwise, it will act just like your old one without Tkinter (and in fact, it *is* your old one).

19.1.3 Client/Server Architecture—Take Two

In the earlier chapter on network programming, we introduced the notion of client/server computing. A windowing system is another example of a software server. These run on a machine with an attached display, such as a monitor of some sort. There are clients, too—programs that require a windowing environment to execute, also known as GUI applications. Such applications cannot run without a windows system.

The architecture becomes even more interesting when networking comes into play. Usually when a GUI application is executed, it displays to the machine that it started on (via the windowing server), but it is possible in some networked windowing environments, such as the X Window system on Unix, to choose another machine's window server to display to. In such situations, you can be running a GUI program on one machine, but have it displayed on another!

19.2 Tkinter and Python Programming

19.2.1 Tkinter Module: Adding Tk to your Applications

So what do you need to do to have Tkinter as part of your application? Well, first of all, it is not necessary to have an application already. You can create a pure GUI if you want, but it probably isn't too useful without some underlying software that does something interesting.

There are basically five main steps that are required to get your GUI up and running:

1. Import the `Tkinter` module (or **from** `Tkinter` **import** *).
2. Create a top-level windowing object that contains your entire GUI application.

3. Build all your GUI components (and functionality) on top (or "inside") of your top-level windowing object.
4. Connect these GUI components to the underlying application code.
5. Enter the main event loop.

The first step is trivial: All GUIs that use Tkinter must import the `Tkinter` module. Getting access to Tkinter is the first step (see Section 19.1.2).

19.2.2 Introduction to GUI Programming

Before going to the examples, we will give you a brief introduction to GUI application development in general. This will provide you with some of the background you need to move forward.

Setting up a GUI application is similar to an artist's producing a painting. Conventionally, there is a single canvas onto which the artist must put all the work. The way it works is like this: You start with a clean slate, a "top-level" windowing object on which you build the rest of your components. Think of it as a foundation to a house or the easel for an artist. In other words, you have to pour the concrete or set up your easel before putting together the actual structure or canvas on top of it. In Tkinter, this foundation is known as the top-level window object.

In GUI programming, a top-level root windowing object contains all of the little windowing objects that will be part of your complete GUI application. These can be text labels, buttons, list boxes, etc. These individual little GUI components are known as *widgets*. So when we say create a top-level window, we just mean that you need such a thing as a place where you put all your widgets. In Python, this would typically look like this line:

```
top = Tkinter.Tk() # or just Tk() with "from Tkinter import *"
```

The object returned by `Tkinter.Tk()` is usually referred to as the *root window*, hence the reason why some applications use `root` rather than `top` to indicate as such. Top-level windows are those that show up standalone as part of your application. You may have more than one top-level window for your GUI, but only one of them should be your root window. You may choose to completely design all your widgets first, then add the real functionality, or do a little of this and a little of that along the way. (This means mixing and matching steps 3 and 4 from our list.)

Widgets may be standalone or be containers. If a widget "contains" other widgets, it is considered the *parent* of those widgets. Accordingly, if a widget is "contained" in another widget, it's considered a *child* of the parent, the parent being the next immediate enclosing container widget.

Usually, widgets have some associated behaviors, such as when a button is pressed, or text is filled into a text field. These types of user behaviors are called *events*, and the actions that the GUI takes to respond to such events are known as *callbacks*.

Actions may include the actual button press (and release), mouse movement, hitting the RETURN or Enter key, etc. All of these are known to the system literally as *events*. The entire system of events that occurs from the beginning to the end of a GUI application is what drives it. This is known as event-driven processing.

One example of an event with a callback is a simple mouse move. Let's say the mouse pointer is sitting somewhere on top of your GUI application. If the mouse is moved to another part of your application, something has to cause the movement of the mouse on your screen so that it *looks* as if it is moving to another location. These are mouse move events that the system must process to give you the illusion (and reality) that your mouse is moving across the window. When you release the mouse, there are no more events to process, so everything just sits there quietly on the screen again.

The event-driven processing nature of GUIs fits right in with client/server architecture. When you start a GUI application, it must perform some setup procedures to prepare for the core execution, just as when a network server has to allocate a socket and bind it to a local address. The GUI application must establish all the GUI components, then draw (aka render or paint) them to the screen. Tk has a couple of geometry managers that help position the widget in the right place; the main one that you will use is called Pack, aka the *packer*. Another geometry manager is Grid—this is where you specify GUI widgets to be placed in grid coordinates, and Grid will render each object in the GUI in their grid position. For us, we will stick with the packer.

Once the packer has determined the sizes and alignments of all your widgets, it will then place them on the screen for you. When all of the widgets, including the top-level window, finally appear on your screen, your GUI application then enters a "server-like" infinite loop. This infinite loop involves waiting for a GUI event, processing it, then going back to wait for the next event.

The final step we described above says to enter the main loop once all the widgets are ready. This is the "server" infinite loop we have been referring to. In Tkinter, the code that does this is:

```
Tkinter.mainloop()
```

This is normally the last piece of sequential code your program runs. When the main loop is entered, the GUI takes over execution from there. All other action is via callbacks, even exiting your application. When you pull down the File menu to click on the Exit menu option or close the window directly, a callback must be invoked to end your GUI application.

19.2.3 Top-Level Window: `Tkinter.Tk()`

We mentioned above that all main widgets are built into the top-level window object. This object is created by the `Tk` class in Tkinter and is created via the normal instantiation:

```
>>> import Tkinter
>>> top = Tkinter.Tk()
```

Within this window, you place individual widgets or multiple-component pieces together to form your GUI. So what kinds of widgets are there? We will now introduce the Tk widgets.

19.2.4 Tk Widgets

There are currently 15 types of widgets in Tk. We describe these widgets in Table 19.1.

We won't go over the Tk widgets in detail as there is plenty of good documentation available on them, either from the Tkinter topics page at the main Python Web site or the abundant number of Tcl/Tk printed and online resources (some of which are available in Appendix B). However, we will present several simple examples to help you get started.

CORE NOTE: Default arguments are your friend

GUI development really takes advantage of default arguments in Python because there are numerous default actions in Tkinter widgets. Unless you know every single option available to you for every single widget you are using, it's best to start out by setting only the parameters you are aware of and letting the system handle the rest. These defaults were chosen carefully. If you do not provide these values, do not worry about your applications appearing odd on the screen. They were created with an optimized set of default arguments as a general rule, and only when you know how to exactly customize your widgets should you use values other than the default.

Table 19.1 Tk Widgets

Widget	Description
Button	Similar to a Label but provides additional functionality for mouse overs, presses, and releases as well as keyboard activity/ events
Canvas	Provides ability to draw shapes (lines, ovals, polygons, rectangles); can contain images or bitmaps
Checkbutton	Set of boxes of which any number can be "checked" (similar to HTML checkbox input)
Entry	Single-line text field with which to collect keyboard input (similar to HTML text input)
Frame	Pure container for other widgets
Label	Used to contain text or images
Listbox	Presents user list of choices to pick from
Menu	Actual list of choices "hanging" from a Menubutton that the user can choose from
Menubutton	Provides infrastructure to contain menus (pulldown, cascading, etc.)
Message	Similar to a Label, but displays multi-line text
Radiobutton	Set of buttons of which only one can be "pressed" (similar to HTML radio input)
Scale	Linear "slider" widget providing an exact value at current setting; with defined starting and ending values
Scrollbar	Provides scrolling functionality to supporting widgets, i.e., Text, Canvas, Listbox, and Entry
Text	Multi-line text field with which to collect (or display) text from user (similar to HTML textarea)
Toplevel	Similar to a Frame, but provides a separate window container

---

Example 19.1 Label **Widget Demo** (tkhello1.py)

*Our first Tkinter example is ... what else? "Hello World!" In particular, we introduce
our first widget, the* Label.

```
1   #!/usr/bin/env python
2
3   import Tkinter
4
5   top = Tkinter.Tk()
6   label = Tkinter.Label(top, text='Hello World!')
7   label.pack()
8   Tkinter.mainloop()
```

19.3 Tkinter Examples

19.3.1 Label *Widget*

In Example 19.1, we present tkhello1.py, the Tkinter version of "Hello
World!" In particular, it shows you how a Tkinter application is set up and
highlights the Label widget.

In the first line, we create our top-level window. That is followed by our
Label widget containing the all-too-famous string. We instruct the packer to
manage and display our widget, and finally call mainloop() to run our GUI
application. Figure 19–1 shows what you will see when you run this GUI
application.

19.3.2 Button *Widget*

The next example is pretty much the same as the first. However, instead of a
simple text label, we will create a button instead. In Example 19.2 is the
source code for tkhello2.py.

Unix (twm)

Windows

Figure 19–1   Tkinter Label widget
(tkhello1.py)

Example 19.2 Button Widget Demo (tkhello2.py)

This example is exactly the same as tkhello1.py *except that rather than using a* Label *widget, we create a* Button *widget.*

```
1   #!/usr/bin/env python
2
3   import Tkinter
4
5   top = Tkinter.Tk()
6   quit = Tkinter.Button(top, text='Hello World!',
7       command=top.quit)
8   quit.pack()
9   Tkinter.mainloop()
```

The first few lines are identical. Things differ only when we create the Button widget. Our button has one additional parameter, the Tkinter.quit() method. This installs a callback to our button so that if it is pressed (and released), the entire application will exit. The final two lines are the usual pack() and entering of the mainloop(). This simple button application is shown in Figure 19–2.

19.3.3 Label *and* Button *Widgets*

We combine tkhello1.py and tkhello2.py into tkhello3.py, a script that has both a label and a button. In addition, we are providing more parameters now than before when we were comfortable using all the default arguments that are automatically set for us. The source for tkhello3.py is given in Example 19.3.

Besides additional parameters for the widgets, we also see some arguments for the packer. The fill parameter tells the packer to let the QUIT button take up the rest of the horizontal real estate, and the expand

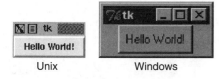

Unix   Windows

Figure 19–2 Tkinter Label widget (tkhello1.py)

Example 19.3 Label and Button Widget Demo
(tkhello3.py)

This example features both a Label *and a* Button *widget. Rather than primarily using default arguments when creating the widget, we are able to specify more now that we know more about* Button *widgets and how to configure them.*

```python
1  #!/usr/bin/env python
2
3  import Tkinter
4  top = Tkinter.Tk()
5
6  hello = Tkinter.Label(top, text='Hello World!')
7  hello.pack()
8
9  quit = Tkinter.Button(top, text='QUIT',
10     command=top.quit, bg='red', fg='white')
11 quit.pack(fill=Tkinter.X, expand=1)
12
13 Tkinter.mainloop()
```

parameter directs the packer to visually fill out the entire horizontal landscape, stretching the button to the left and right sides of the window.

As you can see in Figure 19–3, without any other instructions to the packer, the widgets are placed vertically (on top of each other). Horizontal placement requires creating a new Frame object with which to add the buttons. That frame will take the place of the parent object as a single child object (see the buttons in the listdir.py module, Example 19.6 in Section 19.3.6).

Unix

Windows

Figure 19–3 Tkinter Label and Button widgets (tkhello3.py)

19.3.4 Label, Button, *and* Scale *Widgets*

Our final trivial example, tkhello4.py, involves the addition of a Scale widget. In particular, the Scale is used to interact with the Label widget. The Scale slider is a tool which controls the size of the text font in the Label widget. The greater the slider position, the larger the font, and the same goes for a lesser position, meaning a smaller font. The code for tkhello4.py is given in Example 19.4.

Example 19.4 Label, Button, and Scale **Demo** (tkhello4.py)

Our final introductory widget example introduces the Scale *widget and highlights how widgets can "communicate" with each other using callbacks [such as* resize()*]. The text in the* Label *widget is affected by actions taken on the* Scale *widget.*

```
1   #!/usr/bin/env python
2
3   from Tkinter import *
4
5   def resize(ev=None):
6       label.config(font='Helvetica -%d bold' % \
7           scale.get())
8
9   top = Tk()
10  top.geometry('250x150')
11
12  label = Label(top, text='Hello World!',
13      font='Helvetica -12 bold')
14  label.pack(fill=Y, expand=1)
15
16  scale = Scale(top, from_=10, to=40,
17      orient=HORIZONTAL, command=resize)
18  scale.set(12)
19  scale.pack(fill=X, expand=1)
20
21  quit = Button(top, text='QUIT',
22      command=top.quit, activeforeground='white',
23      activebackground='red')
24  quit.pack()
25
26  mainloop()
```

New features of this script include a `resize()` callback function (lines 5–7), which is attached to the `Scale`. This is the code that is activated when the slider on the `Scale` is moved, resizing the size of the text in the `Label`.

We also define the size (250 × 150) of the top-level window (line 10). The final difference between this script and the first three is that we import the attributes from the `Tkinter` module into our namespace with "**from Tkinter import** *." Although not recommended because it "pollutes" your namespace, we do it here mainly because this application involves a great number of references to Tkinter attributes. This would require use of their fully qualified names for each and every attribute access. By using the undesired shortcut, we are able to access attributes with less typing and have code that is easier to read, at some cost.

As you can see from Figure 19–4, both the slider mechanism as well as the current set value show up in the main part of the window. Figure 19-4 shows the state of the GUI after the user moves the scale/slider to avalue of 36.

Unix

Windows

Figure 19–4 Tkinter `Label`, `Button`, and `Scale` widgets (`tkhello4.py`)

As you can see from the code, the initial setting for the scale when the application starts is 12 (line 18).

19.3.5 Partial Function Application Example

Before looking a longer GUI application, we wanted to review the Partial Function Application (PFA) as introduced back in Section 11.7.3 of Chapter 11.

PFAs were added to Python in version 2.5 and are one piece in a series of significant improvements in functional programming.

2.5

PFAs allow you to "cache" function parameters by effectively "freezing" those predetermined arguments, and then at runtime, when you have the remaining arguments you need, you can thaw them out, send in the final arguments, and have that function called with all parameters.

Best of all, PFAs are not limited to just functions. They will work with any "callable," any object that has a functional interface just by using parentheses, i.e., classes, methods, or callable instances. The use of PFAs fits perfectly into a situation where there are many callables and many of the calls feature the same arguments over and over again.

GUI programming makes a great use case because there is good probability that you want some consistency in GUI widget look-and-feel, and this consistency comes about when the same parameters are used to create like objects. We are now going to present an application where multiple buttons will have the same foreground and background colors. It would be a waste of typing to give the same arguments to the same instantiators every time we wanted a slightly different button: the foreground and background colors are the same, but only the text is slightly different.

We are going to use traffic road signs as our example with our application attempts creating textual versions of road signs by dividing them up into various categories of sign types like critical, warning, or informational (just like logging levels). The type of the sign determines their color layout when the signs are created. For example, critical signs have the text in bright red with a white backdrop, warning signs are in black text on a goldenrod background, and informational or regulatory signs feature black text on a white background. We have the "Do Not Enter" and "Wrong Way" signs, which are both "critical," plus "Merging Traffic" and "Railroad Crossing," both of which are warnings. Finally, we have the regulatory "Speed Limit" and "One Way" signs.

The application creates the "signs," which are just buttons. When users press the buttons, they just pop up the corresponding Tk dialog, critical/error, warning, or informational. It is not too exciting, but how the buttons are built is. You will find our application featured here in Example 19.5.

Example 19.5 Road Signs PFA GUI Application (`pfaGUI2.py`)

Create road signs with the appropriate foreground and background colors based on sign type. Use PFAs to help "templatize" common GUI parameters.

```python
1   #!/usr/bin/env python
2
3   from functools import partial as pto
4   from Tkinter import Tk, Button, X
5   from tkMessageBox import showinfo, showwarning, showerror
6
7   WARN = 'warn'
8   CRIT = 'crit'
9   REGU = 'regu'
10
11  SIGNS = {
12      'do not enter': CRIT,
13      'railroad crossing': WARN,
14      '55\nspeed limit': REGU,
15      'wrong way': CRIT,
16      'merging traffic': WARN,
17      'one way': REGU,
18  }
19
20  critCB = lambda: showerror('Error', 'Error Button Pressed!')
21  warnCB = lambda: showwarning('Warning',
22      'Warning Button Pressed!')
23  infoCB = lambda: showinfo('Info', 'Info Button Pressed!')
24
25  top = Tk()
26  top.title('Road Signs')
27  Button(top, text='QUIT', command=top.quit,
28      bg='red', fg='white').pack()
29
30  MyButton = pto(Button, top)
31  CritButton = pto(MyButton, command=critCB, bg='white', fg='red')
32  WarnButton = pto(MyButton, command=warnCB, bg='goldenrod1')
33  ReguButton = pto(MyButton, command=infoCB, bg='white')
34
35  for eachSign in SIGNS:
36      signType = SIGNS[eachSign]
37      cmd = '%sButton(text=%r%s).pack(fill=X, expand=True)' % (
38          signType.title(), eachSign,
39          '.upper()' if signType == CRIT else '.title()')
40      eval(cmd)
41
42  top.mainloop()
```

Figure 19–5   Road signs PFA GUI application on XDarwin in MacOS X (`pfaGUI2.py`)

When you execute this application, you will get a GUI that will look something like Figure 19.5.

Line-by-Line Explanation

Lines 1–18

We begin our application by importing `functional.partial()`, a few `Tkinter` attributes, and the Tk dialogs (lines 1–5). Next, we define some signs along with their categories (lines 7–18).

Lines 20–28

The Tk dialogs are assigned as button callbacks, which we will use for each button created (lines 20–23). We then launch Tk, set the title, and create a QUIT button (lines 25–28).

Lines 30–33

These lines represent our PFA magic. We use two levels of PFA. The first templatizes the `Button` class and the root window `top`. What this does is that every time we call `MyButton`, it will call `Button` (`Tkinter.Button()` creates a button.) with `top` as its first argument. We have "frozen" this into `MyButton`.

The second level of PFA is where we use our first one, `MyButton`, and templatize *that*. We create separate button types for each of our sign categories. When users create a critical button `CritButton` (by calling it, e.g., `CritButton()`), it will then call `MyButton` along with the appropriate button callback and background and foreground colors, which means calling `Button` with `top`, callback, and colors. Do you see how it unwinds and goes down the layers until at the very bottom, it has the call that you would have originally had to make if this feature did not exist yet? We repeat with `Warn-Button` and `ReguButton`.

Lines 35–42

With the setup completed, we look at our list of signs and create them. We put together a Python evaluatable string consisting of the correct button name, pass in the button label as the text argument, and `pack()` it. If it is a critical sign, then we CAPITALIZE the button text, otherwise we titlecase it. This last bit is done in line 39, demonstrating another feature introduced in Python 2.5, the temporary operator. Then we take each button creation string and execute it with `eval()`, creating the buttons one at a time and resulting in the graphic seen previously. Finally, we start the GUI by entering the main event loop.

This application uses several Python 2.5 features, so you will not be able to run this with an older version.

19.3.6 Intermediate Tkinter Example

We conclude this section with a larger example, `listdir.py`. This application is a directory tree traversal tool. It starts in the current directory and provides a file listing. Double-clicking on any other directory in the list causes the tool to change to the new directory as well as replace the original file listing with the files from the new directory. The source code is given as Example 19.6.

Example 19.6 File System Traversal GUI (`listdir.py`)

This slightly more advanced GUI expands on the use of widgets, adding listboxes, text entry fields, and scrollbars to our repertoire. There are also a good number of callbacks such as mouse clicks, key presses, and scrollbar action.

```
1   #!/usr/bin/env python
2
3   import os
4   from time import sleep
5   from Tkinter import *
6
7   class DirList(object):
8
9       def __init__(self, initdir=None):
10          self.top = Tk()
11          self.label = Label(self.top,
12              text='Directory Lister v1.1')
13          self.label.pack()
14
15  self.cwd = StringVar(self.top)
16
```

Example 19.6 File System Traversal GUI (`listdir.py`) (continued)

```
17   self.dirl = Label(self.top, fg='blue',
18               font=('Helvetica', 12, 'bold'))
19           self.dirl.pack()
20
21           self.dirfm = Frame(self.top)
22           self.dirsb = Scrollbar(self.dirfm)
23           self.dirsb.pack(side=RIGHT, fill=Y)
24           self.dirs = Listbox(self.dirfm, height=15,
25               width=50, yscrollcommand=self.dirsb.set)
26           self.dirs.bind('<Double-1>', self.setDirAndGo)
27           self.dirsb.config(command=self.dirs.yview)
28           self.dirs.pack(side=LEFT, fill=BOTH)
29           self.dirfm.pack()
30
31           self.dirn = Entry(self.top, width=50,
32               textvariable=self.cwd)
33           self.dirn.bind('<Return>', self.doLS)
34           self.dirn.pack()
35
36           self.bfm = Frame(self.top)
37           self.clr = Button(self.bfm, text='Clear',
38               command=self.clrDir,
39               activeforeground='white',
40               activebackground='blue')
41           self.ls = Button(self.bfm,
42               text='List Directory',
43               command=self.doLS,
44               activeforeground='white',
45               activebackground='green')
46           self.quit = Button(self.bfm, text='Quit',
47               command=self.top.quit,
48               activeforeground='white',
49               activebackground='red')
50           self.clr.pack(side=LEFT)
51           self.ls.pack(side=LEFT)
52           self.quit.pack(side=LEFT)
53           self.bfm.pack()
54
55           if initdir:
56               self.cwd.set(os.curdir)
57               self.doLS()
58
59       def clrDir(self, ev=None):
60           self.cwd.set('')
61
62       def setDirAndGo(self, ev=None):
63           self.last = self.cwd.get()
64           self.dirs.config(selectbackground='red')
65           check = self.dirs.get(self.dirs.curselection())
66           if not check:
```

(continued)

Example 19.6 File System Traversal GUI (`listdir.py`) (continued)

```
67                      check = os.curdir
68              self.cwd.set(check)
69              self.doLS()
70
71          def doLS(self, ev=None):
72              error = ''
73              tdir = self.cwd.get()
74              if not tdir: tdir = os.curdir
75
76              if not os.path.exists(tdir):
77                  error = tdir + ': no such file'
78              elif not os.path.isdir(tdir):
79                  error = tdir + ': not a directory'
80
81              if error:
82                  self.cwd.set(error)
83                  self.top.update()
84                  sleep(2)
85                  if not (hasattr(self, 'last') \
86                      and self.last):
87                      self.last = os.curdir
88                  self.cwd.set(self.last)
89                  self.dirs.config(\
90                      selectbackground='LightSkyBlue')
91                  self.top.update()
92                  return
93
94              self.cwd.set(\
95                  'FETCHING DIRECTORY CONTENTS...')
96              self.top.update()
97              dirlist = os.listdir(tdir)
98              dirlist.sort()
99              os.chdir(tdir)
100             self.dirl.config(text=os.getcwd())
101             self.dirs.delete(0, END)
102             self.dirs.insert(END, os.curdir)
103             self.dirs.insert(END, os.pardir)
104             for eachFile in dirlist:
105                 self.dirs.insert(END, eachFile)
106             self.cwd.set(os.curdir)
107             self.dirs.config(\
108                 selectbackground='LightSkyBlue')
109
110 def main():
111     d = DirList(os.curdir)
112     mainloop()
113
114 if __name__ == '__main__':
115     main()
```

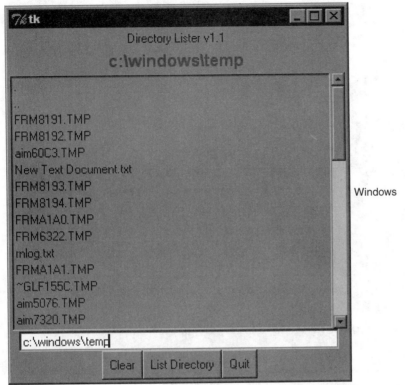

Figure 19–6   List directory GUI application in Windows (`listdir.py`)

In Figure 19–6, we present what this GUI looks like in a Windows environment.

The Unix version of this application is given in Figure 19–7.

Line-by-Line Explanation

Lines 1–5

These first few lines contain the usual Unix startup line and importation of the `os` module, the `time.sleep()` function, and all attributes of the `Tkinter` module.

Lines 9–13

These lines define the constructor for the `DirList` class, an object that represents our application. The first `Label` we create contains the main title of the application and the version number.

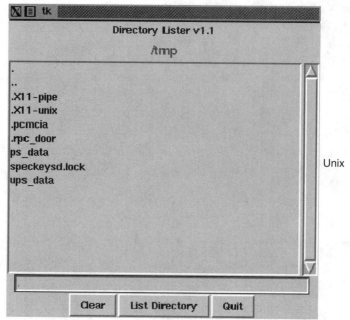

Figure 19-7   List directory GUI application in Unix
(listdir.py)

Lines 15–19

We declare a Tk variable named cwd to hold the name of the directory we
are on—we will see where this comes in handy later. Another Label is created to display the name of the current directory.

Lines 21–29

This section defines the core part of our GUI, (the Listbox) dirs, which
contain the list of files of the directory that is being listed. A Scrollbar is
employed to allow the user to move through a listing if the number of files
exceeds the size of the Listbox. Both of these widgets are contained in a
Frame widget. Listbox entries have a callback (setDirAndGo) tied to
them using the Listbox bind() method.

Binding means to tie a keystroke, mouse action, or some other event to a
callback to be executed when such an event is generated by the user. setDir-
AndGo() will be called if any item in the Listbox is doubleclicked. The
Scrollbar is tied to the Listbox by calling the Scrollbar.config()
method.

Lines 31–34

We then create a text `Entry` field for the user to enter the name of the directory he or she wants to traverse and see its files listed in the `Listbox`. We add a RETURN or Enter key binding to this text entry field so that the user can hit RETURN as an alternative to pressing a button. The same applies for the mouse binding we saw above in the `Listbox`. When the user doubleclicks on a `Listbox` item, it has the same effect as the user's entering the directory name manually into the text `Entry` field and pressing the "go" button.

Lines 36–53

We then define a `Button` frame (bfm) to hold our three buttons, a "clear" button (`clr`), a "go" button (`ls`), and a "quit" button (`quit`). Each button has its own different configuration and callbacks, if pressed.

Lines 55–57

The final part of the constructor initializes the GUI program, starting with the current working directory.

Lines 59–60

The `clrDir()` method clears the `cwd` Tk string variable, which contains the current directory that is "active." This variable is used to keep track of what directory we are in and, more important, helps keep track of the previous directory in case errors arise. You will notice the `ev` variables in the callback functions with a default value of `None`. Any such values would be passed in by the windowing system. They may or may not be used in your callback.

Lines 62–69

The `setDirAndGo()` method sets the directory to traverse to and issues the call to the method that makes it all happen, `doLS()`.

Lines 71–108

`doLS()` is, by far, the key to this entire GUI application. It performs all the safety checks (e.g., is the destination a directory and does it exist?). If there is an error, the last directory is reset to be the current directory. If all goes well, it calls `os.listdir()` to get the actual set of files and replaces the listing in the `Listbox`. While the background work is going on to pull in the new directory's information, the highlighted blue bar becomes bright red. When the new directory has been installed, it reverts to blue.

Lines 110–115

The last pieces of code in `listdir.py` represent the main part of the code. `main()` is executed only if this script is invoked directly, and when `main()` runs, it creates the GUI application, then calls `mainloop()` to start the GUI, which is passed control of the application.

We leave all other aspects of the application as an exercise to the reader, recommending that it is easier to view the entire application as a combination of a set of widgets and functionality. If you see the individual pieces clearly, then the entire script will not appear as daunting.

We hope that we have given you a good introduction to GUI programming with Python and Tkinter. Remember that the best way to get familiar with Tkinter programming is by practicing and stealing a few examples! The Python distribution comes with a large number of demonstration applications that you can study.

If you download the source code, you will find Tkinter demo code in `Lib/lib-tk`, `Lib/idlelib`, and `Demo/tkinter`. If you have installed the Win32 version of Python and `C:\Python2x`, then you can get access to the demo code in `Lib\lib-tk` and `Lib\idlelib`. The latter directory contains the most significant sample Tkinter application: the IDLE IDE itself. For further reference, there are several books on Tk programming, one specifically on Tkinter.

19.4 Brief Tour of Other GUIs

We hope to eventually develop an independent chapter on general GUI development using many of the abundant number of graphical toolkits that exist under Python, but alas, that is for the future. As a proxy, we would like to present a single simple GUI application written using four of the more popular and available toolkits out there: Tix (Tk Interface eXtensions), Pmw (Python MegaWidgets Tkinter extension), wxPython (Python binding to wxWidgets), and PyGTK (Python binding to GTK+). Links to where you can get more information and/or download these toolkits can be found in the reference section at the end of this chapter.

The `Tix` module is already available in the Python standard library. You must download the others, which are third party. Since Pmw is just an extension to Tkinter, it is the easiest to install (just extract into your site packages). wxPython and PyGTK involve the download of more than one file and building (unless you opt for the Win32 versions where binaries are usually available). Once the toolkits are installed and verified, we can begin. Rather than just sticking with the widgets we've already seen in this chapter, we'd like to introduce a few more complex widgets for these examples.

In addition to the Label and Button widgets we have seen before, we would like to introduce the Control or SpinButton and ComboBox. The Control widget is a combination of a text widget with a value inside being "controlled" or "spun up or down" by a set of arrow buttons close by, and the ComboBox is usually a text widget and a pulldown menu of options where the currently active or selected item in the list is displayed in the text widget.

Our application is fairly basic: pairs of animals are being moved around, and the number of total animals can range from a pair to a dozen max. The Control is used to keep track of the total number while the ComboBox is a menu containing the various types of animals that can be selected. In Figure 19–8, each image shows the state of the GUI application immediately after launching. Note that the default number of animals is two, and no animal type has been selected yet.

Things are different once we start to play around with the application, as evidenced in Figure 19–9 after we have modified some of the elements in the Tix application.

Below, you will find the code for all four versions of our GUI. You will note that although relatively similar, each one differs in its own special way. Also, we use the .pyw extension to suppress the popping up of the Dos command or terminal window.

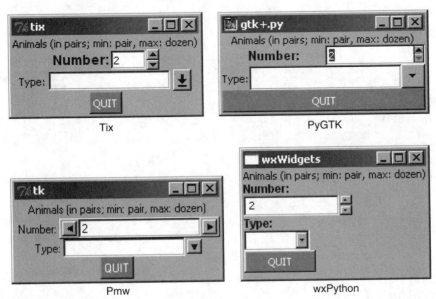

Figure 19–8   Application using various GUIs under Win32 (animal*.pyw)

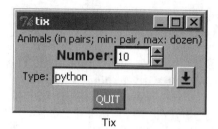

Figure 19–9 After modifying the Tix GUI
version of our application (`animalTix.pyw`)

19.4.1 Tk Interface eXtensions (Tix)

We start with an example (Example 19.7) of using the `Tix` module. Tix is an extension library for Td/T that adds many new widgets, image types, and other commands that keep Tk a viable GUI development todkit. Let's take look at how to use Tix with Python.

Example 19.7 Tix GUI Demo (`animalTix.pyw`)

Our first example uses the `Tix` *module. Tix comes with Python!*

```
1   #!/usr/bin/env python
2
3   from Tkinter import Label, Button, END
4   from Tix import Tk, Control, ComboBox
5
6   top = Tk()
7   top.tk.eval('package require Tix')
8
9   lb = Label(top,
10      text='Animals (in pairs; min: pair, max: dozen)')
11  lb.pack()
12
13  ct = Control(top, label='Number:',
14      integer=True, max=12, min=2, value=2, step=2)
15  ct.label.config(font='Helvetica -14 bold')
16  ct.pack()
17
18  cb = ComboBox(top, label='Type:', editable=True)
19  for animal in ('dog', 'cat', 'hamster', 'python'):
20      cb.insert(END, animal)
21  cb.pack()
22
23  qb = Button(top, text='QUIT',
24      command=top.quit, bg='red', fg='white')
25  qb.pack()
26
27  top.mainloop()
```

Line-by-Line Explanation

Lines 1–7

This is all the setup code, module imports, and basic GUI infrastructure. Line 7 asserts that the `Tix` module is available to the application.

Lines 8–27

These lines create all the widgets: `Label` (lines 9–11), `Control` (lines 13–16), `ComboBox` (lines 18–21), and quit `Button` (lines 23–25). The constructors and arguments for the widgets are fairly self-explanatory and do not require elaboration. Finally, we enter the main GUI event loop in line 27.

19.4.2 Python MegaWidgets (PMW)

Next we take a look at Python MegaWidgets as shown in Example 19.8. This module was created to address the aging Tkinter. It basically helps the extend its longevity by adding more modern widgets to the GUI palette.

The `Pmw` example is so similar to our `Tix` example that we leave line-by-line analysis to the reader. The line of code that differs the most is the constructor for the control widget, the Pmw `Counter`. It provides for entry validation. Instead of specifying the smallest and largest possible values as keyword arguments to the widget constructor, Pmw uses a "validator" to ensure that the values do not fall outside our accepted range.

Now, we are finally going to leave the Tk world behind. Tix and Pmw are extensions to Tk and Tkinter, respectively, but now we are going to change gears to look at completely different toolkits, wxWidgets and GTK+. You will notice that the number of lines of code starts to increase as we start programming in a more object-oriented way when using these more modern and robust GUI toolkits.

19.4.3 wxWidgets and wxPython

wxWidgets (formerly known as wxWindows) is a cross-platform toolkit used to build graphical user applications. It is implemented using C++ and is available on a wide number of platforms to which wxWidgets defines a consistent and common API. The best part of all is that wxWidgets uses the native GUI on each platform, so your program will have the same look-and-feel as all the other applications on your desktop. Another feature is that you are not restricted to developing wxWidgets applications in C++. There are interfaces

Example 19.8 Pmw GUI Demo (`animalPmw.pyw`)

Our second example uses the Python MegaWidgets package.

```python
1   #!/usr/bin/env python
2
3   from Tkinter import Button, END, Label, W
4   from Pmw import initialise, ComboBox, Counter
5
6   top = initialise()
7
8   lb = Label(top,
9       text='Animals (in pairs; min: pair, max: dozen)')
10  lb.pack()
11
12  ct = Counter(top, labelpos=W, label_text='Number:',
13      datatype='integer', entryfield_value=2,
14      increment=2, entryfield_validate={'validator':
15      'integer', 'min': 2, 'max': 12})
16  ct.pack()
17
18  cb = ComboBox(top, labelpos=W, label_text='Type:')
19  for animal in ('dog', 'cat', 'hamster', 'python'):
20      cb.insert(end, animal)
21  cb.pack()
22
23  qb = Button(top, text='QUIT',
24      command=top.quit, bg='red', fg='white')
25  qb.pack()
26
27  top.mainloop()
```

to both Python and Perl. Example 19.9 shows our animal application using wxPython.

Line-by-Line Explanation

Lines 5–37

Here we instantiate a `Frame` class (lines 5–8), of which the sole member is the constructor. This method's only purpose in life is to create our widgets. Inside the frame, we have a `Panel`. Inside the panel we use a `BoxSizer` to contain and layout all of our widgets (lines 10, 36), which consist of a `Label` (lines 12–14), `SpinCtrl` (lines 16–20), `ComboBox` (lines 22–27), and quit `Button` (lines 29–34).

We have to manually add `Label`s to the `SpinCtrl` and `ComboBox` widgets because they apparently do not come with them. Once we have them all,

Example 19.9 wxPython GUI Demo (`animalWx.pyw`)

Our third example uses wxPython (and wxWidgets). Note that we have placed all our widgets inside a "sizer" for organization and the more object-oriented nature of this application.

```python
1   #!/usr/bin/env python
2
3   import wx
4
5   class MyFrame(wx.Frame):
6       def __init__(self, parent=None, id=-1, title=''):
7           wx.Frame.__init__(self, parent, id, title,
8               size=(200, 140))
9           top = wx.Panel(self)
10          sizer = wx.BoxSizer(wx.VERTICAL)
11          font = wx.Font(9, wx.SWISS, wx.NORMAL, wx.BOLD)
12          lb = wx.StaticText(top, -1,
13              'Animals (in pairs; min: pair, max: dozen)')
14          sizer.Add(lb)
15
16          c1 = wx.StaticText(top, -1, 'Number:')
17          c1.SetFont(font)
18          ct = wx.SpinCtrl(top, -1, '2', min=2, max=12)
19          sizer.Add(c1)
20          sizer.Add(ct)
21
22          c2 = wx.StaticText(top, -1, 'Type:')
23          c2.SetFont(font)
24          cb = wx.ComboBox(top, -1, '',
25              choices=('dog', 'cat', 'hamster','python'))
26          sizer.Add(c2)
27          sizer.Add(cb)
28
29          qb = wx.Button(top, -1, "QUIT")
30          qb.SetBackgroundColour('red')
31          qb.SetForegroundColour('white')
32          self.Bind(wx.EVT_BUTTON,
33              lambda e: self.Close(True), qb)
34          sizer.Add(qb)
35
36          top.SetSizer(sizer)
37          self.Layout()
38
39  class MyApp(wx.App):
40      def OnInit(self):
41          frame = MyFrame(title="wxWidgets")
42          frame.Show(True)
43          self.SetTopWindow(frame)
44          return True
45
```

(continued)

> **Example 19.9 wxPython GUI Demo (`animalWx.pyw`) (continued)**
>
> ```
> 46  def main():
> 47      app = MyApp()
> 48      app.MainLoop()
> 49
> 50  if __name__ == '__main__':
> 51      main()
> ```

we add them to the sizer, set the sizer to our panel, and lay everything out. On line 10, you will note that the sizer is vertically oriented, meaning that our widgets will be placed top to bottom.

One weakness of the `SpinCtrl` widget is that it does not support "step" functionality. With the other three examples, we are able to click an arrow selector and have it increment or decrement by units of two, but that is not possible with this widget.

Lines 39–51

Our application class instantiates the `Frame` object we just designed, renders it to the screen, and sets it as the top-most window of our application. Finally, the setup lines just instantiate our GUI application and start it running.

19.4.4 GTK+ and PyGTK

Finally, we have the PyGTK version, which is quite similar to the wxPython GUI (See Example 19.10). The biggest difference is that we use only one class, and it seems more tedious to set the foreground and background colors of objects, buttons in particular.

Line-by-Line Explanation

Lines 1–6

We import three different modules and packages, PyGTK, GTK, and Pango, a library for layout and rendering of text, specifically for I18N purposes. We need it here because it represents the core of text and font handling for GTK+ (2.x).

Lines 8–51

The `GTKapp` class represents all the widgets of our application. The topmost window is created (with handlers for closing it via the window manager), and

Example 19.10 PyGTK GUI Demo (`animalGtk.pyw`)

Our final example uses PyGTK (and GTK+). Like the wxPython example, this one also uses a class for our application. It is interesting to note how similar yet different all of our GUI applications are. This is not surprising and allows programmers to switch between toolkits with relative ease.

```python
1   #!/usr/bin/env python
2
3   import pygtk
4   pygtk.require('2.0')
5   import gtk
6   import pango
7
8   class GTKapp(object):
9       def __init__(self):
10          top = gtk.Window(gtk.WINDOW_TOPLEVEL)
11          top.connect("delete_event", gtk.main_quit)
12          top.connect("destroy", gtk.main_quit)
13          box = gtk.VBox(False, 0)
14          lb = gtk.Label(
15              'Animals (in pairs; min: pair, max: dozen)')
16          box.pack_start(lb)
17
18          sb = gtk.HBox(False, 0)
19          adj = gtk.Adjustment(2, 2, 12, 2, 4, 0)
20          sl = gtk.Label('Number:')
21          sl.modify_font(
22              pango.FontDescription("Arial Bold 10"))
23          sb.pack_start(sl)
24          ct = gtk.SpinButton(adj, 0, 0)
25          sb.pack_start(ct)
26          box.pack_start(sb)
27
28          cb = gtk.HBox(False, 0)
29          c2 = gtk.Label('Type:')
30          cb.pack_start(c2)
31          ce = gtk.combo_box_entry_new_text()
32          for animal in ('dog', 'cat','hamster', 'python'):
33              ce.append_text(animal)
34          cb.pack_start(ce)
35          box.pack_start(cb)
36
37          qb = gtk.Button("")
38          red = gtk.gdk.color_parse('red')
39          sty = qb.get_style()
40          for st in (gtk.STATE_NORMAL,
```

(continued)

Example 19.10 PyGTK GUI Demo (`animalGtk.pyw`) (continued)

```
41            gtk.STATE_PRELIGHT, gtk.STATE_ACTIVE):
42            sty.bg[st] = red
43        qb.set_style(sty)
44        ql = qb.child
45        ql.set_markup('<span color="white">QUIT</span>')
46        qb.connect_object("clicked",
47            gtk.Widget.destroy, top)
48        box.pack_start(qb)
49        top.add(box)
50        top.show_all()
51
52 if __name__ == '__main__':
53     animal = GTKapp()
54     gtk.main()
```

a vertically oriented sizer (VBox) is created to hold our primary widgets. This is exactly what we did in the wxPython GUI.

However, wanting the static labels for the SpinButton and ComboBox-Entry to be next to them (unlike above them for the wxPython example), we create little horizontally oriented boxes to contain the label-widget pairs (lines 18–36), and placed those HBoxes into the all-encompassing VBox.

After creating the quit Button and adding the VBox to our topmost window, we render everything on-screen. You will notice that we create the button with an empty label at first. We do this so that a Label (child) object will be created as part of the button. Then on lines 45–46, we get access to the label and set the text with white font color.

The reason why we do this is because if you set the style foreground, i.e., in the loop and auxiliary code on lines 41–44, the foreground only affects the button's foreground and not the label—for example, if you set the foreground style to white and highlight the button (by pressing TAB until it is "selected") you will see that the inside dotted box identifying the selected widget *is* white, but the label text would still be black if you did not alter it like we did with the markup on line 46.

Lines 53–55

Here we create our application and enter the main event loop.

19.5 Related Modules and Other GUIs

There are other GUI development systems that can be used with Python. We present the appropriate modules along with their corresponding window systems in Table 19.2.

Table 19.2 GUI Systems Available for Python

GUI Module or System	Description
Tk-Related Modules	
Tkinter	TK INTERface: Python's default GUI toolkit http://wiki.python.org/moin/TkInter
Pmw	Python MegaWidgets (Tkinter extension) http://pmw.sf.net
Tix	Tk Interface eXtension (Tk extension) http://tix.sf.net
TkZinc (Zinc)	Extended Tk canvas type (Tk extension) http://www.tkzinc.org
EasyGUI (easygui)	Very simple non-event-driven GUIs (Tkinter extension) http://ferg.org/easygui
TIDE + (IDE Studio)	Tix Integrated Development Environment (including IDE Studio, a Tix-enhanced version of the standard IDLE IDE) http://starship.python.net/crew/mike
wxWidgets-Related Modules	
wxPython	Python binding to wxWidgets, a cross-platform GUI framework (formerly known as wxWindows) http://wxpython.org
Boa Constructor	Python IDE and wxPython GUI builder http://boa-constructor.sf.net
PythonCard	wxPython-based desktop application GUI construction kit (inspired by HyperCard) http://pythoncard.sf.net
wxGlade	another wxPython GUI designer (inspired by Glade, the GTK+/GNOME GUI builder) http://wxglade.sf.net

(continued)

Table 19.2 GUI Systems Available for Python (continued)	
GUI Module **or System**	**Description**
GTK+/GNOME-Related Modules	
PyGTK	Python wrapper for the GIMP Toolkit (GTK+) library http://pygtk.org
GNOME-Python	Python binding to GNOME desktop and development libraries http://gnome.org/start/unstable/bindings http://download.gnome.org/sources/gnome-python
Glade	a GUI builder for GTK+ and GNOME http://glade.gnome.org
PyGUI (GUI)	cross-platform "Pythonic" GUI API (built on Cocoa [MacOS X] and GTK+ [POSIX/X11 and Win32]) http://www.cosc.canterbury.ac.nz/~greg/python_gui
Qt/KDE-Related Modules	
PyQt	Python binding for the Qt GUI/XML/SQL C++ toolkit from Trolltech (partially open source [dual-license]) http://riverbankcomputing.co.uk/pyqt
PyKDE	Python binding for the KDE desktop environment http://riverbankcomputing.co.uk/pykde
eric	Python IDE written in PyQt using QScintilla editor widget http://die-offenbachs.de/detlev/eric3 http://ericide.python-hosting.com/
PyQtGPL	Qt (Win32 Cygwin port), Sip, QScintilla, PyQt bundle http://pythonqt.vanrietpaap.nl
Other Open Source GUI Toolkits	
FXPy	Python binding to FOX toolkit (http://fox-toolkit.org) http://fxpy.sf.net
pyFLTK (fltk)	Python binding to FLTK toolkit (http://fltk.org) http://pyfltk.sf.net
PyOpenGL (OpenGL)	Python binding to OpenGL (http://opengl.org) http://pyopengl.sf.net

Table 19.2 GUI Systems Available for Python (continued)	
GUI Module or System	**Description**
Commercial	
`win32ui`	Microsoft MFC (via Python for Windows Extensions) http://starship.python.net/crew/mhammond/win32
`swing`	Sun Microsystems Java/Swing (via Jython) http://jython.org

You can find out more about all GUIs related to Python from the general GUI Programming page on the Python wiki at http://wiki.python. org/moin/ GuiProgramming.

19.6 Exercises

19–1. *Client/Server Architecture.* Describe the roles of a windows (or windowing) server and a windows client.

19–2. *Object-Oriented Programming.* Describe the relationship between child and parent windows.

19–3. `Label` *Widgets.* Update the `tkhello1.py` script to display your own message instead of "Hello World!"

19–4. `Label` *and* `Button` *Widgets.* Update the `tkhello3.py` script so that there are three new buttons in addition to the QUIT button. Pressing any of the three buttons will result in changing the text label so that it will then contain the text of the `Button` (widget) that was pressed.

19–5. `Label`, `Button`, *and* `Radiobutton` *Widgets.* Modify your solution to the previous problem so that there are three `Radiobuttons` presenting the choices of text for the `Label`. There are two buttons: the QUIT button and an "Update" button. When the Update button is pressed, the text label will then be changed to contain the text of the selected `Radiobutton`. If no `Radiobutton` has been checked, the `Label` will remain unchanged.

19–6.   *Label, Button, and Entry Widgets*. Modify your solution
to the previous problem so that the three Radiobuttons
are replaced by a single Entry text field widget with a
default value of "Hello World!" (to reflect the initial string in
the Label). The Entry field can be edited by the user with
a new text string for the Label which will be updated if the
Update button is pressed.

19–7.   *Label and Entry Widgets and Python I/O*. Create a GUI
application that provides an Entry field where the user can
provide the name of a text file. Open the file and read it, displaying its contents in a Label.

  Extra Credit (Menus): Replace the Entry widget with a
menu that has a File Open option that pops up a window to
allow the user to specify the file to read. Also add an Exit or
Quit option to the menu rather than having a QUIT button.

19–8.   *Simple Text Editor*. Use your solution to the previous
problem to create a simple text editor. A file can be created from scratch or read and displayed into a Text
widget that can be edited by the user. When the user quits
the application (either with the QUIT button or the Quit/
Exit menu option), the user is prompted whether to save
the changes.

  Extra Credit: Interface your script to a spellchecker and
add a button or menu option to spellcheck the file. The words
that are misspelled should be highlighted by using a different
foreground or background color in the Text widget.

19–9.   *Multithreaded Chat Applications*. The chat programs from
Chapters 13, 16, and 17 need completion. Create a fully-
functional multithreaded chat server. A GUI is not really
necessary for the server unless you want to create one as a
front-end to its configuration, i.e., port number, name, connection to a name server, etc. Create a multithreaded chat
client that has separate threads to monitor user input (and
sends the message to the server for broadcast) and another
thread to accept incoming messages to display to the user.
The client front-end GUI should have two portions of the
chat window: a larger section with multiple lines to hold all
the dialog, and a smaller text entry field to accept input
from the user.

19–10. *Using Other GUIs.* The example GUI applications using the various toolkits in Chapter 18.4 are very similar; however, they are not the same. Although it is impossible to make them all look *exactly* alike, tweak them so that they are more consistent than they are now.

19–11. *Using GUI builders.* Download either Boa Constructor (for wxWidgets) or Glade (for GTK+) [or both!], and implement the "animal" GUI by just dragging and dropping the widgets from the corresponding palette. Hook up your new GUIs with callbacks so that they behave just like the sample applications we looked at in that chapter.

WEB
PROGRAMMING

Chapter Topics

- Introduction
- Web Surfing with Python: Simple Web Clients
  - `urlparse` and `urllib` Modules
- Advanced Web Clients
  - Crawler/Spider/Robot
- CGI: Helping Web Servers Process Client Data
- Building CGI Applications
- Using Unicode with CGI
- Advanced CGI
- Creating Web Servers
- Related Modules

Chapter 20

20.1 Introduction

This introductory chapter on Web programming will give you a quick and high-level overview of the kinds of things you can do with Python on the Internet, from Web surfing to creating user feedback forms, from recognizing Uniform Resource Locators to generating dynamic Web page output.

20.1.1 Web Surfing: Client/Server Computing (Again?!?)

Web surfing falls under the same client/server architecture umbrella that we have seen repeatedly. This time, Web *clients* are browsers, applications that allow users to seek documents on the World Wide Web. On the other side are Web *servers*, processes that run on an information provider's host computers. These servers wait for clients and their document requests, process them, and return the requested data. As with most servers in a client/server system, Web servers are designed to run "forever." The Web surfing experience is best illustrated by Figure 20–1. Here, a user runs a Web client program such as a browser and makes a connection to a Web server elsewhere on the Internet to obtain information.

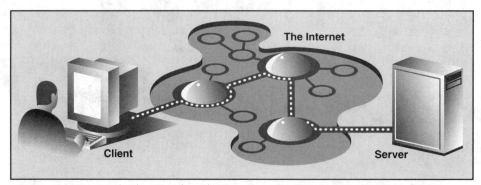

Figure 20-1   Web client and Web server on the Internet. A client sends a request out over the Internet to the server, which then responds with the requested data back to the client.

Clients may issue a variety of requests to Web servers. Such requests may include obtaining a Web page for viewing or submitting a form with data for processing. The request is then serviced by the Web server, and the reply comes back to the client in a special format for display purposes.

The "language" that is spoken by Web clients and servers, the standard protocol used for Web communication, is called *HTTP*, which stands for HyperText Transfer Protocol. HTTP is written "on top of" the TCP and IP protocol suite, meaning that it relies on TCP and IP to carry out its lower-level communication functionality. Its responsibility is not to route or deliver messages—TCP and IP handle that—but to respond to client requests (by sending and receiving HTTP messages).

HTTP is known as a "stateless" protocol because it does not keep track of information from one client request to the next, similar to the client/server architecture we have seen so far. The server stays running, but client interactions are singular events structured in such a way that once a client request is serviced, it quits. New requests can always be sent, but they are considered separate service requests. Because of the lack of context per request, you may notice that some URLs have a long set of variables and values chained as part of the request to provide some sort of state information. Another alternative is the use of "cookies"—static data stored on the client side which generally contain state information as well. In later parts of this chapter, we will look at how to use both long URLs and cookies to maintain state information.

20.1.2 The Internet

The Internet is a moving and fluctuating "cloud" or "pond" of interconnected clients and servers scattered around the globe. Communication between client and server consists of a series of connections from one lily pad on the pond to another, with the last step connecting to the server. As a client user, all this detail is kept hidden from your view. The abstraction is to have a direct connection between you the client and the server you are "visiting," but the underlying HTTP, TCP, and IP protocols are hidden underneath, doing all of the dirty work. Information regarding the intermediate "nodes" is of no concern or consequence to the general user anyway, so it's good that the implementation is hidden. Figure 20–2 shows an expanded view of the Internet.

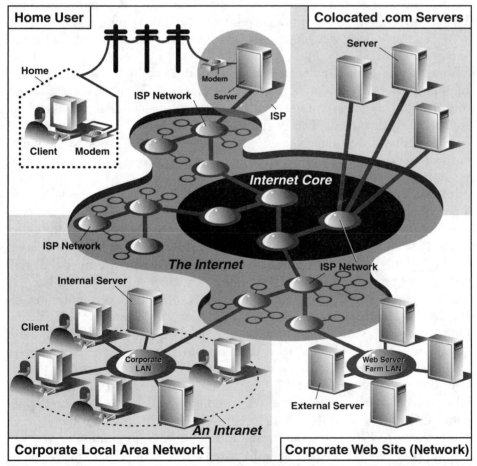

Figure 20–2 A grand view of the Internet. The left side illustrates where you would find Web clients while the right side hints as to where Web servers are typically located.

As you can see from the figure, the Internet is made up of multiply-interconnected networks, all working with some sense of (perhaps disjointed) harmony. The left half of the diagram is focused on the Web clients, users who are either at home dialed-in to their *ISP* (Internet Service Provider) or at work on their company's *LAN* (Local Area Network).

The right-hand side of the diagram concentrates more on Web servers and where they can be found. Corporations with larger Web sites will typically have an entire "Web server farm" located at their ISPs. Such physical placement is called *colocation*, meaning that a company's servers are "co-located" at an ISP along with machines from other corporate customers. These servers are either all providing different data to clients or are part of a redundant system with duplicated information designed for heavy demand (high number of clients). Smaller corporate Web sites may not require as much hardware and networking gear, and hence, may only have one or several colocated servers at their ISP.

In either case, most colocated servers are stored with a larger ISP sitting on a network *backbone*, meaning that they have a "fatter" (meaning wider) and presumably faster connection to the Internet—closer to the "core" of the Internet, if you will. This permits clients to access the servers quickly—being on a backbone means clients do not have to hop across as many networks to access a server, thus allowing more clients to be serviced within a given time period.

One should also keep in mind that although Web surfing is the most common Internet application, it is not the only one and is certainly not the oldest. The Internet predates the Web by almost three decades. Before the Web, the Internet was mainly used for educational and research purposes. Most of the systems on the Internet run Unix, a multi-user operating system, and many of the original Internet protocols are still around today.

Such protocols include telnet (allows users to log in to a remote host on the Internet and still in use today), *FTP* (the File Transfer Protocol that enables users to share files and data via uploading or downloading and also still in use today), *Gopher* (the precursor to the Web search engine—a "gopher"-like piece of software that "tunneled the Internet" looking for the data that you were interested in), *SMTP* or Simple Mail Transfer Protocol (the protocol used for one of the oldest and most widely used Internet applications: electronic mail), and *NNTP* (News-to-News Transfer Protocol).

Since one of Python's initial strengths was Internet programming, you will find support for all of the protocols discussed above in addition to many others. We differentiate between "Internet programming" and "Web programming" by stating that the latter pertains only to applications developed specifically for Web applications, i.e., Web clients and servers, our focus for this chapter.

Internet programming covers a wider range of applications, including some of the Internet protocols we previously mentioned, such as FTP, SMTP, etc., as well as network and socket programming in general, as we discussed in a previous chapter.

20.2 Web Surfing with Python: Creating Simple Web Clients

One thing to keep in mind is that a browser is only one type of Web client. Any application that makes a request for data from a Web server is considered a "client." Yes, it is possible to create other clients that retrieve documents or data off the Internet. One important reason to do this is that a browser provides only limited capacity, i.e., it is used primarily for viewing and interacting with Web sites. A client program, on the other hand, has the ability to do more—it can not only download data, but it can also store it, manipulate it, or perhaps even transmit it to another location or application.

Applications that use the `urllib` module to download or access information on the Web [using either `urllib.urlopen()` or `urllib.urlretrieve()`] can be considered a simple Web client. All you need to do is provide a valid Web address.

20.2.1 Uniform Resource Locators

Simple Web surfing involves using Web addresses called *URLs* (Uniform Resource Locators). Such addresses are used to locate a document on the Web or to call a CGI program to generate a document for your client. URLs are part of a larger set of identifiers known as *URIs* (Uniform Resource Identifiers). This superset was created in anticipation of other naming conventions that have yet to be developed. A URL is simply a URI which uses an existing protocol or scheme (i.e., http, ftp, etc.) as part of its addressing. To complete this picture, we'll add that non-URL URIs are sometimes known as *URNs* (Uniform Resource Names), but because URLs are the only URIs in use today, you really don't hear much about URIs or URNs, save perhaps as XML identifiers.

Like street addresses, Web addresses have some structure. An American street address usually is of the form "number street designation," i.e., 123 Main Street. It differs from other countries, which have their own rules. A URL uses the format:

```
prot_sch://net_loc/path;params?query#frag
```

Table 20.1 Web Address Components

URL Component	Description
prot_sch	Network protocol or download scheme
net_loc	Location of server (and perhaps user information)
path	Slash (/) delimited path to file or CGI application
params	Optional parameters
query	Ampersand (&) delimited set of "key=value" pairs
frag	Fragment to a specific anchor within document

Table 20.1 describes each of the components.

net_loc can be broken down into several more components, some required, others optional. The *net_loc* string looks like this:

    user:passwd@host:port

These individual components are described in Table 20.2.

Of the four, the host name is the most important. The port number is necessary only if the Web server is running on a different port number from the default. (If you aren't sure what a port number is, go back to Chapter 16.)

User names and perhaps passwords are used only when making FTP connections, and even then they usually aren't necessary because the majority of such connections are "anonymous."

Table 20.2 Network Location Components

net_loc Component	Description
user	User name or login
passwd	User password
host	Name or address of machine running Web server [required]
port	Port number (if not 80, the default)

Python supplies two different modules, each dealing with URLs in completely different functionality and capacities. One is `urlparse`, and the other is `urllib`. We will briefly introduce some of their functions here.

20.2.2 `urlparse` Module

The `urlparse` module provides basic functionality with which to manipulate URL strings. These functions include `urlparse()`, `urlunparse()`, and `urljoin()`.

`urlparse.urlparse()`

`urlparse()` breaks up a URL string into some of the major components described above. It has the following syntax:

```
urlparse(urlstr, defProtSch=None, allowFrag=None)
```

`urlparse()` parses `urlstr` into a 6-tuple (`prot_sch`, `net_loc`, `path`, `params`, `query`, `frag`). Each of these components has been described above. `defProtSch` indicates a default network protocol or download scheme in case one is not provided in `urlstr`. `allowFrag` is a flag that signals whether or not a fragment part of a URL is allowed. Here is what `urlparse()` outputs when given a URL:

```
>>>urlparse.urlparse('http://www.python.org/doc/FAQ.html')
('http', 'www.python.org', '/doc/FAQ.html', '', '', '')
```

`urlparse.urlunparse()`

`urlunparse()` does the exact opposite of `urlparse()`—it merges a 6-tuple (`prot_sch`, `net_loc`, `path`, `params`, `query`, `frag`)—`urltup`, which could be the output of `urlparse()`, into a single URL string and returns it. Accordingly, we state the following equivalence:

```
urlunparse(urlparse(urlstr)) ≡ urlstr
```

You may have already surmised that the syntax of `urlunparse()` is as follows:

```
urlunparse(urltup)
```

`urlparse.urljoin()`

The `urljoin()` function is useful in cases where many related URLs are needed, for example, the URLs for a set of pages to be generated for a Web site. The syntax for `urljoin()` is:

```
urljoin(baseurl, newurl, allowFrag=None)
```

Table 20.3 Core `urlparse` Module Functions

urlparse *Functions*	*Description*
urlparse(*urlstr*, *defProtSch*=None, *allowFrag*=None)	Parses *urlstr* into separate components, using *defProtSch* if the protocol or scheme is not given in *urlstr*; *allowFrag* determines whether a URL fragment is allowed
urlunparse(*urltup*)	Unparses a tuple of URL data (*urltup*) into a single URL string
urljoin(*baseurl*, *newurl*, *allowFrag*=None)	Merges the base part of the *baseurl* URL with *newurl* to form a complete URL; *allowFrag* is the same as for urlparse()

urljoin() takes *baseurl* and joins its base path (*net_loc* plus the full path up to, but not including, a file at the end) with *newurl*. For example:

```
>>> urlparse.urljoin('http://www.python.org/doc/FAQ.html', \
... 'current/lib/lib.htm')
'http://www.python.org/doc/current/lib/lib.html'
```

A summary of the functions in `urlparse` can be found in Table 20.3.

20.2.3 `urllib` Module

CORE MODULE: `urllib`

Unless you are planning on writing a more lower-level network client, the `urllib` *module provides all the functionality you need.* `urllib` *provides a high-level Web communication library, supporting the basic Web protocols, HTTP, FTP, and Gopher, as well as providing access to local files. Specifically, the functions of the* `urllib` *module are designed to download data (from the Internet, local network, or local host) using the aforementioned protocols. Use of this module generally obviates the need for using the* `httplib`, `ftplib`, *and* `gopherlib` *modules unless you desire their lower-level functionality. In those cases, such modules can be considered as alternatives. (Note: Most modules named* `*lib` *are generally for developing clients of the corresponding protocols. This is not always the case, however, as perhaps* `urllib` *should then be renamed "internetlib" or something similar!)*

The `urllib` module provides functions to download data from given URLs as well as encoding and decoding strings to make them suitable for including as part of valid URL strings. The functions we will be looking at in this upcoming section include: `urlopen()`, `urlretrieve()`, `quote()`, `unquote()`, `quote_plus()`, `unquote_plus()`, and `urlencode()`. We will also look at some of the methods available to the file-like object returned by `urlopen()`. They will be familiar to you because you have already learned to work with files back in Chapter 9.

`urllib.urlopen()`

`urlopen()` opens a Web connection to the given URL string and returns a file-like object. It has the following syntax:

```
urlopen(urlstr, postQueryData=None)
```

`urlopen()` opens the URL pointed to by *urlstr*. If no protocol or download scheme is given, or if a "file" scheme is passed in, `urlopen()` will open a local file.

For all HTTP requests, the normal request type is "GET." In these cases, the query string provided to the Web server (key-value pairs encoded or "quoted," such as the string output of the `urlencode()` function [see below]), should be given as part of *urlstr*.

If the "POST" request method is desired, then the query string (again encoded) should be placed in the *postQueryData* variable. (For more information regarding the GET and POST request methods, refer to any general documentation or texts on programming CGI applications—which we will also discuss below. GET and POST requests are the two ways to "upload" data to a Web server.

When a successful connection is made, `urlopen()` returns a file-like object as if the destination was a file opened in read mode. If our file object is `f`, for example, then our "handle" would support the expected read methods such as `f.read()`, `f.readline()`, `f.readlines()`, `f.close()`, and `f.fileno()`.

In addition, a `f.info()` method is available which returns the *MIME* (Multipurpose Internet Mail Extension) headers. Such headers give the browser information regarding which application can view returned file types. For example, the browser itself can view *HTML* (HyperText Markup Language), plain text files, and render *PNG* (Portable Network Graphics) and *JPEG* (Joint Photographic Experts Group) or the old *GIF* (Graphics Interchange Format) graphics files. Other files such as multimedia or specific document types require external applications in order to view.

Table 20.4 `urllib.urlopen()` *File-like Object Methods*	
`urlopen()` *Object Methods*	*Description*
`f.read([bytes])`	Reads all or `bytes` bytes from `f`
`f.readline()`	Reads a single line from `f`
`f.readlines()`	Reads a all lines from `f` into a list
`f.close()`	Closes URL connection for `f`
`f.fileno()`	Returns file number of `f`
`f.info()`	Gets MIME headers of `f`
`f.geturl()`	Returns true URL opened for `f`

Finally, a `geturl()` method exists to obtain the true URL of the final opened destination, taking into consideration any redirection that may have occurred. A summary of these file-like object methods is given in Table 20.4.

If you expect to be accessing more complex URLs or want to be able to handle more complex situations such as basic and digest authentication, redirections, cookies, etc., then we suggest using the `urllib2` module, introduced back in the 1.6 days (mostly as an experimental module). It too, has a `urlopen()` function, but also provides other functions and classes for opening a variety of URLs. For more on `urllib2`, see the next section of this chapter.

`urllib.urlretrieve()`

`urlretrieve()` will do some quick and dirty work for you if you are interested in working with a URL document as a whole. Here is the syntax for `urlretrieve()`:

```
urlretrieve(urlstr, localfile=None, downloadSta-
tusHook=None)
```

Rather than reading from the URL like `urlopen()` does, `urlretrieve()` will simply download the entire HTML file located at *urlstr* to your local disk. It will store the downloaded data into *localfile* if given or a temporary file if not. If the file has already been copied from the Internet or if the file is local, no subsequent downloading will occur.

The *downloadStatusHook*, if provided, is a function that is called after each block of data has been downloaded and delivered. It is called with the following three arguments: number of blocks read so far, the block size in bytes, and the total (byte) size of the file. This is very useful if you are implementing "download status" information to the user in a text-based or graphical display.

`urlretrieve()` returns a 2-tuple, (*filename, mime_hdrs*). *filename* is the name of the local file containing the downloaded data. *mime_hdrs* is the set of MIME headers returned by the responding Web server. For more information, see the `Message` class of the `mimetools` module. *mime_hdrs* is `None` for local files.

For a simple example using `urlretrieve()`, take a look at Example 11.4 (`grabweb.py`). A larger piece of code using `urlretrieve()` can be found later in this chapter in Example 20.2.

`urllib.quote()` and `urllib.quote_plus()`

The `quote*()` functions take URL data and "encodes" them so that they are "fit" for inclusion as part of a URL string. In particular, certain special characters that are unprintable or cannot be part of valid URLs acceptable to a Web server must be converted. This is what the `quote*()` functions do for you. Both `quote*()` functions have the following syntax:

```
quote(urldata, safe='/')
```

Characters that are never converted include commas, underscores, periods, and dashes, as well as alphanumerics. All others are subject to conversion. In particular, the disallowed characters are changed to their hexadecimal ordinal equivalents prepended with a percent sign (%), i.e., "%xx" where "xx" is the hexadecimal representation of a character's ASCII value. When calling `quote*()`, the *urldata* string is converted to an equivalent string that can be part of a URL string. The *safe* string should contain a set of characters which should also *not* be converted. The default is the slash (/).

`quote_plus()` is similar to `quote()` except that it also encodes spaces to plus signs (+). Here is an example using `quote()` vs. `quote_plus()`:

```
>>> name = 'joe mama'
>>> number = 6
>>> base = 'http://www/~foo/cgi-bin/s.py'
>>> final = '%s?name=%s&num=%d' % (base, name, number)
>>> final
'http://www/~foo/cgi-bin/s.py?name=joe mama&num=6'
>>>
>>> urllib.quote(final)
'http:%3a//www/%7efoo/cgi-bin/s.py%3fname%3djoe%20mama%26num%3d6'
>>>
>>> urllib.quote_plus(final)
'http%3a//www/%7efoo/cgi-bin/
s.py%3fname%3djoe+mama%26num%3d6'
```

`urllib.unquote()` and `urllib.unquote_plus()`

As you have probably guessed, the `unquote*()` functions do the exact opposite of the `quote*()` functions—they convert all characters encoded in the "%xx" fashion to their ASCII equivalents. The syntax of `unquote*()` is as follows:

```
unquote*(urldata)
```

Calling `unquote()` will decode all URL-encoded characters in url-data and return the resulting string. `unquote_plus()` will also convert plus signs back to space characters.

`urllib.urlencode()`

`urlencode()`, added to Python back in 1.5.2, takes a dictionary of key-value pairs and encodes them to be included as part of a query in a CGI request URL string. The pairs are in "`key=value`" format and are delimited by ampersands (`&`). Furthermore, the keys and their values are sent to `quote_plus()` for proper encoding. Here is an example output from `urlencode()`:

```
>>> aDict = { 'name': 'Georgina Garcia', 'hmdir': '~ggarcia' }
>>> urllib.urlencode(aDict)
'name=Georgina+Garcia&hmdir=%7eggarcia'
```

There are other functions in `urllib` and `urlparse` which we did not have the opportunity to cover here. Refer to the documentation for more information.

Secure Socket Layer support

The `urllib` module was given support for opening HTTP connections using the Secure Socket Layer (SSL) in 1.6. The core change to add SSL is implemented in the `socket` module. Consequently, the `urllib` and `httplib` modules were updated to support URLs using the "https" connection scheme. In addition to those two modules, other protocol client modules with SSL support include: `imaplib`, `poplib`, and `smtplib`.

A summary of the `urllib` functions discussed in this section can be found in Table 20.5.

20.2.4 *urllib2* Module

As mentioned in the previous section, `urllib2` can handle more complex URL opening. One example is for Web sites with basic authentication (login and password) requirements. The most straightforward solution to "getting

Table 20.5 Core `urllib` Module Functions

`urllib` *Functions*	*Description*
`urlopen(urlstr, postQuery-Data=None)`	Opens the URL *urlstr*, sending the query data in *postQueryData* if a POST request
`urlretrieve(urlstr, local-file=None, downloadSta-tusHook=None)`	Downloads the file located at the *urlstr* URL to *localfile* or a temporary file if *localfile* not given; if present, *downloaSta-tusHook* is a function that can receive download statistics
`quote(urldata, safe='/')`	Encodes invalid URL characters of *urldata*; characters in *safe* string are *not* encoded
`quote_plus(urldata, safe='/')`	Same as `quote()` except encodes spaces as plus (+) signs (rather than as `%20`)
`unquote(urldata)`	Decodes encoded characters of *urldata*
`unquote_plus(urldata)`	Same as `unquote()` but converts plus signs to spaces
`urlencode(dict)`	Encodes the key-value pairs of *dict* into a valid string for CGI queries and encodes the key and value strings with `quote_plus()`

past security" is to use the extended `net_loc` URL component as described earlier in this chapter, i.e., `http://user:passwd@www.python.org`. The problem with this solution is that it is not programmatic. Using `urllib2`, however, we can tackle this problem in two different ways.

We can create a basic authentication handler (`urllib2.HTTPBasic-AuthHandler`) and "register" a login password given the base URL and perhaps a *realm*, meaning a string defining the secure area of the Web site. (For more on realms, see RFC 2617 [HTTP Authentication: Basic and Digest Access Authentication]). Once this is done, you can "install" a URL-opener with this handler so that all URLs opened will use our handler.

The other alternative is to simulate typing the username and password when prompted by a browser and that is to send an HTTP client request with the appropriate authorization headers. In Example 20.1 we can easily identify each of these two methods.

Line-by-Line Explanation

Lines 1–7

The usual setup plus some constants for the rest of the script to use.

Lines 9–15

The "handler" version of the code allocates a basic handler class as described earlier, then adds the authentication information. The handler is then used to

---

Example 20.1   HTTP Auth Client (`urlopen-auth.py`)

This script uses both techniques described above for basic authentication.

```python
1   #!/usr/bin/env python
2
3   import urllib2
4
5   LOGIN = 'wesc'
6   PASSWD = "you'llNeverGuess"
7   URL = 'http://localhost'
8
9   def handler_version(url):
10      from urlparse import urlparse as up
11      hdlr = urllib2.HTTPBasicAuthHandler()
12      hdlr.add_password('Archives', up(url)[1], LOGIN, PASSWD)
13      opener = urllib2.build_opener(hdlr)
14      urllib2.install_opener(opener)
15      return url
16
17  def request_version(url):
18      from base64 import encodestring
19      req = urllib2.Request(url)
20      b64str = encodestring('%s:%s' % (LOGIN, PASSWD))[:-1]
21      req.add_header("Authorization", "Basic %s" % b64str)
22      return req
23
24  for funcType in ('handler', 'request'):
25      print '*** Using %s:' % funcType.upper()
26      url = eval('%s_version') (URL)
27      f = urllib2.urlopen(url)
28      print f.readline()
29      f.close()
```

create a URL-opener that is then installed so that all URLs opened will use the given authentication. This code was adapted from the official Python documentation for the `urllib2` module.

Lines 17–22

The "request" version of our code just builds a `Request` object and adds the simple base64-encoded authentication header into our HTTP request. This request is then used to substitute the URL string when calling `urlopen()` upon returning back to "main." Note that the original URL was built into the Request object, hence the reason why it was not a problem to replace it in the subsequent call to `urllib2.urlopen()`. This code was inspired by Mike Foord's and Lee Harr's recipes in the Python Cookbook located at:

http://aspn.activestate.com/ASPN/Cookbook/Python/Recipe/305288
http://aspn.activestate.com/ASPN/Cookbook/Python/Recipe/267197

It would have been great to have been able to use Harr's `HTTPRealm-Finder` class so that we do not need to hardcode it in our example.

Lines 24–29

The rest of this script just opens the given URL using both techniques and displays the first line (dumping the others) of the resulting HTML page returned by the server once authentication has been validated. Note that an HTTP error (and no HTML) would be returned if the authentication information is invalid.

The output should look something like this:

```
$ python urlopen-auth.py
Using handler:
<html>

Using request:
<html>
```

In addition to the official Python documentation for `urllib2`, you may find this companion piece useful: http://www.voidspace.org.uk/python/articles/urllib2.shtml.

20.3 Advanced Web Clients

Web browsers are basic Web clients. They are used primarily for searching and downloading documents from the Web. Advanced clients of the Web are those applications that do more than download single documents from the Internet.

One example of an advanced Web client is a *crawler* (aka *spider*, *robot*). These are programs that explore and download pages from the Internet for different reasons, some of which include:

- Indexing into a large search engine such as Google or Yahoo!
- Offline browsing—downloading documents onto a local hard disk and rearranging hyperlinks to create almost a mirror image for local browsing
- Downloading and storing for historical or archival purposes, or
- Web page caching to save superfluous downloading time on Web site revisits.

The crawler we present below, `crawl.py`, takes a starting Web address (URL), downloads that page and all other pages whose links appear in succeeding pages, but only those that are in the same domain as the starting page. Without such limitations, you will run out of disk space! The source for `crawl.py` appears in Example 20.2.

Line-by-Line (Class-by-Class) Explanation

Lines 1–11

The top part of the script consists of the standard Python Unix start-up line and the importation of various module attributes that are employed in this application.

Lines 13–49

The `Retriever` class has the responsibility of downloading pages from the Web and parsing the links located within each document, adding them to the "to-do" queue if necessary. A `Retriever` instance object is created for each page that is downloaded from the net. `Retriever` consists of several methods to aid in its functionality: a constructor (`__init__()`), `filename()`, `download()`, and `parseAndGetLinks()`.

The `filename()` method takes the given URL and comes up with a safe and sane corresponding filename to store locally. Basically, it removes the "`http://`" prefix from the URL and uses the remaining part as the filename, creating any directory paths necessary. URLs without trailing file-names will be given a default filename of "`index.htm`". (This name can be overridden in the call to `filename()`).

The constructor instantiates a `Retriever` object and stores both the URL string and the corresponding file name returned by `filename()` as local attributes.

Example 20.2   Advanced Web Client: a Web Crawler (`crawl.py`)

The crawler consists of two classes, one to manage the entire crawling process
(`Crawler`), and one to retrieve and parse each downloaded Web page
(`Retriever`).

```
1   #!/usr/bin/env python
2
3   from sys import argv
4   from os import makedirs, unlink, sep
5   from os.path import dirname, exists, isdir, splitext
6   from string import replace, find, lower
7   from htmllib import HTMLParser
8   from urllib import urlretrieve
9   from urlparse import urlparse, urljoin
10  from formatter import DumbWriter, AbstractFormatter
11  from cStringIO import StringIO
12
13  class Retriever(object):# download Web pages
14
15      def __init__(self, url):
16        self.url = url
17        self.file = self.filename(url)
18
19      def filename(self, url, deffile='index.htm'):
20        parsedurl = urlparse(url, 'http:', 0) ## parse path
21        path = parsedurl[1] + parsedurl[2]
22        ext = splitext(path)
23        if ext[1] == '':                  # no file, use default
24            if path[-1] == '/':
25                path += deffile
26            else:
27                path += '/' + deffile
28        ldir = dirname(path)    # local directory
29        if sep != '/':             # os-indep. path separator
30            ldir = replace(ldir, '/', sep)
31        if not isdir(ldir):       # create archive dir if nec.
32            if exists(ldir): unlink(ldir)
33            makedirs(ldir)
34        return path
35
36      def download(self):         # download Web page
37          try:
38              retval = urlretrieve(self.url, self.file)
39          except IOError:
40              retval = ('*** ERROR: invalid URL "%s"' %\
41                  self.url,)
42          return retval
43
44      def parseAndGetLinks(self):# parse HTML, save links
45          self.parser = HTMLParser(AbstractFormatter(\
46              DumbWriter(StringIO())))
47          self.parser.feed(open(self.file).read())
48          self.parser.close()
49          return self.parser.anchorlist
```

(continued)

Example 20.2 Advanced Web Client: a Web Crawler (`crawl.py`) (continued)

```
50
51   class Crawler(object):# manage entire crawling process
52
53     count = 0              # static downloaded page counter
54
55     def __init__(self, url):
56         self.q = [url]
57         self.seen = []
58         self.dom = urlparse(url)[1]
59
60     def getPage(self, url):
61         r = Retriever(url)
62         retval = r.download()
63         if retval[0] == '*': # error situation, do not parse
64             print retval, '... skipping parse'
65             return
66         Crawler.count += 1
67         print '\n(', Crawler.count, ')'
68         print 'URL:', url
69         print 'FILE:', retval[0]
70         self.seen.append(url)
71
72         links = r.parseAndGetLinks() # get and process links
73         for eachLink in links:
74             if eachLink[:4] != 'http' and \
75                     find(eachLink, '://') == -1:
76                 eachLink = urljoin(url, eachLink)
77             print '* ', eachLink,
78
79             if find(lower(eachLink), 'mailto:') != -1:
80                 print '... discarded, mailto link'
81                 continue
82
83             if eachLink not in self.seen:
84                 if find(eachLink, self.dom) == -1:
85                     print '... discarded, not in domain'
86                 else:
87                     if eachLink not in self.q:
88                         self.q.append(eachLink)
89                         print '... new, added to Q'
90                     else:
91                         print '... discarded, already in Q'
92             else:
93                 print '... discarded, already processed'
94
95     def go(self):# process links in queue
96         while self.q:
97             url = self.q.pop()
98             self.getPage(url)
99
100  def main():
101      if len(argv) > 1:
102          url = argv[1]
```

Example 20.2 Advanced Web Client: a Web Crawler (`crawl.py`) (continued)

```
103          else:
104              try:
105                  url = raw_input('Enter starting URL: ')
106          except (KeyboardInterrupt, EOFError):
107                  url = ''
108
109          if not url: return
110          robot = Crawler(url)
111          robot.go()
112
113  if __name__ == '__main__':
114      main()
```

The `download()` method, as you may imagine, actually goes out to the net to download the page with the given link. It calls `urllib.urlretrieve()` with the URL and saves it to the filename (the one returned by `filename()`). If the download was successful, the `parse()` method is called to parse the page just copied from the network; otherwise an error string is returned.

If the `Crawler` determines that no error has occurred, it will invoke the `parseAndGetLinks()` method to parse the newly downloaded page and determine the course of action for each link located on that page.

Lines 51–98

The `Crawler` class is the "star" of the show, managing the entire crawling process for one Web site. If we added threading to our application, we would create separate instances for each site crawled. The `Crawler` consists of three items stored by the constructor during the instantiation phase, the first of which is q, a queue of links to download. Such a list will fluctuate during execution, shrinking as each page is processed and grown as new links are discovered within each downloaded page.

The other two data values for the `Crawler` include seen, a list of all the links that "we have seen" (downloaded) already. And finally, we store the domain name for the main link, dom, and use that value to determine whether any succeeding links are part of the same domain.

`Crawler` also has a static data item named count. The purpose of this counter is just to keep track of the number of objects we have downloaded from the net. It is incremented for every page successfully download.

`Crawler` has a pair of other methods in addition to its constructor, `getPage()` and `go()`. `go()` is simply the method that is used to start the

Crawler and is called from the main body of code. go() consists of a loop that will continue to execute as long as there are new links in the queue that need to be downloaded. The workhorse of this class, though, is the getPage() method.

getPage() instantiates a Retriever object with the first link and lets it go off to the races. If the page was downloaded successfully, the counter is incremented and the link added to the "already seen" list. It looks recursively at all the links featured inside each downloaded page and determines whether any more links should be added to the queue. The main loop in go() will continue to process links until the queue is empty, at which time victory is declared.

Links that are part of another domain, have already been downloaded, are already in the queue waiting to be processed, or are "mailto:" links are ignored and not added to the queue.

Lines 100–114

main() is executed if this script is invoked directly and is the starting point of execution. Other modules that import crawl.py will need to invoke main() to begin processing. main() needs a URL to begin processing. If one is given on the command line (for example, when this script is invoked directly), it will just go with the one given. Otherwise, the script enters interactive mode, prompting the user for a starting URL. With a starting link in hand, the Crawler is instantiated and away we go.

One sample invocation of crawl.py may look like this:

```
% crawl.py
Enter starting URL: http://www.null.com/home/index.html

( 1 )
URL: http://www.null.com/home/index.html
FILE: www.null.com/home/index.html
* http://www.null.com/home/overview.html ... new, added to Q
* http://www.null.com/home/synopsis.html ... new, added to Q
* http://www.null.com/home/order.html ... new, added to Q
* mailto:postmaster@null.com ... discarded, mailto link
* http://www.null.com/home/overview.html ... discarded, already in Q
* http://www.null.com/home/synopsis.html ... discarded, already in Q
* http://www.null.com/home/order.html ... discarded, already in Q
* mailto:postmaster@null.com ... discarded, mailto link
* http://bogus.com/index.html ... discarded, not in domain

( 2 )
URL: http://www.null.com/home/order.html
FILE: www.null.com/home/order.html
* mailto:postmaster@null.com ... discarded, mailto link
* http://www.null.com/home/index.html ... discarded, already processed
```

```
* http://www.null.com/home/synopsis.html ... discarded, already in Q
* http://www.null.com/home/overview.html ... discarded, already in Q

( 3 )
URL: http://www.null.com/home/synopsis.html
FILE: www.null.com/home/synopsis.html
* http://www.null.com/home/index.html ... discarded, already processed
* http://www.null.com/home/order.html ... discarded, already processed
* http://www.null.com/home/overview.html ... discarded, already in Q

( 4 )
URL: http://www.null.com/home/overview.html
FILE: www.null.com/home/overview.html
* http://www.null.com/home/synopsis.html ... discarded, already processed
* http://www.null.com/home/index.html ... discarded, already processed
* http://www.null.com/home/synopsis.html ... discarded, already processed
* http://www.null.com/home/order.html ... discarded, already processed
```

After execution, a `www.null.com` directory would be created in the local file system, with a home subdirectory. Within home, all the HTML files processed will be found.

20.4 CGI: Helping Web Servers Process Client Data

20.4.1 Introduction to CGI

The Web was initially developed to be a global online repository or archive of (mostly educational and research-oriented) documents. Such pieces of information generally come in the form of static text and usually in HTML.

HTML is not as much a *language* as it is a text formatter, indicating changes in font types, sizes, and styles. The main feature of HTML is in its hypertext capability, text that is in one way or another highlighted to point to another document in a related context to the original. Such a document can be accessed by a mouse click or other user selection mechanism. These (static) HTML documents live on the Web server and are sent to clients when and if requested.

As the Internet and Web services evolved, there grew a need to process user input. Online retailers needed to be able to take individual orders, and online banks and search engine portals needed to create accounts for individual users. Thus fill-out forms were invented, and became the only way a Web site can get specific information from users (until Java applets came along). This, in turn, required the HTML now be generated on the fly, for each client submitting user-specific data.

Now, Web servers are only really good at one thing, getting a user request for a file and returning that file (i.e., an HTML file) to the client. They do not have the "brains" to be able to deal with user-specific data such as those which come from fields. Not being their responsibility, Web servers farm out such requests to external applications which create the dynamically generated HTML that is returned to the client.

The entire process begins when the Web server receives a client request (i.e., GET or POST) and calls the appropriate application. It then waits for the resulting HTML—meanwhile, the client also waits. Once the application has completed, it passes the dynamically generated HTML back to the server, who then (finally) forwards it back to the user. This process of the server receiving a form, contacting an external application, and receiving and returning the newly-generated HTML takes place through what is called the Web server's *CGI* (Common Gateway Interface). An overview of how CGI works is illustrated in Figure 20–3, which shows you the execution and data flow, step-by-step, from when a user submits a form until the resulting Web page is returned.

Forms input from the client sent to a Web server may include processing and perhaps some form of storage in a backend database. Just keep in mind that any time there are any user-filled fields and/or a Submit button or image, it most likely involves some sort of CGI activity.

CGI applications that create the HTML are usually written in one of many higher-level programming languages that have the ability to accept user data, process it, and return HTML back to the server. Currently used programming languages include Perl, PHP, C/C++, or Python, to name a few.

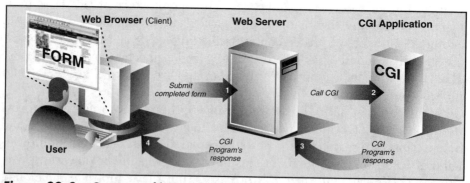

Figure 20–3   Overview of how CGI works. CGI represents the interaction between a Web server and the application that is required to process a user's form and generate the dynamic HTML that is eventually returned.

Before we take a look at CGI, we have to provide the caveat that the typical production Web application is no longer being done in CGI anymore.

Because of its significant limitations and limited ability to allow Web servers to process an abundant number of simultaneous clients, CGI is a dinosaur. Mission-critical Web services rely on compiled languages like C/C++ to scale. A modern-day Web server is typically composed of Apache and integrated components for database access (MySQL or PostgreSQL), Java (Tomcat), PHP, and various modules for Perl, Python, and SSL/security. However, if you are working on small personal Web sites or ones for small organizations and do not need the power and complexity required by mission critical Web services, CGI is the perfect tool for your simple Web sites.

Furthermore, there are a good number of Web application development frameworks out there as well as content management systems, all of which make building CGI a relic of past. However, beneath all the fluff and abstraction, they must still, in the end, follow the same model that CGI originally provided, and that is being able to take user input, execute code based on that input, and provide valid HTML as its final output for the client. Therefore, the exercise in learning CGI is well worth it in terms of understanding the fundamentals in order to develop effective Web services.

In this next section, we will look at how to create CGI applications in Python, with the help of the `cgi` module.

20.4.2 CGI Applications

A CGI application is slightly different from a typical program. The primary differences are in the input, output, and user interaction aspects of a computer program. When a CGI script starts, it needs to retrieve the user-supplied form data, but it has to obtain this data from the Web client, not a user on the server machine nor a disk file.

The output differs in that any data sent to standard output will be sent back to the connected Web client rather than to the screen, GUI window, or disk file. The data sent back must be a set of valid headers followed by HTML. If it is not and the Web client is a browser, an error (specifically, an Internal Server Error) will occur because Web clients such as browsers understand only valid HTTP data (i.e., MIME headers and HTML).

Finally, as you can probably guess, there is no user interaction with the script. All communication occurs among the Web client (on behalf of a user), the Web server, and the CGI application.

20.4.3 `cgi` Module

There is one primary class in the `cgi` module that does all the work: the `FieldStorage` class. This class should be instantiated when a Python CGI script begins, as it will read in all the pertinent user information from the Web client (via the Web server). Once this object has been instantiated, it will consist of a dictionary-like object that has a set of key-value pairs. The keys are the names of the form items that were passed in through the form while the values contain the corresponding data.

These values themselves can be one of three objects. They can be `FieldStorage` objects (instances) as well as instances of a similar class called `MiniFieldStorage`, which is used in cases where no file uploads or multiple-part form data is involved. `MiniFieldStorage` instances contain only the key-value pair of the name and the data. Lastly, they can be a list of such objects. This occurs when a form contains more than one input item with the same field name.

For simple Web forms, you will usually find all `MiniFieldStorage` instances. All of our examples below pertain only to this general case.

20.5 Building CGI Applications
20.5.1 Setting Up a Web Server

In order to play around with CGI development in Python, you need to first install a Web server, configure it for handling Python CGI requests, and then give the Web server access to your CGI scripts. Some of these tasks may require assistance from your system administrator.

If you want a real Web server, you will likely download and install Apache. There are Apache plug-ins or modules for handling Python CGI, but they are not required for our examples. You may wish to install those if you are planning on "going live" to the world with your service. Even this may be overkill.

For learning purposes or for simple Web sites, it may suffice to just use the Web servers that come with Python. In Section 20.8, you will actually learn how to build and configure simple Python-based Web servers. You may read ahead now if you wish to find out more about it at this stage. However, that is not what this section is about.

If you want to just start up the most basic Web server, just execute it directly with Python:

```
$ python -m CGIHTTPServer
```

The -m option is new in 2.4, so if you are using an older version of Python or want to see alternative ways of running it, see section 14.4.3. Anyway, if you eventually get it working. . . .

This will start a Web server on port 8000 on your current machine from the current directory. Then you can just create a Cgi-bin right underneath the directory from which you started the server and put your Python CGI scripts in there. Put some HTML files in that directory and perhaps some .py CGI scripts in Cgi-bin, and you are ready to "surf" directly to this Web site with addresses looking something like these:

> http://localhost:8000/friends.htm
> http://localhost:8000/cgi-bin/friends2.py

20.5.2 Creating the Form Page

In Example 20.3, we present the code for a simple Web form, friends.htm.

As you can see in the code, the form contains two input variables: person and howmany. The values of these two fields will be passed to our CGI script, friends1.py.

You will notice in our example that we install our CGI script into the default cgi-bin directory (see the "Action" link) on the local host. (If this information does not correspond with your development environment, update the form action before attempting to test the Web page and CGI script.) Also, because a METHOD subtag is missing from the form action, all

---

Example 20.3 Static Form Web Page (friends.htm)

This HTML file presents a form to the user with an empty field for the user's name and a set of radio buttons for the user to choose from.

```
1   <HTML><HEAD><TITLE>
2   Friends CGI Demo (static screen)
3   </TITLE></HEAD>
4   <BODY><H3>Friends list for: <I>NEW USER</I></H3>
5   <FORM ACTION="/cgi-bin/friends1.py">
6   <B>Enter your Name:</B>
7   <INPUT TYPE=text NAME=person VALUE="NEW USER" SIZE=15>
8   <P><B>How many friends do you have?</B>
9   <INPUT TYPE=radio NAME=howmany VALUE="0" CHECKED> 0
10  <INPUT TYPE=radio NAME=howmany VALUE="10"> 10
11  <INPUT TYPE=radio NAME=howmany VALUE="25"> 25
12  <INPUT TYPE=radio NAME=howmany VALUE="50"> 50
13  <INPUT TYPE=radio NAME=howmany VALUE="100"> 100
14  <P><INPUT TYPE=submit></FORM></BODY></HTML>
```

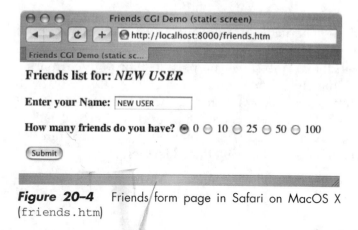

Figure 20–4   Friends form page in Safari on MacOS X
(`friends.htm`)

requests will be of the default type, GET. We choose the GET method because we do not have very many form fields, and also, we want our query string to show up in the "Location" (aka "Address", "Go To") bar so that you can see what URL is sent to the server.

Let us take a look at the screen that is rendered by `friends.htm` in a client (see Figure 20–4 for Safari on MacOS and Figure 20–5 for IE6).

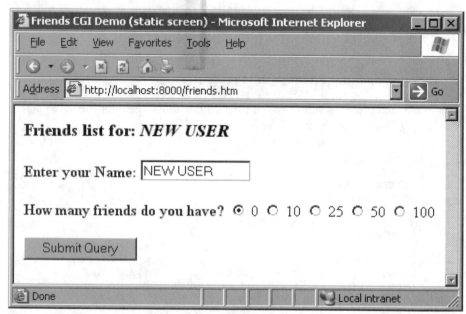

Figure 20–5   Friends form page in IE6 on Win32 (`friends.htm`)

Throughout this chapter, we will feature screenshots from various Web browsers and operating systems over the past few years.

20.5.3 *Generating the Results Page*

The input is entered by the user and the "Submit" button is pressed. (Alternatively, the user can also press the RETURN or Enter key within the text field to cause a similar effect.) When this occurs, the script in Example 20.4, friends1.py, is executed via CGI.

This script contains all the programming power to read the form input and process it, as well as return the resulting HTML page back to the user. All the "real" work in this script takes place in only four lines of Python code (lines 14–17).

The form variable is our FieldStorage instance, containing the values of the person and howmany fields. We read these into the Python who and howmany variables, respectively. The reshtml variable contains the general body of HTML text to return, with a few fields filled in dynamically, the data just read in from the form.

Example 20.4 Results Screen CGI code (friends1.py**)**

This CGI script grabs the person *and* howmany *fields from the form and uses that data to create the dynamically generated results screen.*

```
1   #!/usr/bin/env python
2
3   import cgi
4
5   reshtml = '''Content-Type: text/html\n
6   <HTML><HEAD><TITLE>
7   Friends CGI Demo (dynamic screen)
8   </TITLE></HEAD>
9   <BODY><H3>Friends list for: <I>%s</I></H3>
10  Your name is: <B>%s</B><P>
11  You have <B>%s</B> friends.
12  </BODY></HTML>'''
13
14  form = cgi.FieldStorage()
15  who = form['person'].value
16  howmany = form['howmany'].value
17  print reshtml % (who, who, howmany)
```

CORE TIP: HTTP headers separate from HTML

One thing that always nails CGI beginners is that when sending results back to a CGI script, it must return the appropriate HTTP headers first before any HTML. Furthermore, to distinguish between these headers and the resulting HTML, several NEWLINE characters must be inserted between both sets of data, as in line 5 of our `friends1.py` *example, as well as for the code in the remaining part of the chapter.*

One possible resulting screen appears in Figure 20–6, assuming the user typed in "erick allen" as the name and clicked on the "10 friends" radio button. The screen snapshot this time is represented by the older IE3 browser in a Windows environment.

If you are a Web site producer, you may be thinking, "Gee, wouldn't it be nice if I could automatically capitalize this person's name, especially if they forgot?" This can easily be accomplished using Python CGI. (And we shall do so soon!)

Notice how on a GET request that our form variables and their values are added to the form action URL in the "Address" bar. Also, did you observe that the title for the `friends.htm` page has the word "static" in it while the output screen from `friends.py` has the work "dynamic" in *its* title? We did that for a reason: to indicate that the `friends.htm` file is a static text

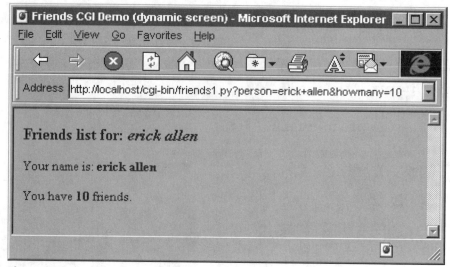

Figure 20–6   Friends results page in IE3 on Win32

file while the results page is dynamically generated. In other words, the HTML for the results page did not exist on disk as a text file; rather, it was generated by our CGI script, which returned it as if it *was* a local file.

In our next example, we will bypass static files altogether by updating our CGI script to be somewhat more multifaceted.

20.5.4 *Generating Form and Results Pages*

We obsolete `friends.html` and merge it into `friends2.py`. The script will now generate both the form page as well as the results page. But how can we tell which page to generate? Well, if there is form data being sent to us, that means that we should be creating a results page. If we do not get any information at all, that tells us that we should generate a form page for the user to enter his or her data.

Our new `friends2.py` script is shown in Example 20.5.

So what did we change in our script? Let's take a look at some of the blocks of code in this script.

Line-by-Line Explanation

Lines 1–5

In addition to the usual startup and module import lines, we separate the HTTP MIME header from the rest of the HTML body because we will use it for both types of pages (form page and results page) returned and we don't want to duplicate the text. We will add this header string to the corresponding HTML body when it comes time for output to occur.

Lines 7–29

All of this code is related to the now-integrated `friends.htm` form page in our CGI script. We have a variable for the form page text, `formhtml`, and we also have a string to build the list of radio buttons, `fradio`. We could have duplicated this radio button HTML text as it is in `friends.htm`, but we wanted to show how we could use Python to generate more dynamic output—see the **for**-loop on lines 22–27.

The `showForm()` function has the responsibility of generating a form for user input. It builds a set of text for the radio buttons, merges those lines of HTML into the main body of `formhtml`, prepends the header to the form, and then returns the entire wad of data back to the client by sending the entire string to standard output.

Example 20.5 Generating Form and Results Pages (`friends2.py`)

Both `friends.html` *and* `friends1.py` *are merged together as* `friends2.py`. *The resulting script can now output both form and results pages as dynamically generated HTML and has the smarts to know which page to output.*

```python
1   #!/usr/bin/env python
2
3   import cgi
4
5   header = 'Content-Type: text/html\n\n'
6
7   formhtml = '''<HTML><HEAD><TITLE>
8   Friends CGI Demo</TITLE></HEAD>
9   <BODY><H3>Friends list for: <I>NEW USER</I></H3>
10  <FORM ACTION="/cgi-bin/friends2.py">
11  <B>Enter your Name:</B>
12  <INPUT TYPE=hidden NAME=action VALUE=edit>
13  <INPUT TYPE=text NAME=person VALUE="NEW USER" SIZE=15>
14  <P><B>How many friends do you have?</B>
15  %s
16  <P><INPUT TYPE=submit></FORM></BODY></HTML>'''
17
18  fradio = '<INPUT TYPE=radio NAME=howmany VALUE="%s" %s> %s\n'
19
20  def showForm():
21      friends = ''
22      for i in [0, 10, 25, 50, 100]:
23          checked = ''
24          if i == 0:
25              checked = 'CHECKED'
26          friends = friends + fradio % \
27              (str(i), checked, str(i))
28
29      print header + formhtml % (friends)
30
31  reshtml = '''<HTML><HEAD><TITLE>
32  Friends CGI Demo</TITLE></HEAD>
33  <BODY><H3>Friends list for: <I>%s</I></H3>
34  Your name is: <B>%s</B><P>
35  You have <B>%s</B> friends.
36  </BODY></HTML>'''
37
38  def doResults(who, howmany):
39      print header + reshtml % (who, who, howmany)
40
41  def process():
42      form = cgi.FieldStorage()
43      if form.has_key('person'):
44          who = form['person'].value
45      else:
46          who = 'NEW USER'
47
```

Example 20.5 Generating Form and Results Pages (`friends2.py`) (continued)

```
48       if form.has_key('howmany'):
49   howmany = form['howmany'].value
50       else:
51           howmany = 0
52
53       if form.has_key('action'):
54           doResults(who, howmany)
55       else:
56           showForm()
57
58   if __name__ == '__main__':
59       process()
```

There are a couple of interesting things to note about this code. The first is the "hidden" variable in the form called `action`, containing the value "edit" on line 12. This field is the only way we can tell which screen to display (i.e., the form page or the results page). We will see this field come into play in lines 53–56.

Also, observe that we set the 0 radio button as the default by "checking" it within the loop that generates all the buttons. This will also allow us to update the layout of the radio buttons and/or their values on a single line of code (line 18) rather than over multiple lines of text. It will also offer some more flexibility in letting the logic determine which radio button is checked—see the next update to our script, `friends3.py` coming up.

Now you may be thinking, "Why do we need an `action` variable when I could just as well be checking for the presence of `person` or `howmany`?" That is a valid question because yes, you could have just used `person` or `howmany` in this situation.

However, the `action` variable is a more conspicuous presence, insofar as its name as well as what it does—the code is easier to understand. The `person` and `howmany` variables are used for their values while the `action` variable is used as a flag.

The other reason for creating `action` is that we will be using it again to help us determine which page to generate. In particular, we will need to display a form *with* the presence of a `person` variable (rather than a results page)—this will break your code if you are solely relying on there being a `person` variable.

Lines 31–39

The code to display the results page is practically identical to that of `friends1.py`.

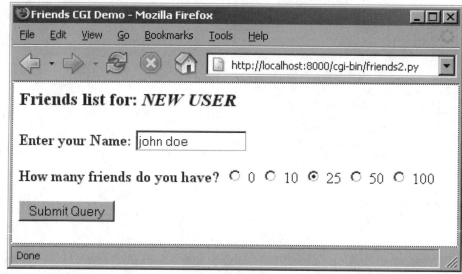

Figure 20–7   Friends form page in Firefox I.x on Win32 (`friends2.py`)

Lines 41–56

Since there are different pages that can result from this one script, we created an overall `process()` function to get the form data and decide which action to take. The main portion of `process()` will also look familiar to the main body of code in `friends1.py`. There are two major differences, however.

Since the script may or may not be getting the expected fields (invoking the script the first time to generate a form page, for example, will not pass any fields to the server), we need to "bracket" our retrieval of the form fields with **if** statements to check if they are even there. Also, we mentioned the `action` field above, which helps us decide which page to bring up. The code that performs this determination is in lines 53–56.

In Figures 20–7 and 20–8, you will see first the form screen generated by our script (with a name entered and radio button chosen), followed by the results page, also generated by our script.

If you look at the location or "Go to" bar, you will not see a URL referring to a static `friends.htm` file as you did in Figure 20–4 or Figure 20–5.

20.5.5 Fully Interactive Web sites

Our final example will complete the circle. As in the past, a user enters his or her information from the form page. We then process the data and output a results page. Now we will add a link to the results page that will allow the

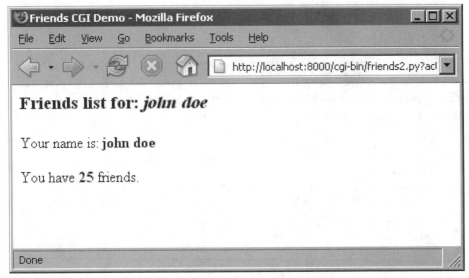

Figure 20–8   Friends results page in Firefox on Win32 (`friends2.py`)

user to go *back* to the form page, but rather than presenting a blank form, we will fill in the data that the user has already provided. We will also add some error processing to give you an example of how it can be accomplished.

We now present our final update, `friends3.py` in Example 20.6.

`friends3.py` is not too unlike `friends2.py`. We invite the reader to compare the differences; we present a brief summary of the major changes for you here.

Abridged Line-by-Line Explanation

Line 8

We take the URL out of the form because we now need it in two places, the results page being the new customer.

Lines 10–19, 69–71, 75–82

All of these lines deal with the new feature of having an error screen. If the user does not select a radio button indicating the number of friends, the how-many field is not passed to the server. In such a case, the show-Error() function returns the error page to the user.

The error page also features a JavaScript "Back" button. Because buttons are input types, we need a form, but no action is needed because we are simply just going back one page in the browsing history. Although our script currently supports (aka detects, tests for) only one type of error, we still use a

Example 20.6   Full User Interaction and Error Processing (`friends3.py`)

By adding a link to return to the form page with information already provided, we have come "full circle," giving the user a fully interactive Web surfing experience. Our application also now performs simple error checking, which notifies the user if no radio button was selected.

```python
1   #!/usr/bin/env python
2
3   import cgi
4   from urllib import quote_plus
5   from string import capwords
6
7   header = 'Content-Type: text/html\n\n'
8   url = '/cgi-bin/friends3.py'
9
10  errhtml = '''<HTML><HEAD><TITLE>
11  Friends CGI Demo</TITLE></HEAD>
12  <BODY><H3>ERROR</H3>
13  <B>%s</B><P>
14  <FORM><INPUT TYPE=button VALUE=Back
15  ONCLICK="window.history.back()"></FORM>
16  </BODY></HTML>'''
17
18  def showError(error_str):
19      print header + errhtml % (error_str)
20
21  formhtml = '''<HTML><HEAD><TITLE>
22  Friends CGI Demo</TITLE></HEAD>
23  <BODY><H3>Friends list for: <I>%s</I></H3>
24  <FORM ACTION="%s">
25  <B>Your Name:</B>
26  <INPUT TYPE=hidden NAME=action VALUE=edit>
27  <INPUT TYPE=text NAME=person VALUE="%s" SIZE=15>
28  <P><B>How many friends do you have?</B>
29  %s
30  <P><INPUT TYPE=submit></FORM></BODY></HTML>'''
31
32  fradio = '<INPUT TYPE=radio NAME=howmany VALUE="%s" %s>
        %s\n'
33
34  def showForm(who, howmany):
35      friends = ''
36      for i in [0, 10, 25, 50, 100]:
37          checked = ''
38          if str(i) == howmany:
39              checked = 'CHECKED'
40          friends = friends + fradio % \
41              (str(i), checked, str(i))
42      print header + formhtml % (who, url, who, friends)
43
44  reshtml = '''<HTML><HEAD><TITLE>
```

Example 20.6 Full User Interaction and Error Processing (`friends3.py`) (continued)

```
45   Friends CGI Demo</TITLE></HEAD>
46   <BODY><H3>Friends list for: <I>%s</I></H3>
47   Your name is: <B>%s</B><P>
48   You have <B>%s</B> friends.
49   <P>Click <A HREF="%s">here</A> to edit your data again.
50   </BODY></HTML>'''
51
52   def doResults(who, howmany):
53     newurl = url + '?action=reedit&person=%s&howmany=%s'%\
54         (quote_plus(who), howmany)
55     print header + reshtml % (who, who, howmany, newurl)
56
57   def process():
58     error = ''
59     form = cgi.FieldStorage()
60
61     if form.has_key('person'):
62         who = capwords(form['person'].value)
63     else:
64         who = 'NEW USER'
65
66     if form.has_key('howmany'):
67         howmany = form['howmany'].value
68     else:
69         if form.has_key('action') and \
70                 form['action'].value == 'edit':
71             error = 'Please select number of friends.'
72         else:
73             howmany = 0
74
75     if not error:
76         if form.has_key('action') and \
77                 form['action'].value != 'reedit':
78             doResults(who, howmany)
79         else:
80             showForm(who, howmany)
81     else:
82             showError(error)
83
84   if __name__ == '__main__':
85     process()
```

generic error variable in case we wanted to continue development of this script to add more error detection in the future.

Lines 27, 38–41, 49, and 52–55

One goal for this script is to create a meaningful link back to the form page from the results page. This is implemented as a link to give the user the ability to return to a form page to update the data he or she entered, in case it was erroneous. The new form page makes sense only if it contains information pertaining to the data that have already been entered by the user. (It is frustrating for users to reenter their information from scratch!)

To accomplish this, we need to embed the current values into the updated form. In line 27, we add a value for the name. This value will be inserted into the name field, if given. Obviously, it will be blank on the initial form page. In Lines 38–41, we set the radio box corresponding to the number of friends currently chosen. Finally, on lines 49 and the updated `doResults()` function on lines 52–55, we create the link with all the existing information, which "returns" the user to our modified form page.

Line 62

Finally, we added a simple feature that we thought would be a nice aesthetic touch. In the screens for `friends1.py` and `friends2.py`, the text entered by the user as his or her name is taken verbatim. You will notice in the screens above that if the user does not capitalize his or her names, that is reflected in the results page. We added a call to the `string.capwords()` function to automatically capitalize a user's name. The `capwords()` function will capitalize the first letter of each word in the string that is passed in. This may or may not be a desired feature, but we thought that we would share it with you so that you know that such functionality exists.

We will now present four screens that show the progression of user interaction with this CGI form and script.

In the first screen, shown in Figure 20–9, we invoke `friends3.py` to bring up the now-familiar form page. We enter a name "foo bar," but deliberately

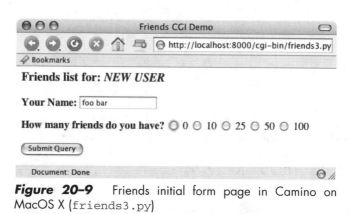

Figure 20–9   Friends initial form page in Camino on MacOS X (`friends3.py`)

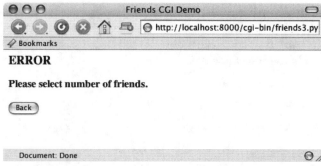

Figure 20–10   Friends error page (invalid user input), also in Camino (`friends3.py`)

avoid checking any of the radio buttons. The resulting error after submitting the form can be seen in the second screen (Figure 20–10).

We click on the "Back" button, check the "50" radio button, and resubmit our form. The results page, shown in Figure 20–11, is also familiar, but now has an extra link at the bottom. This link will take us back to the form page. The only difference between the new form page and our original is that all the data filled in by the user are now set as the "default" settings, meaning that the values are already available in the form. We can see this in Figure 20–12.

Now the user is able to make changes to either of the fields and resubmit his or her form.

You will no doubt begin to notice that as our forms and data get more complicated, so does the generated HTML, especially for complex results pages. If you ever get to a point where generating the HTML text is interfering with your application, you may consider connecting with a Python module such as `HTMLgen`, an external Python module which specializes in HTML generation.

Figure 20–11   Friends updated form page with current information

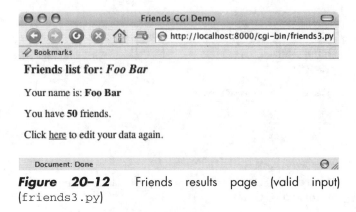

Figure 20–12 Friends results page (valid input) (friends3.py)

20.6 Using Unicode with CGI

In Chapter 6, "Sequences," we introduced the use of Unicode strings. In Section 6.8.5, we gave a simple example of a script that takes a Unicode string, writing it out to a file and reading it back in. In this section, we will demonstrate a simple CGI script that has Unicode output and how to give your browser enough clues to be able to render the characters properly. The one requirement is that you must have East Asian fonts installed on your computer so that the browser can display them.

To see Unicode in action we will build a CGI script to generate a multilingual Web page. First of all we define the message in a Unicode string. We assume your text editor can only enter ASCII. Therefore the non-ASCII characters are input using the \u escape. In practice the message can also be read from a file or from database.

```
# Greeting in English, Spanish,
# Chinese and Japanese.
UNICODE_HELLO = u"""
Hello!
\u00A1Hola!
\u4F60\u597D!
\u3053\u3093\u306B\u3061\u306F!
"""
```

The first output the CGI generates is the content-type HTTP header. It is very important to declare here that the content is transmitted in the UTF-8 encoding so that the browser can correctly interpret it.

```
print 'Content-type: text/html; charset=UTF-8\r'
print '\r'
```

Example 20.7   Simple Unicode CGI Example (uniCGI.py)

This script outputs Unicode strings to your Web browser.

```
1    #!/usr/bin/env python
2
3    CODEC = 'UTF-8'
4    UNICODE_HELLO = u'''
5    Hello!
6    \u00A1Hola!
7    \u4F60\u597D!
8    \u3053\u3093\u306B\u3061\u306F!
9    '''
10
11   print 'Content-Type: text/html; charset=%s\r' % CODEC
12   print '\r'
13   print '<HTML><HEAD><TITLE>Unicode CGI Demo</TITLE></HEAD>'
14   print '<BODY>'
15   print UNICODE_HELLO.encode(CODEC)
16   print '</BODY></HTML>'
```

Then output the actual message. Use the string's `encode()` method to translate the string into UTF-8 sequences first.

```
    print UNICODE_HELLO.encode('UTF-8')
```

Example 20.7 shows the complete program.

If you run the CGI code from your browser, you will get output like that shown in Figure 20–13.

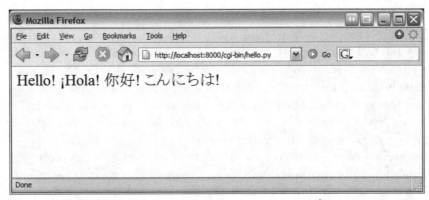

Figure 20–13   Simple Unicode CGI demo output in Firefox (uniCGI.py)

20.7 Advanced CGI

We will now take a look at some of the more advanced aspects of CGI programming. These include the use of *cookies*—cached data saved on the client side—multiple values for the same CGI field and file upload using multipart form submissions. To save space, we will show you all three of these features with a single application. Let's take a look at multipart submissions first.

20.7.1 Multipart Form Submission and File Uploading

Currently, the CGI specifications only allow two types of form encodings, "application/x-www-form-urlencoded" and "multipart/form-data." Because the former is the default, there is never a need to state the encoding in the FORM tag like this:

```
<FORM enctype="application/x-www-form-urlencoded" ...>
```

But for multipart forms, you must explicitly give the encoding as:

```
<FORM enctype="multipart/form-data" ...>
```

You can use either type of encoding for form submissions, but at this time, file uploads can only be performed with the multipart encoding. Multipart encoding was invented by Netscape in the early days but has since been adopted by Microsoft (starting with version 4 of Internet Explorer) as well as other browsers.

File uploads are accomplished using the file input type:

```
<INPUT type=file name=...>
```

This directive presents an empty text field with a button on the side which allows you to browse your file directory structure for a file to upload. When using multipart, your Web client's form submission to the server will look amazingly like (multipart) e-mail messages with attachments. A separate encoding was needed because it just would not be necessarily wise to "urlen-code" a file, especially a binary file. The information still gets to the server, but it is just "packaged" in a different way.

Regardless of whether you use the default encoding or the multipart, the `cgi` module will process them in the same manner, providing keys and corresponding values in the form submission. You will simply access the data through your `FieldStorage` instance as before.

20.7.2 *Multivalued Fields*

In addition to file uploads, we are going to show you how to process fields with multiple values. The most common case is when you have a set of checkboxes allowing a user to select from various choices. Each of the checkboxes is labeled with the same field name, but to differentiate them, each will have a different value associated with a particular checkbox.

As you know, the data from the user are sent to the server in key-value pairs during form submission. When more than one checkbox is submitted, you will have multiple values associated with the same key. In these cases, rather than being given a single `MiniFieldStorage` instance for your data, the `cgi` module will create a list of such instances that you will iterate over to obtain the different values. Not too painful at all.

20.7.3 *Cookies*

Finally, we will use cookies in our example. If you are not familiar with cookies, they are just bits of data information which a server at a Web site will request to be saved on the client side, e.g., the browser.

Because HTTP is a "stateless" protocol, information that has to be carried from one page to another can be accomplished by using key-value pairs in the request as you have seen in the GET requests and screens earlier in this chapter. Another way of doing it, as we have also seen before, is using hidden form fields, such as the action variable in some of the later `friends*.py` scripts. These variables and their values are managed by the server because the pages they return to the client must embed these in generated pages.

One alternative to maintaining persistency in state across multiple page views is to save the data on the client side instead. This is where cookies come in. Rather than embedding data to be saved in the returned Web pages, a server will make a request to the client to save a cookie. The cookie is linked to the domain of the originating server (so a server cannot set or override cookies from other Web sites) and has an expiration date (so your browser doesn't become cluttered with cookies).

These two characteristics are tied to a cookie along with the key-value pair representing the data item of interest. There are other attributes of cookies such as a domain subpath or a request that a cookie should only be delivered in a secure environment.

By using cookies, we no longer have to pass the data from page to page to track a user. Although they have been subject to a good amount of controversy over the privacy issue, most Web sites use cookies responsibly. To prepare you for the code, a Web server requests a client store a cookie by sending the "Set-Cookie" header immediately before the requested file.

Once cookies are set on the client side, requests to the server will automatically have those cookies sent to the server using the HTTP_COOKIE environment variable. The cookies are delimited by semicolons and come in "key=value" pairs. All your application needs to do to access the data values is to split the string several times (i.e., using string.split() or manual parsing). The cookies are delimited by semicolons (;), and each key-value pair is separated by equal signs (=).

Like multipart encoding, cookies originated from Netscape, which implemented cookies and wrote up the first specification, which is still valid today. You can access this document at the following Web site:

> http://www.netscape.com/newsref/std/cookie_spec.html

Once cookies are standardized and this document finally obsoleted, you will be able to get more current information from Request for Comment documents (RFCs). The most current one for cookies at the time of publication is RFC 2109.

20.7.4 Using Advanced CGI

We now present our CGI application, advcgi.py, which has code and functionality not too unlike the friends3.py script seen earlier in this chapter. The default first page is a user fill-out form consisting of four main parts: user-set cookie string, name field, checkbox list of programming languages, and file submission box. An image of this screen can be seen in Figure 20–14.

Figure 20–15 shows another look at the form from another browser. From this form, we can enter our information, such as the sample data given in Figure 20–16. Notice how the text in the button to search for files differs between browsers, i.e., "Browse . . .", "Choose", ". . .", etc.

The data are submitted to the server using multipart encoding and retrieved in the same manner on the server side using the FieldStorage instance. The only tricky part is in retrieving the uploaded file. In our application, we choose to iterate over the file, reading it line by line. It is also possible to read in the entire contents of the file if you are not wary of its size.

Since this is the first occasion data are received by the server, it is at this time, when returning the results page back to the client, that we use the "Set-Cookie:" header to cache our data in browser cookies.

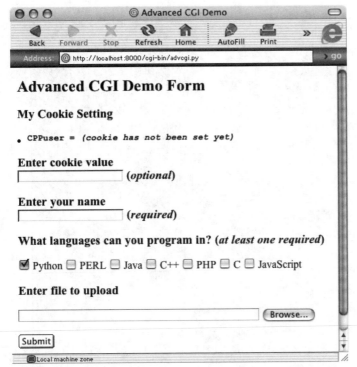

Figure 20–14 Upload and multivalue form page in IE5 on MacOS X

In Figure 20–17, you will see the results after submitting our form data. All the fields the user entered are shown on the page. The given file in the final dialog box was uploaded to the server and displayed as well.

You will also notice the link at the bottom of the results page, which returns us to the form page, again using the same CGI script.

If we click on that link at the bottom, no form data is submitted to our script, causing a form page to be displayed. Yet, as you can see from Figure 20–17, what shows up is anything but an empty form! Information previously entered by the user shows up! How did we accomplish this with no form data (either hidden or as query arguments in the URL)? The secret is that the data are stored on the client side in cookies, two in fact.

The user cookie holds the string of data typed in by the user in the "Enter cookie value" form field, and the user's name, languages they are familiar with, and uploaded files are stored in the info cookie.

When the script detects no form data, it shows the form page, but before the form page has been created, it grabs the cookies from the client

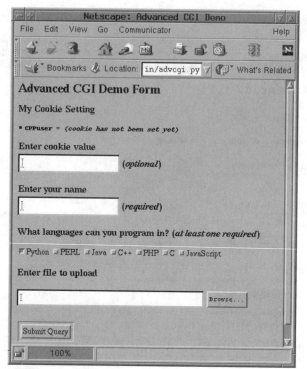

Figure 20–15   The same advanced CGI form but in Netscape4 on Linux

(which are automatically transmitted by the client when the user clicks on the link) and fills out the form accordingly. So when the form is finally displayed, all the previously entered information appears to the user like magic (see Figure 20–18).

We are certain you are eager to take a look at this application, so here it is, in Example 20.8.

`advcgi.py` looks strikingly similar to our `friends3.py` CGI scripts seen earlier in this chapter. It has a form, results, and error pages to return. In addition to all of the advanced CGI features that are part of our new script, we are also using more of an object-oriented feel to our script by using a class with methods instead of just a set of functions. The HTML text for our pages is now static data for our class, meaning that they will remain constant across all instances—even though there is actually only one instance in our case.

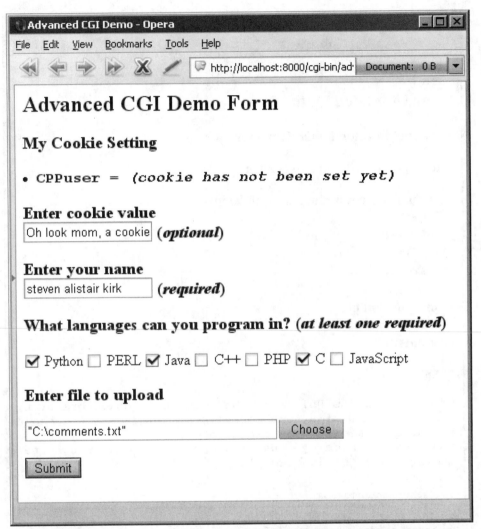

Figure 20-16 Submitting our advanced CGI demo form in Opera8 on Win32

Line-by-Line (Block-by-Block) Explanation

Lines 1–7

The usual startup and import lines appear here. The only module you may not be familiar with is cStringIO, which we briefly introduced at the end of Chapter 10 and also used in Example 20.1. cStringIO.StringIO() creates a file-like object out of a string so that access to the string is similar to opening a file and using the handle to access the data.

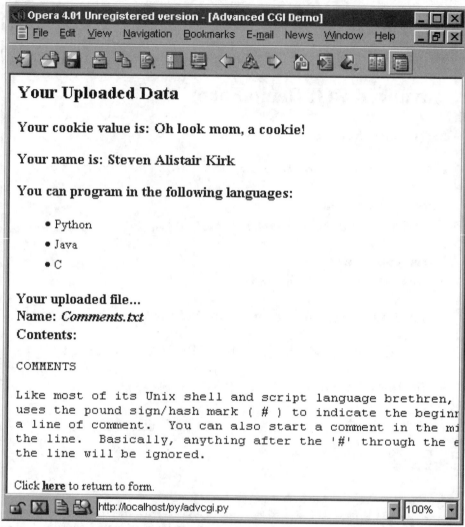

Figure 20–17   Results page generated and returned by the Web server in Opera4 on Win32

Lines 9–12

After the AdvCGI class is declared, the header and url (static class) variables are created for use by the methods displaying all the different pages.

Lines 14–80

All the code in this block is used to generate and display the form page. The data attributes speak for themselves. getCPPCookies() obtains cookie

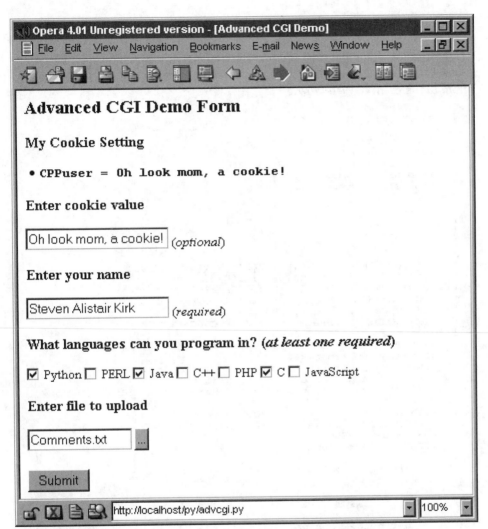

Figure 20-18 Form page with data loaded from the Client cookies

information sent by the Web client, and showForm() collates all the information and sends the form page back to the client.

Lines 82-91

This block of code is responsible for the error page.

Lines 93-144

The results page is created using this block of code. The setCPPCookies() method requests that a client store the cookies for our application, and the

Example 20.8 Advanced CGI Application (`advcgi.py`)

This script has one main class that does everything, `AdvCGI`. *It has methods to show either form, error, or results pages as well as those that read or write cookies from/to the client (a Web browser).*

```python
1   #!/usr/bin/env python
2
3   from cgi import FieldStorage
4   from os import environ
5   from cStringIO import StringIO
6   from urllib import quote, unquote
7   from string import capwords, strip, split, join
8
9   class AdvCGI(object):
10
11      header = 'Content-Type: text/html\n\n'
12      url = '/py/advcgi.py'
13
14      formhtml = '''<HTML><HEAD><TITLE>
15  Advanced CGI Demo</TITLE></HEAD>
16  <BODY><H2>Advanced CGI Demo Form</H2>
17  <FORM METHOD=post ACTION="%s" ENCTYPE="multipart/form-data">
18  <H3>My Cookie Setting</H3>
19  <LI> <CODE><B>CPPuser = %s</B></CODE>
20  <H3>Enter cookie value<BR>
21  <INPUT NAME=cookie value="%s"> (<I>optional</I>)</H3>
22  <H3>Enter your name<BR>
23  <INPUT NAME=person VALUE="%s"> (<I>required</I>)</H3>
24  <H3>What languages can you program in?
25  (<I>at least one required</I>)</H3>
26  %s
27  <H3>Enter file to upload</H3>
28  <INPUT TYPE=file NAME=upfile VALUE="%s" SIZE=45>
29  <P><INPUT TYPE=submit>
30  </FORM></BODY></HTML>'''
31
32      langSet = ('Python', 'PERL', 'Java', 'C++', 'PHP',
33                          'C', 'JavaScript')
34      langItem = \
35          '<INPUT TYPE=checkbox NAME=lang VALUE="%s"%s> %s\n'
36
37      def getCPPCookies(self):   # read cookies from client
38          if environ.has_key('HTTP_COOKIE'):
39              for eachCookie in map(strip, \
40                      split(environ['HTTP_COOKIE'], ';')):
41                  if len(eachCookie) > 6 and \
42                          eachCookie[:3] == 'CPP':
43                      tag = eachCookie[3:7]
44                      try:
45                          self.cookies[tag] = \
46                              eval(unquote(eachCookie[8:]))
47                      except (NameError, SyntaxError):
48                          self.cookies[tag] = \
49                              unquote(eachCookie[8:])
50          else:
51              self.cookies['info'] = self.cookies['user'] = ''
52
53          if self.cookies['info'] != '':
54              self.who, langStr, self.fn = \
```

Example 20.8 Advanced CGI Application (`advcgi.py`) (continued)

```
55                       split(self.cookies['info'], ':')
56              self.langs = split(langStr, ',')
57          else:
58              self.who = self.fn = ' '
59              self.langs = ['Python']
60
61      def showForm(self):          # show fill-out form
62          self.getCPPCookies()
63          langStr = ''
64          for eachLang in AdvCGI.langSet:
65              if eachLang in self.langs:
66                  langStr += AdvCGI.langItem % \
67                      (eachLang, ' CHECKED', eachLang)
68              else:
69                  langStr += AdvCGI.langItem % \
70                          (eachLang, '', eachLang)
71
72          if not self.cookies.has_key('user') or \
73                  self.cookies['user'] == '':
74              cookStatus = '<I>(cookie has not been set yet)</I>'
75              userCook = ''
76          else:
77              userCook = cookStatus = self.cookies['user']
78
79          print AdvCGI.header + AdvCGI.formhtml % (AdvCGI.url,
80              cookStatus, userCook, self.who, langStr, self.fn)
81
82      errhtml = '''<HTML><HEAD><TITLE>
83  Advanced CGI Demo</TITLE></HEAD>
84  <BODY><H3>ERROR</H3>
85  <B>%s</B><P>
86  <FORM><INPUT TYPE=button VALUE=Back
87  ONCLICK="window.history.back()"></FORM>
88  </BODY></HTML>'''
89
90      def showError(self):
91          print AdvCGI.header + AdvCGI.errhtml % (self.error)
92
93      reshtml = '''<HTML><HEAD><TITLE>
94  Advanced CGI Demo</TITLE></HEAD>
95  <BODY><H2>Your Uploaded Data</H2>
96  <H3>Your cookie value is: <B>%s</B></H3>
97  <H3>Your name is: <B>%s</B></H3>
98  <H3>You can program in the following languages:</H3>
99  <UL>%s</UL>
100 <H3>Your uploaded file...<BR>
101 Name: <I>%s</I><BR>
102 Contents:</H3>
103 <PRE>%s</PRE>
104 Click <A HREF="%s"><B>here</B></A> to return to form.
105 </BODY></HTML>'''
106
107     def setCPPCookies(self):# tell client to store cookies
108         for eachCookie in self.cookies.keys():
109             print 'Set-Cookie: CPP%s=%s; path=/' % \
110                 (eachCookie, quote(self.cookies[eachCookie]))
111
```

(continued)

Example 20.8 Advanced CGI Application (`advcgi.py`) (continued)

```
112     def doResults(self):# display results page
113         MAXBYTES = 1024
114         langlist = ''
115         for eachLang in self.langs:
116           langlist = langlist + '<LI>%s<BR>' % eachLang
117
118         filedata = ''
119         while len(filedata) < MAXBYTES:# read file chunks
120             data = self.fp.readline()
121             if data == '': break
122             filedata += data
123          else:                      # truncate if too long
124             filedata += \
125              '... <B><I>(file truncated due to size)</I></B>'
126         self.fp.close()
127         if filedata == '':
128             filedata = \
129         <B><I>(file upload error or file not given)</I></B>'
130         filename = self.fn
131
132         if not self.cookies.has_key('user') or \
133                 self.cookies['user'] == '':
134             cookStatus = '<I>(cookie has not been set yet)</I>'
135             userCook = ''
136         else:
137             userCook = cookStatus = self.cookies['user']
138
139         self.cookies['info'] = join([self.who, \
140             join(self.langs, ','), filename], ':')
141         self.setCPPCookies()
142         print AdvCGI.header + AdvCGI.reshtml % \
143                 (cookStatus, self.who, langlist,
144                 filename, filedata, AdvCGI.url)
145
146     def go(self):              # determine which page to return
147         self.cookies = {}
148         self.error = ''
149         form = FieldStorage()
150         if form.keys() == []:
151             self.showForm()
152             return
153
154         if form.has_key('person'):
155             self.who = capwords(strip(form['person'].value))
156             if self.who == '':
157                 self.error = 'Your name is required. (blank)'
158         else:
159             self.error = 'Your name is required. (missing)'
160
161         if form.has_key('cookie'):
162             self.cookies['user'] = unquote(strip(\
163                             form['cookie'].value))
164         else:
165             self.cookies['user'] = ''
166
167         self.langs = []
```

Example 20.8 Advanced CGI Application (`advcgi.py`) (continued)

```
168     if form.has_key('lang'):
169         langdata = form['lang']
170         if type(langdata) == type([]):
171             for eachLang in langdata:
172                 self.langs.append(eachLang.value)
173             else:
174                 self.langs.append(langdata.value)
175         else:
176             self.error = 'At least one language required.'
177
178     if form.has_key('upfile'):
179         upfile = form["upfile"]
180         self.fn = upfile.filename or ''
181         if upfile.file:
182             self.fp = upfile.file
183         else:
184             self.fp = StringIO('(no data)')
185     else:
186         self.fp = StringIO('(no file)')
187         self.fn = ''
188
189     if not self.error:
190         self.doResults()
191     else:
192         self.showError()
193
194 if __name__ == '__main__':
195     page = AdvCGI()
196     page.go()
```

`doResults()` method puts together all the data and sends the output back to the client.

Lines 146–196

The script begins by instantiating an `AdvCGI` page object, then calls its `go()` method to start the ball rolling, in contrast to a strictly procedural programming process. The `go()` method contains the logic that reads all incoming data and decides which page to show.

The error page will be displayed if no name was given or if no languages were checked. The `showForm()` method is called to output the form if no input data were received, and the `doResults()` method is invoked otherwise to display the results page. Error situations are created by setting the `self.error` variable, which serves two purposes. It lets you set an error reason as a string and also serves as a flag to indicate that an error has occurred. If this value is not blank, the user will be forwarded to the error page.

Handling the person field (lines 154–159) is the same as we have seen in the past, a single key-value pair; however, collecting the language information is a bit trickier since we must check for either a (Mini)FieldStorage instance or a list of such instances. We will employ the familiar type() built-in function for this purpose. In the end, we will have a list of a single language name or many, depending on the user's selections.

The use of cookies (lines 161–165) to contain data illustrates how they can be used to avoid using any kind of CGI field pass-through. You will notice in the code that obtains such data that no CGI processing is invoked, meaning that the data do not come from the FieldStorage object. The data are passed to us by the Web client with each request and the values (user's chosen data as well as information to fill in a succeeding form with pre-existing information) are obtained from cookies.

Because the showResults() method receives the new input from the user, it has the responsibility of setting the cookies, i.e., by calling setCPP-Cookies(). showForm(), however, must read in the cookies' values in order to display a form page with the current user selections. This is done by its invocation of the getCPPCookies() method.

Finally, we get to the file upload processing (lines 178–187). Regardless of whether a file was actually uploaded, FieldStorage is given a file handle in the file attribute. On line 180, if there was no filename given, then we just set it to a blank string. If the value attribute is accessed, the entire contents of the file will be placed into value. As a better alternative, you can access the file pointer—the file attribute—and perhaps read only one line at a time or other kind of slower processing.

In our case, file uploads are only part of user submissions, so we simply pass on the file pointer to the doResults() function to extract the data from the file. doResults() will display only the first 1K of the file for space reasons and to show you that it is not necessary (or necessarily productive/useful) to display a four-megabyte binary file.

20.8 Web (HTTP) Servers

Until now, we have been discussing the use of Python in creating Web clients and performing tasks to aid Web servers in CGI request processing. We know (and saw earlier in Sections 20.2 and 20.3) that Python can be used to create both simple and complex Web clients. Complexity of CGI requests goes without saying.

However, we have yet to explore the creation of Web *servers*, and that is the focus of this section. If the Firefox, Mozilla, IE, Opera, Netscape, AOL, Safari, Camino, Epiphany, Galeon, and Lynx browsers are among the most popular Web clients, then what are the most common Web servers? They are Apache, Netscape, IIS, thttpd, Zeus, and Zope. In situations where these servers may be overkill for your desired application, Python can be used to create simple yet useful Web servers.

20.8.1 Creating Web Servers in Python

Since you have decided on building such an application, you will naturally be creating all the custom stuff, but all the base code you will need is already available in the Python Standard Library. To create a Web server, a base server and a "handler" are required.

The base (Web) server is a boilerplate item, a must have. Its role is to perform the necessary HTTP communication between client and server. The base server class is (appropriately) named `HTTPServer` and is found in the `BaseHTTPServer` module.

The handler is the piece of software that does the majority of the "Web serving." It processes the client request and returns the appropriate file, whether static or dynamically generated by CGI. The complexity of the handler determines the complexity of your Web server. The Python standard library provides three different handlers.

The most basic, plain, vanilla handler, named `BaseHTTPRequestHandler`, is found in the `BaseHTTPServer` module, along with the base Web server. Other than taking a client request, no other handling is implemented at all, so you have to do it all yourself, such as in our `myhttpd.py` server coming up.

The `SimpleHTTPRequestHandler`, available in the `SimpleHTTPServer` module, builds on `BaseHTTPRequestHandler` by implementing the standard GET and HEAD requests in a fairly straightforward manner. Still nothing sexy, but it gets the simple jobs done.

Finally, we have the `CGIHTTPRequestHandler`, available in the `CGIHTTPServer` module, which takes the `SimpleHTTPRequestHandler` and adds support for POST requests. It has the ability to call CGI scripts to perform the requested processing and can send the generated HTML back to the client.

The three modules and their classes are summarized in Table 20.6.

To be able to understand how the more advanced handlers found in the `SimpleHTTPServer` and `CGIHTTPServer` modules work, we will implement simple GET processing for a `BaseHTTPRequestHandler`.

Table 20.6 Web Server Modules and Classes	
Module	*Description*
`BaseHTTPServer`	Provides the base Web server and base handler classes, `HTTPServer` and `BaseHTTPRequestHandler`, respectively
`SimpleHTTPServer`	Contains the `SimpleHTTPRequestHandler` class to perform GET and HEAD requests
`CGIHTTPServer`	Contains the `CGIHTTPRequestHandler` class to process POST requests and perform CGI execution

In Example 20.9, we present the code for a fully working Web server, `myhttpd.py`.

This server subclasses `BaseHTTPRequestHandler` and consists of a single `do_GET()` method, which is called when the base server receives a GET request. We attempt to open the path passed in by the client and if present, return an "OK" status (200) and forward the downloaded Web page. If the file was not found, it returns a 404 status.

The `main()` function simply instantiates our Web server class and invokes it to run our familiar infinite server loop, shutting it down if interrupted by ^C or similar keystroke. If you have appropriate access and can run this server, you will notice that it displays loggable output, which will look something like this:

```
# myhttpd.py
Welcome to the machine... Press ^C once or twice to quit
localhost - - [26/Aug/2000 03:01:35] "GET /index.html HTTP/1.0" 200 -
localhost - - [26/Aug/2000 03:01:29] code 404, message File Not Found: /x.html
localhost - - [26/Aug/2000 03:01:29] "GET /dummy.html HTTP/1.0" 404 -
localhost - - [26/Aug/2000 03:02:03] "GET /hotlist.htm HTTP/1.0" 200 -
```

Of course, our simple little Web server is so simple, it cannot even process plain text files. We leave that as an exercise for the reader, which can be found at the end of the chapter.

As you can see, it doesn't take much to have a Web server up and running in pure Python. There is plenty more you can do to enhance the handlers to customize it to your specific application. Please review the Library Reference for more information on the modules (and their classes) discussed in this section.

Example 20.9 Simple Web Server (myhttpd.py)

This simple Web server can read GET requests, fetch a Web page (.html file) and return it to the calling client. It uses the `BaseHTTPRequestHandler` *found in* `BaseHTTPServer` *and implements the* `do_GET()` *method to enable processing of GET requests.*

```python
1  #!/usr/bin/env python
2
3  from os import curdir, sep
4  from BaseHTTPServer import \
5              BaseHTTPRequestHandler, HTTPServer
6
7  class MyHandler(BaseHTTPRequestHandler):
8
9      def do_GET(self):
10         try:
11             f = open(curdir + sep + self.path)
12             self.send_response(200)
13             self.send_header('Content-type',
14                             'text/html')
15             self.end_headers()
16             self.wfile.write(f.read())
17             f.close()
18         except IOError:
19             self.send_error(404,
20                 'File Not Found: %s' % self.path)
21
22 def main():
23     try:
24         server = HTTPServer(('', 80), MyHandler)
25         print 'Welcome to the machine...',
26         print 'Press ^C once or twice to quit.'
27         server.serve_forever()
28     except KeyboardInterrupt:
29         print '^C received, shutting down server'
30         server.socket.close()
31
32 if __name__ == '__main__':
33     main()
```

20.9 Related Modules

In Table 20.7, we present a list of modules which you may find useful for Web development. You may also wish to look at the Internet Client Programming in Chapter 17, as well as the Web services section of Chapter 23 for other modules that may be useful for Web applications.

Table 20.7 Web Programming Related Modules

Module/Package	Description
Web Applications	
cgi	Gets Common Gateway Interface (CGI) form data
cgitb[c]	Handles CGI tracebacks
htmllib	Older HTML parser for simple HTML files; HTML-Parser class extends from sgmllib.SGMLParser
HTMLparser[c]	Newer non-SGML-based parser for HTML and XHTML
htmlentitydefs	HTML general entity definitions
Cookie	Server-side cookies for HTTP state management
cookielib[e]	Cookie-handling classes for HTTP clients
webbrowser[b]	Controller: launches Web documents in a browser
sgmllib	Parses simple SGML files
robotparser[a]	Parses robots.txt files for URL "fetchability" analysis
httplib[a]	Used to create HTTP clients
XML Processing	
xmllib	(Outdated/deprecated) original simple XML parser
xml[b]	XML package featuring various parsers (some below)
xml.sax[b]	Simple API for XML (SAX) SAX2-compliant XML parser
xml.dom[b]	Document Object Model [DOM] XML parser
xml.etree[f]	Tree-oriented XML parser based on the Element flexible container object
xml.parsers.expat[b]	Interface to the non-validating Expat XML parser
xmlrpclib[c]	Client support for XML Remote Procedure Call (RPC) via HTTP

Table 20.7 Web Programming Related Modules (continued)

Module/Package	Description
XML Processing	
SimpleXMLRPCServer[c]	Basic framework for Python XML-RPC servers
DocXMLRPCServer[d]	Framework for self-documenting XML-RPC servers
Web Servers	
BaseHTTPServer	Abstract class with which to develop Web servers
SimpleHTTPServer	Serve the simplest HTTP requests (HEAD and GET)
CGIHTTPServer	In addition to serving Web files like SimpleHTTPS-ervers, can also process CGI (HTTP POST) requests
wsgiref[f]	Standard interface between Web servers and Python Web application
3rd party packages (not in standard library)	
HTMLgen	CGI helper converts Python objects into valid HTML http://starship.python.net/crew/friedrich/HTMLgen/html/main.html
BeautifulSoup	HTML and XML parser and screen-scraper http://crummy.com/software/BeautifulSoup
Mail Client Protocols	
poplib	Use to create POP3 clients
imaplib	Use to create IMAP4 clients
Mail and MIME Processing and Data Encoding Formats	
email[c]	Package for managing e-mail messages, including MIME and other RFC2822-based message
mailbox	Classes for mailboxes of e-mail messages
mailcap	Parses mailcap files to obtain MIME application delegations

(continued)

Table 20.7 Web Programming Related Modules (continued)

Module/Package	Description
Mail and MIME Processing and Data Encoding Formats	
mimetools	Provides functions for manipulating MIME-encoded messages
mimetypes	Provides MIME-type associations
MimeWriter	Generates MIME-encoded multipart files
multifile	Can parse multipart MIME-encoded files
quopri	En-/decodes data using quoted-printable encoding
rfc822	Parses RFC822-compliant e-mail headers
smtplib	Uses to create SMTP (Simple Mail Transfer Protocol) clients
base64	En-/decodes data using base64 encoding
binascii	En-/decodes data using base64, binhex, or uu (modules)
binhex	En-/decodes data using binhex4 encoding
uu	En-/decodes data using uuencode encoding
Internet Protocols	
httplib[a]	Used to create HTTP clients
ftplib	Used to create FTP (File Transfer Protocol) clients
gopherlib	Used to create Gopher clients
telnetlib	Used to create Telnet clients
nntplib	Used to create NNTP (Network News Transfer Protocol [Usenet]) clients

a.   New in Python 1.6.
b.   New in Python 2.0.
c.   New in Python 2.2.
d.   New in Python 2.3.
e.   New in Python 2.4.
f.   New in Python 2.5.

20.10 Exercises

20–1. *urllib Module and Files*. Update the `friends3.py` script so that it stores names and corresponding number of friends into a two-column text file on disk and continues to add names each time the script is run.

Extra Credit: Add code to dump the contents of such a file to the Web browser (in HTML format). Additional Extra Credit: Create a link that clears all the names in this file.

20–2. *urllib Module*. Write a program that takes a user-input URL (either a Web page or an FTP file, i.e., http://python.org or ftp://ftp.python.org/pub/python/README), and downloads it to your machine with the same filename (or modified name similar to the original if it is invalid on your system). Web pages (HTTP) should be saved as .htm or .html files, and FTP'd files should retain their extension.

20–3. *urllib Module*. Rewrite the `grabWeb.py` script of Example 11.,4, which downloads a Web page and displays the first and last non-blank lines of the resulting HTML file so that you use `urlopen()` instead of `urlretrieve()` to process the data directly (as opposed to downloading the entire file first before processing it).

20–4. *URLs and Regular Expressions*. Your browser may save your favorite Web site URLs as a "bookmarks" HTML file (Mozilla-flavored browsers do this) or as a set of .URL files in a "favorites" directory (IE does this). Find your browser's method of recording your "hot links" and the location of where and how they stored. Without altering any of the files, strip the URLs and names of the corresponding Web sites (if given) and produce a two-column list of names and links as output, and storing this data into a disk file. Truncate site names or URLs to keep each line of output within 80 columns in size.

20–5. *URLs, urllib Module, Exceptions, and REs*. As a follow-up problem to the previous one, add code to your script to test each of your favorite links. Report back a list of dead links (and their names), i.e., Web sites that are no longer active or a Web page that has been removed. Only output and save to disk the still-valid links.

20–6. *Error Checking*. The `friends3.py` script reports an error if
no radio button was selected to indicate the number of friends.
Update the CGI script to also report an error if no name (e.g.,
blank or whitespace) is entered.

Extra Credit: We have so far explored only server-side error
checking. Explore JavaScript programming and implement
client-side error checking by creating JavaScript code to check
for both error situations so that these errors are stopped before
they reach the server.

Problems 20–7 to 20–10 below pertain to *Web server access log files and
regular expressions*. Web servers (and their administrators) generally have to
maintain an access log file (usually `logs/access_log` from the main
Web, server directory) which tracks requests file. Over a period of time, such
files get large and either need to be stored or truncated. Why not save only
the pertinent information and delete the files to conserve disk space? The
exercises below are designed to give you some exercise with REs and how
they can be used to help archive and analyze Web server data.

20–7. Count how many of each type of request (GET versus POST)
exist in the log file.

20–8. Count the successful page/data downloads: Display all links
that resulted in a return code of 200 (OK [no error]) and how
many times each link was accessed.

20–9. Count the errors: Show all links that resulted in errors
(return codes in the 400s or 500s) and how many times each
link was accessed.

20–10. Track IP addresses: For each IP address, output a list of each
page/data downloaded and how many times that link was
accessed.

20–11. *Simple CGI*. Create a "Comments" or "Feedback" page for
a Web site. Take user feedback via a form, process the data in
your script, and return a "thank you" screen.

20–12. *Simple CGI*. Create a Web guestbook. Accept a name, an
e-mail address, and a journal entry from a user and log it to
a file (format of your choice). Like the previous problem,
return a "thanks for filling out a guestbook entry" page. Also
provide a link that allows users to view guestbooks.

20–13. *Web Browser Cookies and Web site Registration*. Update
your solution to Exercise 20–4. So your user-password information should now pertain to Web site registration instead of
a simple text-based menu system.

Extra Credit: familiarize yourself with setting Web browser cookies and maintain a login session for 4 hours from the last successful login.

20–14. *Web Clients*. Port Example 20.1, `crawl.py`, the Web crawler, to using the `HTMLParser` module or the BeautifulSoup parsing system.

20–15. *Errors*. What happens when a CGI script crashes? How can the `cgitb` module be helpful?

20–16. *CGI, File Updates, and Zip Files*. Create a CGI application that not only saves files to the server's disk, but also intelligently unpacks Zip files (or other archive) into a subdirectory named after the archive file.

20–17. *Zope, Plone, TurboGears, Django*. Investigate each of these complex Web development platforms and create one simple application in each.

20–18. *Web Database Application*. Think of a database schema you want to provide as part of a Web database application. For this multi-user application, you want to provide everyone read access to the entire contents of the database, but perhaps only write access to each individual. One example may be an "address book" for your family and relatives. Each family member, once successfully logged in, is presented with a Web page with several options, add an entry, view my entry, update my entry, remove or delete my entry, and view all entries (entire database).

Design a `UserEntry` class and create a database entry for each instance of this class. You may use any solution created for any previous problem to implement the registration framework. Finally, you may use any type of storage mechanism for your database, either a relational database such as MySQL or some of the simpler Python persistent storage modules such as `anydbm` or `shelve`.

20–19. *Electronic Commerce Engine*. Use the classes created for your solution to Exercise 13–11 and add some product inventory to create a potential electronic commerce Web site. Be sure your Web application also supports multiple customers and provides registration for each user.

20–20. *Dictionaries and `cgi` module*. As you know, the `cgi.FieldStorage()` method returns a dictionary-like object containing the key-value pairs of the submitted CGI variables. You can use methods such as `keys()` and has_key() for such objects. In Python 1.5, a get() method was added to dictionaries which returned the value of the requested key, or the default value for a non-existent key. FieldStorage objects do not have such a method. Let's say we grab the form in the usual manner of:

```
form = cgi.FieldStorage()
```

Add a similar get() method to class definition in cgi.py (you can rename it to mycgi.py or something like that) such that code that looks like this:

```
if form.has_key('who'):
    who = form['who'].value
else:
    who = '(no name submitted)'
```

. . . can be replaced by a single line which makes forms even more like a dictionary:

```
howmany = form.get('who', '(no name submitted)')
```

20–21. *Creating Web Servers.* Our code for myhttpd.py in Section 20.7 is only able to read HTML files and return them to the calling client. Add support for plain text files with the ".txt" ending. Be sure that you return the correct MIME type of "text/plain."

Extra credit: add support for JPEG files ending with either ".jpg" or ".jpeg" and having a MIME type of "image/jpeg."

20–22. *Advanced Web Clients.* URLs given as input to crawl.py must have the leading "http://" protocol indicator and top-level URLs must contain a trailing slash, i.e., http://www.prenhallprofessional.com/. Make crawl.py more robust by allowing the user to input just the hostname (without the protocol part [make it assume HTTP]) and also make the trailing slash optional. For example, www.prenhallprofessional.com should now be acceptable input.

20–23. *Advanced Web Clients.* Update the crawl.py script in Section 20.3 to also download links that use the "ftp:" scheme. All "mailto:" links are ignored by crawl.py. Add support to ensure that it also ignores "telnet:", "news:", "gopher:", and "about:" links.

20–24. *Advanced Web Clients.* The crawl.py script in Section 20.3 only downloads .html files via links found in Web pages at the same site and does not handle/save images that are also valid "files" for those pages. It also does not handle servers that are susceptible to URLs that are missing the trailing slash (/). Add a pair of classes to `crawl.py` to deal with these problems.

A `My404UrlOpener` class should subclass `urllib.FancyURLOpener` and consist of a single method, `http_error_404()` which determines if a 404 error was reached using a URL without a trailing slash. If so, it adds the slash and retries the request again (and only once). If it still fails, return a real 404 error. You must set `urllib._urlopener` with an instance of this class so that `urllib` uses it.

Create another class called `LinkImageParser`, which derives from `htmllib.HTMLParser`. This class should contain a constructor to call the base class constructor as well as initialize a list for the image files parsed from Web pages. The `handle_image()` method should be overridden to add image filenames to the image list (instead of discarding them like the current base class method does).

DATABASE PROGRAMMING

Chapter Topics

- Introduction
- Databases and Python RDBMSs, ORMs, and Python
- Database Application Programmer's Interface (DB-API)
- Relational Databases (RDBMSs)
- Object-Relational Mappers (ORMs)
- Related Modules
- Exercises

Chapter 21

I n this chapter, we discuss how to communicate with databases from Python. Earlier, we discussed simplistic persistent storage, but in many cases, a full-fledged relational database management system (RDBMS) is required for your application.

21.1 Introduction

21.1.1 Persistent Storage

In any application, there is a need for persistent storage. Generally, there are three basic storage mechanisms: files, a relational database system (RDBMS), or some sort of hybrid, i.e., an API (application programmer interface) that "sits on top of" one of those existing systems, an object relational mapper (ORM), file manager, spreadsheet, configuration file, etc.

In an earlier chapter, we discussed persistent storage using both plain file access as well as a Python and DBM overlay on top of files, i.e., *dbm, dbhash/bsddb files, shelve (combination of pickle and DBM), and using their dictionary-like object interface. This chapter will focus on using RDBMSs for the times when files or writing your own system does not suffice for larger projects.

21.1.2 Basic Database Operations and SQL

Before we dig into databases and how to use them with Python, we want to present a quick introduction (or review if you have some experience) to some elementary database concepts and the Structured Query Language (SQL).

Underlying Storage

Databases usually have a fundamental persistent storage using the file system, i.e., normal operating system files, special operating system files, and even raw disk partitions.

User Interface

Most database systems provide a command-line tool with which to issue SQL commands or queries. There are also some GUI tools that use the command-line clients or the database client library, giving users a much nicer interface.

Databases

An RDBMS can usually manage multiple databases, e.g., sales, marketing, customer support, etc., all on the same server (if the RDBMS is server-based; simpler systems are usually not). In the examples we will look at in this chapter, MySQL is an example of a server-based RDBMS because there is a server process running continuously waiting for commands while neither SQLite nor Gadfly have running servers.

Components

The *table* is the storage abstraction for databases. Each *row* of data will have fields that correspond to database *columns*. The set of table definitions of columns and data types per table all put together define the database *schema*.

Databases are *created* and *dropped*. The same is true for tables. Adding new rows to a database is called *inserting*, changing existing rows in a table is called *updating*, and removing existing rows in a table is called *deleting*. These actions are usually referred to as database *commands* or *operations*. Requesting rows from a database with optional criteria is called *querying*.

When you query a database, you can *fetch* all of the results (rows) at once, or just iterate slowly over each resulting row. Some databases use the concept of a *cursor* for issuing SQL commands, queries, and grabbing results, either all at once or one row at a time.

SQL

Database commands and queries are given to a database by SQL. Not all databases use SQL, but the majority of relational databases do. Here are some examples of SQL commands. Most databases are configured to be case-insensitive, especially database commands. The accepted style is to use CAPS for database keywords. Most command-line programs require a trailing semicolon (;) to terminate a SQL statement.

Creating a Database

```
CREATE DATABASE test;
GRANT ALL ON test.* to user(s);
```

The first line creates a database named "test," and assuming that you are a database administrator, the second line can be used to grant permissions to specific users (or all of them) so that they can perform the database operations below.

Using a Database

```
USE test;
```

If you logged into a database system without choosing which database you want to use, this simple statement allows you to specify one with which to perform database operations.

Dropping a Database

```
DROP DATABASE test;
```

This simple statement removes all the tables and data from the database and deletes it from the system.

Creating a Table

```
CREATE TABLE users (login VARCHAR(8), uid INT, prid INT);
```

This statement creates a new table with a string column `login` and a pair of integer fields `uid` and `prid`.

Dropping a Table

```
DROP TABLE users;
```

This simple statement drops a database table along with all its data.

Inserting a Row

```
INSERT INTO users VALUES('leanna', 311, 1);
```

You can insert a new row in a database with the INSERT statement. Specify the table and the values that go into each field. For our example, the string 'leanna' goes into the login field, and 311 and 1 to uid and prid, respectively.

Updating a Row

```
UPDATE users SET prid=4 WHERE prid=2;
UPDATE users SET prid=1 WHERE uid=311;
```

To change existing table rows, you use the UPDATE statement. Use SET for the columns that are changing and provide any criteria for determining which rows should change. In the first example, all users with a "project ID" or prid of 2 will be moved to project #4. In the second example, we take one user (with a UID of 311) and move them to project #1.

Deleting a Row

```
DELETE FROM users WHERE prid=%d;
DELETE FROM users;
```

To delete a table row, use the DELETE FROM command, give the table you want to delete rows from, and any optional criteria. Without it, as in the second example, all rows will be deleted.

Now that you are up to speed on basic database concepts, it should make following the rest of the chapter and its examples much easier. If you need additional help, there are plenty of database books out in the market that you can check out.

21.1.3 Databases and Python

We are going to cover the Python database API and look at how to access relational databases from Python, either directly through a database interface, or via an ORM, and how you can accomplish the same task but without necessarily having to give explicitly commands in SQL.

Topics such as database principles, concurrency, schema, atomicity, integrity, recovery, proper complex left JOINs, triggers, query optimization, transactions, stored procedures, etc., are all outside the scope of this text, and we will not be discussing these in this chapter other than direct use from a Python application. There are plenty of resources you can refer to for general information. Rather, we will present how to store and retrieve data to/from RDBMSs while playing within a Python framework. You can then decide which is best for your current project or application and be able to study sample code that can get you started instantly. The goal is to get you up to speed as quickly as possible if you need to integrate your Python application with some sort of database system.

We are also breaking out of our mode of covering only the "batteries included" features of the Python standard library. While our original goal was to play only in that arena, it has become clear that being able to work with databases is really a core component of everyday application development in the Python world.

As a software engineer, you can probably only make it so far in your career without having to learn something about databases: how to use one (command-line and/or GUI interfaces), how to pull data out of one using the Structured Query Language (SQL), perhaps how to add or update information in a database, etc. If Python is your programming tool, then a lot of the hard work has already been done for you as you add database access to your Python universe. We first describe what the Python "DB-API" is, then give examples of database interfaces that conform to this standard.

We will give some examples using popular open source relational database management systems (RDBMSs). However, we will not include discussions of open source vs. commercial products, etc. Adapting to those other RDBMS systems should be fairly straightforward. A special mention will be given to Aaron Watters's Gadfly database, a simple RDBMS written completely in Python.

The way to access a database from Python is via an *adapter*. An adapter is basically a Python module that allows you to interface to a relational database's client library, usually in C. It is recommended that all Python adapters conform to the Python DB-SIG's Application Programmer Interface (API). This is the first major topic of this chapter.

Figure 21.1 illustrates the layers involved in writing a Python database application, with and without an ORM. As you can see, the DB-API is your interface to the C libraries of the database client.

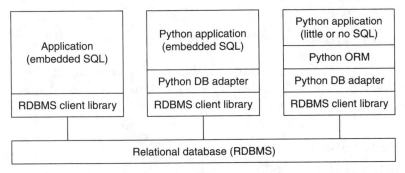

Figure 21-1 Multitiered communication between application and database. The first box is generally a C/C++ program while DB-API compliant adapters let you program applications in Python. ORMs can simplify an application by handling all of the database-specific details.

21.2 Python Database Application Programmer's Interface (DB-API)

Where can one find the interfaces necessary to talk to a database? Simple. Just go to the database topics section at the main Python Web site. There you will find links to the full and current DB-API (version 2.0), existing database modules, documentation, the special interest group, etc. Since its inception, the DB-API has been moved into PEP 249. (This PEP obsoletes the old DB-API 1.0 specification which is PEP 248.) What is the DB-API?

The API is a specification that states a set of required objects and database access mechanisms to provide consistent access across the various database adapters and underlying database systems. Like most community-based efforts, the API was driven by strong need.

In the "old days," we had a scenario of many databases and many people implementing their own database adapters. It was a wheel that was being reinvented over and over again. These databases and adapters were implemented at different times by different people without any consistency of functionality. Unfortunately, this meant that application code using such interfaces also had to be customized to which database module they chose to use, and any changes to that interface also meant updates were needed in the application code.

A special interest group (SIG) for Python database connectivity was formed, and eventually, an API was born . . . the DB-API version 1.0. The API provides for a consistent interface to a variety of relational databases, and porting code between different databases is much simpler, usually only requiring tweaking several lines of code. You will see an example of this later on in this chapter.

21.2.1 Module Attributes

The DB-API specification mandates that the features and attributes listed below must be supplied. A DB-API-compliant module must define the global attributes as shown in Table 21.1.

Data Attributes

apilevel

This string (not float) indicates the highest version of the DB-API the module is compliant with, i.e., "1.0", "2.0", etc. If absent, "1.0" should be assumed as the default value.

Table 21.1 DB-API Module Attributes	
Attribute	*Description*
apilevel	Version of DB-API module is compliant with
threadsafety	Level of thread safety of this module
paramstyle	SQL statement parameter style of this module
connect()	Connect() function
(Various exceptions)	*(See Table 21.4)*

threadsafety

This an integer with these possible values:

- 0: Not threadsafe, so threads should not share the module at all
- 1: Minimally threadsafe: threads can share the module but not connections
- 2: Moderately threadsafe: threads can share the module and connections but not cursors
- 3: Fully threadsafe: threads can share the module, connections, and cursors

If a resource is shared, a synchronization primitive such as a spin lock or semaphore is required for atomic-locking purposes. Disk files and global variables are not reliable for this purpose and may interfere with standard mutex operation. See the threading module or the chapter on multithreaded programming (Chapter 16) on how to use a lock.

paramstyle

The API supports a variety of ways to indicate how parameters should be integrated into an SQL statement that is eventually sent to the server for execution. This argument is just a string that specifies the form of string substitution you will use when building rows for a query or command (see Table 21.2).

Function Attribute(s)

connect() Function access to the database is made available through Connection objects. A compliant module has to implement a connect() function, which creates and returns a Connection object. Table 21.3 shows the arguments to connect().

Table 21.2 `paramstyle` Database Parameter Styles

Parameter Style	Description	Example
numeric	Numeric positional style	`WHERE name=:1`
named	Named style	`WHERE name=:name`
pyformat	Python dictionary `printf()` format conversion	`WHERE name=%(name)s`
qmark	Question mark style	`WHERE name=?`
format	ANSI C `printf()` format conversion	`WHERE name=%s`

You can pass in database connection information as a string with multiple parameters (DSN) or individual parameters passed as positional arguments (if you know the exact order), or more likely, keyworded arguments. Here is an example of using `connect()` from PEP 249:

```
connect(dsn='myhost:MYDB',user='guido',password='234$')
```

The use of DSN versus individual parameters is based primarily on the system you are connecting to. For example, if you are using an API like ODBC or JDBC, you would likely be using a DSN, whereas if you are working directly with a database, then you are more likely to issue separate login parameters. Another reason for this is that most database adapters have not implemented support for DSN. Below are some examples of non-DSN

Table 21.3 `connect()` Function Attributes

Parameter	Description
user	Username
password	Password
host	Hostname
database	Database name
dsn	Data source name

`connect()` calls. Note that not all adapters have implemented the specification exactly, e.g., `MySQLdb` uses `db` instead of `database`.

- `MySQLdb.connect(host='dbserv', db='inv', user='smith')`
- `PgSQL.connect(database='sales')`
- `psycopg.connect(database='template1', user='pgsql')`
- `gadfly.dbapi20.connect('csrDB', '/usr/local/database')`
- `sqlite3.connect('marketing/test')`

Exceptions

Exceptions that should also be included in the compliant module as globals are shown in Table 21.4.

21.2.2   *Connection* **Objects**

Connections are how your application gets to talk to the database. They represent the fundamental communication mechanism by which commands are sent to the server and results returned. Once a connection has been established (or a pool of connections), you create cursors to send requests to and receive replies from the database.

Table 21.4 DB-API Exception Classes

Exception	*Description*
`Warning`	Root warning exception class
`Error`	Root error exception class
`InterfaceError`	Database interface (not database) error
`DatabaseError`	Database error
`DataError`	Problems with the processed data
`OperationalError`	Error during database operation execution
`IntegrityError`	Database relational integrity error
`InternalError`	Error that occurs within the database
`ProgrammingError`	SQL command failed
`NotSupportedError`	Unsupported operation occurred

Methods

`Connection` objects are not required to have any data attributes but should define the methods shown in Table 21.5.

When `close()` is used, the same connection cannot be used again without running into an exception.

The `commit()` method is irrelevant if the database does not support transactions or if it has an auto-commit feature that has been enabled. You can implement separate methods to turn auto-commit off or on if you wish. Since this method is required as part of the API, databases that do not have the concept of transactions should just implement "pass" for this method.

Like `commit()`, `rollback()` only makes sense if transactions are supported in the database. After execution, `rollback()` should leave the database in the same state as it was when the transaction began. According to PEP 249, "Closing a connection without committing the changes first will cause an implicit rollback to be performed."

If the RDBMS does not support cursors, `cursor()` should still return an object that faithfully emulates or imitates a real cursor object. These are just the minimum requirements. Each individual adapter developer can always add special attributes specifically for their interface or database.

It is also recommended but not required for adapter writers to make all database module exceptions (see above) available via a connection. If not, then it is assumed that `Connection` objects will throw the corresponding module-level exception. Once you have completed using your connection and cursors closed, you should `commit()` any operations and `close()` your connection.

Table 21.5 `Connection` **Object Methods**

Method Name	Description
`close()`	Close database connection
`commit()`	Commit current transaction
`rollback()`	Cancel current transaction
`cursor()`	Create (and return) a cursor or cursor-like object using this connection
`errorhandler(cxn, cur, errcls, errval)`	Serves as a handler for given connection cursor

21.2.3 *Cursor* Objects

Once you have a connection, you can start talking to the database. As we mentioned above in the introductory section, a cursor lets a user issue database commands and retrieve rows resulting from queries. A Python DB-API cursor object functions as a cursor for you, even if cursors are not supported in the database. In this case, the database adapter creator must implement CURSOR objects so that they act like cursors. This keeps your Python code consistent when you switch between database systems that have or do not have cursor support.

Once you have created a cursor, you can execute a query or command (or multiple queries and commands) and retrieve one or more rows from the results set. Table 21.6 shows data attributes and methods that cursor objects have.

Table 21.6 Cursor Object Attributes

Object Attribute	Description
arraysize	Number of rows to fetch at a time with fetchmany(); defaults to 1
connection	Connection that created this cursor (optional)
description	Returns cursor activity (7-item tuples): (name, type_code, display_size, internal_size, precision, scale, null_ok); only name and type_code are required
lastrowid	Row ID of last modified row (optional; if row IDs not supported, default to None)
rowcount	Number of rows that the last execute*() produced or affected
callproc(func[, args])	Call a stored procedure
close()	Close cursor
execute(op[, args])	Execute a database query or command
executemany(op, args)	Like execute() and map() combined; prepare and execute a database query or command over given arguments

Table 21.6 Cursor **Object Attributes (continued)**

Object Attribute	Description
fetchone()	Fetch next row of query result
fetchmany ([*size*=cur- sor.arraysize])	Fetch next size rows of query result
fetchall()	Fetch all (remaining) rows of a query result
__iter__()	Create iterator object from this cursor (optional; also see next())
messages	List of messages (set of tuples) received from the database for cursor execution (optional)
next()	Used by iterator to fetch next row of query result (optional; like fetchone(), also see __iter__())
nextset()	Move to next results set (if supported)
rownumber	Index of cursor (by row, 0-based) in current result set (optional)
setinput- sizes(*sizes*)	Set maximum input size allowed (required but imple- mentation optional)
setoutput- size(*size*[,*col*])	Set maximum buffer size for large column fetches (required but implementation optional)

The most critical attributes of cursor objects are the execute*() and the fetch*() methods . . . all the service requests to the database are performed by these. The arraysize data attribute is useful in setting a default size for fetchmany(). Of course, closing the cursor is a good thing, and if your data-base supports stored procedures, then you will be using callproc().

21.2.4 Type Objects and Constructors

Oftentimes, the interface between two different systems are the most fragile. This is seen when converting Python objects to C types and vice versa. Similarly, there is also a fine line between Python objects and native database objects. As a programmer writing to Python's DB-API, the parameters you send to a database are given as strings, but the database may need to convert it to a variety of different, supported data types that are correct for any particular query.

For example, should the Python string be converted to a VARCHAR, a TEXT, a BLOB, or a raw BINARY object, or perhaps a DATE or TIME object if that is what the string is supposed to be? Care must be taken to provide database input in the expected format, so because of this another requirement of the DB-API is to create constructors that build special objects that can easily be converted to the appropriate database objects. Table 21.7 describes classes that can be used for this purpose. SQL NULL values are mapped to and from Python's NULL object, `None`.

Table 21.7 Type Objects and Constructors

Type Object	Description
Date(*yr,mo,dy*)	Object for a date value
Time(*hr,min,sec*)	Object for a time value
Timestamp(*yr,mo,dy,hr,min,sec*)	Object for a timestamp value
DateFromTicks(*ticks*)	Date object given number of seconds since the epoch
TimeFromTicks(*ticks*)	Time object given number of seconds since the epoch
TimestampFromTicks(*ticks*)	Timestamp object given number of seconds since the epoch
Binary(*string*)	Object for a binary (long) string value
STRING	Object describing string-based columns, e.g., VARCHAR
BINARY	Object describing (long) binary columns, i.e., RAW, BLOB
NUMBER	Object describing numeric columns
DATETIME	Object describing date/time columns
ROWID	Object describing "row ID" columns

Changes to API Between Versions

Several important changes were made when the DB-API was revised from version 1.0 (1996) to 2.0 (1999):

- Required dbi module removed from API
- Type objects were updated
- New attributes added to provide better database bindings
- callproc() semantics and return value of execute() redefined
- Conversion to class-based exceptions

Since version 2.0 was published, some of the additional optional DB-API extensions that you read about above were added in 2002. There have been no other significant changes to the API since it was published. Continuing discussions of the API occur on the DB-SIG mailing list. Among the topics brought up over the last 5 years include the possibilities for the next version of the DB-API, tentatively named DB-API 3.0. These include the following:

- Better return value for nextset() when there is a new result set
- Switch from float to Decimal
- Improved flexibility and support for parameter styles
- Prepared statements or statement caching
- Refine the transaction model
- State the role of API with respect to portability
- Add unit testing

If you have strong feelings about the API, feel free to participate and join in the discussion. Here are some references you may find handy.

- http://python.org/topics/database
- http://www.linuxjournal.com/article/2605
- http://wiki.python.org/moin/DbApi3

21.2.5 Relational Databases

So, you are now ready to go. A burning question must be, "Interfaces to which database systems are available to me in Python?" That inquiry is similar to, "Which platforms is Python available for?" The answer is, "Pretty much all of them." Following is a list that is comprehensive but not exhaustive:

Commercial RDBMSs

- Informix
- Sybase
- Oracle
- MS SQL Server
- DB/2
- SAP
- Interbase
- Ingres

Open Source RDBMSs

- MySQL
- PostgreSQL
- SQLite
- Gadfly

Database APIs

- JDBC
- ODBC

To find a current list of what databases are supported, check out:

http://python.org/topics/database/modules.html

21.2.6 Databases and Python: Adapters

For each of the databases supported, there exists one or more adapters that let you connect to the target database system from Python. Some databases, such as Sybase, SAP, Oracle, and SQLServer, have more than one adapter available. The best thing to do is to find out which ones fit your needs best. Your questions for each candidate may include: how good its performance is, how useful is its documentation and/or Web site, whether it has an active community or not, what the overall quality and stability of the driver is, etc. You have to keep in mind that most adapters provide just the basic necessities to get you connected to the database. It is the extras that you may be looking for. Keep in mind that you are responsible for higher-level code like threading and thread management as well as management of database connection pools, etc.

If you are squeamish and want less hands-on—for example, if you wish to do as little SQL or database administration as much as possible—then you may wish to consider object-relational mappers, covered later on in this chapter.

Let us now look at some examples of how to use an adapter module to talk to a relational database. The real secret is in setting up the connection. Once you have this and use the DB-API objects, attributes, and object methods, your core code should be pretty much the same regardless of which adapter and RDBMS you use.

21.2.7 Examples of Using Database Adapters

First, let us look at a some sample code, from creating a database to creating a table and using it. We present examples using MySQL, PostgreSQL, and SQLite.

MySQL

We will use MySQL as the example here, along with the only MySQL Python adapter: MySQLdb, aka MySQL-python. In the various bits of code, we will also show you (deliberately) examples of error situations so that you have an idea of what to expect, and what you may wish to create handlers for.

We first log in as an administrator to create a database and grant permissions, then log back in as a normal client.

```
>>> import MySQLdb
>>> cxn = MySQLdb.connect(user='root')
>>> cxn.query('DROP DATABASE test')
Traceback (most recent call last):
  File "<stdin>", line 1, in ?
_mysql_exceptions.OperationalError: (1008, "Can't drop
database 'test'; database doesn't exist")
>>> cxn.query('CREATE DATABASE test')
>>> cxn.query("GRANT ALL ON test.* to ''@'localhost'")
>>> cxn.commit()
>>> cxn.close()
```

In the code above, we did not use a cursor. Some adapters have Connection objects, which can execute SQL queries with the query() method, but not all. We recommend you either not use it or check your adapter to make sure it is available.

The commit() was optional for us as auto-commit is turned on by default in MySQL. We then connect back to the new database as a regular user, create a table, and perform the usual queries and commands using SQL to get our job done via Python. This time we use cursors and their execute() method.

The next set of interactions shows us creating a table. An attempt to create it again (without first dropping it) results in an error.

```
>>> cxn = MySQLdb.connect(db='test')
>>> cur = cxn.cursor()
>>> cur.execute('CREATE TABLE users(login VARCHAR(8), uid INT)')
0L
```

Now we will insert a few rows into the database and query them out.

```
>>> cur.execute("INSERT INTO users VALUES('john', 7000)")
1L
>>> cur.execute("INSERT INTO users VALUES('jane', 7001)")
1L
>>> cur.execute("INSERT INTO users VALUES('bob', 7200)")
1L
>>> cur.execute("SELECT * FROM users WHERE login LIKE 'j%'")
2L
>>> for data in cur.fetchall():
...     print '%s\t%s' % data
...
john    7000
jane    7001
```

The last bit features updating the table, either updating or deleting rows.

```
>>> cur.execute("UPDATE users SET uid=7100 WHERE uid=7001")
1L
>>> cur.execute("SELECT * FROM users")
3L
>>> for data in cur.fetchall():
...     print '%s\t%s' % data
...
john    7000
jane    7100
bob     7200
>>> cur.execute('DELETE FROM users WHERE login="bob"')
1L
>>> cur.execute('DROP TABLE users')
0L
>>> cur.close()
>>> cxn.commit()
>>> cxn.close()
```

MySQL is one of the most popular open source databases in the world, and it is no surprise that a Python adapter is available for it. Keep in mind that no database modules are available in the Python standard library—all adapters are third-party packages that have to be downloaded and installed separately from Python. Please see the References section toward the end of the chapter to find out how to download it.

PostgreSQL

Another popular open source database is PostgreSQL. Unlike MySQL, there are no less than three current Python adapters available for Postgres: psycopg, PyPgSQL, and PyGreSQL. A fourth, PoPy, is now defunct, having contributed its project to combine with that of PyGreSQL back in 2003. Each of the three remaining adapters has its own characteristics, strengths, and weaknesses, so it would be a good idea to practice due diligence to determine which is right for you.

The good news is that the interfaces are similar enough that you can create an application that, say, measures the performance between all three (if that is a metric that is important to you). Here we show you the setup code to get a `Connection` object for each:

psycopg

```
>>> import psycopg
>>> cxn = psycopg.connect(user='pgsql')
```

PyPgSQL

```
>>> from pyPgSQL import PgSQL
>>> cxn = PgSQL.connect(user='pgsql')
```

PyGreSQL

```
>>> import pgdb
>>> cxn = pgdb.connect(user='pgsql')
```

Now comes some generic code that will work for all three adapters.

```
>>> cur = cxn.cursor()
>>> cur.execute('SELECT * FROM pg_database')
>>> rows = cur.fetchall()
>>> for i in rows:
...   print i
>>> cur.close()
>>> cxn.commit()
>>> cxn.close()
```

Finally, you can see how their outputs are slightly different from one another.

PyPgSQL

```
sales
template1
template0
```

psycopg

```
('sales', 1, 0, 0, 1, 17140, '140626', '3221366099',
'', None, None)
('template1', 1, 0, 1, 1, 17140, '462', '462', '', None,
'{pgsql=C*T*/pgsql}')
('template0', 1, 0, 1, 0, 17140, '462', '462', '', None,
'{pgsql=C*T*/pgsql}')
```

PyGreSQL

```
['sales', 1, 0, False, True, 17140L, '140626',
'3221366099', '', None, None]
['template1', 1, 0, True, True, 17140L, '462', '462',
'', None, '{pgsql=C*T*/pgsql}']
['template0', 1, 0, True, False, 17140L, '462',
'462', '', None, '{pgsql=C*T*/pgsql}']
```

SQLite

For extremely simple applications, using files for persistent storage usually suffices, but the most complex and data-driven applications demand a full relational database. SQLite targets the intermediate systems and indeed is a hybrid of the two. It is extremely lightweight and fast, plus it is serverless and requires little or no administration.

SQLite has seen a rapid growth in popularity, and it is available on many platforms. With the introduction of the `pysqlite` database adapter in Python 2.5 as the `sqlite3` module, this marks the first time that the Python standard library has featured a database adapter in any release.

2.5

It was bundled with Python not because it was favored over other databases and adapters, but because it is simple, uses files (or memory) as its backend store like the DBM modules do, does not require a server, and does not have licensing issues. It is simply an alternative to other similar persistent storage solutions included with Python but which happens to have a SQL interface.

Having a module like this in the standard library allows users to develop rapidly in Python using SQLite, then migrate to a more powerful RDBMS such as MySQL, PostgreSQL, Oracle, or SQL Server for production purposes if this is their intention. Otherwise, it makes a great solution to stay with for those who do not need all that horsepower.

Although the database adapter is now provided in the standard library, you still have to download the actual database software yourself. However, once you have installed it, all you need to do is start up Python (and import the adapter) to gain immediate access:

```
>>> import sqlite3
>>> cxn = sqlite3.connect('sqlite_test/test')
>>> cur = cxn.cursor()
>>> cur.execute('CREATE TABLE users(login VARCHAR(8), uid
        INTEGER)')
>>> cur.execute('INSERT INTO users VALUES("john", 100)')
>>> cur.execute('INSERT INTO users VALUES("jane", 110)')
>>> cur.execute('SELECT * FROM users')
>>> for eachUser in cur.fetchall():
...     print eachUser
...
(u'john', 100)
(u'jane', 110)
>>> cur.execute('DROP TABLE users')
<sqlite3.Cursor object at 0x3d4320>
>>> cur.close()
>>> cxn.commit()
>>> cxn.close()
```

Okay, enough of the small examples. Next, we look at an application similar to our earlier example with MySQL, but which does a few more things:

- Creates a database (if necessary)
- Creates a table
- Inserts rows into the table
- Updates rows in the table
- Deletes rows from the table
- Drops the table

For this example, we will use two other open source databases. SQLite has become quite popular of late. It is very small, lightweight, and extremely fast for all the most common database functions. Another database involved in this example is Gadfly, a mostly SQL-compliant RDBMS written entirely in Python. (Some of the key data structures have a C module available, but Gadfly can run without it [slower, of course].)

Some notes before we get to the code. Both SQLite and Gadfly require the user to give the location to store database files (while MySQL has a default area and does not require this information from the use). The most current incarnation of Gadfly is not yet fully DB-API 2.0 compliant, and as a result, is missing some functionality, most notably the cursor attribute `rowcount` in our example.

Database Adapter Example Application

In the example below, we want to demonstrate how to use Python to access a database. In fact, for variety, we added support for three different database systems: Gadfly, SQLite, and MySQL. We are going to create a database (if one does not already exist), then run through various database operations such as creating and dropping tables, and inserting, updating, and deleting rows. Example 21.1 will be duplicated for the upcoming section on ORMs as well.

Line-by-Line Explanation

Lines 1–18

The first part of this script imports the necessary modules, creates some global "constants" (the column size for display and the set of databases we are supporting), and features the `setup()` function, which prompts the user to select the RDBMS to use for any particular execution of this script.

The most notable constant here is `DB_EXC`, which stands for DataBase EXCeption. This variable will eventually be assigned the database exception module for the specific database system that the users chooses to use to run this application with. In other words, if users choose MySQL, `DB_EXC` will be `_mysql_exceptions`, etc. If we developed this application in more of an object-oriented fashion, this would simply be an instance attribute, i.e., `self.db_exc_module` or something like that.

Lines 20–75

The guts of consistent database access happens here in the `connect()` function. At the beginning of each section, we attempt to load the requested database modules. If a suitable one is not found, `None` is returned to indicate that the database system is not supported.

Once a connection is made, then all other code is database and adapter independent and should work across all connections. (The only exception in our script is `insert()`.) In all three subsections of this set of code, you will notice that a valid connection should be passed back as `cxn`.

If SQLite is chosen (lines 24–36), we attempt to load a database adapter. We first try to load the standard library's `sqlite3` module (Python 2.5+). If that fails, we look for the third-party `pysqlite2` package. This is to support 2.4.x and older systems with the pysqlite adapter installed. If a suitable adapter

Example 21.1   Database Adapter Example (`ushuffle_db.py`)

This script performs some basic operations using a variety of databases (MySQL, SQLite, Gadfly) and a corresponding Python database adapter.

```python
1    #!/usr/bin/env python
2
3    import os
4    from random import randrange as rrange
5
6    COLSIZ = 10
7    RDBMSs = {'s': 'sqlite', 'm': 'mysql', 'g': 'gadfly'}
8    DB_EXC = None
9
10   def setup():
11       return RDBMSs[raw_input('''
12   Choose a database system:
13
14   (M)ySQL
15   (G)adfly
16   (S)QLite
17
18   Enter choice: ''').strip().lower()[0]]
19
20   def connect(db, dbName):
21       global DB_EXC
22       dbDir = '%s_%s' % (db, dbName)
23
24       if db == 'sqlite':
25           try:
26               import sqlite3
27           except ImportError, e:
28               try:
29                   from pysqlite2 import dbapi2 as sqlite3
30               except ImportError, e:
31                   return None
32
33           DB_EXC = sqlite3
34           if not os.path.isdir(dbDir):
35               os.mkdir(dbDir)
36           cxn = sqlite.connect(os.path.join(dbDir, dbName))
37
38       elif db == 'mysql':
39           try:
40               import MySQLdb
41               import _mysql_exceptions as DB_EXC
42           except ImportError, e:
43               return None
44
45           try:
46               cxn = MySQLdb.connect(db=dbName)
47           except _mysql_exceptions.OperationalError, e:
```

Example 21.1 Database Adapter Example (`ushuffle_db.py`) (continued)

```
48                    cxn = MySQLdb.connect(user='root')
49                    try:
50                            cxn.query('DROP DATABASE %s' % dbName)
51                    except DB_EXC.OperationalError, e:
52                            pass
53                    cxn.query('CREATE DATABASE %s' % dbName)
54                    cxn.query("GRANT ALL ON %s.* to ''@'localhost'" % dbName)
55                cxn.commit()
56                cxn.close()
57                cxn = MySQLdb.connect(db=dbName)
58
59        elif db == 'gadfly':
60            try:
61                    from gadfly import gadfly
62                    DB_EXC = gadfly
63            except ImportError, e:
64                    return None
65
66            try:
67                    cxn = gadfly(dbName, dbDir)
68            except IOError, e:
69                    cxn = gadfly()
70                    if not os.path.isdir(dbDir):
71                        os.mkdir(dbDir)
72                    cxn.startup(dbName, dbDir)
73        else:
74            return None
75        return cxn
76
77  def create(cur):
78      try:
79          cur.execute('''
80            CREATE TABLE users (
81                login VARCHAR(8),
82                uid INTEGER,
83                prid INTEGER)
84          ''')
85      except DB_EXC.OperationalError, e:
86          drop(cur)
87          create(cur)
88
89  drop = lambda cur: cur.execute('DROP TABLE users')
90
91  NAMES = (
92      ('aaron', 8312), ('angela', 7603), ('dave', 7306),
93      ('davina',7902), ('elliot', 7911), ('ernie', 7410),
94      ('jess', 7912), ('jim', 7512), ('larry', 7311),
95      ('leslie', 7808), ('melissa', 8602), ('pat', 7711),
96      ('serena', 7003), ('stan', 7607), ('faye', 6812),
97      ('amy', 7209),
98  )
99
```

(continued)

Example 21.1 Database Adapter Example (`ushuffle_db.py`) (continued)

```
100 def randName():
101     pick = list(NAMES)
102     while len(pick) > 0:
103         yield pick.pop(rrange(len(pick)))
104
105 def insert(cur, db):
106     if db == 'sqlite':
107         cur.executemany("INSERT INTO users VALUES(?, ?, ?)",
108             [(who, uid, rrange(1,5)) for who, uid in randName()])
109     elif db == 'gadfly':
110         for who, uid in randName():
111             cur.execute("INSERT INTO users VALUES(?, ?, ?)",
112                 (who, uid, rrange(1,5)))
113     elif db == 'mysql':
114         cur.executemany("INSERT INTO users VALUES(%s, %s, %s)",
115             [(who, uid, rrange(1,5)) for who, uid in randName()])
116
117 getRC = lambda cur: cur.rowcount if hasattr(cur,
    'rowcount') else -1
118
119 def update(cur):
120     fr = rrange(1,5)
121     to = rrange(1,5)
122     cur.execute(
123         "UPDATE users SET prid=%d WHERE prid=%d" % (to, fr))
124     return fr, to, getRC(cur)
125
126 def delete(cur):
127     rm = rrange(1,5)
128     cur.execute('DELETE FROM users WHERE prid=%d' % rm)
129     return rm, getRC(cur)
130
131 def dbDump(cur):
132     cur.execute('SELECT * FROM users')
133     print '\n%s%s%s' % ('LOGIN'.ljust(COLSIZ),
134         'USERID'.ljust(COLSIZ), 'PROJ#'.ljust(COLSIZ))
135     for data in cur.fetchall():
136         print '%s%s%s' % tuple([str(s).title().ljust(COLSIZ) \
137             for s in data])
138
139 def main():
140     db = setup()
141     print '*** Connecting to %r database' % db
142     cxn = connect(db, 'test')
143     if not cxn:
144         print 'ERROR: %r not supported, exiting' % db
145         return
146     cur = cxn.cursor()
147
148     print '\n*** Creating users table'
```

Example 21.1 Database Adapter Example (`ushuffle_db.py`) (continued)

```
149       create(cur)
150
151       print '\n*** Inserting names into table'
152       insert(cur, db)
153       dbDump(cur)
154
155       print '\n*** Randomly moving folks',
156       fr, to, num = update(cur)
157       print 'from one group (%d) to another (%d)' % (fr, to)
158       print '\t(%d users moved)' % num
159       dbDump(cur)
160
161       print '\n*** Randomly choosing group',
162       rm, num = delete(cur)
163       print '(%d) to delete' % rm
164       print '\t(%d users removed)' % num
165       dbDump(cur)
166
167       print '\n*** Dropping users table'
168       drop(cur)
169       cur.close()
170       cxn.commit()
171       cxn.close()
172
173 if __name__ == '__main__':
174       main()
```

is found, we then check to ensure that the directory exists because the database is file based. (You may also choose to create an in-memory database.) When the `connect()` call is made to SQLite, it will either use one that already exists or make a new one using that path if it does not.

MySQL (lines 38–57) uses a default area for its database files and does not require this to come from the user. Our code attempts to connect to the specified database. If an error occurs, it could mean either that the database does not exist or that it does exist but we do not have permission to see it. Since this is just a test application, we elect to drop the database altogether (ignoring any error if the database does not exist), and re-create it, granting all permissions after that.

The last database supported by our application is Gadfly (lines 59–75). (At the time of writing, this database is mostly but not fully DB-API–compliant, and you will see this in this application.) It uses a startup mechanism similar to that of SQLite: it starts up with the directory where the database files should be. If it is there, fine, but if not, you have to take a roundabout way to start up a new database. (Why this is, we are not sure. We believe that the `startup()` functionality should be merged into that of the constructor `gadfly.gadfly()`.)

Lines 77–89

The `create()` function creates a new users table in our database. If there is an error, that is almost always because the table already exists. If this is the case, drop the table and re-create it by recursively calling this function again. This code is dangerous in that if the recreation of the table still fails, you will have infinite recursion until your application runs out of memory. You will fix this problem in one of the exercises at the end of the chapter.

The table is dropped from the database with the one-liner `drop()`.

Lines 91–103

This is probably the most interesting part of the code outside of database activity. It consists of a constant set of names and user IDs followed by the generator `randName()` whose code can be found in Chapter 11 (Functions) in Section 11.10. The `NAMES` constant is a tuple that must be converted to a list for use with `randName()` because we alter it in the generator, randomly removing one name at a time until the list is exhausted. Well, if `NAMES` was a list, we would only use it once. Instead, we make it a tuple and copy it to a list to be destroyed each time the generator is used.

Lines 105–115

The `insert()` function is the only other place where database-dependent code lives, and the reason is that each database is slightly different in one way or another. For example, both the adapters for SQLite and MySQL are DB-API–compliant, so both of their cursor objects have an `execute-many()` function, whereas Gadfly does not, so rows have to be inserted one at a time.

Another quirk is that both SQLite and Gadfly use the `qmark` parameter style while MySQL uses `format`. Because of this, the format strings are different. If you look carefully, however, you will see that the arguments themselves are created in a very similar fashion.

What the code does is this: for each name-userID pair, it assigns that individual to a project group (given by its project ID or `prid`). The project ID is chosen randomly out of four different groups (`randrange(1,5)`).

Line 117

This single line represents a conditional expression (read as: Python ternary operator) that returns the rowcount of the last operation (in terms of rows altered), or if the cursor object does not support this attribute (meaning it is not DB-API–compliant), it returns –1.

Conditional expressions were added in Python 2.5, so if you are using 2.4.x or older, you will need to convert it back to the "old-style" way of doing it:

2.5

```
getRC = lambda cur: (hasattr(cur, 'rowcount') \
    and [cur.rowcount] or [-1])[0]
```

If you are confused by this line of code, don't worry about it. Check the FAQ to see why this is, and get a taste of why conditional expressions were finally added to Python in 2.5. If you *are* able to figure it out, then you have developed a solid understanding of Python objects and their Boolean values.

Lines 119–129

The update() and delete() functions randomly choose folks from one group. If the operation is update, move them from their current group to another (also randomly chosen); if it is delete, remove them altogether.

Lines 131–137

The dbDump() function pulls all rows from the database, formats them for printing, and displays them to the user. The **print** statement to display each user is the most obfuscated, so let us take it apart.

First, you should see that the data were extracted after the SELECT by the fetchall() method. So as we iterate each user, take the three columns (login, uid, prid), convert them to strings (if they are not already), titlecase it, and format the complete string to be COLSIZ columns left-justified (right-hand space padding). Since the code to generate these three strings is a list (via the list comprehension), we need to convert it to a tuple for the format operator (%).

Lines 139–174

The director of this movie is main(). It makes the individual functions to each function described above that defines how this script works (assuming that it does not exit due to either not finding a database adapter or not being able to obtain a connection [lines 143–145]). The bulk of it should be fairly self-explanatory given the proximity of the **print** statements. The last bits of main() close the cursor, and commit and close the connection. The final lines of the script are the usual to start the script.

21.3 Object-Relational Managers (ORMs)

As seen in the previous section, a variety of different database systems are available today, and most of them have Python interfaces to allow you to harness their power. The only drawback to those systems is the need to know SQL. If you are a programmer who feels more comfortable with manipulating Python objects instead of SQL queries, yet still want to use a relational database as your data backend, then you are a great candidate to be a user of ORMs.

21.3.1 Think Objects, Not SQL

Creators of these systems have abstracted away much of the pure SQL layer and implemented objects in Python that you can manipulate to accomplish the same tasks without having to generate the required lines of SQL. Some systems allow for more flexibility if you do have to slip in a few lines of SQL, but for the most part, you can avoid almost all the general SQL required.

Database tables are magically converted to Python classes with columns and features as attributes and methods responsible for database operations. Setting up your application to an ORM is somewhat similar to that of a standard database adapter. Because of the amount of work that ORMs perform on your behalf, some things are actually more complex or require more lines of code than using an adapter directly. Hopefully, the gains you achieve in productivity make up for a little bit of extra work.

21.3.2 Python and ORMs

The most well-known Python ORMs today are SQLAlchemy and SQLObject. We will give you examples of SQLAlchemy and SQLObject because the systems are somewhat disparate due to different philosophies, but once you figure these out, moving on to other ORMs is much simpler.

Some other Python ORMs include PyDO/PyDO2, PDO, Dejavu, PDO, Durus, QLime, and ForgetSQL. Larger Web-based systems can also have their own ORM component, i.e., WebWare MiddleKit and Django's Database API. Note that "well-known" does not mean "best for your application." Although these others were not included in our discussion, that does not mean that they would not be right for your application.

21.3.3 Employee Role Database Example

We will port our user shuffle application `ushuffle_db.py` to both SQLAlchemy and SQLObject below. MySQL will be the backend database server for both. You will note that we implement these as classes because there is more of an object "feel" to using ORMs as opposed to using raw SQL in a database adapter. Both examples import the set of NAMES and the random name chooser from `ushuffle_db.py`. This is to avoid copying-and-pasting the same code everywhere as code reuse is a good thing.

SQLAlchemy

We start with SQLAlchemy because its interface is somewhat closer to SQL than SQLObject's interface. SQLAlchemy abstracts really well to the object world but does give you more flexibility in issuing SQL if you have to. You will find both of these ORMs (Examples 21.2 and 21.3) very similar in terms of setup and access, as well as being of similar size, and both shorter than `ushuffle_db.py` (including the sharing of the names list and generator used to randomly iterate through that list).

Line-by-Line Explanation

Lines 1–10

As expected, we begin with module imports and constants. We follow the suggested style guideline of importing Python Standard Library modules first, followed by third-party or external modules, and finally, local modules to our application. The constants should be fairly self-explanatory.

Lines 12–31

The constructor for our class, like `ushuffle_db.connect()`, does everything it can to make sure that there is a database available and returns a connection to it (lines 18–31). This is the only place you will see real SQL, as such activity is typically an operational task, not application-oriented.

Lines 33–44

The `try-except` clause (lines 33–40) is used to reload an existing table or make a new one if it does not exist yet. Finally, we attach the relevant objects to our instance.

Example 21.2 SQLAlchemy ORM Example (`ushuffle_sa.py`)

This "user shuffle" application features SQLAlchemy paired up with the MySQL database as its backend.

```
1   #!/usr/bin/env python
2
3   import os
4   from random import randrange as rrange
5   from sqlalchemy import *
6   from ushuffle_db import NAMES, randName
7
8   FIELDS = ('login', 'uid', 'prid')
9   DBNAME = 'test'
10  COLSIZ = 10
11
12  class MySQLAlchemy(object):
13      def __init__(self, db, dbName):
14          import MySQLdb
15          import _mysql_exceptions
16          MySQLdb = pool.manage(MySQLdb)
17          url = 'mysql://db=%s' % DBNAME
18          eng = create_engine(url)
19          try:
20              cxn = eng.connection()
21          except _mysql_exceptions.OperationalError, e:
22              eng1 = create_engine('mysql://user=root')
23              try:
24                  eng1.execute('DROP DATABASE %s' % DBNAME)
25              except _mysql_exceptions.OperationalError, e:
26                  pass
27              eng1.execute('CREATE DATABASE %s' % DBNAME)
28              eng1.execute(
29              "GRANT ALL ON %s.* TO ''@'localhost'" % DBNAME)
30              eng1.commit()
31              cxn = eng.connection()
32
33          try:
34              users = Table('users', eng, autoload=True)
35          except exceptions.SQLError, e:
36              users = Table('users', eng,
37                  Column('login', String(8)),
38                  Column('uid', Integer),
39                  Column('prid', Integer),
40                  redefine=True)
41
42          self.eng = eng
43          self.cxn = cxn
44          self.users = users
45
46      def create(self):
47          users = self.users
```

Example 21.2   SQLAlchemy ORM Example (`ushuffle_sa.py`) (continued)

```
48              try:
49                  users.drop()
50              except exceptions.SQLError, e:
51                  pass
52              users.create()
53
54      def insert(self):
55          d = [dict(zip(FIELDS,
56              [who, uid, rrange(1,5)])) for who,uid in randName()]
57          return self.users.insert().execute(*d).rowcount
58
59      def update(self):
60          users = self.users
61          fr = rrange(1,5)
62          to = rrange(1,5)
63          return fr, to, \
64      users.update(users.c.prid==fr).execute(prid=to).rowcount
65
66      def delete(self):
67          users = self.users
68          rm = rrange(1,5)
69          return rm, \
70      users.delete(users.c.prid==rm).execute().rowcount
71
72      def dbDump(self):
73          res = self.users.select().execute()
74          print '\n%s%s%s' % ('LOGIN'.ljust(COLSIZ),
75              'USERID'.ljust(COLSIZ), 'PROJ#'.ljust(COLSIZ))
76          for data in res.fetchall():
77              print '%s%s%s' % tuple([str(s).title().ljust
(COLSIZ) for s in data])
78
79      def __getattr__(self, attr):
80          return getattr(self.users, attr)
81
82      def finish(self):
83          self.cxn.commit()
84          self.eng.commit()
85
86  def main():
87      print '*** Connecting to %r database' % DBNAME
88      orm = MySQLAlchemy('mysql', DBNAME)
89
90      print '\n*** Creating users table'
91      orm.create()
92
93      print '\n*** Inserting names into table'
94      orm.insert()
95      orm.dbDump()
96
```

(continued)

Example 21.2 SQLAlchemy ORM Example (`ushuffle_sa.py`) (continued)

```
 97        print '\n*** Randomly moving folks',
 98        fr, to, num = orm.update()
 99        print 'from one group (%d) to another (%d)' % (fr, to)
100        print '\t(%d users moved)' % num
101        orm.dbDump()
102
103        print '\n*** Randomly choosing group',
104        rm, num = orm.delete()
105        print '(%d) to delete' % rm
106        print '\t(%d users removed)' % num
107        orm.dbDump()
108
109        print '\n*** Dropping users table'
110        orm.drop()
111        orm.finish()
112
113 if __name__ == '__main__':
114        main()
```

Lines 46–70

These next four methods represent the core database functionality of table creation (lines 46–52), insertion (lines 54–57), update (lines 59–64), and deletion (lines 66–70). We should also have a method for dropping the table:

```
def drop(self):
    self.users.drop()
```

or

```
drop = lambda self: self.users.drop()
```

However, we made a decision to give another demonstration of *delegation* (as introduced in Chapter 13, Object-Oriented Programming). Delegation is where missing functionality (method call) is passed to another object in our instance which has it. See the explanation of lines 79–80.

Lines 72–77

The responsibility of displaying proper output to the screen belongs to the dbDump() method. It extracts the rows from the database and pretty-prints the data just like its equivalent in `ushuffle_db.py`. In fact, they are nearly identical.

Lines 79–80

We deliberately avoided creating a drop() method for the table since it would just call the table's drop method anyway. Also, there is no added

Example 21.3 SQLObject ORM Example (`ushuffle_so.py`)

This "user shuffle" application features SQLObject paired up with the MySQL database as its backend.

```
1   #!/usr/bin/env python
2
3   import os
4   from random import randrange as rrange
5   from sqlobject import *
6   from ushuffle_db import NAMES, randName
7
8   DBNAME = 'test'
9   COLSIZ = 10
10  FIELDS = ('login', 'uid', 'prid')
11
12  class MySQLObject(object):
13      def __init__(self, db, dbName):
14          import MySQLdb
15          import _mysql_exceptions
16          url = 'mysql://localhost/%s' % DBNAME
17
18          while True:
19              cxn = connectionForURI(url)
20              sqlhub.processConnection = cxn
21              #cxn.debug = True
22              try:
23                  class Users(SQLObject):
24                      class sqlmeta:
25                          fromDatabase = True
26                      login = StringCol(length=8)
27                      uid = IntCol()
28                      prid = IntCol()
29                  break
30              except _mysql_exceptions.ProgrammingError, e:
31                  class Users(SQLObject):
32                      login = StringCol(length=8)
33                      uid = IntCol()
34                      prid = IntCol()
35                  break
36              except _mysql_exceptions.OperationalError, e:
37                  cxn1 = sqlhub.processConnection=
connectionForURI('mysql://root@localhost')
38                  cxn1.query("CREATE DATABASE %s" % DBNAME)
39                  cxn1.query("GRANT ALL ON %s.* TO ''@'
   localhost'" % DBNAME)
40                  cxn1.close()
41          self.users = Users
42          self.cxn = cxn
43
44      def create(self):
45          Users = self.users
```

(continued)

Example 21.3 SQLObject ORM Example (`ushuffle_so.py`) (continued)

```
46              Users.dropTable(True)
47              Users.createTable()
48
49      def insert(self):
50          for who, uid in randName():
51              self.users(**dict(zip(FIELDS,
52                  [who, uid, rrange(1,5)])))
53
54      def update(self):
55          fr = rrange(1,5)
56          to = rrange(1,5)
57          users = self.users.selectBy(prid=fr)
58          for i, user in enumerate(users):
59              user.prid = to
60          return fr, to, i+1
61
62      def delete(self):
63          rm = rrange(1,5)
64          users = self.users.selectBy(prid=rm)
65          for i, user in enumerate(users):
66              user.destroySelf()
67          return rm, i+1
68
69      def dbDump(self):
70          print '\n%s%s%s' % ('LOGIN'.ljust(COLSIZ),
71              'USERID'.ljust(COLSIZ), 'PROJ#'.ljust(COLSIZ))
72          for usr in self.users.select():
73              print '%s%s%s' % (tuple([str(getattr(usr,
74                  field)).title().ljust(COLSIZ) \
75                  for field in FIELDS]))
76
77      drop = lambda self: self.users.dropTable()
78      finish = lambda self: self.cxn.close()
79
80  def main():
81      print '*** Connecting to %r database' % DBNAME
82      orm = MySQLObject('mysql', DBNAME)
83
84      print '\n*** Creating users table'
85      orm.create()
86
87      print '\n*** Inserting names into table'
88      orm.insert()
89      orm.dbDump()
90
91      print '\n*** Randomly moving folks',
92      fr, to, num = orm.update()
93      print 'from one group (%d) to another (%d)' % (fr, to)
```

Example 21.3 SQLObject ORM Example (`ushuffle_so.py`) (continued)

```
94       print '\t(%d users moved)' % num
95       orm.dbDump()
96
97       print '\n*** Randomly choosing group',
98       rm, num = orm.delete()
99       print '(%d) to delete' % rm
100      print '\t(%d users removed)' % num
101      orm.dbDump()
102
103      print '\n*** Dropping users table'
104      orm.drop()
105      orm.finish()
106
107 if __name__ == '__main__':
108      main()
```

functionality, so why create yet another function to have to maintain? The __getattr__() special method is called whenever an attribute lookup fails.

If our object calls `orm.drop()` and finds no such method, getattr (orm, 'drop') is invoked. When that happens, __getattr__() is called and delegates the attribute name to self.users. The interpreter will find that self.users has a `drop` attribute and pass that method call to it: self.users.drop()!

Lines 82–84

The last method is `finish()`, which commits the transaction.

Lines 86–114

The `main()` function drives our application. It creates a MySQLAlchemy object and uses that for all database operations. The script is the same as for our original application, `ushuffle_db.py`. You will notice that the database parameter `db` is optional and does not serve any purpose here in `ushuffle_sa.py` or the upcoming SQLobject version `ushuffle_so.py`. This is a placeholder for you to add support for other RDBMSs in these applications (see Exercises at the end of the chapter).

Upon running this script, you may get output that looks like this:

```
$ ushuffle_sa.py
*** Connecting to 'test' database

*** Creating users table

*** Inserting names into table

LOGIN      USERID     PROJ#
Serena     7003       4
Faye       6812       4
Leslie     7808       3
Ernie      7410       1
Dave       7306       2
Melissa    8602       1
Amy        7209       3
Angela     7603       4
Jess       7912       2
Larry      7311       1
Jim        7512       2
Davina     7902       3
Stan       7607       4
Pat        7711       2
Aaron      8312       2
Elliot     7911       3


*** Randomly moving folks from one group (1) to another (3)
          (3 users moved)

LOGIN      USERID     PROJ#
Serena     7003       4
Faye       6812       4
Leslie     7808       3
Ernie      7410       3
Dave       7306       2
Melissa    8602       3
Amy        7209       3
Angela     7603       4
Jess       7912       2
Larry      7311       3
Jim        7512       2
Davina     7902       3
Stan       7607       4
Pat        7711       2
Aaron      8312       2
Elliot     7911       3
```

```
*** Randomly choosing group (2) to delete
       (5 users removed)
LOGIN      USERID    PROJ#
Serena     7003      4
Faye       6812      4
Leslie     7808      3
Ernie      7410      3
Melissa    8602      3
Amy        7209      3
Angela     7603      4
Larry      7311      3
Davina     7902      3
Stan       7607      4
Elliot     7911      3
*** Dropping users table
$
```

Line-by-Line Explanation

Lines 1–10

This modules imports and constant declarations are practically identical to those of ushuffle_sa.py except that we are using SQLObject instead of SQLAlchemy.

Lines 12–42

The constructor for our class does everything it can to make sure that there is a database available and returns a connection to it, just like our SQLAlchemy example. Similarly, this is the only place you will see real SQL. Our application, as coded here, will result in an infinite loop if for some reason a Users table cannot be created in SQLObject.

We are trying to be clever in handling errors by fixing the problem and retrying the table (re)create. Since SQLobject uses metaclasses, we know that special magic is happening under the covers, so we have to define two different classes—one for if the table already exists and another if it does not.

The code works something like this:

1. Try and establish a connection to an existing table; if it works, we are done (lines 23–29)
2. Otherwise, create the class from scratch for the table; if so, we are done (lines 31–36)
3. Otherwise, we have a database issue, so try and make a new database (lines 37–40)
4. Loop back up and try all this again

Hopefully it (eventually) succeeds in one of the first two places. When the loop is terminated, we attach the relevant objects to our instance as we did in ushuffle_sa.py.

Lines 44–67, 77–78

The database operations happen in these lines. We have table create (lines 44–47) and drop (line 77), insert (lines 49–52), update (lines 54–60), and delete (lines 62–67). The finish() method on line 78 is to close the connection. We could not use delegation for table drop like we did for the SQLAlchemy example because the would-be delegated method for it is called dropTable() not drop().

Lines 69–75

This is the same and expected dbDump() method, which pulls the rows from the database and displays things nicely to the screen.

Lines 80–108

This is the main() function again. It works just like the one in ushuffle_sa.py. Also, the db argument to the constructor is a placeholder for you to add support for other RDBMSs in these applications (see Exercises at the end of the chapter).

Here is what your output may look like if you run this script:

```
$ ushuffle_so.py

*** Connecting to 'test' database

*** Creating users table

*** Inserting names into table

LOGIN      USERID    PROJ#
Jess       7912      1
Amy        7209      4
Melissa    8602      2
Dave       7306      4
Angela     7603      4
Serena     7003      2
Aaron      8312      1
Leslie     7808      1
Stan       7607      3
Pat        7711      3
Jim        7512      4
Larry      7311      3
Ernie      7410      2
```

```
Faye       6812      4
Davina     7902      1
Elliot     7911      4
*** Randomly moving folks from one group (2) to another (3)
        (3 users moved)

LOGIN      USERID    PROJ#
Jess       7912      1
Amy        7209      4
Melissa    8602      3
Dave       7306      4
Angela     7603      4
Serena     7003      3
Aaron      8312      1
Leslie     7808      1
Stan       7607      3
Pat        7711      3
Jim        7512      4
Larry      7311      3
Ernie      7410      3
Faye       6812      4
Davina     7902      1
Elliot     7911      4
*** Randomly choosing group (3) to delete
        (6 users removed)

LOGIN      USERID    PROJ#
Jess       7912      1
Amy        7209      4
Dave       7306      4
Angela     7603      4
Aaron      8312      1
Leslie     7808      1
Jim        7512      4
Faye       6812      4
Davina     7902      1
Elliot     7911      4
*** Dropping users table
$
```

21.3.4 Summary

We hope that we have provided you with a good introduction to using relational databases with Python. When your application's needs go beyond those offered by plain files, or specialized files like DBM, pickled, etc., you have many options. There are a good number of RDBMSs out there, not to mention one completely implemented in Python, freeing one from having to install, maintain, or administer a real database system. Below, you will find information on many of the Python adapters plus database and ORM systems out there. We also suggest checking out the DB-SIG pages as well as the Web pages and mailing lists of all systems of interest. Like all other areas of software development, Python makes things easy to learn and simple to experiment with.

21.4 Related Modules

Table 21.8 lists most of the common databases out there along with working Python modules and packages that serve as adapters to those database systems. Note that not all adapters are DB-API–compliant.

Table 21.8   Database-Related Modules and Websites

Name	Online Reference or Description
Databases	
Gadfly	http://gadfly.sf.net
MySQL	http://mysql.com or http://mysql.org
MySQLdb a.k.a. MySQL-python	http://sf.net/projects/mysql-python
PostgreSQL	http://postgresql.org
psycopg	http://initd.org/projects/psycopg1
psycopg2	http://initd.org/software/initd/psycopg/
PyPgSQL	http://pypgsql.sf.net
PyGreSQL	http://pygresql.org
PoPy	Deprecated; merged into PyGreSQL project
SQLite	http://sqlite.org
pysqlite	http://initd.org/projects/pysqlite
`sqlite3`[a]	`pysqlite` integrated into Python Standard Library; use this one unless you want to download the latest patch
APSW	http://rogerbinns.com/apsw.html

Table 21.8 Database-Related Modules and Websites (continued)	
Name	*Online Reference or Description*
Databases	
MaxDB (SAP)	http://mysql.com/products/maxdb
sdb	http://dev.mysql.com/downloads/maxdb/ 7.6.00.html#Python
sapdb	http://sapdb.org/sapdbPython.html
Firebird (InterBase)	http://firebird.sf.net
KInterbasDB	http://kinterbasdb.sf.net
SQL Server	http://microsoft.com/sql
pymssql	http://pymssql.sf.net (requires FreeTDS [http:// freetds.org])
adodbapi	http://adodbapi.sf.net
Sybase	http://sybase.com
sybase	http://object-craft.com.au/projects/sybase
Oracle	http://oracle.com
cx_Oracle	http://starship.python.net/crew/atuining/cx_Oracle
DCOracle2	http://zope.org/Members/matt/dco2 (older, for Oracle8 only)
Ingres	http://ingres.com
Ingres DBI	http://ingres.com/products/ Prod_Download_Python_DBI.html
ingmod	http://www.informatik.uni-rostock.de/~hme/software/
ORMs	
SQLObject	http://sqlobject.org
SQLAlchemy	http://sqlalchemy.org
PyDO/PyDO2	http://skunkweb.sf.net/pydo.html

a. `pysqlite` added to Python 2.5 as `sqlite3` module.

21.5 Exercises

21–1. *Database API*. What is the Python DB-API? Is it a good thing? Why (or why not)?

21–2. *Database API*. Describe the differences between the database module parameter styles (see the `paramstyle` module attribute).

21–3. *Cursor Objects*. What are the differences between the cursor `execute*()` methods?

21–4. *Cursor Objects*. What are the differences between the cursor `fetch*()` methods?

21–5. *Database Adapters*. Research your RDBMS and its Python module. Is it DB-API compliant? What additional features are available for that module that are extras not required by the API?

21–6. *Type Objects*. Study using Type objects for your database and DB-API adapter and write a small script that uses at least one of those objects.

21–7. *Refactoring*. In the `create()` function of Example 21.1 (`ushuffle_db.py`), a table that already exists is dropped and re-created by recursively calling `create()` again. This is dangerous in case the re-creation of the table fails (again) because you will then have infinite recursion. Fix this problem by creating a more practical solution that does not involve copying the create query (`cur.execute()`) again in the exception handler. Extra Credit: Try to recreate the table a maximum of three times before returning failure back to the caller.

21–8. *Database and HTML*. Take any existing database table, and use the knowledge you developed from Chapter 20 and output the contents of a database table into an HTML table.

21–9. *Web Programming and Databases*. Take our "user shuffle" example (`ushuffle_db.py`), and create a Web interface for it.

21–10. *GUI Programming and Databases*. Take our "user shuffle" example (`ushuffle_db.py`), and throw a GUI for it.

21–11. *Stock Portfolio Class*. Update the stock database example from Chapter 13 to use a relational database.

21–12. *Switching ORMs to a Different RDBMS*. Take either the SQLAlchemy (`ushuffle_sa.py`) or SQLObject (`ushuffle_so.py`) application and swap out MySQL as the backend RDBMS for another one of your choice.

EXTENDING PYTHON

Chapter Topics

- Introduction/Motivation
- Extending Python
  - Create Application Code
  - Wrap Code in Boilerplate
  - Compile
  - Import and Test
  - Reference Counting
  - Threading and the GIL
- Related Topics

Chapter 22

I n this chapter, we will discuss how to take code written externally and integrate that functionality into the Python programming environment. We will first give you motivation for doing this, then take you through the step-by-step process on how to do it. We should point out, though, that because extensions are primarily done in the C language, all of the example code you will see in this section is pure C but is easily portable to C++.

22.1 Introduction/Motivation

22.1.1 What Are Extensions?

In general, any code that you write that can be integrated or imported into another Python script can be considered an extension. This new code can be written in pure Python or in a compiled language like C and C++ (or Java for Jython and C# or VisualBasic.NET for IronPython).

One great feature of Python is that its extensions interact with the interpreter in exactly the same way as the regular Python modules. Python was designed so that the abstraction of module import hides the underlying implementation details from the code that uses such extensions. Unless the client programmer searches the file system, he or she simply cannot tell whether a module is written in Python or in a compiled language.

CORE NOTE: Creating extensions on different platforms

We will note here that extensions are generally available in a development environment where you compile your own Python interpreter. There is a subtle relationship between manual compilation versus obtaining the binaries. Although compilation may be a bit trickier than just downloading and installing binaries, you have the most flexibility in customizing the version of Python you are using. If you intend to create extensions, you should perform this task in a similar environment.

The examples in this chapter are built on a Unix-based system (which usually comes with a compilers), but, assuming you do have access to a C/C++ (or Java) compiler and a Python development environment in C/C++ (or Java), the only differences are in your compilation method. The actual code to make your extensions usable in the Python world is the same on any platform.

If you are developing on a Win32 platform, you will need Visual C++ "Developer Studio." The Python distribution comes with project files for version 7.1, but you may use older versions of VC++. More information on building extensions on Win32 can be found at:

http://docs.python.org/ext/building-on-windows.html

Caution: Although we know enough not to move binaries between different hosts, it is also a good idea just to compile on the same box and not move extensions between boxes either, even if they are of the same architecture. Sometimes slight differences of compiler or CPU will cause code not to work consistently.

22.1.2 Why Extend Python?

Throughout the brief history of software engineering, programming languages have always been taken at face value. What you see is what you get; it was impossible to add new functionality to an existing language. In today's programming environment, however, the ability to customize one's programming environment is now a desired feature; it also promotes code reuse. Languages such as TCL and Python are among the first languages to provide the ability to extend the base language. So why would you want to extend a language like Python, which is already feature-rich? There are several good reasons:

- **Added/extra (non-Python) functionality**
  One reason for extending Python is the need to have new functionality not provided by the core part of the language. This can be accomplished in either pure Python or as a compiled extension,

but there are certain things such as creating new data types or embedding Python in an existing application which must be compiled.

- **Bottleneck performance improvement**
  It is well known that interpreted languages do not perform as fast as compiled languages due to the fact that translation must happen on the fly and during runtime. In general, moving a body of code into an extension will improve overall performance. The problem is that it is sometimes not advantageous if the cost is high in terms of resources.

  Percentage-wise, it is a wiser bet to do some simple profiling of the code to identify what the bottlenecks are, and move *those* pieces of code out to an extension. The gain can be seen more quickly and without expending as much in terms of resources.

- **Keep proprietary source code private**
  Another important reason to create extensions is due to one side effect of having a scripting language. For all the ease-of-use such languages bring to the table, there really is no privacy as far as source code is concerned because the executable *is* the source code.

  Code that is moved out of Python and into a compiled language helps keep proprietary code private because you ship a binary object. Because these objects are compiled, they are not as easily reverse-engineered; thus, the source remains more private. This is key when it involves special algorithms, encryption or software security, etc.

  Another alternative to keeping code private is to ship pre-compiled .pyc files only. It serves as a good middle ground between releasing the actual source (.py files) and having to migrate that code to extensions.

22.2 Extending Python by Writing Extensions

Creating extensions for Python involves three main steps:

1. Creating application code
2. Wrapping code with boilerplates
3. Compilation and testing

In this section, we will break out all three pieces and expose them all to you.

22.2.1 Create Your Application Code

First, before any code becomes an extension, create a standalone "library." In other words, create your code keeping in mind that it is going to turn into a Python module. Design your functions and objects with the vision that Python code will be communicating and sharing data with your C code and vice versa.

Next, create test code to bulletproof your software. You may even use the "Pythonic" development method of designating your `main()` function in C as the testing application so that if your code is compiled, linked, and loaded into an executable (as opposed to just a shared object), invocation of such an executable will result in a regression test of your software library. For our extension example below, this is exactly what we do.

The test case involves two C functions that we want to bring to the world of Python programming. The first is the recursive factorial function, `fac()`. The second, `reverse()`, is a simple string reverse algorithm, whose main purpose is to reverse a string "in place," that is, to return a string whose characters are all reversed from their original positions, all without allocating a separate string to copy in reverse order. Because this involves the use of pointers, we need to carefully design and debug our code before bringing Python into the picture.

Our first version, `Extest1.c`, is presented in Example 22.1.

This code consists of a pair of functions, `fac()` and `reverse()`, which are implementations of the functionality we described above. `fac()` takes a single integer argument and recursively calculates the result, which is eventually returned to the caller once it exits the outermost call.

The last piece of code is the required `main()` function. We use it to be our tester, sending various arguments to `fac()` and `reverse()`. With this function, we can actual tell whether our code works (or not).

Now we should compile the code. For many versions of Unix with the `gcc` compiler, we can use the following command:

```
$ gcc Extest1.c -o Extest
$
```

To run our program, we issue the following command and get the output:

```
$ Extest
4! == 24
8! == 40320
12! == 479001600
reversing 'abcdef', we get 'fedcba'
reversing 'madam', we get 'madam'
$
```

Example 22.1 Pure C Version of Library (Extest1.c)

The following code represents our library of C functions which we want to wrap so that we can use this code from within the Python interpreter. main() *is our tester function.*

```c
1   #include <stdio.h>
2   #include <stdlib.h>
3   #include <string.h>
4
5   int fac(int n)
6   {
7       if (n < 2) return(1); /* 0! == 1! == 1 */
8       return (n)*fac(n-1); /* n! == n*(n-1)! */
9   }
10
11  char *reverse(char *s)
12  {
13      register char t,                  /* tmp */
14               *p = s,                  /* fwd */
15               *q = (s + (strlen(s)-1));   /* bwd */
16
17      while (p < q)              /* if p < q */
18      {                          /* swap & mv ptrs */
19          t = *p;
20          *p++ = *q;
21          *q-- = t;
22      }
23      return s;
24  }
25
26  int main()
27  {
28      char s[BUFSIZ];
29      printf("4! == %d\n", fac(4));
30      printf("8! == %d\n", fac(8));
31      printf("12! == %d\n", fac(12));
32      strcpy(s, "abcdef");
33      printf("reversing 'abcdef', we get '%s'\n", \
34          reverse(s));
35      strcpy(s, "madam");
36      printf("reversing 'madam', we get '%s'\n", \
37          reverse(s));
38      return 0;
39  }
```

We stress again that you should try to complete your code as much as possible, because you do not want to mix debugging of your library with potential bugs when integrating with Python. In other words, keep the debugging of your core code separate from the debugging of the integration. The closer you write your code to Python interfaces, the sooner your code will be integrated and work correctly.

Each of our functions takes a single value and returns a single value. It's pretty cut and dried, so there shouldn't be a problem integrating with Python. Note that, so far, we have not seen any connection or relationship with Python. We are simply creating a standard C or C++ application.

22.2.2 Wrap Your Code in Boilerplate

The entire implementation of an extension primarily revolves around the "wrapping" concept that we introduced earlier in Section 13.15.1. You should design your code in such a way that there is a smooth transition between the world of Python and your implementing language. This interfacing code is commonly called "boilerplate" code because it is a necessity if your code is to talk to the Python interpreter.

There are four main pieces to the boilerplate software:

1. Include Python header file
2. Add `PyObject* Module_func()` Python wrappers for each module function
3. Add `PyMethodDef ModuleMethods[]` array/table for each module function
4. Add **void** init*Module*() module initializer function

Include Python Header File

The first thing you should do is to find your Python include files and make sure your compiler has access to that directory. On most Unix-based systems, this would be either `/usr/local/include/python2.x` or `/usr/include/python2.x`, where the "2.x" is your version of Python. If you compiled and installed your Python interpreter, you should not have a problem because the system generally knows where your files are installed.

Add the inclusion of the `Python.h` header file to your source. The line will look something like:

```
#include "Python.h"
```

That is the easy part. Now you have to add the rest of the boilerplate software.

Add `PyObject* ` *`Module_func()`* **Python Wrappers for Each Function**

This part is the trickiest. For each function you want accessible to the Python environment, you will create a **static** `PyObject*` function with the module name along with an underscore (_) prepended to it.

For example, we want `fac()` to be one of the functions available for import from Python and we will use Extest as the name of our final module, so we create a "wrapper" called `Extest_fac()`. In the client Python script, there will be an "**import** Extest" and an "`Extest.fac()`" call somewhere (or just "`fac()`" for "**from** Extest **import** fac").

The job of the wrapper is to take Python values, convert them to C, then make a call to the appropriate function with what we want. When our function has completed, and it is time to return to the world of Python, it is also the job of this wrapper to take whatever return values we designate, convert them to Python, and then perform the return, passing back any values as necessary.

In the case of `fac()`, when the client program invokes `Extest.fac()`, our wrapper will be called. We will accept a Python integer, convert it to a C integer, call our C function `fac()` and obtain another integer result. We then have to take that return value, convert it back to a Python integer, then return from the call. (In your head, try to keep in mind that you are writing the code that will proxy for a "**def** fac(n)" declaration. When you are returning, it is as if that imaginary Python `fac()` function is completing.)

So, you're asking, how does this conversion take place? The answer is with the `PyArg_Parse*()` functions when going from Python to C, and `Py_BuildValue()` when returning from C to Python.

The `PyArg_Parse*()` functions are similar to the C `sscanf()` function. It takes a stream of bytes, and, according to some format string, parcels them off to corresponding container variables, which, as expected, take pointer addresses. They both return 1 on successful parsing and 0 otherwise.

`Py_BuildValue()` works like `sprintf()`, taking a format string and converting all arguments to a single returned object containing those values in the formats that you requested.

You will find a summary of these functions in Table 22.1.

A set of conversion codes is used to convert data objects between C and Python; they are given in Table 22.2.

These conversion codes are the ones given in the respective format strings that dictate how the values should be converted when moving between both languages. Note: The conversion types are different for Java since all data types are classes. Consult the Jython documentation to obtain the corresponding Java types for Python objects. The same applies for C# and VB.NET.

Table 22.1 Converting Data Between Python and C/C++

Function	Description
Python to C	
int PyArg_ParseTuple()	Converts (a tuple of) arguments passed from Python to C
int PyArg_ParseTupleAndKeywords()	Same as PyArg_ParseTuple() but also parses keyword arguments
C to Python	
PyObject* Py_BuildValue()	Converts C data values into a Python return object, either a single object or a single tuple of objects

Table 22.2 Common Codes to Convert Data Between Python and C/C++

Format Code	Python Type	C/C++ Type
s	str	**char***
z	str/None	**char***/NULL
i	int	**int**
l	long	**long**
c	str	**char**
d	float	**double**
D	complex	Py_Complex*
O	(any)	PyObject*
S	str	PyStringObject

Here we show you our completed `Extest_fac()` wrapper function:

```
static PyObject *
Extest_fac(PyObject *self, PyObject *args) {

    int res;                    // parse result
    int num;                    // arg for fac()
    PyObject* retval;           // return value

    res = PyArg_ParseTuple(args, "i", &num);
    if (!res) {                 // TypeError
        return NULL;
    }
    res = fac(num);
    retval = (PyObject*)Py_BuildValue("i", res);
    return retval;

}
```

The first step is to parse the data received from Python. It should be a regular integer, so we use the "i" conversion code to indicate as such. If the value was indeed an integer, then it gets stored in the num variable. Otherwise, `PyArg_ParseTuple()` will return a NULL, in which case we also return one. In our case, it will generate a `TypeError` exception that tells the client user that we are expecting an integer.

We then call `fac()` with the value stored in num and put the result in res, reusing that variable. Now we build our return object, a Python integer, again using a conversion code of "i." `Py_BuildValue()` creates an integer Python object which we then return. That's all there is to it!

In fact, once you have created wrapper after wrapper, you tend to shorten your code somewhat to avoid extraneous use of variables. Try to keep your code legible, though. We take our `Extest_fac()` function and reduce it to its smaller version given here, using only one variable, num:

```
static PyObject *
Extest_fac(PyObject *self, PyObject *args) {
    int num;
    if (!PyArg_ParseTuple(args, "i", &num))
        return NULL;
    return (PyObject*)Py_BuildValue("i", fac(num));
}
```

What about `reverse()`? Well, since you already know how to return a single value, we are going to change our `reverse()` example somewhat, returning two values instead of one. We will return a pair of strings as a tuple, the first element being the string as passed in to us, and the second being the newly reversed string.

To show you that there is some flexibility, we will call this function `Extest.doppel()` to indicate that its behavior differs from `reverse()`. Wrapping our code into an `Extest_doppel()` function, we get:

```
static PyObject *
Extest_doppel(PyObject *self, PyObject *args) {
    char *orig_str;
    if (!PyArg_ParseTuple(args, "s", &orig_str)) return NULL;
    return (PyObject*)Py_BuildValue("ss", orig_str, \
        reverse(strdup(orig_str)));
}
```

As in `Extest_fac()`, we take a single input value, this time a string, and store it into `orig_str`. Notice that we use the "s" conversion code now. We then call `strdup()` to create a copy of the string. (Since we want to return the original one as well, we need a string to reverse, so the best candidate is just a copy of the string.) `strdup()` creates and returns a copy, which we immediate dispatch to `reverse()`. We get back a reversed string.

As you can see, `Py_BuildValue()` puts together both strings using a conversion string of "ss." This creates a tuple of two strings, the original string and the reversed one. End of story, right? Unfortunately, no.

We got caught by one of the perils of C programming: the memory leak, that is, when memory is allocated but not freed. Memory leaks are analogous to borrowing books from the library but not returning them. You should always release resources that you have acquired when you no longer require them. How did we commit such a crime with our code (which looks innocent enough)?

When `Py_BuildValue()` puts together the Python object to return, it makes copies of the data it has been passed. In our case here, that would be a pair of strings. The problem is that we allocated the memory for the second string, but we did not release that memory when we finished, leaking it. What we really want to do is to build the return object and then free the memory that we allocated in our wrapper. We have no choice but to lengthen our code to:

```
static PyObject *
Extest_doppel(PyObject *self, PyObject *args) {
    char *orig_str;                    // original string
    char *dupe_str;                    // reversed string
    PyObject* retval;
    if (!PyArg_ParseTuple(args, "s", &orig_str)) return NULL;
    retval = (PyObject*)Py_BuildValue("ss", orig_str, \
        dupe_str=reverse(strdup(orig_str)));
    free(dupe_str);
    return retval;
}
```

We introduce the `dupe_str` variable to point to the newly allocated string and build the return object. Then we `free()` the memory allocated and finally return back to the caller. Now we are done.

Add PyMethodDef *Module*Methods[] Array/Table for Each Module Function

Now that both of our wrappers are complete, we want to list them somewhere so that the Python interpreter knows how to import and access them. This is the job of the *Module*Methods[] array.

It is made up of an array of arrays, with each individual array containing information about each function, terminated by a NULL array marking the end of the list. For our `Extest` module, we create the following Extest-Methods[] array:

```
static PyMethodDef
ExtestMethods[] = {
    { "fac", Extest_fac, METH_VARARGS },
    { "doppel", Extest_doppel, METH_VARARGS },
    { NULL, NULL },
};
```

The Python-accessible names are given, followed by the corresponding wrapping functions. The constant METH_VARARGS is given, indicating a set of arguments in the form of a tuple. If we are using `PyArg_ParseTuple-AndKeywords()` with keyworded arguments, we would logically OR this flag with the METH_KEYWORDS constant. Finally, a pair of NULLs properly terminates our list of two functions.

Add void init*Module*() Module Initializer Function

The final piece to our puzzle is the module initializer function. This code is called when our module is imported for use by the interpreter. In this code, we make one call to `Py_Init`*Module*`()` along with the module name and the name of the *Module*Methods[] array so that the interpreter can access our module functions. For our `Extest` module, our `initEx-test()` procedure looks like this:

```
void initExtest() {
        Py_InitModule("Extest", ExtestMethods);
}
```

We are now done with all our wrapping. We add all this code to our original code from `Extest1.c` and merge the results into a new file called `Extest2.c`, concluding the development phase of our example.

Another approach to creating an extension would be to make your wrapping code first, using "stubs" or test or dummy functions which will, during the course of development, be replaced by the fully functional pieces of implemented code. That way you can ensure that your interface between Python and C is correct, and then use Python to test your C code.

22.2.3 Compilation

Now we are on to the compilation phase. In order to get your new wrapper Python extension to build, you need to get it to compile with the Python library. This task has been standardized (since 30) across platforms to make life a lot easier for extension writers. The `distutils` package is used to build, install, and distribute modules, extensions, and packages. It came about back in Python 2.0 and replaced the old 1.x way of building extensions using "makefiles." Using `distutils`, we can follow this easy recipe:

1. Create `setup.py`
2. Compile and link your code by running `setup.py`
3. Import your module from Python
4. Test function

Create `setup.py`

The next step is to create a `setup.py` file. The bulk of the work will be done by the `setup()` function. All the lines of code that come before that call are preparatory steps. For building extension modules, you need to create an `Extension` instance per extension. Since we only have one, we only need one `Extension` instance:

```
Extension('Extest', sources=['Extest2.c'])
```

The first argument is the (full) extension name, including any high-level packages if necessary. The name should be in full dotted-attribute notation. Ours is standalone, hence the name "Extest." `sources` is a list of all the source files. Again, we only have the one, `Extest2.c`.

Now we are ready to call `setup()`. It takes a name argument for what it is building and a list of the items to build. Since we are creating an extension, we set it a list of extension modules to build as `ext_modules`. The syntax will be like this:

```
setup('Extest', ext_modules=[...])
```

Example 22.2 The Build Script (`setup.py`)

This script compiles our extension into the `build/lib.*` *subdirectory.*

```
1   #!/usr/bin/env python
2
3   from distutils.core import setup, Extension
4
5   MOD = 'Extest'
6   setup(name=MOD, ext_modules=[
7       Extension(MOD, sources=['Extest2.c'])])
```

Since we only have one module, we combine the instantiation of our extension module into our call to `setup()`, setting the module name as "constant" `MOD` on the preceding line:

```
MOD = 'Extest'
setup(name=MOD, ext_modules=[
    Extension(MOD, sources=['Extest2.c'])])
```

There are many more options to `setup()`, which are too numerous to list here. You can find out more about creating `setup.py` and calling `setup()` in the official Python documentation that we refer to at the end of this chapter. Example 22.2 shows the complete script that we are using for our example.

Compile and Link Your Code by Running `setup.py`

Now that we have our `setup.py` file, we can build our extension by running it with the "build" directive, as we have done here on our Mac (your output will differ based on the version of the operating system you are running as well as the version of Python you are using):

```
$ python setup.py build
running build
running build_ext
building 'Extest' extension
creating build
creating build/temp.macosx-10.x-fat-2.x
gcc -fno-strict-aliasing -Wno-long-double -no-cpp-
precomp -mno-fused-madd -fno-common -dynamic -DNDEBUG -g
-I/usr/include -I/usr/local/include -I/sw/include -I/
usr/local/include/python2.x -c Extest2.c -o build/
temp.macosx-10.x-fat-2.x/Extest2.o
creating build/lib.macosx-10.x-fat-2.x
gcc -g -bundle -undefined dynamic_lookup -L/usr/lib -L/
usr/local/lib -L/sw/lib -I/usr/include -I/usr/local/
include -I/sw/include build/temp.macosx-10.x-fat-2.x/
Extest2.o -o build/lib.macosx-10.x-fat-2.x/Extest.so
```

22.2.4 Import and Test

Import Your Module from Python

Your extension module will be created in the `build/lib.*` directory from where you ran your `setup.py` script. You can either change to that directory to test your module or install it into your Python distribution with:

```
$ python setup.py install
```

If you do install it, you will get the following output:

```
running install
running build
running build_ext
running install_lib
copying build/lib.macosx-10.x-fat-2.x/Extest.so ->
/usr/local/lib/python2.x/site-packages
```

Now we can test out our module from the interpreter:

```
>>> import Extest
>>> Extest.fac(5)
120
>>> Extest.fac(9)
362880
>>> Extest.doppel('abcdefgh')
('abcdefgh', 'hgfedcba')
>>> Extest.doppel("Madam, I'm Adam.")
("Madam, I'm Adam.", ".madA m'I ,madaM")
```

Test Function

The one last thing we want to do is to add a test function. In fact, we already have one, in the form of the `main()` function. Now, it is potentially dangerous to have a `main()` function in our code because there should only be one `main()` in the system. We remove this danger by changing the name of our `main()` to `test()` and wrapping it, adding `Extest_test()` and updating the `ExtestMethods` array so that they both look like this:

```
static PyObject *
Extest_test(PyObject *self, PyObject *args) {
    test();
    return (PyObject*)Py_BuildValue("");
}
static PyMethodDef
ExtestMethods[] = {
```

```
        { "fac", Extest_fac, METH_VARARGS },
        { "doppel", Extest_doppel, METH_VARARGS },
        { "test", Extest_test, METH_VARARGS },
        { NULL, NULL },
};
```

The `Extest_test()` module function just runs `test()` and returns an empty string, resulting in a Python value of `None` being returned to the caller.

Now we can run the same test from Python:

```
>>> Extest.test()
4! == 24
8! == 40320
12! == 479001600
reversing 'abcdef', we get 'fedcba'
reversing 'madam', we get 'madam'
>>>
```

In Example 22.3, we present the final version of `Extest2.c` that was used to generate the output we just witnessed.

In this example, we chose to segregate our C code from our Python code. It just kept things easier to read and is no problem with our short example. In practice, these source files tend to get large, and some choose to implement their wrappers completely in a different source file, i.e., `ExtestWrappers.c` or something of that nature.

22.2.5 *Reference Counting*

You may recall that Python uses reference counting as a means of keeping track of objects and deallocating objects no longer referenced as part of the garbage collection mechanism. When creating extensions, you must pay extra special attention to how you manipulate Python objects because you must be mindful of whether or not you need to change the reference count for such objects.

There are two types of references you may have to an object, one of which is an *owned reference*, meaning that the reference count to the object is incremented by one to indicate your ownership. One place where you would definitely have an owned reference is where you create a Python object from scratch.

When you are done with a Python object, you must dispose of your ownership, either by decrementing the reference count, transferring your ownership by passing it on, or storing the object. Failure to dispose of an owned reference creates a memory leak.

You may also have a *borrowed reference* to an object. Somewhat lower on the responsibility ladder, this is where you are passed the reference of an

Example 22.3 Python-Wrapped Version of C Library (Extest2.c)

```
1    #include <stdio.h>
2    #include <stdlib.h>
3    #include <string.h>
4
5    int fac(int n)
6    {
7        if (n < 2) return(1);
8        return (n)*fac(n-1);
9    }
10
11   char *reverse(char *s)
12   {
13       register char t,
14                     *p = s,
15                     *q = (s + (strlen(s) - 1));
16
17       while (s && (p < q))
18       {
19           t = *p;
20           *p++ = *q;
21           *q-- = t;
22       }
23       return s;
24   }
25
26   int test()
27   {
28       char s[BUFSIZ];
29       printf("4! == %d\n", fac(4));
30       printf("8! == %d\n", fac(8));
31       printf("12! == %d\n", fac(12));
32       strcpy(s, "abcdef");
33       printf("reversing 'abcdef', we get '%s'\n", \
34           reverse(s));
35       strcpy(s, "madam");
36       printf("reversing 'madam', we get '%s'\n", \
37           reverse(s));
38       return 0;
39   }
40
41   #include "Python.h"
42
43   static PyObject *
44   Extest_fac(PyObject *self, PyObject *args)
45   {
46       int num;
47       if (!PyArg_ParseTuple(args, "i", &num))
48           return NULL;
49       return (PyObject*)Py_BuildValue("i", fac(num));}
50   }
51
52   static PyObject *
```

Example 22.3   Python-Wrapped Version of C Library (`Extest2.c`) (continued)

```
53  Extest_doppel(PyObject *self, PyObject *args)
54  {
55      char *orig_str;
56      char *dupe_str;
57      PyObject* retval;
58
59      if (!PyArg_ParseTuple(args, "s", &orig_str))
60          return NULL;
61      retval = (PyObject*)Py_BuildValue("ss", orig_str, \
62          dupe_str=reverse(strdup(orig_str)));
63      free(dupe_str);
64      return retval;
65  }
66
67  static PyObject *
68  Extest_test(PyObject *self, PyObject *args)
69  {
70      test();
71      return (PyObject*)Py_BuildValue("");
72  }
73
74  static PyMethodDef
75  ExtestMethods[] =
76  {
77      { "fac", Extest_fac, METH_VARARGS },
78      { "doppel", Extest_doppel, METH_VARARGS },
79      { "test", Extest_test, METH_VARARGS },
80      { NULL, NULL },
81  };
82
83  void initExtest()
84  {
85      Py_InitModule("Extest", ExtestMethods);
86  }
```

object, but otherwise do not manipulate the data in any way. Nor do you have to worry about its reference count, as long as you do not hold on to this reference after its reference count has decreased to zero. You may convert your borrowed reference to an owned reference simply by incrementing an object's reference count.

Python provides a pair of C macros which are used to change the reference count to a Python object. They are given in Table 22.3.

In our above `Extest_test()` function, we return `None` by building a `PyObject` with an empty string; however, it can also be accomplished by becoming an owner of the `None` object, `PyNone`, incrementing your reference

Table 22.3 Macros for Performing Python Object Reference Counting	
Function	*Description*
Py_INCREF(*obj*)	Increment the reference count to *obj*
Py_DECREF(*obj*)	Decrement the reference count to *obj*

count to it, and returning it explicitly, as in the following alternative piece of code:

```
static PyObject *
Extest_test(PyObject *self, PyObject *args) {
        test();
        Py_INCREF(Py_None);
        return PyNone;
}
```

Py_INCREF() and Py_DECREF() also have versions that check for NULL objects. They are Py_XINCREF() and Py_XDECREF(), respectively.

We strongly urge the reader to consult the Python documentation regarding extending and embedding Python for all the details with regard to reference counting (see the documentation reference in the Appendix).

22.2.6 Threading and the GIL

Extension writers must be aware that their code may be executed in a multithreaded Python environment. Back in Section 18.3.1, we introduced the Python Virtual Machine (PVM) and the Global Interpreter Lock (GIL) and described how only one thread of execution can be running at any given time in the PVM and that the GIL is responsible for keeping other threads from running. Furthermore, we indicated that code calling external functions such as in extension code would keep the GIL locked until the call returns.

We also hinted that there was a remedy, a way for the extension programmer to release the GIL, for example before performing a system call. This is accomplished by "blocking" your code off to where threads may (and may not) run safely using another pair of C macros, Py_BEGIN_ALLOW_THREADS and Py_END_ALLOW_THREADS. A block of code bounded by these macros will permit other threads to run.

As with the reference counting macros, we urge you to consult with the documentation regarding extending and embedding Python as well as the Python/C API reference manual.

22.3 Related Topics

SWIG

There is an external tool available called SWIG, which stands for Simplified Wrapper and Interface Generator. It was written by David Beazley, also the author of *Python Essential Reference*. It is a software tool that can take annotated C/C++ header files and generate wrapped code, ready to compile for Python, Tcl, and Perl. Using SWIG will free you from having to write the boilerplate code we've seen in this chapter. You only need to worry about coding the solution part of your project in C/C++. All you have to do is create your files in the SWIG format, and it will do the background work on your behalf. You can find out more information about SWIG from its main Web site located at the following Web address (URL):

> http://swig.org

Pyrex

One obvious weakness of creating C/C++ extensions (raw or with SWIG) is that you have to write C/C++ (surprise, surprise), with all of its strengths, and, more importantly, its pitfalls. Pyrex gives you practically all of the gains of writing extensions but not the headache. Pyrex is a new language created specifically for writing Python extensions. It is a hybrid of C and Python, leaning much more toward Python: in fact, the Pyrex Web site goes as far as saying that, "Pyrex is Python with C data types." You only need to write code in the Pyrex syntax and run the Pyrex compiler on the source. Pyrex creates C files, which can then be compiled and used as a normal extension would. Some have sworn off C programming forever upon discovering Pyrex. You can get Pyrex at its home page:

> http://cosc.canterbury.ac.nz/~greg/python/Pyrex

Psyco

Pyrex gives us the advantage that you no longer have to write pure C; however, do you need to learn its syntax, "yet another language." In the end, your Pyrex code turns into C anyway. You use C/C++, C/C++ with SWIG, or Pyrex because you still want that performance boost you are looking for. What if you can obtain performance gains without changing your Python code?

Psyco's concept is quite different from those other approaches. Rather than writing C code, why not just make your existing Python code run faster?

Psyco serves as a just-in-time (JIT) compiler so you do not have to change to your source other than importing the Psyco module and telling it to start optimizing your code (during runtime).

Psyco can also profile your code to see where it can make the most significant improvements. You can even enable logging to see what Psyco does while optimizing your code. For more information, go to its main Web site:

http://psyco.sf.net

Embedding

Embedding is another feature available in Python. It is the inverse of an extension. Rather than taking C code and wrapping it into Python, you take a C application and wrap a Python interpreter inside it. This has the effect of giving a potentially large, monolithic, and perhaps rigid, proprietary, and/or mission-critical application the power of having an embedded Python interpreter. Once you have Python, well, it's like a whole new ball game.

For extension writer, there is a set of official docs that you should refer to for additional information.

Here are links to some of the Python documentation related to this chapter's topics:

Extending and Embedding

http://docs.python.org/ext

Python/C API

http://docs.python.org/api

Distributing Python Modules

http://docs.python.org/dist

22.4 Exercises

22–1.   *Extending Python.* What are some of the advantages of Python extensions?

22–2.   *Extending Python.* Can you see any disadvantages or dangers of using extensions?

22–3.   *Writing Extensions.* Obtain or find a C/C++ compiler and write a small program with it to (re)familiarize yourself with C/C++ programming. Find your Python distribution directory and locate the `Misc/Makefile.pre.in` file. Take the program you just wrote and wrap it in Python. Go through the steps necessary to create a shared object. Access that module from Python and test it.

22–4. *Porting from Python to C.* Take several of the exercises you did in earlier chapters and port them to C/C++ as extension modules.

22–5. *Wrapping C Code.* Find a piece of C/C++ code, which you may have done a long time ago, but want to port to Python. Instead of porting, make it an extension module.

22–6. *Writing Extensions.* In Exercise 13–3, you created a `dollar-ize()` function as part of a class to convert a floating point value to a financial numeric string with embedded dollar signs and commas. Create an extension featuring a wrapped `dollarize()` function and integrate a regression testing function, i.e., `test()`, into the module. Extra credit: In addition to creating a C extension, also rewrite `dollar-ize()` in Pyrex.

22–7. *Extending versus Embedding.* What is the difference between extending and embedding?

MISCELLANEOUS

Chapter Topics

- Introduction
- Web Services
- Programming Microsoft Office with Win32 COM
- Python and Java Programming with Jython
- Exercises

Chapter 23

I n this chapter, we will give brief preview introductions to miscellaneous areas of Python programming we did not have time to explore more fully. We hope to eventually develop these into full chapters for future editions of this book.

23.1 Web Services

There are many Web services and applications on the Net, providing a wide variety of services. You will find application programmer interfaces (APIs) from most of the big players today, i.e., Yahoo!, Google, eBay, and Amazon, to name a few. In the past, APIs have been used just to access data using these services; however, today's APIs are different. They are rich and fully featured, and you are able to actually integrate services into your own personal Web sites and Web pages, commonly known as "Mash-ups."

This is an area of active interest that we will continue to explore (REST, XML, RSS, etc.), but for now, we are going to take a trip back in time to play around with an older interface that is both useful and has longevity, the stock quote server from Yahoo! at http://finance.yahoo.com.

23.1.1 Yahoo! Finance Stock Quote Server

If you visit the Web site and pull up a quotation for any stock, you will find a Uniform Resource Locator (URL) link under the basic quote data labeled "Download Data," which lets users download a CSV file suitable for importing into Microsoft Excel or Intuit Quicken:

> http://finance.yahoo.com/d/
> quotes.csv?s=GOOG&f=sl1d1t1c1ohgv&e=.csv

If your browser's MIME settings are set correctly, your browser will actually launch Excel with the resulting data. This is due primarily to the final variable (key-value) pair found in the link, `e=.csv`. This variable is actually not used by the server as it always sends back data in CSV format anyway.

If we use our friend `urllib.urlopen()`, we see that for any stock ticker symbol, one CSV string is returned:

```
>>> from urllib import urlopen
>>> u = urlopen('http://quote.yahoo.com/d/
    quotes.csv?s=YHOO&f=sl1d1t1c1ohgv')
>>> for row in u:
...     print 'row'
...
'"YHOO",30.76,"5/23/
    2006","4:00pm",+0.30,31.07,31.63,30.76,28594020\r\n'
>>> f.close()
```

The string would then have to be manually parsed (by stripping the trailing whitespace and splitting on the comma delimiter). As an alternative to parsing the data string ourselves, we can use the `csv` module, introduced in Python 2.3, which does both the string split and the whitespace strip. Using `csv`, we can replace the **for** loop above with the following assuming all other lines are left intact:

2.3

```
>>> import csv
>>> for row in csv.reader(u):
...     print row
...
['YHOO', '30.76', '5/23/2006', '4:00pm', '+0.30',
    '31.07', '31.63', '30.76', '28594020']
```

By analyzing the argument field `f` passed to the server and from reading Yahoo!'s online help for this service, you will see that the symbols (`sl1d1t1c1ohgv`) correspond to: ticker symbol, last price, date, time, change, open price, daily high, daily low, and volume.

You can get more information by checking the Yahoo! Finance Help pages—just search for "download data" or "download spreadsheet format."

Further analysis of the API reveals a few more options such as the previous closing price, the percentage change of the current price to the previous close, the 52-week high and low, etc. All in all, the options can be summarized in Table 23.1 along with the formats of the returned components.

The field names are given in the order you want them from the server. Just concatenate them together as a single argument to the field parameter f as part of the requesting URL. As mentioned in the returned value footnote,

Table 23.1 Yahoo! Finance Stock Quote Server Parameters

Stock Quotation Data	Field Name[a]	Format Returned[b]
Stock ticker symbol	s	`"YHOO"`
Price of last trade	l1	`328`
Last trade date	d1	`"2/2/2000"`
Time of last trade	t1	`"4:00pm"`
Change from previous close	c1	`+10.625`
Percentage change from previous close	p2	`"+3.35%"`
Previous closing price	p	`317.375`
Last opening price	o	`321.484375`
Daily high price	h	`337`
Daily low price	g	`317`
52-week range	w	`"110 - 500.125"`
Volume for the day	v	`6703300`
Market capitalization	j1	`86.343B`
Earnings per share	e	`0.20`
Price-to-earnings ratio	r	`1586.88`
Company name	n	`"YAHOO INC"`

a. First character of field name is alphabetic; the second, if any, is numeric.
b. Some values returned quoted although all are returned in one CSV string.

some of components returned are quoted separately. It is up to the parser to properly extract the data. Observe the resulting (sub)strings when parsed manually vs. using the `csv` module in our example above. If a value is not available, the quote server returns "N/A" (separately quoted since that field is, which makes it consistent . . . a good thing).

For example, if we give the server a field request of `f=s11d1c1p2`, we get a string like the following returned for a valid stock ticker:

```
"YHOO",166.203125,"2/23/2000",+12.390625,"+8.06%"
```

For the case where the stock is no longer publicly traded, we get something like this instead (note again how fields that come back quoted still do, even if N/A):

```
"PBLS.OB",0.00,"N/A",N/A,"N/A"
```

The quote server will also allow you to specify multiple stock ticker symbols, as in `s=YHOO,GOOG,EBAY,AMZN`. You will get back one row of data like the above for each company. Just keep in mind that "[any] redistribution of quotes data displayed on Yahoo! is strictly prohibited," as quoted in the Yahoo! Finance Help pages, so you should only be using these data for personal reasons. Also be aware that all of the quotes you download are delayed.

Using what we know now, let us build an example (Example 23.1) application that will read and display some stock quote data for some of our favorite Internet companies.

Example 23.1 Yahoo! Finance Stock Quote Example (`stock.py`)

This script downloads and displays stock prices from the Yahoo! quote server.

```
1   #!/usr/bin/env python
2
3   from time import ctime
4   from urllib import urlopen
5
6   ticks = ('YHOO', 'GOOG', 'EBAY', 'AMZN')
7   URL = 'http://quote.yahoo.com/d/quotes.csv?s=%s&f=s11c1p2'
8
9   print '\nPrices quoted as of:', ctime()
10  print '\nTICKER'.ljust(9), 'PRICE'.ljust(8), 'CHG'.ljust(5), '%AGE'
11  print '------'.ljust(8), '-----'.ljust(8), '---'.ljust(5), '----'
12  u = urlopen(URL % ','.join(ticks))
13
14  for row in u:
15      tick, price, chg, per = row.split(',')
16      print eval(tick).ljust(7), \
17              ('%.2f' % round(float(price), 2)).rjust(6), \
18              chg.rjust(6), eval(per.rstrip()).rjust(6)
19
20  f.close()
```

If we run this script, we will get output that looks like the following:

```
$ stock.py

Prices quoted as of: Sat May 27 03:25:56 2006

TICKER   PRICE    CHG    %AGE
------   -----    ---    ----
YHOO     33.02   +0.10  +0.30%
GOOG    381.35   -1.64  -0.43%
EBAY     34.20   +0.32  +0.94%
AMZN     36.07   +0.44  +1.23%
```

23.2 Programming Microsoft Office with Win32 COM

One of the most useful things that you can do in an everyday business environment is to integrate support for Win32 applications. Being able to read data from and write data to such applications can often be very handy. Your department may not be necessarily be running in a Win32 environment, but chances are, your management and other project teams are. Mark Hammond's Windows Extensions for Python allows programmers to interact natively with Win32 applications in their native environment. (It can be downloaded at the book's Web site.)

The Win32 programming universe is expansive. Most of it available from the Windows Extensions for Python package, i.e., Windows API, processes, Microsoft Foundation Classes (MFC) Graphical User Interface (GUI) development, Windows multithreaded programming, services, remote access, pipes, server-side COM programming, and events. And don't forget about IronPython (http://codeplex.com/Wiki/View.aspx?ProjectName=IronPython), an implementation of the Python language in C# for the .NET/Mono development environment. In this section, we are going to focus on one part of the Win32 programming universe, which easily has practical applications for client-side, COM programming.

23.2.1 Client-Side COM Programming

We can use Component Object Model, better known as COM (or its marketing name, ActiveX), to communicate with tools such as Outlook and Excel. For programmers, the pleasure comes with being able to "control" a native Office application directly from their Python code.

Specifically, when discussing the use of a COM object, e.g., launching of an application and allowing code to access methods and data of that applications, this is referred to as COM *client-side* programming. Server-side COM programming is where you are implementing a COM object for clients to access.

CORE NOTE: Python and Microsoft COM (Client-Side) Programming

Python on the Windows 32-bit platform contains connectivity to COM, a Microsoft interfacing technology that allows objects to talk to one another, or more higher-level applications to talk to one another, without any language- or format-dependence. We will see in this section how the combination of Python and COM (client programming) presents a unique opportunity to create scripts that can communicate directly with Microsoft Office applications such as Word, Excel, PowerPoint, and Outlook.

The prerequisites to this section include running on a Win32 platform with both Python and the Windows Extensions for Python installed. You must also have one or more Microsoft applications available to try the examples with. The download instructions for the Windows Extensions should be adequate to get your system ready to go. Since PythonWin comes with the Extensions distribution, we recommend IDE for building and testing your Win32 scripts.

In this section, we will show you how you can interact with an Office application. We will present a few examples, some of them quite useful, and describe how they work in detail. You will also find several of these at the "Python Cookbook" Web site. We confess to readers that we are not COM or VisualBasic experts and we are well aware that our examples can be vastly improved. We would like to solicit the readership to drop us a line and send us any comments, suggestions, or improvements that you would consider for the general audience.

Let us start with very simple examples of how to launch and interact with Microsoft Excel, Word, PowerPoint, and Outlook. Before we show you examples of all we have discussed, we want to point out that client-side COM applications all follow similar steps in execution. The typical way in which you would interact with these applications is something like this:

1. Launch application
2. Add appropriate document to work on (or load one from disk)
3. Make application visible (if desired)
4. Perform all desired work on document
5. Save or discard document
6. Quit

Enough talking . . . let us take a look at some code. Below are a series of scripts that control a different Microsoft application. All import the `win32com.client` module as well as a couple of Tk modules to control the launching (and completion) of each application. Also like we did in Chapter 19, we use the `.pyw` file extension to suppress the unneeded DOS command window.

23.2.2 Microsoft Excel

Our first example is a demonstration using Excel. Of the entire Office suite, we find Excel to be the most programmable. It is quite useful to pass data to Excel so that you can both take advantage of the spreadsheet's features as well as viewing data in a nice printable format. It is also useful to be able to read data from a spreadsheet and process data with the power of a real programming language like Python. We will present a more complex example using Excel at the end of this section, but we have to start somewhere. So, we start with Example 23.2.

Example 23.2 Excel Example (`excel.pyw`)

This script launches Excel and writes data to spreadsheet cells.

```
1  #!/usr/bin/env python
2
3  from Tkinter import Tk
4  from time import sleep
5  from tkMessageBox import showwarning
6  import win32com.client as win32
7
8  warn = lambda app: showwarning(app, 'Exit?')
9  RANGE = range(3, 8)
10
11 def excel():
12     app = 'Excel'
13     xl = win32.gencache.EnsureDispatch('%s.Application' % app)
14     ss = xl.Workbooks.Add()
15     sh = ss.ActiveSheet
16     xl.Visible = True
17     sleep(1)
18
19     sh.Cells(1,1).Value = 'Python-to-%s Demo' % app
20     sleep(1)
21     for i in RANGE:
22         sh.Cells(i,1).Value = 'Line %d' % i
23         sleep(1)
24     sh.Cells(i+2,1).Value = "Th-th-th-that's all folks!"
25
26     warn(app)
27     ss.Close(False)
28     xl.Application.Quit()
29
30 if __name__=='__main__':
31     Tk().withdraw()
32     excel()
```

Line-by-Line Explanation

Lines 1–6, 31

We import `Tkinter` and `tkMessageBox` only to use the `showwarning` message box upon termination of the demonstration. We `withdraw()` the Tk top-level window to suppress it (line 31) before bringing up the dialog box (line 26). If you do not initialize the top level beforehand, one will automatically be created for you; it won't be withdrawn and will be an annoyance on-screen.

Lines 11–17

After the code starts (or "dispatches") Excel (an application), we add a *workbook* (a spreadsheet that contains *sheets* that the data are written to; these sheets are organized as tabs in a workbook), and grab a handle to the *active sheet*, meaning the sheet that is displayed. Do not get all worked up about the terminology, which may be confusing mostly because a "spreadsheet contains sheets."

CORE NOTE: Static and dynamic dispatch

On line 13, we use what is known as static dispatch. *Before starting up the script, we ran the Makepy utility from PythonWin. (Start the IDE, select* Tools ⇒ COM Makepy utility *and choose the appropriate application object library.) This utility program creates and caches the objects that are needed for the application. Without this prep work, the objects and attributes will have to be built during runtime; this is known as* dynamic dispatch. *If you want to run dynamically, then use the regular* Dispatch() *function:*

```
xl = win32com.client.Dispatch('%s.Application' % app)
```

The `Visible` flag must be set to `True` to make the application visible on your desktop, then pause so that the user can see each step in the demonstration (line 16). For an explanation of the `sleep()` call on line 17, just read the next paragraph.

Lines 19–24

In the application portion of the script, we write out the title of our demonstration to the first and upper leftmost cell, (A1) or (1, 1). We then skip a row and then write "Line *N*" where *N* is numbered from 3 to 7, pausing 1 second in between each row so that users can see our updates happening live. (The cell updates would occur too quickly without the delay.)

Lines 26–32

A warning dialog box comes up after the demo letting the user know that he or she can quit this demo once they have observed the output. The spreadsheet is closed without saving, `ss.Close([SaveChanges=]False)`, and the application exits. Finally, the "main" part of the script just initializes Tk and runs the core part of the application.

Running this script results in an Excel application window, which should look similar to Figure 23–1.

23.2.3 Microsoft Word

The next demonstration is with Word. Using Word for documents is not as applicable to the programming world as there is not much data involved. One could consider using Word for generating form letters, however. In Example 23.3, we create a document by simply writing one line of text after another.

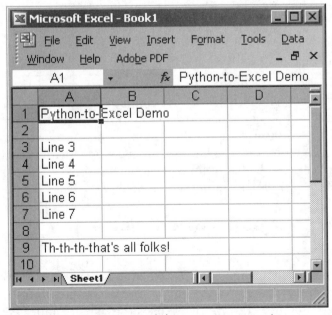

Figure 23–1   Python-to-Excel demonstration script (`excel.pyw`)

Example 23.3 Word Example (`word.pyw`)

This script launches Word and writes data to the document.

```python
1  #!/usr/bin/env python
2
3  from Tkinter import Tk
4  from time import sleep
5  from tkMessageBox import showwarning
6  import win32com.client as win32
7
8  warn = lambda app: showwarning(app, 'Exit?')
9  RANGE = range(3, 8)
10
11 def word():
12     app = 'Word'
13     word = win32.gencache.EnsureDispatch('%s.Application' % app)
14     doc = word.Documents.Add()
15     word.Visible = True
16     sleep(1)
17
18     rng = doc.Range(0,0)
19     rng.InsertAfter('Python-to-%s Test\r\n\r\n' % app)
20     sleep(1)
21     for i in RANGE:
22         rng.InsertAfter('Line %d\r\n' % i)
23         sleep(1)
24     rng.InsertAfter("\r\nTh-th-th-that's all folks!\r\n")
25
26     warn(app)
27     doc.Close(False)
28     word.Application.Quit()
29
30 if __name__=='__main__':
31     Tk().withdraw()
32     word()
```

The Word example follows pretty much the same script as the Excel example. The only difference is that instead of writing in cells, we have to insert the strings into the text "range" of our document and move the cursor forward after each write. We also have to manually provide the line termination characters of carriage RETURN following by NEWLINE (\r\n).

If we run *this* script, a resulting screen might look like Figure 23–2.

23.2.4 *Microsoft PowerPoint*

Applying PowerPoint in an application may not seem commonplace, but you could consider using it when you are rushed to make a presentation. You can create your bullet points in a text file on the plane, then upon arrival at the hotel that evening, use a script that parses the file and auto-generates a set of slides. You can further enhance those slides by adding in a background,

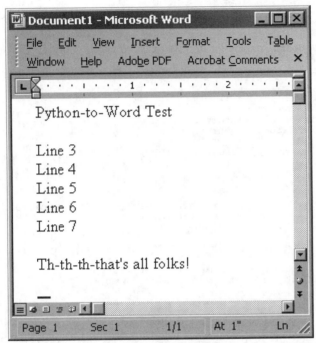

Figure 23-2 Python-to-Word demonstration script (`word.pyw`)

animation, etc., all of which are possible through the COM interface. Another use case would be if you had to auto-generate or modify new or existing presentations. You can create a COM script controlled via a shell script to create and tweak each presentation generated. Okay, enough speculation . . . now let us take a look at our PowerPoint example (i.e., Example 23.4).

Again, you will notice similarities to both the Excel and Word demonstrations above. Where PowerPoint differs is in the objects you write data to. Instead of a single active sheet or document, PowerPoint is somewhat trickier because each presentation slide can have a different layout. With a presentation, you have multiple slides, and each slide can have a different layout. (Recent versions of PowerPoint have 30 different layouts!) The actions you can perform on a slide depend on which layout you have chosen for each page.

In our example, we just use a (title and) text layout (line 17) and fill in the main title (lines 19–20), `Shape[0]` or `Shape(1)`—Python sequences begin at index 0 while Microsoft software starts at 1—, and the text portion (lines 22–26), `Shape[1]` or `Shape(2)`. To figure out which constant to use, you will need a list of all the ones available to you. For example, `ppLayoutText` is defined as a constant with a value of 2 (integer), `ppLayoutTitle` is 1, etc. You can

Example 23.4 PowerPoint Example (`ppoint.pyw`)

This script launches PowerPoint and writes data to the "shapes" on a slide.

```
1  #!/usr/bin/env python
2
3  from Tkinter import Tk
4  from time import sleep
5  from tkMessageBox import showwarning
6  import win32com.client as win32
7
8  warn = lambda app: showwarning(app, 'Exit?')
9  RANGE = range(3, 8)
10
11 def ppoint():
12     app = 'PowerPoint'
13     ppoint = win32.gencache.EnsureDispatch('%s.Application' % app)
14     pres = ppoint.Presentations.Add()
15     ppoint.Visible = True
16
17     s1 = pres.Slides.Add(1, win32.constants.ppLayoutText)
18     sleep(1)
19     s1a = s1.Shapes[0].TextFrame.TextRange
20     s1a.Text = 'Python-to-%s Demo' % app
21     sleep(1)
22     s1b = s1.Shapes[1].TextFrame.TextRange
23     for i in RANGE:
24         s1b.InsertAfter("Line %d\r\n" % i)
25         sleep(1)
26     s1b.InsertAfter("\r\nTh-th-th-that's all folks!")
27
28     warn(app)
29     pres.Close()
30     ppoint.Quit()
31
32 if __name__=='__main__':
33     Tk().withdraw()
34     ppoint()
```

find the constants in most Microsoft VB/Office programming books or online by just searching on the names. Alternatively, you can just use the integer constants without having to name them via `win32.constants`.

The PowerPoint screenshot is shown in Figure 23–3.

23.2.5 Microsoft Outlook

Finally, we give an Outlook demonstration, which uses even more constants than PowerPoint. As a fairly common and versatile tool, use of Outlook in an application makes sense, like it does for Excel. There are always e-mail addresses, messages, and other data that can be easily manipulated in a Python program. Example 23.5 is an Outlook example that does a little bit more than our previous examples.

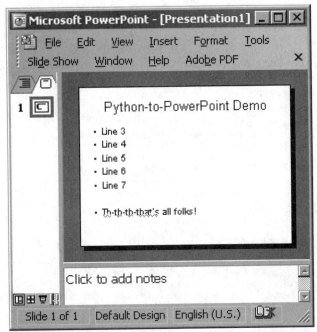

Figure 23–3 Python-to-PowerPoint demonstration script (`ppoint.pyw`)

In this example, we use Outlook to send an e-mail to ourselves. In order to make the demonstration work, you need to turn off your network access so that you do not really send the message, and thus are able to view it in your `Outbox` folder (and delete it if desired after viewing it). After launching Outlook, we create a new mail message and fill out the various fields such as recipient, subject, and body (lines 15–21). We then call the `send()` method (line 22) to spool the message to the `Outbox` where it will be moved to "Sent Mail" once the message has actually been transmitted to the mail server.

Like PowerPoint, there are many constants available . . . `olMailItem` (with a constant value of 0) is the one used for e-mail messages. Other popular Outlook items include `olAppointmentItem` (1), `olContactItem` (2), and `olTaskItem` (3). Of course, there are more, so you will have to find a VB/Office programming book or search for the constants and their values online.

In the next section (lines 24–27), we use another constant, `olFolder-Outbox` (4), to open the `Outbox` folder and bring it up for display. We find the most recent item (hopefully the one we just created) and display it as well. Other popular folders include: `olFolderInbox` (6), `olFolder-Calendar` (9), `olFolderContacts` (10), `olFolderDrafts` (16), `olFolderSentMail` (5), and `olFolderTasks` (13). If you use dynamic

Example 23.5 Outlook Example (`olook.pyw`)

This script launches Outlook, creates a new message, "sends" it, and lets you view it by opening and displaying both the `Outbox` *and the message itself.*

```
1   #!/usr/bin/env python
2
3   from Tkinter import Tk
4   from time import sleep
5   from tkMessageBox import showwarning
6   import win32com.client as win32
7
8   warn = lambda app: showwarning(app, 'Exit?')
9   RANGE = range(3, 8)
10
11  def outlook():
12      app = 'Outlook'
13      olook = win32.gencache.EnsureDispatch('%s.Application' % app)
14
15      mail = olook.CreateItem(win32.constants.olMailItem)
16      recip = mail.Recipients.Add('you@127.0.0.1')
17      subj = mail.Subject = 'Python-to-%s Demo' % app
18      body = ["Line %d" % i for i in RANGE]
19      body.insert(0, '%s\r\n' % subj)
20      body.append("\r\nTh-th-th-that's all folks!")
21      mail.Body = '\r\n'.join(body)
22      mail.Send()
23
24      ns = olook.GetNamespace("MAPI")
25      obox = ns.GetDefaultFolder(win32.constants.olFolderOutbox)
26      obox.Display()
27      obox.Items.Item(1).Display()
28
29      warn(app)
30      olook.Quit()
31
32  if __name__=='__main__':
33      Tk().withdraw()
34      outlook()
```

dispatch, you will likely have to use the numeric values instead of the constants' names (see previous Core Note).

Figure 23–4 shows a screen capture of just the message window.

Before we get this far, however, from its history we know that Outlook has been vulnerable to all kinds of attacks, so Microsoft has built some protection into Outlook for restricting access to your address book and being able to send mail on your behalf. When attempting to access your Outlook data, the screen shown in Figure 23–5 pops up where you must explicitly give permission to an outside program.

Then when you are trying to send a message from an external program, you get the warning dialog shown in Figure 23–6, where you have to wait until the timer expires before you are allowed to select "Yes."

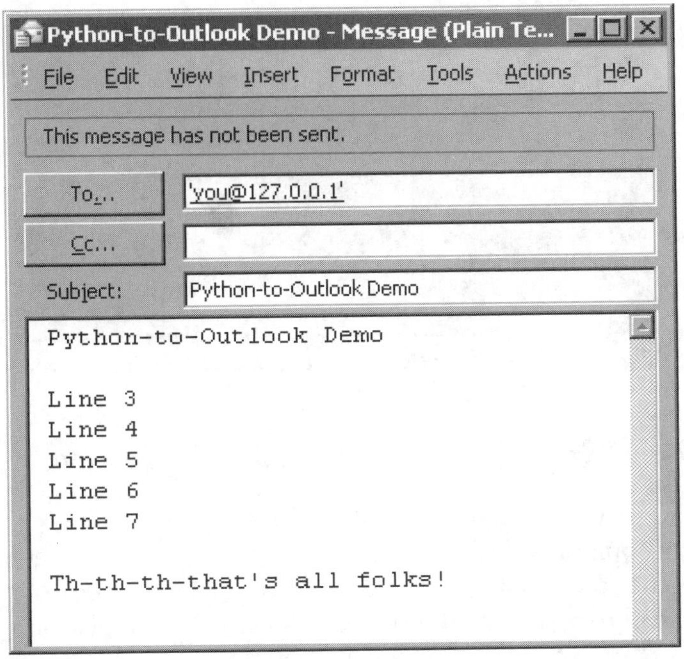

Figure 23–4 Python-to-Outlook demonstration script (`olook.pyw`)

Once you pass all the security checks, everything else should work smoothly. There is software available to help get you around these checks but they have to be downloaded and installed separately.

On this book's Web site at http://corepython.com, you will find an alternative script that combines these four smaller ones into a single application that lets users choose which of these demonstrations to run.

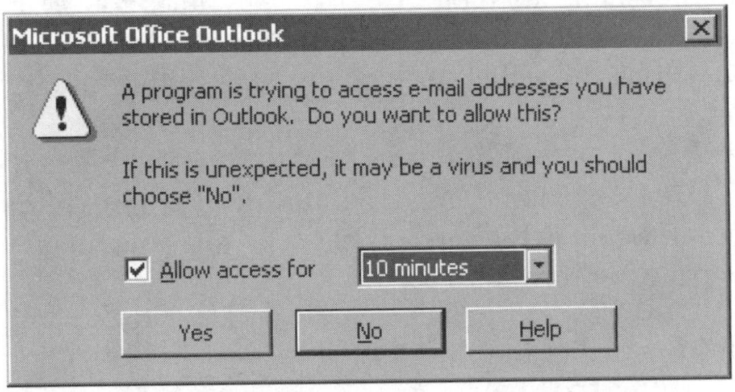

Figure 23–5 Outlook address book access warning

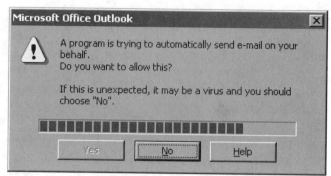

Figure 23–6 Outlook e-mail transmission warning

23.2.6 Intermediate Example

Now that we have gotten a good taste of Office programming, let us build a more useful application by combining the material from this section with that of the Web Services section. If we were to combine the stock quote example with our Excel demonstration script, we would get an application that would download stock quotes from the net and pop them directly into Excel without having to create or use CSV files as a medium (see Example 23.6).

Line-by-Line Explanation

Lines 1–13

We import all of the attributes from both the original Web services stock quote (stock.py) above and Excel scripts here as well as define the same constants.

Lines 15–32

The first part of the core function launches Excel as seen earlier (lines 17–21). The title and timestamp are then written to cells (lines 23–29), along with the column headings, which are then bolded (line 30). The remaining cells are dedicated to writing the actual stock quote data, starting in row 6 (line 32).

Lines 34–43

We open the URL as before (line 34), but instead of just writing the data to standard output, we fill in the spreadsheet cells, one column of data at a time, and one company per row (lines 35–42).

Lines 45–51

The remaining lines of our script mirror code that we have seen before.

Example 23.6 Stock Quote and Excel Example (`estock.pyw`)

This script downloads stock quotes from Yahoo! and writes the data to Excel.

```python
1  #!/usr/bin/env python
2
3  from Tkinter import Tk
4  from time import sleep, ctime
5  from tkMessageBox import showwarning
6  from urllib import urlopen
7  import win32com.client as win32
8
9  warn = lambda app: showwarning(app, 'Exit?')
10 RANGE = range(3, 8)
11 TICKS = ('YHOO', 'GOOG', 'EBAY', 'AMZN')
12 COLS = ('TICKER', 'PRICE', 'CHG', '%AGE')
13 URL = 'http://quote.yahoo.com/d/quotes.csv?s=%s&f=sl1c1p2'
14
15 def excel():
16     app = 'Excel'
17     xl = win32.gencache.EnsureDispatch('%s.Application' % app)
18     ss = xl.Workbooks.Add()
19     sh = ss.ActiveSheet
20     xl.Visible = True
21     sleep(1)
22
23     sh.Cells(1, 1).Value = 'Python-to-%s Stock Quote Demo' % app
24     sleep(1)
25     sh.Cells(3, 1).Value = 'Prices quoted as of: %s' % ctime()
26     sleep(1)
27     for i in range(4):
28         sh.Cells(5, i+1).Value = COLS[i]
29     sleep(1)
30     sh.Range(sh.Cells(5, 1), sh.Cells(5, 4)).Font.Bold = True
31     sleep(1)
32     row = 6
33
34     u = urlopen(URL % ','.join(TICKS))
35     for data in u:
36         tick, price, chg, per = data.split(',')
37         sh.Cells(row, 1).Value = eval(tick)
38         sh.Cells(row, 2).Value = ('%.2f' % round(float(price), 2))
39         sh.Cells(row, 3).Value = chg
40         sh.Cells(row, 4).Value = eval(per.rstrip())
41         row += 1
42         sleep(1)
43     f.close()
44
45     warn(app)
46     ss.Close(False)
47     xl.Application.Quit()
48
49 if __name__=='__main__':
50     Tk().withdraw()
51     excel()
```

Figure 23–7 shows a window with real data after executing our script.

Note that the data columns lose the original formatting of the numeric strings because Excel stores them as numbers using the default cell format. We lose the formatting of the numbers to two places after the decimal point,

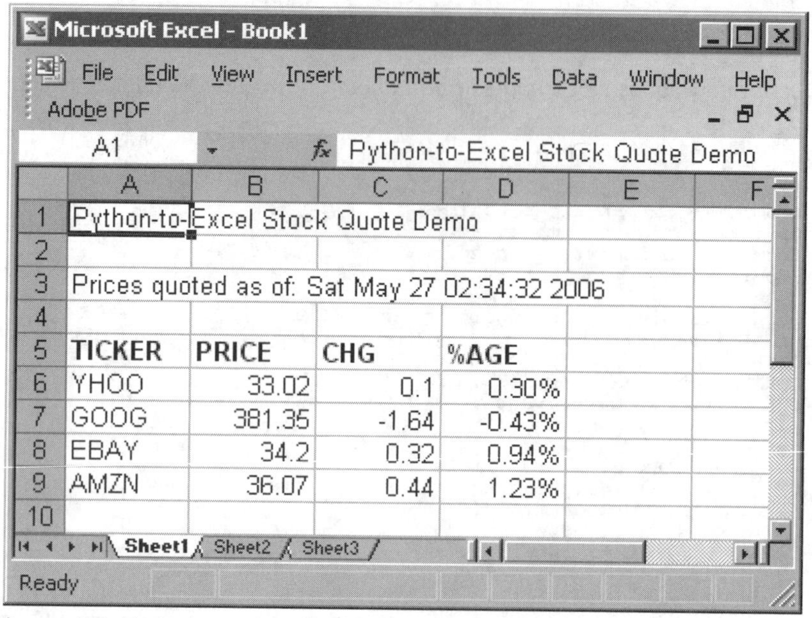

Figure 23–7   Python-to-Excel stock quote demonstration script (`estock.pyw`)

e.g., "34.2" is displayed even though Python passed in "34.20"; and for the "change from previous close column," we lose not only the decimal places but also the plus sign (+) indicating a positive change in value. (Compare the output in Excel to the output from the original text version [`stock.py`]. These problems will be addressed by an exercise at chapter's end.)

23.3 Python and Java Programming with Jython

23.3.1 What Is Jython?

Jython is one of those tools that can unite two diverse programming populations. For one, it caters to Python programmers embedded in a Java development environment and gives them the ability to rapidly prototype solutions that seamlessly integrate into an existing Java platform. Another reason is that it helps simplify the lives of millions of Java programmers out there by giving Java a scripting language environment. No longer do Java programmers have to write a test harness or driver application to simply test a class they have just written.

Jython gives you most of what Python has to offer along with the ability to instantiate and interact with Java classes too! Jython code is dynamically compiled into Java bytecode, plus you can extend Java classes in Jython. You can also extend Python using Java. It is quite easy to write a class in Python and then use it as a Java class. You can always statically compile a Jython script into Java bytecode.

Jython can be downloaded from the book's Web site or at http://jython.org. After installation and seeing some default startup notices of processing new .jar files, starting up Jython's interactive interpreter looks eerily like you're using Python. And yes, Virginia, you can still do the same old "Hello World!" in Python:

```
$ jython
Jython 2.2a1 on java1.4.2_09 (JIT: null)
Type "copyright", "credits" or "license" for more
    information.
>>> print 'Hello World!'
Hello World!
>>>
>>> import sys
>>> sys.stdout.write('Hello World!\n')
Hello World!
```

The only difference is that you now have (to wait for) Java's long startup time. Once you have accepted that inevitability, you can move on to greater things. The more interesting thing about the Jython interactive interpreter is that now you can do "Hello World!" using Java(!):

```
>>> from java.lang import System
>>> System.out.write('Hello World!\n')
Hello World!
```

Java gives Python users the added bonuses of native exception handling (not available in standard Python, or "CPython" as it is called, when being referred to among other implementations) as well as use of Java's own garbage collector (so Python's did not have to be [re]implemented for Java).

23.3.2 Swing GUI Development (Java or Python!)

By having access to all Java classes, we have a much broader universe of what is possible. One example is GUI development. In Python, we have the default GUI of Tk via the Tkinter module, but Tk is not a native Python toolkit. However, Java does have Swing, and it is native. With Jython, we can actually write a GUI application using Swing components . . . not with Java, but using Python.

A simple "Hello World!" GUI written in Java followed by its equivalent in Python is given in Examples 23.7 and 23.8, respectively, both of which mimic the Tk examples `tkhello3.py` found earlier in the GUI programming chapter. These programs are called `swhello.java` and `swhello.py`, respectively.

Example 23.7 Swing "Hello World" in Java (`swhello.java`)

This program creates a GUI just like `tkhello3.py` *but uses Swing instead of Tk. It is written in Java.*

```java
1  import java.awt.*;
2  import java.awt.event.*;
3  import javax.swing.*;
4  import java.lang.*;
5
6  public class swhello extends JFrame {
7      JPanel box;
8      JLabel hello;
9      JButton quit;
10
11     public swhello() {
12         super("JSwing");
13         JPanel box = new JPanel(new BorderLayout());
14         JLabel hello = new JLabel("Hello World!");
15         JButton quit = new JButton("QUIT");
16
17         ActionListener quitAction = new ActionListener() {
18             public void actionPerformed(ActionEvent e) {
19                 System.exit(0);
20             }
21         };
22         quit.setBackground(Color.red);
23         quit.setForeground(Color.white);
24         quit.addActionListener(quitAction);
25         box.add(hello, BorderLayout.NORTH);
26         box.add(quit, BorderLayout.SOUTH);
27
28         addWindowListener(new WindowAdapter() {
29             public void windowClosing(WindowEvent e) {
30                 System.exit(0);
31             }
32         });
33         getContentPane().add(box);
34         pack();
35         setVisible(true);
36     }
37
38     public static void main(String args[]) {
39         swhello app = new swhello();
40     }
41 }
```

Example 23.8 Swing "Hello World" in Python (`swhello.py`)

This is an equivalent Python script to the above Java program and executed with the Jython interpreter.

```
1   #!/usr/bin/env jython
2
3   from pawt import swing
4   import sys
5   from java.awt import Color, BorderLayout
6
7   def quit(e):
8        sys.exit()
9
10  top = swing.JFrame("PySwing")
11  box = swing.JPanel()
12  hello = swing.JLabel("Hello World!")
13  quit = swing.JButton("QUIT", actionPerformed=quit,
14        background=Color.red, foreground=Color.white)
15
16  box.add("North", hello)
17  box.add("South", quit)
18  top.contentPane.add(box)
19  top.pack()
20  top.visible = 1      # or True for Jython 2.2+
```

The code for both matches that of `tkhello3.py` except they use Swing instead of Tk. The hallmark of the Python version is the significant reduction in the number of lines of code necessary to do the same thing in Java. The Python code is more expressive, with each line of code having more significance. In short, there is less "white noise." Java code tends to have a lot more boilerplate code to get work done, while Python lets you concentrate on the important parts of your application: the solution to the problem you are trying to solve.

Since both applications are compiled to Java bytecode, it is no surprise that both applications look exactly alike when executing on the same platform (see Figure 23–8).

Jython is a great development tool because you get the expressiveness of Python plus the rich API in the Java libraries. If you are a current Java developer, we hope that we have whet your appetite in terms of what you can now do with the power of Python behind you. If you are new to Java, Jython will be able to ease you in gently. You can prototype in Jython, then port easily to Java as necessary.

Figure 23-8 Swing Hello World Demonstration Scripts (`swhello.{java,py}`)

23.4 Exercises

Web Services

23–1. *Web Services*. Take the Yahoo! stock quote example (`stock.py`) and change the application to save the quote data to a file instead of displaying it to the screen. Optional: You may change the script so that users can choose to display the quote data or save it to a file.

23–2. *Web Services*. Update the Yahoo! stock quote example (`stock.py`) to download other stock quote data given the additional parameters listed above. Optional: You may add this feature to your solution to the above exercise.

23–3. *Web Services and the* `csv` *Module*. Convert `stock.py` to using the `csv` module to parse the incoming data, like we did in the example code snippet. Extra Credit: Do the same thing to the Excel version of this script (`estock.py`).

23–4. *REST and Web Services*. Study how REST and XML are used in more modern-day Web services APIs and applications. Describe the additional functionality you get over older systems like the Yahoo! quote server, which uses URL parameters.

23–5. *REST and Web Services*. Build an application framework using Python's support for REST and XML that will allow you to share and reuse this code when writing applications that use any of the newer Web services and APIs available today. Display your code using APIs from Yahoo!, Google, eBay, and/or Amazon.

Microsoft Office Programming

23–6. *Microsoft Excel and Web Pages*. Create an application that will read data from an Excel spreadsheet and map all of it to an equivalent HTML table. (You may use the third-party `HTMLgen` module if desired.)

23–7. *Microsoft Office Applications and Web Services*. Interface to any existing Web service, whether REST- or URL-based, and write data to an Excel spreadsheet or format the data nicely into a Word document. Format them properly for printing. Extra Credit: Support both Excel *and* Word.

23–8. *Microsoft Outlook and Web Services*. Similar to the previous problem, do the same thing, but put the data into a new e-mail message that you send with Outlook. Extra Credit: Do the same thing but send the e-mail with regular SMTP instead. (You may wish to refer to Chapter 17 on Internet Client Programming.)

23–9. *Microsoft PowerPoint*. Design a presentation slide creator. Design the specification of a text file that users will create with Word or a normal text editor. Using the specification format, read in the presentation data and create the appropriate PowerPoint slides all as part of a single presentation.

23–10. *Microsoft Outlook, Databases, and Your Address Book*. Write a program that will extract the contents of an Outlook address book and store the desired fields into a database. The database can be a text file, DBM file, or even an RDBMS. (You may wish to refer to Chapter 21, Database Programming.) Extra Credit: Do the reverse . . . read in contact information from a database (or allow for direct user input) and create or update records in Outlook.

23–11. *Microsoft Outlook and E-mail*. Develop a program that backs up your e-mail by taking the contents of your Inbox and/or other important folders and saves them in (as close to) regular "box" format to disk.

23–12. *Microsoft Outlook Calendar*. Write a simple script that creates new Outlook appointments. Take at least the following as user input: start date and time, appointment name or subject, and duration of appointment.

23–13. *Microsoft Outlook Calendar*. Build an application that dumps the contents of your appointments to a destination of your choice, i.e., to the screen, to a database, to Excel, etc. Extra Credit: Do the same thing to your set of Outlook tasks.

23–14. *Multithreading.* Update the Excel version of the stock quote download script (`estock.pyw`) so that the downloads of data happen "concurrently" using multiple Python threads. Optional: You may also try this exercise with Visual C++ threads using `win32process.beginthreadex()`.

23–15. *Excel Cell Formatting.* In the spreadsheet version of the stock quote download script (`estock.pyw`), we saw in Figure 23–7 how the stock price does not default to two places after the decimal point even if we pass in a string with the trailing zero(s). When Excel converts it to a number, it uses the default setting for the number format.

(a) Change the numeric format to correctly go out to two decimal places by changing the cell's `NumberFormat` attribute to "`0.00`."

(b) We can also saw that the "change from previous close" column loses the "+" in addition to the decimal point formatting. However, we discover that making the correction in part (a) to both columns only solves the decimal place problem... the plus sign is automatically dropped for any number. The solution here is to change this column to be text instead of a number. You can do this by changing the cell's `NumberFormat` attribute to "`@`."

(c) By changing the cell's numeric format to text, however, we lose the right alignment that comes automatically with numbers. In addition to your solution to part (b), you must also now set the cell's `HorizontalAlignment` attribute to the Win32 Excel constant `xlRight`. After you come up with the solutions to all three parts, your output will now look more acceptable, as shown in Figure 23–9.

Java, Python, Jython

23–16. *Jython.* What is the difference between Jython and CPython?

23–17. *Java and Python.* Take an existing Java application and port it to Python. Write down your experience in a journal. When complete, give an executive summary of what has to be accomplished, what some of the important steps are, and what common operations you have to perform to make it happen.

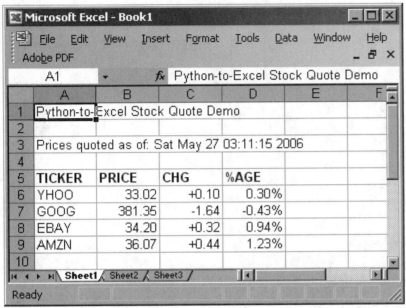

Figure 23-9 Improving the Python-to-Excel stock quote script (`estock.pyw`)

23–18. *Java and Python.* Study the Jython source code. Describe how some of Python standard types are implemented in Java.

23–19. *Java and Python.* Extend Python by writing an extension in Java. What are the necessary steps? Demonstrate your working solution by showing how it works in with the Jython interactive interpreter.

23–20. *Jython and Databases.* Find an interesting exercise from the Chapter 21 and port it to Jython. One of the best things about Jython is that starting in 2.1, it now comes with a JDBC database module called zxJDBC that is nearly Python DB-API 2.0–compliant.

23–21. *Python and Jython.* Find a Python module not available in Jython (yet) and port it. Consider submitting it as a patch to the Jython distribution.

Appendix A

Answers to Selected Exercises

Chapter 2

5. Loops and numbers
   a)
   ```
   i = 0
   while i < 11:
       i += 1
   ```
   b)
   ```
   for i in range(11):
       pass
   ```

6. Conditionals
   ```
   n = int(raw_input('enter a number: '))
   if n < 0:
       print 'negative'
   elif n > 0:
       print 'positive'
   else:
       print 'zero'
   ```

7. Loops and strings

```
s = raw_input('enter a string: ')
for eachChar in s:
    print eachChar    # (does not print index)
```

or

```
for i in range(len(s)):
    print i, s[i]
```

or

```
i = 0
slen = len(s)
while i < slen:
    print i, s[i]
```

or

```
for i, x in enumerate(s):
    print i, x
```

8. Loops and operators

```
subtot = 0
for i in range(5):
    subtot += int(raw_input('enter a number: '))
print subtot
```

or

```
# uses sum() BIF and generator expressions
print sum(int(raw_input('enter a number: ')) for i in range(5))
```

Chapter 3

4. Statements
   Use ;

5. Statements
   Use \ (unless part of a comma-separated sequence in which case \ is optional)

7. Identifiers

40XL	number
$saving$	symbol
print	keyword
0x40L	number
big-daddy	symbol
2hot2touch	number
thisIsn'tAVar	symbol
if	keyword
counter-1	symbol

Chapter 4

1. Python objects

All Python objects have three attributes: type, ID, and value. All are read-only with a possible exception of the value (which can be changed only if the object is mutable).

5. `str()` vs. `repr()`

`repr()` is a built-in function while `str()` was a built-in function that changed to a factory function in Python 2.2. They will both return a string representation of an object; however, `str()` returns a *printable* string representation while `repr()` (and the backquote operator ` `` `) return an *evaluatable* string representation of an object, meaning that it is a string that represents a (valid) Python object that would be created if passed to `eval()`.

6. Object equality

`type(a) == type(b)`	whether the value of `type(a)` is the same as the value of `type(b)` . . . `==` is a value compare
`type(a)` **is** `type(b)`	whether the type objects returned by `type(a)` and `type(b)` are the same object

Since there exists only one (type) object for each built-in type, there is no need to check their values; hence, only the latter form should be used.

Chapter 5

8. Geometry

```python
import math

def sqcube():
    s = float(raw_input('enter length of one side: '))
    print 'the area is:', s ** 2., '(units squared)'
    print 'the volume is:', s ** 3., '(cubic units)'

def cirsph():
    r = float(raw_input('enter length of radius: '))
    print 'the area is:', math.pi * (r ** 2.),
    '(units squared)'
    print 'the volume is:', (4. / 3.) * math.pi * (r **
3.), '(cubic units)'

sqcube()
cirsph()
```

11. Modulus

a)

```
for i in range(0, 22, 2):      # range(0, 21, 2) okay too
    print i
```

or

```
for i in range(22):            # range(21) okay too
    if i % 2 == 0:
        print i
```

b)

```
for i in range(1, 20, 2):      # range(1, 21, 2) okay too
    print i
```

or

```
for i in range(20):            # range(21) okay too
    if i % 2 != 0:
        print i
```

c)

When i % 2 == 0, it's even (divisible by 2), otherwise it's odd.

Chapter 6

1. Strings

find(), rfind(), index(), rindex(); can also use the **in** operator.

2. Identifiers

```
import string
alphas = string.letters + '_'
alnums = alphas + string.digits

iden = raw_input('Identifier to check? ')

if len(iden) > 0:
    if iden[0] not in alphas:
        print "Error: first char must be alphabetic"
    else:
        if len(iden) > 1:
            for eachChar in iden[1:]:
                if eachChar not in alnums:
                    print "Error: others must be alnum"
                    break
            else:
                import keyword
                if iden not in keyword.kwlist:
                    print 'ok'
                else:
                    print 'Error: keyword name'
else:
    print 'Error: no identifier entered'
```

Chapter 7

1. Dictionary methods

```
dict.update()
```

3. Dictionary methods

a)

```
keys = dict.keys()
keys.sort()
```

or

```
sorted(dict.keys())
```

4. Creating dictionaries

```
# assumes  and list2 are the same length
d = {}
for i in range(len(list1)):
    d[list1[i]] = list2[i]
```

or

```
d = {}
for i, x in enumerate(list1):
    d[x] = list2[i]
```

or

```
d = dict(map(None, list1, list2))
```

or

```
d = dict(zip(list1, list2))
```

7. Inverting dictionaries

```
list1 = oldDict.values()
list2 = oldDict.keys()
```

Now apply the solutions to Problem 4.

Note that these solutions are destructive, meaning that for one-to-many dictionaries, keys that share the same values will only have the latest installed value for the value that is now a key. Extra Credit: Come up with a non-destructive solution where keys that share the same values in the old dictionary are now stored inside a list as the value for the corresponding key in the new dictionary.

Chapter 8

3. `range()` built-in function
   a)

   ```
   range(10)
   ```

4. Prime numbers

   ```python
   import math
   def isprime(num):
       count = int(math.sqrt(num))
       while count > 1:
           if num % count == 0:
               return False
           count -= 1
       else:
           return True
   ```

Chapter 9

2. File access

   ```python
   f = open(raw_input('enter filename: '))
   i = 0
   num = int(raw_input('enter number of lines: '))
   for eachLine in f:
       if i == num:
           break
       print eachLine,         # suppress NEWLINE
       i += 1
   f.close()
   ```

13. Command-line arguments
    b)

    ```python
    import sys
    print "# of args", len(sys.argv)    # argc
    print "args:", sys.argv             # argv
    ```

Chapter 10

1. Raising exceptions
   e)

2. Raising exceptions
   d)

4. Keywords

try-except monitors the **try** clause for exceptions and execution jumps to the matching **except** clause. However, the **finally** clause of a **try-finally** will be executed regardless of whether or not an exception occurred. How does the **try-except-finally** statement work?

5. Exceptions (we'll provide the solution, but you have to determine why):

a) SyntaxError

b) IndexError

c) NameError

d) ZeroDivisionError

e) ValueError

f) TypeError

Chapter 11

2. Functions

```
def sumtimes(x, y):
    return (x+y, x*y)
```

6. Variable-length arguments

```
def printf(string, *args):
    print string % args
```

Chapter 12

2. Importing attributes

a)

```
import mymodule ⇒ mymodule.foo()
```

and

```
from mymodule import foo ⇒ foo()
```

b)

If you use the **import** statement, the module name is brought into the local namespace, and foo() is only accessible from the module's namespace.

If you use the **from-import** statement, "foo()" itself is brought into the local namespace. In this case, you do not need to use the module's namespace to access it.

Chapter 13

2. Functions versus methods
Methods are basically functions but tied to a specific class object type. They are defined as part of a class and are executed as part of an instance of that class.

15. Delegation
It makes no difference whether we use `open()` or `capOpen()` to read our file because in `capOpen.py`, we delegated all of the reading functionality to the Python system defaults, meaning that no special action is ever taken on reads. The same code would be executed, i.e., none of `read()`, `readline()`, or `readlines()` are overridden with any special functionality.

Chapter 14

1. Callable objects
Functions, methods, classes, callable class instances

3. `input()` vs. `raw_input()`
`raw_input()` returns user input as a string; `input()` returns the evaluation of the user input as a Python expression. In other words:

```
input() ≡ eval(raw_input())
```

Chapter 15

Regular expressions
1. Matching strings
bat, hat, bit, etc.

```
[bh][aiu]t
```

2. First name last
```
[A-Za-z-]+ [A-Za-z-]+
```

(Any pair of words separated by a single space, e.g., first and last names, hyphens allowed)

3. Last name first
```
[A-Za-z-]+, [A-Za-z]
```

(Any word and single letter separated by a comma and single space, e.g., last name, first initial)

```
[A-Za-z-]+, [A-Za-z-]+
```

(Any pair of words separated by a comma and single space, e.g., last, first names, hyphens allowed)

8. Python longs

```
\d+[lL]
```

(Decimal [base 10] integers only)

9. Python floats

```
[0-9]+(\.[0-9]*)?
```

(Describes a simple floating point number, that is, any number of digits followed optionally by a single decimal point and zero or more numeric digits, as in "0.004," "2," "75.," etc.)

Chapter 16

3. Sockets
   TCP

6. Daytime service

```
>>> import socket
>>> socket.getservbyname('daytime', 'udp')
13
```

Chapter 17

20. Identifiers
    pass is a keyword, so it cannot be used as an identifier. The common idiom in all such cases is to append an underscore (_) to the name of the offending variable.

Chapter 18

2. Python threads
   I/O-bound . . . why?

Chapter 19

1. Client/server architecture
   Window(ing) clients are GUI events generated usually by users which must be processed by the window(ing) system that acts as the server; it is responsible for making timely updates to the display as to be apparent to the user.

Chapter 20

15. CGI errors

The Web server returns either no data or error text, which results in an HTTP 500 or Internal Server Error in your browser because that (returned data) is not valid HTTP or HTML data. The `cgitb` module captures the Python traceback and returns it as valid data through CGI, which gets displayed to the user . . . a great debugging tool.

Chapter 21

1. Extending Python
   - Performance improvement
   - Protecting source code
   - New or desired change of functionality
   - And more!

Chapter 22

1. DB-API

The DB-API is a common interface specification for all Python database adapters. It is good in that it forces all adapter writers to code to the same specification so that end-user programmers can write consistent code that can be (more) easily ported to other databases with the minimum amount of effort.

Chapter 23

3. Web services and the `csv` module

Replace the **for** loop in `stock.py` with the following:

```
import csv
for tick, price, chg, per in csv.reader(f):
    print tick.ljust(7), ('%.2f' % round(float(price),
2)).rjust(6), chg.rjust(6), per.rjust(6)
```

Appendix B

Reference Tables

Python Keywords

Table B.1 lists Python's keywords.

Table B.1 Python Keywords[a]

and	as[b]	assert[c]	break
class	continue	def	del
elif	else	except	exec
finally	for	from	global
if	import	in	is
lambda	not	or	pass
print	raise	return	try
while	with[b]	yield[d]	None[e]

a. **access** keyword obsoleted in Python 1.4.
b. New in Python 2.6.
c. New in Python 1.5.
d. New in Python 2.3.
e. Not a keyword but made a constant in Python 2.4.

Python Standard Operators and Functions

Table B.2 represents the operators and (built-in and factory) functions that can be used with most standard Python objects as well as user-defined objects in which you have implemented their corresponding special methods.

Table B.2 Standard Type Operators and Functions

Operator/function	Description	Result[a]
String representation		
` `	Evaluatable string representation	str
Built-in and factory functions		
cmp(*obj1*, *obj2*)	Compares two objects	int
repr(*obj*)	Evaluatable string representation	str
str(*obj*)	Printable string representation	str
type(*obj*)	Object type	type

Table B.2 Standard Type Operators and Functions (continued)

operator/function	Description	Result[a]
Value comparisons		
<	Less than	bool
>	Greater than	bool
<=	Less than or equal to	bool
>=	Greater than or equal to	bool
==	Equal to	bool
!=	Not equal to	bool
<>	Not equal to	bool
Object comparisons		
is	The same as	bool
is not	Not the same as	bool
Boolean operators		
not	Logical negation	bool
and	Logical conjunction	bool
or	Logical disjunction	bool

a. Boolean comparisons return either True or False.

Numeric Type Operators and Functions

Table B.3 represents the operators and (built-in and factory) functions that apply to Python's numeric objects.

Table B.3 Operators and Built-in Functions for All Numeric Types

Operator/ built-in	Description	int	long	float	complex	Result[a]
abs()	Absolute value	•	•	•	•	number[a]
chr()	Character	•	•			str

(continued)

Table B.3 Operators and Built-in Functions for All Numeric Types (continued)

Operator/built-in	Description	int	long	float	complex	Result[a]
coerce()	Numeric coercion	•	•	•	•	tuple
complex()	Complex factory function	•	•	•	•	complex
divmod()	Division/modulo	•	•	•	•	tuple
float()	Float factory function	•	•	•	•	float
hex()	Hexadecimal string	•	•			str
int()	Int factory function	•	•	•	•	int
long()	Long factory function	•	•	•	•	long
oct()	Octal string	•	•			str
ord()	Ordinal			(string)		int
pow()	Exponentiation	•	•	•	•	*number*
round()	Float rounding			•		float
**[b]	Exponentiation	•	•	•	•	*number*
+[c]	No change	•	•	•	•	*number*
-[c]	Negation	•	•	•	•	*number*
~[c]	Bit inversion	•	•			int/long
**[b]	Exponentiation	•	•	•	•	*number*
*	Multiplication	•	•	•	•	*number*
/	Classic or true division	•	•	•	•	*number*
//	Floor division	•	•	•	•	*number*
%	Modulo/remainder	•	•	•	•	*number*

Table B.3 Operators and Built-in Functions for All Numeric Types (continued)

Operator/built-in	Description	int	long	float	complex	Result[a]
+	Addition	•	•	•	•	*number*
–	Subtraction	•	•	•	•	*number*
<<	Bit left shift	•	•			int/long
>>	Bit right shift	•	•			int/long
&	Bitwise AND	•	•			int/long
^	Bitwise XOR	•	•			int/long
|	Bitwise OR	•	•			int/long

a. A result of "number" indicates any of the numeric types, perhaps the same as the operands.
b. **has a unique relationship with unary operators; see Section 5.5.3 and Table 5.2.
c. Unary operator.

Sequence Type Operators and Functions

Table B.4 contains the set of operators, (built-in and factory) functions, and built-in methods that can be used with sequence types.

Table B.4 Sequence Type Operators, Built-in Functions, and Methods

Operator, built-in function or method	str	list	tuple
[] (list creation)		•	
()			•
""	•		
append()		•	

(continued)

Table B.4 Sequence Type Operators, Built-in Functions, and Methods (continued)

Operator, built-in function or method	str	list	tuple
capitalize()	•		
center()	•		
chr()	•		
cmp()	•	•	•
count()	•	•	
decode()	•		
encode()	•		
endswith()	•		
expandtabs()	•		
extend()		•	
find()	•		
hex()	•		
index()	•	•	
insert()		•	
isdecimal()	•		
isdigit()	•		
islower()	•		
isnumeric()	•		
isspace()	•		
istitle()	•		
isupper()	•		
join()	•		

Table B.4 Sequence Type Operators, Built-in Functions, and Methods (continued)

Operator, built-in function or method	str	list	tuple
len()	•	•	•
list()	•	•	•
ljust()	•		
lower()	•		
lstrip()	•		
max()	•	•	•
min()	•	•	•
oct()	•		
ord()	•		
pop()		•	
raw_input()	•		
remove()		•	
replace()	•		
repr()	•	•	•
reverse()		•	
rfind()	•		
rindex()	•		
rjust()	•		
rstrip()	•		
sort()		•	
split()	•		

(continued)

Table B.4 Sequence Type Operators, Built-in Functions, and Methods (continued)

Operator, built-in function or method	str	list	tuple
splitlines()	•		
startswith()	•		
str()	•	•	•
strip()	•		
swapcase()	•		
split()	•		
title()	•		
tuple()	•	•	•
type()	•	•	•
upper()	•		
zfill()	•		
. (attributes)	•	•	
[] (slice)	•	•	•
[:]	•	•	•
*	•	•	•
%	•		
+	•	•	•
in	•	•	•
not in	•	•	•

String Format Operator Conversion Symbols

Table B.5 lists the formatting symbols that can be used with the string format operator (%).

String Format Operator Directives

When using the string format operator (see Table B.5), you may enhance or fine-tune the object display with the directives shown in Table B.6.

Table B.5 String Format Operator Conversion Symbols

Format Symbol	Conversion
%c	Character (integer [ASCII value] or string of length 1)
%r[a]	String conversion via `repr()` prior to formatting
%s	String conversion via `str()` prior to formatting
%d / %i	Signed decimal integer
%u[b]	Unsigned decimal integer
%o[b]	(Unsigned) octal integer
%x[b] / %X[b]	(Unsigned) hexadecimal integer (lower/UPPERcase letters)
%e / %E	Exponential notation (with lowercase 'e'/UPPERcase 'E')
%f / %F	Floating point real number (fraction truncates naturally)
%g / %G	The shorter of %e and %f/%E% and %F%
%%	Percent character (%) unescaped

a. New in Python 2.0; likely unique only to Python.
b. %u/%o/%x/%X of negative int will return a signed string in Python 2.4+.

Table B.6 Format Operator Auxiliary Directives

Symbol	Functionality
*	Argument specifies width or precision
-	Use left justification
+	Use a plus sign (+) for positive numbers
<sp>	Use space-padding for positive numbers
#	Add the octal leading zero (′ 0 ′) or hexadecimal leading ′ 0x ′ or ′ 0X ′ , depending on whether ′ x ′ or ′ X ′ were used
0	Use zero-padding (instead of spaces) when formatting numbers
%	′ %% ′ leaves you with a single literal ′ % ′
(var)	Mapping variable (dictionary arguments)
m.n	*m* is the minimum total width and *n* is the number of digits to display after the decimal point (if applicable)

String Type Built-in Methods

The descriptions for the string built-in methods listed above are given in Table B.7.

Table B.7 String Type Built-in Methods

Method Name	Description
string.capitalize()	Capitalizes first letter of *string*
string.center(*width*)	Returns a space-padded *string* with the original *string* centered to a total of *width* columns
string.count(*str*, *beg*=0, *end*=len(*string*))	Counts how many times *str* occurs in *string*, or in a substring of *string* if starting index *beg* and ending index *end* are given

Table B.7 String Type Built-in Methods (continued)

Method Name	*Description*
string.decode(*encoding*='UTF-8', *errors*='strict') [** ed. add FN: New in Python 2.2]	Returns decoded string version of string; on error, default is to raise a ValueError unless *errors* is given with 'ignore' or 'replace'
string.encode(*encoding*='UTF-8', *errors*='strict')[a]	Returns encoded string version of string; on error, default is to raise a ValueError unless *errors* is given with 'ignore' or 'replace'
string.endswith(*str*, *beg*=0, *end*=len(*string*))[b]	Determines if *string* or a substring of *string* (if starting index *beg* and ending index *end* are given) ends with *str*; returns True if so, and False otherwise
string.expandtabs(*tabsize*=8)	Expands tabs in *string* to multiple spaces; defaults to 8 spaces per tab if *tabsize* not provided
string.find(*str*, *beg*=0 *end*=len(*string*))	Determines if *str* occurs in *string*, or in a substring of *string* if starting index *beg* and ending index *end* are given; returns index if found and −1 otherwise
string.index(*str*, *beg*=0, *end*=len(*string*))	Same as find(), but raises an exception if *str* not found
string.isalnum()[a,b,c]	Returns True if *string* has at least 1 character and all characters are alphanumeric and False otherwise
string.isalpha()[a,b,c]	Returns True if *string* has at least 1 character and all characters are alphabetic and False otherwise
string.isdecimal()[b,c,d]	Returns True if *string* contains only decimal digits and False otherwise
string.isdigit()[b,c]	Returns True if *string* contains only digits and False otherwise
string.islower()[b,c]	Returns True if *string* has at least 1 cased character and all cased characters are in lowercase and False otherwise

(continued)

Table B.7 String Type Built-in Methods (continued)

Method Name	*Description*
string.isnumeric() [b,c,d]	Returns True if *string* contains only numeric characters and False otherwise
string.isspace() [b,c]	Returns True if *string* contains only whitespace characters and False otherwise
string.istitle() [b,c]	Returns True if *string* is properly "titlecased" (see title()) and False otherwise
string.isupper() [b,c]	Returns True if *string* has at least one cased character and all cased characters are in uppercase and False otherwise
string.join(*seq*)	Merges (concatenates) the string representations of elements in sequence *seq* into a string, with separator *string*
string.ljust(*width*)	Returns a space-padded *string* with the original string left-justified to a total of *width* columns
string.lower()	Converts all uppercase letters in *string* to lowercase
string.lstrip()	Removes all leading whitespace in *string*
string.replace(*str1*, *str2*, num=*string*.count(*str1*))	Replaces all occurrences of *str1* in *string* with *str2*, or at most *num* occurrences if *num* given
string.rfind(*str*, beg=0, end=len(*string*))	Same as find(), but search backwards in *string*
string.rindex(*str*, beg=0, end=len(*string*))	Same as index(), but search backwards in *string*
string.rjust(*width*)	Returns a space-padded *string* with the original string right-justified to a total of *width* columns

Table B.7 String Type Built-in Methods (continued)

Method Name	*Description*
`string.rstrip()`	Removes all trailing whitespace of *string*
`string.split(str="",` `num=string.count(str))`	Splits *string* according to delimiter *str* (space if not provided) and returns list of substrings; split into at most *num* substrings if given
`string.splitlines(` `num=string.count('\n'))`[b,c]	Splits *string* at all (or *num*) NEWLINEs and returns a list of each line with NEWLINEs removed
`string.startswith(str, beg=0,` `end=len(string))`[b]	Determines if *string* or a substring of *string* (if starting index *beg* and ending index *end* are given) starts with substring *str*; returns `True` if so, and `False` otherwise
`string.strip([obj])`	Performs both `lstrip()` and `rstrip()` on *string*
`string.swapcase()`	Inverts case for all letters in *string*
`string.title()`[b,c]	Returns "titlecased" version of *string*, that is, all words begin with uppercase, and the rest are lowercase (also see `istitle()`)
`string.translate(str, del="")`	Translates *string* according to translation table *str* (256 chars), removing those in the *del* string
`string.upper()`	Converts lowercase letters in *string* to uppercase
`string.zfill(width)`	Returns original *string* left-padded with zeros to a total of *width* characters; intended for numbers, `zfill()` retains any sign given (less one zero)

a. Applicable to Unicode strings only in 1.6, but to all string types in 2.0.
b. Not available as a `string` module function in 1.5.2.
c. New in Python 2.1.
d. Applicable to Unicode strings only.

List Type Built-in Methods

In Table B.8, we present full descriptions and usage syntax for the list built-in methods given above.

Dictionary Type Built-in Methods

In Table B.9, we list the full description and usage syntax for the dictionary built-in methods listed below.

Table B.8 List Type Built-in Methods

List Method	Operation
`list.append(obj)`	Adds *obj* to the end of *list*
`list.count(obj)`	Returns count of how many times *obj* occurs in *list*
`list.extend(seq)`[a]	Appends contents of *seq* to *list*
`list.index(obj, i=0, j=len(list))`	Returns lowest index *k* where `list[k]` == *obj* and $i <= k < j$; otherwise `ValueError` raised
`list.insert(index, obj)`	Inserts *obj* into *list* at offset *index*
`list.pop(index=-1)`[a]	Removes and returns *obj* at given or last *index* from *list*
`list.remove(obj)`	Removes object *obj* from *list*
`list.reverse()`	Reverses objects of *list* in place
`list.sort(func=None, key=None, reverse=False)`	Sorts list members with optional comparison *func*tion; *key* is a callback when extracting elements for sorting, and if *reverse* flag is `True`, then list is sorted in reverse order

a.   New in Python 1.5.2.

Table B.9 Dictionary Type Methods

Method Name	*Operation*
`dict.clear`[a]`()`	Removes all elements of `dict`
`dict.copy`[a]`()`	Returns a (shallow[b]) copy of `dict`
`dict.fromkeys`[c]`(seq, val=None)`	Creates and returns a new dictionary with the elements of `seq` as the keys and `val` as the initial value (defaults to `None` if not given) for all keys
`dict.get(key, default=None)`[a]	For key `key`, returns value or `default` if `key` not in `dict` (note that `default`'s default is `None`)
`dict.has_key(key)`	Returns `True` if `key` is in `dict`, `False` otherwise; partially deprecated by the **in** and **not in** operators in 2.2 but still provides a functional interface
`dict.items()`	Returns a list of the (key, value) tuple pairs of `dict`
`dict.keys()`	Returns a list of the keys of `dict`
`dict.iter*`[d]`()`	`iteritems()`, `iterkeys()`, `itervalues()` are all methods that behave the same as their non-iterator counterparts but return an iterator instead of a list
`dict.pop`[c]`(key[, default])`	Similar to `get()` but removes and returns `dict[key]` if key present and raises `KeyError` if key not in `dict` and `default` not given
`dict.setde-fault(key, default=None)`[e]	Similar to `get()`, but sets `dict[key]=default` if key is not already in `dict`
`dict.update(dict2)`[a]	Adds the key-value pairs of `dict2` to `dict`
`dict.values()`	Returns a list of the values of `dict`

a. New in Python 1.5
b. More information regarding shallow and deep copies can be found in Section 6.19.
c. New in Python 2.3.
d. New in Python 2.2.
e. New in Python 2.0.

Set Types Operators and Functions

Table B.10 outlines the various operators, (built-in and factory) functions, and built-in methods that apply to both set types (`set` [mutable] and `frozenset` [immutable]).

Table B.10 Set Type Operators, Functions, and Methods

Function/Method Name	Operator Equivalent	Description
All Set Types		
`len(s)`		Set cardinality: number of elements in s
`set([obj])`		Mutable set factory function; if *obj* given, it must be iterable, new set elements taken from *obj*; if not, creates an empty set
`frozenset([obj])`		Immutable set factory function; operates the same as `set()` except returns immutable set
	obj **in** *s*	Membership test: is *obj* an element of *s*?
	obj **not in** *s*	Non-membership test: is *obj* not an element of *s*?
	s == *t*	Equality test: do *s* and *t* have exactly the same elements?
	s != *t*	Inequality test: opposite of ==
	s < *t*	(Strict) subset test; *s* != *t* and all elements of *s* are members of *t*
`s.issubset(t)`	*s* <= *t*	Subset test (allows improper subsets): all elements of s are members of t
	s > *t*	(Strict) superset test: *s* != *t* and all elements of *t* are members of *s*
`s.issuperset(t)`	*s* >= *t*	Superset test (allows improper supersets): all elements of t are members of *s*

Table B.10 Set Type Operators, Functions, and Methods (continued)

Function/Method Name	Operator Equivalent	Description
All Set Types		
`s.union(t)`	`s	t`	Union operation: elements in *s* or *t*
`s.intersection(t)`	`s & t`	Intersection operation: elements in *s* and *t*
`s.difference(t)`	`s - t`	Difference operation: elements in *s* that are not elements of *t*
`s.symmetric_difference(t)`	`s ^ t`	Symmetric difference operation: elements of either *s* or *t* but not both
`s.copy()`		Copy operation: return (shallow) copy of *s*
Mutable Sets Only		
`s.update(t)`	`s |= t`	(Union) update operation: members of *t* added to *s*
`s.intersection_update(t)`	`s &= t`	Intersection update operation: *s* only contains members of the original *s* and *t*
`s.difference_update(t)`	`s -= t`	Difference update operation: *s* only contains original members who are not in *t*
`s.symmetric_difference_update(t)`	`s ^= t`	Symmetric difference update operation: *s* only contains members of *s* or *t* but not both
`s.add(obj)`		Add operation: add *obj* to *s*
`s.remove(obj)`		Remove operation: remove *obj* from *s*; `KeyError` raised if *obj* not in *s*
`s.discard(obj)`		Discard operation: friendlier version of `remove()`—remove *obj* from s if *obj* in *s*
`s.pop()`		Pop operation: remove and return an arbitrary element of *s*
`s.clear()`		Clear operation: remove all elements of *s*

File Object Methods and Data Attriobutes

Table B.11 lists the built-in methods and data attributes of file objects.

Table B.11 Methods for File Objects

File Object Attribute	Description
`file.close()`	Closes `file`
`file.fileno()`	Returns integer file descriptor (FD) for `file`
`file.flush()`	Flushes internal buffer for `file`
`file.isatty()`	Returns True if `file` is a tty-like device and False otherwise
`file.next`[a]`()`	Returns the next line in the file [similar to `file.readline()`] or raises Stop-Iteration if no more lines are available
`file.read(size=-1)`	Reads `size` bytes of file, or all remaining bytes if `size` not given or is negative, as a string and return it
`file.readinto`[b]`(buf, size)`	Reads `size` bytes from `file` into buffer `buf` (unsupported)
`file.readline(size=-1)`	Reads and returns one line from `file` (includes line-ending characters), either one full line or a maximum of `size` characters
`file.readlines(sizhint=0)`	Reads and returns all lines from `file` as a list (includes all line termination characters); if `sizhint` given and > 0, whole lines are returned consisting of approximately `sizhint` bytes (could be rounded up to next buffer's worth)
`file.xreadlines`[c]`()`	Meant for iteration, returns lines in `file` read as chunks in a more efficient way than `readlines()`

Table B.11 Methods for File Objects (continued)

File Object Attribute	*Description*
`file.seek(off, whence=0)`	Moves to a location within `file`, `off` bytes offset from `whence` (0 == beginning of file, 1 == current location, or 2 == end of file)
`file.tell()`	Returns current location within `file`
`file.truncate(size=file.tell())`	Truncates `file` to at most `size` bytes, the default being the current file location
`file.write(str)`	Writes string `str` to `file`
`file.writelines(seq)`	Writes `seq` of strings to `file`; `seq` should be an iterable producing strings; prior to 2.2, it was just a list of strings
`file.closed`	`True` if `file` is closed and `False` otherwise
`file.encoding`[d]	Encoding that this file uses—when Unicode strings are written to file, they will be converted to byte strings using `file.encoding`; a value of `None` indicates that the system default encoding for converting Unicode strings should be used
`file.mode`	Access mode with which `file` was opened
`file.name`	Name of `file`
`file.newlines`[d]	`None` if no line separators have been read, a string consisting of one type of line separator, or a tuple containing all types of line termination characters read so far
`file.softspace`	0 if space explicitly required with `print`, 1 otherwise; rarely used by the programmer—generally for internal use only

a. New in Python 2.2.
b. New in Python 1.5.2 but unsupported.
c. New in Python 2.1 but deprecated in Python 2.3.
d. New in Python 2.3.

Python Exceptions

Table B.12 lists exceptions in Python.

Table B.12 Python Built-In Exceptions

Exception Name	Description
BaseException[a]	Root class for all exceptions
SystemExit[b]	Request termination of Python interpreter
KeyboardInterrupt[c]	User interrupted execution (usually by typing ^C)
Exception[d]	Root class for regular exceptions
StopIteration[e]	Iteration has no further values
GeneratorExit[a]	Exception sent to generator to tell it to quit
SystemExit[f]	Request termination of Python interpreter
StandardError[d]	Base class for all standard built-in exceptions
ArithmeticError[d]	Base class for all numeric calculation errors
FloatingPointError[d]	Error in floating point calculation
OverflowError	Calculation exceeded maximum limit for numerical type
ZeroDivisionError	Division (or modulus) by zero error (all numeric types)
AssertionError[d]	Failure of **assert** statement
AttributeError	No such object attribute
EOFError	End-of-file marker reached without input from built-in

Table B.12 Python Built-In Exceptions(continued)

Exception Name	Description
EnvironmentError	Base class for operating system environment errors
IOError	Failure of input/output operation
OSError	Operating system error
WindowsError	MS Windows system call failure
ImportError	Failure to import module or object
KeyboardInterrupt[f]	User interrupted execution (usually by typing ^C)
LookupError[d]	Base class for invalid data lookup errors
IndexError	No such index in sequence
KeyError	No such key in mapping
MemoryError	Out-of-memory error (non-fatal to Python interpreter)
NameError	Undeclared/uninitialized object (non-attribute)
UnboundLocalError	Access of an uninitialized local variable
ReferenceError	Weak reference tried to access a garbage-collected object
RuntimeError	Generic default error during execution
NotImplementedError	Unimplemented method
SyntaxError	Error in Python syntax
IndentationError	Improper indentation
TabError[g]	Improper mixture of TABs and spaces
SystemError	Generic interpreter system error

(continued)

Table B.12 Python Built-In Exceptions(continued)

Exception Name	Description
TypeError	Invalid operation for type
ValueError	Invalid argument given
UnicodeError[h]	Unicode-related error
UnicodeDecodeError	Unicode error during decoding
UnicodeEncodeError	Unicode error during encoding
UnicodeTranslate Error[i]	Unicode error during translation
Warning[j]	Root class for all warnings
DeprecationWarning[j]	Warning about deprecated features
FutureWarning[i]	Warning about constructs that will change semantically in the future
OverflowWarning[k]	Old warning for auto-long upgrade
PendingDeprecation Warning[i]	Warning about features that will be deprecated in the future
RuntimeWarning[j]	Warning about dubious runtime behavior
SyntaxWarning[j]	Warning about dubious syntax
UserWarning[j]	Warning generated by user code

a.   New in Python 2.5.
b.   Prior to Python 2.5, SystemExit subclassed Exception.
c.   Prior to Python 2.5, KeyboardInterrupt subclassed StandardError.
d.   New in Python 1.5, the release when class-based exceptions replaced strings.
e.   New in Python 2.2.
f.   Only for Python 1.5 through 2.4.x.
g.   New in Python 2.0.
h.   New in Python 1.6.
i.   New in Python 2.3.
j.   New in Python 2.1.
k.   New in Python 2.2 but removed in Python 2.4.

Special Methods for Classes

Table B.13 represents the set of special methods that can be implemented to allow user-defined objects to take on behaviors and functionality of Python standard types.

Table B.13 Special Methods for Customizing Classes	
Special Method	*Description*
Basic Customization	
`C.__init__(self[, arg1, ...])`	Constructor (with any optional arguments)
`C.__new__(self[, arg1, ...])`[a]	Constructor (with any optional arguments); usually used for setting up subclassing of immutable data types
`C.__del__(self)`	Destructor
`C.__str__(self)`	Printable string representation; `str()` built-in and **print** statement
`C.__repr__(self)`	Evaluatable string representation; `repr()` built-in and ` `` ` operator
`C.__unicode__(self)`[b]	Unicode string representation; `unicode()` built-in
`C.__call__(self, *args)`	Denote callable instances
`C.__nonzero__(self)`	Define `False` value for object; `bool()` built-in (as of 2.2)
`C.__len__(self)`	"Length" (appropriate for class); `len()` built-in
Object (Value) Comparison[c]	
`C.__cmp__(self, obj)`	Object comparison; `cmp()` built-in
`C.__lt__(self, obj)` and `C.__le__(self, obj)`	Less than/less than or equal to; `<` and `<=` operators
`C.__gt__(self, obj)` and `C.__ge__(self, obj)`	Greater than/greater than or equal to; `>` and `>=` operators
`C.__eq__(self, obj)` and `C.__ne__(self, obj)`	Equal/not equal to; `==`, `!=` and `<>` operators

(continued)

Table B.13 Special Methods for Customizing Classes (continued)

Special Method	Description
Attributes	
`C.__getattr__(self, attr)`	Get attribute; `getattr()` built-in
`C.__setattr__(self, attr, val)`	Set attribute; `setattr()` built-in
`C.__delattr__(self, attr)`	Delete attribute; **del** statement
`C.__getattribute__(self, attr)`[a]	Get attribute; `getattr()` built-in
`C.__get__(self, attr)`	Get attribute; `getattr()` built-in
`C.__set__(self, attr, val)`	Set attribute; `setattr()` built-in
`C.__delete__(self, attr)`	Delete attribute; **del** statement
Customizing Classes/Emulating Types	
Numeric Types: binary operators[d]	
`C.__*add__(self, obj)`	Addition; + operator
`C.__*sub__(self, obj)`	Subtraction; – operator
`C.__*mul__(self, obj)`	Multiplication; * operator
`C.__*div__(self, obj)`	Division; / operator
`C.__*truediv__(self, obj)`[f]	True division; / operator
`C.__*floordiv__(self, obj)`[e]	Floor division; / / operator
`C.__*mod__(self, obj)`	Modulo/remainder; % operator
`C.__*divmod__(self, obj)`	Division and modulo; `divmod()` built-in
`C.__*pow__(self, obj[, mod])`	Exponentiation; `pow()` built-in; ** operator
`C.__*lshift__(self, obj)`	Left shift; << operator
`C.__*rshift__(self, obj)`	Right shift; >> operator
`C.__*and__(self, obj)`	Bitwise AND; & operator
`C.__*or__(self, obj)`	Bitwise OR; | operator
`C.__*xor__(self, obj)`	Bitwise XOR; ^ operator
Numeric Types: unary operators	
`C.__neg__(self)`	Unary negation
`C.__pos__(self)`	Unary no-change

Table B.13 Special Methods for Customizing Classes (continued)

Special Method	Description
Numeric Types: unary operators	
`C.__abs__(self)`	Absolute value; `abs()` built-in
`C.__invert__(self)`	Bit inversion; `~` operator
Numeric Types: numeric conversion	
`C.__complex__(self, com)`	Convert to complex; `complex()` built-in
`C.__int__(self)`	Convert to int; `int()` built-in
`C.__long__(self)`	Convert to long; `long()` built-in
`C.__float__(self)`	Convert to float; `float()` built-in
Numeric Types: base representation (string)	
`C.__oct__(self)`	Octal representation; `oct()` built-in
`C.__hex__(self)`	Hexadecimal representation; `hex()` built-in
Numeric Types: numeric coercion	
`C.__coerce__(self, num)`	Coerce to same numeric type; `coerce()` built-in
Sequence Types[d]	
`C.__len__(self)`	Number of items in sequence
`C.__getitem__(self, ind)`	Get single sequence element
`C.__setitem__(self, ind, val)`	Set single sequence element
`C.__delitem__(self, ind)`	Delete single sequence element
`C.__getslice__(self, ind1, ind2)`	Get sequence slice
`C.__setslice__(self, i1, i2, val)`	Get sequence slice
`C.__delslice__(self, ind1, ind2)`	Delete sequence slice
`C.__contains__(self, val)`[f]	Test sequence membership; **in** keyword
`C.__*add__(self, obj)`	Concatenation; `+` operator

(continued)

Table B.13 Special Methods for Customizing Classes (continued)

Special Method	Description
Sequence Types[d]	
C.__*mul__(*self, obj*)	Repetition; * operator
C.__iter__(*self*)[e]	Create iterator class; iter() built-in
Mapping Types	
C.__len__(*self*)	Number of items in mapping
C.__hash__(*self*)	Hash function value
C.__getitem__(*self, key*)	Get value with given key
C.__setitem__(*self, key, val*)	Set value with given key
C.__delitem__(*self, key*)	Delete value with given key

a. New in Python 2.2; for use with new-style classes only.
b. New in Python 2.3.
c. All except cmp() new in Python 2.1.
d. "*" either nothing (self OP obj), "r" (obj OP self), or "i" for in-place operation (new in Python 2.0), i.e., __add__, __radd__, or __iadd__.
e. New in Python 2.2.
f. New in Python 1.6.

Python Operator Summary

Table B.14 represents the complete set of Python operators and to which standard types they apply. The operators are sorted from highest-to-lowest precedence, with those sharing the same shaded group having the same priority.

Table B.14 Python Operators († - unary)

Operator[a]	int[b]	long	float	complex	str	list	tuple	dict	set, frozenset[c]
[]					•	•	•		
[:]					•	•	•		
**	•	•	•	•					
+†	•	•	•	•					

Table B.14 Python Operators († - unary) (continued)

Operator[a]	int[b]	long	float	complex	str	list	tuple	dict	set, frozenset[c]
-†	•	•	•	•					
~†	•	•							
*	•	•	•	•	•	•	•		
/	•	•	•	•					
//	•	•	•	•					
%	•	•	•	•	•				
+	•	•	•	•	•	•	•		
-	•	•	•	•					•
<<	•	•							
>>	•	•							
&	•	•							•
^	•	•							•
|	•	•							•
<	•	•	•	•	•	•	•	•	•
>	•	•	•	•	•	•	•	•	•
<=	•	•	•	•	•	•	•	•	•
>=	•	•	•	•	•	•	•	•	•
==	•	•	•	•	•	•	•	•	•
!=	•	•	•	•	•	•	•	•	•
<>	•	•	•	•	•	•	•	•	•
is	•	•	•	•	•	•	•	•	•

(continued)

Table B.14 Python Operators († - unary) (continued)

Operator[a]	int[b]	long	float	complex	str	list	tuple	dict	set, frozenset[c]
is not	•	•	•	•	•	•	•	•	•
in					•	•	•		•
not in					•	•	•		•
not †	•	•	•	•	•	•	•	•	•
and	•	•	•	•	•	•	•	•	•
or	•	•	•	•	•	•	•	•	•

a.   May also include corresponding augmented assignment operators.

b.   Operations involving Boolean types will be performed on the operands as `ints`.

c.   (Both) set types new in Python 2.4.

Index

About the Author

Wesley Chun was initiated into the world of computing in high school. There he learned BASIC and 6502 Assembly on Commodore PET/CBM systems, Pascal on the Apple IIe, and FORTRAN on punch cards. He also helped the journalism department convert from typewriters to CP/M-based Osborne 1s running MicroPro WordStar and served as a student-instructor teaching BASIC programming to 4th, 5th, and 6th graders, and their parents.

Wesley then went on to the University of California, Berkeley, as a California Alumni Scholar. He nearly completed a triple major, finally graduating with an A.B. in applied math (computer science) and a minor in music (classical piano). While at Cal he coded in Pascal, Logo, and C. One of his summer internships involved programming in a 4GL and writing an entire "Getting Started" user manual. Also at Cal, he took a course on tutoring undergraduates that featured videotape training and psychological counseling. Several years later at the University of California, Santa Barbara, Wesley continued his studies in computer science (networking) and taught C programming for UCSB Extension. A paper based on his master's thesis was nominated for the Best Paper award at the 29th HICSS conference and a later version appeared in the University of Singapore's *Journal of High Performance Computing*.

After graduation, Wesley went on to Sun Microsystems where he worked on the Solaris operating system. He also continued to teach for UC Extension, this time for the Santa Cruz campus in Silicon Valley, instructing courses in Unix and C (and later, Python). When the Internet finally went mainstream, he joined a start-up named Four11 (later acquired by Yahoo!) where he was exposed to Python. He was on the Yahoo!Mail development team, rearchitecting the original spellchecker and address book, and was also the lead engineer for Yahoo! People Search. After leaving Yahoo!, he wrote the first edition of this book, then traveled around the world. He then came back to do something (almost) completely different for Synarc: spinal fracture radiology software for doctors in a clinical trials setting. Then he went to IronPort to help keep spam and viruses out of your inbox.

Wesley is now an independent Python consultant and technical trainer (www.cyberwebconsulting.com). In his spare time, his non-computer-related hobbies include: bowling, basketball, bicycling, yoga, ultimate frisbee, playing poker online and with friends, traveling, playing the piano, and spending time with his wife and kids. He is a coordinator for the Silicon Valley-San Francisco Bay Area Python users group (www.baypiggies.net) and a volunteer for the Python Tutor mailing list. He is also responsible for creating and maintaining the online "Monster Discography" for musical artists, including, The Alan Parsons Project, Alan Parsons (solo band), Eric Woolfson (and his projects), and Andrew Powell and the Philharmonia Orchestra. (If you think you're a fan but don't have *Freudiana*, you had better find it.)

PRENTICE HALL

informIT

YOUR GUIDE TO IT REFERENCE

Articles

Keep your edge with thousands of free articles, in-depth features, interviews, and IT reference recommendations – all written by experts you know and trust.

Online Books

Answers in an instant from **InformIT Online Book's** 600+ fully searchable on line books. For a limited time, you can get your first 14 days **free**.

POWERED BY
Safari
TECH BOOKS ONLINE

Catalog

Review online sample chapters, author biographies and customer rankings and choose exactly the right book from a selection of over 5,000 titles.